Ha
International Relations

Handbook of India's International Relations

Edited by David Scott

 Routledge
Taylor & Francis Group
LONDON AND NEW YORK

First edition 2011
Routledge
2 Park Square, Milton Park, Abingdon, Oxfordshire OX14 4RN

711 Third Avenue, New York, NY 10017

First issued in paperback 2014

Routledge is an imprint of the Taylor and Francis Group, an informa business

ISBN 978-1-85743-552-8 (hbk)
ISBN 978-1-85743-800-0 (pbk)
ISBN 978-0-203-82886-1 (ebk)

Europa Development Editor: Cathy Hartley

Typeset in Bembo and Minion by Taylor & Francis Books

The publishers make no representation, express or implied, with regard to the accuracy of the information contained in this book and cannot accept any legal responsibility for any errors or omissions that may take place.

Contents

Contents

Tables

Contributors

Arpita Anant is an Associate Fellow at the Institute for Defence Studies and Analyses (IDSA), New Delhi, which she joined in 2007. Previously she had worked for the National Centre of International Security and Defence Analysis (NISDA), University of Pune (2005–07), and for the Strategic Foresight Group, Mumbai (2004–05), after being awarded a PhD in International Politics by the Jawaharlal Nehru University. Her current research interests include identity and conflict in Kashmir and non-state armed groups in Asia. Among her publications are: 'Security in the Post-Cold War World' (*NISDA Occasional Paper Series*, Paper No. 1, March 2006); 'Terrorism: The Matrix of Regional Security Perspectives and Responses' (*NISDA Occasional Paper Series*, No. 7, March 2007); and 'Identity and Conflict: Perspectives from the Kashmir Valley' (*Strategic Analysis*, Vol. 33, Issue No. 5, 2009).

Anindya Batabyal is a Senior Lecturer at the University of Kalyani. His research is on the theoretical and empirical domains of international relations with special reference to the South-East Asian region. It was from this convergence and theory that his well-received study, 'Balancing China in Asia: A Realist Assessment of India's Look East Strategy' (2006), came out, as well as 'ASEAN's Quest for Security: A Theoretical Explanation' (2004), which appeared in *International Studies*. Other articles have appeared, like 'Will the Nuclear Deal be Finally Operationalized?' (IPCS, 2008).

Sreeram Chaulia is Vice Dean of the Jindal School of International Affairs (JSIA) and Executive Director of the Centre for Global Governance and Policy (CGGP) at the OP Jindal Global University in Sonipat, India. He is the co-author of *People Who Influenced the World Over the Past 100 Years* (Murray Books, 2005) and the author of over 390 articles and reviews in scholarly journals, newspapers and magazines. His forthcoming book, *International Organisations and Civilian Protection: Power, Ideas and Humanitarian Aid in Conflict Zones*, will be published by I.B. Tauris, London. He is a leading columnist on international current affairs for the Hong Kong-based *Asia Times* and the New Delhi-based *Financial Express*. Having been a humanitarian and a civilian peacekeeper for international organizations in three continents, he combines activism with academic scholarship.

Ajay Dubey has a PhD in International Studies and is Director of the Area Studies Programme on Africa at the School of International Studies, Jawaharlal Nehru University. He is a former chairperson of the Centre for West Asian and African Studies at the School of International Studies. He is also General Secretary of the African Studies Association of India (ASA India) and managing editor of two peer-reviewed journals: *Africa Review* and

Insight on Africa. Professor Dubey's primary research areas include India-Africa relations and the role of the Indian diaspora. Apart from various articles on these themes, he is also the author of *Indian Diaspora Global Identity* (2003), *Trends in Indo-African Relations* (2010) and *Indian Diaspora in Africa: A Comparative Perspective* (2010).

James R. Holmes is an Associate Professor of Strategy at the US Naval War College. The views presented here are his alone. He has been a visiting scholar at the Institute of International Relations, National Chengchi University, Taipei, and the Institute for Defence Studies and Analyses (IDSA) in New Delhi. A former US Navy surface warfare officer, he is co-author of *Chinese Naval Strategy in the 21st Century: The Turn to Mahan* (2007) and of *Indian Naval Strategy in the 21st Century* (2009); and co-editor of *Asia Looks Seaward: Power and Maritime Strategy* (2007). He has written a wide range of other works, which have included various articles on the Indian Ocean maritime politics of India, China and the USA.

Rajendra K. Jain is Jean Monnet Chair and Professor of European Studies at the School of International Studies, Jawaharlal Nehru University. He was President of the European Union Studies Association – Asia Pacific (EUSA-Asia Pacific) (2009–10). He has been Visiting Professor at Freiburg, Leipzig and Tübingen universities in Germany, the Maison des Sciences de l'Homme, Paris, and the Asia-Europe Institute, University of Malaya (2010). He was formerly Humboldt Fellow at the University of Konstanz and the School of Slavonic and East European Studies, University of London, and Visiting International Fellow, Monash Europe and EU Centre, Melbourne (2009). He is the editor of *India and the European Union in the 21st Century* (2002), co-editor of *India, the European Union and the WTO* (2006) and of *India, Europe and the Changing Dimensions of Security* (2006), and editor of *India and the European Union: Building a Strategic Partnership* (2007). Various India-EU articles also continue to appear, such as 'The European Union and SAARC: The First Enlargement and After' (*Asia-Pacific Journal of EU Studies*, 2008) and 'The European Union in the Eyes of India' (*Asia Europe Journal*, 2010).

Emilian Kavalski is Lecturer in Politics and International Relations at the University of Western Sydney, Australia. In 2008 he gained the Andrew Mellon Fellowship at the American Institute for Indian Studies in Delhi. He is the author of *India and Central Asia: The Mythmaking and International Relations of a Rising Power* (2010), and has edited *China and the Global Politics of Regionalization* (2009). Apart from a variety of books, he has also written articles looking at the interactions of India, China and the European Union (EU) in Central Asia, and on the India-EU relationship, exemplified by his articles 'Partnership or Rivalry between the EU, India and China in Central Asia' (2007), and 'Venus and the Porcupine: Assessing the Strategic Partnership between the EU and India' (2008).

Satish Kumar is a Senior Lecturer at MMH College, Ghaziabad. He has published various Institute of Peace and Conflict Studies (IPCS) articles, such as 'Rapprochement with Nepal: India's Concerns', 'Pakistan's "Great Game" in Central Asia', 'India and WTO: Some Critical Concerns', 'Myanmar: Contending hegemonies between India and China', 'Nuclearisation of Tibetan Plateau and its Implications for India', and 'India Between America and Russia: Need to Tilt Towards U.S.'

P.R. Kumaraswamy is a Professor at the Jawaharlal Nehru University. He is also the Honorary Director of the Middle East Institute at New Delhi (www.mei.org.in). He has written widely on the Middle East in general and on India's role in and surrounding the region, including

'India's Interests Collide Over Iran' (2005) and 'India can Live without the Lankan Quagmire' (2006), and has co-authored 'India Struggles to Negotiate a Settlement in Nepal' (2006). He has just written a definitive book on *India's Israel Policy* (Columbia University Press, 2010).

Walter C. Ladwig, III is a doctoral candidate in International Relations at Merton College, Oxford and a former pre-doctoral fellow at the Miller Center of Public Affairs at the University of Virginia. His scholarly publications have appeared in *International Security, Comparative Strategy, Small Wars & Insurgencies, Asian Security, Military Review, Strategic Insights, War in History, Seminar* and *Joint Force Quarterly,* in addition to half a dozen chapters in edited volumes. He has commented on international affairs for the BBC and his commentaries have appeared in the *Wall Street Journal,* the *San Diego Union-Tribune,* the *Baltimore Sun* and the *Indian Express.*

Mukund Narvenkar is a Lecturer in the Department of Political Science, Fr Agnel College of Arts and Commerce, Goa. He has given various presentations on maritime security issues, one on 'India's Relations with the Gulf' to the Maritime Security Conference held at the Combined Services College (United Kingdom) in September 2008, and another on 'Maritime Terrorism as the new threat to India's Security' at the National Seminar on Globalization, Religious Fundamentalism and Terrorism Issues in South India in April 2010.

Chris Ogden is a Lecturer in Asian Security at the University of St Andrews. His 2010 PhD thesis, 'Gear Shift: Hindu Nationalism and the Evolution of Indian Security' (University of Edinburgh), sought to show how domestic policy sources directly impact upon a state's external security policies – work explicitly concerned with constructed identities in International Relations. His other research interests relate to identity and security politics in East Asia, as well as the analytical uses of social psychology in international relations. Dr Ogden has recently published articles on 'Norms, Indian Foreign Policy and 1998–2004 National Democratic Alliance' (2010), 'Post-Colonial, Pre-BJP: The Normative Parameters of India's Security Identity, 1947–98' (2009), and 'Diaspora Meets IR's Constructivism: An Appraisal' (2008). He is also a Research Associate with the Foreign Policy Centre (FPC) in London.

Brian Orland graduated from Davidson College in 2007 with a BA in Political Science, before going on to internships at the Institute of Peace and Conflict Studies (IPCS) in New Delhi, and then with the Strategic Foresight Group (SFG) in September 2008, which involved writing on Tamil and Sri Lankan issues. Currently he is completing postgraduate work at the Johns Hopkins University, at the School of Advanced International Studies (SAIS). He is the author of various pieces, including a substantive IPCS Research Paper, 'India's Sri Lanka Policy: Towards Economic Engagement' (2008).

Harsh V. Pant teaches at King's College London in the Department of Defence Studies. He is also an Associate with the King's Centre for Science and Security Studies and an Affiliate with the King's India Institute. His current research is focused on Asia-Pacific security and defence issues. His most recent books include *Contemporary Debates in Indian Foreign and Security Policy* (Palgrave Macmillan, 2008), *Indian Foreign Policy in a Unipolar World* (Routledge, 2009) and *The China Syndrome. Grappling with an Uneasy Relationship* (HarperCollins, 2010).

S. Vijayasekhara Reddy is Reader in Political Science at the Indira Gandhi National Open University. His interests lie in development studies, international studies and South Asian studies. In addition, his interest in India's space programme saw him writing one of the few academic treatments of the issue, 'India's Forays into Space: The Evolution of India's Space Program', which appeared in *International Studies* in 2008.

Gulshan Sachdeva is Associate Professor at the Centre for European Studies, School of International Studies, Jawaharlal Nehru University in New Delhi. Prior to March 2010 he worked as a Regional Co-operation Adviser with The Asia Foundation project (funded by the British Government) at the Afghanistan Ministry of Foreign Affairs. Frequent appearances at conferences and workshops on India–Afghanistan are one feature of his current activities. A prolific writer, his recent publications have included book chapters on 'Indian Perspectives on Energy Security' (2009), as well as articles including 'India & the EU: Time to De-Bureaucratize Strategic Partnership' (*Strategic Analysis*, 2009) and 'India's Attitude towards China's Growing Influence in Central Asia' (*China and Eurasia Forum Quarterly*, 2006). He is also the author of *The Economy of North-East: Policy, Present Conditions and Future Possibilities* (2000) and is working on another book, *Globalizing Indian North-East* (forthcoming).

David Scott is Lecturer at Brunel University, where his interests and teaching focus on the rise of India and China in the international system. Varied India-related articles have appeared, including 'India's "extended neighbourhood" concept' (*India Review* 2009); 'Sino-Indian security predicaments for the 21st century' (*Asian Security*, 2008); 'The Great Power "Great Game" between China and India – the "logic of geography"' (*Geopolitics*, 2008); 'India's drive for a "Blue Water" navy' (*Journal of Military and Strategic Studies*, 2008); 'Strategic imperatives of India as an emerging player in Pacific Asia' (*International Studies*, 2007); 'India's "Grand Strategy" for the Indian Ocean: Mahanian visions' (*Asia-Pacific Review*, 2006); and 'Indian "footprints" in the Indian Ocean: power projection for the 21st century' (*Indian Ocean Survey*, 2006).

Raghav Sharma studied History at St Stephen's College, Delhi University and International Relations at the Central European University, Budapest. He is the author of *Pakistan as a Nation State and Flag Bearer of Islam* (2009), and 'India & Afghanistan: Charting a Future' (2009), a Research Paper for the Institute of Peace and Conflict Studies (IPCS), where he has been an intern and Research Officer. This has led to other IPCS writings such as 'Afghanistan: Evolving an Indo-Pak Strategy. Perspectives from India' (2009), and 'India in Central Asia. The Way Ahead' (2009).

Uttam Kumar Sinha is Research Fellow at the Institute for Defence Studies and Analyses (IDSA), New Delhi. Before joining IDSA in 2001, he worked for *The Pioneer* and wrote the weekly column 'Strategic Eye'. His research areas focus on non-traditional aspects of security, with particular attention to climate change and transboundary water issues. He co-authored the IDSA Report on *Security Implications of Climate Change for India* (2009) and is also the principal author of the IDSA Report on *India and Water Security: External Dynamics*.

Robert Stewart-Ingersoll and **Derrick V. Frazier** are Assistant Professors in the Department of International Studies at the American University of Sharjah (Stewart-Ingersoll), and in the Department of Political Science at the University of Illinois (Frazier). They have jointly authored *Regional Powers and Security Orders* (Routledge, 2011). Their joint work has involved them in wider articles on international stability issues, but also on 'India as a Regional Power', which sought to identify the impact of roles and foreign policy orientation on the South Asian Security Order, a study which appeared in *Asian Security* in 2010.

Abbreviations

ACP	African, Caribbean and Pacific
ADB	Asian Development Bank
ADC	Aerospace Defence Command
AFRICA	Action for Resisting Invasion, Colonialism and Apartheid
AIADMK	All-India Anna Dravida Munnetra Kazhagam
aka	also known as
ANC	African National Congress
APEC	Asia-Pacific Economic Cooperation
APP	Asia-Pacific Partnership for Clean Development and Climate
APPLE	Ariane Passenger Payload Experiment
ARF	ASEAN Regional Forum
ASAT	anti-satellite
ASEAN	Association of Southeast Asian Nations
ASEM	Asia Europe Meeting
ASLV	Augmented Satellite Launch Vehicle
BAPCO	Bahrain Petroleum Company
BASIC	Brazil, South Africa, India and China
BBC	British Broadcasting Corporation
BEE	Bureau of Energy Efficiency
BIMSTEC	BIMSTEC Bay of Bengal Initiative for Multi-Sectoral Technical and Economic Cooperation (formerly Bangladesh, India, Myanmar, Sri Lanka, Thailand Economic Cooperation)
BJP	Bharatiya Janata Party (Indian People's Party)
BNP	Bangladesh Nationalist Party
BOAD	West African Development Bank
BRIC	Brazil, Russia, India and China
BSF	Border Security Force
CARs	Central Asian republics
CASE	Commission for Additional Sources of Energy
CBI	Central Bureau of Investigation (India)
CCA	Commercial Cooperation Agreement
CCIT	Comprehensive Convention for Combating International Terrorism
CDM	Clean Development Mechanism
CDS	Chief of Defence Staff
CECA	Comprehensive Economic Cooperation Agreement

CEIB	Central Economic Intelligence Bureau
CEPA	Comprehensive Economic Partnership Agreement
CHOGM	Commonwealth Heads of Government Meeting
CIC	China Investment Corporation
cm	centimetre(s)
CMEA	Council for Mutual Economic Assistance
CNG	compressed natural gas
CNPC	China National Petroleum Corporation
COMESA	Common Market for Eastern and Southern Africa
COPUOS	United Nations Committee on the Peaceful Uses of Outer Space
COSPAR	Committee on Space Research
COTER	Council Working Group on Terrorism
CPI(M)	Communist Party of India (Marxist)
CPN(M)	Communist Party of Nepal (Maoist)
CSCs	China Study Centres
CTBT	Comprehensive Nuclear Test Ban Treaty
CTC	United Nations Counter-Terrorism Committee
CTED	United Nations Counter-Terrorism Committee Executive Directorate
cu	cubic
DAE	Department of Atomic Energy
DCA	Defence Co-operation Agreement
DMK	Dravida Munnetra Kazhagam
DoP	Declaration of Principles
DOS	Department of Space
DPJ	Democratic Party of Japan
DRDO	Defence Research and Development Organization
DSB	Dispute Settlement Body
EAC	East African Community; East Asian Community
EAS	East Asian Summit
ECOWAS	Economic Community of West African States
EEZ	Exclusive Economic Zone
EHP	Early Harvest Programme
EIA	Energy Information Administration
ESCES	Experimental Satellite Communication Station
ETF	Ecological Task Force
EU	European Union
FATF	Financial Action Task Force
FBA	Federal Investigation Agency
FDI	foreign direct investment
FENC	Far Eastern Naval Command
FIU-IND	Financial Intelligence Unit
FMCT	Fissile Material Cutoff Treaty
Fr	Father
ft	feet
FTAs	Free Trade Agreements
FTO	Foreign Terrorist Organizations list
GAIL	Gas Authority of India Limited
GCC	Gulf Cooperation Council

GDI	Global Democracy Initiative
GDP	gross domestic product
GHG	greenhouse gas(es)
GLONASS	Global Navigation Satellite System
GNPOC	Greater Nile Petroleum Operating Company
GOPIO	Global Organisation of the People of Indian Origin
GSLV	Geo-synchronous Satellite Launch Vehicle
GSP	Generalised System of Preferences
Gt	gigaton(s)
IAEA	International Atomic Energy Agency
IAF	Indian Air Force
IAFS	India-Africa Forum Summit
IBSA	India, Brazil and South Africa
ICPs	integrated check posts
IDSA	Institute for Defence Studies and Analyses
IEDs	improvised explosive devices
IGAD	Intergovernmental Authority on Development
IGMDP	Integrated Guided Missile Development Programme
IGY	International Geophysical Year
IIF	International Islamic Front
IM	Indian mujahideen
IMASRCON	International Maritime Search and Rescue Conference
IMF	International Monetary Fund
IMU	Islamic Movement of Uzbekistan
INC	Indian National Congress party
INCOSPAR	Indian National Committee for Space Research
INRSA	Indian National Remote Sensing Agency
INSATs	Indian National Satellites
INSC	International North-South Corridor
INSTC	International North-South Trade Corridor
IOC	Indian Oil Corporation
IONS	Indian Ocean Naval Symposium
IOR	Indian Ocean Region
IOR-ARC	Indian Ocean Rim–Association for Regional Cooperation
IPCC	Intergovernmental Panel on Climate Change
IPCS	Institute of Peace and Conflict Studies
IPE	International Political Economy
IPI	Iran-Pakistan-India
IPKF	Indian Peace-keeping Forces
IR	International Relations
IRBM	intermediate range ballistic missile
IRIGC-TEC	India–Russia Inter-Governmental Commission on Trade, Economic, Scientific, Technological and Cultural Cooperation
IRS	Indian Remote Sensing
ISF-IM	Indian Security Force—Indian Mujahideen
ISI	Inter-Services Intelligence
ISL	international shipping lane
ISLA	Indo-Sri Lankan Accord

ISLFTA	India-Sri Lanka Free Trade Agreement
ISPS	International Ship and Port Facility Security
ISRO	Indian Space Research Organization
ITEC	Indian Technical and Economic Cooperation
JAFZ	Jebel Ali Free Zone
JAP	Joint Action Plan
JeM	Jaish-e-Mohammed
JWG	Joint Working Group
kg	kilogram(s)
kgOE	kilogram(s) of oil equivalent
km	kilometre(s)
KMG	KazMunaiGaz
KMT	Kuomintang
LAC	Line of Actual Control
Lanka IOC	Lanka Indian Oil Corporation
LDP	Liberal Democratic Party
LeT	Lashkar-e-Taiba
LNG	liquefied natural gas
LTTE	Liberation Tigers of Tamil Eelam
m	metre(s)
m.	million
MAC	Multi-Agency Centre
MDMK	Marumalarchi Dravida Munnetra Kazhagam
MEH	Marine Electronic Highway
MFN	most favoured nation
MGC	Mekong-Ganga Cooperation
MNRE	Ministry of New and Renewable Energy
MOEA	Ministry of External Affairs
MoEF	Ministry of Environment and Forests
MOIA	Ministry of Overseas Indian Affairs
MTCR	Missile Technology Control Regime
MW	megawatts
NAM	Non-Aligned Movement
NAPCC	National Action Plan on Climate Change
NASA	National Aeronautic and Space Administration
NCA	Nuclear Command Authority
NDA	National Democratic Alliance
NDFB	National Democratic Front of Bodoland
NDMA	National Disaster Management Authority
NEFA	North-East Frontier Agency
NEPAD	New Partnership for Africa's Development
NNWS	Non-Nuclear Weapons States
No.	Number
NORAD	North American Aerospace Defence Command
NPT	Nuclear Non-Proliferation Treaty
NRI	non-resident Indians
NSA	National Security Adviser
NSAB	National Security Advisory Board

NSC	National Security Council
NSCN	National Socialist Council of Nagaland
NSG	Nuclear Suppliers Group
NSSP	Next Steps in Strategic Partnership
NWS	Nuclear Weapons States
OCI	Overseas Citizenship of India
OECD	Organisation for Economic Co-operation and Development
OIC	Organization of the Islamic Conference
OIL	Oil India Ltd
OMEL	ONGC Mittal Energy Limited
ONGC	Oil and Natural Gas Corporation
OVL	ONGC Videsh Limited
P-5	the five Permananent Members of the United Nations Security Council
PBSA	Pravasi Bharatiya Samman Award
PGR	Persian Gulf Residency
PIF	Pacific Islands Forum
PIO	people of Indian origin; Popular International Organization
PLA	People's Liberation Army
PLO	Palestine Liberation Organization
PMK	Pattali Makkal Katchi
PNE	Peaceful Nuclear Explosion
PoK	Pakistan-occupied Kashmir
POTO	Prevention of Terrorism Ordinance
PPO	purchasing power parity
PSLV	Polar Satellite Launch Vehicle
PTAs	Preferential Trade Agreements
R&D	research and development
RAW	Research and Analysis Wing
RCI	Russia, China and India
RIC	Russia-India-China
RSC	Regional Security Complex
SAARC	South Asian Association for Regional Cooperation
SADC	Southern African Development Community
SAIS	School of Advanced International Studies
SAP	Structural Adjustment Programme
SAPTA	SAARC Preferential Trading Arrangement
SCO	Shanghai Cooperation Organization
SCOMET	special chemicals, organisms, materials, equipment and technologies
SDGT	Specially Designated Global Terrorists
SEATO	South-East Asian Treaty Organization
SFG	Strategic Foresight Group
SIMI	Students' Islamic Movement of India
SITE	Satellite Instructional Television Experiment
SLOCs	Sea Lines of Communication
sq	square
SSTC	Space Science and Technology Centre
St	Saint
SWAPO	South-West African People's Organization

TAC	Treaty of Amity and Cooperation in Southeast Asia
TAPI	Turkmenistan-Afghanistan-Pakistan-India
TEAM-9	Techno-Economic Approach for Africa India Movement
TEL	Terrorist Exclusion List
TERLS	Thumba Equatorial Rocket Launching Station
UAE	United Arab Emirates
UK	United Kingdom
ULFA	United Liberation Front of Assam
UN	United Nations
UNCTAD	United Nations Conference on Trade and Development
UNDOF	United Nations Disengagement Observer Force
UNDP	United Nations Development Programme
UNEP	United Nations Environmental Programme
UNFCCC	United Nations Framework Convention on Climate Change
UNHCHR	United Nations High Commissioner for Human Rights
UNIFIL	United Nations Interim Force in Lebanon
UNMOGIP	United Nations Military Observer Group
UNSC	United Nations Security Council
UNSCOP	United Nations Special Committee on Palestine
UPA	United Progressive Alliance
US(A)	United States (of America)
USSR	Union of Soviet Socialist Republics
Vol.	volume
WANA	West Asia and North Africa
WMD	weapons of mass destruction
WPNS	West Pacific Naval Symposium
WTO	World Trade Organization

Preface: Setting the scene

Introduction

This book serves as a survey of India's international relations. Consideration of this topic is of ever increasing interest to politicians, planners and analysts inside and outside India. The sense is palpable that the 21st century is witnessing the 'rise' of India within the international system.[1] There is a degree of impatience in India and a sense of surprise outside India, but it does point to India's emergence as a pole of power, one of the Great Powers in the making.[2] India's rise is underpinned, but it is also a perquisite for its aspirations, 'it is no longer a mere pawn on the world stage; it is also a player [...] it aspires to a place at the head table [...] it has the ambition and the confidence that India can be a major player in the emerging global scenario. Therein lie the challenges', for India and for the international system.[3] In such a shift, India shares much with the People's Republic of China; but whereas China's rise has attracted frequent attention, India has attracted less, at times something that perhaps can irritate or frustrate Indian opinion. This *Handbook of India's International Relations* aims to redress this imbalance.

Consequently, two sections follow in this introductory chapter, to set the scene, as it were. First, discussion of the structure of the *Handbook*, a structure that reflects the way in which India itself talks about the structure of its foreign policy. Second, discussion of the role of International Relations (IR) theories and paradigms, which will help shed light on and across the varied relationships and settings within which India operates.

Structure of the *Handbook*

The book is centred on India's own description of its foreign policy as operating in *concentric circles*. In 2002 it was the Bharatiya Janata Party (BJP—Indian People's Party) administration talking of how, 'just as Kautilya talked of the Circle of States, a useful conceptual framework for the consideration of India's foreign policy would be to view it as consisting of three concentric circles around a central axis – the first of our immediate region, the second of the larger world and the third of over arching global issues'.[4] In 2007 it was a Congress party administration talking of how, 'from the broader perspective, we regard our security as lying in a neighborhood of widening concentric circles'.[5] This 'concentric circles' concept gives the book a clear overarching five-fold division, which is reflected in five sections: Part 1 deals with 'India'; Part 2 deals with India's 'immediate neighbourhood'; Part 3 deals with India's 'extended neighbourhood'; Part 4 deals with India's relations with other Great Powers; and Part 5 deals with India's stance on key international 'global issues'. Underpinning themes across the *Handbook* are 'challenge and response' and 'perceptions'. With regard to 'challenge and response', this involves the challenge from and response by India to other countries and to international issues, as well as the response by others to the challenge posed by India. With regard to 'perceptions', this is about how India sees its own position in the world – in other words, its hopes and fears, its aspirations – as well as how other actors perceive and thus respond to India.

Part 1: India

Part 1 of this *Handbook* looks at the world from India's own initial setting, the very centre of the 'concentric circles' framework. Thus, Chapter 1 considers India's national *aspirations*: is there a national consensus or are there very different aspirational currents within India? How coherent is India's Grand Strategy and foreign policy direction? In a word, what does India want, how does it propose getting there (and where), what does it hope and fear? Chapter 2 considers India's past attitudes to war and peace, its *strategic culture* and its legacy thereon. Chapter 3 considers what sort of *power* India has, power that shapes how far aspirations may be realized. Such power is considered in terms of its 'hard power' (military and economic terms). It is also considered in terms of *soft power* ideas and image assets: 'deploying soft-power assets will be as important as "hard power" assets'.[6] Chapter 4 considers the sense of how Indian politicians have reckoned that 'the logic of geography is unrelenting', i.e. *geopolitics*.[7] Here the Government has seen what it considers the 'geopolitical realities and imperatives' at play for India; where 'its location at the base of continental Asia and the top of the Indian Ocean gives it a vantage point in relation to both West, Central, continental and South-East Asia, and the littoral States of the Indian Ocean from East Africa to Indonesia'.[8] Such 'logic of geography' ranges from considerations of the very shape of India and its island possessions and to the location of others vis-à-vis India, as well as moving into critical geopolitics' concern with rightful space and rightful position (for India) within its neighbourhood/s. Finally, in Chapter 5, geopolitics gives way to the *geoeconomics* at play in India's economic rise, which brings with it, in particular, the growing 'challenge that India faces in seeking energy security' outside India.[9]

Part 2: India's 'immediate neighbourhood'

Part 2 considers India's relations in what it dubs its *immediate neighbourhood*, in other words South Asia, as reflected in the members of the South Asian Association for Regional Cooperation (SAARC). An underlying concern here is how far the Indian sub-continent is seen as India's sub-continent, its own sphere in which to exert regional leadership and power. To the immediate north-west, Chapter 6 opens the section by considering India's problematic neighbour, Pakistan, with analysis of the various levels of what Ganguly famously dubbed the 'unending conflict'.[10] To the immediate north, Chapter 7 looks at the Himalayan states of Nepal and Bhutan (and Sikkim), all of which involve China-related complications for India. Further to the immediate east comes Chapter 8 and India's other large local neighbour, Bangladesh, a neighbour born with Indian help in 1971, yet one that has posed problems for India through its geopolitical location, ambiguous and porous borders, turn to Islamist tendencies and links with China. Continuing in that vein, Chapter 9 looks to India's immediate south, to Sri Lanka, and with it the overlapping Tamil factor between the two states, as well as China-background complications again for India. The final bilateral relation with which this section deals is in Chapter 10, Afghanistan, in which competition with Pakistan and stances towards Islamist *jihadist* overspill southwards is one motif, whilst Afghanistan's links to Central Asia pull India further northwards, out of its *immediate neighbourhood* into its *extended neighbourhood*. Before leaving India's immediate neighbourhood, Chapter 11 looks at India's role in regional integration, initially in South Asia, with its regional organization SAARC's relative failures which are perhaps pushing India to seek more beneficial regional structures for co-operation outside South Asia.

Part 3: India's 'extended neighbourhood'

Part 3 looks beyond India's *immediate neighbourhood* of South Asia, into the areas beyond South Asia, areas dubbed by India as its *extended neighbourhood*. The significance of this framework is clear enough and was first clearly announced by India in 1999, 'our concerns and interactions go well beyond South Asia. They include other neighbours, and countries immediately adjoining this region – our "extended neighbourhood" [...] in relation to the large issues of development, and security', with *extended neighbourhood* being both a concept and a policy.[11]

The first manifestation of extended neighbourhood frameworks in this section is Chapter 12, with what India has called its 'Look East' policy operating towards South-East Asia, in which economic ties, institutional linkages with the Association of Southeast Asian Nations (ASEAN), and a degree of competition with China (including in the South China Sea) are apparent. Chapter 13 carries this eastwards thrust forward with regard to what India has called its 'Look East 2' policy, India's further outreach into East Asia/Australasia, which involves economic links with the Republic of Korea (South Korea), security links with Australia and, above all, economic-security links with Japan. The extended neighbourhood focus then turns in Chapter 14 to India's southerly drive, for some Indians the hope to make the Indian Ocean 'India's Ocean'. The next aspect of the extended neighbourhood, in Chapter 15, brings in India's emerging 'Look West' strategy, which is evident with regard to India's strategic partnership with Iran, where constraining Pakistan and energy motifs feature uncomfortably alongside links with the USA; and with regard to the Gulf, where energy access entwines with emerging military-naval links with actors like Oman and Qatar. This westerly involvement is developed further in Chapter 16 and its consideration of India's wider links with the Middle East, which brings in the ongoing energy situation seen with Saudi Arabia, the political approach taken towards the Palestinian issue, potential links with Turkey and access to Central Asian oil, the military-security partnership with Israel, and India's own naval outreach into the Gulf of Aden through the Red Sea into the Eastern Mediterranean. Chapter 17 continues this westwards thrust by considering India's growing presence in Africa. Last, but certainly not least, portrayed in Chapter 18 is what has been called India's 'Look North' outreach towards Central Asia, in part the military links seen with Tajikistan (and even Mongolia) and even more so the energy linkages with Turkmenistan and Uzbekistan; an outreach that brings India into its ambivalent relationship with the vehicle of regional integration, the Shanghai Cooperation Organisation (SCO) and latent rivalry with China.

Part 4: India's Great Power relations

This section considers India's relations, as an emerging Great Power with other major states in the international system, in which the relationships cuts across the global/extended-immediate neighbourhood divides. This reflects the sense of opportunity and challenge felt by India's leadership: 'India too is reciprocating positively to overtures of other major players in the global balance of power. No doubt this involves sophisticated bargaining with each of them', for, 'international relations are in the final analysis, power relations. This balance of power politics in international relations is more sophisticated than during the Cold War era. We must learn to deal with this new reality'.[12] Chapter 19 looks at Russia, and its earlier incarnation as the USSR, including their diplomatic and military relationship and their mutual interests in

Afghanistan and Central Asia and vis-à-vis China. Chapter 20 considers the strategic partnership proclaimed with the European Union, and with it the extent to which economic trade is becoming more strategic security-minded in an emerging multipolar framework. Chapter 21 moves to consideration of India's biggest neighbour, China, its biggest trade partner, yet a country which territorial disagreements and past war have brought into South Asia and around ('strategic encirclement?') India, has witnessed growing naval rivalry, and has generated wider Sino–Indian contest and rivalry in India's extended neighbourhood.[13] Chapter 22 discusses India's relationship with the most powerful state in the world, the USA, with its consideration of the extent to which their 'strategic partnership' represents a balance vis-à-vis China and an of India's emerging pre-eminence in the Indian Ocean.

Part 5: India and global issues

Earlier sections having focused on India's relations with various states and regions, section 5 looks at issues of global importance, in which India's role is of some wider significance. The first global theme tackled is in Chapter 23, the Indian diaspora scattered around the world. Chapter 24 considers India's response to what has been called 'internationalism terrorism', brought into high relief with the attacks on Mumbai in November 2008. Chapter 25 looks at global governance, represented by the United Nations, in which India's role as a prominent provider of peace-keeping forces goes hand in hand with its quest to achieve a permanent seat on the UN Security Council. The next issue, in Chapter 26, is that of nuclear power, in which India's nuclear rivalry with Pakistan and China can be fruitfully compared and put into the wider context of nuclear proliferation. Such a traditional security arena can be complemented by the new soft security issue of climate change, discussed in Chapter 27, in which India's role, like China's, as a new industrializing power is of central importance for achieving any global breakthrough over the next couple of decades. From climate change in the atmosphere to still further outwards into outer space is the theme of Chapter 28, where India's emergence as a space power is discussed, including the extent to which it is in competition with China. A final postscript is then given in Chapter 29.

International Relations theories and paradigms to apply

As India emerges from the Third World and seeks to play a part as one of the Great Powers for the 21st century, IR theory can be examined to see how far India's reality fits it. This represents what Rana calls 'slicing' into IR theory, necessary since 'the Indian study of IR is seriously flawed because it takes little or no cognizance of related theoretical and disciplinary developments'.[14]

Some analysts argue that traditional IR paradigms are derived from the West, and so are not necessarily applicable to countries like India.[15] This would suggest that there are distinctive, uniquely Indian theoretical perspectives to be taken into account.[16] Behera's argument on the need for 'Re-imaging IR in India' states that IR has by its Western nature 'acquired a Gramscian hegemony over the epistemological foundations' of IR and maintained 'disciplinary gate-keeping practices'.[17] This study refuses to follow this Indo-centric epistemological argument, though it uses Indian settings. It does not seem that there are features of Indian international position for the coming century that are not explicable through existing IR paradigms. Admittedly, in general IR theory examples are often taken from Western practice, the criticism by Neuman and Behera. However, in itself, a Western example does not show that the underlying theory is inherently limited to the West. Kautilya, for example, showed vigorous IR realism-realpolitik in action many centuries before modern realists like Morgenthau and others.[18] The lesson to be derived from Behera is not one of whether IR realism is applicable, but rather one of what sorts of sources are used to illustrate and validate its universal application.

However, whilst arguing that IR theory is universal rather than particular, this work refuses to take any one IR line of interpretation. Any individual model is by definition a limited 'construct', only part of the bigger picture. This is not sloppy relativism, but rather methodological scepticism towards any nomothetic, often sweeping, paradigm. Instead, flexibility in using IR theory is proposed. The advice by Katzenstein and Okawara for Japan and Asia–Pacific security seems just as applicable for considering India's future relationship in the international system, namely to follow a degree of 'analytical eclecticism', given that 'the complex links between power, interest, and norms defy analytical capture by any one' exclusive methodological approach or 'grand paradigm'.[19] Let us turn to theories and explanatory paradigms.

One very influential theory has been that of IR *realism*, with its emphasis on state-centred sovereignty and inherent competition between states; Kenneth Waltz's 'anarchic' international society riddled with social Darwinian competition, the law of the jungle and the survival of the fittest. It is of significance that Kanti Bajpai argues that IR realism 'assumptions, analyses, and prescriptions are rife in India'.[20] Consequently,

> states' [...] unbending and jealous attachment to boundaries and territories, the fragility of inert-state cooperation and institutions in a competitive international system, the tendency towards power balancing, the centrality of military strength, and the reliance of force to regulate international relations [are] the staples of Indian thinking on international affairs. It is not just the foreign policy and security community that thinks this way; it is also the common sense of many ordinary Indians.[21]

Thus, IR *balance of power* shifts and calculations, the *defensive/structural realism* represented by Kenneth Waltz, have relevance for India.[22] Rajesh Rajagopalan sees Waltz's *structural realism* as very applicable to the ongoing India–Pakistan conflict, where, in this anarchic power-driven game, *realpolitik* adjustments may be common as states seek to defend their own interests, making and remaking alliances and agreements to suit their own sovereign interests.[23] Girja Bajpai, the first Secretary-General of the Ministry of External Affairs, began his 1952 essay, 'India and the Balance of Power', with the famous quotation from Thucydides, 'the powerful exact what they can, and the weak grant what they must'. Bajpai reckoned that power considerations could not be avoided, and that 'balance-of-power is not an ethical principle [...] it is a product of circumstances which the righteous and the upright may dislike but cannot afford to ignore'.[24]

India has had its own balance of power imperatives emerge with regard to Pakistan and China. With regard to India's immediate neighbourhood of South Asia, Pardesi sees that, 'it is evident that India's foreign/security policy has supported the main tenets of offensive realism' with regard to maximizing her power, curtailing Pakistan and trying to establish regional hegemony.[25] On the other hand, with regard to China it has not so much been hard balancing in the vein of John Mearsheimer's *offensive realism* explicit in containment structures and military alliance formation, but rather *internal balancing* through building up India's own strength and *softer balancing* through more fluid implicit understandings and arrangements with other states like the USA and Japan, which are also concerned about China.

Such balancing considerations point towards India following a *balance of threat* rather than *balance of power* logic towards China. A *balance of power* logic would suggest India aligning with China against the more powerful USA; however, Walt's *balance of threat* criteria (aggregate power, offensive capabilities, (perceived) offensive intentions, and geographical proximity) push

India to align more with the USA to constrain China.[26] Whilst Walt applied and took his threat framework from Middle Eastern and then European examples, we can apply it to India's strategic situation. There, with regard to China, it is not only her power capability, but also China's geopolitical relational position and positioning that make it a perceived threat for many in India. Pakistan is a threat to India, not through Pakistan's own power, but through Pakistan's balancing against India manifested in Pakistan's alignment with China.

Of course, *balance of power* considerations and shifts can trigger negative bilateral responses between states, in a mutually reinforcing negative downward spiral, IR's famous *security dilemma*. Each state sees itself as carrying out defensive moves; each sees the other as carrying out offensive threatening moves; each feeds off the fears of the other; each cannot afford not to act, yet their very actions make the situation worse. India's relations with China have manifested this 'security dilemma' process in the late 20th century.[27] The India-Pakistan nuclear/missile race also shows this security dilemma spiral.

There are alternatives to these rather grim IR *realism*-related pictures of an anarchic competitive international system. Individuals, and thus states, are not necessarily antagonistic or inherently competitive as IR *realism* posits. Instead, common interest and co-operation can naturally emerge between states.

IR *institutionalist theory* emphasizes how international organizations soften national edges and provide frameworks for state sovereignty to be modified, with India's entry into the World Trade Organization (WTO) in 1995 being one such example. The question remains of how far India will be shaped by globalization, or how far local Indian conditions will be maintained, *glocalization*.

Meanwhile, there has been a growing Indian involvement in multilateral settings, regional membership and links with acronym-laden organizations like SAARC, BIMSTEC, ARF, SCO, EAS, as well as global frameworks like the WTO. India's involvement in UN activities has been noticeable in terms of providing troops for peace-keeping operations, and in her drive to gain Great Power P-5 Permanent Member status on the UN Security Council.

In contrast to IR realism, IR *liberalism-functionalism* takes a more positive view of economic processes in the international system, with trade fostering international links between states. Karl Marx's focus on economics as the key determinant of power in the international arena remains pertinent for India, as do related *dependency* models. Processes in the International Political Economy (IPE) interact with processes in the international system, where India can construct development- and trade-related coalitions with other countries and blocs.[28] Hard-edged economic factors are certainly apparent for India, where economic growth underpins India's foreign policy, the so-called *Manmohan Doctrine*:

> Ultimately, foreign policy is the outcome of economic policy [...] shaped by our commitment to our economic development [...] it is shaped by our yearning to recover our lost space in the global economy and our economic status in the comity of Nations [...] and our economic partners.[29]

India reckons that in any assessment of balance of power, 'as we approach the sixtieth anniversary of our independence, India's international prospects have never looked better. The new optimism about India's future, within the nation and the wider world, is not necessarily an irrational exuberance. It is based on sustained high economic growth rates that have touched eight per cent and more per annum in recent years'.[30]

Control of and access to resources, *geoeconomics*, has become a frequently evoked concept for the late 20th century, and in the case of India, her growing economic needs and her soaring industrialization have made questions of energy security particularly noticeable as a key geoe-conomic issue, as something increasingly affecting Indian foreign policy, 'energy diplomacy' and military deployments.

Geoeconomics, the control of and access to resources by the state, is closely linked to *geopolitics*, the location, shape and size of a state. Typical of this linkage were comments by Mani Shankar Aiyar, India's oil minister: 'geopolitics brings one to the interface between foreign policy and quest of energy security [...] We are fortunate to be placed at the vortex of an extended neighbourhood which has some of the largest gas [and oil] resources in the world'.[31] In India, politicians have frequently used geopolitical frameworks in describing Indian foreign policy. As ministers for external affairs, Jaswant Singh asked, 'how do you alter geography?', and Shyam Saran considered that 'the logic of geography is unrelenting'.[32] An even blunter implication was admitted by Pranab Mukherjee: 'India's primacy in South Asia is based on demography and geography [...] that reality will not change'.[33]

Geopolitical paradigms still pose questions for India's priorities and pulls, in the shape of Mackinder's Eurasian 'heartland', Spykman's 'rimland' and Mahan's Pacific 'seapower' paradigms. India looks both ways, to land and to sea. The story of the 21st century will be, in part, the story of which way and where India turns her attention. Within the Indian Ocean, India is able to pose a particular shadow over Sea Lines of Communication (SLOCs) through her land projection deep into the Indian Ocean, and by her middle position there. She also faces geopolitical challenges in South Asia. Previously this was on both her flanks, from West and East Pakistan. Currently it is with respect to perceptions of Chinese 'encirclement' of India to the north by Tibet, to the east by Myanmar and Bangladesh, to the south by Sri Lanka and the Maldives, and to the west by Pakistan. At the micro level, the ability of China to cut the Siliguri corridor, and with it India's links with its north-eastern states, remains evident. India is faced with other geopolitical challenges: it remains sensitive to control of the energy choke points out of the Indian Ocean, namely the Strait of Malacca, the Strait of Hormuz and the Bab el Mandeb at the head of the Red Sea.

Questions of economic power drives take one to Paul Kennedy's magisterial survey in 1988, in *The Rise and Fall of the Great Powers*, crucially subtitled *Economic Change and Military Conflict from 1500 to 2000*. His argument was that, ultimately and in the longer term, it was economic factors like size, population, resources and exploitation that have generally determined a country's rise and fall. It is no coincidence that Kennedy's book started by pinpointing powers at their zenith like Mughal India, which then went into decline and colonial occupation, and it was also no surprise that his book concluded by looking at new rising powers for the coming century, an economics-driven rise of India and China.[34] The implications for India are direct, given her underlying potential and current drive to economic and technological modernization, like China by the middle of the 21st century. Great Power rise is a well-established theme in international relations. As Pardesi argues, 'a rising India will try to establish regional hegemony just like all the other rising Great Powers have since Napoleonic times, with the long term goal of achieving Great Power status on an Asian and perhaps global scale'.[35]

So far, *hard power* military and economic dimensions have both been mentioned as IR tools. A third swathe of IR models and paradigms can be seen with *soft power* socio-cultural-ideational aspects. The divide is not absolute. After all, globalization is a cultural as well as an economic phenomenon, to which India responds in both arenas. Iriye has long advocated consideration of culture in foreign policy analysis, alongside security and economics, 'international relations as intercultural relations'.[36] As such, *geoculture* can be put alongside geopolitics and geoeconomics.

One worrying inter-cultural scenario has, indeed, been Samuel Huntington's *Clash of Civilizations* thesis. Amidst his sense of how 'India's power could grow substantially in the early twenty-first century', he also pinpointed conflictual faultlines with respect to a Hindu India vis-à-vis Islamic and Sinic (Chinese) blocks, of no little importance given how one civilizational war scenario for Huntington was between India and Pakistan, proposed for 2010![37] Huntington's talk of a Hindu India may have seemed alarmist in the mid-1990s, but the election of a BJP government in 1998–2004 put *Hindutva* ('Hindu-ness') at the centre of Indian politics. In Hindutva circles this involved a 'civilisational understanding of what constitutes the basis for international relations and what it means to be a regional power [in which] India is a Hindu nation and will seek to control its immediate neighborhood and influence the Asian continent to defend Hindu territory and protect Hindu interests. Serious threats to Hindus and their territory is posed by jehadi Islam'.[38]

A very different *soft power* challenge is posed by the question of how far, as the world's largest democracy, India is, and should be, seeking to actively foster democratic values in other states.[39] Proponents of the IR *democracy = peace* linkage would, of course, see India as naturally tending towards peaceful relations with other democracies, but not necessarily with other non-democratic states – something of particular relevance for suggesting continuing structural friction with an undemocratic Pakistan and China.

One soft way to consider India's position is look at the constructed *images* and *perceptions* surrounding India, where IR *constructivism* challenges both IR *realism* and *liberalism-functionalism*, and to some extent runs alongside much of the *soft power* socio-cultural aspects of analysis. It remains true that from perceptions, and misperceptions, come actions and responses.

National culture is all about *national identity* and from that *international identity* – again a key theme for India in the 21st century. Ignoring for the moment the problem of exactly defining 'India', the broad question remains: who does India think it is, what does India think it stands for, where does India think it should be going? This is an attitude and a state of mind, which perhaps can be dubbed *geopsychology*. Of course, perceptions can also be *misperceptions*, at which point we come close to the IR 'security dilemma' triggers seen in the political 'hard power' domain. Talk of 'images' and 'perceptions' can be brought in not only through IR's 'constructivism', but also in history through the Annales school's concern with *mentalités*, not so much with regard to domestic settings, but with regard to India's *weltanschauung*, or 'world view'. Talk of the Annales school takes one back to its founder, Braudel, and his concern with time and long-term structural change, *longue durée*, in IR terms *Long Cycle* theory of 'long-term change' for the 21st century surrounding India's rise, which was where this preface started.

David Scott

Notes

1 For example, S. Gordon, *India's Rise to Power in the Twentieth Century and Beyond*, New York: St Martin's, 1995; N. Rajadhyaksha, *The Rise of India: Its Transformation from Poverty to Prosperity*, New Delhi: Wiley India, 2006; M. Kamdar, *Planet India: The Turbulent Rise of the World's Largest Democracy*, London: Simon & Schuster Ltd, 2007; H. Pant, *Contemporary Debates in Indian Foreign and Security Policy: India Negotiates its Rise in the International System*, New York: Palgrave Macmillan, 2008; S. Sanyal, *The Indian Renaissance: India's Rise After a Thousand Years of Decline*, New Delhi: Penguin, 2008; D. Rothermund, *India: The Rise of an Asian Giant*, New Haven: Yale University Press, 2009.

2 For example, S. Cohen, *India: Emerging Power*, Washington: Brookings Institution Press, 2001; B. Buzan, 'South Asia Moving Towards Transformation: Emergence of India as a Great Power', *International Studies*, Vol. 39, No. 1, 2002; S. Ganguly (ed.), *India as an Emerging Power*, London: Frank Cass, 2003; B. Nayar and T. Paul, *India in the World Order: Searching for Major Power Status*, Cambridge: Cambridge University Press, 2003; N. Subramanian, 'India's Great Power Plans', *The Diplomat*, 29 March 2010.

3 R. Sikri, *Challenge and Strategy. Rethinking India's Foreign Policy*, New Delhi: Sage, 2009, p.15.

4 Y. Sinha, 'Future Directions of India's Foreign Policy', www.mea.gov.in, 30 October 2002.

5 S. Menon, 'India and International Security', www.indianembassy.org, 3 May 2007.

6 Ibid.

7 Ibid.

8 P. Mukherjee, 'India's Strategic Perspective', Carnegie Institute, 27 June 2005, www.indianembassy.org.

9 Menon, 'India and International Security', op. cit.

10 S. Ganguly, *Conflict Unending: India-Pakistan Tensions Since 1947*, New York: Oxford University Press, 2002.

11 MEA (Government of India), *Annual Report 1998–1999*, New Delhi: Ministry of External Affairs, 1999, mealib.nic.in. See D. Scott, 'India's "Extended Neighbourhood" Concept: Power Projection for a Rising Power', *India Review*, Vol. 8, No. 2, 2009.

12 Manmohan Singh, 'Extracts from the Speech of the Prime Minister', Combined Commanders Conference, pmindia.nic.in, 20 October 2005. See also R. Rajagopalan and V. Sahni, 'India and the Great Powers: Strategic Imperatives, Normative Necessities', *South Asian Survey*, Vol. 15, No. 1, 2008.

13 J. Garver, *Protracted Contest: Sino-Indian Rivalry in the Twentieth Century*, Seattle: University of Washington Press, 2001.

14 A. Rana, 'Understanding International Conflict in the Third World: A Conceptual Enquiry', in K. Bajpai and S. Mallavarapu (eds), *International Relations in India. Theorising the Region and Nation*, New Delhi: Orient Longman, 2004, p.13.

15 S. Neuman (ed.), *International Relations Theory and the Third World. An Oxymoron?* New York: St Martin's Press, 1998, p.2.

16 A. Acharya and B. Buzan, 'On the Possibility of a Non-Western IR Theory in Asia', *International Relations of the Asia-Pacific*, Vol. 7, No. 3, 2007, p.433.

17 N. Behera, 'Re-imaging IR in India', *International Relations of the Asia-Pacific*, Vol. 7, No. 3, 2007, p.341. Also Behera (ed.), *International Relations in South Asia: Search for an Alternative Paradigm*, New Delhi: Sage Publications, 2008.

18 R. Zaman, 'Kautilya: The Indian Strategic Thinker and Indian Strategic Culture', *Comparative Strategy*, Vol. 25, No. 3, 2006.

19 P. Katzenstein and N. Okawara, 'Japan, Asian-Pacific Security, and the Case for Analytical Eclecticism', *International Security*, 26.3, 2001–02.

20 K. Bajpai, 'Introduction', in K. Bajpai and S. Mallavarapu (eds), *International Relations in India. Theorising the Region and Nation*, New Delhi: Orient Longman, 2004, p.2.

21 Ibid.

22 D. Hagerty, 'India and the Global Balance of Power: A Neorealist Snapshot', in H. Pant (ed.), *Indian Foreign Policy in a Unipolar World*, New Delhi: Routledge, 2009.

23 R. Rajagopalan, 'Neorealist Theory and the India-Pakistan Conflict', in K. Bajpai and S. Mallavarapu (eds), *International Relations in India. Theorising the Region and Nation*, New Delhi: Orient Longman, 2004.

24 G. Bajpai, 'India and the Balance of Power', in *The Indian Year Book of International Affairs*, Madras: Indian Study Group of International Affairs, 1952, p.1. See also C. Raja Mohan, 'India and the Balance of Power', *Foreign Affairs*, Vol. 85, No. 4, 2006.

25 M. Pardesi, 'Deducing India's Grand Strategy of Regional Hegemony from Historical and Regional Perspectives', *Working Paper* (Institute of Defence and Strategic Studies, Singapore), No. 76, 2005, p.50.

26 S. Walt, *The Origin of Alliances*, Ithaca: Cornell University Press, 1987, with regard to the Middle East. See also S. Walt, 'The Progressive Power of Realism', in J. Vasquez and C. Elman (eds), *Realism and the Balance of Power. A New Debate*, Upper Saddle River: Prentice Hall, 2003.

27 J. Garver, 'The Security Dilemma in Sino-Indian Relations', *India Review*, Vol. 1, No. 4, 2002; J. Holslag, 'The Persistent Military Security Dilemma between China and India', *Journal of Strategic Studies*, Vol. 32, No. 6, 2009.

28 J. Patnaik, 'International Political Economy and Regime Analysis: A Developing-Country Perspective', in K. Bajpai and S. Mallavarapu (eds), *International Relations in India. Theorising the Region and Nation*, New Delhi: Orient Longman, 2004.

29 M. Singh, 'Speech by Prime Minister Dr. Manmohan Singh at India Today Conclave, New Delhi', meaindia.nic.in, 25 February 2005.

30 P. Mukherjee, 'India and the Global Balance of Power', www.meaindia.nic.in, 16 January 2007.

31 M. Aiyar, 'What Lies Beneath: Getting to All that Oil and Gas', *Indian Express*, 25 February 2006.

32 J. Singh, 'Interview with External Affairs Minister Jaswant Singh', www.indianembassy.org, 14 March 1999; S. Saran, 'Present Dimensions of the Indian Foreign Policy', meaindia.nic.in, 11 January 2006.

33 P. Mukherjee, 'Indian Foreign Policy: A Road Map for the Decade Ahead', www.meaindia.nic.in, 15 November 2006.

34 P. Kennedy, *The Rise and Fall of the Great Powers*, London: Unwin Hyman, 1988, pp.12–13, 455.

35 Pardesi, 'Deducing India's Grand Strategy of Regional Hegemony from Historical and Regional Perspectives', op. cit., p.55.

36 A. Iriye, 'Culture and Power: International Relations as Intercultural Relations', *Diplomatic History*, Vol. 3, No. 2, 1979.

37 S. Huntington, *The Clash of Civilizations and the Remaking of World Order*, New York: Simon & Schuster, 1996, pp.244–45, 314.

38 R. Rajan, 'The RSS Should Have a Foreign Policy', *Organiser*, 29 January 2006.

39 C. Raja Mohan, 'Balancing Interests and Values: India's Struggle with Democracy Promotion', *Washington Quarterly*, Vol. 30, No. 3, 2007.

Part 1
India

International 'aspirations' of a rising power

Chris Ogden

A free India, with her vast resources, can be a great service to the world and to humanity. India will always make a difference to the world; fate has marked us for big things.[1]

(Jawaharlal Nehur)

Introduction

This chapter investigates the roots of India's Great Power aspiration and how it has become normalized and conditioned by events in India's foreign and domestic relations, becoming part of India's self-perception and global self-image. By aspiration, I refer to the underlying aims, goals and interests that have continued to drive Indian foreign policy across different political generations and political parties. For India, these aspirations have been based upon a consensus of ensuring India's emergence as a Great Power that is fully autonomous, influential and respected in the global comity of nations. Most commonly, such aspirations are based upon gaining parity with other great (and super) powers such as the People's Republic of China, Russia (formerly the USSR) and the USA, and most typically include gaining a permanent seat on the United Nations Security Council (UNSC). Underlying such desires are also fears of Indian influence being limited to South Asia, of India being used as a pawn in the international politics of other states (as was particularly apparent during the Cold War), and of losing her strategic autonomy.

Whilst not representing a pre-ordained Grand Strategy, these aspirations are instead deeply entrenched beliefs formulated across time among India's strategic community of bureaucrats and diplomats (especially those in India's Ministry of External Affairs), political thinkers, politicians, journalists and academics. As such, they have been a consistent and normalized presence throughout India's post-independence history. As both India's political and economic power continues to increase within the international system, this aspiration will continue to temper and drive its actions and status as a rising power. While broadly seen as reflective of her large physical landmass, having a sixth of the world's population, and an extensive and diverse civilizational heritage, some differences in approach concerning how India's rise as a Great Power will be achieved are apparent. These differences predominantly occur between the widely perceived

3

idealism of earlier Indian leaders (especially Jawaharlal Nehru) and more *realist* and *realpolitik* (practical rather than ideological) attitudes that emerged in the 1990s.

Reflective of these differing views, on one hand India's autonomy in international affairs is based upon positive neutralism and *purna swaraj* (complete independence) from Great Power politics. This approach in the Cold War period encompassed specific policies of non-alignment, self-reliance, *ahimsa* (non-violence) and nuclear disarmament.[2] Furthermore, Indian conduct was based upon the idealistic internationalism of a Nehruvian world order that strove for peace, harmony, co-operation and development, whereby all countries were treated equally, regardless of status or position. The legacies of colonialism (and Partition) played into this logic by instilling an inherent distrust of any outside (and therefore imperialistic) forces. In sum, this Nehruvian approach to security represented, for the doyen of Indian strategic thought, K. Subrahmanyam, a 'strategy of balance of power for a militarily weak but large and self-confident nation in a bipolar world'.[3] Other core characteristics included equilibrating balances within Indian society, namely tolerance, equality and general detachment.[4]

Set against this idealism, there was also a deep-seated belief that India was inherently destined to achieve Great Power status. This aspiration was rooted in the perceived standing of earlier Indian empires, the various conquering powers that had sought control of India (from the Greeks and Muslim invaders to the French and the British) and also India's physical location as the meeting point of Asia.[5] These beliefs combined with India's struggle for independence, which India's leaders interpreted as part of an 'Asian Renaissance' with a dynamic and pro-active India at the helm. A nuclear capacity was additionally regarded as part of this aim in terms of developing both independent capabilities and national self-worth. Despite these more forceful approaches that explicitly called for the world to recognize India's future position, such aspirations continued to be peaceful, dominated by the understanding 'that power-seeking provokes power-seeking, force begets force'.[6] Indian policy consequently led to her neither pre-emptively invading nor conquering other states.

In order to lay out how these different viewpoints have become solidified into India's strategic thinking as core underlying aspirations, the chapter is split into three sections. Drawing out the major principles central to India's Great Power aspiration, the first section deals with the colonial legacies inherited by India and the guiding force of Nehru in the first decades of independence. The next section looks at how India's aspirations evolved during the Cold War as India interacted and was socialized into the international system through its contact with other countries. The third section then discusses how the nuclear tests of 1998 matured and accelerated India's aspiration to Great Power status and inspired her increasingly influential geostrategic relationships. The chapter concludes with some observations on the future trajectory of India's search for Great Power status.

Colonial legacies and Nehruvian principles

India's aspiration to Great Power status begins with the perceived greatness of earlier Indian empires dating back several millennia as often personified in classical Indian texts, such as the *Mahabharata* and Kautilya's realpolitik-evoking *Arthashastra*. In turn, India's historical exposure to various empires also emphasized the physical and strategic position of India as both a meeting point and a bridge between the Middle East and East Asia. As external Great Powers continued to want India for both its geopolitical location and material resources, a sense of national self-importance and prestige was inculcated within India's elite, leading to an urge and expectation to play a major role in the world.[7] The raw nature of such an aspiration was tempered by ancient Hindu practice, which instilled itself into Indian psyches as pragmatism, patience and autonomous separation. Furthermore, the ascriptive and hierarchical criteria of the Hindu caste system reinforced an expectancy of greatness among the country's elite whereby 'India's status is a given, not earned'.[8]

When colonial rule ended, India was left with territorial issues as a legacy of the Partition of British India into India and Pakistan. The demarcation of India's northern borders through the Curzon and the McMahon lines, and disputes concerning their validity, directly led to border issues with China and territorial claims over Jammu and Kashmir with Pakistan. These issues initially confined India's interaction within the global system to South Asia, made successive Indian governments fearful of their country's Balkanization and resulted (directly and indirectly) in wars with China in 1962, and with Pakistan in 1947, 1965, 1971 and 1999. Partition therefore instilled an inherent distrust of outside forces that had formed the new borders of India and Pakistan, an action seemingly undertaken to inspire instability in the region by failing to synchronize with ethnic and state borders. The creation of a lasting legacy of multiple cross-border and internal security problems evidenced this perception. A resultant anti-imperialist attitude would go on to manifest itself into both anti-Chinese and anti-US sentiments (over their roles in Pakistan), and even anti-UN sentiment (over any attempts at mediating the Kashmir issue). These suspicions furthermore tempered a desire for India to independently gain Great Power status.

Since he was both India's first Prime Minister and first Minister of Defence, the beliefs of Jawaharlal Nehru dominated the making of Indian foreign policy from 1947 until his death in 1964. Central to these beliefs was that India had 'special rights and duties in the management of international society based on its status as one of the world's major civilisations'.[9] In turn, India's international interaction was to be a form of positive neutralism based upon *purna swaraj* (complete independence), consisting of an independent foreign policy and separation from big power games, also often termed as enlightened national self-interest. Such a policy was central to establishing India as an inherently self-determining, powerful and stable nation on the international stage. Mahatma Gandhi's principles of *ahimsa* (non-violence) further imbued India with an aversion to pure power approaches, influencing how she wished to achieve Great Power status. *Ahimsa* was linked to ideas of an emerging alternative world order after the Second World War, in which the use of force was minimal, racialism was repudiated and countries were emancipated from imperialism.

India's leadership of the Non-Aligned Movement (NAM)—which it co-founded in Belgrade in 1961—endeavoured to counteract the rigid dichotomies of a Cold War world dominated by the USA and USSR. Non-alignment also generated moral influence for India and reinforced arguments that to ally with either of the two superpower blocs would effectively mortgage India's future rise and emergence as a Great Power. In the first decades of her independence, this belief existed 'regardless of the realities of what India is',[10] as India's leaders saw Great Power status as based upon moral idealism rather than territorial, economic or military indicators. Employment of this language also helped to portray India as a self-assured and thoroughly independent power. As such, the NAM created a powerful forum for Indian interests and goals in international politics, where it became the second largest multilateral diplomatic organization after the UN. Overall, non-alignment became an article of faith for India's leaders and strategic community that allowed the nation to become established as an independent voice in international politics.

Non-alignment was neither isolationist nor neutral as India criticized various states over their policies in Korea, Congo, Suez and Viet Nam. Reflecting India's own experiences, such criticism targeted expansionist powers rather than specific ideologies. The policy of economic self-reliance (*swadeshi*)—often based upon socialist five-year plans and limited internal investment

5

from outside powers—also backed-up non-alignment aims of stability and self-sufficiency. So critical was *swadeshi* that Nehru stated that 'we would rather delay our development [...] than submit to any kind of economic domination to any country'.[11] These notions were under-pinned and exemplified by the implementation of an economic and science-and-technology policy, which included nuclear power through the establishment of the Atomic Energy Com-mission in 1948 and the Department of Atomic Energy in 1954. Furthermore, eschewing arms races allowed what would have been military spending to be concentrated on economic development. By leading the NAM, Indian leaders also wanted to overcome the view com-monly held by external powers (such as the USA, the United Kingdom and China) of supposed India-Pakistan equality, in an attempt to free India from being purely associated with South Asia.

India's aspirations evolve: interaction and socialization

India's misgivings about the role of both regional and global powers towards it were sustained in 1954 when Pakistan aligned itself with the USA in the Mutual Defence Assistance Pact and the US-backed South-East Asian Treaty Organization (SEATO). Perceived US aims of creating Indo-Pakistani parity, in order to cancel out each other's influence through mutual animosity, facilitated and confirmed an Indian elite distrust of the USA as a core threat to her long-term status aspirations. Although the USA had encouraged Indian independence, the region's poverty and colonial past marginalized India in the post-Second World War global hierarchy. Further-more, the USA regarded the NAM's role in the international system as a liability that cir-cumvented its influence, leading to the US unilateral arming of Pakistan—also in part to contain the USSR and to protect the Gulf. Additionally, following Indian state visits to Moscow and Beijing in the 1950s, US officials became convinced that India was part of the Soviet bloc. India's prior recognition of the communist government in China in 1949 only underlined this opinion, as did India's socialistic orientations.

A historical spirit of civilizational amity between India and China continued in the immediate aftermath of the Second World War, with India consistently voting in China's favour at the UN.[12] However, as the Cold War began to solidify into different power blocs, Indian leaders became fearful of the superpowers using China against it. As China began to see India threa-tening its perceived leadership of the Third World, relations between the two countries became more fraught, especially concerning the annexation of Tibet and Chinese aid to the nascent Mizo and Naga insurrections in India's north-east. This tension became personified by ongoing border disputes between the two sides and proved to be the stimuli for armed conflict in 1962, in which India was humiliated.[13] This defeat forced India to accept 'that the pursuit of a major power role in the absence of hard power or military capabilities was a chimera'.[14] As such, the 1962 experience 'socialized' India into the international order, as Indian leaders and strategic community learnt the limits of their conception of Great Power status. It also questioned the efficacy of non-alignment, diminished India's international standing, and led to pronounced and increased military spending. Increased Sino-Pakistani ties during the same period (including arms and technology transfers), as well as continued US-Pakistan links, amplified these factors. Much of India's newly accepted military aid also came from the two superpowers, diminishing her fully autonomous foreign policy outlook. India's humiliation was compounded when she was compelled to institute limited economic liberalization in order to develop her heavy industry and infrastructure.

Despite the 1962 setback, the belief in pursuing Great Power status remained and India's 1965 victory versus Pakistan strengthened her self-sufficiency. India's growing awareness of Great Power politics was again shown before the 1971 war with Pakistan, when she signed a

20-year Treaty of Peace, Friendship and Co-operation with the USSR. This treaty protected India from UN censure by the USA, balanced against the Islamabad–Beijing–Washington line-up, and acted as a socializing experience in Great Power *realpolitik*. The 1971 conflict with Pakistan and India's consequent 'liberation' of East Pakistan into Bangladesh showed India capable of successfully fighting a limited conflict and of redefining her strategic environment. Subsequently, post-1971, India emerged as the foremost power on the subcontinent; 1971 furthermore confirmed the ongoing morality present within India's aspiration to Great Power status and remains as a rare case of successful state-to-state humanitarian intervention. These events also emboldened India's acquisition of nuclear weapons, achieved through the Peaceful Nuclear Explosion (PNE) of May 1974. The tests were emblematic of its criticism of the permanent vetoes of the P-5 (China, France, the USA, the then-USSR and the United Kingdom) Permanent Members of the UN Security Council and the Non-Nuclear Proliferation Treaty (NPT) of 1968 that protected their exclusive nuclear status.

Assuring India's regional hegemony was a key step to achieving Great Power status and was primarily carried out by denying external powers any influence in South Asia. This policy is often referred to as the Indira/Rajiv Doctrine, named after two prime ministers who led India in the 1960s, 1970s and 1980s. As part of this doctrine, Indian military power was used as a deterrent and as an interventionist force in the region, with India engaging in bilateral peace-keeping operations in Sri Lanka (1971 and 1987–90) and in the Maldives (1988), as well as an economic blockade of Nepal in 1989–90. While not always wholly successful—as with the 1987–90 peace-keeping operations in Sri Lanka—India embraced such interventionist policies towards South Asia, which it abhorred if applied to itself. In the face of heightening energy needs and deeper economic relations, Indian policy towards the region changed in the 1990s, mainly through the actions of Prime Minister I.K. Gujral, who effectively gave up reciprocity in bilateral affairs. Regarded as necessary to counter the influence of states such as Pakistan, China and the USA, the Gujral Doctrine instead based regional relations upon goodwill and benevolence.[15]

Building on its paramount subcontinent status and pre-existing treaty-based security relationships with Bhutan and Nepal dating from 1949–50, Indian leaders also attempted to initiate some forms of Asian multilateralism. These efforts dated from Nehru's Asian Relations Conference in March 1947 and calls in 1967 for an Asian Council. As such, India stepped up multilateral links within the region in order to improve her stability and trade links and most importantly to increase her global standing. This policy included joining various multilateral bodies such as the South Asian Association for Regional Cooperation (SAARC) in 1985, and BIMSTEC (Bay of Bengal Initiative for Multi-Sectoral Technical and Economic Cooperation—formerly Bangladesh, India, Myanmar, Sri Lanka, Thailand Economic Cooperation) in 1997, and links with the Association of Southeast Asian Nations (ASEAN) from 1992 onwards. These latter links rested upon India creating further military, economic and diplomatic ties with South-East Asia through the 'Look East' policy, which built upon her religious, artistic, linguistic and political legacies to the region. Through such policies India steadily extended her regional dominance beyond South Asia, emboldening her global Great Power aspirations. In general (and by the 1990s), such eastern-looking policies held greater importance for India's policy-makers than her relations towards West Asia.

India's aspirations to achieve Great Power status also contained engrained beliefs of her natural supremacy in the Indian Ocean Region (IOR). Apart from inheriting the British colonialists' Curzonian arc from Aden to Singapore, this domination rested upon historical elements whereby British, Dutch and French colonialists had all invaded India from the sea. As such, India insisted that the Great Powers leave the Indian Ocean, and in the 1960s and 1970s endeavoured to declare the IOR a Zone of Peace. After this approach failed, India joined the Indian Ocean Rim Association for Regional Co-operation (IOR-ARC) in 1995, a trade association composed of 18 member states. By the 1990s the security importance of the IOR was underscored as India became the biggest consumer of natural gas from the Gulf, Central Asia and South-East Asia. Corresponding increases in her economic growth ameliorated her Great Power prospects. Rising strategic competition with Pakistan and China increased this importance, and was underpinned by India having the most developed navy in the Indian Ocean.[16]

On a wider spectrum, India remained suspicious of foreign investment, multinational corporations and a gradually globalizing economic order. Such external financial mechanisms were regarded as threatening *swadeshi* through coercive and restrictive multilateral organizations such as the International Monetary Fund (IMF) and the World Trade Organization (WTO). However, the 1980s were also marked by selective foreign capital and technological investment in India as the ties of non-alignment were re-defined by Prime Minister Indira Gandhi to indicate the basis for a new international economic order. Such changes took advantage of India's largely apolitical relationships with Africa and Latin America and the legacy of the NAM. India's gradual liberalization would be resolutely spurred on by the 1991 balance of payments crisis.

In these ways, the advantages of economic liberalization in terms of status acquisition were gradually being acknowledged by India's leaders, especially as a way to engage with the international system's Great Powers, such as the USA. Such understandings also recognized the realities of a post-Cold War world, which had disrupted existing Indo-USSR links, increasingly made the NAM irrelevant and demanded new foreign policy dimensions if Great Power status was to be achieved. However, anti-US sentiments remained, as India's perception of the USA directly acting against her interests continued during the 1980s, particularly as the USA sent arms via Pakistan to counter the Soviet invasion of Afghanistan in 1979. As the Cold War ended, US strategic disinterest grew, in conjunction with the Soviet withdrawal from Afghanistan in 1989. China would, however, continue to support Pakistan throughout this period and its aid indirectly helped Pakistan, in turn, to support the insurgency that erupted in Indian-controlled Kashmir during the 1980s.

Overall, by the 1990s India was steadily increasing her regional and international status en route to her goal of acquiring Great Power status. In response to its interaction internationally, India's core belief in becoming a Great Power remained in place, now characterized by an injection of *realpolitik* and continued anti-imperialism towards the USA and China. These attitudes had enabled India's successful dominance of South Asia, and a gradual spreading of her influence eastwards into South-East Asia and the Indian Ocean. On a wider scale, however, she remained an outlier in the international system, separated from the supremacy of the P-5 powers of the UN Security Council.

Post-1998: India's aspirations evolve

The 1990s witnessed the emergence of Hindu nationalism under the Bharatiya Janata Party (BJP) as India's domestic politics shifted away from the dominance of the Indian National Congress (INC) Party. In 1998 the BJP-led National Democratic Alliance (NDA) coalition gained power, breaking decades of INC rule. Through a *Hindutva* emphasis on regaining India's glorious Hindu past, the BJP wished to reverse the perceived failure of India to successfully impose itself regionally and globally, and they resuscitated calls for India to reclaim her rightful place in the world. Explicit nuclear weapons testing was deemed necessary to fulfil these aims and to ensure for India, as BJP manifestos stated, 'a role in world affairs commensurate with its size and capability'.[17]

From these perspectives, BJP policy fitted with voices within India's strategic community who believed that the pre-eminence of the UN Security Council P-5 was only guaranteed by their exclusive possession of strategic nuclear forces. BJP leaders and this elite contended that India would only be heard (and gain a permanent veto on the UNSC) when she explicitly had nuclear weapons capability, something that had not been achieved with her earlier tests. An additional background of continued US sanctions from India's 1974 PNE and sustained nuclear discrimination against her from the P-5 powers concerning the NPT and Comprehensive Nuclear Test Ban Treaty (CTBT), contributed to pressures to test. As such, and barely two months after the BJP had formed a new government in March 1998, a series of nuclear tests were carried out in the Pokhran desert bordering Pakistan on 11 and 13 May, 'nuclear nationalism' and 'nuclear imagination' in operation.[18] Pakistan responded with her own nuclear tests shortly afterwards at Chaghai Hills in Baluchistan on 28 and 30 May.

The impact of the Pokhran tests on India's desire for Great Power status was immense and transformed much of its foreign diplomacy. In particular, the far more pragmatic and single-minded outlook of the BJP concerning foreign policy made India proactive and expectant in its Great Power status acquisition by forcing international engagement. As BJP Prime Minister Atal Behari Vajpayee stated at the time, 'India is now a nuclear weapon state [...] it is not a conferment that we seek; nor is it a status for others to grant [...] it is India's due, the right of one-sixth of humankind'.[19] This greater sense of International Relations (IR) realism and *realpolitik* supplanted the earlier idealism and *ahimsa* typical of Nehru and the Congress Party, yet maintained the core principles of India gaining Great Power status, namely the protection of India's autonomy and independence. BJP beliefs in an emergent and strong India were underpinned by elite recognition of India's increased economic power and international significance by 1998. As such, India could withstand the pressure of sanctions, as her financial linkages to international corporations and other countries would protect her from complete economic isolation. Indeed, while the USA (and Japan) issued sanctions in the aftermath of the tests, Russia, France, China and the United Kingdom did not. By questioning the dominant global nuclear consensus (and being the first country to proclaim a new nuclear status since China in 1964), the Pokhran tests brought India into the global political, economic and strategic mainstream.

High levels of Indian diplomacy also came to characterize India's mainstream re-integration, as Indian officials and leaders endeavoured to maintain the momentum of the tests to make India a global power. Thus, Indian government and Ministry of External Affairs officials undertook a policy of 'total diplomacy' with all states.[20] Through this approach, and the catalyst of the 1998 tests, India aimed to inculcate new and deeper relationships across the world. Such a proactive approach often involved reference to an emergent ranked hierarchy in Indian diplomacy, whereby greater attention was given to the P-5 powers and second/middle-tier powers such as Japan, Australia, the European Union (EU) and Israel. This ranking differed from earlier Indian policy-makers, who had given equal status to all countries, regardless of (current or potential) political and economic relations. New diplomatic groupings (often with countries also striving for increased international status) also began to emerge, such as the Russia-China-India (RCI), Brazil-Russia-India-China (BRIC), and India-Brazil-South Africa (IBSA) formations. Such pragmatic and strategic developments were now a signal to other states 'that India's strategic frontier may not be coterminous with its political borders'.[21]

By the beginning of the 21st century, India's Great Power aspiration was ascendant as her political, diplomatic and trade links increased exponentially: 'India matters', in a phrase.[22] As such, India's international relations improved across the board, especially those with the USA, as the two countries' leaders talked of India and the USA as 'natural allies', a phrase first used by India's Prime Minister Atal Bihari Vajpayee in his speech, 'India, USA and the World', made in

New York to the Asia Society in September 1998. While this change was not straightforward to achieve and while Indian elite distrust of the USA remained, the 1998 nuclear tests forced US attention onto South Asia—particularly given India's significance as the largest military (and now nuclear) power between the USA's two major military presences in the Persian Gulf and East Asia. Critically, the USA began to accept the new consequences of India in terms of her economy, nuclear capabilities, stable democracy and large middle class. Such respect and acceptance increased India's international standing and made closer US ties a new pillar of India's foreign policy. In turn, India became a key strategic partner of the USA, witnessed in their bilateral Defence Agreement drawn up in 2005.[23]

As India's international profile increased, heightened trade levels and greater military-to-military links (including the signing of 'strategic partnerships' with many major and high-level powers) personified her international interaction. Such ties have helped expand and strengthen India's links to the international community and international economy, confirming her status as a rising international force. Typical of this expansion, Indian policy-makers broadened the scope of India's security horizons, with officials talking of India's 'extended neighbourhood' (Central Asia, South-East Asia and Africa), 'Look East Phase 2' (towards East Asia and Australasia), and a more even-handed approach to West Asia (between Israel and the Arab states), as well as better links with the EU. A rising presence in the IOR has underlined this expansion of Indian diplomacy along with a more explicit emphasis on combating terrorism and piracy, and protecting international trade routes.[24] While regional problems still exist (especially territorial disputes with Pakistan over Kashmir and China over Arunachal Pradesh), India's political and economic links with her neighbourhood have become more stable.[25]

Conclusions

Over the last 60 years, an aspiration to achieve Great Power status has become a normalized feature of Indian foreign policy. Through the legacies of colonial powers and Nehru, this aspiration developed through continued international interaction. Much of this development came from learning the lessons of systemic *realpolitik*, such as India's defeat by China in 1962, wars in 1965 and 1971 with Pakistan, and forcing the world's attention towards India with the nuclear tests of 1998. From these events we can expect India's Great Power aspiration to continue and to become more heightened, while being tempered by a suspicion of outside powers and the maintenance of Indian autonomy in all areas. The core sentiments within India's Great Power aspiration—anti-imperialism, self-reliance and being unaligned—will remain integral to such a disposition. As such, the very nature of India's Great Power aspiration may be potentially debilitating to its full integration into the global economy (for fear of losing self-reliance), and will certainly militate against any all-weather alliances. Instead, strategic partnerships will flourish where the political and economic gains for India are clear. Of note here is that despite different political parties being in power in India, this consensus on Great Power status has remained unchanged, suggesting a normative durability in the belief and approach to the acquisition of Great Power status.

According to Nayar, *power* has 10 features.[26] Four of these are 'hard' features: the military; the economy; technology; and demographics. Six of these are 'soft' features: norms (which can be defined as beliefs, hopes, fears); leadership of international forums; culture; state capacity; strategy and diplomacy; and national leadership. In symbiosis, these virtues translate into power and influence within the international system concerning security provision, the determination and style of financial institutions, and the control of knowledge acquisition and dissemination. Currently the USA is the only complete power in regard of all these power virtues.

In comparison with other states—both the P-5 powers and other second-tier (and aspirant great) powers from each continent—how does India measure up? A cursory comparison can be seen in Table 1.1, below, which shows India's relative strength in terms of 'hard' virtues—its physical landmass, population, economic performance and military expenditure. While looking certain to surpass Japan in the next decade to become the world's third largest economy, maintaining current rates of growth indicates that by the middle of the 21st century the size of the Indian economy will surpass that of the USA and perhaps eventually China. It is India's comparatively younger (and in the future, given current growth rates, larger) population and continued growth in gross domestic product (GDP) that are essential to this surpassing of other Great Powers.

In turn, India has the eighth highest rate of military expenditure, and the world's fourth largest army. This expenditure can rise in line with her economic expansion, which is dominated by India's expertise in software, but also her growing strength in industrial production, satellite technology and arms manufacture.

Growth will also be aided by the preponderance of English language usage in India and its increasing cultural exports in terms of film, cuisine, music, dance and literature—all 'soft' power attributes. A democratic tradition additionally increases India's international legitimacy. In turn, it is important to note that 'Great Powers are not just made by their material capacities but also by their dispositions, that is, by their willingness to articulate a vision of a preferred world and to accept the burdens of shaping that vision'.[27] Here, India needs to achieve more, to be more proactive in its global interaction and to lead debates in international forums on topics such as global warming and energy security. Such leadership may often appear paradoxical in the face of India's economic needs and will demand new, innovative yet balanced diplomatic approaches. Having a clearer national security strategy would also facilitate India's international rise, and a nascent National Security Council (NSC) and National Security Advisory Board (NSAB) (both founded in 1998), as well as a Draft Nuclear Doctrine (first issued on 17 August 1999) are all steps that ameliorate this factor.

Table 1.1 India in comparison with P-5 and other candidate Great Powers

	land (sq km)	population (million, 2009)	GDP (PPP) (US$) (2009)		military expenditure	
			total (billion)	per capita	GDP (%) (2007)	US$ (billion) (2009)
China	9,569,901	1,338.61	8,767	6,500	2.0	98.80
France	640,053	64.06	2,113	32,800	2.3	67.32
Russia	16,377,742	140.04	2,103	15,200	3.5	61.00
UK	241,930	61.11	2,165	35,400	2.4	69.28
US	9,161,966	307.21	14,260	46,400	4.0	663.26
Brazil	8,459,417	198.74	2,024	10,200	1.5	27.12
EU	4,324,782	491.59	14,520	32,700	n/a	n/a
Germany	348,672	82.33	2,812	34,200	1.3	48.02
India	**2,973,193**	**1,157.00**	**3,548**	**3,100**	**2.6**	**36.60**
Japan	364,485	127.08	4,141	32,600	0.9	46.86
S. Africa	1,214,470	49.05	488.6	10,000	1.3	3.93

Source: *CIA World Factbook*, https://www.cia.gov; Stockholm International Peace Research Institute (SIPRI) database, http://www.sipri.org.

While India is accurately seen as a candidate Great Power, her border issues are stumbling blocks to her wider influence in the international system. These issues (and ongoing fractious relations with Pakistan, China and often Bangladesh) are continued influences on separatists within India, especially the Naxalites who early in the 21st century were active in a third of the country, as well as other groups in her north-east. India's population is also India's potential Achilles' heel as it modernizes, a population that currently remains generally highly illiterate, unskilled and impoverished, draining resources. The challenge to ameliorate such conditions seems even harder when comparisons with other major powers are made, and it will take some time to achieve higher living standards. High incidences of corruption, bureaucratic lethargy and apathy in law implementation all exacerbate these factors. However, as India's economy continues to expand and investment continues to filter out through the country's states to its vast population, it is reasonable to expect that, with time, many of these issues can and will be resolved. Although India may never achieve a permanent seat on the UNSC (given that the P-5 would have to implement any reforms, which would by definition diminish their own influence), we can expect India to emerge as one of the major poles, and hence Great Powers, of the 21st century.

Notes

1 Nehru, 1939, as quoted in S. Gordon, *India's Rise to Power in the Twentieth Century and Beyond*, New York: St Martin's Press, 1995, p.1.

2 V. Dutt, *India's Foreign Policy*, New Delhi: Vikas, 1984; K.P. Misra (ed.), *Foreign Policy of India: A Book of Readings*, New Delhi: Thomson, 1977; B. Prasad (ed.), *India's Foreign Policy: Studies of Continuity and Change*, New Delhi: Vikas, 1979.

3 Quoted in L. Mansingh, 'Foreign Policy Imperatives for a Post-Nuclear India', in N.S. Sisodia and C. Bhaskar (eds), *Emerging India: Security and Foreign Policy Perspectives*, Delhi: Institute for Defence Studies and Analyses, 2005, p.46.

4 P. Panda, *Making of India's Foreign Policy: Prime Ministers and Wars*, Delhi: Raj Publications, 2003, p.48; D.E. Smith, *India as a Secular State*, Princeton: Princeton University Press, 1963, p.40.

5 See M. Pardesi, 'Deducing India's Grand Strategy of Regional Hegemony from Historical and Comparative Perspectives', *RSIS Working Paper* (Singapore: Institute of Defence and Strategic Studies), No. 76, 2005.

6 K. Bajpai, 'India: Modified Structuralism', in M. Alagappa (ed.), *Asian Security Practice: Material and Ideational Influences*, Stanford: Stanford University Press, 1999, p.195.

7 M. Alagappa, 'International Politics in Asia: the Historical Context', in M. Alagappa (ed.), *Asian Security Practice: Material and Ideational Influences*, op. cit.; J. Kundra, *Indian Foreign Policy: 1947–1954*, Groningen: J.B. Wolters, 1956, pp.19–34; R.W. Jones, *India's Strategic Culture*, Defense Threat Reduction Agency SAIC (USA), 2006, p.16, www.dtra.mil.

8 Jones, *India's Strategic Culture*, op.cit., p.7. See also Bajpai, 'India: Modified Structuralism', op. cit., p.8.

9 B. Buzan and O. Wæver, *Regions and Powers: the Structure of International Security*, Cambridge: Cambridge University Press, 2003, p.119; P.K. Panda, *Making of India's Foreign Policy: Prime Ministers and Wars*, Delhi: Raj Publications, 2003. See also B. Buzan, 'South Asia Moving Towards Transformation: Emergence of India as a Great Power', *International Studies*, Vol. 39, No. 1, 2002.

10 J. Dixit, *Makers of India's Foreign Policy: Raja Ram Mohun Roy to Yashwant Sinha*, Delhi: Harper Collins, 2004, p.113. See also D. Mallik, *The Development of Non-Alignment in India's Foreign Policy*, Allahabad: Chaitanya Publishing House, 1967; J. Sengupta, *Non-Alignment: in Search of a Destination*, Calcutta: Naya Prokash, 1979.

11 Cited in R. Singh, *India's Foreign Policy: The First Study in Continuity and Change*, New Delhi: Samiksha Prakashan, 2001, p.11.

12 B. Nanda, 'Introduction', in B.R. Nanda (ed.), *Indian Foreign Policy: The Nehru Years*, New Delhi: Vikas, 1976, p.16; S.S. Patil, 'India's China Policy in the 1950s: Threat Perceptions and Balances', *South Asian Survey*, Vol. 14, No. 2, 2007, p.289; S. Swamy, *India's China Perspective*, New Delhi: Konrak Publishers, 2001, p.20.

13 S. Shirk, 'One-Sided Rivalry: China's Perceptions and Policies towards India', in F. Frankel and H. Harding, *The India-China Relationship: Rivalry and Engagement*, Oxford: Oxford University Press, 2004, p.126. N. Maxwell, *India's China War*, London: Jonathan Cape, 1970 remains an authoritative study; as does J. Garver, *Protracted Contest: Sino-Indian Rivalry in the Twentieth Century*, London: University of Washington Press, 2001.

14 B. Nayar and T. Paul, *India in the World Order: Searching for Major Power Status*, Cambridge: Cambridge University Press, 2003, p.19.

15 I.K. Gujral, *A Foreign Policy for India*, Delhi: External Publicity Division, 1998. Also C.R. Mohan, 'The Gujral Doctrine', in *Crossing the Rubicon: The Shaping of India's New Foreign Policy*, Delhi: Penguin, 2003, pp.241–44.

16 G. Hiranandani, 'The Indian End of the Telescope: India and its Navy', in *Naval War College Review* (US Naval War College), Vol. 55, No. 2, 2002.

17 BJP, '1998 Manifesto', in *Bharatiya Janata Party 1980–2005: Party Document – Volume 1, Election Manifestoes*, New Delhi: BJP HQ, 2005, p.156.

18 S. Chaturvedi, 'Representing Post-Colonial India: Inclusive/Exclusive Geopolitical Imaginations', in K. Dodds and D. Atkinson (eds), *Geopolitical Traditions: A Century of Geopolitical Thought*, London: Routledge, 2000, pp.226–29, for section 'Geopolitics of "Nuclear Nationalism": Exploding Geopolitical Imagination'.

19 A.B. Vajpayee, '*Suo Motu* Statement by Prime Minister Shri Atal Behari Vajpayee in Parliament', 27 May 1998, www.indianembassy.org.

20 Y. Sinha, 'Diplomacy in the 21st Century', in A. Gupta, M. Chaturvedi and A. Joshi (eds), *Security and Diplomacy*, New Delhi: Manas Publications, 2004, p.188.

21 S. Cohen, *India: Emerging Power*, Washington: Brookings Institution Press, 2001, p.44.

22 A. Mohammed, 'India Matters', *Washington Quarterly*, Vol. 21, No. 1, 2000.

23 P.K. Das, *New Heights in Indo-US Relations*, Jaipur: Raj Publishing House, 2005; N. Gaan, *India and the United States: From Estrangement to Engagement*, Delhi: Kalpaz, 2007; S. Ganguly, 'The Start of a Beautiful Friendship? The United States and India', *World Policy Journal*, Vol. 20, No. 1, 2003; S. Ganguly, B. Shoup and A. Scobell (eds), *US-Indian Strategic Cooperation into the 21st Century: More than Words*, London: Routledge, 2006.

24 For example, A. Acharya, 'India and Southeast Asia in the Age of Terror: Building Partnerships for Peace', *Contemporary Southeast Asia*, Vol. 28, No. 2, 2006; A. Batabyal, 'Balancing China in Asia: A Realist Assessment of India's Look East Strategy', *China Report*, Vol. 42, No. 2, 2006; S. Blank, 'India's Rising Profile in Central Asia', *Comparative Strategy*, Vol. 22, 2003, p.143; C. Fair, 'India and Iran: New Delhi's Balancing Act', *Washington Quarterly*, Vol. 30, No. 3, 2007; C. Grant, 'India's Role in the New World Order', Briefing Note (Centre for European Reform), September 2008; B. Pradhan, 'Changing Dynamics of India's West Asia Policy', *International Studies*, Vol. 41, No. 1, 2004.

25 S. Muni and C. Raja Mohan, 'Emerging Asia: India's Options', *International Studies*, Vol. 41, No. 3, 2004; R. Sikri, 'India's Foreign Policy in the Coming Decade', *Working Paper* (Institute of South Asian Studies—ISAS), No. 25, September 2007.

26 Nayar and Paul, *India in the World Order*, op. cit., pp.24–64.

27 K. Bajpai, 'India's Global Role in the 21st Century: Politics of Community, Order and Cooperation', in L. Mansingh (ed.), *Indian Foreign Policy: Agenda for the 21st Century*, Vol. 1, New Delhi: Konark Publishers, 2000, p.19.

2

Indian strategic culture: the debate and its consequences

Harsh V. Pant

Introduction

Time and again, India's behaviour in the realm of foreign and security policy has confounded observers, deviating as it does from the 'norm' set by other major powers. Indian foreign and security policy has been deemed incoherent and inconsistent.[1] As India's weight has grown in the international system in recent years, there is a perception that India is on the cusp of achieving Great Power status. It is repeated *ad nauseum* in the Indian and often in global media, and India is already being asked to behave like one. In the past, non-alignment was the broader framework through which India had viewed its relationship with the outside world. The idea of retaining 'strategic autonomy' was seen as crucial by the Indian elite and non-alignment was an instrument towards that end.

Today, when India wants to shape the international system as opposed to being merely its referent object, it should be expected that its foreign policy will be anchored on a planned augmentation of the power of the nation as a whole. Some are indeed suggesting that, after years of rejecting *power politics* and emphasizing the importance of international *norms*, India has now 'begun to lean towards greater strategic realism'.[2] Yet, much like in the past, Indian adversaries seem to have been successful in limiting India's strategic options even at a time when Indian capabilities—economic and military—seem to be at an all-time high. A state can promulgate law and pursue strategy once it has not only achieved a legitimate monopoly on violence but when it is also free of the coercive violence of other states.[3] This brings to the fore the issue of Indian strategic culture and its impact on shaping Indian foreign and security policy. This chapter examines the debate on Indian strategic culture and the consequences it has had on Indian foreign and security policies.

Scholars of international politics have increasingly focused on *culture* as an important variable determining state behaviour in the international realm. Culture is an amorphous concept and scholars using the term have often been blamed for being vague in defining the boundaries of this term. Culture can refer both to a set of evaluative standards, such as norms or values, and to cognitive standards, such as rules or models defining what entities and actors exist in a system and how they operate and inter-relate.[4] It has been argued that the cultural environment affects not only the incentives for different kinds of state behaviour but also how states perceive themselves, what is called a state identity.[5] Cultural elements of a state's domestic environment, thereby, become an important factor shaping the national security interests and the security policies of states.

While critics have argued that culture does not matter in global politics and foreign policy, and cultural effects can be reduced to epiphenomena of the distribution of power and capabilities, one can surely examine culture as one of the variables shaping a state's foreign policy even if there are reasons to be cautious about using culture to explain political outcomes.

Strategic culture deficit

India's ability to think strategically on issues of national security has been considered at best questionable. George Tanham, in his landmark study on Indian strategic thought, pointed out that the Indian elite have shown little evidence of having thought coherently and systematically about national strategy. He argued that this lack of long-term planning and strategy derives from India's historical and cultural developmental patterns. These include the Hindu view of life as largely unknowable, thereby being outside man's control, and the Hindu concept of time as eternal, thereby discouraging planning. As a consequence, Tanham argued that India has been on the strategic defensive throughout its history, reluctant to assert itself except within the subcontinent.[6] In a similar vein, Sandy Gordon suggests that 'the hierarchical nature of caste naturally leads to a propensity towards compartmentalization and exclusivity', which 'undermines seriously coordination and planning'.[7]

India's former Minister of External Affairs, Jaswant Singh, also examined the evolution of strategic culture in Indian society and in its political decision-making class, with a particular reference to post-independence India. He considered the Indian political elite as not thinking strategically about foreign policy and defence issues; with his guns particularly trained on India's first Prime Minister, Jawaharlal Nehru, he pointed to Nehru's 'idealistic romanticism' and his unwillingness to institutionalize strategic thinking, policy formulation and implementation.[8]

It is ironic, however, that even when Singh was himself Minister of External Affairs in 1998–2002, there was little evidence that anything of substance really changed in so far as the strategic dimension of India's foreign policy is concerned. For all the blame that Singh laid at Nehru's door, even he and the Bharatiya Janata Party (BJP)-led government in which he served did not move towards the institutionalization of strategic thinking, policy formulation and implementation. Perhaps the Indian strategic culture became too powerful a constraint for even him to overcome?

Critics of these views have argued that claims made by Tanham and others regarding India's lack of strategic culture can not only be refuted easily but such arguments also lack methodological rigour.[9] Others have suggested that Tanham is being ethnocentric in his claims about the impact of culture on Indian thinking.[10] In response to Tanham's argument that India lacks a tradition of strategic thinking, it has been suggested that 'India has had strategy and grand strategy, and one could distil these from Indian pronouncements and behaviour, but it cannot produce a canon of strategic thought of any great lineage, and certainly not comparable to Europe's'.[11] Others see bureaucratic inertia, political ineptitude and the state of civil-military relations as factors responsible for the absence of strategic thinking in India.[12]

However, contra Tanham, an analysis of the strategic behaviour of five pan-Indian powers spanning over two millennia—the Mauryas, the Guptas, the Mughals, British India and the Republic of India—suggests a remarkable continuity. These five powers, according to this argument, seem to have followed a similar grand strategic paradigm that includes a drive towards power maximization under the veneer of morality, striving for regional hegemony in

15

the subcontinent, use of war as part of the statecraft, a defensive strategic orientation against extra-regional states, and rapid adaptation to changing political and military trends.[13]

Yet, with the exception of the *Arthasastra*, attributed to the ancient Indian scholar Kautilya, there is no major written text that has actually recorded Indian strategic thinking. Before India's emergence as a nation-state in 1947, Indian strategic culture was projected through Lord Wellesly's *Subsidiary Alliance* system, whereby various Indian rulers were prepared to outsource their security to the British Raj and live under its protection. Unlike China, which has a tradition of a strong central state dominating the lives of the people, in India Society has always been more important than the State. This was one of the reasons why India welcomed Queen Victoria's famous proclamation in 1858 that the British Raj would not interfere in the functioning of Indian society, disclaiming 'the right and the desire to impose our convictions on any of our subjects'.

Jawaharlal Nehru dominated the Indian foreign and security policy landscape in the immediate aftermath of Indian independence till his death in 1964. It was his *worldview* that shaped Indian foreign policy priorities, and Indian strategic culture can be viewed through the prism of Nehruvian predilections. Nehru was a strategic thinker and his non-alignment was a classic 'balance of power' policy in a bipolar world where the two superpowers could not go to war because of nuclear weapons. He was an internationalist. However, non-alignment was reduced to a dogma and an ideology after him and became in effect isolationism. India was forced to alter its economic and foreign policies because of the grave economic crisis in the early 1990s. Isolationism did not lead to a careful assessment of the dynamic international security situation and exploration of options for India.

For a long time there was a myth propagated by the political elite in the country that there was a general consensus across political parties on major foreign policy issues. Aside from the fact that such a consensus has been more a result of intellectual apathy than any real attempt to forge a coherent grand strategy that cuts across ideological barriers, this is most certainly an exaggeration, as until the early 1990s the Congress Party's dominance over the Indian political landscape was almost complete and there was no political organization of an equal capacity that could bring to bear its influence on foreign and security policy issues in the same measure. It was the rise of the Hindu nationalist BJP that gave India a significantly different voice on foreign policy, but more importantly it was changes in the international environment that forced Indian policy-makers to challenge some of the assumptions underlying their approach to the outside world.

If we define *strategic culture* more narrowly in terms of its three basic components—political military culture (civil-military relations), domestic attitudes towards the use of force, and domestic political culture—then it becomes easier to identify how these three have shaped Indian foreign policy and security behaviour.[14]

Marginalization of the military

Indian politicians after independence in 1947 viewed the Indian Army with suspicion as the last supporters of the British Raj and did their best to isolate the military from policy and influence. This attitude was further reinforced by the views of two giants of the Indian nationalist movement, Mahatma Gandhi and Jawaharlal Nehru. Gandhi's ardent belief in non-violence (*ahimsa*) left little room for accepting the role of the use of force in an independent India. It also shaped the views on military and defence of the first generation of post-independence political leaders in India. More important, though, has been the legacy of Nehru, India's first Prime Minister, who laid the institutional foundations for civil-military relations in India. His obsession with economic development was only matched by his disdain and distrust of the military, resulting in the sidelining of defence planning in India.[15]

By institutionalizing civilian supremacy over the country's military apparatus, Nehru also ensured that the experiences in neighbouring Pakistan, where military had become the dominant political force soon after independence, would not be repeated in India. The Indian civilian elite also did not want the emergence of a rival military elite with direct access to political leadership. Two significant changes immediately after independence that reduced the influence of the military and strengthened civilian control were the abolition of the post of Commander-in-Chief, which had hitherto been the main military adviser to the government, and the strengthening of the civilian-led Ministry of Defence.[16] Other organizational changes followed that further strengthened civilian hold over the armed forces. The Indian national security decision-making system was devised by Lord Ismay, Mountbatten's Chief of Staff during Partition in 1947, and handed over to a civilian government and military leaderships, both of which were amateurs in matters of national security. The Army, Navy and Air Force Acts passed during 1947–50 made those forces independent juridical entities outside the government, leading to the creation of a civilian Ministry of Defence with Armed Forces Commands staying outside the government. It has been argued that, as a consequence, India is among only a handful of nations where civilian administrations wield so much power over the military.[17]

Along with Nehru, another civilian who left a lasting impact on the evolution of civil-military relations was V.K. Krishna Menon, India's Minister of Defence in 1957–62. During his tenure, which has been described as the most controversial stewardship of the Indian defence ministry, he heralded a number of organizational changes that were not very popular with the armed forces.[18] The first major civil-military clash in independent India also took place under his watch, when B.K. Thimayya, the then well-respected Chief of Army, decided to bypass Menon in 1959 and went straight to the Prime Minister with his litany of complaints, which included, among others, Menon's interference in the administration of the armed forces. The situation was so precarious that Thimayya even submitted his resignation to Nehru, which he was per-suaded to withdraw later.[19] While this episode demonstrated the strength of civil-military relations in India insofar as Thimayya used the due process to challenge his civilian superior, it also revealed the dangers of civilian intervention in matters that the military feels belong to its domain. The consequences of such civil-military friction was to be grave for India in the 1962 war with China.

Despite lackiing any military experience, Nehru and Menon were actively involved in operational-level planning before the outbreak of the Sino–Indian war of 1962. They 'directly supervised the placement of individual brigades, companies, and even platoons, as the Chinese and Indian forces engaged in mutual encirclement of isolated outposts'.[20] As a consequence, when China won the war decisively, the blame was laid at the doors of Menon and Nehru. Menon resigned, while Nehru's reputation suffered lasting damage. It also made it clear, both to the civilians and the military, that purely operational matters were best left to the military. Some have argued that since then a convention has been established whereby, while the operational directive is laid down by the political leadership, the actual planning of operations is left to the chiefs of staff.[21]

Stephen Rosen, in his study of the impact of societal structures on the military effectiveness of a state, argues that the separation of the Indian military from Indian society, while preserving the coherence of the Indian army, has led to a reduction in the effective military power of the Indian state.[22] While India has been successful in evolving a sustained tradition of strict civilian control over the military since its independence, unlike its immediate neighbours, India has been unable to evolve institutions and procedures that would allow the military to substantially participate in the national security decision-making processes. This has significantly reduced the effectiveness with which India can wield its military as an instrument of national power.

Inability to use force effectively

A nation's vital interests, in the ultimate analysis, can only be preserved and enhanced if the nation has sufficient power capabilities at its disposal. Not only must a nation possess such capabilities, there must also be a willingness to employ the required forms of power in pursuit of those interests. India's lack of an instinct for power is most palpable in the realm of the military, where, unlike other major global powers of the past and the present, India has failed to master the creation, deployment and use of its military instruments in support of its national objectives.[23] Nehru envisioned making India a global leader without any help from the nation's armed forces, arguing, 'the right approach to defence is to avoid having unfriendly relations with other countries—to put it differently, war today is, and ought to be, out of the question'.[24] War has been systematically factored out of Indian foreign policy and the national security matrix, with resulting ambiguity about India's ability to withstand major wars of the future. The modern state system, in fact the very nature of the state itself, has been determined to a significant degree by the changing demands of war and it has developed through a series of what Philip Bobbitt called 'Epochal Wars'.[25] A defining feature of any state is its ability to make war and keep peace.

Military power, more often than not, affects the success with which other instruments of statecraft are employed, as it always lurks in the background of inter-state relations, even when nations are at peace with each other. Military power remains central to the course of international politics as force retains its role as the final arbiter among states in an anarchical international system.[26] States may not always need to resort to the actual use of force, but military power vitally affects the manner in which states deal with each other even during peace time, despite what the protagonists of globalization and liberal institutionalism might claim. A state's diplomatic posture will lack effectiveness if it is not backed by a credible military posture. In the words of Thomas Schelling, 'like the threat of a strike in industrial relations, the threat of divorce in a family dispute, or the threat of bolting the party at a political convention, the threat of violence continuously circumscribes international politics'.[27] Even in the age of nuclear weapons, contrary to suggestions in some quarters that the utility of force has declined, military strategy has merely morphed into the art of coercion, of intimidation, a contest of nerves and risk-taking and what has been termed 'the diplomacy of violence'.

Few nations face the kind of security challenges that confront India. Yet, since independence military was never seen as a central instrument in the achievement of Indian national priorities, with the tendency of the Indian political elite being to downplay the importance of military power. India ignored the defence sector after independence and paid inadequate attention to its defence needs. Even though the policy-makers themselves had little knowledge of critical defence issues, the defence forces had little or no role in the formulation of defence policy until 1962.[28] Divorcing foreign policy from military power was a recipe for disaster, as India realized in 1962 when even Nehru was forced to concede that 'military weakness has been a temptation, and a little military strength may be a deterrent'.[29] In recent times, this phenomenon was exemplified when, after the terrorist attacks on Mumbai in 2008, India found that it no longer had the capability of imposing quick and effective retribution on Pakistan and that it no longer enjoyed the kind of conventional superiority vis-à-vis its regional adversary that it had enjoyed for the past five decades.[30] This was a surprising conclusion for a nation that the international community regarded as a major global economic and military power, pursuing a defence modernization programme estimated at over US $50,000m. over the next five years.

A state's legitimacy is tied to its ability to monopolize the use of force and operate effectively in an international strategic environment, and India had lacked clarity on this relationship between the use of force and its foreign policy priorities.

Discomfort with power

A fundamental quandary that has long dogged India in the realm of foreign affairs, which has become even more acute with India's ascent in the international order, is the need, as Sunil Khilnani put it, to 'instruct ourselves on the new necessities and responsibilities of world power—to instil in our elites an instinct for power'.[31] Power lies at the heart of international politics. It affects the influence that states exert over one another, thereby shaping political outcomes. The success and failure of a nation's foreign policy is largely a function of its power and the manner in which that power is wielded. The exercise of power can be shocking and at times corrupting, but power is absolutely necessary to fight the battles that must be fought. India's ambivalence about power and its use has resulted in a situation where, even as India's economic and military capabilities have gradually expanded, it has failed to evolve a commensurate strategic agenda and requisite institutions so as to be able to mobilize and use its resources optimally.

Hans Morgenthau, the arch-advocate of International Relations (IR) *realism*, once famously wrote, 'The prestige of a nation is its reputation for power. That reputation, the reflection of the reality of power in the mind of the observers, can be as important as the reality of power itself. What others think about us is as important as what we actually are'.[32] India faces a unique conundrum: its political elite desperately wants global recognition for India as a major power and all the prestige and authority associated with it. Yet, they continue to be reticent about the acquisition and use of power in foreign affairs. Most recently, this ambivalence was expressed by the Indian Minister of Commerce in a speech when he suggested that, 'this word power often makes me uncomfortable'.[33] Though he was talking about the economic rise of India and the challenges that India faced as it continued to strive for sustained economic growth, his discomfort with the notion of India as a rising power was indicative of a larger reality in Indian polity. This ambivalence about the use of power in international relations, where 'any prestige or authority eventually rely upon traditional measures of power, whether military or economic', is curious, as the Indian political elite have rarely shied away from the maximization of power in the realm of domestic politics, thereby corroding the institutional fabric of liberal democracy in the country.[34]

In what has been diagnosed as a 'mini-state syndrome', those states that do not have the material capabilities to make a difference to the outcomes at the international level often denounce the concept of power in foreign policy-making.[35] India had long been one such state, viewing itself as an object of the foreign policies of a small majority of powerful nations. As a consequence, the Indian political and strategic elite developed a suspicion of power politics, with the word 'power' itself acquiring a pejorative connotation in so far as foreign policy was concerned. The relationship between power and foreign policy was never fully understood, leading to a progressive loss in India's ability to wield power effectively in the international realm.

Lack of institutionalization

A major consequence of this lack of an Indian strategic culture has been a perceptible lack of institutionalization of foreign policy-making in India. At its very foundation, Indian democracy is sustained by a range of institutions from the more formal ones of the executive, legislative and judiciary, to the less formal ones of broader civil society. It is these institutions that in large measure have allowed Indian democracy to thrive and flourish for more than 50 years now, despite a number of constraints that have led to the failure of democracy in many other societies. However, in the realm of foreign policy it is the lack of institutionalization that has allowed a drift to set in without any long-term orientation.

Some have laid the blame on Nehru for his unwillingness to construct strategic planning architecture because he single-handedly shaped Indian foreign policy during his tenure.[36] Even his successors, however, have failed to pursue institutionalization in a consistent manner. The BJP-led National Democratic Alliance (NDA) came to power in 1999 promising that it would establish a National Security Council (NSC) to analyse the military, economic and political threats to the nation and to advise the government on meeting these challenges effectively. While it did set up the NSC in the late 1990s and defined its role in policy formulation, the BJP neglected the institutionalization of the NSC and the building up of its capabilities to play the role assigned to it, thereby failing to underpin national security by structural and systematic institutional arrangements. Important national security decisions were taken in an *ad hoc* manner without utilizing the Cabinet Committee on Security, the Strategic Policy Group (comprising key secretaries, service chiefs and heads of intelligence agencies), and officials of the National Security Advisory Board. Moreover, as has been rightly pointed out, the way the NSC is structured makes long-term planning impossible, thereby negating the very purpose of its formation, and its effectiveness remains hostage to the weight of the National Security Adviser (NSA) in national politics.[37] The NSA has become the most powerful authority on national security, sidelining the institution of the NSC.

While the Congress-led United Progressive Alliance came to power in 2004 promising that it would make the NSC a professional and effective institution and blaming the NDA for making only cosmetic changes in the institutional arrangements, it too has failed to make it work in an optimal manner whereby the NSC anticipates national security threats, co-ordinates the management of national security, and engenders long-term planning by generating new and bold ideas. An effective foreign policy institutional framework would not only identify the challenges, but would also develop a coherent strategy to deal with them, organize and motivate the bureaucracy, and persuade and inform the public. The NSC, by itself, is not a panacea, particularly in light of the inability of the NSC in the USA to successfully mediate in the bureaucratic wars and effectively co-ordinate policy. However, the lack of an effective NSC in India is reflective of India's *ad hoc* decision-making process in the realm of foreign policy. If there is any continuity in India's approach to foreign policy and national security, it is the inability and unwillingness of policy-makers across political ideologies to give a strategic vision to their nation's foreign policy priorities.

Conclusions

There is clearly an appreciation in Indian policy-making circles of India's rising capabilities. It is reflected in a gradual expansion of Indian foreign policy activity in recent years, in India's attempt to reshape its defence forces, in its desire to seek greater global influence. As India has risen in the global inter-state hierarchy in recent years, three different streams of thinking have been identified in the Indian strategic discourse: Nehruvianism, neoliberalism and hyper-realism.[38] It is not entirely clear if these three 'schools' of Indian strategic thinking can generate long-term direction for the country. Indian grand strategy continues to be marked by its absence.

Since foreign policy issues do not tend to win votes, there is little incentive for political parties to devote serious attention to them and the result is *ad hoc* responses to various crises as they emerge. It is possible that, with faster economic growth and increased interaction with the international community, Indian strategic culture will undergo a change in the coming years. If the past is any guide, then this process might take much longer than expected.

Notes

1 S. Gordon, *India's Rise to Power in the Twentieth Century and Beyond*, New York: St Martin's Press, 1995.
2 C. Raja Mohan, 'India's Strategic Challenges in the Indian Ocean and the Gulf', in *India's Grand Strategy in the Gulf*, Washington: The Nixon Center, 2009, p.57.
3 P. Bobbitt, *The Shield of Achilles: War, Peace, and the Course of History*, New York: Anchor Books, 2003, p.336.
4 This definition is borrowed from R. Jepperson, A. Wendt and P. Katzenstein, 'Norms, Identity, and Culture in National Security', in P. Katzenstein (ed.), *The Culture of National Security: Norms and Identity in World Politics*, New York: Columbia University Press, 1996, p.56.
5 Ibid., p.32. See also Y. Lapid and F. Kratochhwl, *The Return of Culture and Identity in IR Theory*, Boulder: Lynne Rienner, 1996.
6 G. Tanham, *Indian Strategic Thought: An Interpretive Essay*, Santa Monica, CA: RAND, 1992.
7 Gordon, *India's Rise to Power*, op. cit., p.7.
8 J. Singh, *Defending India*, New York: St Martin's Press, 1999, pp.1–58.
9 R. Basrur, 'Nuclear Weapons and Indian Strategic Culture', *Journal of Peace Research*, Vol. 38, No. 2, 2001, p.183.
10 W. Sidhu, 'Of Oral Traditions and Ethnocentric Judgements', in K. Bajpai and A. Mattoo (eds), *Securing India: Strategic Thought and Practice*, New Delhi: Manohar Publishers, 1996.
11 K. Bajpai, 'State, Society, Strategy', in Bajpai and Mattoo (eds), *Securing India*, op. cit., p.141.
12 A. Mattoo, 'Raison d'Etat or Adhocism?', in Bajpai and Mattoo (eds), *Securing India*, op. cit.
13 M. Pardesi, 'Deducing India's Grand Strategy of Regional Hegemony from Historical and Comparative Perspectives', *RSIS Working Paper* (Singapore: Institute of Defence and Strategic Studies), No. 76, 2005, p.ii.
14 R. Zaman, 'Strategic Culture: A "Cultural" Understanding of War', *Comparative Strategy*, Vol. 28, No. 1, 2009.
15 S. Cohen, *India: Emerging Power*, New Delhi: Oxford University Press, 2001, pp.127–30.
16 S. Cohen, *The Indian Army: Its Contribution to the Development of a Nation*, New Delhi: Oxford University Press, 1990, pp.17–173.
17 V. Kukreja, *Civil-Military Relations in South Asia: Pakistan, Bangladesh, and India*, New Delhi: Sage Publications, 1991, p.212.
18 P. Chari, 'Civil-Military Relations in India', *Armed Forces and Society*, Vol. 4, No. 1, 1977, pp.13–15.
19 Ibid., pp.15–17.
20 Cohen, *The Indian Army*, op. cit., p.176.
21 P. Chari, 'Civil-Military Relations of India', *Link*, 15 August 1977, p.75.
22 S. Rosen, *Societies and Military Power: India and its Armies*, Ithaca: Cornell University Press, 1996, pp.250–53.
23 This point has been eloquently elaborated in A. Tellis, 'Future Fire: Challenges Facing Indian Defense Policy in the New Century', *India Today* Conclave, New Delhi, 13 March 2004, www.ceip.org.
24 Quoted in P. Rao, *India's Defence Policy and Organisation Since Independence*, New Delhi: The United Services Institution of India, 1977, pp.5–6.
25 Bobbitt, *The Shield of Achilles*, op. cit.
26 R. Art, 'To What Ends Military Power', *International Security*, Vol. 4, Spring 1980, pp.4–35.
27 T. Schelling, 'The Diplomacy of Violence', in R. Art and R. Jervis (eds), *International Politics: Enduring Concepts and Contemporary Issues*, New York: Longman, 2003, p.179.
28 K. Subrahmanyam, *Perspectives in Defence Planning*, New Delhi: Abhinav, 1972, pp.126–33.
29 L. Kavic, *India's Quest for Security: Defence Policies, 1947–1965*, Berkeley: University of California Press, 1967, p.192.
30 S. Gupta, 'No First Use Options', *Indian Express*, 17 January 2009. The problem for India was the advice from its military figures that India could not face a two-front war against China and Pakistan,

which might be sparked by any Indian action against Pakistan; see S. Srivastava, 'India Army "Backed Out" of Pakistan Attack', *Asia Times*, 21 January 2009. Ironically, India's military planners did, in 2010, move towards accepting such a two-front war against Pakistan and China simultaneously—see S. Kapila, 'China-Pakistan Military Nexus Formally Recognized in Indian Strategic Planning', Plainspeak (*Boloji*), 24 January 2010, www.boloji.com.

31 S. Khilnani, 'Hard, Soft and Bridging Power', *India Today*, 29 March 2004.

32 Hans J. Morgenthau, 'Vietnam: Shadow and Substance', *New York Review of Books*, 16 September 1965.

33 K. Nath, 'Dinner Address' (India as a Rising Great Power: Challenges and Opportunities, IISS), 18–20 April 2008, www.iiss.org.uk.

34 M. Sheehan, *The Balance of Power: History and Theory*, London: Routledge, 1996, p.7.

35 K. Subrahmanyam, *Indian Security Perspectives*, New Delhi: ABC Publishing House, 1982, p.127.

36 Ibid., p.34.

37 A. Tellis, *India's Emerging Nuclear Posture: Between Recessed Deterrent and Ready Arsenal*, New York: Oxford University Press, 2001, p.658.

38 K. Bajpai, 'Indian Strategic Culture', in M. Chambers (ed.), *South Asia in 2020: Future Strategic Balances and Alliances*, Carlisle: US Army War College, 2002.

3

India's 'power' attributes

Sreeram Chaulia

As the economic power, cultural reach, and political influence of India increase, it is assuming a more influential role in global affairs.

(US Department of Defense, *Quadrennial Defence Review*, 2010)

India can't actually compete with China in a number of areas, like international influence, overall national power and economic scale. India apparently has not yet realised this.

('India's Unwise Military Moves', *Global Times*, 11 June 2009)

Introduction: knocking on the door

Power in the international system has always remained concentrated in a select few hands instead of being equally or equitably distributed among all its constituent actors. While the normative domain of International Relations (IR) terminology contains concepts like equality of all sovereign nation-states in terms of status and dignity, the realm of *power politics* accepts and promotes hierarchy and vertical positioning of states within environments likened euphemistically to totem poles or food chains.

In this world of haves and have-nots, high tables and low tables, big leagues and small fries, consequential and trivial, gaining admittance into the sanctum sanctorum of accepted elite states is an ambition that several nurture but very few succeed in achieving. The failure rate is high because of the ultra-competitive nature of the struggle to rise up the ranks and to be acknowledged as already 'arrived' on the scene. Aspirants ('wannabes') of every era and different levels of vanity have tried knocking on the door of the hallowed portals of the Great Powers, but only the most capable and strategically astute players have crossed the threshold and remained inside on a sustainable basis.

Thanks to IR *realism* theory, the term 'capabilities' looms large in any discussion of a state's chances of making it into the charmed circle. Without taking stock of a state's arsenal of power attributes, i.e. the component strengths that make it a contender for the title of a crucial mover and shaker in world affairs, one cannot rationally assess claims and counter-claims about who really matters in a given international system. IR *realist* scholars have devoted ample space to classifying, categorizing and measuring states' core capabilities, giving us a rich (though incomplete) framework to begin evaluating countries on the power barometer.

This chapter draws on both IR *realist* literature as well as other theoretical camps, to size up the elements that constitute the might of one of the most currently talked-about states in world politics: India. Since the turn of the century, academics, practitioners and journalists commenting on the subject of which countries occupy the power list or are on their way onto it have tended to progressively give India a customary mention.[1] The world's largest democracy has frequently, somewhat to the consternation of Indians proud of their liberal political system, also been paired up with the People's Republic of China as the 'other' big mentionable Asian success story that must be reckoned with in international affairs.[2] The fact that both these Asian giants rode out practically unscathed from the global economic downturn since 2008 has only increased attention and focus on India as a special case, and a leader the power and presence of which are on the way up.[3] Observers interested in the changing global power configuration from *unipolarity* to *multipolarity* also regularly cite India as one among a few new centres of influence that are transforming the structure and processes of conducting international relations.[4]

What exactly has India done by way of steady accumulation of different elements of national power that is causing these bouts of expectation and optimism about its enhanced importance in the scheme of world politics? India's inventory of muscle must be counted and valued using theoretical measures of power to judge whether announcements of its indispensability to international relations in the contemporary age are premature, overblown or just right. This chapter argues that India's *hard* and *soft power* attributes have improved over the last decade, but that it suffers from internal and external bottlenecks that threaten to leave it permanently frozen in the 'not quite there' category of aspirants to the annals of Great Powers.

Military underdog to credible deterrent

In IR *realist* literature and the rulebooks of practical exponents of *realpolitik*, a state's capabilities are synonymous with its military sinews. To them, all roads in measuring power attributes lead to military potential because war is an ever-present reality in a competitive world with no world government and numerous latent or active strategic threats. Defence indicators hold the key to grading a self-interested state's power for realists, who envisage an international system that approximates 'state of nature' (Thomas Hobbes), where preparation for war is the best solution to optimize security and be respected or feared by other selfish states. To cite IR *neorealism* guru John Mearsheimer, 'I define power largely in military terms because offensive realism emphasises that force is the *ultima ratio* of world politics'.[5]

Conflictual mapping of the world, where another state may exploit relatively weak military or national security systems of one's own state and either launch an actual armed attack or engage in long-term destabilization, remains the hallmark of different variants of IR *realism*. Self-help doctrines that reflect IR *security dilemma* dynamics therefore insist that there is no short cut to constant military modernization and improvement of national security apparatuses to keep pace with or one step ahead of anticipated or surprise threats. In grand strategy, a true Great Power should have a strong and self-sufficient military with adept offensive and defensive abilities that have wide outreach to project power and meet political objectives far beyond one's own geographic confines.

The former Soviet strongman and instinctive realist, Joseph Stalin, once famously quipped that the Pope could hardly gain admission onto the main chess board of world politics because he lacked large, well-armed, trained and penetrative military 'divisions' under his command.

The Indian strategic elite woke up to this truism in 1962, when the people's Republic of China ambushed and vanquished the poorly equipped and under-prepared Indian army in a humiliating border war that Chairman Mao Zedong likened to a 'lesson' in gunpowder politics to a state he deemed a pushover.[6] Since this calamity, which still rankles in the memories of Indian nationalists, successive civilian governments and their advisers have stressed the imperative of continuous military renovation and upgrading of different segments of India's national defence architecture and doctrine. India's Cold War closeness to the USSR came in handy since the mid-1960s for raising the quality of its weapons systems, as Moscow had geopolitical incentives to offer New Delhi rupee payment-based 'sweetheart' import deals. In a foreign exchange and cash-strapped developing country saddled with a socialist 'Hindu rate of economic growth' and huge welfare state commitments to social sectors, the Soviet hand was crucial for India to match the military expansions in Pakistan and China, the two traditional continental foes, the relative capabilities of which were most cautiously watched by India. Concessionary imports of state-of-the-art Soviet weaponry during certain periods of spurts helped New Delhi assuage domestic critics and pressures about the foregone opportunity costs in terms of social sector budgetary allocations. However, the classic 'guns versus butter' dilemma of whether a poor democratic country could afford to 'crowd out' scarce resources to the military has often dragged down the Indian state's commitment to robust defence spending. Prominent economists and civil society groups have consistently demanded attention to the 'social costs of militarism',[7] especially in light of very low human development indices in the country.

A glance at the ebbs and flows in India's defence spending in the 1990s shows that the lows correspond with tight economic conditions, balance of payments crises and dependence on conditional foreign aid. IR *realists* from Hans Morgenthau to Kenneth Waltz have insisted that a sound and growing economy is essential to maintaining strong military capability. As long as India was economically growing at a snail's speed and remained a bound elephant, both purchasing power and domestic production infrastructure in the military sphere were limited due to pocketbook shortages. The remarkable surge in the Indian gross domestic product (GDP) rate since 2003, however, has eased the pecuniary restrictions somewhat and provided justification for greater investment in building the military into a potent 21st-century force befitting India's self-image as a future superpower. None the less, despite media-labelled 'whopping' increases in defence spending over the last several years, India continues to have relatively moderate military expenditure averaging around 2% of GDP. Laments from strategists and long-range planners that such outlays are 'grossly inadequate' and need to be reaching 3.5% of GDP by 2015[8] do not always find favour among civilian politicians, who tend to be reactive on national security needs and are more amenable to opening the purse immediately after a war or a major terrorist attack.

Electoral compulsions of ruling parties, including the urge to spend largesse on populist welfare schemes to win votes, have also held back India from keeping the defence spending-to-GDP ratio on a par with undemocratic China or Pakistan. The lobbying power and valid arguments of the three wings of the Indian military—army, navy and air force—and of their civilian counterparts in the Ministry of Defence to increase allocations for hardware purchases, research and development, and personnel costs[9] does not fully convince India's crafty civilian political top brass. The irony here is that India, which unlike many of its neighbours in South Asia has remained stubbornly democratic and free of armed *coups d'état*, has a civil-military relations problem when it comes to critical issues like army pay scales, creating an integrated Chief of Defence Staff (CDS), decisions about materiel procurement, etc.[10] Serious lacunae continue to also hinder the growth of a self-sufficient military industrial complex in India that integrates civilian politicians, the armed forces and the private sector. Unlike Great Powers like

25

the P-5 Permanent Members of the UN Security Council (China, France, Russia, the USA and the United Kingdom), India does not have a cutting edge domestic military manufacturing base of its own. Lack of an indigenous military technical base has often been exposed like a sore thumb whenever prestigious models of combat equipment that were conceived for home-based production failed to be delivered, under-performed in battle or underwent cost and time overruns. Patronage-style politics in awarding contracts only to parastatals have survived in the touch-me-not defence sector, even though the rest of Indian industry has enjoyed the benefits of economic liberalization since 1991.[11] The 'commanding heights' argument to defend closure of defence production from competitive private bidders has come in for criticism from Indian analysts concerned about over-dependence of the military on foreign suppliers like Russia, Israel, France, the United Kingdom and the USA, but to no avail. Huge kickbacks in opaque defence import deals have created a permanent vested interest within the Indian bureaucratic machine for buying weapons rather than encouraging the rise of transparent domestically made alternatives.[12] As with other ills that often defeat India's hope of climbing the ladder of world power, the glaring inability to establish a competent local arms industry for use and export can be blamed on the country's notorious lack of good governance, a structural malaise that percolates through the body politic.

One of the bright spots for which India does get noticed world-wide for military prowess is its navy, the value of which as a force multiplier for the country's global power projection has risen with foreign policy shifts of the last two decades. Some Indian policy specialists have bemoaned the country's ossified 'continental mentality' that is obsessed with meeting land-based threats, primarily from Pakistan and China, and have sought strategic reorientation that capitalizes on the vast oceanic reach of a true world-class 'blue water' navy.[13] Given that all landed territory on the planet is demarcated and parcelled out into sovereign boundaries that are not to be legally trespassed by state armies, and the extreme sensitivity and zealousness with which national airspaces are monitored and protected, the only relatively free spaces in which a state's military can stretch far beyond its immediate environs are the high seas. Extension by means of a navy into 'out of area' waters has been an old strategy of empires world-wide, including the medieval-era south Indian Cholas who spread their vast political influence from Sri Lanka to Indonesia, Cambodia and Viet Nam through advanced naval formations.

It is these very South-East Asian pastures that were rediscovered by New Delhi in the 1990s as valuable for furthering India's trade and strategic interests. Dubbed the 'Look East' policy, India entered into sustained involvement in building military and economic agreements with South-East Asian countries with an implicit objective of acting as a strategic counterweight to a menacingly powerful China. The Indian Navy is central to this policy and has been deployed for joint exercises and patrols along with likeminded partner states in the South China Sea, which have a host of island disputes with China and are nervous about becoming subservient to the dragon. India's navy was also a principal in five-nation exercises in the Bay of Bengal between 2007 and 2009 that included participation from the navies of Japan, Australia and the USA, which were also eager to balance the rising Chinese sphere of influence in South-East and East Asia. On the westward horizon, too, India's navy grabbed world attention in the last few years by dispatching naval ships to the Gulf of Aden off Yemen and Somalia to try and help rein in the international scourge of piracy through strong-arm methods.[14] How successfully India's diplomats and navy can ward off China's so-called 'string of pearls' strategy of building naval bases in and around the Indian Ocean will be another theatre that will be closely scrutinized as a mark of Great Power-like behaviour.

India's de facto nuclear weapons power status since 1998 is another factor that has earned it grudging recognition as a major player in international relations. By shedding a decades-long ambiguous closet nuclear power position and testing atomic devices, India crossed a Rubicon and stoically endured Western sanctions, Pakistani tit-for-tat tests and Chinese condemnation. With a reported arsenal of 60 to 70 nuclear warheads and a capacity to build bombs with yields of up to 200 kilotons, India has managed to raise hackles both in Islamabad and Beijing for steadfastly pursuing a burning 'desire to become a world power'.[15] Admittedly, possession of nuclear weapons has not shielded India from sub-threshold war with Pakistan in 1999 or a barrage of non-conventional terrorist threats from Islamist *jihadist* outfits. The psychological impact of a New Delhi that keeps and updates a credible nuclear deterrent, including a retaliatory strike capability deliverable from a 'triad' of land-, air- and sea-based platforms, is bound to dissuade the conventionally superior Chinese military in the context of a long drawn-out border dispute and intense strategic competition between the two Asian colossi. To preserve moving goalposts of deterrence, New Delhi has resisted US calls to sign the Comprehensive Test Ban Treaty by forwarding the precondition of Beijing and Washington inking the dotted line first. Whether India can convert its nuclear weapons capability into concrete security and political gains in the international arena remains a key subject area of interest in the coming decades.

Neither Hans Morgenthau's 'elements of national power', nor Kenneth Waltz's 'determinants of state capabilities' were compiled during times when terrorism by state-backed or independent violent non-state actors had become a national security nightmare in the West. India's self-description as one of the world's longest suffering victims of cross-border terrorism emanating from Pakistan (and secondarily, Bangladesh) necessitates evaluation of counter-terrorism capacity as an integral ingredient of its overall military power. Securing India's disputed borders with antagonistic neighbour Pakistan has been an ordeal in peacetime since independence because of the latter's resort to non-regular Islamist *mujahideen* (holy warriors) infiltrators who are ideologically zealous about 'freeing' Kashmir and are unafraid of death.[16] India's armed forces and paramilitaries have, over time, learnt lessons and managed to stem the flow and movement of *jihadists* from Pakistan-controlled Kashmir into the Indian-controlled part, but not a year goes by without fresh reports of successful ingress and brutal slayings of innocent civilians by terrorists who sneak into Indian territory, often under cover of artillery shelling by the regular Pakistani army.[17] While the defensive shields against Pakistani *jihadists* are being beefed-up, especially since the completion of a protective fence along the border in Kashmir and efforts to improve domestic policing, India's counter-offensive capability to deter terrorist outfits based in Pakistan has not materialized at all. While there is no dearth of Indian intelligence penetration in Pakistani society and the state apparatus,[18] India has been unable to penetrate Pakistan's state-backed *Lashkar-e-Taiba* (LeT) and *Jaish-e-Muhammad* (JeM) conglomerates. Although an Indian military head claimed after a deadly Pakistan-abetted terrorist attack in early 2002 that his forces had concrete information of training camps and hideouts of Pakistani *jihadist* groups on Pakistani soil, and could destroy them with a barrage of missiles or aerial bombardment if they got the political green light,[19] no concrete action has been undertaken to raise the costs of *jihad*. After the outrage caused by the Mumbai terror attacks of December 2008 and demands for prompt retaliation, this option of covert, plausibly deniable and targeted anti-terror strikes was again spoken about in strategic circles,[20] but nothing seems to have come of it. India habitually wrings its hands that wanted terrorist ringleaders roam about freely in Pakistan (and to a lesser extent in Bangladesh and Nepal) with state cover and patronage, but this does not succeed in changing the behaviour of nettlesome neighbours. In this context, it is doubtful whether an Indian state 'that is repeatedly defenceless against the infiltration and impunity of religious zealots from across its border [can] be considered a Great Power'.[21] A 'flabby state' that keeps muddling through with routine intelligence and security failures and presents itself like a sitting duck for terrorists to raid and destroy at will is not going to be taken seriously in its own backyard, not to mention on the wider world stage.[22]

One of the ironies of India's external image as an Information Technology superpower is that it has been subjected to several waves of cyber attacks by 'hacktivists' from Pakistan and China, who intend to wage a propaganda war, spy on sensitive diplomatic data and disrupt the communication infrastructure. This author was informed by senior Indian intelligence officials in charge of cyber-defence and counter-attack operations that China is by far the most sophisticated threat in this realm and that Beijing is further ahead in the game than New Delhi. On numerous occasions in the past few years, hackers traceable to mainland China have managed to breach the information systems of India's elite governmental circles, including the Ministry of External Affairs, the Office of the National Security Adviser and the Prime Minister's Office.[23] China's lead in this powerful new capability is owing to an uncharacteristically liberal environment fostered by the communist authorities for strategically minded cyber-criminals to set up base and operate on the world-wide web without fear of repercussions. India was relatively slower to start down this path, due to inbuilt techno-illiteracy and the wariness of ageing bureaucrats who man the national security structure, as well as turf battles among different ministries over which agency should be leading the cyber-war programme. An infusion of young blood, however, especially from among the brainy IT 'whiz kids' in the country's private sector, has begun to raise the level of India's capability to thwart Chinese and other cyber attackers from wreaking havoc. The realization that 21st-century warfare will rely greatly on information domination has grown in Indian strategic thinking, and plenty of budgetary resources have been placed at the command of the country's cyber sentinels to tap into the nation's vast pool of talented computer engineers and 'netizens' for intercepting threats and also turning them on the perpetrators.

The unbound elephant

Economic growth and vitality are universally viewed as quintessential power attributes of a state, and underpin the Manmohan Doctrine on Indian foreign policy. IR *realist* scholars from Morgenthau and Waltz up to Mearsheimer accord prime place to economic factors in measuring the total power of states, because a bouncing and competitive economy can devote more resources to the defence sector and convert healthy GDP into relatively greater military might. IR *liberal* figures like Robert Keohane concur with IR *realists* on this point and emphasize that 'economic strength is ultimately the basis for economic and military power'.[24] The economy has also been the central explanatory variable for the genre of 'declinism' (Samuel Huntington, Paul Kennedy) in IR, which attempts to identify general theoretical laws for the rise and fall of Great Powers throughout history. The collective wisdom of rationalist IR traditions is also shared by the mass media and popular perceptions that a rising or accomplished Great Power can be identified by its inherent economic dynamism, productivity, and ability to keep growing in size and quality. Much of the commentary about the increasing power of the BRIC countries (Brazil, Russia, India and China) and the concomitant decline of the Organisation for Economic Co-operation and Development (OECD) countries stems from the former's increasing share in the world economy and the latter's stagnation and recessionary crises that seem to be structurally incorrigible.[25]

India itself began to be re-evaluated in much of global consciousness as a powerful state only after it entered a higher economic growth trajectory of over 8% per annum since 2003, touching 10.1% in the third quarter of 2006.[26] To be spoken of in the same league as China, India had to raise and then sustain GDP growth at such a fast rate. That has been achieved due to a combination of two phases of liberalization of state controls on the economy, inflow of vast amounts of foreign investment, and exposure of Indian producers to foreign competition. A surge in the manufacturing sector and continued expansion in the service sectors (finance, insurance, real estate, telecoms, software and IT-enabled services) have underpinned the post-2003 boom,[27] which slowed during the initial shock of the global financial crisis in 2008–09, but recovered during 2009–10 to reach 7.4% for the whole year, having accelerated still further back up to 8.8% in the second quarter of 2010. Because domestic consumption drove the bulk of the Indian economy, most of its sectors succeeded in weathering the post-2008 global contagion of steep falls in foreign consumer demand and loss of export markets.

Economists are bullish about India's long-term prospects because it is widely perceived to possess the appropriate 'fundamentals'. For instance, researchers at Credit Suisse reckon that the country's 'favourable demographics, a low urbanization rate and still rising savings and investment rates', will ensure that 'capital stock (machinery, physical infrastructure etc), labour and their productivity, will grow rapidly over the next decade, sustaining high real GDP growth rates'.[28] Population profile is, in particular, propitious for the Indian economy because the country's dependency ratio (proportion of non-working to working people) is likely to fall further, triggering a virtuous cycle of even higher domestic savings, capital accumulation and investment. With an ageing population, China's economic growth is predicted to slow down by 2020, while India 'will be the locomotive of the future [...] until the middle of this century'.[29]

Yet, it is clear that simply enjoying a preponderance of young, productive workers in the labour force does not automatically generate positives unless India goes into public policy overdrive to train and equip its teeming millions with skills. Skills shortfalls in the vocational and technical spheres have been described as an ugly 'underbelly of India's demographic dividend', with as many as 80% of workers lacking the qualities consistent with job market requirements.[30] While India gets praised for highly qualified human capital in the applied sciences like medicine and engineering, the supply of skilled manpower still falls short of the demands of what is touted as the second fastest growing economy in the world. Massive private and public investment in the education system and reorienting its basics are imperatives for upgrading young Indians' skill sets and increasing their productivity. The yield-per-worker stands to gain impressively if various government- and industry-proposed reforms to give education a practical tinge are effectively implemented.

The other big lacuna that holds India's economy back is the substandard condition of its infrastructure, which raises the costs of economic transactions, and lowers efficiency and profitability. India's roads, bridges, airports, seaports, electricity grids and clean water utilities are chronically under-supplied, deficient, crumbling or outright non-existent, especially in rural areas. Economist Jagdish Bhagwati has calculated that GDP growth could easily go two percentage points higher if the country built up 'decent roads, railways and power'.[31] Chronic paucity of electricity is a blight that brooks no short-term solution because of surging demand, depleting coal resources and limited hydro electric power potential. The much-touted India-US civilian nuclear deal was sold by the Manmohan Singh Government as one of the solutions to power shortages, but nuclear power may well remain only a small speck in India's overall energy mix for decades to come. Unless terms for private investment in the infrastructure sector are made more lucrative, the gap between aspiration to world-class amenities and the moribund reality will keep haunting India's self-image as an emerging powerhouse.

Unlike China, which has taken long strides in recent years by investing in alternative fuels that are green-tinted, India seems to remain in the familiar territory of failing to fully grasp future trends and then having to play catch-up with global leaders. China has moved from sixth

(2007) and fourth (2008) to second (2009) in an Ernst & Young ranking of countries for attractiveness for investment in renewable energy, while India fell to fourth position (2009) from a high of third (2008).[32] Competition for investing early in green technologies is tight and India is not doing badly, but it remains to be seen if its relatively weaker industrial base compared with China will in the long run also leave India behind in the capacity to produce for its own domestic energy needs and to export Indian innovations world-wide. It is possible that China's 'Green Leap Forward' will outdistance India by a wide margin, just as it has done in the overall economic growth race.[33]

India has been held up by liberals as a shining counter-example to the 'Asian values' theory of former Singaporean strongman Lee Kuan Yew that authoritarian political systems and social values facilitate rapid economic growth.[34] India's spectacular economic achievements since 2003, in spite of a resilient and contentious democracy, reconfirm the country's exceptional status as an outlier that does not neatly fit positivist social science explanations. Yet, the compulsions of electoral politics in a hard-fought democracy have sometimes held back necessary market-based economic reforms which could have set the growth rate at a gallop. Inflexible labour laws, high fiscal deficits due to large agrarian subsidies, and resistance to privatization of public sector firms have been identified by scholars as hurdles to speeding up economic growth that remain unaddressed due to their political sensitivity and short-term vote-loss ramifications for India's elected representatives.[35] One exponent of quickening the pace of economic reforms commented nearly a decade ago that 'too much democracy and not enough capitalism', and 'placing politics before economics' were two big obstacles to unleashing the full potential of India's economic capabilities.[36] Tremendous social churning, redistributive impulses and opportunities presented by the ballot box are indeed paradoxically the causes of India's stable polity and imperfect economy. Since coalition politics, where no single party is capable of forming governments at the central level on its own, has become a permanent feature on the Indian scene, demands for 'liberalizing with a human face' and protecting uncompetitive sectors of the economy to avoid painful adjustment costs will act as speed breakers on the growth rate until long-term shifts occur in the class structure of Indian society itself.

One actionable growth-catalysing strategy that is not structurally precluded by domestic political compulsions is the execution of creative foreign economic diplomacy, an arena in which India has been found to be relatively wanting. New Delhi has always maintained friendly relations with oil-rich Arab countries in the Middle East and taken a pro-Palestinian stand in the Arab–Israeli conflict because of its heavy dependence on remittances and imported petroleum products from that region.[37] Newer energy fountainheads emerged in recent decades in Africa, Central Asia and Latin America, though, demanding a focused effort on India's part to approach these hitherto neglected regions with the right mix of economic incentives and geostrategic selling points. 'Energy security' became a buzz phrase as the Indian economy grew, but the alacrity and thoroughness with which one had to make a timely entry in targeted markets to lock in assured supplies of hydrocarbons was missing. By the time the Indian Government had appointed an Advisory Committee on Oil Diplomacy for Energy Security in late 2004, China had already zeroed-in on African oil giants like Angola and Nigeria with the full might of bilateral foreign aid and infrastructure-building promises as a cushion for Chinese petroleum majors to go on acquiring exclusive extraction rights and reserving oil blocks at a dizzying rate. In 2007 Beijing formed a giant sovereign wealth fund, the China Investment Corporation (CIC), to help state-run companies aggressively acquire oil, coal and metal assets abroad. India was again late in discovering the benefits of this public-private partnership model to enhance its economic footprint and secure assured energy channels. It was only in March 2010 that the Ministry of Petroleum floated the idea of a sovereign fund by setting aside part of India's

US $254,000m. in foreign exchange reserves to assist Indian energy majors 'take on competition from their Chinese counterparts'.[38] The spectacle of India losing bids to China or not even figuring in competition for energy rights in countries as far ranging as Iran and Kazakhstan to Argentina is a dampener for economic expansion and a reality check of how far-reaching New Delhi's global ambit is. In 2003 former banker Percy Mistry wrote that economic diplomacy was 'becoming a much more important plank in overall foreign policy than countries like India (and their rigid bureaucratic and ignorant political establishments) have as yet recognised, although countries like China have done so some time ago'.[39] That gap in alertness to seizing economic opportunities at the international level with *savoir faire* still persists between India and China and accentuates the latter's lead in striking deals for a flurry of regional/preferential trading agreements and market-opening opportunities for Chinese corporations.[40]

Lovable Asian hulk?

Of the categories of power that add up to the collective national strength of a state, *soft power* has received increasing attention ever since the liberal scholar Joseph Nye invented the concept in 1990. The ability of a state to influence and lead other states through attraction and good will has been central to the hegemony of the USA in the post-Second World War and post-Cold War eras. The belief that the USA and its socio-economic institutions, like Wall Street and Hollywood, worked not only for their own interests but in the general interests of world order by spreading public good like security, free markets and universal entertainment, underpinned US global leadership until the disastrous 'war on terrorism' and the collapse of the financial sector. The noticeable fall in favourability ratings of the USA in international public opinion over the last decade, the decade of President George W. Bush, was a critical factor in ending the unipolar moment since 1991 and taking the world towards *multipolarity*. If the traditional analysis of the waxing and waning of dominant states is overloaded with *hard power* variables like military and economic strength, the media- and opinion-saturated information age is bound to elevate the importance of *soft power* in the overall power calculations for any state.

India began its journey as a self-determining state in 1947 with a *soft power* bang that faded away after its greatest exponent, the country's first Prime Minister Jawaharlal Nehru, died in 1964. In the Nehru years, India was a pygmy in *hard power* indices, but a giant in *soft power*, in which Indian foreign policy was global in scope and based on universally appealing concepts such as peaceful co-existence and distributional equity in the world economy. The number of diplomatic forays Nehru made into distant conflicts around the world was dizzying and brought instant liking and recognition for India as a responsible Asian country that was trying to solve global problems.[41] However, a narrowing of India's domain of foreign policy interest due to generational change in political leadership and the harsh realities of war with China and Pakistan reduced the country's *soft power* range and limited it, at best, to the status of a South Asian hegemon. Ironically, even as India practically disappeared as an actor with influence in far-flung regions of the Global South like Africa and Latin America by the turn of the century, it began to improve its *hard power* attributes by logging higher economic growth and military prowess. Counter-factually, if only India's current leadership and strategic elite corps had the global vision of a Nehru, they could work wonders for the country's image and reputation because they sit atop ever-accumulating *hard power* of which Nehru could only dream. The attitudinal change required in India's foreign policy bureaucracy to reorient itself and redefine India's sphere of interest in global rather than regional or continental proportions has not yet occurred, however. The status quo is riddled with an obsession for happenings in the immediate neighbourhood, neglect of political developments in geographically distant parts of the world and their potential impact on India's fundamental long-term projected foreign policy ambitions. A paucity of endogenous knowledge accumulation in IR theory and application in Indian academia and policy-making has also condemned the strategic discourse in the country to be a mere recipient of new thinking about statecraft from overseas rather than producing its own recognizable brand of action in world politics that could be admired or emulated by others. Unlike China, for instance, which has coined the catchy phrase 'peaceful rise' to portray its own ascent in international power standings and has built a coherent literature and narrative to go with it, India finds itself intellectually handicapped in confecting long-term foreign policy planning mantras that would set it apart as a desirable state the upward mobility of which is mostly welcomed, not feared.

India has bristled in recent years at being depicted as a spoiler state on keystone issues underpinning the international system such as nuclear non-proliferation, climate change and multilateral trade, but an image problem has persisted that India is a country that flouts global norms and acts exclusively for narrow self-interest.[42] To an extent, India can claim to be victim of a vilification campaign by Western media houses that are unable to digest the ongoing power shift to Asia, but the country's rulers have not given enough thought to branding India's foreign policy and unique domestic social attributes like pluralism, democracy and tolerance to the level that authoritarian China has done through its masterful 'charm offensive'.[43] India has not leveraged its core strength, its vast pool of English-speaking mathematics, engineering and medical graduates, to good effect when they could easily spearhead the country's overseas aid missions and earn much-needed international empathy. India's vibrant cultural exports like Bollywood films, yoga, spirituality and the *Kamasutra* definitely count in slowly rebuilding its *soft power* points tally, but there does not appear to be a methodical plan co-ordinating state and civil society to purposefully expand them on a global scale in the way China has managed through its burgeoning Confucius Institutes. Better utilization of the country's finest minds for public relations and diplomacy overseas remains one of the many items in India's overflowing 'to do' list.

Conclusions

In 2003 the nuclear specialist George Perkovich concluded on the basis of an itemized checklist that India, 'must make great strides before it can attain significant power over other states and thus in the international system at large'.[44] Since that time, the Indian economy has been a flag bearer for the national quest to be accepted as a genuine Great Power. Economic growth remains India's main claim for entry into the hallowed portals of influential states, and this attribute is likely to keep impressing itself on the rest of the world with even bigger voice in decades to come. Should infrastructure revamping and skilling of the population succeed, the sky's the limit for India's entrepreneurial energies, as outlined in former President Abdul Kalam's writings.[45] Simultaneous enhancements are warranted for India's *soft power*, which can be augmented by harnessing the country's talented sections of the labour force and introducing an element of creativity, flexibility and global vision into foreign policy. India's military has a silver lining, but will have to undergo revolutionary upgrade in capacity and sharpness before becoming a compelling force that advances strategic goals and has systemic impact on international peace and security. The dreadful epithet of a 'soft state' that cannot determine its own security environment and is always at the mercy of external powers is a burdensome one that India has borne shamefacedly without attempting to forcefully shake it off. Movement in a direction where India bends the international system to suit its preferences is still not on the horizon. This is, of course, also dependent on the relative power of other states, but if one accepts the realist picturization of a self-help world where each state builds its own capacity to the maximum and hopes that its accumulation of power proves sufficient, India has to pull up its socks in the different realms of practice and policy outlined in this essay and there is still some way to go. To recall the historic mission outlined by Kautilya, the ancient Indian advocate of *realpolitik*, 'always endeavour to augment power and elevate happiness'.[46]

Notes

1 Some have given India serious 'power' consideration, like S. Cohen, *India: Emerging Power*, Washington, DC: Brookings Institution Press, 2001; A. Tellis, 'India as a New Global Power: An Action Agenda for the United States', Washington, DC: Carnegie Endowment for International Peace, 2005; 'India a Rising and Responsible Global Power: Obama', *Indo-Asian News Service*, 25 November 2009.
2 R. Meredyth, *The Elephant and the Dragon: The Rise of India and China, and What it Means for the Rest of Us*, New York: W.W. Norton, 2007; P. Engardio (ed.), *Chindia: How China and India are Revolutionising Global Business*, Columbus: McGraw-Hill, 2006.
3 K. Brown, 'China and India Lead Asian Recovery', *Financial Times*, 4 January 2010.
4 K. Mahbubani, *The New Asian Hemisphere: The Irresistible Shift of Global Power to the East*, New York: PublicAffairs, 2008; F. Zakaria, *The Post-American World*, New York: W.W. Norton, 2008.
5 J. Mearsheimer, *The Tragedy of Great Power Politics*, New York: W.W. Norton, 2003, p.56.
6 C. Arpi, *Tibet: The Lost Frontier*, New Delhi: Lancer Publishers, 2008.
7 Cf. J. Dreze and A. Sen, *India: Development and Participation*, New Delhi: Oxford University Press, 2002, ch. 8.
8 V. Raghuvanshi, 'India Eyes Fund Hike, Returns Revenues', *Defense News*, 22 September 2008.
9 'Antony Favours Defence Budget at 3 Percent of GDP', *Indo-Asian News Service*, 10 June 2008.
10 For instance, there is simmering mistrust between civilian authorities and military thinkers on the question of usurpation of the former's powers if the office of a CDS is instituted. See S.K. Sinha, 'The Chief of Defence Staff', *Journal of Defence Studies*, Vol. 1, No. 1, 2007.
11 A. Shukla, 'DRDO: More Failures than Successes', *Business Standard*, 9 May 2006.
12 N. Kaushal, 'India's Defense Budget: Can it be Reduced?', *Occasional Paper* (University of Illinois at Urbana-Champaign), 1995.
13 A. Prakash, *From the Crow's Nest: A Compendium of Speeches and Writings on Maritime and Other Issues*, New Delhi: Lancer Publishers, 2007. Also D. Scott, 'India's Drive for a "Blue Water" Navy', *Journal of Military and Strategic Studies*, Vol. 10, No. 2, 2007–08.
14 S. Chaulia, 'Indian Navy Comes of Age', *The Hindu*, 21 November 2008.
15 S. Wei and X. Pingting, 'India Raises Nuclear Stakes with 200-Kiloton Bombs', *Global Times*, 29 September 2009.
16 P. Swami, *India, Pakistan and the Secret Jihad: The Covert War in Kashmir, 1947–2004*, London: Routledge, 2007.
17 'Infiltration from Pakistan Increased in 2009: Army Chief', *Indo-Asian News Service*, 14 January 2010.
18 See, for instance, M.K. Dhar, *Mission to Pakistan – An Intelligence Agent in Pakistan*, New Delhi: Manas Publications, 2002.
19 'Army Chief's Warning to Islamabad', *News Behind the News*, 14 January 2002.
20 S. Srivastava, 'India Army "Backed Out" of Pakistan Attack', *Asia Times*, 21 January 2009.
21 S. Chaulia, 'India: Great Power or Not?', *The Globalist*, 9 December 2008.
22 S. Chaulia, 'India Caught in a Terror Tangle', *Asia Times*, 11 December 2009.
23 R. Beeston and J. Page, 'China Tried to Hack Our Computers, Says India's National Security Chief M.K. Narayanan', *The Times*, 18 January 2010.
24 R. Keohane, *Power and Governance in a Partially Globalised World*, London: Routledge, 2002, p.63.
25 M. Deen, 'The West's Share of Global GDP Set to Fall', *Financial Express*, 3 June 2009.
26 T. Poddar and E. Yi, 'India's Rising Growth Potential', in *BRICS and Beyond*, Washington, DC: Goldman Sachs, 2007.
27 C. Chandrasekhar and J. Ghosh, 'What Explains the High GDP Growth?', *Business Line*, 11 September 2007.
28 'Resilient India to Grow at an Average of 8 pc Till 2014', *Deccan Herald*, 13 January 2010.
29 I. Png, 'Watch India – It May Outgrow China', *Straits Times*, 23 February 2010.
30 A. Palit, 'Let's Get Technical', *Financial Express*, 26 December 2009.

31 'The Trouble With India', *Business Week*, 19 March 2007.
32 *Renewable Energy Country Attractiveness Indices*, London: Ernst & Young, November 2009.
33 T. Friedman, 'Who's Sleeping Now?', *International Herald Tribune*, 9 January 2010.
34 A. Waldman, 'In India, Economic Growth and Democracy Do Mix', *New York Times*, 23 May 2004.
35 A. Varshney, 'India's Democratic Challenge', *Foreign Affairs*, Vol. 86, No. 2, 2007.
36 G. Das, *The Elephant Paradigm – India Wrestles With Change*, New Delhi: Penguin, 2001.
37 'India, Arab World Boost Ties, Sign Pact', *Indo-Asian News Service*, 2 December 2008.
38 N. Mohammad, 'Sovereign Wealth for Energy Assets?', *Financial Express*, 24 March 2010.
39 P. Mistry, 'Rethinking India's International Economic Diplomacy', *Economic and Political Weekly*, Vol. 38, No. 28, 2003, p.2947.
40 N. Batra, 'Bullish in China Shop', *Times of India*, 15 October 2009.
41 S. Chaulia, 'India's Soft Power: Lessons from Nehru', *Indo-Asian News Service*, 12 March 2007.
42 See, for instance, B. Crossette, 'The Elephant in the Room', *Foreign Policy,* January/February 2010.
43 J. Kurlantzick, *Charm Offensive: How China's Soft Power is Transforming the World*, Connecticut: Yale University Press, 2007. See C. Raja Mohan, 'Balancing Interests and Values: India's Struggle with Democracy Promotion', *Washington Quarterly*, Vol. 30, No. 3, 2007, for juggling of imperatives by India.
44 G. Perkovich, 'Is India a Major Power?', *Washington Quarterly*, Vol. 27, No. 1, 2003.
45 A. Kalam, *Ignited Minds: Unleashing the Power Within India*, New Delhi: Penguin, 2002; A. Kalam and Y. Rajan, *India 2020: A Vision for the New Millennium*, New Delhi: Penguin Books India, 2003. His emphasis on technological creativity being the gateway for an 'empowered nation' was a feature of his *Addresses to the Nation* speeches during 2003–07. See also A. Kalam, *Envisioning an Empowered Nation: Technology for Societal Transformation*, Noida: Tata McGraw-Hill, 2004.
46 Kautilya, *Kautilya's Arthasastra*, tr. R. Shamasastry, Bangalore: Government Press, 1915, Book VI, p.325.

4

Geopolitics for India

Robert Stewart-Ingersoll and Derrick V. Frazier

Introduction

After experiencing relatively slow and erratic economic growth for most of its post-independence history, India has now grabbed the attention of the world with its rapid rise over the past two decades. When its economic growth is combined with its size, its critically important location and its self-perception as the 'natural hegemon' of South Asia[1] (and indeed the Indian Ocean for India's maritime exponents), India's geopolitical and strategic importance within regional and global politics appears to be moving on a steep upward trajectory.

Here, 'geopolitics' uses Kristof's sense of 'strategic writings' (like India's 2007 *Maritime Military Strategy*), in which 'the element of space, the distribution of raw materials and populations, strategic routes, and other similar factors of national power potential and military strength are taken into consideration and evaluated in terms of certain known political objectives'.[2] Examination here of the geopolitics of India thus focuses on the strategic incorporation of territorial and maritime interests and resources into its foreign policy, as well as considering the implications of India's rise and expansion with respect to the strategic interests of other significant actors that geographically interact and impinge on India's political horizons. An important wider trend to note is the increasing importance of regional systems (the Regional Security Complex—RSC) as venues within which many of the most critical security dynamics operate, and within which are located the most pressing securitized issues for most members of the international system.[3]

In this chapter, we address the territorially based interests upon which India is focused both within its own borders as well as with regard to the South Asian RSC. After a brief general discussion about its strategic relationship with its own RSC, we consider two specifically geopolitical issue areas that are relevant to India's strategic position within South Asia and beyond, namely the relevance of India's internal separatist movements and territorial disputes with neighbouring states. Second, we explore the expansion of India's power and strategic interests beyond South Asia, focusing on its increasing strategic interest and 'footprint' within the Indian Ocean littoral. It is in this area that India has the most salience as an emerging power, and in which its strategic interests are coming into direct contact with those of external Great Powers. In any drive to make the Indian subcontinent India's continent, and to shape the Indian Ocean as India's Ocean, geopolitics are involved.

Indian geopolitics within South Asia

India as a regional power

The strategic interactions and security concerns of the vast majority of states are focused upon their immediate neighbourhoods. This is true for small and Great Powers alike, and is the result of a decidedly geographical factor: distance. In the first place, power degrades as distance increases. The capacity of most state and non-state actors to project capabilities is most pronounced within close range. In the second place, most security threats emerge from proximate areas. This is particularly true with regard to those threats dealing directly with geography, such as territorial or water disputes. Thus, space matters, and particularly with respect to geopolitics.

Our contention is that the South Asian region reflects a unipolar system in which no other member comes close to possessing the power capabilities of India.[4] Further, India perceives itself to be the natural and de facto 'hegemon' within the Indian subcontinent.[5] Nevertheless, India has not behaved as a regional power, for it has not consistently, effectively, or comprehensively played a role in developing a means through which regional security problems are prepared for and addressed within South Asia. Nor has it consistently, effectively, or comprehensively been able to manage security problems that have arisen within the region—even those which directly affect its own geopolitical interests and which it has attempted to manage. Finally, it has been unable, in spite of a clear desire to do so, to deflect external Great Powers from significant interventions in its region.

We can now focus on two specific issue areas that are reflective of these contentions, and which directly relate to geopolitics: India's internal militant movements and border disputes. They represent but do not exhaust the areas in which India lacks command of its region. This broader issue is connected to the geopolitics of India, though in the sense that it not only deals in many cases with geographically related strategic issues, but it also calls into question the capacity and/or willingness of India to effectively project its power across a space that is the most proximate and in which it has no peer. If it does not or cannot effectively do this within the South Asian confines, the merit of its claim to be a Great Power is called into question.

Internal militant movements

The first critical overlap between geography and politics that can be considered is the integrity of the Indian state itself. Not only does this involve a link between geography and politics at the most fundamental level, but the resolution of India's internal geopolitical problems is to a large extent a prerequisite for its capacity to effectively project its influence across still greater distances. In the Indian case, this integrity involves the maintenance of the existing sovereign borders, the capacity of the government to project order and govern within these borders, and arguably the maintenance of the nation's government as one that operates according to a democratic system. None of these criteria are firmly secure. Harsh Pant argues that 'India is witnessing a gradual collapse in the authority of the state. From left-wing extremism to right-wing religious fundamentalism, the nation is facing multiple challenges that threaten to derail the story of a rising India'.[6]

Internal insurgencies might not typically be considered central to an exploration of geopolitics; they do not seem to reflect examples of the sort of strategic thinking that was identified above as being representative of geopolitics. However, overlooking these internal challenges within such a chapter on geopolitics would be a mistake for at least three reasons. First, the consolidation of control within the state's borders is essentially related to the connection between geography and politics, and the effective projection of power. Second, the relationship between some insurgency and terrorist groups within India to other states (notably Pakistan and Bangladesh) points to a connection between internal struggles and India's efforts to project power and pursue broader strategies outside of its borders. Finally, the potential for these challenges to undermine India's sustained growth is intimately related to India's interest in being recognized as a Great Power in and outside its region.

While India's enormous Muslim population (the second largest in the world) long remained largely uninvolved in transnational terrorism, this has not recently been the case. Rather, Indian Muslims have become active in terrorist organizations, and India has become a central target of terrorist attacks.[7] Groups such as the Indian *mujahideen* (IM), the Indian Security Force—Indian *mujahideen* (ISF-IM), and the Students' Islamic Movement of India (SIMI) have claimed responsibility for numerous attacks in recent years.[8] This increasing internal activity presents a threat to each of the above criteria for maintenance of state integrity. Further, the radicalization of these groups is coinciding and associated with the rise of radical right-wing Hindu groups, as well as the undermining of certain bedrock principles of Indian democracy, such as tolerance, dissent and limits on government action.[9]

It would be a mistake to contend, however, that the internal threat to India's integrity and ascent toward Great Power status is limited to Islamist terrorist groups. India also confronts a number of separatist groups, as well as Maoist (referred to as Naxalite) insurgencies. The most notable examples of recent separatist conflicts within India have been within the north-eastern states of Manipur and Assam, where various groups within these territories wish to establish independent homelands based upon tribal and ethnic identity. The insurgency campaigns by the United Liberation Front of Assam (ULFA) and the National Socialist Council of Nagaland (NSCN) have led to 20,000 fatalities since the mid-1980s. The ULFA, in particular, has been the beneficiary of financial and military support from Bangladeshi and Pakistani intelligence agencies. While there has been a relatively high level of violence in recent years associated with these conflicts, there is hope of progress. For instance, a formal cease-fire has been put into place with the National Democratic Front of Bodoland (NDFB). Additionally, several top leaders of the ULFA were arrested in Dhaka in 2009. This resulted from the co-operative efforts of the Indian and Bangladeshi Governments, indicating a shift in the orientation of Bangladesh towards its previous support for such movements. Finally, there was a slight decrease in the fatality rates in 2008–09 in these conflicts, adding a degree of optimism.

The same cannot be said with regard to the ideologically motivated Naxalite movement, which has been expanding in recent years.[10] Since the two largest Maoist factions (the People's War Group and the Maoist Communist Centre) merged in 2004, they have rapidly extended their influence and operations into the very heartland of India. In 2006 Prime Minister Manmohan Singh called it the 'single biggest internal-security challenge' that India has faced.[11] While roughly 700,000 Indian troops are stationed in Kashmir, the police and military forces deployed to counter this growing Naxalite insurgency are surprisingly low. A 'dismal security presence in states of the so-called red corridor, which stretches from the Deccan Plateau to the Himalayan foothills', is shown whereby 'in Bihar, there are 54 police officers for every 100 square kilometers, compared to 31 in Jharkand, and 17 in Chattisgargh. It's far worse in Bastar, where less than four policemen are on the ground for every 100 square kilometers, probably half being teenage irregulars'.[12] Such deployments indicate a lack of prioritization and/or recognition on the part of the Indian Government of the scale of the threat.

Border disputes with neighbouring states

The second principal geopolitical issue that is explored with regard to India, and which continues our extension outwards from India's centre, is the existence of several disputed border areas with neighbouring states. While India has problematic border issues with Bangladesh, Nepal and Myanmar, the focus here will be specifically on the long-standing Sino–Indian border dispute and the Kashmir conflict with Pakistan, as, in terms of their impact upon its broader strategic interests, these geopolitical conflicts are of paramount importance.

In 1962 India experienced a decisive defeat by the Chinese military over the disputed territory that stands between India and Tibet. The legacy of the war is of importance to Indian geopolitics in several ways. First, it represents an explicitly geographical conflict over the location of the dividing line between the two states: geopolitics of the most obvious order.[13] As the Minister of External Affairs (2004–06), Shyam Saran, put it: 'geopolitical reality' was in play 'where the interests of both India and China intersect. It is said that the logic of geography is unrelenting. Proximity is the most difficult and testing among diplomatic challenges a country faces. To those who harbour any skepticism about this fact, it would suffice to remind that we share one of the longest [and most disputed] land borders in the world with China.'[14] Second, the mistrust of the People's Republic of China and widely held perception of its aggressive intentions generates a sense of fear in India, which underlies the rivalry between the two Asian giants. Given the size of these two states and their potential for strategic competition over the longer term, this is arguably the more important of the two border conflicts focused on here.[15] Third, this experience and India's perception of China's aggressive intentions provided the rhetorical basis for its 1998 detonation of a nuclear weapon. Fourth, the advantageous position that China holds along the border forms a critical component in its strategy of encircling India.

With respect to the first point, the Sino–Indian territorial dispute, Shyam Saran's 'logic of geography' revolves primarily around two areas: Assam Himalaya and Aksai Chin. The former was designated Indian territory according to the McMahon Line that was agreed at the Simla Conference of 1913–14 by British and Tibetan officials. China's position since has been that Tibet, in spite of its four decades of de facto independence, was in no position to make such a deal, since, given China's suzerainty, only the Chinese Government could make such an agreement.[16] When the independent Government of India took power, it interpreted the territorial boundaries delineated under the Simla Agreement rather broadly, including the area of Aksai Chin located to the north.[17] The Chinese position since the 1950s has been that it would likely accept the territory demarcated by the McMahon Line (and encompassing the Indian state of Arunachal Pradesh) through diplomatic negotiations if India were willing to cede its claims to Aksai Chin.

The disputes over these territories, and the lack of willingness by the two sides to arrive at a diplomatic resolution, led to their 1962 war. While China immediately withdrew from most of the territory it occupied in Arunachal Pradesh, it did not withdraw from 14,000 square miles of territory in Aksai Chin. Neither side has accepted the validity of the areas of control by the other since this time, leading to intermittent skirmishes. The most promising marks of progress occurred during the 1990s when two confidence-building agreements were signed: The Agreement on Maintaining Peace and Tranquillity in the Border Areas along the Line of Actual Control (1993) and the Agreement on Confidence-Building Measures in the Military Field along the Line of Actual Control in the India-China Border (1996).[18] Amicable language was also contained in their Joint Declaration on Principles for Relations and Comprehensive Cooperation (2003), and Prime Minister Singh's and Premier Wen Jiabao's A Shared Vision for the Twenty-First Century (2008). However, these statements have not been accompanied by any substantive negotiations or any sovereignty agreements. Moreover, the disputed Himalayan region was the scene of increasing tension between 2008 and 2009, including infrastructure races, heightened military deployments, base renewals and 'incursion' incidents. The Sino–Indian border remains actively disputed and represents a direct geographic challenge for Indian foreign policy-makers.

Second, the overwhelming defeat at the hands of the Chinese had a long-lasting impact on Indian 'perceptions' of its northern neighbour, with, of course, perceptions being the stamping ground of International Relations (IR) *constructivism*. There is a common perception that the war resulted from unprovoked Chinese actions and came as a surprise to Prime Minister Jawaharlal Nehru. While the veracity of this narrative has been called into question, its internalization by Indian society and its impact on Indian views is unmistakable.[19] Koch elaborates on this point:

> The scar on India's national psyche left by the 1962 defeat cannot be underestimated. There is a legacy of humiliation and grievance that remains a central component of Indian thinking about China. As a result, the notion has crystallized within India that the only language China understands and respects is one based on national strength. One of the most important lessons that India drew from the border conflict was that it would be extremely damaging for India to let down its guard. India assumes that while Pakistan represents the more immediate short-term threat, only China possesses the ability to threaten Indian vital interests.[20]

The 1962 war shapes India's view both in terms of its inability to prevent China's external penetration of its own sphere, and how the relationship is likely to develop at the broader Indian Ocean and global level.

The third geopolitical legacy of the 1962 war is related. On 11 and 13 May 1998 India openly became a nuclear weapons state by the successful detonation of five nuclear devices. While the immediate attention of the international community focused on the implications of this move for the Indian–Pakistani rivalry (particularly given Pakistan's own nuclear tests on 28 and 30 May 1998), New Delhi argued that the move was more a response to the security threat from China. As India's Prime Minister explained to the US President:

> I have been deeply concerned at the deteriorating security environment, specially the nuclear environment, faced by India for some years past. We have an overt nuclear weapon state on our borders, a state which committed armed aggression against India in 1962. Although our relations with that country have improved in the last decade or so, an atmosphere of distrust persists mainly due to the unresolved border problem.[21]

Given the continued dispute over territory, the 1962 experience, the steady rise of both states and the nuclear capacity of China, it had become strategically important for India to also become a nuclear power. Such status would improve its relative strategic position vis-à-vis China.

The fourth important geopolitical factor in this border dispute is the advantageous position that China holds over India along its northern frontier, where China's positioning along the border contributes substantially to its seemingly wider game of 'encirclement' of India.[22] By maintaining its positions since 1962, deploying medium-range missile systems in the area, and significantly developing the highway and rail lines into Tibet (significantly improving its mobilization capacity), China is in a stronger position than India. While the strategy of encirclement is broader than the Sino–Indian border, this use of the area connects it to the broader geopolitical relationship between India and China.

The second border conflict that we can now address is the conflict with Pakistan over Kashmir. Again, there are four primary implications of this conflict that need to be considered within the overall evaluation of the geopolitics of India. The first (as with the Sino–Indian border conflict) is the fact that, as a conflict over territory, it is focused on an explicitly geographical dispute. Second, it is a central conflict within the broader Indian–Pakistani rivalry, which has both shaped and limited the strategic potential of India since independence. Third, given the history, the capacity of both parties and the relationship of the underlying issue in Kashmir to other areas, the stakes of the conflict are exceedingly high. Fourth, the Indian–Pakistani rivalry is an access point through which the Sino–Indian relationship plays out, and through which China is seen as pursuing a strategy of encirclement of India.

The first implication of the Kashmir conflict for India's geopolitics is its explicit connection to geography. Since the accession of the Muslim-majority Kashmir to India by the Hindu maharajah, Hari Singh, in 1947, the two states have fought three wars and engaged in numerous other crises and lower-level skirmishes. While much of the population of Kashmir seeks secession from India, allowing this would mean India sacrificing a sizable piece of territory—something states are generally loath to do, the more so if it means territory being transferred to Pakistan. Beyond this, the direct geopolitical implications of ceding the territory also would be significant. An independent Kashmir could become a zone of strategic competition for China, India and Pakistan. Furthermore, it would mean ceding strategic control over the rivers that provide both the potential for much-needed hydro-electric power to India and access to essential irrigation water for Pakistan. An independent Kashmir with control over these resources might mean the undermining of the *Indus Water Treaty*, which has guided both states' access to the six-river Indus system since its signing in 1969.[23]

This geographical significance mixed with the identity component of the Kashmir conflict raises the second implication. In short, this dispute is a central issue in the broader Indian–Pakistani rivalry. While it is an error to call it the sole basis for the rivalry, three of the four wars that have been fought between India and Pakistan, and most of the battles and crises that have fallen short of outright war between the two states since independence, have revolved around Kashmir. In recent years the situation in Kashmir has stabilized to some extent, and violence has diminished. Nevertheless, the lack of resolution of the conflict and its connection to the broader relationship with Pakistan links it to a rivalry that occupies a great deal of India's strategic focus and limits its ability to broaden its regional and global influence.

Beyond the fact that this has been a long-term source of internal instability and a core issue in Indian–Pakistani rivalry, the stakes of the conflict are also exceedingly high. The most obvious way in which this is true is the potential for an Indo–Pakistani conflict to escalate to use of nuclear weapons. Still, there is another fundamental issue at stake that also relates to the geopolitical coherence of the Indian state and its continued rise as an international power. Those in the liberal camp within India who call for allowing Kashmir to gain independence do not adequately consider the implications of such a precedent for other conflicts. As Pant argues, 'clearly, no Indian government is in a position to allow Kashmir's secession from India for fear of triggering a new spate of separatist struggles in the multi–ethnic, multinational nation'.[24]

The final point to be made about the geopolitical implications of the Kashmir conflict is that it provides another point through which India's rivalry with China operates. Mitra argues that one cannot really understand the overall Indian–Pakistani rivalry without considering it to be subsumed within the larger China-India-Pakistan triad, in which Chinese military and diplomatic support to Pakistan has been a long-standing feature of regional security.[25] This Sino-Pakistani relationship provides a second front along which China's strategy of encircling India is implemented. It is through this often proclaimed 'all-weather friendship' with Pakistan that China is able to extend its land threat along the western boundaries of India, partly through China's commitment of military and financial support, but also partly through the upgrading of the Karakorum Highway, which provides a corridor for more rapid and effective projection of Chinese land power. Thus, the Kashmir conflict, and the broader rivalry between Pakistan and India, is a critical strategic issue that figures in the geopolitics of India.

The extension of Indian geopolitics

India as a Great Power

India's footprint in world politics is expanding, particularly so its 'footprints' in the Indian Ocean and its littoral.[26] This expansion of strategic interests and presence can be seen in two broad ways. The first is in India's projection of military and diplomatic influence into, and indeed beyond, the Indian Ocean area. This extension places India directly into contact with the interests and presence of China; consequently, much of the discussion below focuses on this. However, it is clearly worth considering how India's expanding interests alter its strategic relationships with the USA and a number of states within the surrounding RSCs. The second area we examine is India's effort to deepen economic interactions with neighbouring regions and to secure access to critical natural resources, which involve issues of secure SLOCs (Sea Lines of Communication). There is clear overlap between this and its politico-military expansion, but we dedicate a section to geoeconomics as it has a critical relationship to India's ability to sustain economic growth over the long term, and to fully enter the category of Great Power.

The Indian Ocean and Great Power politics

The extension of India's strategic posture into the Indian Ocean littoral creates opportunities and challenges associated with its increasing contact and influence across a broader area. As described above, China appears to be pursuing a policy of encirclement of India, relying upon its military advantage along the Sino–Indian border and its 'all-weather friendship' with Pakistan. To the south, China attempts to complete the circle by sea. Its so-called 'string of pearls' strategy is a three-pronged approach to check US naval power in the Indian Ocean and to achieve strategic maritime advantage over India. Meanwhile, India's posture involves the construction of a series of naval bases/berthing points along its sea lanes to the Middle East, the improvement of its diplomacy throughout the Indian Ocean area, and the rapid attempt to build a 'blue water' navy to project power effectively.[27] In recent years China has notably increased its presence in the Bay of Bengal and the Arabian Sea. Chinese and Indian analysts continue to cite Mahan's supposed geopolitical comment, 'Whoever controls the Indian Ocean, controls Asia. The Indian Ocean is the gateway to the world's seven seas. The destiny of the world in the 21st century will be determined by the Indian Ocean.'[28] The Indian Ocean Region (IOR) is becoming an important front in China's naval strategy, and India's presence at the centre creates a clear challenge with which China must deal.

India also understands the central importance of the IOR to its own strategic interests, with a Grand Strategy and strategy leanings that reflect Mahanian-style tenets of *seapower* and *geopolitics*.[29] India's response has been to work at developing its diplomacy throughout the area, building and modernizing its military capacity, and developing its ability to project power more effectively. India's self-proclaimed strategic security perimeter runs from the choke points of the

Strait of Hormuz to the Strait of Malacca, and from the east coast of Africa to the west coast of Australia.

In military terms, India has embarked upon a massive military development programme. Much of this military development is focused upon projecting power throughout the Indian Ocean. It includes the addition of a sea-based leg to its nuclear posture, substantial air force development (including combat aircraft, Il-78 tanker aircraft for in-air refuelling, and AWACS systems), and major investment in the expansion of its surface and submarine naval capacities. Most significantly, it awaits delivery of the refurbished Kiev-class Admiral Gorshkov aircraft carrier (renamed INS Vikramaditya), due in late 2012, and it is building an indigenous 40,000-ton Vikrant-class aircraft carrier, due to be launched by the end of 2010 and commissioned by 2014, a development picked up in China.[30]

India's official *Maritime Military Strategy* (2007), a good example of Kristof's 'strategic writings', which are a vehicle for geopolitical formulations, show a keen sense of location and position in play for India in the Indian Ocean. Its entire chapter 3 was titled 'The Indian Ocean and its Geopolitics', in which 'whatever happens in the IOR can affect our national security and is of interest to us'.[31] At a basic level, it argued that:

> India is singularly blessed in terms of maritime geography. We have unimpeded access to the Indian Ocean on both our coasts besides two advantageously located island groups, in the east and the west, which permit forward deployment. The Maritime Military Strategy exploits these geographical advantages available to India by adopting an oceanic approach to its strategy, rather than a coastal one.[32]

India's own area of 'primary strategic interest' was defined as: a) 'The Arabian Sea and the Bay of Bengal'; b) 'The choke points leading to and from the Indian Ocean—principally the Strait of Malacca, the Strait of Hormuz, the Strait of Bab-el-Mandeb and the Cape of Good Hope'; c) 'the island countries'; d) 'the Persian Gulf'; and e) 'the principle ISLs [International Shipping Lanes] crossing the IOR'.[33] The South China Sea was designated as a further, though secondary, area of strategic interest.

India perceives two broad categories of threats to which it is responding. The first is the increasing importance of non-traditional threats like terrorism, weapons proliferation, and piracy. They require that India increase attention to the effective policing of large sea areas. The surveillance and projection capacities that are part of this build-up contribute to India's ability to do so. The second threat is the presence of rival navies. Here, China was flagged as a state engaged in an 'ambitious modernisation' programme to create a 'blue water' navy with attendant 'attempts to gain strategic toe-hold in the IOR'.[34] The *Maritime Military Strategy* clearly indicates a focus on the extension of Indian influence by sea, rather than land. It recognizes the relative strengths that China and India have over one another, the well-suited geographical position of India at the heart of critical SLOCs, and the importance that they play in its continued rise.

The final element of India's reciprocal strategy of encirclement of China involves the development of a base structure throughout the region. The introduction of two new purely naval deep-sea port facilities on the south-west coast at Kawar and on the south-east coast some 50 kilometres south of Visakhapatnam, 'will enable Indian power to be felt further around the Indian Ocean, and thereby enable India to more easily cut China's Sea Lanes of Communication between the Persian Gulf and Straits of Malacca'. Elsewhere, the extension and build-up of Campbell Airport on Great Nicobar island 'gives India the chance to strike against the southern and central Chinese zones, avoiding the geographical problems for India of trans-Himalayan operations'. The year 2005 saw the setting-up of India's Far Eastern Naval Command (FENC), at Port Blair in the Andaman Islands: 'the islands look westwards back to India and the Eastern Naval Command at Visakhapatnam, thereby securing the whole Bay of Bengal as a consequence. They also look eastwards, to Southeast Asia and the South China Sea; indeed they geographically pull India into Southeast Asia'.[35]

All in all, India is making a push to modernize and expand its naval presence throughout the Indian Ocean littoral, partially in a bid to contain China's own growing presence. This modernization and expansion is coupled with an extension of its basing structure and diplomatic ties throughout the region as well. While China is clearly of concern in this regard, so is the USA. India is aware of the US naval primacy in Asia and still stings from the Seventh Fleet's intervention in the Bay of Bengal during the 1971 Indo–Pakistani War. The important geopolitical position played by the US base at Diego Garcia has caused concern for Indian strategists in previous decades. Given India's discomfort with playing a secondary role in Asia and the Indian Ocean to China and its other shared interests in the Middle East with the USA, greater security co-operation between the two states is a reasonable expectation. Certainly, there has been increasing co-ordination between the US and Indian navies within the region. The 2007 joint exercise between the Indian, US, Japanese, Australian and Singaporean navies in the Bay of Bengal, MALABAR-2, was one example. Such developments indicate that the USA and India are developing, albeit strictly based upon each state's strategic interests, a co-operative relationship that could assist each in addressing strategic concerns relating to China.

Geoeconomics and resource acquisition

The second area of examination regarding the extension of India's strategic presence in the Indian Ocean region deals with the necessity of deepening economic partnerships with states throughout the region and securing the supply of energy resources. It was again no coincidence that an entire chapter—chapter 4—was devoted to 'Maritime and Energy Security' in the *Maritime Military Strategy*. Such a focus on economics and energy within foreign policy follows the strategic vision that has been referred to as the Manmohan Doctrine.[36]

Seeking to expand trade ties with states and organizations throughout the Indian Ocean region is central to India's 'Look East' policy. This lies behind India's *Maritime Military Strategy* sense that:

> Geographically, India is in a unique position in the geopolitics of IOR, with its interests and concerns straddling across the sub-regions of IOR. This geopolitical reality and India's belief that enhanced regional cooperation is mutually advantageous, is driving the active participation in the SAARC, the ASEAN, the East Asia Summit and the Shanghai Cooperation Organisation.[37]

Such engagement can be seen in all directions of the Indian Ocean and beyond, which reflects India's so-called '360 degrees diplomacy'.

In an eastwards direction, India has promoted Bay of Bengal Co-operation through BIM-STEC (Bay of Bengal Initiative for Multi-Sectoral Technical and Economic Cooperation—formerly Bangladesh, India, Myanmar, Sri Lanka, Thailand Economic Cooperation). There is an ongoing discussion between the Governments of India, Bangladesh and Myanmar to build a joint pipeline in order to transport liquefied natural gas from Myanmar to India.[38] India has pushed bilateral links with Singapore and Indonesia, and economic links with the Association of Southeast Asian Nations (ASEAN), with which it became an official Dialogue Partner in 1992, and a member of the ASEAN Regional Forum (ARF) in 1996, and signed a Comprehensive Economic Co-operation Agreement (CECA) in 2003, and a Free Trade Agreement in 2009. This positioning with regard to ASEAN and other regional institutions also reflects a set of moves by China and India to enter into organizations within each other's backyards.[39]

In a westwards direction, India's relations with Israel have developed strongly since normalization of relations in 1992. Israel has become one of India's largest investors. In addition, India has acquired a number of important defence systems from Israel, has built complementary programmes of weapons systems development, and seems to have engaged in unofficial maritime co-operation around the Red Sea area.[40] India has taken a broad approach to securing energy resources, fostering a series of relationships in energy-rich regions nearby, notably Saudi Arabia and the Gulf. Relations with Iran have involved some military co-operation, but most importantly for India is Iran's potential as a significant and proximate supplier of energy resources. The effort with Iran to develop the port complex at Chabahar as a conduit for accessing Central Asia is also intended to assist India's resource acquisition. Chabahar (and its Indian support) stands in competition with Pakistan's Gwadar (and its Chinese support) as an energy corridor link point.

In a southerly direction India's efforts have seen active maritime diplomacy and bilateral arrangements with various island (Mauritius, Seychelles, Madagascar) and littoral (e.g. Mozambique, South Africa) states, with India taking a leading position in setting up the IONS (Indian Ocean Naval Symposium) in 2009, to which China was not invited. Maintaining secure transit through the choke points and across the Indian Ocean remains a key concern for India, which receives over 90% of its trade by sea. As India's *Maritime Military Strategy* put it, 'being the major maritime power in the IOR, a large part of the responsibility for ensuring the safety of ISLs devolves upon the Indian Navy'.[41]

Conclusions

It seems likely that India's interests and impact will continue to extend further into the broader Asian and Indian Ocean space. It possesses the latent resources to emerge as an enormous power. To conclude, we reiterate a few points. First, the resolution of its own internal threats and its border disputes with neighbouring countries would improve India's position to further extend its influence. The relevance of South Asian security problems for India and others implies that an increased capacity and willingness to manage South Asian security would reduce threats to India and increase its recognition as a significant power. Second, its growth and expansion clearly put it into significant strategic contact with the other rising Asian power—China. While we would not say that this necessitates a conflictual relationship, the evidence seems to point towards at least a highly competitive one. Thus, the geopolitics of the Indian Ocean region will continue to evolve in a way that involves both states' growing power and interests. Finally, India's relationship with the USA and other states throughout this region will be driven by its own strategic interests in the coming years, which will be in large part driven by the Sino-Indian relationship.

Notes

1 D. Hagerty and H. Hagerty, 'India's Foreign Relations', in D. Hagerty (ed.), *South Asia in World Politics*, Oxford: Rowman and Littlefield, 2005, p.41.
2 L. Kristof, 'The Origins and Evolution of Geopolitics', *Journal of Conflict Resolution*, Vol. 4, No. 1, 1960, pp.37–38. Also O. Osterud, 'Review: The Uses and Abuses of Geopolitics', *Journal of Peace Research*, Vol. 25, No. 2, 1988.

3 For example, B. Buzan and O. Waever, *Regions and Powers: The Structure of International Security*, Cambridge: Cambridge University Press, 2003; and D. Frazier and R. Stewart-Ingersoll, 'Regional Powers and Security: A Framework for Understanding Order within Regional Security Complexes', *European Journal of International Relations*, Vol. 16, No. 3, 2010.

4 R. Stewart-Ingersoll and D. Frazier, 'India as a Regional Power: Identifying the Impact of Roles and Foreign Policy Orientation on the South Asian Security Order', *Asian Security*, Vol. 6, No. 1, 2010.

5 D. Hagerty and H. Hagerty, 'India's Foreign Relations', op. cit., p.41.

6 H. Pant, 'Indian Foreign and Security Policy: Beyond Nuclear Weapons', *Brown Journal of World Affairs*, Vol. 25, No. 2, 2009, p.229.

7 Ibid., p.230.

8 L. Curtis, 'After Mumbai: Time to Strengthen U.S.-India Counterterrorism Cooperation', *Backgrounder Paper*, No. 2217, 9 December 2008, www.heritage.org.

9 K. Bajpai, 'The Effects of Terrorism on Indian Democracy', in S. Khatri and G. Kueck (eds), *Terrorism in South Asia: Impact on Development and Democratic Process*, Delhi: Shipra Publications, 2009, p.188.

10 A. Mehta, 'Countering India's Maoist Insurgency', *RSIS Commentaries*, No. 74/2010, 5 July 2010.

11 M. Singh, 'PM's Speech at the Chief Minister's Meet on Naxalism', 13 April 2006, pmindia.nic.in. Also, 'Ending the Red Terror', *Economist*, 27 February 2010.

12 J. Motlagh, 'The Maoists in the Forest: Tracking India's Separatist Rebels', *Virginia Quarterly Review*, Vol. 84, No. 3, 2008, p.103.

13 E. Anderson, 'Geopolitics: International Boundaries as Fighting Places', in C. Gray and G. Sloan (eds), *Geopolitics: Geography and Strategy,* London: Frank Cass, 1999.

14 S. Saran, 'Present Dimensions of the Indian Foreign Policy', 11 January 2006, meaindia.nic.in.

15 On the other hand, it could be argued that the dispute with Pakistan is more critical, given that it is viewed in terms of Great Power conflict for India while the other is not. Thus, stalemate or negotiations with China are viewed differently than those with Pakistan, the latter to which India perceives itself as superior. In other words, losing vis-à-vis Pakistan is much more devastating to Great Power status than a stalemate with or even losing to China.

16 S. Hoffman, 'Rethinking the Linkage between Tibet and the China-India Border Conflict: A Realist Approach', *Journal of Cold War Studies*, Vol. 8, No. 3, 2006.

17 N. Maxwell, 'Sino-Indian Border Dispute Reconsidered', *Economic and Political Weekly*, Vol. 34, No. 15, 1999.

18 W. Sidhu and J. Yuan, 'Resolving the Sino-Indian Border Dispute: Building Confidence through Cooperative Monitoring', *Asian Survey*, Vol. 41, No. 2, 2001.

19 N. Maxwell, 'Forty Years of Folly: What Caused the Sino-Indian Border War and Why the Dispute is Unresolved', *Critical Asian Studies*, Vol. 35, No. 1, 2003.

20 C. Koch, 'China and Regional Security in South Asia', in Emirates Center for Strategic Studies and Research (ed.), *The Balance of Power in South Asia*, Reading: Ithaca Press, 2000, p.82.

21 A.B. Vajpayee, 'Letter' [to William Clinton], *New York Times*, 13 May 1998.

22 D. Scott, 'The Great Power "Great Game" between India and China: "The Logic of Geography"', *Geopolitics*, Vol. 13, No. 1, 2008.

23 R. Wirsing, 'The Kashmir Territorial Dispute: The Indus Runs Through It', *Brown Journal of International Affairs*, Vol. 25, No. 1, 2008.

24 H. Pant, 'Indian Foreign and Security Policy', op. cit., p.232.

25 S. Mitra, 'War and Peace in South Asia: A Revisionist View of India-Pakistan Relations', *Contemporary South Asia*, Vol. 10, No. 3, 2001.

26 D. Scott, 'Indian "Footprints" in the Indian Ocean: Power Projection for the 21st Century', *Indian Ocean Survey*, Vol. 2, No. 2, 2006; D. Berlin, 'India in the Indian Ocean', *Naval War College Review*, Vol. 59, No. 2, 2006.

27 D. Scott, 'India's Drive for a "Blue Water" Navy', *Journal of Military and Strategic Studies*, Vol. 10, No. 2, 2007–08.

28 J. Holmes, A. Winner and T. Yoshihara, *Indian Naval Strategy in the 21st Century*, London: Routledge, 2009, p.132. The authors note that the authenticity of the quote is dubious. Nevertheless, its frequent use by Chinese and Indian strategists to accentuate the increasing importance that each country places on building its naval presence within the Indian Ocean is quite real and relevant.

29 For example, D. Scott, 'India's "Grand Strategy" for the Indian Ocean: Mahanian Visions', *Asia-Pacific Review*, Vol. 13, No. 2, 2006.

30 'India to get First Indigenous Aircraft Carrier by 2014', *People's Daily*, 11 January 2010.

31 Indian Navy, *Freedom to Use the Seas: India's Maritime Military Strategy*, New Delhi: Ministry of Defence, 2007, p.59.
32 Ibid., pp.10–11.
33 Ibid., pp.59–60.
34 Ibid., p.41.
35 D. Scott, 'The Great Power "Great Game" Between India and China', op. cit., p.9, for all three quotations.
36 Manmohan Doctrine, enunciated by M. Singh, 'Speech by Prime Minister Dr. Manmohan Singh at *India Today* Conclave, New Delhi', 25 February 2005, meaindia.nic.in.
37 Indian Navy, *Freedom to Use the Seas: India's Maritime Military Strategy*, op. cit., p.29.
38 A. Sharma, 'India and Energy Security', *Asian Affairs*, Vol. 38, No. 2, 2007.
39 D. Scott, 'The Great Power "Great Game" Between India and China', op. cit., talks about these developments. In particular, it points toward both states' moves to closer relations with ASEAN, China's attainment of observer status in the South Asian Association for Regional Cooperation (SAARC) and India's attainment of observer status in the Shanghai Cooperation Organisation (SCO).
40 P. Kumaraswamy, 'India and Israel: Emerging Partnership', in S. Ganguly (ed.), *India as an Emerging Power*, Portland: Frank Cass, 2003.
41 Indian Navy, *Freedom to Use the Seas: India's Maritime Military Strategy*, op. cit., p.54.

5

Geoeconomics and energy for India

Gulshan Sachdeva

Introduction

Geopolitics arose in the 19th century, and throughout the 20th century it explained how the global power map was shaped. Power equations were formed by imperialism in the early part of the century; by the East–West divide and Cold War after the Second World War; and by the forces of globalization during the last decade of the century.[1] Since the publication of the 1990 article by Edward Luttwak, 'From Geopolitics to Geoeconomics', the term 'geoeconomics' has been used quite frequently by writers and policy-makers.[2] It is explained as 'the intersection of economics and finance with global political and security considerations'.[3] Earlier it was thought that geoeconomics might replace geopolitics, but now it is accepted that 'geo-economics recasts rather than simply replaces geopolitical calculation'.[4] In other words, geoeconomics 'links the "big picture" with the practical realm of markets'.[5]

Since the early 1990s India has been adapting itself simultaneously to economic globalization and to the emerging balance of power. Changes in India's internal and external economic policies also coincided with the end of the Cold War. Accelerated growth and policies of trade and investment liberalization have also influenced India's foreign policy. The strategic consequences of its economic performance are clearly evident. Growth and outward orientation have helped India to forge new relationships with its neighbours in Asia and with major powers.[6] More than a decade ago some analysts predicted that 'India will be forced to calculate its energy security requirements within more general geo-political environment that is characterized by rapid change and unpredictability'.[7] Consequently, India has launched its integrated energy policy and 'oil diplomacy' in search of new energy assets to fulfil the energy requirements of its high economic growth, with *energy security* emerging as a 'crucial' component of its foreign policy.[8] In a speech at the Constituent Assembly in December 1947, Jawaharlal Nehru had argued that in 'talking about foreign policies, the House must remember that these are not just empty struggles on a chess board. Behind them lie all manner of things. Ultimately foreign policy is the outcome of economic policy, and until India has properly evolved her economic policy, her foreign policy will be rather vague, rather inchoate, and will be groping'.[9] In Manmohan Singh repeating these very same words over half a century later, amidst his annunciation of the economics-driven *Manmohan Doctrine*, such sentiments have become clearer to Indian policy-makers than at any time in the recent past.[10]

Changing economic engagements

India is making a successful transition from an excessively inward-oriented economy to a more globally integrated economy. As a result of new policies in the early 1990s, it has become one of the fastest growing economies in the world. Despite some serious challenges, like energy security, poverty, infrastructure, regional disparities and internal security, there are strong indications that rapid growth will continue. Notwithstanding global recession, the Indian economy continues to be one of the highest growing economies in the world. Due to increasing global linkages, the growth rate in 2008/09 came down to 6.7% from the average 8.8% achieved between 2003/04 and 2007/08, though recovering to 7.4% for 2009/10, and accelerating to 8.8% in the second quarter of 2010. With US $185,000m. in exports, India's merchantable trade reached $490,000m. in 2008/09. It has been growing at an average annual rate of about 26% in the last four years (between 2005/06 and 2008/09). In addition, the services sector, which accounts for about 55% of the Indian economy, continues to perform well and contribute to growing service exports, which touched $102,000m. in 2008/09. Within the services sector, IT and Business Process Outsourcing (BPO) industries have been growing quickly and were responsible for $50,000m. in exports of IT and related services.[11]

Apart from expansion, the Indian economy is also becoming more diversified. Traditionally, Western countries were main markets for Indian exports. In recent years significant diversification has taken place. India's trade relations with the USA and the European Union (EU) may have increased in absolute terms, but relatively speaking as a percentage of India's total trade, trade with the EU and the USA has declined in the last decade. In comparison, there has been rapid integration of the Indian economy within Asia, which has been reinforced by India's 'Look East' policy, which was initiated in the early 1990s. This is clearly evident from the figures of India–China trade (average trade growth was 53% per year between 2003/04 and 2007/08), as well as India–Association of Southeast Asian Nations (ASEAN) trade. Studies have shown that India's qualitative and quantitative engagement with the Asian economies is far deeper than commonly perceived.[12] India's economic linkage with the West Asian countries has been traditionally quite strong, and more so now due to energy imports, a 2.5m. Indian diaspora, and good trade relations.

It is now becoming clear that, along with the People's Republic of China and Japan, India would be playing an important role in an evolving Asian economic architecture. However, it is also realized that India's role will be less effective if its economic relations within South Asia and with the Central Asian region remain marginal. In this case, India needs to work for an economic policy framework, in which Pakistan, Afghanistan and the Central Asian republics view the partnership as benefiting them too. This policy framework will also improve India's energy security as it may finally get more substantive access to some of the energy resources in the Eurasian region. It can also fundamentally change India's sea-based continental trade.[13] Indians can also find tremendous investment opportunities in Central Asia, which in turn can transform their small and medium industries as well as agriculture. The growing realization of these opportunities has influenced policy-makers not just in India, but also in Pakistan and Afghanistan, as witnessed in Afghanistan's membership of the South Asian Association for Regional Cooperation (SAARC), the signing of the South Asian Free Trade Area (SAFTA), the Regional Economic Co-operation Conferences on Afghanistan, the emerging India-Kazakhstan partnership, the continuous interest in Turkmenistan-Afghanistan-Pakistan-India (TAPI) and Iran-Pakistan-India (IPI) gas pipelines, and India's $1,300m. contribution to Afghanistan's reconstruction.

In the early and mid-1990s, when the whole world was going for regional economic groupings, Indian policy-makers were concerned that India's major participation was only in

SAARC, which was going nowhere. Under new policy initiatives, a major effort was made to move closer to the Association of Southeast Asian Nations (ASEAN) and gain membership of the Asia-Pacific Economic Cooperation (APEC), in which India's objectives were both economic as well as foreign policy and strategic. After limited success with ASEAN, but frustration with APEC (where a moratorium on new members was put in place in 1997), India started looking for alternatives. It started developing other regional arrangements, specifically Indian Ocean Rim initiatives and arrangements with immediate neighbours in South Asia. Efforts made at various forums resulted in the establishment of the Indian Ocean Rim Association for Regional Co-operation (IOR-ARC) in 1997.[14] Other major regional initiatives taken by India were the establishment of the Bay of Bengal Initiative for Multi-Sectoral Technical and Economic Cooperation (BIMSTEC—formerly Bangladesh, India, Myanmar, Sri Lanka, Thailand Economic Cooperation) and the Ganga-Mekong Cooperation programme. In the late 1990s there were also discussions on establishing a growth quadrangle involving south-western China, north-eastern India, northern Myanmar and Bangladesh.[15]

The collapse of the Doha development round of the World Trade Organization (WTO) negotiations pushed many countries, including India, to look for alternatives to multilateral negotiations to improve their trade positions. Since 2005 India has put its proposed regional trade agreements on the fast track. In the past, India had adopted a cautious approach to regionalism and was engaged in only a few bilateral/regional initiatives, mainly through Preferential Trade Agreements (PTAs) or through open regionalism.[16] In recent years, it has started concluding Comprehensive Economic Co-operation Agreements (CECAs) with many countries. The CECAs cover Free Trade Agreements (FTAs) in goods (which means a zero customs duty regime within a fixed time frame on items covering substantial trade, and a relatively small negative list of sensitive items with no or limited duty concessions), services, investment and other identified areas of economic co-operation. India has already signed an agreement on a South Asian Free Trade Area (SAFTA) as well as individual trade agreements with Afghanistan, Bhutan, Sri Lanka and Nepal. The India-Singapore CECA, India-ASEAN FTA, India-Chile PTA, and an India-Southern Common Market (MERCOSUR) PTA have also been signed. In addition, trade and investment deals are being negotiated with the Gulf Cooperation Council (GCC), the Republic of Korea (South Korea), Malaysia and Mauritius. India-EU and India-Japan negotiations are also at a very advanced stage. Similarly, India-Israel, India-Brazil, IBSA (India, Brazil, South Africa), and India-Russia joint study groups have been set up.

Border trade

So far the majority of India's trade has been conducted by sea. Border trade with China was stopped after the India–China war in 1962. Similarly, very little official trade happens by road with Pakistan, Bangladesh and Myanmar. Since 1995 some positive developments in the area of border trade have taken place. Still, the policy initiatives were limited to a few border points with a small number of commodities exchanged by local communities living on both sides of the borders, mainly with Bangladesh and Myanmar. These initiatives were intended to stop the large amount of 'unauthorized trade' that was already taking place across borders in the north-eastern states.[17] Encouraged by rapidly growing India-China trade, a limited opening has also been made through Nathu La pass in Sikkim. To give a new thrust to border trade, the Union Cabinet gave approval for the *Land Ports Authority Bill* in 2008.

The new Land Ports Authority will oversee the construction, management and maintenance of integrated check posts (ICPs) on land borders; it will regulate the functioning of various agencies and co-ordinate several concerned ministries and departments. The ICPs will have the regulatory agencies like immigration, customs and border security, as well as support facilities like banking and cargo terminals, hotels, etc. The Indian Government has approved the establishment of 13 ICPs at borders with Bangladesh, Pakistan, Nepal, Bhutan and Myanmar over a period of three years. Of these, four ICPs will be set up in the first phase, at Petrapole (West Bengal), Moreh (Manipur), Raxaul (Bihar) and Attari (Punjab). If successful, this policy initiative has the potential to transform landlocked northern and north-eastern border regions of India.

Energy security issues

The era of high economic growth in the Western world between 1945 and the first oil crisis of 1973 coincided with a period of cheap oil prices. The second oil crisis, triggered by the Iranian revolution of 1979, further complicated the situation. Recent years of high economic growth in countries like India and China have coincided with periods of increased oil price uncertainty. India's oil requirements for its 8%–9% growth every year since 2003 have been financed at increasing global oil prices. The oil shock of July 2008, when oil prices reached a record high of $147 a barrel, set off alarm signals among Indian policy-makers and reminded them of the earlier crises. Being a country dependent on oil imports for about 80% of its requirements, India scrambled for a solution as high oil prices resulted in inflation and threatened to undo the gains of high economic growth achieved in the previous two decades. Immediate fire-fighting responses also exposed the weaknesses of a still developing national energy strategy.

Just before the global economy went into recession, the US Energy Information Administration (EIA) projected that global energy consumption would increase by 50% from 2005 to 2030. It was evident that emerging economies would account for much of this projected growth over the next 25 years. Among the emerging economies, the highest demand was expected to occur in Asia, particularly in China and India. Despite slowdowns in 2008 and 2009, their economic projections remain high in the medium-to-long term. During this period, fossil fuels (oil, natural gas and coal) will continue to supply much of the energy, with oil continuing to be important.

Despite fairly low per capita energy consumption, India is the fifth largest energy consumer and is likely to become the third largest by 2030. The country is also a major producer and is currently the world's seventh largest producer of energy. Primary commercial energy demand grew almost three-fold at an annual rate of 6% between 1981 and 2001. To catch up with the rest of dynamic Asia and to remove poverty, it has become essential for India to continue growing at about 8%–10% or more over the next 25 years. Its energy requirements for a sustained 8%–9% annual growth rate pose a major challenge. According to the government integrated energy policy, India needs to increase its primary energy supply by three to four times its 2004 levels, and its electricity generation capacity/supply by five to six times. With 2004 as the base, its commercial energy supply needs to grow at 4.3%–5.1% annually. By 2030, power generation capacity must increase to nearly 800,000 megawatts (MW) from the 2004 capacity of around 160,000 MW. In addition, the requirement of coal, the dominant fuel in India's mix, will also need to expand to 2,000m. tons a year.[18]

India's energy basket has a mix of all the resources available including renewables. The importance of oil in India's energy mix can be seen from the fact that it accounts for about 33% of India's primary commercial energy, alongside other sources like coal (54%), gas (9%), nuclear (1%), hydro electricity (2.5%) and wind (0.25%).[19] The Government's *Hydrocarbon Vision 2025* released in 2000 indicated that by 2025 India's energy mix would probably be dominated by coal (50%), with the rest being made up of oil (25%), gas (20%), hydro (2%) and nuclear (3%).[20]

Estimates show that India's energy consumption between 2007 and 2035 will grow at an average annual rate of 2.2%, with consumption of natural gas and nuclear energy averaging higher annual increases of 4.1% and 9.5 %, respectively.[21] Since India is relatively poor in oil and gas resources, it has to depend on imports to meet its energy supplies. With already about 80% of its crude oil requirements met by imports, its oil import bill was close to $90,000m. in 2008/09. The Organisation for Economic Co-operation and Development (OECD) estimated that in 2005 India imported about 70% of its crude oil requirements and consumed about 3% of world oil supply. Liquefied Natural Gas (LNG) imports in 2005 made up 17% of total gas supply. India also imported about 12% of its coal supply.[22]

The Indian economy relies heavily on coal, which also accounts for about 70% of its electricity generation. After China and the USA, India is the world's third largest coal user. As a result of a government policy of diversifying the energy mix, the share of natural gas has increased to just over 9%. Other sources, such as wind, solar and nuclear power, still account for very small shares. Although coal will still be a very important source of energy, the alternative policy scenario of the Government visualizes reduction in its demand by 2030. In the alternative scenario, coal demand will grow much slower and oil demand will also decrease somewhat due to the introduction of Compressed Natural Gas (CNG) and fuel efficiency. Similarly, the role of nuclear power is envisaged to increase still further. Even if all these changes are implemented, India will still be importing between 29% and 59% of its total commercial primary energy from outside. The latest government projections, in the Five Year Plan 2007–12, indicate that by 2030 India may be importing 90%–95% of its oil, one-half of its gas and one-third of its coal requirements.[23] Although India has been a net oil importer since the 1970s, LNG imports started only in 2004.

Currently, India imports oil from about 25 countries, with nearly two-thirds of imports coming from four countries: Saudi Arabia, Nigeria, Kuwait and Iran (see Table 5.1).

Most analysts in India believe that the Middle East region (or West Asia as it is called in India) will remain the source of the overwhelming proportion of India's oil and gas imports, accounting for around two-thirds of Indian exports (Table 5.1). In addition, every oil shock in this region has had an adverse impact on the Indian economy.[24] Due to this dependence, Indian policy-makers are worried about oil price volatility, and its impact on inflation, economic growth and foreign exchange reserves. In addition, overwhelming dependence on the Gulf region has its own political implications. Compared with other major states in the world, India is more vulnerable to any disruption in oil supplies from the Gulf. However, it could be argued that India's dependence should not be seen as a vulnerability, as encouragement of growing interdependence between India and the Gulf contributes stability to energy markets.

Government energy policy

As over one-half of the country's population does not have access to electricity or any other form of commercial energy, availability and access to energy is considered crucial for sustained economic growth by the Government.[25] The Government of India's expert committee on integrated energy policy argued that India would be 'energy secure when we can supply lifeline energy to all our citizens irrespective of their ability to pay for it as well as meet their effective demand for safe and convenient energy to satisfy their various needs at competitive prices, at all times and with a prescribed confidence level considering shocks and disruptions that can be reasonably expected'.[26] The major issues discussed in the context of Indian energy security by the expert committee were reducing energy requirements, substituting imported energy with domestic alternatives, diversifying supply sources, expanding resource bases, developing

Gulshan Sachdeva

Table 5.1 Sources of India's oil imports, 2004/05 and 2007

Middle East				Other regions			
	2004/05		2007		2004/05		2007
Country	Oil imports (mmt)	% of total imports	% of total imports	Country	Oil imports (mmt)	% of total imports	% of total imports
Iran	9.61	10.03	17	Angola	2.44	2.55	–
Iraq	8.33	8.69	10	Brazil	0.29	0.30	–
Kuwait	11.46	11.85	9	Brunei	0.81	0.84	–
Neutral zone	0.15	0.15	–	Cameroon	0.35	0.36	–
Oman	0.14	0.14	–	Congo	0.14	0.14	–
Qatar	1.19	1.24	–	Egypt	2.12	2.21	–
Saudi Arabia	23.93	24.96	23	Ecuador	0.15	0.16	–
United Arab Emirates	6.43	6.71	9	Equatorial Guinea	1.66	1.73	–
Yemen	3.51	3.66	3	Gabon	0.28	0.29	–
				Libya	1.47	1.53	–
				Malaysia	3.43	3.58	4
				Mexico	2.28	2.38	–
				Nigeria	15.08	15.73	11
				Russia	0.16	0.16	–
				Sudan	0.33	0.34	–
				Thailand	0.27	0.28	–
Sub-total	64.64	67.43		Sub-total	31.23	32.57	–

Note: mmt = million metric tons.
Source: *Integrated Energy Policy: Report of the Expert Committee*, New Delhi: Planning Commission, 2006, p.59; 2007 figures (rounded) from author; US Energy Information Administration, www.eia.doe.gov.

alternative energy sources, increasing the ability to withstand supply shocks and increasing the ability to import energy and face market risks. Overall, it is believed that India's energy security can be increased by a) diversifying both energy mix and sources of energy imports; b) seriously pursuing overseas acquisitions of energy assets; and c) initiating policy reforms to attract foreign investment as well as improving domestic production, distribution and consumption. In order to safeguard against short-term supply disruptions, the Indian Government is also in the process of setting up 5m. metric tons (36.6m. barrels) of strategic crude oil storage reserves at Manglore, Vishshapatnam and Padur. This strategic reserve will be in addition to the existing storage facilities of various public sector oil companies. These stores are located along the coast so that reserves could be easily exported during disruptions.

Energy diplomacy

In the last decade, 'energy diplomacy' has also become one of the main agendas of the country's foreign and security policy. India is seriously considering its nuclear energy option as well as importing sources beyond the Middle East. Bilateral nuclear agreements with the USA, France, Russia and Canada, as well as consistent engagements with the countries of Eurasia, Africa and Latin America, could be seen from this perspective. The external dimension of energy efforts by India include: a) acquisition of assets abroad through acquiring equity participation in developed fields, and obtaining exploration-production contracts in different parts of the world; b) entering into long-term LNG supply contracts; c) pursuing transnational gas pipeline proposals; and d) promoting partnerships with foreign entities in the downstream sector, both in India and abroad.[27]

In an attempt to diversify oil and gas imports, Indian companies are trying hard to get a strong foothold in the Eurasian region. Investment in Russia's Sakhalin-1 field, and the purchase of Imperial Energy by the Indian public sector company Oil and Natural Gas Corporation (ONGC) in 2009 were efforts in this direction. India views Kazakhstan as an important energy player in Central Asia. Kazakhstan's onshore and offshore proven hydrocarbon reserves have been estimated at 30,000m.–40,000m. barrels; production figures were 1.45m. barrels a day in 2007, expected to touch 1.9m. barrels a day in 2010 and about 2.9m. barrels in 2020. Competition in this region is very fierce as China is also pursuing the same strategy. At the same time, rapidly growing trade and economic relationships between India and China may also compel them to talk of building partnerships in other areas. Both have declared their intentions of co-operation in oil and gas biddings. India also mooted the idea of Asian regional co-operation in energy, and initiated a dialogue between principal Asian suppliers (Saudi Arabia, United Arab Emirates (UAE), Kuwait, Iran, Qatar and Oman) and principal Asian buyers (India, China, Japan and South Korea). These efforts showed some results when China National Petroleum Corporation (CNPC) and India's ONGC mounted a successful $573m. joint bid to acquire Petro-Canada's 37% stake in the al-Furat oil and gas fields in Syria. Earlier, they worked as joint operators in Sudan. India and China may be co-operating in other areas, but when it comes to Central Asian energy, cash-rich China has shown that it can outmanoeuvre India in energy deals. This was clearly illustrated in late 2005 when China outbid India to acquire PetroKazakhstan, Kazakhstan's third-largest oil producer with CNPC raising its bid to $4,180m.

After trying for many years, India may finally be getting into the energy scene in Kazakhstan. During the 2009 visit of the Kazakhstani president to India, ONGC Mittal Energy Limited (OMEL) and KazMunaiGaz (KMG, National Oil Company of Kazakhstan) signed an agreement for exploration of oil and gas in Satpayev block in the Caspian Sea. The Satpayev block covers an area of 1,582 sq km and is at a water depth of 5 m–10 m. It is situated in a highly prospective region of the north Caspian Sea and is in close proximity to major fields, like Karazhanbas, Kalamkas, Kashagan and Donga, where significant quantities of oil have been discovered. It has estimated reserves of 1,850m. barrels. The Indian company will have a 25% stake and the remaining 75% will be with KMG.[28] OMEL also holds a 45.5% share in block OPL 279 and a 64.3% share in OPL 285 in Nigeria, where they had invested more than $200m. up to March 2009. OMEL also had exploration blocks in Turkmenistan, which it has surrendered due to limited hydrocarbon potential. Similar efforts are being pursued in Latin America and Africa as well.

In 2008 ONGC Videsh (OVL) signed an agreement with the Corporación Venezolana del Petróleo and acquired a 40% participating interest in the San Cristobal project. During the same year OVL signed deals in Brazil and Colombia. Earlier, the company had acquired some new assets in Cuba, Colombia, Congo, Sudan and Egypt. With about 40 oil and gas projects, OVL has a presence in 17 countries. It has production of oil and gas from Sudan, Viet Nam, Syria, Russia and Colombia, with various projects under development in Iran, Brazil, Myanmar, Egypt, Venezuela and Kazakhstan. In addition, its subsidiary company, ONGC Nile Ganga BV (ONGBV), has invested $669m. in the Greater Nile Oil Project in Sudan and $223m. in the al-Furat project in Syria. ONGBV has also invested about $300m. in different blocks in Brazil. ONGC's wholly owned subsidiary ONGC Amazon Alaknanda Limited (OAAL) has invested $437 in Colombia, while its subsidiary ONGC Narmada Limited (ONL) has invested in Nigeria.[29]

Gas pipelines

India is also exploring the possibility of importing gas through pipelines from Turkmenistan, Iran, Myanmar and Bangladesh. Since 2002 there has been a lot of discussion on the $7,600m. Turkmenistan-Afghanistan-Pakistan-India (TAPI) gas pipeline. There have been some uncertainties over gas reserves in Turkmenistan, over the security situation in Afghanistan, and over the endemic strained relations between India and Pakistan. Still, all parties are considering the proposal very seriously. This 1,680-km pipeline would run from the Dauletabad gas field in Turkmenistan to Afghanistan, from where it would be constructed alongside the highway running from Herat to Kandahar, and then via Quetta and Multan in Pakistan. The final destination of the pipeline would be Fazilka in Indian Punjab. India was formally invited to join the project in 2006, having earlier participated as an observer.[30]

The Asian Development Bank (ADB) has already proposed various structures of the pipeline for attracting investors, contractors and financial institutions. In 2006 Turkmenistan informed the members that an independent firm, De Golyer & McNaughton, had confirmed reserves of over 2,300 billion cu m of gas at the Daulatabad field. Additional reserves of about 1,200 billion cu m are expected after drilling in the adjacent area. The gas production capacity of the field could be increased to about 125m. cu m per day (cu m/d) from the current 80m. cu m/d. Turkmenistan has committed to providing sovereign guarantees for long-term uninterrupted supplies to Pakistan and India.[31] In May 2006 the Indian Government officially approved its participation in the TAPI project and authorized the Ministry of Petroleum and Natural Gas to put up a formal request for joining the project. In April 2008 Afghanistan, India and Pakistan signed a Framework Agreement to buy gas from Turkmenistan.[32] The participating countries also planned to discuss soon the issues of payments of transit to Afghanistan and Pakistan, taxation structure and consortium issues. For the last few years, TAPI has also been discussed at almost every important meeting on Afghanistan's reconstruction.

Despite many obstacles, the $7,500m., 2,300-km Iran-Pakistan-India (IPI) gas pipeline is still on the agenda. The proposed IPI pipeline will initially transport 60m. cu m of Iranian gas a day, split between India and Pakistan equally. In Pakistani territory an 800-km pipeline will be carrying gas for both Pakistan and India. Iran and Pakistan have already finalized gas sale agreements, with Iran committing itself to supplying 21m. cu m of natural gas daily to Pakistan from 2014. In 2010 the Minister of External Affairs made a statement in the Indian parliament that India was still party to the IPI project and various issues concerning pricing of gas, delivery point of gas, project structure, assured supplies and security of the pipeline, transportation tariffs and transit fees for passage of natural gas through Pakistan, etc., were being discussed between participating countries. As in other parts of the world, the USA is also trying to inject its own geopolitical interests in the Asian energy competition. It has discouraged India from sourcing gas from Iran and instead promoted the TAPI pipeline.[33] After more than a decade of engagement with these two pipeline proposals, it is becoming clear to Indian policy-makers that none of these two projects may take off in the near future, as the security situation in Afghanistan and Pakistan has deteriorated further and India-Pakistan relations have not improved either.[34] Still, if any of these projects materializes in the near future, it will be a game changer in regional geopolitics and geoeconomics.

A final pipeline project, importing gas from Myanmar, was also struck due to regional geopolitics. India and Myanmar signed a deal in 2006 to build a 900-km pipeline that would have crossed Bangladesh. Indecision from Bangladesh delayed the project and another pipeline proposal between Myanmar and China further complicated the matter. There were also reports of India and Myanmar discussing alternative proposals linking the pipeline directly with the Indian north-eastern states. Since the beginning of 2010, there have been reports that the new Bangladeshi Government has agreed to a tri-nation gas pipeline.[35] In this case, the Myanmar--Bangladesh-India gas pipeline may materialize in the next couple of years.

Conclusions

At this stage of economic modernization, India is adapting to economic globalization and to the emerging Asian and global balance of power. Its accelerated economic performance has impacted upon its foreign policy in general, and on its engagement within Asia and with Great Powers. It is aggressively pursuing regional trade arrangements and also has started policy reforms to improve border trade. For India, development within the last two decades has shown that geoeconomics has not replaced geopolitics. However, potential new economic opportunities, if realized, may influence regional geopolitics. India is vulnerable due to its insufficient energy resources. Accelerated growth has also forced India to synchronize its energy security issues within its foreign and security policy. In the coming years, actions and commitments on the energy front will shape India's relations with countries like the USA, Russia, China and Iran. In the past, external energy policy meant securing reliable supplies from the Gulf. More recently it included multiple strategies of diversification, acquiring assets abroad and pipeline politics. In future, protecting supplies from different sources as well as assets abroad will also become part of national security. Despite all ambitious efforts, coal will continue to be India's main energy source and the Gulf region will continue to be its main source of oil and gas. On the domestic front, we can witness major policy changes in the area of coal production, with private-sector participation, power sector reforms, rationalization of fuel prices, efforts in the direction of energy efficiency and demand management. It is also expected that nuclear and hydro electric power as well as renewables will be playing a relatively bigger role. Therefore, the major action will be in the creation of a legal and institutional framework to implement all these policies.

Notes

1 *Governance in the 21st Century*, Paris: OECD, 2001.
2 E. Luttwak, 'From Geopolitics to Geo-economics: Logic of Conflict, Grammar of Commerce', *The National Interest*, No. 20, 1990.
3 R. Kubaych, 'Geo-economics Injects New Uncertainties into Troubled Markets', 20 May 2004, www.cfr.org.
4 D. Cowen and N. Smith, 'After Geopolitics? From Geopolitical Social to Geo-economics', *Antipode*, Vol. 41, No. 1, 2009. Also see D. Scott, 'The Great Power "Great Game" Between India and China: "The Logic of Geography"', *Geopolitics*, Vol. 13, No. 1, 2008.
5 Kubaych, 'Geo-economics Injects New Uncertainties into Troubled Markets', op. cit.
6 S. Baru, *Strategic Consequences of India's Economic Performance*, New Delhi: Academic Foundation, 2006.
7 J. McDonald and S. Wimbush, 'India's Energy Security', *Strategic Analysis*, Vol. 23, No. 5, 1999, p.826.
8 M. Pardesi and S. Ganguly, 'India and Energy Security: A Foreign Policy Priority', in H. Pant (ed.), *Indian Foreign Policy in a Unipolar World*, New Delhi: Routledge, 2009. Also S. Dadwal, 'Energy Security: India's Options', *Strategic Analysis*, Vol. 23, No. 4, 1999.
9 J. Nehru, 'India's Foreign Policy', 4 December 1947, *Independence and After: A Collection of Speeches, 1946–1949*, New York: John Day Company, 1950, p.201.
10 'The idea that economic considerations play a role in shaping a Nation's foreign policy is not new. We in India were alerted to this reality at our very birth as a Republic when Panditji [Nehru] first articulated his vision of Indian foreign policy in the Constituent Assembly legislature in December 1947. Panditji had said, and I quote: "talking of Foreign policies, the House must remember that these are not just empty struggles on a chess board. Behind them lie all manner of things. Ultimately, foreign

policy is the outcome of economic policy." I submit to you that India has indeed developed this argument in the economic field', M. Singh, 'PM's Speech at India Today Conclave', 25 February 2005, pmindia.nic.in.

11 Figures used are taken from various publications of the Ministry of Finance, and Ministry of Commerce and Industry of the Government of India.

12 See J. Ramesh, 'India's Economic Integration with Asia', Seminar Series on Regional Economic Integration, 24 November 2008, www.icainstitute.org; M. Asher, 'India's Rising Role in Asia', Discussion Paper (RIS, New Delhi), No. 121, 2007.

13 G. Sachdeva, 'Regional Economic Linkages', in N. Joshi (ed.), *Reconnecting India & Central Asia: Emerging Security & Economic Dimensions*, Washington, DC: Central Asia Caucasus Institute (Johns Hopkins University), 2010.

14 G. Sachdeva, 'India Ocean Region: Present Economic Trends & Future Possibilities', *International Studies*, Vol. 41, No. 1, 2004.

15 G. Sachdeva, 'India-China Economic Cooperation Through Growth Quadrangle', in K. Bajpai and A. Mattoo (eds), *The Peacock and the Dragon: India-China Relations in the 21st Century*, New Delhi: Har-Anand, 2000.

16 There is no single definition of open regionalism. The concept was mainly developed by APEC countries where members of a trade bloc undertook trade liberalization together and extended it world-wide on a 'most favoured nation' basis.

17 G. Sachdeva, *Economy of the Northeast: Policy, Present Conditions and Future Possibilities*, New Delhi: Konark Publishers, 2000.

18 Government of India, *Integrated Energy Policy: Report of the Expert Committee*, New Delhi: Planning Commission, 2006.

19 Planning Commission, planningcommission.nic.in/sectors/energy.html, percentage figures for 2007/08, rounded.

20 Government of India, *India: Hydrocarbon Vision 2025*, New Delhi: Ministry of Petroleum and Natural Gas, 2000. Wind is less than 0.5%. See also G. Pant, *India: The Emerging Energy Player*, New Delhi: Pearson Longman, 2008, p.43, for coal domination.

21 US Department of Energy, *International Energy Outlook 2010*, Washington, DC: Department of Energy, 2010. These projections may change depending on higher or lower growth than the reference rate. Upward or downward prices of energy may also change these scenarios.

22 For details see *Energy Outlook 2007*, Paris: IEA/OECD, 2007.

23 Government of India, *Eleventh Five Year Plan: 2007–12*, Vol. 3, 2008, www.planningcommission.nic.in, p.343.

24 G. Dietl, 'New Threats to Oil and Gas in West Asia: Issues in India's Energy Security', *Strategic Analysis*, Vol. 28, No. 3, 2004.

25 Government of India, *Eleventh Five Year Plan: 2007–12*, Vol. 3, p.343.

26 Government of India, *Integrated Energy Policy: Report of the Expert Committee*, New Delhi: Planning Commission, 2006, p.54.

27 T. Ahmad, 'Geopolitics of Oil', *Seminar*, No. 555, November 2005.

28 'ONGC Mittal Signs Deal to Take 25% Stake in Kazakh Oilfield', *Times of India*, 24 January 2009.

29 *Annual Report 2008–09*, New Delhi: ONGC Videsh, 2009.

30 'India Invited to Join TAPI Project', *The Hindu*, 17 March 2006.

31 'Delhi Invited to Join TAPI Project', *The Dawn*, 16 March 2006, www.dawn.com.

32 M. Khan, 'Basic Accord for Turkmen Gas Project Signed', *The Dawn*, 25 April 2008, www.dawn.com.

33 B. Chellaney, *Asian Juggernaut: The Rise of China, India and Japan*, New Delhi: HarperCollins, 2006, p.89.

34 India also has interest in the International North-South Corridor (INSC) project, perhaps as a safer alternative, linking the Caspian/Turkmenistan fields to Iran down to Chabahar.

35 U. Bhaskar, 'Bangladesh Agrees to Tri-nation Gas Pipeline', 28 February 2010, www.livemint.com.

Part 2
India's 'immediate neighbourhood'

6

India's relations with Pakistan

David Scott

Introduction

Of all India's relations, that with Pakistan has been the most problematic and highly charged, over the longest period of time, a relationship accurately described by Inder Gujral as a 'tormented' one.[1] Such has been this ongoing, generally negative relationship that for each country the other now looms large as something of an existential bogeyman, the 'Other'. Even as India looks beyond South Asia in its international rise, relations with Pakistan continue to remain embedded like a thorn in India's foreign policy, both within its *immediate neighbourhood*, and also in India's *extended neighbourhood*. An 'unending' tension and conflict has characterized their relationship as neighbouring independent states.[2]

An initial moment in time illustrates this well, namely the Simla Agreement, drawn up in July 1972 in the aftermath of yet another war between these two neighbours.[3] This came a quarter of a century after their emergence as independent successor states to British India. The Agreement's preamble asserted that 'The Government of India and the Government of Pakistan are resolved that the two countries put an end to the conflict and confrontation that have hitherto marred their relations and work for the promotion of a friendly and harmonious relationship and the establishment of durable peace in the subcontinent'. To talk of conflict and confrontation as having marred their relations was indeed accurate. Unfortunately, a friendly and harmonious relationship had failed to operate before 1972, but equally well has also failed to establish itself since 1972.

Within the Simla Agreement some technical details were established over the return of Prisoners of War, but little else. It stated that 'the two countries are resolved to settle their differences by peaceful means through bilateral negotiations or by any other peaceful means mutually agreed upon between them'. Their differences have not been resolved. The Simla Agreement talked of how 'the basic issues and causes of conflict which have bedevilled the relations between the two countries for the last 25 years shall be resolved by peaceful means', but those basic issues and causes of conflict still remain pretty intact, unresolved by peaceful or indeed non-peaceful means. Within that range of issues, the Agreement talked of working to bring about 'a final settlement of Jammu and Kashmir', but almost 40 years on, the issue of Kashmir remains a confrontational bone of contention between them.

Meanwhile, the Simla Agreement talked of interim measures, of a practical *modus vivendi*: 'both Governments will take all steps within their power to prevent hostile propaganda directed against each other', a still-born piece of rhetoric. The Agreement may have expressed the hope that 'pending the final settlement of any of the problems between the two countries, neither side shall unilaterally alter the situation and both shall prevent the organization, assistance or encouragement of any acts detrimental to the maintenance of peaceful and harmonious relations', but each side accuses the other of detrimental acts and encouragement of hostile forces. The Agreement may have asserted that 'the pre-requisite for reconciliation, good neighborliness and durable peace between them is a commitment by both the countries to peaceful coexistence, respect for each other's territorial integrity and sovereignty and non-interference in each other's internal affairs', yet interference and destabilization continued to be perceived by each against the other. Pakistan accuses India of supporting Baluchi separatism; India accuses Pakistan of supporting Kashmir *jihadist* breakaway groups.

The Simla Agreement talked of 'basic issues and causes of conflict which have bedevilled the relations between the two countries for the last 25 years'. These basic issues and causes of conflict can be organized into the following: national identity, Kashmir, terrorism, strategic culture and the legacy of war, missile–nuclear arms race, wider alliances, and economic linkages. Three Pakistan levels are involved, the role of Pakistan's governments, the role of Pakistan's Inter-Services Intelligence (ISI), and the role of Pakistan-based *jihadist* groups.

National identity

One of the interesting things in international relations has been the way in which perceptions of culture and identity have indeed returned to the front of international relations analysis.[4] The date 22 February 1941 was a fateful one in the history of British India and for the future shape of the sub-continent. On that day the force of Muhammad Ali Jinnah's 'two-nation theory' took decisive shape with the Lahore Declaration, the formal call by the Muslim League for Partition: 'the areas in which the Muslims are numerically in majority as in the North-Western and Eastern zones of India should be grouped to constitute independent states in which the constituent units shall be autonomous and sovereign'. In bald terms, this led to the creation of Pakistan, divided into two wings, West Pakistan and East Pakistan.

The rationale for this was the two-nation theory propounded vigorously by Jinnah, whose forceful personality and determination played a key part in getting this, and hence his being called the *Quaid-I Azam* 'Father of the Nation'. In this case, his sense of nation was religiously based, even if his personal life was not, namely Islam.

> It is a dream that the Hindus and Muslims can ever evolve a common nationality and this misconception of one Indian nation has gone far beyond the limits and is the cause of most of your troubles and will lead India to destruction if we fail to revise our notions in time. The Hindus and Muslims belong to two different religious philosophies, social customs, literatures. They neither inter-marry nor inter-dine together and, indeed, they belong to two different civilizations which are based mainly on conflicting ideas and conceptions [...] To yoke together two such nations under a single State, one as a numerical minority and the other as a majority, must lead to growing discontent and final destruction of any fabric that may be so built up for the government of such a state.[5]

Samuel Huntington's *Clash of Civilization* thesis had indeed been predated in this analysis by Jinnah half a century earlier, a 'fractured fraternity' predating Huntington's 'fracture lines of conflict'.[6] In successfully pushing through this vision of religious-cum-political division, the question then arose as to what legacy such nation-formation has had on the two successor states, the Islamic Republic of Pakistan, and the (secular) Republic of India.

The irony is that Jinnah seemed to think that dividing India up on different nation grounds would not damage subsequent inter-nation relations between two such diametrically created states:

> The problem in India is not of an inter-communal character but manifestly of an international one, and it must be treated as such [...] There is no reason why these states should be antagonistic to each other [...] It will lead more towards natural good will by international pacts between them, and they can live in complete harmony with their neighbours. This will lead further to a friendly settlement all the more easily with regard to Minorities by reciprocal arrangements and adjustments between Muslim India and Hindu India, which will far more adequately and effectively safeguard the rights and interests of Muslims and various other Minorities.[7]

However, this has most certainly not been the case. For over half a century these two neighbours emerging from British India have polarized the subcontinent and taken their arguments against each other inside *and* outside the region.

Part of the legacy has been the reverberating effects of the political polemics surrounding Partition, and the very tangible human suffering caused as Partition was implemented on the ground amidst population transfers and sectarian killings on a significant scale during that summer of 1947. In terms of national psyche, this historical memory is still strong.

In addition, there is a political legacy. The problem has been that the political foundations of the one challenge the very foundations and legitimacy of the other, through being based on diametrically opposite principles. On the one hand stands Pakistan, the very case for the political independence of which is based on a sense of nationalism based on religious allegiance. Without religion, Pakistan made no sense, especially in its split geographical position between East and West Pakistan. Islam was the ideological glue used to justify its very national existence, based on the claim that Hindus and Muslims could not get along in a common national framework. On the other hand the Republic of India rejected the very foundations of the two-nation theory and, refusing to see itself a Hindu India, it proclaimed and rejoiced in religious pluralism supported by a secular state ideology and for a geographical sense of what India was. India's secular-political claims cut across and in a way continue to undermine Pakistan's legitimacy, whilst Pakistan's religious-political claims cut across and in a way continue to undermine India's secular legitimacy. In effect, 'the underlying basis of the Indo-Pakistani conflict is really an argument about the fundamentals of state-construction', an argument over 'primordial conceptions of identity' that continues to shape antagonistic inter-state relations vis-à-vis each other.[8]

The reverberations of this have continued down the decades. Pakistan has a continuing sense, with some reason for some Indian quarters, of being seen as an aberration, as an inherently flawed national project that is doomed to failure, an unviable national ideology which will eventually give way to a reincorporation into the bigger Indian neighbour, thereby restoring the unity of the Indian sub-continent, but on New Delhi's terms. After all, the Bharatiya Janata Party (BJP—Indian People's Party) 2004 manifesto was blunt in how 'the BJP unflinchingly holds that differences in faith cannot challenge the idea of India as One Nation or undermine our millennia-old identity as One People. This is why we rejected the two-nation theory on the basis of which our Motherland was tragically partitioned in 1947'.[9] India has the sense of Pakistan wanting to undermine her secular stability, to vindicate the two-nation theory of Hindu-Muslim divide, and to incorporate Muslim majority areas that are presently under the control of India. This, of course, takes us on to the issue of Kashmir, where intangible concerns and claims over national formation have created ongoing territorial dispute and military conflicts on a regular basis.

Kashmir

Kashmir is the fulcrum on which intangible matters of national formation have developed into tangible matters of international conflict. In the months of Partition in 1947, generally Hindu-majority states went to India, and Muslim-majority states went to Pakistan. However, there were a few exceptions where local rulers did not reflect the religious identity of their states. In the case of Junagadh, a coastal enclave, its Muslim ruler, counselled by his adviser Shah Nawaz Bhutto, the father of Pakistan's later Prime Minister Zulfikar Bhutto, opted for Pakistan, but was swept away by a blockade, military intervention and a successful plebiscite imposed by India. In the case of Hyderabad, totally surrounded by Indian territory, its Muslim ruler opted for independence before Indian troops intervened in September 1947.

In the case of Kashmir the lines went the other way, with a Hindu ruler sitting atop a Muslim majority population. Further ambiguity was caused by strong independence sentiments being muffled, and with the majority Muslim opinion being reflected not by Jinnah's Muslim League but by Sheikh Abdullah's National Conference that had co-operative links with the Congress Party. Suffice to say that, amidst temporization by the Kashmir ruler, growing instability and appearance of irregular forces from the Pakistan side wass followed by the decision of the ruler to call for Indian assistance, which in turn brought formal Pakistan intervention as well. The results were two-fold. There was a de facto partition of Kashmir between the India-held central valley (Muslim-dominated) as well as Jammu (Hindu) and Ladakh (Buddhist), whilst Pakistan held onto the western fringes of Kashmir (renamed *Azad Kashmir*, 'Free Kashmir') and the northerly mountainous area of Baltistan. In the wake of military stalemate and recourse to the UN, vague promises were given on a plebiscite at some point, but this was shelved subsequently, as Sheikh Abdullah lent support to Kashmir's accession to India, and Pakistan strengthened its grip on Azad Kashmir/Baltistan.

Since then, conflict, 'unending war', has raged, with indeterminate outcomes merely entrenching divided outlooks between the two neighbours.[10] War in 1947–49 focused on Kashmir, whilst the wider conflicts in 1965 and 1971 brought in collateral fire in Kashmir. Within Kashmir the Kargil mini-war of 1999 was of course Kashmir-based, with the Siachin glacier proving another spot within Kashmir over which the two countries clashed. The Kargil dispute was the last time that the states employed their military forces directly against each other, but cross-fire along the Line of Control continues down to the present.

Post-Kargil, Kashmir has not disappeared as an issue.[11] Instead of state-to-state conflict, Kashmir has developed its sub-state and trans-state conflict dynamics as the growth of local operatives in Kashmir was given support by Pakistan. This is labelled by India as little more than Pakistan 'sponsoring' terrorism, a subject to which we can turn.

Terrorism

A constant refrain from India is the country's sense of Pakistan being a state that sponsors 'terrorism'. Initially, this was associated with Pakistani support given to Kashmir and Sikh insurgents in the 1970s, part of Zulfiqar Ali Bhutto's strategy for forward strategic depth, an instrument to substitute for the lack of strategic depth and early warning capabilities of a Pakistan that had been truncated in two following the 1971 war with India. Internal Kashmir developments, including the death of Sheikh Abdullah in 1982 and harder-line coercive policies by Indira Gandhi, had sparked a growing insurgency in the valley of Kashmir in 1989. In Pakistan the political leadership, now headed by Benazir Bhutto, gave political support to the Kashmir cause, whilst the ISI gave material and substantial support to the insurgent groups, funnelling aid across the ceasefire Line of Control leading from Pakistan-controlled Azad Kasmir/Baltistan into the Indian-controlled valley of Kashmir.

The results were clear enough: growing identification and denunciation of Pakistan as a terrorist-sheltering state. Typical was India's Ministry of External Affairs *Annual Report 1998–1999*:

> Our concerns regarding Pakistan's continued, and active involvement in instigating and sponsoring terrorism in J&K and other parts of India, were made clear to them on several occasions during the year – and reiterated during the composite dialogue, and conclusive evidence to this effect was also presented. It was emphasised that our resolve to defeat cross-border terrorism and to safeguard our security interests was total. We have advised them that abandonment of this activity, and full respect for their commitments under the Simla Agreement, including avoidance of provocative acts across the LOC and hostile propaganda, were essential steps.[12]

Such Pakistan-sponsored support for insurgency groups was further strengthened by the ending of the ISI-supported *mujahideen* groups that had been operating against Soviet forces in Afghanistan. In the wake of the Soviet withdrawal, such Afghanistan-conflict *mujahideen* veterans, based in Pakistan, turned their attentions eastwards to Kashmir. Instead of formal state–state war (as in 1947–49, 1965 and 1971), Kashmir was the scene for 'covert war' waged by *jihadist* groups aided and abetted by Pakistan's ISI.

However a further problem for India has been the readiness of such Pakistan-sponsored groups to take the fight to other parts of India. In 1993 'Pakistan's complicity in the planning and execution of the bomb blasts in Bombay resulted in an increased perception of the public in India of Pakistan's designs to interfere in India's internal affairs and to engineer conditions of instability'.[13] In 2001 it was the bombing of the Indian parliament, which brought large-scale 'near-war' mobilization of Indian forces along the border with Pakistan. It also brought detailed analysis by the Indian Government:

> The abortive terrorist attack against Parliament on 13 December, by elements of the Pakistan-based Lashkar-e-taiba (LeT) and JeM [Jaish-e-Muhammad], was undoubtedly the most audacious, as also the most alarming act of terrorism in the nearly two decades of Pak-sponsored terrorism in India. This time, the Pakistani-based terrorists and their mentors across the border had the temerity to try and wipe out the entire political leadership of India. Much thought and reflection have been given as to why Pakistan based terrorist groups and their mentors decided to raise the stakes so high [...] The only answer that satisfactorily addresses this query is that Pakistan – a product of the indefensible Two Nation Theory, a theocratic state with an extremely tenuous tradition of democracy – is unable to reconcile itself with the reality of a secular, democratic, self-confident and steadily progressing India, whose standing in the international community is getting inexorably higher with the passage of time.[14]

What is striking is the rejection of Pakistan's very foundations, the two-nations theory, as being indefensible, not only then in Pakistan's 1947 formation, but also logically for its continuation

63

in the 21st century. What is also noticeable is this sense of Pakistan dragging India down from its otherwise straightforward international rise.

In 2008 it was the Mumbai bombings again. India was clear on the Pakistani provenance of the attackers:

> The more fragile a Government, the more it tends to act in an irresponsible fashion. Pakistan's responses to our various demarches on terrorist attacks is an obvious example [...] Those in charge of the terrorist infrastructure in Pakistan have resorted to other stratagems to infiltrate terrorists into India. Infiltration is occurring via Nepal and from Bangladesh, though it has not totally ceased via the Line of Control in J&K. We are aware that the sea route is another option that is now being exercised. A few interceptions have taken place, though we failed to intercept the 10 Pakistani terrorists who came by sea from Karachi on November 26. The terrorist attack in Mumbai in November last year was clearly carried out by a Pakistan-based outfit, the Lashkar-e-Taiba. On the basis of the investigations carried out, including the Agencies of some foreign countries whose nationals were killed in the attack, there is enough evidence to show that, given the sophistication and military precision of the attack it must have had the support of some official agencies in Pakistan.[15]

Talk of 'some official agencies in Pakistan' is another word for the ISI. What is noticeable is India's sense of terrorist attacks circumventing India's military hold on Kashmir, through operating from Nepal and Bangladesh.

Strategic culture, the legacy of war and military arms race dynamics

Amidst such ideological and territorial divides, Pakistan and India have come to blows several times. India may stress its *ahimsa* (non-violence) tradition, but it has been prepared to take the battle to Pakistan. With both claiming moral justification over their respective causes, and with both claiming to have fought defensive wars against each other, the fact remains that conflict has been endemic since independence in 1947. Just over a century has seen successive wars, namely full-scale conflicts in 1947–49, 1965 and 1971, the mini-war over Kargil in 1999, ongoing skirmishes over the inhospitable Siachin glacier, near-war in 2001–02 (*Operation Prakaram* mobilization), and cross-fire border incidents which are a continuing fact of life.[16] For each country, their most obvious military enemy has been the other; they have become used to thinking of the other as the military foe.

Pakistan has long sought strategic parity with India, with a sense of cultural élan compensating for numeric inferiority, the feeling that 'one Pakistani soldier is equal to 10 Indian soldiers'. India has long sought to establish superiority over Pakistan, militarily and diplomatically. Its *Cold Start* military doctrine, introduced in 2004, was 'aimed militarily at Pakistan and is offensive-operations specific', involving rapid deployment forces able to strike into Pakistan and crush both the Pakistani Army and terrorist groups operating on Pakistani soil.[17]

Given such adversarial mindsets, there has also been an ongoing arms race competition, within which classic IR 'security dilemma' dynamics operate as each tries to match and cap the other, in a spiral of spending and mistrust. From Pakistan's point of view, it has long sought military equipment from more powerful allies to enable competition with India. Initially such arms transfers were mainly from the USA, but in more recent years the People's Republic of China has also provided Pakistan with ongoing military assistance. From India's point of view, its military links with the Soviet Union and later Russia have partly been aimed at redressing the imbalance with China, but have been aimed also at attaining/maintaining military superiority over Pakistan. Fighter aircraft have been one aspect of their arms race, with India keen in recent years to see that US arms sales to India are not matched by similar sales to Pakistan.[18]

Missiles have been another feature of this arms race and build-up. Pakistan's arsenal was steadily built up during 1989–2000 in terms of numbers and range. It consists of *Hatf-I* (60 km–80 km range), *Haft-II* (aka *Abdali*), *Hatf-III* (aka *Ghaznavi*, 290 km range), *Hatf-IV* (aka *Shaheen-I*, 750 km range), *Hatf-V* (aka *Ghauri*, 1,500 km range and payload capacity of 700 kg), *Ghauri-II* (2,300 km range), and *Hatf-VI* (2,500 km range). These are all India-centric in terms of range and purpose. Meanwhile, India's own missile programme has developed over the years, with its Integrated Guided Missile Development Programme (IGMDP) set up in 1983. This has led to *Prithvi-I* (150 km range), *Prithvi-II* (250 km range), *Prithvi-III* (aka *Dhanush*, 350 km range), *Agni-I* (700 km range), and *Agni-II* (2,000 km range). The *Prithvi* and *Agni-I* missiles are all Pakistan-centric, while the longer range of *Agni-II* gives it China- as well as Pakistan-centric purposes, with the subsequent longer range *Agni-III* missile being China-centric alone.

The increasing range but also increasing payload of Pakistani and Indian missiles has also been entwined with their nuclear weapons programme, which indeed provides the nuclear payload for such missiles. India's nuclear weapons programme was sparked by China's nuclear advances in the 1960s. The 1971 defeat with India, followed by India's own nuclear explosion in 1974 (Pokhran-I, *Operation Smiling Buddha*) was the spur for Pakistan to develop its own nuclear weapons programme, to try to re-establish military-strategic parity.

Such developments came to a head in 1998, when in April of that year Pakistan tested its most powerful missile to date, the *Hatf-V* (aka *Ghauri*) missile, with a 1,500 km range and payload capacity of 700 kg. India's response was immediate: the Pokhran-II, *Operation Shakti*, nuclear tests in May 1998, which were immediately matched by Pakistan's own nuclear tests, *Operation Chagai*, later in the month. Both sides have built up a small nuclear arsenal, with Pakistan spending proportionally more to try and match India's bigger economic capacity.[19]

India's logic at the time involved Pakistan. As Prime Minister Vajpayee's letter to the US President pointed out:

> I have been deeply concerned at the deteriorating security environment, specially the nuclear environment, faced by India for some years past. We have an overt nuclear weapon state [China] on our borders, a state which committed armed aggression against India in 1962. Although our relations with that country have improved in the last decade or so, an atmosphere of distrust persists mainly due to the unresolved border problem. To add to the distrust, that country has materially helped another neighbour of ours [Pakistan] to become a covert nuclear weapons state. At the hands of this bitter neighbour [Pakistan] we have suffered three aggressions in the last 50 years. And for the last ten years we have been the victim of unremitting terrorism and militancy sponsored by it [Pakistan] in several parts of our country, specially Punjab and Jammu and Kashmir.[20]

What, of course, is evident are the China-centric strands of the argument, as well as the reiteration of having to face ongoing military conflicts and sponsorship of terrorism against India by Pakistan. In addition, though Pakistan's close links with China were of concern to India, specifically with regard to the crucial Chinese help given to Pakistan's nuclear programme,[21] so was Pakistan's role as a proxy for China, as a surrogate state.

Pakistan links with China

One China-Pakistan irritant for India was the readiness of Pakistan to give up to China its claims to the Trans-Karakorum Tract (Shaksgam valley) in 1963. This was greeted with dismay by India, which of course claimed that the Shaksgam valley was part of India through India's wider claims to Kashmir. Further reports of Pakistan allowing entry of Chinese forces into Pakistan-occupied Kashmir, in Gilgit and Baltistan, were of concern to India in the summer of 2010.[22]

In wider terms, it is true that India may on its own have an undoubted power advantage over Pakistan, whose hopes of maintaining any strategic parity with India disappeared after defeat in the 1971 war and the division of Pakistan. Pakistan's response to its diminishing power position *vis-à-vis* India has been to develop its own nuclear weapons programme (with the assistance of China) and to strengthen its foreign policy alignment with China in general. This so-called 'all-weather friendship' between Pakistan and China operates as a more sinister 'nexus' in Indian eyes, in which 'China thus operates as a "force multiplier" for Pakistan vis-à-vis India'.[23] New Delhi increasingly sees Pakistan as not so important in its own right, but as offering dangerous opportunities for China's attempt to encircle India, coming, as it were, down from the Himalayas, down the Indus to the Indian Ocean, in effect blocking India along its north-western flanks. China's links with Pakistan are also seen as threatening with the build-up of the deep water port of Gwadar, opened in 2008 with Chinese funding, and offering berthing potential for a growing Chinese naval presence in the Indian Ocean. Pakistan's links with China do constrain India to some extent. This did not stop India from military action in 1971 (Bangladesh) and 1999 (Kargil), but the dangers of facing a two-front war against Pakistan and China did stop India from taking military action against Pakistan in the wake of the Mumbai bombings of 2008.[24] Ironically, India's military planners did, in 2010, move towards accepting such a two-front war against Pakistan and China simultaneously.[25]

Positive linkages?

So far, the relationship of India with Pakistan has been portrayed in generally negative terms. National ideologies, territorial disputes, terrorism, a military arms race, and differing diplomatic alignments (the Pakistan-China nexus) have generated entrenched ongoing friction and negative relations between Indian and Pakistan. International Relations (IR) *constructivism*, geopolitics and *realism*[26] power imperatives are all in play in such negative dynamics. However, are there any IR strands that can, or could, ease their situation? The IR *democracy = peace* framework would suggest one avenue for easing tensions. However, Pakistan's democracy has been fragile, often swept away by recurring bouts of military rule, or sidelined by the presence of the ISI.

The other main IR framework has been IR liberalism-functionalism, the idea of increasing economic trade across borders. There should indeed be 'security spill-overs' from economic co-operation between these two neighbours.[27] The only problem here is that Indian-Pakistani economic links have been so low as to be virtually non-existent. Infrastructure links are the exception rather than the rule, hence the fuss over Atal Vajpayee and Nawaz Sharif re-establishing the Delhi–Lahore bus route in 1999. After the Indo-Pakistan war in 1965, trade was almost negligible for a period of nine years. Bilateral trade did resume in 1975/76, following the 1974 protocol for the restoration of commercial relations on a government-to-government basis, signed by the two countries after the 1971 war, but it remained at an insignificant level till very recently. It stood at around US $150m. in 1992/93. Since 1996 trade between the two countries has been generally increasing, though subject to erratic variations reflecting political hiccups between the two countries, following India's granting of most favoured nation (MFN) status to Pakistan. Pakistan, in turn, increased its list of permissible items to 600, adding another 78 items in 2003, and another 72 items in 2004. The latter year also saw the two countries signing the South Asia Free Trade Agreement (SAFTA). Trade stood at $180m. in 1996, but has been increasing in quantity terms to $616m. in 2004/05, $869m. in 2005/06, $1,674m. in 2006/07, to reach a peak of $2,239m. in 2007/08, before slipping back to $1,810m. in 2008/09 (a decline of almost 20%, partly caused by the global recession but also by the post-Mumbai bombing deterioration in relations).[28] It remained down at $1,849m. for 2009/10. From India's point of view, Pakistan is still an unimportant trade partner. Pakistan's share of India's total trade remained small at 0.24% in 2003/04, 0.32% in 2004/05, 0.34% in 2005/06, 0.54% in 2006/07, 0.54% in 2007/08, 0.37% in 2008/09 and 0.40% in 2009/10. Admittedly, illegal trade might push these figures up, but then illegal, unofficial trade is unlikely to improve official relations.

Indeed, some specific trade issues are problematic. Two important pipeline projects are the TAPI (Turkmenistan-Afghanistan-Pakistan-India) and IPI (Iran-Pakistan-India) projects. Having crucial energy concerns vulnerable to Pakistan (turning the taps off, as it were), interruption is something that is pushing India to seek alternatives, i.e. establishing links from Afghanistan to Iran's port of Chabahar, rebuilt with Indian financial assistance, or routing Turkmenistani oil via the International North South Corridor (INSC) route from the Caspian Sea down to Chabahar.

Conclusions

Anyone speculating on Indian-Pakistani relations faces a quandary. The most tangible issue may be resolvable, perhaps with a status quo partition along the current Line of Control, with soft borders and decentralization of power away from India and Pakistan. Something on those lines seemed to have 'almost' been agreed in 2004, before the fall from power of Pervez Musharraf. However, ideologically they remain poles apart, with an inherent readiness to assume the worst of each other and to seek to constrain the other country, in the case of Pakistan with the help of China. IR *security dilemmas* continue to operate between these two neighbours. Trade will probably grow, though, as after all their remaining low level of trade means there is sizeable potential for increased trade.[29] However, India may well be focusing its economic interest elsewhere, eastwards to the Bay of Bengal (BIMSTEC), South-East Asia (ASEAN) and East Asia (EAS) frameworks.

Of course, the internal character of each state remains problematic. Pakistan faces two challenges: one is to avoid the 'Talibanization of Pakistan', the scenario whereby rising Islamist forces take control of Pakistan (and its nuclear forces) ready to unleash *jihadist* cadres against India in Kashmir and elsewhere.[30] This would be a nightmare scenario for New Delhi. The other challenge is surviving intact.[31] Some Indian commentators see Pakistan as an inherently flawed creation, and something that is either doomed to eventual re-absorption back into a still-rising India, undoing Partition as it were. An alternative variant is the disintegration of Pakistan into constituent Baluchi, Pashtun, Sindhi and Punjabi parts, smaller units that would be unable to pose such a challenge to India as Pakistan has. The example of 1971 lies before Pakistan and India, the eruption of Bengali nationalism generating the creation (with Indian help) of Bangladesh, thereby undercutting the whole logic of the two-nation theory and its underpinning of Pakistan's continuing existence. Meanwhile, what of India?

India faces some similar challenges. First, there could be a Hindu equivalent of the 'Talibanization of Pakistan', overturning the secular direction of post-Independence India. The possibility is there: the *Hindutva* forces restrained by Nehru's Congress Party did, after all, achieve power in 1998, under the BJP, the first act of which was to conduct nuclear tests at Pokhran-II, 'the Hindu bomb' as some called it. Though the BJP lost the 2004 and 2008 general elections, a return to power could see a *Hindutva* resurgence. The irony for Pakistan would be that this would echo Jinnah's own two-nation theory analysis of a Muslim India (Pakistan) and a Hindu India. Such a development would probably be detrimental to India-Pakistan relations. Second, India might fragment. This was the notorious suggestion by one Chinese think tank, an India fragmenting into 30 pieces.[32] Such fragmented post-India successor states would be unable to pose the existential threat to Pakistan in the structural way that the Republic of India has managed to do through its sheer size and numbers, at almost 10:1.

Notes

1   I. Gujral, 'Significance of an Independent Foreign Policy', 14 October 1996, in I. Gujral, *Continuity and Change. India's Foreign Policy*, London: Macmillan, 2003, p.109.
2   S. Ganguly, *Conflict Unending. India-Pakistan Tensions Since 1947*, New York: Columbia University Press, 2001; P. Chander, *India & Pakistan Unending Conflict*, 3 vols, New Delhi: Aph Publishing Corporation, 2002; T.V. Paul (ed.), *The India-Pakistan Conflict: An Enduring Rivalry*, Cambridge: Cambridge University Press, 2005. Also D. McLeod, *India and Pakistan: Friends, Rival or Enemies?* Aldershot: Ashgate, 2008; A. Misra, *India-Pakistan Coming to Terms*, London: Macmillan, 2010.
3   India-Pakistan, *Simla Agreement*, 2 July 1972, mea.gov.in/jk/sim-ag.htm.
4   Y. Lapid and F. Kratochwl, *The Return of Culture and Identity in IR Theory*, Boulder: Lynne Rienner, 1996.
5   M. Jinnah, 22 March 1940 (Lahore), rep. 'An International Problem', in W. de Bary (ed.), *Sources of Indian Tradition*, Vol. II, New York: Columbia University Press, 1958, pp.284–85.
6   M. Ajithkumar, *India Pakistan Relations: The Story of a Fractured Fraternity*, New Delhi: Kalpaz Publications, 2006.
7   M. Jinnah, 'An International Problem', op. cit., p.284.
8   Ganguly, *Conflict Unending. India-Pakistan Tensions Since 1947*, op. cit., p.5.
9   Bharatiya Janata Party, *Vision Document 2004*, 2004, www.bjp.org.
10 V. Schofield, *Kashmir in Conflict: India, Pakistan and the Unending War*, London: I.B. Tauris & Company, 2003. Also R. Wirsing, *India, Pakistan, and the Kashmir Dispute*, New York: St Martin's Press, 1998; K. Gupta (ed.), *India-Pakistan Relations with Special Reference to Kashmir*, 4 Vols, New Delhi: Atlantic Publishers & Distributors (P) Ltd, 2006; S. Kapur, 'The Kashmir Dispute. Past, Present and Future', in S. Ganguly, A. Scobell and J. Liow (eds), *The Routledge Handbook of Asian Security Studies*, London: Routledge, 2010.
11 ICS, 'India, Pakistan and Kashmir: Stabilising a Cold Peace', *Briefing Paper* (International Crisis Group), No. 51, 15 June 2006.
12 Ministry of External Affairs, *Annual Report 1998–1999*, New Delhi: Ministry of External Affairs, 1999, mealib.nic.in.
13 Ministry of External Affairs, *Annual Report 1993–1994*, New Delhi: Ministry of External Affairs, 1994, p.6.
14 Ministry of External Affairs, *Annual Report 2001–2002*, p.9. Also V. Khanna, 'Continuation of Terrorism by Pakistan', 13 March 2003, Rajya Sabha, meaindia.nic.in; S. Noor, 'Pakistan-India Relations and Terrorism', *Pakistan Horizon*, Vol. 60, No. 2, 2007.
15 M. Singh, 'Address by Prime Minister at CM's Conference', 6 January 2009.
16 S. Ganguly, *The Origins of War in South Asia: Indo-Pakistani Conflicts Since 1947*, Boulder: Westview Press, 1994.
17 S. Kapila, 'India's New "Cold Start" War Doctrine Strategically Reviewed', *Papers* (SAAG), No. 991, 4 May 2004. Also S. Kapila, 'Indian Army Validates its Cold Start War Doctrine', *Papers* (SAAG), No. 1408, 7 June 2005.
18 'US Supply of Sophisticated Weapons to Pakistan Concerns India, says Antony', 6 March 2010, www.thaindian.com.
19 S. Kapur, 'India and Pakistan's Unstable Peace: Why Nuclear South Asia is Not Like Cold War Europe', *International Security*, Vol. 30, No. 2, 2005. Also S. Ganguly and D. Hagerty, *Fearful Symmetry: India-Pakistan Crises in the Shadow of Nuclear Weapons*, Seattle: University of Washington Press, 2006; R. Basrur, 'Nuclear Weapons and India-Pakistan Relations', *Strategic Analysis*, Vol. 33, No. 3, 2009; S. Ganguly and S. Kapur, *India, Pakistan, and the Bomb: Debating Nuclear Stability in South Asia*, New York: Columbia University Press, 2010.

20 A.B. Vajpayee, 'Letter' [to William Clinton], *New York Times*, 13 May 1998.

21 L. Dittmer (ed.), *South Asia's Nuclear Security Dilemma: India, Pakistan, and China*, Armonk: M.E. Sharpe, 2005.

22 'India to Verify Reports of Chinese Presence in PoK, Says Govt', *Times of India*, 30 August 2010; the Ministry of External Affairs spokesman Vishnu Prakas commented: 'If true, it would be a matter of serious concern and we would do all that is necessary to ensure safety and security of the nation.'

23 R. Mishra, 'Nuclear and Missile Threats to India: China-Pakistan Nexus in South Asia', *Papers* (South Asia Analysis Group), No. 296, 17 August 2001; B. Raman, 'Pakistan as China's Force-multiplier Against India', *Papers* (SAAG), No. 3918, 11 July 2010. Also M. Bhattacharjea, 'India-China-Pakistan: Beyond Kargil – Changing Equations', *China Report*, Vol. 35, No. 4, 1999.

24 S. Srivastava, 'India Army "Backed Out" of Pakistan Attack', *Asia Times*, 21 January 2009.

25 S. Kapila, 'China-Pakistan Military Nexus Formally Recognized in Indian Strategic Planning', *Plainspeak* (Boloji), 24 January 2010, www.boloji.com.

26 R. Rajagopalan, 'Neorealist Theory and the India-Pakistan Conflict', in K. Bajpai and S. Mallavarapu (eds), *International Relations in India: Theorising the Region and Nation*, New Delhi: Orient Longman, 2004.

27 E. Sridharan, 'Economic Cooperation and Security Spill-Overs: The Case of India and Pakistan', in M. Krepon and C. Gagne (eds), *Economic Confidence-Building and Regional Security*, Washington: Henry L. Stimson Center, 2000; S. Zaidi, 'Economic Confidence Building Measures in South Asia: Trade as a Precursor to Peace with India', in M. Ahmar (ed.), *The Challenge of Confidence Building in South Asia*, New Delhi: Har-Anand Publications, 2001; East Asia Forum, 'Improving India-Pakistan Relations Through Trade', 19 April 2010, www.eastasiaforum.org.

28 In this book, figures for India's trade are generally taken, unless otherwise indicated, from India's Department of Commerce Import Export Data Bank, at commerce.nic.in/eidb/default.asp.

29 M. Khan, 'India-Pakistan Trade: A Roadmap for Enhancing Economic Relations', *Policy Brief* (Peterson Institute for International Economics), July 2009.

30 A. Mir, *Talibanisation of Pakistan: From 9/11 to 26/11*, New Delhi: Pentagon Security International, 2009.

31 C. Raja Mohan, 'What If Pakistan Fails? India Isn't Worried…Yet', *Washington Quarterly*, Vol. 28, No. 1, 2004–05.

32 D. Rajan, 'China Should Break up the Indian Union, Suggests a Chinese Strategist', *Papers* (SAAG), No. 3342, 10 August 2009.

7

India and the Himalayan states

Satish Kumar

Introduction

The Himalayan kingdoms of Nepal and Bhutan and the Indian state of Sikkim have occupied an important place in India's foreign policy scheme.[1] The importance of these Himalayan actors for India can be visualized from two different angles: a) the strategic importance of these Himalayan actors for India's national security; and b) the place of these Himalayan actors in India's own role perception in international politics. The Himalayas have become the southern border of the People's Republic of China, but they do not occupy such an important place in the Chinese life and culture as they do in India. The Himalayan kingdoms of Nepal, Bhutan and the erstwhile kingdom (now Indian state) of Sikkim were considered an integral part of the Indian regional system. As such, these three units are right in the middle of India's whole 'Himalayan frontiers', its northern 'borderland' flanks.[2]

Himalayan frontiers after Indian independence

The Himalayas were the arena for competition between British India and China in imperial times, with important buffer considerations being in play. The foreign policy of British rulers of India had been directed towards securing the alliance, integrity, or neutralization of the borderlands and minor states covering the Himalayan land approaches to the Indian empire, and blocking countervailing Chinese competition.[3] The 'ring fence' system operated by Britain resulted in an independent but friendly and co-operative Nepal, with Sikkim and Bhutan as Indian protectorates, and with Tibet as an autonomous buffer state guaranteeing India's commercial and strategic interests there. On this 'imperial chessboard', the British Government sent a strong note of warning to a weak China on 11 April 1910, which informed China that no interference in the affairs of the Himalayan states would be tolerated.[4] At the time these areas indeed formed 'the Gates of India [...] mountain ways which have aforetime let in the irrepressible Chinaman'.[5] One hundred years later and similar dynamics and similar concerns were in play for India. India was, though, in an enviable position on gaining independence in 1947, so far as security in the north was concerned, with 'Forward Rights' inherited in Tibet and a weak China still mired in civil war.

Jawaharlal Nehru, India's architect of foreign policy, wanted to continue the British policy towards the Himalayan states, but he failed to do so. It might have happened due to the lack of long-term strategic vision or excessive idealistic structures of Indian foreign policy. The fault lines started with the Indian policy on Tibet. From 1946 to 1951 the Tibet policy of Nehru and his associates reflected that of the British: treating Tibet as an autonomous buffer state between that of India and China, recognizing vague Chinese suzerainty but *not* sovereignty over Tibet. Thus, in March 1947 a Tibetan delegation was invited to the Asian Relations Conference in Delhi, despite protests from Chinese (Kuomintang) delegates.

When the Chinese People's Liberation Army (PLA) marched into Tibet in 1950, Indians (including Nehru), vociferously protested against the invasion. Such actions indicated India's preference for continuing the British policy towards Tibet. Nehru wanted to protect the Indian security interests in the Himalayan regions. As the Chinese communists neared their revolutionary victory, Nehru rushed through a series of defence treaties with Bhutan (August 1949), Nepal (July 1950) and Sikkim (December 1950). These countries constituted Nehru's definition of a redrawn security zone. Throughout the 1950s Nehru demonstrated his serious commitment to this Himalayan doctrine. In February 1951 he established the North and North-Eastern Defence Committee, and visited the North-East Frontier Agency (NEFA), Sikkim and Bhutan. In public statements in August and December 1959, Nehru offered support in the defence of Nepal, Bhutan and Sikkim in case of Chinese invasion.

Gradually, though, India started losing ground in the Himalayan regions vis-à-vis China. Neither India's vital interests in the Himalayas nor its stand on the border problem were recognized in writing or respected in practice by China. Nor was the autonomy of Tibet respected by China. Ironically, Nepal seems to have had a firmer sense of this. When Nehru was faced with the Nepalese Government's argument that 'they had not recognised the sovereignty of China over Tibet which for them was an autonomous state', this was met by Nehru's rejoinder that 'it was well known that Tibet is part of Chinese State and the Chinese exercised full sovereignty there. This fact has inevitably to be recognized'.[6] In recognizing full Chinese control of Tibet, as a 'region of China' in the 1954 *Agreement on Trade and Intercourse between the Tibet Region of China and India*, strategically India surrendered its outer ring of defence without gaining anything substantial in return from China. Ginsburg and Mathos, in their study on *Communist China and Tibet* (1964) clearly brought out the geographical importance of Tibet in this domino-theory type logic: 'he who holds Tibet dominates; he who dominates the Himalayan piedmont threatens the Indian sub-continent; and he who threatens the Indian sub-continent may well have all of south-east Asia within its reach, and with it, all of Asia'.[7] The Chinese occupation of Tibet brought home to India the urgency of taking effective steps to safeguard its national security in the north. The occupation of Tibet by China was in itself a grave threat to India's security. To add to India's woes, the Chinese claimed that the Himalayan kingdoms of Nepal, Bhutan and Sikkim were in fact Chinese 'Middle Kingdom' territories that China had lost to the imperialist in her bad days and now that China had acquired strength it would try to regain the 'lost territories'. Occupation of Tibet by a strong China exposed the Himalayan states and India's northern frontier to a grave potential threat, with Nepal-Bhutan-Sikkim constituting what Dawa Norbu described as a 'new buffer zone', after the old buffer (Tibet) had fallen under China's sovereign political-military control in 1951.[8] It is to Nepal, Bhutan and Sikkim that we now turn.

Nepal

Strategic location of Nepal

Of the three Himalayan units, Nepal is the largest, covering an area of 140,797 sq km (54,362 sq miles). Bounded on the north by China (the Tibetan region) and on the south, east and west by India, Nepal is a land-locked state, smaller in size than several states of the Indian Union. Nepal is separated from the Tibet region of China by the great Himalayan range. Except for 8,000 sq miles of the southern plain strip, 80% of the total area of Nepal is mountainous. The three principal river systems of Nepal (the Karnali, the Gandak and the Kosi) all have their sources in Tibet, and enter Nepal through three gorges that cut across the Himalayas. Bhattacharya has been clear on Nepal's geopolitical significance. For him, Nepal's

> [s]trategic importance can be fathomed not only from its geo-political location, being sandwiched between the two rising Asian giants but also from its transformation into a new buffer zone between India and China in the 1950s. This buffer has assumed even more importance in the current times with Royal Nepal being transformed into a People's Nepal in the aftermath of the Maoist victory in the election to the Constituent Assembly on April 10, 2008. The victory of the Communist Party of Nepal (Maoist) CPN(M) a one-time rebel group, has significant geopolitical repercussions for the region.[9]

If one stands back, then 'Indian-Chinese rivalry in Nepal' indeed continues to provide the main strategic feature surrounding Nepal.[10]

Changed status of Tibet and its implications for Nepal

The withdrawal of Britain from the Indian subcontinent in 1947 brought India's inheritance of British pre-eminence in Nepal. Nehru's sense in 1948–49 was that 'politically our interest in Nepal is so important', and that Indian policy was 'to prevent the exploitation of Nepal by [other] foreign interests', but to 'help in developing Nepal to the mutual advantage of Nepal and India'.[11] However, one new 'foreign interest' raising its head was the conclusion of the Chinese civil war, and with it the emergence of a strong People's Republic of China. On 6 December 1950, summing up India's security concerns *vis-à-vis* Nepal, Nehru had said to parliament: 'from time immemorial the Himalayas have provided us with magnificent frontiers. We cannot allow that barrier to be penetrated because it is also the principal barrier to India. Therefore, as much as we appreciate the independence of Nepal, we cannot allow anything to go wrong in Nepal or permit that barrier to be crossed or weakened, because that would be a risk to our own country'.[12] The Indo-Nepalese Treaty of Peace and Friendship (July 1950) had the two states 'agree mutually to acknowledge and respect the complete sovereignty, territorial integrity and independence of each other' (Article 1).[13] However, with regard to sensitive military-defence matters, Article 5 gave India an important role: 'the Government of Nepal shall be free to import, from or through the territory of India, ammunition or warlike material and equipment necessary for the security of Nepal. The procedure for giving effect to this arrangement shall be worked out by the two governments acting in consultation'. Consequently, a close consultative relationship settled down on commerce, defence and foreign relations, with Indian military missions deployed during the 1950s. India has subsequently maintained that any attack on Nepal would be regarded as an aggression against India. However, the 1950 Treaty's military-consultative clause faced some resentment in Nepal, which began seeing it as an encroachment of its sovereignty and an unwelcome extension of Indian influence.

China's occupation of Tibet in 1950–51 completely changed Nepal's status for India. India's status in Nepal became vulnerable, since India accepted Tibet as an integral part of China under the 1954 *Agreement on Trade and Intercourse between the Tibet Region of China and India*. Once this had occurred, China began to claim territory along the Indo-Tibetan border, using the provisions of the 1954 Treaty as its rationale. The following year, China began to compete with India for a sphere of influence in Nepal. The changed strategic status of Nepal provided an opportunity to the Nepalese rulers to swing from one posture to another.[14]

Changing foreign policy of Nepal

The first significant foreign policy shift by Nepal was the establishment of diplomatic relations with China in 1955. Shortly after his return to Nepal, King Mahendra, to the great surprise of all (and more so of the Indian leaders) announced the formation of a cabinet headed by Tanka Prasad Acharya. Just after assuming office in 1956, Acharya declared at a press conference that Nepal would pursue a policy of equal friendship with all countries, and accept economic and other help from all friendly countries, including China and Russia. King Mahendra set for Nepal the ultimate foreign policy objective of balancing the external influences in order to minimize their capacity to restrict Nepal's freedom of action. The Nepalese Government embarked upon the policy of diversifying its relations, but alienated and antagonized India. Nepal made an informal request to India suggesting the revision of the Indo-Nepalese Treaty of trade and commerce of 1950 and is reported to have secured an assurance from her. Shortly after the conclusion of the agreement, in September 1956, Acharya paid a visit to Beijing to become the first Nepalese prime minister to visit the People's Republic of China. Significantly, he went to China *before* going over to India.

China gave aid to Nepal as part of its policy of detaching Nepal from India's embrace. It built the Kathmandu–Kodari road, the construction of which started in 1963 and was completed in 1965. The road provided a direct strategic connection between China and Nepal via the difficult Tibetan route. If Nepal was not able to resist an attack through this road, the Indian heartland would be easily accessible. For India, these developments were a cause of grave concern. The nature of this proximity was all the more troubling for India in wake of its defeat in the Sino-Indian war of 1962.

Nepal is the only one of the three Himalayan kingdoms with enough power to play an autonomous role between China and India. China openly exhorted the Nepalese assertion of independence throughout the 1970s. Intense anti-India propaganda was directed by China towards Nepal. When India annexed Sikkim in 1974, Chinese propagandists argued that Nepal might be India's next target.

The expanding role of China in Nepal and its implications for India

In India, the growing friendship between Nepal and China produced concern and anxiety, the more so in the arrival of the CPN(M) as the largest party in the 2008 general elections, and formation of a Maoist-led government under Pushpa Kamal Dahal (Prachanda), which held office until May 2009. The talks held by his defence minister, Ram Bahadur Thapa, heading a three-member delegation to witness the PLA's 'Warrior 2008' military exercise with China's defence minister, Gen. Li Guanglie, raised yet more concerns for India. The Chinese PLA wanted to extend its relations with the Maoist PLA in Nepal.

Meanwhile, the Chinese presence in Nepal grew in size. Apart from road and rail linkages, there was a sudden proliferation of China Study Centres (CSCs) all along the Indo-Nepalese border, with their number rising from seven in 2005 to 19 by February 2008. Whilst they were initially set up in 2000 as civil society groups to promote cultural interaction, they have become effective enough tools for advancing Chinese perspectives concerning Nepal. These centres also distribute materials to undermine India's predominance in Nepal, to stress 'the benign role of China and caution the Nepalis about India's hegemonic intentions'.[15] One indication of this growing Chinese influence in and on Nepal is the latter's crackdown on Tibetan protests in April 2008 at the behest of China, with Beijing deploying security officials inside Nepal to help detect fleeing Tibetans and keep a lid on unrest. Trans-border considerations are important here, China seeing Tibetan unrest as being stimulated by international forces operating from Nepal. Thus, in order to secure its southern Tibetan periphery, which it considers most vulnerable, it feels the need to monitor clandestine activities in Nepal.

China can also hope to capitalize on moves by land-locked Nepal to reduce its economic dependency on India. It has been mooting the extension of the China–Tibet railway line down into Nepal. India is Nepal's largest trading partner, accounting for more than 60% of its trade, and 12 of the 13 trade routes for Nepal are via India. About 50% of Nepal's remittances come from India. Thus, for strategic *and* economic reasons, the Maoists feel the urgent need to cultivate deeper ties with China on the one hand, and reduce their dependence on India on the other. This, therefore, also explains why the Maoists called for renegotiating the 1950 Treaty between India and Nepal.

The collapse in May 2009 of the Maoist-led government of Prachanda has, though, given India the chance to regain some ground *vis-à-vis* China in Nepal. Indeed, faced with new intelligence-sharing arrangements between India and Nepal, and talks of an Indian air base being set up in Nepal, worried Chinese sources were warning in March 2010 that 'India has resumed military cooperation with Nepal [...] the struggle between pro-India and pro-China forces in Nepal is at a critical stage and China needs to pay more attention to its interests there'.[16]

Changing contours of Indo-Nepalese relations

India-Nepal relations have been special from the very beginning, with 'interdependence' often used in connection with its Hindu monarchy.[17] In recent years India's 'uneasy partner' has presented uncertainties for India, which in turn has had a somewhat 'rickety roadmap' to follow.[18]

During the 1950s the monarchy in Nepal for its own self-interests initiated an anti-India campaign. The *Citizenship Act* of 1952, which allowed Indians to emigrate to Nepal and acquire Nepalese citizenship with ease, fanned this resentment. Mahendra succeeded his father in March 1955. His desire to reduce the special relationship with India to an equal one by increasing Nepal's strategic options led to moves to circumvent the 1950 Treaty. Nepal signed an agreement to maintain friendly relations with China in 1956. It had already become a member of the UN in December 1955. It sought aid from Britain, the USA, France and the Soviet Union, besides India. All in all, during the last 50 years, powerful vested interests have injected an anti-India ethos into Nepalese nationalism to serve their narrow political and economic interests during the monarchy. Even the kingdom's socio-economic and ethnic divide between the hills and the plains have been linked to anti-India feelings.

Such anti-India sentiments were further strengthened under the Maoist Government in Nepal, the outbursts of which have systematically created an anti-India wave in Nepal. While calling for reconsideration of India's present policies towards smaller neighbours, Prachanda said that India sought to intimidate, interfere with, expand its influence over and dictate terms to its neighbours. His wish list against India is indeed long and includes, among other items, the regulation of the Nepal–India border, banning entry of Indian vehicles into Nepal, and the end of Gurkha recruitments in the Indian armed forces. The Nepalese Maoists have tended to maintain a staunch anti-India posture from the very beginning. Prachanda said, 'Nepal after signing the Sugauli Treaty of 1816 with the then British India entered into the era of a partial-colonial and feudal system which continues to date', and stated further, 'we are yet to liberate ourselves from the partial colonial and feudal system with the dawn of the republican order'.[19] Outside players are involved in this process, with China keen to end the Nepalese over-dependence on India. Another active player in fanning anti-India feelings in Nepal has been Pakistan. As Chengappa notes, there has been a convergence of interests there against India: 'over the years India has been the primary focus of Pakistan-Nepal relations [...] Pakistan has striven to exploit the irritants in India's relationship with Nepal and thereby strengthen her stature vis-à-vis India in the subcontinent. Nepal sought to develop ties with Pakistan, so as to reduce its dependence on India'.[20]

Consistent ideological feeding against India among the Nepalese youth has been taking place for the last many years. Covertly and overtly it was started under the monarchy of King Mahendra, whilst the Prachanda Government cemented this still further into official policy-making. An anti-India wave in Pakistan was the result of the ideological fermentation by political leaders there. If Nepal moves on the same line, it will pose a similar security threat to India.

India's concerns loom large on the revision of 1950 India-Nepal Treaty. Should the controversial clause concerning arms sales change? If that happens, would Nepal choose China as a new supplier of weapons? Furthermore, access to energy from China will challenge India's almost complete current monopoly on energy exports to Nepal. If India is to prevent Nepal from slipping into China's hands completely, which economically and strategically it can ill afford, then it can no longer view Nepal as a subordinate partner and northern backyard of India. This may force India to rearrange the Himalayan frontiers policy.

Emerging cross-border threats to India from Nepal

As much as an 821-km stretch of the 1,664-km Indo-Nepalese border adjoins Uttar Pradesh. Of this, around 391 km is spread across Poorvanchal's five sensitive districts: Maharajganj, Sidharthanagar, Balrampur, Shravasti and Bahraich. The Union Minister of Home Affairs, Sriprakash Jaiswal, stated that, in view of Pakistani militants using Nepalese territory as a hideout and base for infiltration into India, the Government might re-draft its extradition treaty with Nepal. He said Pakistani militants had 'found a safe hideout in Nepal and it is a safe passage for coming to India'.[21] The Minister's statement confirmed a fact well-documented over the years, that Nepalese territory has long been used by the Pakistani Inter-Services Intelligence (ISI) as a launching pad for its activities against India.

The ISI is trying to exploit anti-India groups with the utilization of Nepalese soil as a springboard for launching terrorist strikes against India with the help of Kashmir extremists. A large number of *madrasas* (religious schools) have mushroomed along the Indo-Nepalese border. Most of the new mosques and *madrasas* went up after 1988, in the Nepalese districts of Bardia, Kapilvastu and Nawalparsi bordering Kheri West, Siddhartnagar and Maharanjanj in Uttar Pradesh, and in Parsa, Bara and Saptari bordering East Champaran, Sitamarhi and Supaul in Bihar. There are also anti-India campaigns being run by the Nepal Muslim Ettehand Sangh,

Islamic Sangh Nepal and Muslim Youth Organization. The Ministry of Home Affairs *Annual Report 1999–2000* highlighted this Pakistani involvement in Nepal:

> Pakistani intelligence agencies have started exploiting India's open border with Nepal for infiltration of militants along with arms, ammunition and explosives to carry out terrorist strikes in various parts of India with the help of certain Indian extremist groups as well as Pakistan based fundamentalist groups like Harku-uk Mujahideen. Since the 1990s, Pakistani intelligence agencies have been very active in Nepal for helping anti-India elements to infiltrate into India.[22]

The arrest of several militants and their subsequent interrogation added to evidence on the growing ISI network in Nepal. Dawood Ibrahim is reported to have visited Kathmandu at least half a dozen times since 1998. He is believed to be using his connections with the ISI and Nepal's leading politicians, business houses and the underworld for large-scale smuggling and questionable *hawala* (remittance) transactions.

With the weak political situation in Nepal during the late 1990s and early part of the new century, not much attention was able to be paid to the porous 1,751-km Indo-Nepalese border. Some 20 Indian districts and 26 districts of Nepal are situated on each side of the border and although there were 15 check pointposts between the two countries to monitor human traffic, only seven were functional. In the absence of a secure control apparatus along the border, Maoists, aided and abetted by the ISI, have formed a common front and have been working hard to smuggle narcotics and arms. Drugs and mafia on the India–Nepal border pose a serious challenge to the Indian security apparatus, in which most of the criminals find safe passage to Nepal and a safe refuge too. The Nepalese border has been a road to heaven for smugglers, who have been able to smuggle drugs and arms to India without hindrance.

Finally, a further concern, of late, within the Indian security establishment, is the nightmare scenario of the Nepalese Maoists carving out a Compact Revolutionary Zone, a 'Revolutionary Corridor' spreading from Nepal through Bihar and the Dandkaranya region to Andhra Pradesh and the Naxalite insurgency. As one Nepalese Maoist figure, C.P. Gajurel, put it in 2009, 'we have extended our full support and cooperation to the Indian Maoists, who are launching armed revolt'.[23] Thus India's external and internal challenges converge, and make ties with Nepal of extreme importance, yet also of extreme delicacy for India.

Bhutan

Bhutan, the *durk yul* 'land of thunder dragons', is the second largest of the Himalayan kingdoms, with an area of around 38,394 sq km that is less than one-quarter of the size of Nepal's area of around 140,797 sq km. Two-thirds of Bhutan is covered with forest and everywhere there are mountains and strong water flows. Bhutan is bounded on the north (like Nepal) by the Tibetan region of China, and on the south and the east by the Indian union territory of Arunachal Pradesh. Geopolitically, the location of Bhutan between the Tibetan plateau and the Assam–Bengal plains of India makes it important for India; as one Indian analyst summarized, 'Bhutan occupies a strategic position on our northern border'.[24] In terms of external boundaries, Bhutan has a border of 605 km with India and 470 km with China; the two countries 'collide' in and over Bhutan.[25] Bhutan, therefore, emerges as a crucial buffer state between India and China in the eastern Himalayas in the military sense. Western Bhutan borders the sensitive Chumbi valley, and therefore guards any possible Chinese ingress routes in any possible future conflict. The Indian state of Sikkim, adjoining western Bhutan, until recently was being disputed by China. Similarly, eastern Bhutan adjoins vital Indian Army defences in Arunachal Pradesh, an Indian state still wholly claimed by China.

Bhutan's special relationship with India

On the one hand, Bhutan has cultural affinities with Tibet, as 80% of Bhutan's population was of Tibetan stock, and their language, customs and religion were much like those of the Tibetans. On the other hand, Bhutan is geographically a part of the Indian subcontinent, and has extremely close political ties to India. Under the 1949 Treaty of Friendship and Neighbourliness, 'The Government of India undertakes to exercise no interference in the internal administration of Bhutan. On its part the Government of Bhutan agrees to be guided by the advice of the Government of India in regard to its external relations' (Article 2).[26] That particular 'guidance' clause was removed in the revised 2007 Treaty, however.[27]

Between 1951 and 1958 India's relations with Bhutan and Sikkim were by and large harmonious. Various visits were quickly made by the Bhutanese rulers to India in 1952, 1954 and 1955, reflecting the close relations between the two countries. Nehru, the architect of Indian foreign policy, fully realized the importance of Bhutan for Indian security. Nehru's description of Bhutan in 1954 was sanguine:

> Our relations with Bhutan are friendly. Bhutan is a semi-independent State whose foreign policy has to be conducted in consultation with us. The State receives a subsidy from us also. They are very anxious to preserve their independence, but realise that they have to rely on India. We have no desire to interfere internally in Bhutan but we have made it clear that, so far as external matters are concerned or any defence matters, India is intensely interested and must have a say. This is the position.[28]

Such perceptions remain the position for India. The persistent Indian effort to persuade Bhutan to become a partner yielded some result, and by 1958 Bhutan was persuaded to embark on the gradual modernization of the country and link its fate with India. Nehru was the first foreign dignitary ever to visit Bhutan. During his 1958 stay in Bhutan, Nehru had discussions with the Maharaja and other high officials of the kingdom. The visit was not only a landmark in Bhutan's relations with India, but also a step in the gradual opening of Bhutan for India. It also brought assurances from Nehru in the Indian parliament, on 29 August 1959, that any (Chinese) aggression against Bhutan, and Sikkim, would be considered an act of aggression against India. A team of Indian military officers visited Bhutan in 1961 in order to make the necessary arrangements with Bhutan for its defence. Half a century later and such linkages are still very evident between India and Bhutan.

Military and economic assistance

India's continuing military assistance to Bhutan was reciprocated in 2003 when Bhutanese military forces took action in *Operation All Clear* against some 30 camps of Indian insurgent groups (such as the United Liberation Front of Assam—ULFA—the National Democratic Front of Bodoland, and the Kamtapur Liberation Organization), which had set-up training camps on Bhutanese territory.[29] India has assured Bhutan of its continued support for military and development projects, and is currently preparing a comprehensive modernization package for the Bhutanese army. It has agreed to sell low-tech arms to Bhutan—5.56-mm INSAS assault rifles, 51-mm or 81-mm mortars, night vision devices, winter clothing for the army, and military vehicles. It has also agreed to increase the military training of Bhutanese army officers in India. India will also establish a joint military grid to patrol against Indian militants.[30]

India is the single largest donor to Bhutan; in fact, it has flooded Bhutan with economic aid. Eight Five Year Plans in Bhutan have been completed since 1961, the first two of which were totally financed by India. Indian contributions to Bhutan's Five Year Plans remain significant. The Indian contribution to the 7th Five Year Plan for 1992–97 was 750 crores; to the 8th Five Year Plan for 1997–2002 it was 1,050 crores (26% of the total plan outlay); to the 9th Five Year Plan for 2002–07 it was 2,600 crores. India has also contributed to Bhutan's development outside the scope of the Five Year Plans, through megaprojects on infrastructure and power supplies. Bhutan also enjoys complete free trade with India, and remains dependent on India for most of its imports and exports. During 2008 imports from India were of the order of Rs17,330m. and constituted 74% of Bhutan's total imports. Bhutan's exports to India in 2008 amounted to Rs21,480m. and constituted 95% of its total exports.

Manmohan Singh's visit to Bhutan in May 2008, the previous visit being by Narashima Rao in 1993, brought a raft of economic and hydro electric energy deals, with India also again agreeing to fund nearly one-quarter of Bhutan's 10th Five Year Plan, with an outlay of 3,400 crores. In his speech to the Bhutanese parliament, the Indian Prime Minister reckoned that India's wider total bilateral economic engagement with Bhutan over the next five years was to be of the order of Rs100,000m. (10,000 crores). In terms of security, he flagged up new security issues, where 'India and Bhutan are well placed to create a new paradigm for inter-governmental cooperation in the areas of water security and environmental integrity. The Himalayan glaciers are our common asset and we can do much more together to devise strategies to combat global warming'.[31] Interestingly, though, he avoided any mention of Bhutan's security problems with China, though he did announce the construction of the first railway linkage between Bhutan and India, perhaps a response to China's construction of a direct railway line to Lhasa and its moves to extend it to the borders of Nepal and Bhutan. Bhutan's moves against terrorist groups and its common problems with China have moved Bhutan's relationship with India 'from development cooperation to strategic partnership', albeit between two partners with very different power.[32]

The Chinese stand on Bhutan

The July 1958 issue of *China Pictorial* published a map of China in which the Sino-Indian border was indicated by a thick brown line. This map once again included a large chunk of Indian territory within the territorial limits of China. A considerable area of eastern and north-eastern Bhutan was also portrayed as part of China. China had always claimed rights in Nepal, Bhutan and Sikkim on grounds of traditional, ethnic, cultural and religious affinity between the populations of these lands and China's Tibetan region, in which the chief aim of the Government's current manipulations in the region seemed to be to detach these territories from India and integrate them into the Chinese orbit by any means short of war.[33] It came to the notice of the Bhutanese and Indian authorities that the Chinese had occupied eight villages on the Bhutan–Tibet border in 1959. In accordance with the Article 2 provisions of the 1949 India-Bhutan Treaty, India took up the border matter with China on behalf of Bhutan. In a letter dated 22 March 1959, Nehru wrote to the Chinese premier that the publication of Chinese maps showing parts of Indian and Bhutanese territory as parts of China were not in accordance with long-established usage as well as treaties. Even though Nehru firmly adhered to the view that the security of Bhutan and Sikkim was the concern of India, Zhou Enlai refused to recognize any 'special relation' of Bhutan and Sikkim with India. Since 1984 some 19 rounds of border talks have been held between Bhutan and China, but with little result.[34]

Recent developments in Bhutan and concerns for India

India assumed the responsibility for the defence of Bhutan because of what it considered to be China's ruthless actions in Tibet and its aggressive posture along the disputed borders. Bhutan has also become concerned about China's road-building ventures on its immediate northern borders in recent times. In November 2004 Bhutan lodged a formal protest to Beijing stating that some of China's road-building programme violated the Bhutan-China *Agreement on the Maintenance of Peace and Tranquillity Along the Sino-Bhutanese Border Areas* (1998). The agreement stipulates that China and Bhutan will maintain peace and tranquillity on the borders, uphold the status quo of the boundary prior to March 1959 and not resort to unilateral action to alter the status quo of the border. China purportedly agreed to suspend the construction work until the next round of border talks in 2005, but then resumed activity, amidst inconclusive border talks and cross-border incursions. This all led to Indian accusations of China's 'bullying and teasing tactics'.[35] Chinese troop movements in late 2007 into the disputed Chumbi valley tri-junction between Bhutan, China (Tibet) and India (Sikkim) brought immediate Indian reinforcements, and pointed attention towards Sikkim's role in Himalayan politics.

Sikkim

Sikkim is the smallest of the three Himalayan kingdoms, with an area of 7,096 sq km (2,739 sq miles). The relatively short, but strategically important, Sikkim–China frontier lies between the Nepal–China and Bhutan–China borders. There are several easily traversable passes on this border, the most important being Nathu La. During British rule Sikkim was not considered part of British India, either as an allied princely state or as a colonial territory. Instead, relations between Sikkim and British India were handled under a separate set of treaties. Those agreements did, however, establish British administrative control over Sikkim, which was considered a protectorate. Following Indian independence, India's role increased when an Indian official was loaned to Sikkim to serve as prime minister and reorganize the region's administrative system. Sikkim-India relations became closer still in 1950, as the Chinese occupation of Tibet destroyed India's Tibetan buffer. China's move prompted India's leaders to debate the proper approach to Sikkim.

Sikkim came under India's umbrella with the India-Sikkim Peace Treaty, signed in December 1950.[36] Under the Treaty, politically 'Sikkim shall continue to be a Protectorate of India, and subject to the provisions of this Treaty, shall enjoy autonomy in regard to its internal affairs' (Article II). Militarily, 'the Government of India will be responsible for the defence and integrity of Sikkim. It shall have the right to take such measures as it considers necessary for the defence of Sikkim or the security of India, whether preparatory or otherwise, and within or outside Sikkim. In particular, the Government of India shall have the right to station troops anywhere within Sikkim' (Article III). Diplomatically, 'the external relations of Sikkim, whether political, economic or financial, shall be conducted and regulated solely by the Government of India; and the Government of Sikkim shall have no dealings with any foreign power' (Article IV). India's argument was that such arrangements were 'dictated by the facts of geography'.[37]

Sikkim remained ethnically divided. The eruption of serious ethnic rioting and anti-Chogyal (Sikkim's ruler) demonstrations in early 1973 provided India with an opportunity to act, with policy inspired by a belief that India must act or China would take advantage of the situation.

Units of the Indian army and the paramilitary central reserve police force were deployed to Sikkim to re-establish order.[38] In September 1974 the Indian parliament adopted a constitutional amendment making Sikkim an 'associate state' of (i.e. within) India. China's ministry of foreign affairs 'strongly condemned' this as 'outright expansionism' and 'colonialism' on the part of India.

Foreign support encouraged the Chogyal to attempt to use foreign influence to limit India's embrace of Sikkim. In March 1975 the Chogyal attended the coronation of Nepal's King Birendra in Kathmandu. While there, he met with Chinese and Pakistani representatives, seeking their support. He also gave a press conference in Kathmandu criticizing India's moves and challenging the legality of Sikkim's new status as an Indian territory. The meeting with Chinese and Pakistani representatives sealed the Chogyal's fate and provided the pretext for which India had been waiting to move ahead with the full incorporation of Sikkim. Consequently, Sikkim's assembly called for the Chogyal's removal and a full merger with India. A referendum was quickly organized, resulting in overwhelming support for both moves. On 29 April 1975 Sikkim was incorporated into the Republic of India as a full state. Sikkim's monarchy was abolished and the region became a state of India, operating under the administrative and constitutional rules applicable to other Indian states.

China's recognition of this incorporation by India was not forthcoming at the time, though indirect Chinese recognition seemed to be implied with the designation in 2003 of Nathu La as an official border trade post between India and China. Nevertheless, Sikkim's disputed border with China continues to be an issue. The bloodiest Sino-Indian clashes since the 1962 war occurred on Sikkim's borders in 1967, at Nathu La pass, rousing Indian concerns about China's intentions regarding Sikkim. Rising 'incursion' incidents into Sikkim during 2008 by Chinese troops undermined Wen Jiabao's assertions in 2005 that 'Sikkim is no longer the problem between China and India'.[39]

Conclusions

Garver's sense remains persuasive, that 'taken together, and placed in the context of their particular location and terrain, the status of Nepal, Sikkim and Bhutan are highly significant. The political-military regime regulating the three areas is a significant component in the overall correlation of forces between India and China'.[40] India's starting point in looking at and dealing with these two areas is geography, and the perceived role that geography plays in maintaining the integrity of India's defensive barrier in the Himalayan ranges—in other words, geopolitical. From the Indian perspective, China's approach is difficult to understand. China has taken for itself the largest buffer, the vast area of Tibet, destroying Tibet's culture in the process and ignoring persistent Indian protests. India desires for itself a much smaller buffer in the three Himalayan units of Nepal, Bhutan and Sikkim, and does not seek to alter the traditional cultures of these areas. Having consolidated its hold over Tibet, China now seeks to erode India's special position in the Himalayas. The last 60 years of Indian foreign policy have seen India lose its privileged status in much of the Himalayan sphere. Although India has incorporated Sikkim, Nepal has already moved from India's clutches. Could Bhutan be next?

Notes

1 R.K. Jha, *The Himalayan Kingdoms in Indian Foreign Policy*, New Delhi: Maitryee Publications, 1986.
2 R. Rahul, *The Himalayan Borderland*, Delhi: Vikas Publishing House, 1970; K. Warikoo (ed.), *Himalayan Frontiers of India: Historical, Geo-political and Strategic Perspectives*, London: Routledge, 2009.

3 D. Woodman, *Himalayan Frontiers. A Political Review of British, Chinese, Indian and Russian Rivalries*, London: Barrie and Rockliff, 1969.
4 P. Addy, *Tibet on the Imperial Chessboard. The Making of British Policy Towards Lhasa*, New Delhi: Academic Publishers, 1984, p.210. The note said 'His Majesty's Government cannot allow any administrative change in Tibet to affect or prejudice the integrity of Nepal or of the two smaller states of Bhutan and Sikkim, and that they are prepared if necessary to protect the interests and rights of these three states', discussed in S. Dutt, 'India and the Himalayan States', *Asian Affairs*, Vol. 11, No. 1, 1984.
5 T. Holdich, *The Gates Of India*, London: Macmillan, 1910, p.4.
6 J. Nehru, 'Coordination of Foreign Policy With Nepal', 7 May 1954, in *Selected Works of Jawaharlal Nehru*, Second Series, Vol. 25, New Delhi: Jawaharlal Nehru Memorial Fund, 1999, p.461.
7 Originally coined in G. Gingsburg and M. Mathos, *Communist China and Tibet*, The Hague: Martinul Nijhoff, 1964; frequently cited, e.g. S. Kumar, 'Nuclearisation of Tibetan Plateau and its Implications for India', *Article* (ICPS), No. 482, 13 March 2001; D. Norbu, 'Chinese Strategic Thinking on Tibet and the Himalayan Region', *Strategic Analysis,* 32.4, 2008.
8 D. Norbu, 'Chinese Strategic Thinking on Tibet and the Himalayan Region', op. cit.
9 A. Bhattacharya, 'China and Maoist Nepal: Challenges for India', *IDSA Comment*, 23 May 2008.
10 J. Garver, 'Indo-Chinese Rivalry in Nepal', in *Protracted Contests. Sino-Indian Rivalry in the Twentieth Century*, Seattle: University of Washington Press, 2001, pp.138–66.
11 J. Nehru, 'Help to Nepal in Mineral Development', 23 January 1949 (p.477), and 'Letter to Rafi Ahmed Kidwai', 21 December 1948 (p.475), both in *Selected Works of Jawaharlal Nehru*, Second Series, Vol. 25, New Delhi: Jawaharlal Nehru Memorial Fund, 1999.
12 J. Nehru, 6 December 1950, cited in Leo E. Rose, *Nepal: Strategy for Survival*, Berkeley, Los Angeles: University of California Press, 1970, p.192.
13 India-Nepal, *Treaty of Peace and Friendship*, 31 July 1950, untreaty.un.org.
14 M. Dabhade and H. Pant, 'Coping with Challenges to Sovereignty: Sino-Indian Rivalry and Nepal's Foreign Policy', *Contemporary South Asia*, Vol. 13, No. 2, 2004.
15 Bhattacharya, 'China and Maoist Nepal: Challenges for India', op. cit.
16 Dai Bing, 'India Building a Security Barrier Against China', 8 February 2010, www.china.org.cn; picked up in India by S. Dasgupta, 'India Aid to Bhutan, Russia Ties with Russia Worrying China', *Times of India*, 8 February 2010.
17 Ramakant and B. Upreti (eds), *India and Nepal: Aspects of Interdependent Relations*, Delhi: Kalinga Publications, 2001.
18 S. Jha, *Uneasy Partners: India and Nepal in the Post-colonial Era*, New Delhi: Manas, 1975; P. Singh, 'India-Nepal Relations: Rickety Roadmap', *World Focus*, Vol. 317, No. 27, 2003.
19 'Nepal Faces Threats Not Only From India: PM Dahal', *Telegraph Weekly* (Kathmandu), 17 October 2008.
20 B. Chengappa, 'Pakistan's Foreign Policy and Nepal', in *Pakistan, Islamisation, Army and Foreign Policy*, New Delhi: APH, 2004, p. 115.
21 Ajit Singh, 'Subversion Sans Borders', *Outlook*, 20 November 2006.
22 Ministry of Home Affairs, 'Effective Management of the Indo-Nepal Border', in *Annual Report 1999–2000*, New Delhi: Ministry of Home Affairs, 2000. See also S. Pattanaik, 'Indo-Nepal Open Border: Implications for Bilateral Relations and Security', *Strategic Analysis*, Vol. 22, No. 3, 1998.
23 'Nepal Maoists Admit Link with Indian Naxals', *Times of India*, 3 November 2009.
24 S.S. Gupta, 'Indo–Bhutan Relations', in Ramakant and Ramesh C. Misra, *Bhutan Society and Polity*, New Delhi: Indus Publishing, 1998, p.292.
25 M. Balaji, 'In Bhutan, China and India Collide', *Asia Times*, 12 January 2008.
26 India-Bhutan, 'Treaty Between India and Bhutan 1949', 8 August 1949, www.indianembassythimphu.bt/treaty.htm.
27 S. Ramachadran, 'India, Bhutan: No More Unequal Treaties', *Asia Times*, 17 January 2007.
28 J. Nehru, 'Coordination of Foreign Policy With Nepal', op. cit., p.464.
29 'Bhutan: Counterinsurgency a Strategic Window for India', *Stratfor Report*, 18 December 2003; D. Banerjee and B. Laishram, 'Bhutan's "Operation All Clear": Implications for Insurgency and Security Cooperation', *Issue Brief* (IPCS), No. 18, January 2004; A. Mazumdar, 'Bhutan's Military Action against Indian Insurgents', *Asian Survey*, Vol. 45, No. 4, 2005.
30 B. Chandramohan, 'Indo-Bhutan Joint Action Against Insurgents', *IDSA Comment*, 5 October 2009.
31 M. Singh, 'Speech by the Prime Minister at the National Assembly of Bhutan', 17 May 2008, meaindia.nic.in.

32 M. Bisht, 'India-Bhutan Relations: From Developmental Cooperation to Strategic Partnership', *Strategic Analysis*, Vol. 33, No. 3, 2010.

33 See L. Yadav, *Indo Bhutan Relations and China Interventions*, New Delhi: Anmol, 1998, for triangle dynamics.

34 M. Bisht, 'Sino-Bhutan Boundary Negotiations: Complexities of the "Package Deal"', *IDSA Comment*, 19 January 2010.

35 S. Chandrasekharan, 'Bhutan's Northern Border: China's Bullying and Teasing Tactics', *Notes* (SAAG), No. 564, 14 January 2010.

36 India-Sikkim, 'The Text of the India-Sikkim Peace Treaty', 5 December 1950, in S. Sharma and U. Sharma (eds), *Documents on Sikkim and Bhutan*, New Delhi: Anmol Publications, 1998, pp.66–69.

37 'Press Note of the Ministry of External Affairs', 20 March 1950, in Sharma and Sharma (eds), *Documents on Sikkim and Bhutan*, op. cit., p.65.

38 B. Grover, *Sikkim and India: Storm and Consolidation*, Delhi: Jain Brothers, 1974.

39 'Premier Wen Jiabao Meets with Journalists, Talking about 3 Achievements of His Visit to India', 12 April 2005, www.fmprc.gov.cn. Also 'China Hopes to Have Border Trade Cooperation with Sikkim at an Early Date: Premier', *People's Daily*, 13 April 2005.

40 Garver, *Protracted Contests*, op. cit., p.186.

8

India's relations with Bangladesh

Harsh V. Pant

Introduction

Begum Khaleda Zia's first visit to India came in March 2006, only at the end of her term as Prime Minister of Bangladesh, and head of the Bangladesh Nationalist Party (BNP)-led administration. A visit to India—Bangladesh's most important neighbour—was probably viewed as either unnecessary or too problematic, resulting in it being relegated to the very end of her tenure. In contrast, her successor, Sheikh Hasina Wajed, visited India in January 2010, just a year into her term as the nation's Prime Minister, in which, overcoming formidable hurdles, Wajed's Awami League had swept to a decisive electoral victory in December 2008. New Delhi rolled out the red carpet to welcome Hasina as its first state guest of the decade, as talk was of the two countries looking to 'turn a corner' in their bilateral relations.[1]

This tale of two visits is a reflection of how India's relationship with Bangladesh, a relationship in search of meaning, seems to have become hostage to domestic political imperatives in Dhaka. It is ironic that this should happen to Indo-Bangladesh ties, given India's central role in helping to establish the independent state of Bangladesh and the close cultural affinities, geographic ties and ethnic linkages they share. However, friends are as temporary as enemies in international politics. Instead, it is a state's national interests that determine the contours of its foreign policy. In the case of India and Bangladesh, these interests have been diverging for some years now; theirs has been 'a relationship adrift', with a bilateral relationship highly susceptible to the domestic political narratives in New Delhi and Dhaka.[2]

This chapter examines the factors that are shaping India–Bangladesh relations and argues that a host of structural and domestic political variables are pulling the two states in opposite directions. It will require more than routine diplomatic posturing to restore amicable ties. Unless some serious efforts are made by both sides, there is little hope of significant improvement. Such deterioration would have important consequences not only for the two states involved, but also for the entire South Asian region and, indeed, the international community at large.

Historical overview: a long road from 1947 to 2010

India and Bangladesh are historically, geographically and culturally so tied to each other that they cannot escape having significant bilateral interaction. Before achieving independence in

1971, the modern state of Bangladesh was part of a larger, non-contiguous Pakistan. It must be noted that Bangladeshis (then known as 'East Pakistanis') comprised a major part of the movement to establish the independent state of Pakistan in 1947. As a result, many of the grievances that resulted in the original Partition of 1947 remain a part of the collective historical memory of modern-day Bangladesh. However, India's role in establishing an independent Bangladesh in 1971 meant that, at least for a few years, India enjoyed a privileged relationship with the new state.[3] India's assistance to refugees from East Pakistan, as well as its relief and reconstruction aid, went a long way toward setting the foundations of the new country. New Delhi, by pulling its troops out of Bangladesh quickly after the 1971 Indo–Pakistani war, acknowledged the new state's sovereignty. India, not surprisingly, was also the first state to grant recognition to Bangladesh. In 1972 the two states signed a Treaty of Friendship and Peace for a term of 25 years, declaring that both sides would respect their mutual independence, sovereignty and territorial integrity while refraining from interfering in each other's internal affairs.

However, the assassination of Mujib-ur-Rahman in 1975 (Sheikh Hasina's husband) and the assumption of power by General Zia-ur-Rahman (Begum Khaleda Zia's husband) in 1977, disrupted the friendly enough evolution of India-Bangladesh ties. It did not take long for relations to deteriorate as Bangladesh started moving away from the linguistic nationalism that had been the focal point of its national liberation from Pakistan. Instead, Islam became the new symbol and binding force of the emerging form of Bangladeshi national identity. From a four-pronged state policy of nationalism, democracy, secularism and socialism, Bangladesh began moving rapidly toward embracing Islamic ideology, which has been used by subsequent Bangladeshi governments to legitimate their rule.[4] In fact, India's attempt to emphasize its common ethnic and cultural affinities with Bangladesh backfired as this supposedly threatened to dilute the status of hard-earned Bangladeshi national identity. Much like other states in South Asia, Bangladesh also started resenting India's overwhelming regional presence and India eventually became one of the central issues around which domestic politics in Bangladesh revolved. Opposing India became the most effective way of burnishing one's nationalist credentials in Bangladesh, and political parties made full use of this tactic, with the possible exception of the Awami League, Sheikh Mujib-ur-Rahman's party that was now led by his widow Sheikh Hasina Wajed.

It has been correctly observed that bilateral relations have been characterized by belligerence and insensitivity on India's part, and oversensitivity and suspicion on the part of Bangladesh.[5] Despite this, both states recognized that they needed to co-operate in order to address mutual problems. Thus, India agreed in 1992 to grant Bangladesh a perpetual lease over the Tin Bigha corridor, covering an area of 1.5 hectares, which had long separated an enclave of Bangladeshi nationals from their homeland, in accordance with the promises of a pact signed between India and Bangladesh in 1974. This happened despite Indian concerns that the land had become a haven for illegal immigrants to cross over to India and was being used by terrorist groups to infiltrate Indian territory. The return of Sheikh Hasina Wajed's Awami League to power in 1996–2001 saw the signing of the Ganges Water Sharing Treaty in 1996, valid for 30 years.

The coming to power of the Bharatiya Janata Party (BJP) in 1998 in India was, though, viewed with suspicion in Bangladesh. Dhaka had concerns that certain sections of the Hindu nationalist BJP might desire to re-establish the 'sub-continental India' that existed during the British rule, including territories stretching from the Khyber Pass in the north-west to Chittagong in the east. Thus, the return to power in 2004 of the more 'secular' Congress Party-led United Progressive Alliance (UPA) was cautiously welcomed by Bangladesh, which sent its foreign minister to India immediately for a four-day visit as a special envoy of Prime Minister

Khaleda Zia, who had come back into power in 2001. However, bilateral relations nosedived after New Delhi refused to attend the South Asia Association for Regional Cooperation (SAARC) summit in Dhaka in February 2005, citing law and order problems in Bangladesh and Nepal. Given Bangladesh's special attachment to SAARC, it found India's attitude particularly insulting. India's ties with Bangladesh touched their nadir under the Khaleda Zia administration in Dhaka.

Overcoming formidable constraints, Sheikh Hasina Wajed, daughter of Sheikh Mujib-ur-Rahman, led the Awami League to an absolute majority in the December 2008 elections, displacing the openly anti-India BNP. Since then, both sides have made attempts to address each other's concerns, though it still remains unclear how significant a mere change in administration is going to be in transforming India-Bangladesh ties. Each state still perceives that the issues most important to it are being taken lightly by the other side. The factors that inhibit better relations can be categorized into three broad types: structural, institutional and bilateral. Each will be discussed separately below.

Structural: balancing India's predominance

Bangladesh is surrounded on three sides by India along a 4,094-km land border. This results in near total geographical domination by India except for the 193-km land border that Bangladesh shares with Myanmar. India's overarching presence in South Asia, in fact, has been a cause for concern for all of its smaller neighbours. Bangladesh is no exception. For India, the struggle against Pakistan in 1971 was a strategic imperative, in which India further marginalized Pakistan by cutting it in half with the emergence of Bangladesh. India may have expected Bangladesh to remain indebted to it for its role in assisting Bangladesh to achieve independence, but this did not happen. Structural constraints are the most important determinant of state behaviour in international politics and Bangladesh soon began 'balancing' against Indian preponderance in the region. Like other states in South Asia, Bangladesh has tried to counter India's regional hegemony through a variety of means.

Bangladesh's relations with Pakistan in the years immediately after independence were severely strained for obvious reasons, but their ties eventually began to improve quite dramatically. A major impetus for this was the desire of both countries to balance India's power and influence in the region. In 1974 Pakistan and Bangladesh signed an accord to recognize each other and two years later established formal diplomatic relations. The two states have maintained high-level contacts ever since. It has been correctly observed that popular fears of Indian domination in both countries outweigh any lingering animosity between them, resulting in closer Pakistan-Bangladesh ties.[6] Thus Bangladesh started cultivating Pakistan in an effort to counterbalance India because it sees India as its main potential threat. In contrast, India's foreign policy obsession with Pakistan has led it to ignore Bangladesh. There is some suspicion that Pakistani President General Pervez Musharraf used his 2003 visit to Bangladesh to forge covert military ties with Dhaka and obtain authorization for Pakistan's premier intelligence agency, the Inter-Services Intelligence (ISI), to operate from Bangladeshi territory.

More significant are Bangladesh's attempts to woo an extra-regional power, namely China, to prevent New Delhi from asserting regional supremacy in its relations with Dhaka—something for which other states in the region, including both Pakistan and Nepal, have also frequently used China. For its part, China has been quite willing to play this role because it not only enhances Beijing's influence in South Asia, but also keeps India bogged down in regional affairs and hobbled in its efforts to become a major global player.

Since China and Bangladesh established ties in 1976, their bilateral relationship has grown steadily, culminating in the signing of a Defence Co-operation Agreement in 2002 that covers military training and defence production.[7] China has also provided Bangladesh with substantial resources to bolster its civil service and law enforcement agencies. The two states have signed an agreement on peaceful uses of nuclear energy in the fields of medicine, agriculture and bio-technology. Energy-hungry China views Bangladesh's large natural gas reserves as a potential asset to be tapped. Much to India's discomfort, Bangladesh supports China's full entry into SAARC. China is also helping Bangladesh in the construction of a deep water port at Chittagong, further heightening Indian fears of 'encirclement'.

In this context, it is interesting to note the proposal to revive the Stilwell Road (also known as the 'Old Burma Road'), which stretches from the Indian state of Assam through Bangladesh and Myanmar, extending all the way to Yunnan Province in southern China. In 1999 China, India, Myanmar and Bangladesh all came together in what is known as the 'Kunming Initiative' to push this proposal forward, mainly because of the potential trade advantages that would derive from linking those countries to South-East Asia via a long land route.[8] However, India has been reconsidering this proposal, fearing that it might give a fillip to insurgents in north-eastern India who receive support from Bangladesh and might also allow Chinese goods to potentially flood Indian markets.

Institutional: domestic politics and the 'other'

A nation's foreign policy is also a function of domestic political institutions. India has emerged as a major factor in domestic Bangladeshi politics. It would not be an exaggeration to say that, in many ways, India is the central issue around which Bangladeshi political parties define their foreign policy agenda. This should not be a surprise given India's geographic, linguistic and cultural linkages to Bangladesh. Over the years political parties opposing the Awami League have tended to define themselves in opposition to India, in effect portraying Awami League as India's 'stooge'. Moreover, radical Islamist groups in Bangladesh have tried to buttress their own 'Islamic identity' by attacking India.

India realizes that it is perceived in Bangladesh as being close to the Awami League; conse-quently, New Delhi has made some efforts to rectify this situation. When the BNP-led coali-tion of Begum Khaleda Zia assumed office in 2001, Indian officials sent a special emissary to Dhaka to assure the new government that New Delhi had no political favourites in Ban-gladesh and that its internal affairs were not India's concern. However, this failed to make any long-term impact on the new political alignment in Bangladesh. Some in India argue that India should separate its relationship with Bangladesh from the latter's domestic politics and pursue greater engagement.[9] However, the harsh reality is that political parties in Bangladesh invariably drag India into the nation's domestic politics in order to criticize each other. By visiting India just before the 2008 elections and showing that she, too, could do business with India, Khaleda Zia was hoping to marginalize her long-time rival in Bangladeshi politics, Sheikh Hasina Wajed.

Since she came to power in December 2008, Sheikh Hasina Wajed has faced challenges to her authority from right-wing parties as well as the fundamentalist organizations such as *Jamat-e-Islami* and *Jamat-ul-Mujahideen*, which enjoy Pakistan's support. These groups are united in undermining efforts to improve ties with New Delhi. The greatest challenge that Sheikh Hasina overcame in her first year was the mutiny by the paramilitary Bangladesh Rifles, which erupted in February 2009. It soon became clear that the mutineers were being instigated by supporters of the opposition led by the BNP and others connected to the *Jamat-e-Islami*. India supported

Hasina's crackdown on the mutineers by sealing its borders with Bangladesh and forcing back mutineers attempting to cross over.

The army in Bangladesh has also made periodic forays into politics, further preventing democratic institutions from consolidating. General Zia-ur-Rahman seized power in 1975 in the turbulent aftermath of the massacre of ruling Awami League leaders including Sheikh Mujib-ur-Rahman (Sheikh Hasina Wajed's husband). To give his military regime increased legitimacy, Zia actively wooed domestic Islamist fundamentalists and the Islamic regimes of the Middle East. In essence, he transformed Bangladesh from a secular to an Islamic republic. This transformation continued under his successor, General Hussain Mohammed Ershad, who ruled from 1982 to 1990, thereby ensuring that the military held an entrenched position in Bangladeshi politics. The army's role is less active today, but it still remains a powerful force with its own deep-seated interests. Elements in Bangladesh's army continue to hold a strong anti-Indian outlook, in part because of the military's institutional Pakistani legacy.

The inability of civilian state institutions to govern Bangladesh effectively has not only raised serious concerns about the future viability of democracy there but has also undermined relations with India. In the immediate aftermath of the 2001 elections there were concerted attacks by ruling-party activists against Hindus, who were perceived to be supporters of the opposition Awami League. The weakness of governmental institutions has emboldened non-state actors such as the radical Islamist groups that are attempting to make Bangladesh into another frontier in their global struggle against the 'infidels'.[10] Religion has succeeded in so dominating political institutions that *The Economist* called the 2001 parliamentary elections in effect 'a vote for Bin Laden', given the overwhelming presence of Osama Bin Laden's visage in campaign posters.[11] By 2005 there were estimated to be around 50,000 Islamist militants belonging to more than 40 groups controlling large areas of Bangladesh with the assistance of *Jamat-e-Islami* and a section of the BNP.[12] The emergence of Bangladesh as a 'weak state with fragile institutions' unable to tackle internal security and governance has also given rise to problems in India–Bangladesh relations on a whole range of issues.[13]

Domestic politics in India have also played a role in shaping bilateral relations. The issue of illegal immigration (or infiltration) into India from Bangladesh has been part of the BJP election manifesto for several years, while the other national political parties tend to avoid this sensitive issue in their agendas. When operating in opposition, Congress Party leaders often criticized the BJP foreign policy towards Bangladesh as being driven by sectarian purposes. In this view, the BJP's anti-Muslim posture in domestic politics largely shapes its antagonistic posture towards Bangladesh. For its part, the BJP has argued that Bangladesh maintains a lackadaisical attitude on illegal migration and when dealing with anti-India elements within its borders. The BJP's aggressive foreign policy posture was often considered to be reckless and overbearing by other political parties. They argued that it does not behove a government to project Bangladesh as a bastion of Islamist fundamentalism when the BJP itself often callously tries to polarize Indian society on communal lines for the purposes of gaining domestic political mileage.

In turn, the BJP, in opposition, has argued that the Congress-led UPA's policy towards Bangladesh and illegal immigration is driven by the need to appease minorities rather than India's own national interests.[14] It has jumped upon the Indian Supreme Court's ruling that 'there can be no manner of doubt that the state of Assam is facing external aggression and internal disturbance on account of large scale illegal migration of Bangladesh nationals'.[15] Instead of addressing illegal immigration in a judicious manner, both Congress and the BJP have ended up making a 'political football' of the issue even as the problems it engenders continue to fester and the India–Bangladesh relationship continues to deteriorate.

Bilateral issues between India and Bangladesh

Water concerns

Bangladesh is heavily dependent on India for the flow of water from the 54 rivers that the two countries share. Bangladesh has complained that its share of river waters, in comparison with India's, remains unfair. The construction by India of the Farakka Barrage—a low dam in West Bengal Province designed to increase water supply in the Hoogli River—was a major bone of contention between the two countries. India has built a feeder canal at Farakka where the Ganges divides into two branches; this has allowed India to control the flow of Ganges water by re-channelling it on the Indian side of the river. This dispute was resolved in 1996 with the mutual signing of a 30-year water-sharing agreement for the Ganges. This happened after earlier short-term agreements had lapsed.

However, differences between the two countries have re-emerged after India announced a plan to link 30 major international rivers in order to divert the flow of water toward its own drought-prone regions. This has generated concern in Bangladesh about potential economic and environmental problems emanating from this plan, whereas India continues to insist that its project to integrate the rivers will not harm Bangladeshi interests. India's project is currently aimed only at peninsular rivers and officials have indicated that Bangladesh would be consulted when northern rivers were to be interconnected. As the upper riparian state India clearly dominates the management of water resources. Dhaka's bigger grievance is that although a water-sharing accord exists for the Ganges, similar agreements are needed for the remaining 53 shared rivers. Officials in the capital assert that many rivers and canals have dried up because of India's denial of water to Bangladesh. During Sheikh Hasina's visit to New Delhi in January 2010, the two sides decided to resolve the issue of the sharing of the waters of the river Teesta after Bangladesh agreed to joint hydrological observations. The construction by India of the Tipai-mukh Dam across the Barak river has also been addressed.

Migration and its discontents

Another kind of flow has also become a serious bilateral issue: the stream of illegal Bangladeshi immigrants into India. India shares a border with Bangladesh running through the Indian states of West Bengal, Assam, Meghalaya, Tripura and Mizoram. This border is longer than the one that India shares with China. Indian officials have alleged that continued illegal immigration from Bangladesh has altered the demography of India's border areas resulting in ethnic imbalance, electoral irregularity, and loss of employment opportunities for Indian nationals.[16] In fact, in the late 20th century the massive influx of refugees fleeing persecution in East Pakistan (as Bangladesh was known before independence) was one of the major reasons India assisted the Mukti Bahini guerrillas fighting for liberation from Pakistan. According to some estimates around 15m.–20m. illegal immigrants from Bangladesh have crossed over to India over the last several decades.

The north-eastern states in India are particularly vulnerable to population movement: less than 1% of the region's external boundaries are contiguous with the rest of India whereas 99% are international boundaries. Bangladesh has complained that the overwhelming numerical superiority of Indian security forces along their long common border has spurred the killing of innocent Bangladeshi nationals by India's paramilitary Border Security Force (BSF). According to some estimates the ratio of Indian to Bangladeshi security forces deployed along the border is 2.5:1. Exchanges of fire between the BSF and its counterpart, the Bangladeshi Rifles, are now a regular feature along the border, often resulting in inhumane treatment of each other's forces. Bangladesh also argues that the land boundary delimitation agreement signed in 1974 between Indira Gandhi and Mujib-ur-Rahman has yet to be implemented, with 6.5 km of unmarked borderland in need of clear demarcation.

Ineffective border management has also emerged as a major irritant in India-Bangladesh relations because of concerns about smuggling, illegal immigration, trafficking in women and children, and insurgency. India's plan to erect a 2,886-km fence along its border with Bangladesh, with an additional 400 km in the state of Mizoram, is nearing completion. However, there is no evidence that fencing will be effective in checking infiltration in the area, where for historical reasons there are around 57 Bangladeshi enclaves in Indian territory and around 111 Indian enclaves inside Bangladesh. In many ways the border with Bangladesh is more difficult for India to manage than the border with Pakistan. The Indian army has little presence on the eastern border which is patrolled almost exclusively by Indian paramilitary forces. New Delhi's concerns are not only about demographic changes but also about the security threat posed by anti-India radicals and insurgents who sneak in along with economically deprived Bangladeshi migrants. As mentioned earlier, Indian domestic politics further complicate this issue, making an amicable bilateral solution difficult.

Bangladeshis, for their part, are apprehensive that India has the resources and inclination to re-ignite ethnic rebellion in the Chittagong Hill Tracts area of Bangladesh. India had been accused of helping Chakma tribal insurgents there with resources and training from 1975 to 1997, when the Dhaka Government finally signed a peace treaty with the Chakmas. Part of this accord allowed for the return to Bangladesh of tribal refugees who had fled to India in the 1980s to escape violence caused by the insurgency. However, suspicions about Indian motives and potential political leverage remain strong in Bangladesh.

Islamist fundamentalism

The rise of Islamist fundamentalism in Bangladesh has further aggravated India's relations with its neighbour, with Indians like Sengupta 'concerned' about Bangladesh's role as the 'next terror frontier'.[17] After independence, Bangladesh not only had declared secularism to be one of its founding principles, but it had also banned religious political parties. As the military became a major political force in Bangladesh over the years, it used the country's Islamic identity to give its rule increased legitimacy, whilst mainstream political parties started using Islam for their own partisan purposes as well. As a result, religion has come to occupy a central place in Bangladeshi political discourse.[18] Islamist radicals are no longer shy of openly declaring their ambitions. After the US invasion of Afghanistan in 2001 the members of IOJ—one of the constituents of the then ruling coalition led by the BNP—took to the streets chanting, 'We will be the Taliban, and Bangladesh will be Afghanistan'.[19]

Bangladesh has the third-largest Muslim population out of any country in the world, but of its 144m. population, 70m. live on less than US $10 a day.[20] This has made the country an easy target for Islamist radical groups with global pretensions believing in the unity of *ummah* (the Islamic community of believers) against the West and other non-believers. Militant groups have percolated into all sections of Bangladeshi society, including mosques, seminaries, educational institutions, the judiciary, mass media and the armed forces. The Awami League, while in opposition, tried to draw the attention of the international community toward the 'Talibanization' of Bangladesh.[21] Not only did anti-India rhetoric reached an all-time high in Bangladesh, but Pakistan's ISI had been making full use of growing radical Islam for furthering its own activities against India. The BNP leader Begum Khaleda Zia, while in opposition, had been quoted as saying that the insurgents in India's north-east were 'freedom fighters' and that Bangladesh should help them instead of curbing their activities.[22] The BNP also went all out to burnish its Islamic credentials with an eye on the elections. For example, a bridge was even named after Hezbollah by a government minister, who claimed that this was being done 'because of our love for the Lebanese resistance group'.[23] Indian fears were that 'the growing trend of Islamisation in Bangladesh is the fall out of its Pakistanisation, which would ultimately turn it also in the category of a second terrorist state neighbouring India'.[24]

There is a consensus in India that Bangladesh cannot continue to deny the anti-India terrorist and insurgent activities that emanate from Bangladeshi territory and that Dhaka should be forced to take concerted, verifiable action against anti-India actors within its borders. Bangladesh, in fact, has long been a willing host to militant outfits operating in north-east India.[25] Even before the emergence of Bangladesh as an independent state, the Chittagong Hill Tracts were used by the Pakistani army to train and shelter Mizo and Naga insurgents fighting against India. It has been suspected that Bangladesh and Pakistan's ISI has been co-ordinating anti-India activities along with outfits like the United Liberation Front of Assam, the National Socialist Council of Nagaland, the National Liberation Front of Tripura and the All Tripura Tiger Force.

There have been concerns in recent years that as Pakistan comes under increasing scrutiny for its role in sponsoring terrorism, some Pakistan-based terrorist groups have moved their training camps to Bangladesh. Indian intelligence agencies also claimed that the ISI and various militant organizations based in Pakistan had changed their *modus operandi* and were now using Bangladesh as a transit point for pushing terrorists into India. Bangladeshi nationals who are part of terrorist groups are often asked to illegally enter India and set up bases in different parts of the country. They subsequently provide safe hideouts to more incoming terrorists, and act as couriers of explosives and finance.

The rise of the *Jamat-ul-Mujahideen* in Bangladesh is a testament to the country's growing Islamist radicalization. As a consequence, Islam in Bangladesh—which has traditionally been tolerant and syncretic in nature—has come to be dominated by the radical strain in more recent years. Although the *Jamat-ul-Mujahideen* in Bangladesh was finally banned by the Dhaka Government in early 2005 following threats of withdrawal of aid by the West, the group still managed to set off serial bomb blasts during August 2005 in 63 out of the 64 districts of Bangladesh.[26]

Suicide bombings have also emerged as another tool in the arsenal of radical Islamists, suggesting that militants in Bangladesh are adopting the tactics and techniques of their counterparts in the Middle East. Bangladesh is now viewed as a safe haven by *jihadists*, who use its friendly government and infrastructure to regroup and for training purposes. A number of recent terrorist attacks in India have been traced back to Bangladeshi nationals working on behalf of *Harkat-ul-Jihad-al-Islami*, which is suspected of being an al-Qaeda front and also has links with the *Jaish-e-Mohammed* and *Lashkar-e-Taiba jihadist* groups based in Pakistan. *Harkat-ul-Jihad-al-Islami* is now one of the fastest growing fundamentalist organizations in Bangladesh and has been designated a 'terrorist organization' by the US Government. Islamist radicals from across Asia, including India, Myanmar, Thailand, Indonesia, Afghanistan and the Philippines, have gravitated toward Bangladesh for military training and refuge from their home governments, under the protection of *Harkat-ul-Jihad-al-Islami*.

Despite the fact that the international community, including India, has long been asking Dhaka to take action against the presence of Taliban remnants along with various other militant groups in its territory, it was only in February 2005 that the Government of Bangladesh finally decided to act by banning two groups, the *Jamat-ul-Mujahideen* and Jagrata Muslim Janata Bangladesh, and taking additional action against some others. Even these steps seemed half-hearted on the part of the BNP Government. It is under the Awami League Government, which regained power after the December 2008 elections, that Dhaka has stepped up its activities against Islamist extremists. The Awami League Government of Sheikh Hasina Wajed cracked down on the *Lashkar-e-Taiba* and *Jagrata Muslim Janata Bangladesh* groups, with the chief of the *Jamat-ul-Mujahideen*, Said-ur-Rahman, being finally arrested in Dhaka on 26 May 2010 after a pursuit of three years. The Bangladeshi Government has also acted to pre-empt cross-border attacks on India and on the Indian establishments in Dhaka, which has effectively curtailed the ability of Pakistan to use Bangladesh as a springboard for terrorism against India.

Weak economic ties

The economic basis of bilateral ties between India and Bangladesh remains weak and lacks any constructive agenda, making it even more difficult for the two states to move forward on other issues. This is despite the fact that India and Bangladesh are members of both SAARC and the Bay of Bengal Initiative for Multi-Sectoral Technical and Economic Cooperation (BIM-STEC—formerly Bangladesh, India, Myanmar, Sri Lanka, Thailand Economic Cooperation). The Indo-Bangladeshi Joint Working Group on Trade Issues was established in 2003 and has held regular meetings ever since. None the less, it has failed to re-orient economic ties between the two states in a meaningful way. Bilateral trade may have increased to $3,180m. (a 0.71% share of India's overall trade) by 2007/08, but it had slipped back to $2,810m. by 2008/09 and $2,690m. by 2009/10 (a 0.58% share). Illegal trade, amounting to about three-quarters of the regular trade, has been the bigger winner. India's efforts to secure transit and trans-shipment facilities for accessing north-east states through the territory of Bangladesh have been rebuffed by Dhaka.

The BNP Government also reneged on its earlier commitment, via the tripartite agreement, for the transportation of natural gas from Myanmar to India via a pipeline running through Bangladesh. India wants to pursue this project because it is deemed to be its most economical option. The India-Bangladesh-Myanmar pipeline idea was initially seen as a landmark in Indo-Bangladeshi relations, in which Bangladesh would have agreed to let its territory be used for the transport of an economic commodity to the Indian market for the first time in 30 years. Although India appeared willing to pay a $125m. transit fee to Bangladesh, Dhaka also wanted additional concessions before concluding this agreement. These included a transit facility through India for hydro electric power from Nepal and Bhutan to Bangladesh, a Nepal-Bhutan trade corridor, and measures to reduce the bilateral trade imbalance. The Indian corporate giant, the Tata Group, has proposed massive investments in Bangladesh to the tune of $2,500m. in the steel, fertilizer and power sectors, but this agreement has been stuck over differences regarding the price of the natural gas that Bangladesh has insisted be used. The Tata Group finally decided to put its investment plans for Bangladesh on hold, citing Dhaka's insufficient progress in assessing and responding to the firm's revised investment offer.

India has also proposed concluding a Free Trade Agreement (FTA) with Bangladesh. Many Bangladeshis are asking the Government to consider this seriously in the light of Sri Lanka, which has operated an FTA with India since 2001.[27] Concluding an FTA would strengthen the economic basis of bilateral ties between India and Bangladesh and go a long way toward solving the problem of illegal trade. However, India's scepticism of Bangladesh's testing procedures for its food exports remains a constraining factor and it has asked for the codes to be harmonized and classifications to be made standard in order to come to a 'rules of origin' agreement to give Bangladesh greater access to Indian markets. Many in Bangladesh view this as another sign of India's protectionist tendencies. India has assured Dhaka that it would bring down some of its existing non-tariff barriers to exports from Bangladesh and assist Bangladesh in ensuring that its exports met Indian quality standards. Both countries are working to ensure that long delays experienced by traders on cross-border trade are minimized by trade facilitation measures.

Dhaka has also been asking for unilateral tariff concessions on select items of export interest to help reduce its trade deficit with India. In contrast, India feels that Indian investments in Bangladesh, such as the one proposed by the Tata Group, are another way of solving this problem. With India's economic growth at an all-time high, its investments in the region will increase in coming years and there is no reason for Bangladesh to exclude itself from a process that will benefit it immensely. After all, Bangladesh is set to become the second largest economy in South Asia, behind only India. Bangladesh's economic development is also in India's best interests, both to help curb illegal immigration and to make it more difficult for terrorist groups in Bangladesh to find fresh recruits.

India is undertaking actions to meet Bangladesh's immediate energy requirements by selling 250 megawatts of electric power. Indian companies will find investment opportunities in the development of power infrastructure in Bangladesh as the power deficit in the country is set to increase further in coming years.

It is clear that the SAARC agenda—including regional free trade, upgrading of the transport and communication infrastructure, and energy co-operation—cannot be fully realized unless India-Bangladesh relations are improved. This is also essential for the integration of the eastern part of the sub-continent, including Nepal and Bhutan, into a regional framework. India realizes that the success of its 'Look East' policy depends on Bangladesh acting as an effective bridge between north-east India and South-East Asia. The need has long been apparent for development of closer transport and communication links between India and Bangladesh in order to achieve the full potential of regional economic integration, but so far progress has only been lacklustre.

Although a regular bus service between Kolkata and Dhaka started in 2003, it continues to face management problems, primarily because Dhaka insists on levying high travel taxes. Proposals to commence bus service from other Indian cities such as Shillong, Guwahati and Siliguri to Dhaka have not progressed significantly. Regular passenger train services have yet to start between India and Bangladesh, despite their signing an agreement to this effect in 2001. However, in a move that could have long-term benefits for the north-east, the countries have agreed to allow each other's territory to be used for transporting goods via waterways, roadways and railways, both for commerce and trans-shipment. This is an emerging bright spot in bilateral relations that could be the basis for even further co-operation in the future. By extending a line of credit of $1,000m. for the development of infrastructure, India has cleared the way for its involvement in the development of rail and road communications linking its land-locked north-east with the rest of the country. India is also planning to invest in the development of Chittagong and Mongla ports, which will provide access for goods from Nepal and Bhutan to these ports, furthering regional economic integration.

Conclusions

The consequences of strained bilateral relations are far reaching for both India and Bangladesh. India is witnessing rising turmoil all around its borders and therefore a stable, moderate Bangladesh as a partner is in its long-term interest. Constructive Indo-Bangladeshi ties could be a major stabilizing factor for the South Asian region as a whole. The instability in Pakistan, Afghanistan, Nepal, Sri Lanka and Myanmar is a significant inhibiting factor for India to realize its dream of becoming a major global player. India is surrounded by several weak states that view New Delhi's hegemonic status in the region with suspicion. The structural position of

India in the region makes it highly likely that Indian predominance will continue to be resented by its smaller neighbours, even as instability nearby continues to have the potential of upsetting its own delicate political balance. However, a policy of 'splendid isolation' is not an option and India's desire to emerge as a major global player will remain just that—a desire—unless it engages its *immediate neighbourhood* more meaningfully.

The present constraints that impinge upon this India-Bangladesh relationship make it imperative for both sides to reduce the mutual 'trust deficit' that has crept into their bilateral ties. This is a necessary first step before any meaningful relationship can emerge. India, being the bigger and economically more powerful of the two, can and should take the lead in this process by taking generous and constructive steps to improve relations with Bangladesh. In this context, recent initiatives by the Indian Government allowing easy access to Bangladeshi goods represents a significant step.

However, Bangladesh also needs to return to the more secular, tolerant traditions of Islam that it used to espouse, and to oppose Islamist radicalism more forcefully. It has been rightly observed that the unchecked rise of religious extremism currently underway in Bangladesh bodes ill for the country, its neighbours and the world. A failed state in Bangladesh is in no one's interest. India and the rest of the international community can lend a hand, but the bulk of the burden for extricating itself from the morass into which it has sunk will have to be borne by Bangladesh itself.

Notes

1 S. Srivastava, 'India, Bangladesh Look to Turn a Corner', *Asia Times*, 16 January 2010. Her visit to China in March 2010 brought further concerned, albeit muted, Indian comments.

2 See H. Pant, 'India and Bangladesh: A Relationship Adrift', in M. Chatterji and B. Jain (eds), *Conflict and Peace in South Asia*, London: Emerald Publishers, 2008. Also H. Pant, 'India and Bangladesh: Will the Twain Ever Meet?', *Asian Survey*, Vol. 47, No. 2, 2007.

3 A useful account of the 1971 war can be found in S. Ganguly, *The Origins of War in South Asia: Indo-Pakistani Conflicts Since 1947*, Boulder: Westview Press, 1994, pp.81–116.

4 T. Hashmi, 'Islam in Bangladesh Politics', in M. Hussin and T. Hashmi (eds), *Islam, Muslims and the Modern State*, New York: St Martin's Press, 1994, pp.100–38.

5 K. Jacques, *Bangladesh, India, and Pakistan: International Relations and Regional Tensions in South Asia*, New York: St Martin's Press, 2000, pp.3–24.

6 Ibid., p.161.

7 S. Kapila, 'Bangladesh-China Defence Co-operation Agreement's Strategic Implications', *Papers* (SAAG), No. 582, 14 January 2003.

8 R. Maitra, 'Prospects Brighten for Kunming Initiative', *Asia Times*, 12 February 2003.

9 See, for example, C. Raja Mohan, 'Five Fold Embrace for Khaleda', *Indian Express*, 20 March 2006.

10 M. Hossain, 'The Rising Tide of Islamism in Bangladesh', *Current Trends in Islamist Ideology*, Vol. 3, 2006.

11 'A Vote for Bin Laden?', *The Economist*, 27 September 2001.

12 K. Lakshman, 'Islamist Extremist Mobilization in Bangladesh', *Terrorism Monitor*, Vol. 13, No. 12, 2005, p.6.

13 Iftekharuzzaman, 'Bangladesh: A Weak State and Power', in M. Alagappa, *Asian Security Practice: Material and Ideational Influences*, Stanford, CA: Stanford University Press, 1998, p.317.

14 'Bangladeshi Infiltration Deeply Affecting Assam: BJP', *Hindustan Times*, 27 March 2006.

15 'Assam Facing External Aggression. SC', *Indian Express*, 15 July 2005.

16 R. Sengupta, 'Why India is Concerned About Bangladesh', *India Abroad*, 22 December 2005.

17 Ibid.; Sengupta, 'Bangladesh: Next Terror Frontier?', *India Abroad*, 19 December 2005.

18 A. Riaz, 'God Willing: The Politics and Ideology of Islamism in Bangladesh', *Comparative Studies of South Asia, Africa, and Middle East*, Vol. 23, No. 1/2, 2003, pp.310–20.

19 E. Griswold, 'The Next Islamist Revolution', *New York Times*, 23 January 2005.

20 A. Perry, 'Rebuilding Bangladesh', *Time* (Asia), 3 April 2006.

21 See, for example, the 74-page report, 'Growing Fanaticism and Extremism in Bangladesh: Shades of the Taliban', on the official website of the Awami League, www.albd.org/aldoc/growing/growing. fanaticism.pdf. Also S. Kapila, 'Bangladesh Government in Denial Mode on Country's Talibanisation', Papers (SAAG), No. 1062, 15 July 2004.

22 H. Karlekar, 'Cautious Tango', *South Asia Intelligence Review*, Vol. 1, No. 42, 2003.

23 'An Ugly Alliance', *The Economist*, 12 August 2006.

24 R. Upadhyay, 'De-Pakistanisation of Bangladesh', *Papers* (SAAG), No. 2199, 7 April 2007.

25 P. Tarapot, *Insurgency Movement in North Eastern India*, New Delhi: Vikas Publishing House, 1993, pp. 127–46.

26 '459 Blasts in 63 Districts in 30 Minutes', *The Daily Star*, 18 August 2005.

27 This view has been articulated very forcefully by a former Foreign Secretary of Bangladesh, Farooq Sobhan. See his paper, 'India–Bangladesh Relations: The Way Forward', 2005, www.bei-bd.org. Also World Bank, 'India–Bangladesh Bilateral Trade and Potential Free Trade Agreement', *Bangladesh Development Series Paper*, No. 13, 2006.

9

India's relations with Sri Lanka

Brian Orland

Introduction

Since a low point in 1990 when the Indian Peace-Keeping Forces (IPKF) withdrew from Sri Lanka, the relationship between India and Sri Lanka has undergone a period of significant recuperation. In the late 1980s and early 1990s the bilateral relationship suffered from bitterness and mistrust on both sides. Today the relationship is much healthier, and the two countries maintain close economic and defence co-operation. How did this positive transformation in their relationship occur, and what challenges and issues constrain the development of an even stronger bilateral relationship?

India's economic-led foreign policy, exemplified in the Manmohan Doctrine, found a way to foster a close relationship with its neighbour. India emphasized economic relations and backed away from the highly contentious political issues of conflict intervention. Since the India-Sri Lanka Free Trade Agreement (ISLFTA) became operational in 2000, increased trade and investment have been the impetus for the improvement in bilateral relations.

India's decision to offer Sri Lanka favourable terms in a free trade agreement yielded not only greater economic engagement, but political and strategic benefits as well. A significant reduction in the trade balance, which had been heavily lopsided toward India, helped diminish the Sri Lankan perception of India as the region's hegemonic bully. Burgeoning trade and investment between India and Sri Lanka, including in the strategic energy sector, have woven economic inter-dependency into the bilateral relationship. This helped India and Sri Lanka push past the mistrust and resentment that had characterized the deterioration in their relationship during the late 1980s and early 1990s.

This chapter begins with a look at India's strategic interests in Sri Lanka to understand the motivations driving India's behaviour. It then gives a brief historical account of India's Sri Lanka policy from the beginning of the conflict in 1983 until the IPKF withdrew in 1980. After the historical section, the chapter examines the central dilemma in India's policy stemming from the political compulsions of its Tamil Nadu constituency. The chapter then turns to defence relations followed by a look at how economic engagement spurred the positive turn-around in the relationship. The chapter ends by addressing India's concerns about Chinese influence in Sri Lanka.

India's strategic interests in Sri Lanka

After the Cold War India's interests in Sri Lanka shifted from geostrategic power balancing to pragmatic security considerations. During the 1980s and early 1990s India's strategy to avoid the Cold War power struggle eclipsed efforts to support Sri Lanka's peace and stability. In the post-Cold War period, however, India's economic and pragmatic security interests led it to emphasize Sri Lanka's peace and security in an effort to control the externalities of the conflict threatening to undermine India's own security and internal stability. Thus, today, Sri Lanka's unity, peace and stability are India's primary concern. Additionally, maritime security in the Indian Ocean and between India and Sri Lanka has developed into a prominent concern for Indian policy-makers. Sri Lanka is located at an important point for projecting naval power into the Indian Ocean, and is an enviable berth for major naval powers with interests in the region. Within this, the influence of the People's Republic of China and Pakistan in Sri Lanka is also worrisome for India's security interests.

During the Cold War India pursued a policy of non-alignment, intended to guide Cold War geostrategic struggles away from its borders. While this was not possible along India's northern borders, near its southern border Indian policy-makers saw an opening in Sri Lanka to expel the troubling US encroachment. With the terms of the 1987 Indo-Sri Lankan Accord (ISLA), India sought to gain Sri Lanka's allegiance as a way to eliminate the USA's strategic presence in Sri Lanka, considerations reflecting the Indira Doctrine notion of India's regional pre-eminence. Under the ISLA, Sri Lanka had to scrap the American contract for the Trincomalee oil storage facilities, and remove the *Voice of America* outlet with which the USA broadcast radio messages into Soviet-friendly territory and transmitted intelligence reports. This geostrategic thinking reflected the Indian policy-makers' aim to push the USA's Cold War meddling a safe distance from India's borders.

The onset of the post-Cold War period diminished Sri Lanka's strategic importance in regional politics.[1] India's major strategic concern shifted to Sri Lanka's instability because of the effects it was having on India's own stability. Sri Lanka's decline of strategic importance to India reflected much stronger Indo-US relations. In the post-Cold War 1990s the USA accorded India a prominent place in American foreign policy initiatives in South Asia. Subsequently, Indo-US relations became highly developed and close. Instead of US encroachment, it has been negative externalities of the conflict that have irritated the relationship since the end of the Cold War.

Sri Lanka's ethnic violence increased maritime security concerns in the Palk Strait and adjacent water. India has a large economic stake in a secure and manoeuvrable Indian Ocean environment, and Sri Lanka plays a significant role in this. Sri Lanka occupies a critical location in the Indian Ocean's strategic environment, as international shipping lanes flow right by Sri Lanka's southern coast. The port of Colombo is used as an entry and exit point for regional goods, bound for or incoming from the East and the West. The Indian Ocean accommodates half the world's containerized freight, one-third of its bulk cargo, and two-thirds of its oil shipments.[2] Thus its security is an essential consideration for all economies with significant sea-based trade and energy demands.

India, especially, has important economic reasons for ensuring a stable security situation in and around the Indian Ocean. Sea trade dominates India's overall transnational trade, and nearly 89% of oil imports to India arrive by sea. Sri Lanka plays a particularly important role in India's maritime trade: over 70% of Indian imports arrive through the port of Colombo for bulk-breaking before they are shipped on local vessels to Indian ports. In the post-Cold War period, and especially since India passed trade-oriented economic reforms in 1991, India's dependence on the Indian Ocean as a maritime trading zone and transit-way for oil trade has meant that securing the Indian Ocean is crucial to its continued engagement with the international market-place. The waters adjacent to Sri Lanka assume special significance in these security arrangements.

Sri Lanka's strategic importance as a maritime power base in the Indian Ocean has historical roots. Sri Lanka's colonizers—the Portuguese, the Dutch and the British—recognized Sri Lanka's value as a trading port and naval base. The British occupied the island, then called Ceylon, not only for strategic maritime purposes (as the Portuguese and Dutch had done), but also for the protection of neighbouring British India. After independence India continued to recognize and treat Sri Lanka as strategically important in the regional maritime environment.

With strong motivations for major powers to gain economic and military access on the island, Sri Lanka finds itself vulnerable to major power penetration. In the 1980s the USA gained a listening post into the USSR from the island, irking Indian policy-makers. Since then, China's and Pakistan's engagement with Sri Lanka's defence and economic activity has worried Indian policy-makers. Foreign power penetration in Sri Lanka is inimical to Indian interests.

The 1980s: India meddles and then intervenes in Sri Lankan conflict

In July 1983 an attack by the nascent Tamil militant group, the Liberation Tigers of Tamil Eelam (LTTE), provoked a violent backlash against Sri Lankan Tamils by the Sinhalese-dominated Sri Lankan state. Sombrely referred to as 'Black July', these events marked the beginning of full-scale ethnic conflict that would vitiate the next 25 years of Sri Lankan history. The conflict would also put a damper on relations with Sri Lanka's closest neighbour and regional power—India.

Two major influences pushed India's policy response to the Sri Lankan conflict: the active engagement of foreign influence by the Sri Lankan Government and the demands of India's own Tamil population for India to act on behalf of the Sri Lankan Tamils. Sri Lanka pushed for a military solution to the conflict by seeking external support from countries that India was not comfortable with a presence so close to its southern border. As the scholar S.D. Muni pointed out in his authoritative account of India's peace-keeping venture, Sri Lanka 'wanted to isolate India in the region by facilitating the strategic presence of the forces inimical to India's perceived security interests'.[3]

Also of concern to India was the backlash among kin Tamils in Tamil Nadu. India's Tamil population in Tamil Nadu, then some 50m.-strong, felt India had a responsibility to control the Sri Lankan state's harsh response against Sri Lankan Tamils. For India, the July 1983 events in Sri Lanka were alarming, and the Government of India, then under Prime Minister Indira Gandhi, asserted its influence on the situation as a regional power, kin state, and close neighbour.

Mrs Gandhi's policy featured a multi-pronged approach. She persuaded the Sri Lankan President Jayewardene to open negotiations with Tamil groups,[4] and India facilitated direct talks between the Sri Lankan Government and Tamil leadership (the Tamil United Liberation Front, not the LTTE), producing the Annexure 'C' proposals for the devolution of power. Even as she beckoned Jayewardene to dialogue with the Tamils, however, Indian government officials voiced strong concerns and sympathy for the sufferings of the Sri Lankan Tamils. For the Sri Lankan Sinhalese population, India's rhetorical support for the Tamils biased India's support for a negotiated settlement. By focusing attention in Western capitals on the Sri Lankan military's aggression towards the Tamils, India further fortified the Sinhalese perception that India was prejudiced against the Sri Lankan state.[5] It was also during this time that India's external intelligence agency, the Research and Analysis Wing (RAW), began supplying Tamil militant groups with military training, cash and arms in an attempt to draw them under India's influence and to use that influence as leverage against the Sri Lankan state. RAW's support for the nascent Tamil militant groups gave them an important source of strength in their early days of violent resistance against the Sri Lankan state.

When Rajiv Gandhi succeeded his assassinated mother as Prime Minister, he changed tack on his mother's Sri Lanka policy. Rajiv drew closer to the Sri Lankan state and toughened India's position on the LTTE. He reversed his predecessor's policy on negotiations by adopting the Sri Lankan Government's position to hold negotiations only after, as opposed to before, cessation of violence. At this time as well, India, in co-operation with the Sri Lankan Navy, started patrolling the Palk Straits in earnest, to counter Tamil militant groups which were transporting supplies and rebels between the southern coast of India and northern Sri Lanka. The policy shift, under Rajiv, pushed for a resolution of the conflict at the cost of alienating the Tamil militants.

Rajiv's policy failed to end the conflict or resolve the ethnic issue. By the end of 1985 the Tamil militants had established international connections and received supplies and sanctuary in Tamil Nadu now without Indian intelligence covert support. To make matters worse, Colombo was showing no proclivity toward granting basic regional autonomy and devolution of powers to the Tamil community. After failed peace talks between the Sri Lankan Government and Tamil leaders in the Bhutanese capital, Thimphu in 1985, the Sri Lankan Government resumed its military solution against the Tamil insurgency. By 1987 the Tamils on the Jaffna Peninsula faced a humanitarian crisis caused by the Sri Lankan offensive, pushing India to intervene. After sending relief supplies by boat, which Sri Lanka turned away, India launched Operation Poomalai dropping 'bread bombs' (relief packages) on the Peninsula from Indian Air Force planes. Critics complained that India had impinged on Sri Lanka's sovereignty, but India was unapologetic since it held that its intervention had helped limit Tamil suffering at the hands of the Sri Lankan Government. Sri Lanka's military offensive had challenged India's tolerance for state violence against the Tamil population, and India responded with a more active policy.

Operation Poomalai served as the launching pad for deeper and formalized Indian intervention in Sri Lanka. In June 1987 Sri Lanka's Minister of External Affairs stated that by involving itself through the use of 'bread bombs', India now had a 'moral obligation' to resolve the ethnic dispute. The Minister's statement, while beckoning India's further involvement, also indicated India's loss of credibility as a mediator on the ethnic issue, as it made clear India's bias in favour of the Tamil cause.[6] Its humanitarian intervention did, in fact, signal India's openness to greater intervention, prompting Sri Lanka, then under President J.R. Jayewardene, to initiate talks with Rajiv Gandhi, resulting in the signing of the ISLA on 29 July 1987.

The ISLA was signed between India and Sri Lanka with only a dubious 'go-ahead' from the LTTE. When the ISLA was implemented, the lack of LTTE 'buy-in' to the agreement proved disastrous. Under the terms of the ISLA, the Sri Lankan Government agreed to make constitutional changes for devolving powers, the essential moderate Tamil demand, in exchange for India enforcing an arms collection from the rebel groups. India's obligation essentially made it the guarantor of peace. The LTTE briefly stopped fighting, but did not hand over its weapons, and soon resumed violent insurgency—this time against Indian troops. The provisions of the ISLA compelled the IPKF to engage the LTTE, which Indian intelligence had earlier helped train.

The IPKF transformed from a peace-keeping mission into a counter-insurgency campaign, which India was ill-equipped to fight on unfamiliar territory. The IPKF suffered failure and substantial casualties (over 1,200 fatalities), causing resentment and mistrust on all sides—India, Sri Lanka and the LTTE. There was a backlash in Sri Lanka to Indian troops on Sri Lankan soil, with the Sinhalese nationalist Janatha Vimukthi Peramuna launching a short-lived violent insurrection. Tamils in India resented India for turning its troops on Sri Lankan Tamils in what they saw as an unjust war against their ethnic kin population. Two years before the end of the

Cold War, in 1989, then Sri Lankan President Ranasinghe Premadasa started pushing for IPKF withdrawal from Sri Lanka, embarrassing India on the world stage. When power changed hands in Colombo and India, there was a consensus in India to withdrawal and the last IPKF soldiers returned to India in early 1990.

India's involvement in Sri Lanka's ethnic conflict transformed from heavy meddling, with both state and non-state actors, starting in 1983, to failed 'boots on the ground' intervention in the late 1980s. This pushed Indo-Sri Lankan relations to a new low. In 1991, after the IPKF withdrawal was complete and the LTTE had assassinated former Indian Prime Minister Rajiv Gandhi, India brought its involvement in Sri Lanka's internal ethnic conflict to a complete halt. After 1991 India reversed its policy of active involvement, distancing itself from an interventionist role that in the past it had felt compelled to play.

Tamil Nadu influence on India's policy

The central dilemma in India's Sri Lanka policy since IPKF withdrawal was trying to balance the Sri Lankan Government's needs with the sensitivities of its own domestic Tamil population. This proved particularly difficult during the latter part of the protracted conflict in Sri Lanka when India could not supply the Sri Lankan military with its arms and munitions needs. To India's chagrin, Sri Lanka turned to China to supply its military. With the military defeat of the LTTE in May 2009, India can now step closer to the Sri Lankan state. However, it still must contend with encroachment of foreign powers through economic avenues of influence.

Tamil Nadu's political parties, to a significant degree, have the power to translate Tamil Nadu's sympathies for its kin population into Indian government policy. Over 60m. Tamils in Tamil Nadu have kin, community and cultural ties with the Tamil community in Sri Lanka. Tamil Nadu politicians, particularly in election years, take a 'stand' in support of Sri Lankan Tamils to play on the sympathies in its own Tamil population. Tamil Nadu's political representation in coalitions at the Centre, as is the case in the present coalition, gives it formidable influence on the Centre's policy. This means that India's policy decisions on matters involving Sri Lanka have to take into consideration Tamil Nadu's likely reactions to the effects such decisions may have on the Sri Lankan Tamil population.

Tamil Nadu's sympathies for the Tamil population in Sri Lanka remain a prominent aspect of India's Sri Lanka policy. In the 1980s organizations and political parties in Tamil Nadu sourced, trained and harboured Tamil militants fighting against the Sri Lankan state. After the IPKF experience and Rajiv Gandhi's assassination, public opinion of the LTTE throughout India dropped precipitously, including in Tamil Nadu. Ganguly writes, 'the little public sympathy which the LTTE enjoyed in Tamil Nadu was also eroded when it became clear that the LTTE was responsible for the assassination of Rajiv Gandhi'.[7] Still, Tamils in Tamil Nadu retain sympathy for their kin ethnic group in Sri Lanka.

The parties in Tamil Nadu take different positions on the LTTE and the Tamil cause. Jayaram Jayalilitha's All-India Anna Dravida Munnetra Kazhagam (AIADMK) has been unequivocally against the LTTE, in sharp contrast to the historical support of the Dravida Munnetra Kazhagam (DMK) political party. However, the DMK, under Chief Minister Karuninidhi, has grown colder in its support for the LTTE during its current phase of leadership in the state. Karuninidhi's previously supportive position especially came under challenge when the LTTE's relationship with south Indian fishermen soured following a rise in LTTE violence against the fishermen. The Marumalarchi Dravida Munnetra Kazhagam (MDMK) party and the Pattali Makkal Katchi (PMK) continue to run on platforms of support for the LTTE, championing the case of a Tamil Eelam—a separate homeland for Tamils in north-east Sri Lanka.

There are a few recurring issues in the Sri Lankan conflict that spark controversy and protests in Tamil Nadu. Chief among these issues is the refugee inflow from Sri Lanka into southern India. Today, over 100,000 Sri Lankan refugees who have escaped the violent ethnic conflict live in over 100 government-run camps in southern India, for the most part in Tamil Nadu. During peaks in violence, refugee flows to southern India rose dramatically, crowding camps and unofficial refugee communities. Often the inflow unsettled an already fragile political environment and frail economic situation in the south Indian state. Tamil Nadu's sympathies are also sensitive to any support given by India to the Sri Lankan military. Similarly, the proposed India-Sri Lanka Defence Co-operation Agreement, discussed below, has reportedly been held up by political parties from Tamil Nadu.

'Hands off' the conflict

India's policy of simultaneously supporting a political solution to the conflict and tacitly condoning Sri Lanka's clampdown on LTTE terrorists allowed India to pragmatically respond to the LTTE terrorist threat and maintain a safe, albeit removed, position from the conflict vis-à-vis support for the peace process. India's tacit support for Sri Lanka's defence measures against the LTTE, though far from whole-hearted, encouraged Sri Lankan military co-operation on threats to Indian security and ensured that the LTTE did not overpower Sri Lanka's state defences. As for support to the failed Norway-led peace process, Indian leaders were apprised of developments by reports of Sri Lankan government officials and other governments involved, particularly Norway, the United Kingdom and the USA. Its limited response to the developments, however, enabled it to keep a safe distance from the controversial political issues involved. Critics characterized India's policy as a 'do-nothing stance', arguing, alongside other observers, that India should move to a 'more active role' in facilitating discussions between the two sides.[8]

India's policy of simultaneously supporting Sri Lanka's 'unity and integrity' and a 'negotiated settlement' to the ethnic conflict, raises questions about where India stands. For instance, will the Indian Government resist pressures from its own Tamil Nadu constituency to intervene if Sri Lanka's Tamil populations face mass suffering? For the Indian Government, the two positions articulated as one—valuing Sri Lanka's 'unity and integrity' and pressing for a 'negotiated settlement'—allow for a flexible policy under which it can tailor responses to developments in Sri Lankan politics and the ethnic conflict. India's policy remains at times a frustrating balancing act between domestic political pressures from Tamil Nadu and pragmatic security concerns.

The Indian Government officially maintains that the ethnic conflict is a Sri Lankan problem that only Sri Lankans and their government can solve on their own. This Indian response was a knee-jerk reaction to the embittering IPKF experience, suggesting a parallel with the USA's 'Viet Nam syndrome'—that is, since intervention did not work and came at a great cost, to prevent any chance of its re-occurrence one would go to the other extreme: 'hands off'. India's 'hands-off' policy, though formulated through a political response to failed military intervention, has been sustained on account of its success in repairing relations with Sri Lanka and avoiding contentious loyalty issues surrounding the conflict. However, Sri Lanka's ethnic conflict continued to irritate relations with spillover effects negatively impacting on India.

Defence relations

India's defence relationship with Sri Lanka was minimal throughout the 1990s, and it continues to remain rather limited, despite Sri Lanka's proximity to India and their mutual security concerns. However, there are some areas of assistance and co-ordination between the two militaries, particularly concerning maritime and, recently, aerial security threats posed by the LTTE. These areas include training of Sri Lankan officers at Indian Defence Universities, which has taken place uninterrupted for decades, and the sharing of intelligence on the LTTE's maritime movements to aid the Sri Lankan Navy in intercepting rogue vessels.

The Indian Navy's intelligence-sharing with the Sri Lankan Navy bolstered the latter's ability to track LTTE supplies and attack its vessels operating around the island. During the final phase of the Sri Lankan war, India helped the Sri Lankan Navy identify suspicious vessels off the coast of Sri Lanka. Thus, in September 2007, the Sri Lankan Navy, possibly acting off information from Indian intelligence, sunk three LTTE supply vessels 600 nautical miles south-east of Sri Lanka.[9] Co-operation between the Indian Coast Guard and Navy and the Sri Lankan Navy involves a frequent exchange of information, expedited by co-ordinating the procedures of operation and ensuring open channels of communication. Every six months the officers of the Indian Coast Guard and Navy meet with their counterparts in the Sri Lankan Navy at the International Boundary Line to discuss logistical issues of co-ordination and communication. Such co-operation reflects India and Sri Lanka's shared strategic interests in maintaining maritime security throughout their bordering waterways and has been expanding since the conflict against LTTE ended. Shortly after the war ended in May 2009, India gave the Sri Lankan Navy a high-tech offshore patrol vessel surveillance ship. The Indian and Sri Lankan navies engaged in joint training exercises in October 2009 and again in April 2010.[10] This post-conflict trend of greater co-operation is likely to continue with more joint exercises meant to develop a collaborative approach to maritime security.

Each year, officers in the Sri Lankan military study at Indian Defence Universities on the invitation of the Indian Government. India's invitation has been extended for decades, and its importance to the quality of the Sri Lankan Armed Forces is duly noted by Sri Lankan leaders. Such education is a modest way in which India can support its neighbour's military strength without risking domestic and international political repercussions.

Weaponry requests form a large part of Sri Lanka's bid for defence support from India, but India has been reluctant to significantly arm the Sri Lankan military. Under President Mahinda Rajapakse's tenure, the urgency of Sri Lanka's requests fell on unresponsive ears in New Delhi, and India's refusal to arm Sri Lanka's military led critics to accuse India of an inconsistent and uncommitted stand on the LTTE. India placed greater importance on controlling the risk of domestic political repercussions in its Tamil constituency than maintaining a consistent stance on the LTTE. For the six years preceding 2002 India had actually banned transfer of any military supplies to Sri Lanka. From 2002 India's military equipment assistance to the Sri Lankan Armed Forces was limited to 'defensive and non-lethal' equipment, precluding any chance of Indian weaponry contributing to Sri Lankan Tamil casualties in the Sri Lankan Government's military operations. India would not supply offensive or lethal weaponry to Sri Lanka (there was speculation of covert arms transfers) until Sri Lanka conceded basic devolution of powers to the Tamil population.

Even with India's reluctance to supply Sri Lanka with weaponry, in late October 2003 Sri Lankan Prime Minister Ranil Wickremesinghe and Indian Prime Minister A.B. Vajpayee issued a joint statement indicating mutual interest in working towards a Defence Co-operation Agreement (DCA). The DCA sought to formalize existing supply of equipment, troop training, intelligence exchange and joint naval patrolling.[11] After power in both New Delhi and Colombo changed hands, Prime Minister Mahinda Rajapakse's state visit to New Delhi in June 2004 garnered rhetorical support from both sides for expediting the DCA proposed by the previous administrations.[12] Kumaratunga and Indian Prime Minister Manmohan Singh even announced that they agreed to sign not only the DCA, but also a Memorandum of Understanding on joint rehabilitation of the Palaly Air Force Base. Access to Palaly Air Force Base would offer India greater aerial reach in the Bay of Bengal and Indian Ocean region. However, political hurdles in India's coalition government, most likely on account of opposition from the Tamil Nadu's political parties, have prevented India from signing the DCA with Sri Lanka. Even so, the DCA, presumably still on the table, would only formalize existing defence ties.

Economic relations

The island of Sri Lanka and the Indian subcontinent engaged in trade dating back to the pre-colonial era. After independence in the late 1940s both countries pursued inward-looking economic development strategies that stifled trade between the two countries despite their close proximity. Sri Lanka opened its economy in 1978—becoming the first South Asian economy to do so—but trade between Sri Lanka and India did not pick up until India started opening its economy in the 1980s and early 1990s.

After India's 1991 economic reforms, trade between India and Sri Lanka jumped. Two-way trade between 1993 and 1996 doubled. This growth reflected an explosion of Indian exports into the Sri Lankan market, increasing over 500% between 1990 and 1996. In 1995 India eclipsed Japan as the largest source of imports for Sri Lanka. However, Sri Lankan exports to the Indian market grew much less impressively, and this lopsided growth drew criticism that the economic relationship heavily favoured India. This pattern of trade fed the Sri Lankan perception of India as a regional hegemon: the large Indian economy was preying on its smaller and weaker neighbours.

Still, both countries recognized the benefits of free trade with one another. When the SAARC Preferential Trading Arrangement (SAPTA) failed to significantly reduce tariffs after it was launched in 1996, India and Sri Lanka made a bilateral trade agreement. In 1998 India and Sri Lanka signed their bilateral India-Sri Lanka Free Trade Agreement (ISLFTA) with the agreement coming into operation by 2001. The ISLFTA granted duty-free and duty-preference access to goods produced in the two countries and laid out practical steps for a time-bound creation of a free trade area in the near future.

Since the ISLFTA, bilateral trade has markedly increased, accompanied by a surge of Indian investment in Sri Lanka. In 2001 trade doubled. By 2004/05 bilateral trade reached US $1,690m.; by 2005/06 their trade of $2,600m. was five times the amount 10 years earlier. By 2007/08 it had reached a peak of $3,470m., leaving Sri Lanka as India's biggest trade partner in South Asia. Amidst the global recession, figures for 2008/09 showed some reduction, back to $2,780m., with a further reduction to $2,580m. in 2009/10. An increase in Indian investment in Sri Lanka reinforced India's commitment to long-term economic engagement on the island. From a meagre $4m. in the late 1990s, Indian direct investment in Sri Lanka jumped to $150m. in 2006. By 2005 Indian investment in Sri Lanka accounted for 50% of total Indian investment in South Asian Association for Regional Cooperation (SAARC) countries, making India the fourth highest source of investment in the island, thereby further interweaving the fates of India and Sri Lanka.[13] By 2008 Indian investment increased to $125.9m., making it the second largest investor in Sri Lanka after Malaysia.[14] The most prominent investments have been in the Lanka Indian Oil Corporation (Lanka IOC), TATAs (Taj Hotels, VSNL, Watawala tea plantations), Apollo Hospitals, LIC, L&T (now Aditya Birla Group), Ambujas, Rediffusion, Ceat, Nicholas Piramal, Jet Airways, Sahara, Indian Airlines and Ashok Leyland. In 2007 some 63% of Indian investment was in the services sector, which contributed to job growth in the struggling Sri Lankan economy.

The ISLFTA was much more than just an economic success. Bilateral economic engagement on the back of the ISLFTA is the hallmark of and impetus for improved Indo-Sri Lankan relations. The benefits of these prospering economic ties extend beyond economic gains to political and strategic relations. The resultant goodwill and increased interaction within the institutional framework and enthusiasm from enhanced economic engagement has helped repair political wounds and advance overall bilateral relations. Most importantly, it helped change the Sri Lankan perception of India as just a regional hegemon.

The trigger for this turn-around was a conscious decision by the Indian policy establishment, outlined in the Gujral Doctrine, to offer its smaller neighbours asymmetrical advantages in trade.[15] This decision foresaw the propitious effects of greater economic engagement in India's strategic relationships with its neighbours. Following the Gujral Doctrine principles, tariff concessions under the ISLFTA signed in 1998, favouring Sri Lanka, significantly reduced the imbalance in Sri Lanka-bound Indian exports to India-bound Sri Lankan exports.

Sri Lankan exports to India boomed under the improved trade arrangements favouring Sri Lankan produced goods. India's 'negative list' (goods not subject to tariff reduction or elimination) included 429 goods compared with Sri Lanka's 1,180, and India had three years to reach zero-tariff level against Sri Lanka's eight. The new arrangements worked to even the trade imbalance. Just two years after the ISLFTA was put into effect, Sri Lankan exports to India increased by 342%. The advantage given to Sri Lanka under the Gujral Doctrine principles had narrowed the trade imbalance to 5:1 by 2002; in 1998 it had stood at 16:1. Since 2003 India has been Sri Lanka's third highest export destination.

In April 2003 the two countries set up a Joint Study Group to enhance the ISLFTA with a Comprehensive Economic Partnership Agreement (CEPA).[16] The much-anticipated CEPA would further remove tariff barriers on trade, create greater market access in the services sector, as well as stimulate greater Indian investment in Sri Lanka through an institutional framework. After more than a dozen rounds of negotiations, CEPA was supposed to be signed by India and Sri Lanka at the SAARC summit in Colombo in August 2008. However, it has been subject to delay, and as of August 2010 had still not been signed even though negotiations seemed to have been pretty well concluded. The India-Sri Lanka Joint Declaration, drawn up in the wake of President Rajapaksa's state visit in June 2010, was rather circumspect on the matter:

> Recognizing the considerable benefits from greater economic cooperation between the two countries, the two Leaders noted the progress achieved under the India–Sri Lanka Free Trade Agreement. They agreed that it would be timely to build on this achievement through a more comprehensive framework of economic cooperation, best suited to the two countries. In this context, they directed the concerned officials of the two countries to hold intensive consultations towards developing a framework for sustainable economic partnership between the two countries and addressing outstanding issues.[17]

Sri Lankan business interests concerned with Indian goods overrunning Sri Lankan markets are most likely the cause of the hold-up.

Nevertheless, in the broader view, the growth in trade and investment between India and Sri Lanka marks a shift in India's engagement with Sri Lanka towards the economic realm. Of the three major agreements between India and Sri Lanka, the ISLFTA was the first treaty that was economic in nature.[18] Whereas India's previous Sri Lanka policy focused—and eventually floundered—on controversial political issues, the thrust of the ISLFTA was economic engagement, and its positive spillover effects in political relations. Since the ISLFTA took effect in

March 2000, expanded economic engagement has become the backbone of the India-Sri Lanka relationship, which has reached new levels of co-operation and trust.

Bolstered economic engagement between India and Sri Lanka, particularly since the ISLFTA came into effect, produced propitious political effects favouring better Indo-Sri Lankan relations. Most importantly, greater equality in terms of benefits from the economic relationship helped overcome Sri Lankan perceptions of subservience to Indian interests. Whereas the attitude toward Indian presence in Sri Lanka turned hostile in the late 1980s, benefits from economic engagement with India have made Sri Lankans, even those among the nationalist ranks, eager for India to play a greater economic role in Sri Lanka. Sri Lankans have been much more receptive to India's economic involvement than they were to its military intervention.

Sri Lankan receptiveness to India's economic involvement opened up an avenue for communication on a broader set of issues. The India-Sri Lanka Joint Commission, reformulated and expanded in 1991 from an earlier joint committee, has institutionalized a framework for economic integration from which the ISLFTA emerged. Formed primarily to address economic issues like 3 educational and cultural programmes to mutual security concerns like terrorism. Thus, while economic engagement served as the impetus for and continues to drive this institutionalized bilateral framework, the framework also serves as a forum for a wider scope of issues.

India and Sri Lanka are strongly engaging in the strategic energy sector. Indian companies are serving Sri Lanka's energy market and exploring the island's offshore oil resources. Lanka IOC took over a 30% market share in Sri Lanka's retail petrol market in 2005, operating 151 retail outlets on the island. Lanka IOC is building and operating storage facilities at the Trincomalee Tank farm, which, as stated earlier, is of critical importance in the maritime strategic environment. India also has a significant stake in the exploration of oil resources off Sri Lanka's coast. India's Oil and Natural Gas Corporation (ONGC) has been promised one of the five drilling blocks in the Mannar basin.[19] The Mannar basin, thought to contain the equivalent of 1,000m. barrels of oil, has three remaining blocks up for auction; besides the one promised to India, the second of the five has been granted to China.

Most importantly, India is developing port facilities at one of the world's largest deep-water harbours, Trincomalee. Ancient Sri Lankan kings through to the colonial powers used Trincomalee harbour as a naval base and trading port, since it is the only port in Sri Lanka where ships of all sizes can dock in any kind of weather. For India, Trincomalee offers both economic and strategic advantages. The port is an entry and exit point for goods travelling in and out of India, and India is currently refurbishing the infrastructure of an oil tank farm near the harbour that was built by the British in the 1930s. Sri Lanka has a naval base at Trincomalee, and it is likely that if Indian and Sri Lankan naval co-operation continues, the Indian Navy will have some amount of access to the harbour.

China and Sri Lanka

India has perceived Chinese economic interaction with Sri Lanka as encroachment into its strategic territory; they are both there in what Harsh Pant sees as a 'great game' in the Indian Ocean.[20] The supply of defence equipment to a Sri Lankan military at war provided one of the major inroads for China (and Pakistan) to gain strategic influence within Sri Lanka.[21] China was willing to provide Sri Lanka with the defence support it needed to pursue a military solution against the LTTE. India was aware of the nature and development of these relationships, though it had no power to stop China from meeting Sri Lanka's defence needs. India's domestic political compulsions prevented it from challenging the roles played by China and Pakistan— the restraints of coalition politics allowed for lesser defence 'carrots' than Sri Lanka needed, and the bitter memory of the failed IPKF experience lingered. India's political compulsions worked against its strategic imperative to keep major powers from gaining inroads into Sri Lanka.

During the war, Sri Lanka and China made multiple defence deals centred on arms transfers. These deals included a $37.6m. contract between Sri Lanka and China's Poly Technologies, signed in April 2007. Sri Lanka's debt to Norinco, another defence supplier, was reportedly $200m. Sri Lanka gained large amounts of mortar shells, artillery shells, mortar bombs, JY 11 3D radars, anti-aircraft guns and Jian-17 fighter jets. China also helped fulfil the Sri Lankan Navy's 'shopping list' of weaponry and munitions needs. Such military help was seen by many as having been crucial in enabling the Sri Lankan Government to achieve military victory and crush the Tamil Tigers in 2009: 'an unfettered China is supporting Colombo and, in the process, authenticating India's fears about Beijing extending its influence in the Indian Ocean'.[22]

Indian concern has focused around the Chinese developing the Hambantota port on the southern tip of Sri Lanka. Chinese contractors are currently working to finish Phase One of the project by the end of 2010, at a cost of $76.5m. The work includes building a 1.3-km jetty to shelter the harbour, and an oil refinery. At the end of the initial phase, the facility will be a bunker terminal (bunker fuels are used to power ships) with a capacity of 500,000 metric tons. The Sri Lanka Ports Authority indicated that it would rent out storage space to private domestic and foreign firms, and presumably this will include Chinese firms. The entire project has four phases, with the contract for Phase Two signed in June 2010 with the China Harbour Engineering Company Ltd. It is all expected to be completed by 2022, some 15 years after it was started, though the economic success or failure of the first stages will determine if the entire plan is carried out.

China's interest in the Hambantota port is consistent with its desire to supply ample refuelling terminals along Indian Ocean shipping lanes to support an increasing amount of sea-based trade. It has also partnered with other neighbouring states to develop port facilities in Gwadar (Pakistan), Chittagong (Bangladesh) and Sitwe (Myanmar).[23] For China, this is a strategic imperative rather than just a foreign investment to bolster its growing economy. The majority of China's oil travels this Sea Line of Communication, in which any increasing maritime security concerns off the coast of Somalia and in the Malacca Straits threaten China's energy security.

Though China's 'blue water' Navy is below the US Navy, and (in some areas) the Indian Navy, it is placing a lot of resources into developing greater capabilities so that it can eventually exert greater control over its maritime trade routes. India worries that a Chinese presence in Hambantota will one day include the Chinese Navy. Both China and Sri Lanka deny any plans for a Chinese naval base in Sri Lanka, but India continues to worry about the possibility. India's fear is that if Sri Lanka were to grant naval access on the island to China, Chinese encirclement of India with a 'string of pearls' (ports) in the Indian Ocean region would become a reality.[24]

Conclusions

The end of the Sri Lankan conflict in May 2009 provides an opening for closer Indo-Sri Lankan relations. Will there be a large jump in bilateral co-operation between 2010 and 2015 and beyond? The answer likely depends most on whether the Sri Lankan majority Sinhalese and minority Tamils achieve political reconciliation. The Government of Sri Lanka militarily defeated the LTTE, so the conflict ended without political reconciliation. The grievances of the Tamil minority that originally inspired popular support for the insurgency have for the most part not been addressed. Until the Government of Sri Lanka addresses Tamil demands for minority rights and equal educational and economic opportunities, the underlying ethnic tension of the

Brian Orland

conflict will remain. For India, this means that its policy dilemma discussed above will continue to constrain its relationship with Sri Lanka.

Notes

1 P. Sahadevan, 'India's Policy of Non-Intervention in Sri Lanka', in A. Raju (ed.), *India-Sri Lanka Partnership in the 21st Century*, New Delhi: Kalpaz Publications, 2007.
2 S. Ramachandran, 'Delhi All Ears in the Indian Ocean', *Asia Times*, 3 March 2006.
3 S.D. Muni, *Pangs of Proximity*, New Delhi: Sage Publications, 1993, p.52.
4 Ibid., p.73.
5 Ibid.
6 Ibid., p.102.
7 R. Ganguly, *Kin State Intervention in Ethnic Conflicts: Lessons From South Asia*, New Delhi: Sage Publications, 1998, p.218.
8 P. Jayaram, 'India May Rethink its Stand on Sri Lanka: New Delhi Fears a Flood of Tamil Refugees if Violence Worsens in its Southern Neighbour', *Straits Times*, 3 June 2006.
9 B. Reddy, 'Three LTTE Ships Destroyed: Navy', *The Hindu*, 12 September 2007.
10 B. Reddy, 'India, Sri Lanka to Hold Naval Training', *The Hindu*, 6 October 2009; 'India to Train 100 Sri Lankan Naval Officers', *Indo-Asian News Service*, 9 April 2010.
11 I. Athas, 'The Unfolding Indian Role in Sri Lanka', *The Hindu*, 1 November 2003.
12 S. Cherian, 'Tilting the Balance', *South Asia Intelligence Review*, Vol. 3, No. 18, 2004.
13 S. Kelegama, 'India, Sri Lanka Agreement is an Example to Follow', *Financial Express*, 5 October 2005.
14 D. Daniel, 'Indo-Lanka FTA is 10 Years Old', *The Island*, 15 March 2010.
15 In 1996 India's Prime Minister, Inder Kumar Gujral, explicated five principles of what he termed the 'Gujral Doctrine' to guide how India conducted foreign relations with its immediate neighbours. The first of these principles says that 'India does not ask for reciprocity, but gives and accommodates what it can in good faith and trust', cited in I. Gujral, 'Significance of an Independent Foreign Policy', 14 October 1996, in *Continuity and Change. India's Foreign Policy*, London: Macmillan, 2003, pp.108–09.
16 'India-Sri Lanka Forum to Discuss Economic Pact', *The Hindu*, 2 November 2006.
17 India-Sri Lanka, *Joint Declaration*, 9 June 2010, www.hcicolombo.org.
18 D. Roy, 'Indo-Sri Lanka Trade: Hype and Reality', *Asia Times*, 12 March 2004.
19 G. Warushamana, 'Oil Exploration in Mannar Basin Will Take Time', *Sunday Observer*, 11 November 2007.
20 H. Pant, 'China and India Competing Over Sri Lanka', *Japan Times*, 29 June 2010.
21 R. Bedi, 'Sri Lanka Turns to Pakistan, China for Military Needs', *Indo-Asian News Service*, 6 February 2007.
22 'India Upset with China over Sri Lanka Crisis', *Times of India*, 26 April 2009.
23 B. Raman, 'Gwadar, Hanbantota and Sitwe: China's Strategic Triangle', *Papers* (SAAG), No. 2158, 6 March 2007.
24 D.R. Chaudhury, 'Boosting Maritime Capabilities in the Indian Ocean', www.worldpress.org, 23 August 2007.

10

India's relations with Afghanistan

Raghav Sharma

Introduction

The camaraderie that characterizes India-Afghanistan relations both at the political and popular level is not merely a product of modern geopolitics but is also a testimony to the historico-cultural linkages that have existed between Afghanistan and the Indian subcontinent since ancient times.[1] The partition of British India in 1947 ruptured India's geographical contiguity with Afghanistan, but not the warmth that characterized their relations; this stood in sharp contrast to Pakistan, which, in spite of its geographical contiguity as well as religious and ethnic congruity, has seen its relations with Kabul for most of its history being clouded by bitterness and a deep sense of distrust. India's role in Afghanistan has re-emerged into importance not just for Afghanistan and the region, but also as 'a test case for a rising power'—India.[2] Afghanistan's importance for India and others is largely geopolitical, as Afghanistan faces southwards down from the Hindu Kush into the Indian subcontinent, India's *immediate neighbourhood*. Yet it also looks northwards down from the Hindu Kush into India's *extended neighbourhood*, in which 'Afghanistan is the fractious gateway to and from Central Asia, which defines the way other powers grapple and circumvent the complexities of the region', as well as being part of what has been called the 'Greater Middle East'.[3]

India's interaction with Afghanistan: 1947–2009

Afghanistan's stance on the question of the creation of *Pakhtunistan*, its 1948 vote opposing Pakistan's entry into the UN—making it the only country to do so—and its refusal to toe Pakistan's line on the question of Kashmir, laid the foundations for forging close links quite early on with the new Republic of India that took over the reins of power from the British. India's gradual drift towards Moscow and Kabul's increasing dependence on the Soviets for aid further complemented India-Afghanistan bilateral ties. Relations between the two states remained warm and both sides maintained deep cultural and modest economic links.

The first formidable challenge to India's Afghanistan policy came in the wake of the Soviet military intervention in Afghanistan in December 1979 to help prop up a pro-Soviet communist regime that had usurped power through a bloody coup christened the 'Saur Revolution'.

The challenge at hand for New Delhi became more pronounced in light of its proclaimed policy of non-alignment. The then Prime Minister, Chaudhary Charan Singh, categorically opposed Soviet intervention and called for an immediate withdrawal of Soviet troops. However, this stand was short lived and was reversed when Indira Gandhi made a dramatic political comeback and was re-elected to office in January 1980.[4] She stated that Soviet troops were introduced into Afghanistan 'only after Pakistan started training Afghan rebels and sending them in to topple the government there [...] nevertheless India was opposed to the USSR's presence and it had told that country so'.[5] However, despite its discomfort with Soviet military presence in its neighbourhood, India, while steering clear of an unequivocal endorsement of Soviet military intervention, consistently chose to abstain on key UN resolutions calling for Soviet withdrawal from Afghanistan.

India's response to the Soviet intervention in Afghanistan was essentially conditioned by the following four key factors: first, Washington's economic aid, supply of sophisticated arms and F-16 fighter aircrafts to Pakistan; second, Washington's rapprochement with Beijing in which Islamabad had played a key role; third, a US naval build-up in the Indian Ocean region;[6] and fourth, a fear of *mujahideen* victory giving Pakistan clear strategic leverage in Afghanistan. Given these complex geopolitical realities, India could not afford to jeopardize its partnership with the USSR, which had emerged as its major supplier of defence equipment and space technology, and which played a key role in extending support to India at key international forums on critical issues such as Kashmir and the Bangladesh war of 1971, in face of stiff opposition from the USA and People's Republic of China.

India's recognition of the pro-Kremlin regime in Kabul—making it the only country outside the Warsaw Pact to do so—did to an extent undermine India's moral stature, especially in the Non-Aligned Movement (NAM), and to an extent also sullied India's image within Afghanistan. Subsequently, New Delhi's decision in 1982 to restore the Indo-Afghan Joint Commission, constituted in the early 1970s for economic and technical assistance and lying in abeyance since the Saur Revolution in 1978, further eroded India's position on the international stage.

India supported all Moscow-backed governments in Kabul and extended modest developmental assistance to the Najibullah regime, in spite of Najibullah's increasingly fragile control over the country. However, within months of the Soviet collapse the Najibullah regime, too, had dramatically unravelled, and was replaced by a fragile coalition of *mujahideen* forces with Badrudin Rabbani at the helm. Given the extremely limited room for political manoeuvring, India cast its lot with Rabbani notwithstanding its apprehensions of Rabbani's own Islamist *Jamat-e-Islami* background and endorsement of Pakistan's position on Kashmir—a clear break from the policy adopted by preceding regimes of Kabul. However, factionalism was rife in Rabbani's *mujahideen*, and this ensured its demise which once again plunged Afghanistan into a brutal civil war.

India suffered its greatest strategic setback in Afghanistan with the rise of the Pakistan-backed Taliban to the political centre stage in 1996. New Delhi refused to recognize the extremist Taliban regime under which Afghanistan, in the now seemingly prophetic words of Dr Najinullah, was to emerge as 'a centre of world smuggling for narcotic drugs. Afghanistan will be turned into a centre for terrorism'.[7] For India, the fallout of the rise of fundamentalism in Afghanistan was ferocious and almost immediate, as it witnessed the rise of what proved to be long and traumatic Islamist insurgency in the Kashmir valley. The participation of 200 soldiers from the Taliban's elite brigade 055 in active combat during the Kargil conflict with Pakistan in 1999,[8] and their more visible role during the landing of the hijacked Indian airliner IC 814 in Kandahar in December 1999 (which led to the freeing of three terrorist including Masood Azhar), foreclosed whatever limited possibility might have existed for exploring the idea of accommodation with the Taliban. India, however, remained sensitive to the plight of the common people in Afghanistan and did indirectly extend limited humanitarian assistance to the country in the form of medicine, vegetable oil, tea and emergency relief material through Dushanbe.[9]

New Delhi's deep antipathy towards the Taliban brought it onto a common platform with Tehran and Moscow, which supported the predominantly Tajik Northern Alliance whose control over Afghanistan was reduced to a mere 10% of the territory in the extreme north. Indian support to the opposition was routed through its base in Farakhor in Tajikistan. The events that ensued in the aftermath of the terrorist attacks on the USA on 11 September 2001 were principally responsible for tilting the scales in favour of the opposition Northern Alliance and unseating the Taliban from power within a matter of weeks. As Ramachandran noted, 'in Afghanistan, Pakistan's loss is India's gain'.[10]

Subsequently, India has managed to effectively claw its way back into Afghanistan's power equations, at least for the near future. The India-educated Hamid Karzai, a Pushtun, came to power first as head of the interim government and has since been re-elected twice as President. Karzai adopted a policy of rekindling Kabul's close ties with New Delhi. This is borne out in particular by two significant symbolic gestures: first, the visit of then foreign minister Abdullah Abdullah and defence minister Mohammad Qasim Fahim to India within three months of the installation of the interim government; and second, the choice of New Delhi as the first destination by national carrier Ariana on its inaugural run, overlooking all the other six geographically contiguous neighbours of Afghanistan. India has attempted to give greater traction to its efforts to secure its interests in Afghanistan by engaging in diplomatic parleys with Kabul at the highest level, Karzai has visited India seven times since taking charge, while in 2005 Prime Minister Manmohan Singh paid a state visit to Kabul, significantly the first such visit by an Indian head of state in three decades.

Today, India is recognized as a key regional player in efforts to stabilize Afghanistan and for the first time there is a broad congruity of Indian and US interests in Afghanistan: both wish to see a stable, democratic and multi-ethnic political solution take root in the country. India moved swiftly to deepen its footprint in Afghanistan by opening its embassy in Kabul and four other consulates in Jalalabad (eastern Afghanistan), Herat (northern Afghanistan), Kandahar (southern Afghanistan) and Mazar-e-Sharif (western Afghanistan). In addition, India also unveiled a US $1,200m. aid programme—a substantial amount for a traditionally non-donor country—making it the largest regional and fifth largest international donor. Indian aid projects spread across various sectors, ranging from offering 500 annual scholarships for Afghan students, provision of vocational training activities for women, construction of roads, dams, transmission lines and telecom networks, to the construction of the new Afghanistan parliament building.[11] Commenting on the Indian aid programme, the Pakistani analyst Ahmed Rashid reckoned that 'India's reconstruction strategy was designed to win over every sector of Afghan society, give India a high profile with Afghans, gain the maximum political advantage and of course, undercut Pakistani influence'.[12]

India's interests in Afghanistan

Indian efforts in Afghanistan are underpinned by the following three key objectives: negating the influence of Pakistani Inter-Services Intelligence (ISI)-backed groups like the Taliban, which are hostile to Indian interests in the neighbourhood; curtailing the spread of drugs-trafficking, which poses a risk to both national and human security in the region; and securing Afghanistan as a trade and energy corridor to Central Asia.

Security interests

Historically, challenges to India's physical security have tended to emanate from its north-western frontier with Afghanistan; serving as a launch pad for invasions into the plains of northern India and Kashmir, the latter region came under a brief but bitterly remembered spell of Afghan rule from 1753–1819.[13] Kashmir's linkage with Afghanistan was rekindled following the Soviet withdrawal in 1989, albeit in a completely different context. The winding down of *jihad* against the atheist Soviets freed up the energies of hundreds of thousands of ideologically motivated *mujahideen,* flush with weapons supplied by the members of the 'free world' (i.e. the USA) who had for the first time in modern history tasted serving on the battlefield for the cause of their religion. Many of the Afghanistan war veterans canalized their energies for waging *jihad* in Kashmir in what was perceived to be a 'holy war'. This linkage was further reinforced with the ascendance of the ISI-backed Taliban in Afghanistan. Commenting on this phenomenon, the Pakistani analyst Ishtiaq Ahmed poignantly noted:

> A Taliban controlled Afghanistan fulfilled military objectives vis-à-vis India: achieving strategic depth for the Pakistan army in case of war with India and ensuring the continuity of Arab and Afghan militancy in Indian Kashmir [...] most of the Islamic militant groups that are now fighting in Kashmir, including Harkat-ul-Mujahideen, are products of the Afghan war. The Taliban are an important external agent in fuelling the fire of Islamic militancy in Kashmir.[14]

The Taliban provided sanctuary for training terrorists for Kashmir and allowed for the establishment of 21 camps across the country.[15] Subsequently, the Taliban's role in the Kargil conflict on the side of Pakistan in the summer of 1999, and later over the course of the negotiations following the landing of the hijacked Indian airliner in the Taliban stronghold of Kandahar in December 1999, further accentuated New Delhi's security concerns.

In light of India's past experiences, it is not surprising that its core security interests in Afghanistan essentially comprise denying reclamation of political and military space to the ISI-backed Taliban in Afghanistan. India sought to achieve this by extending military support to the Tajik-dominated Northern Alliance against the predominantly Pushtun Taliban before 2002, and by extending political, diplomatic and extensive humanitarian support to the Karzai Government from 2002.

Drugs-trafficking

India has the largest opiate-using population in the sub-region (the five Central Asian republics, Iran, Pakistan, Afghanistan and India), accounting for an astounding 3.2m. users out of a total of 5m. users estimated for the entire sub-region. India has also reported the largest cannabis seizures made in Asia, at 108m. tonnes, the bulk of which originated in Afghanistan.[16] Afghanistan's opium makes its way to the Indian market through the Indo–Pakistani border in the Punjab. Opium addiction has grown at an alarming rate, particularly amongst the youth in the border villages, inflicting tremendous damage on the country's social fabric.

The other disconcerting trend for India has been the strengthening linkages between drugs-trafficking and the Taliban insurgency, which has gained tremendous momentum over the last four years. The money generated from drugs-trafficking is being used to fund the supply of sophisticated arms and to win over foot soldiers for the insurgency by paying them a monthly salary of $250–$350, as compared with the paltry sum of $40 being paid to an Afghan National

Army soldier, with the salary only recently being raised to a range of $180–$240. The growing menace of drugs-trafficking poses serious challenges to human security as well as the national security of India.

Energy and commercial interests

A stable Afghanistan has the potential to serve as a key land bridge to facilitate India's energy and commercial interests in hydrocarbon-rich Central Asia, thus facilitating the diversification of oil and gas supplies and reducing India's excessive dependence on supplies from the Middle East. The weight attached to the issue was reflected in a speech by India's then President Dr A. P.J Abdul Kalam: 'my government will give full importance to synchronizing our diplomatic activity with our need for energy to fuel our development needs'.[17] With this objective of enhancing India's energy security, vital to sustain the momentum of its economic growth, India joined the ambitious $7,500m. TAPI (Turkmenistan, Afghanistan, Pakistan and India) pipeline initiative, which was envisaged to carry 30,000m. cu feet of gas from the Dauletabad field in Turkmenistan via Afghanistan and Pakistan, into India.

Afghanistan also has considerable amounts of untapped reserves of oil and natural gas. As per the estimates of Gustavson Associates, the undiscovered gas reserves range between 3.6 trillion and 36.5 trillion cubic feet, while oil reserves are estimated to be between 0.4 billion and 3.6 billion barrels, with 0.1m. to 1.3m. barrels of natural gas liquids.[18] The bulk of these resources are concentrated in the Tajik-dominated north, in the plains and basins next to the Amu Darya, where India has traditionally enjoyed a particularly strong constituency. More recently the discovery of a vast array of industrial metals such as copper, gold, iron, cobalt and lithium, the value of which is estimated at more than $1 trillion, could dramatically transform not only the Afghan economy, but its geopolitical standing in the region if exploited in the right way.[19]

For Indian industry, too, Afghanistan offers a huge untapped market which is presently dominated by Pakistan, Iran and Turkmenistan. It also has the potential to serve as a gateway to penetrate the Central Asian market, which is presently flooded with cheap but low-quality Chinese goods and expensive imports from the West. In particular, both the Afghan as well as the Central Asian markets offer immense potential for Indian tea, pharmaceuticals, food processing, information technology (IT), banking, health, tourism, consumer durables and automobiles industry. India's emergence as a global IT hub, a destination for medical tourism, the remarkable ability of its pharmaceutical industry to make available life-saving drugs at reasonable rates, its expertise in small and medium-sized enterprises, and its emergence as a global automobile manufacturing hub give Indian industry a distinct edge.

In light of Pakistan's refusal to grant trade transit rights, India has worked towards developing an alternative trade corridor going down to Chabahar, christened as the International North South Trade Corridor (INSTC), developed under an agreement that it inked with Russia and Iran in 2000 to access the Central Asian markets. Through the development of the 218-km Zaranj–Delaram road on the Afghanistan–Iran border, at a cost of $150m. and the loss of 11 Indian and 129 Afghan lives, India hopes to achieve two objectives. First, provide land-locked Afghanistan with shorter and alternative access to the sea, thereby reducing its dependency on Pakistan;[20] and second, in light of Pakistan's refusal to grant trade transit rights over land, it envisages by-passing Pakistan and instead shipping its goods from Mumbai port to Chabahar in Iran and then onwards by the Zaranj–Delaram road into Afghanistan and by rail into Central Asia.

The decision to admit Afghanistan as a full member of the South Asia Association for Regional Cooperation (SAARC) at its 14th summit in New Delhi in April 2007 was as much strategic as it was commercial. Strategically, this formally draws Afghanistan into the South Asian regional matrix, where India looms large. On the commercial front, with the passage in 2006 of the South Asia Free Trade Agreement (SAFTA), which eases tariff barriers, sub-continental trade is expected to benefit to the tune of $2,000m., of which $606m. would accrue to Afghanistan.[21]

In addition to the above, a commercial interest with a unique dimension to it is the multi-million dollar Indian entertainment industry. Apart from having huge commercial interests in the Afghanistan market, it also serves as one of the most powerful vehicles for projection of Indian 'soft power'. While Indian films have long been popular with Afghans, with the coming of satellite television a booming Indian television industry has helped India make rapid inroads into the hearts and minds of the people of Afghanistan. A walk down the streets of a bazaar, be it in any major city of Afghanistan or in the dusty countryside, is testimony to India's status as something of a cultural tsar in Afghanistan.[22] Consider, for instance, the immense popularity of the Hindi soap opera *Kyunki Saas Bhi Kabhi Bahu Thi*, broadcast on Tolo TV and enjoying 90% audience penetration.[23] This exponential growth in Indian soft power has been completely independent of any government backing, but it has helped to foster and strengthen con-stituencies of immense goodwill amongst the Afghan people. Instructive in this respect was a 'random national survey', conducted in January 2009, in which 74% of the respondents had a favourable view of India; this was a contrast with Afghan perceptions of Pakistan, where an astounding 91% (up 11 percentage points from the previous year) of respondents viewed Paki-stan's role in a negative light.[24] Although India has no military mission in Afghanistan, it is, as Joseph Nye puts it, 'the side with the better story' in the battle for hearts and minds in Afghanistan.

Challenges facing India

The key challenges facing Indian policy in Afghanistan can broadly be classified under two fronts: security and diplomacy.

Security challenges

The vulnerability of Indian interests within Afghanistan has been demonstrated on numerous occasions by the attacks mounted on Indian personnel engaged in a cross-spectrum of recon-struction efforts in Afghanistan and grenade attacks on the Indian consulate in the border city of Jalalabad. However, the gravity of the threat was forcefully driven home by the car-bombing of the Indian embassy in Kabul in July 2008, which killed, amongst others, two high-ranking Indian officials: the Press Counsellor V.V Rao and Indian Defence Attaché Brigadier Ravi Mehta. The latter had been posted to Kabul as an adviser in Afghanistan's Ministry of Defence, given his substantive counter-insurgency experience in Jammu and Kashmir and the north-east. Credible intelligence reports pointed to the involvement of Pakistan's notorious ISI, which has been covertly supporting Taliban elements to destabilize the growing Indian profile in Afgha-nistan.[25] Some 15 months later, in October 2009, the Kabul embassy was the target of yet another bomb attack. The February 2010 attack on two Kabul guest-houses that primarily housed Indian civilian personnel engaged in reconstruction work further brought to the fore the increasing vulnerability of Indians as soft targets in Afghanistan.[26] Repeated targeting of India both at home and now increasingly in Afghanistan, often claimed and popularly believed to be at the behest of Pakistan's ISI, has given rise to a popular perception among many in Afghani-stan of India being seen as a 'soft state'.[27] There are no signs of the threat to Indian interests abating, with a recent announcement by the Taliban commander Qari Ziaur Rehman stating that 'the operation commanders of the Islamic Emirate are going to meet shortly to finalise a new war strategy under which foreigners working on their national agendas, particularly Indians, will be targeted'.[28]

On the one hand, this magnifying terror threat has been discussed at the ministerial level with the Afghan foreign minister Rangin Spanta, following talks with his Indian counterpart Pranab Mukherjee in 2009, proclaiming that both countries face the 'same terrorism from the same source [read Pakistan]', and efforts will be made to enhance co-operation on terrorism.[29] On the other hand, to date no institutional mechanisms have actually been instituted for sharing of intelligence or information.

The challenges to India's security interests are likely to be magnified in the post-London Conference (2010) scenario. Given the decision of the key players in the Western world to actively support the idea of extending an olive branch to members of the Taliban, many of whom are backed by the ISI, by offering them an intoxicating combination of financial and political power, India faces a complex situation. Repercussions on Indian security interests will play out at three tiers: national security, human security and energy security. First, New Delhi's leverage over Kabul is likely to decrease significantly, which will adversely impact India's ability to shape the regional security dynamics, be it over Kashmir or its efforts to contain the proliferation of radical Islamist ideology. The latter of the two assumes heightened significance as the phenomenon of Islamist militancy is no longer confined to the Kashmir valley; this assumes significance given New Delhi's fears of a radicalization amongst sections of its own community of 140m. Muslims. Second, given the deeply entrenched linkages between terrorism and drugs-trafficking and the latter's growing presence in the Indian market, a political ascendance of the Taliban will multiply the challenge of sapping the channels of financial support to terrorist groups. It will also further challenge the ability of the Indian state to safeguard its human security net that is increasingly coming under strain from a large inflow of Afghan opium. Third, with soaring energy needs, India is expected to import around 94% of its fuel needs by 2030,[30] and its plans to bolster energy security by tapping into hydrocarbon and hydro electric resources of Central Asia, with Afghanistan as a key energy transit hub, appear to be in jeopardy.

Diplomatic challenges

On the diplomatic plane, the challenges before India are threefold: first, India has traditionally been closely identified with the Northern Alliance, which is primarily composed of three ethnic minorities in Afghanistan—the Tajiks who constitute approximately 27% cent of the population, and the Hazaras and Uzbeks who constitute approximately 9% each of the population. It is imperative that India effectively capitalize on some of its key developmental projects located in the Pushtun belt, cultivate links with key Pushtun figures outside the rank and file of the Karzai Government and encourage working towards evolving a multi-ethnic political solution to the Afghan quagmire. Addressing this challenge is crucial if India wishes to counter propaganda of supporting the northern tribes against the Pushtuns, who largely dominate the ranks of the Taliban.

Second, in light of the Taliban insurgency having gained a lethal momentum and with an impatient West willing to negotiate and buy its way out, India will have to find creative ways to retain its relevance as a consequential player in Afghanistan. The changes in the composition of the erstwhile Northern Alliance, the rise in Islamabad's influence as demonstrated at the London Conference and subsequently at the Istanbul security conference on Afghanistan, to which India was not even invited, have further magnified the challenge at hand.

Third, India also needs to effectively leverage its soft power prowess in Afghanistan and reinforce it with a more active role in the country's military sector. This could be done by way of scaling up the very modest levels of training being currently offered to the Afghan National Police and the Afghan National Army. Such an exercise, apart from being far more cost effective than the training programmes being offered by the West, hold out two other distinct advantages: namely, that there is a far greater degree of trust between India and Afghanistan as compared with the West or with any of Afghanistan's neighbouring countries, and also because India is culturally much closer to the Afghans, thus making communication and establishment of bonds with the soldiers far easier. In addition, India has the capacity and capability to offer expertise in counter-insurgency training to Afghan forces at its elite training academies in India. However, for this to materialize, India would have to engage in some tactful diplomacy with Washington and other Western capitals in order to soothe the frayed nerves that such a move would cause in Islamabad.

Finally, pressure on New Delhi from Washington is likely to intensify for not only a resumption of its stalled composite dialogue process with Pakistan, but also for arriving at a solution on the issue of Kashmir. The dominant sentiment prevalent in Western policy circles is underscored by Chief of Staff Admiral Michael Mullen's statement that 'the longstanding animosity and mistrust between Pakistan and India complicates regional efforts [...] we must offer our help to improve confidence and understanding between them in a manner that builds long term stability across the wider region of South Asia'.[31]

Potential developments for India in Afghanistan

The political alignments and re-alignments underway in Afghanistan triggered by an intensifying Taliban insurgency and waning commitment of the West are likely to give rise to four key developments that will have reverberations for India in the near future.

First, with the West accepting Pakistan's offer of using its leverage (especially with the Haqqani group) to broker what appears to be at best a tenuous peace, Islamabad will be tempted to once again look upon Afghanistan as its 'strategic depth' against India and the Taliban as a strategic leverage. The thinking within the Pakistani establishment on this particular issue and the weight attached to it is lucidly demonstrated by the Pakistan army chief's recent statement that 'we want to have strategic depth in Afghanistan'.[32] Former ISI chief Hamid Gul—who both played an instrumental role in propping up the *mujahideen* in Afghanistan, and later supported insurgency in Punjab and Kashmir and was also closely associated with Lashkar-e-Taiba, which was believed to be behind the 2008 terrorist attacks on Mumbai—was even more blunt when publicly proclaiming that, 'America is history, Karzai is history, and the Taliban are the future'.[33] Thus, India's old security concerns emanating from Afghanistan are likely to be rekindled. However, another key point of concern for New Delhi will be that, this time, with a politico-military re-emergence of the Taliban, there also exists a strong possibility of the Taliban using Pakistan's lawless frontier regions as its own strategic depth. This would bring the threat posed by extremist groups much closer to India's geographical as well as psychological frontiers.

Second, with India's political influence being clipped in Afghanistan its efforts to project power, in what New Delhi considers to be its *extended neighbourhood* of energy-rich Central Asia, will suffer a setback, as will its efforts to bolster energy security. Furthermore, as radical Islamist groups such as the Islamic Movement of Uzbekistan (IMU) increasingly forge transnational linkages, particularly with the ISI and Taliban, security challenges on India's western frontiers are likely to multiply. Developments in Afghanistan will inescapably have trans-border reverberations in the Central Asian republics (CARs), three of which, apart from being geographically proximate, have cross-ethnic linkages with Afghanistan. A spillover of Afghan instability in the already fragile CARs could disrupt India's growing interest in the region, especially its growing military co-operation with states like Tajikistan, which is believed to be hosting India's first ever foreign military outpost at Ayni.

Third, as the West utilizes the services of Islamabad to reach out to the Taliban, it will also be attracted to Islamabad's proposition that Kashmir, too, is a major cause for fuelling pan-Islamic radicalism. Thus, major Western capitals will be tempted to put renewed pressure on New Delhi to resolve the issue of Kashmir. India must demonstrate greater dexterity with regard to its policies of engagement with Pakistan if it is to pre-empt efforts being made to hyphenate it with 'Af-Pak'. Moreover, another potential area of concern for India is likely to be the variance of its stance with the USA towards groups such as Lashkar-e-Taiba, which are of immediate concern for New Delhi. This difference in threat perception is underscored by US Secretary of Defence Robert Gates's recent proclamation before the Senate foreign relations committee 'that Al Qaeda is supportive of Lashkar-e-Toiba [...] Al Qaeda is providing them with targeting information and helping them in their plotting in India'.[34] Such a view goes distinctly against the widely held Indian view that the real sponsors of Lashkar-e-Taiba are at the ISI headquarters in Pakistan.

Fourth, the role played by Beijing in Afghanistan in coming years will be closely watched in New Delhi. Beijing's past record of flirting with radical Islamist movements,[35] as also its extremely close alliance with Pakistan through which it hopes to pacify Xinjiang while on the external plane use this alliance to temper a rising Indian profile in both Afghanistan and Central Asia, has all helped deepen suspicions in New Delhi about Beijing's intentions in the region. Indian discomfort can been seen over Beijing's linkages between Pakistan and Afghanistan, Chinese linkages typified in a *People's Daily* editorial that 'the US must ensure a stable domestic and international environment for Pakistan and ease the tension between Pakistan and India[... The] Afghan problem, the Pakistani problem and the Indian-Pakistani problem are all related'.[36] Even more discomforting for India was the fact that this sentiment found echo in the joint statement issued after President Obama's visit to Beijing in November 2009, which said that 'they [the USA and China] support the efforts of Afghanistan and Pakistan to fight terrorism, maintain domestic stability and achieve sustainable economic and social development, and support the improvement and growth of relations between India and Pakistan. The two sides are ready to strengthen communication, dialogue and cooperation on issues related to South Asia and work together to promote peace, stability and development in that region'.[37] Signals like these from Beijing have hardened suspicions of mandarins in New Delhi, who believe that Beijing's real intention is to re-hyphenate India with Pakistan and strengthen the case for India as being part of the problem and not the solution.

Conclusions

As the international community desperately attempts to find a way to extricate itself from the Afghan quagmire, India may increasingly find itself hemmed in by the powers that be. A difficult road lay ahead for India in the summer of 2010 over its Afghanistan policy, in which if India aspired to be a consequential player in Afghan affairs and pre-empt political marginalization, 'New Delhi must recalibrate its strategic calculus in Afghanistan' by playing a proactive role in the political re-alignments taking place in Kabul, as opposed to viewing them with disdain.[38] New Delhi needs to broaden its political engagement outside the ambit of the Kabul Government; this will be imperative if it desires to prevent Pakistan's ISI from once again having a free run. All its attempts to usher in development will be rendered ineffectual if not complemented by a stable political and security paradigm that is not hostile to India. The contours of Indo-Afghan engagement will, to a large extent, be determined by India's ability to effectively respond to the rapidly evolving political dynamics within Afghanistan as well as among the external powers. India's ability to successfully navigate its way through the Afghan matrix in its *immediate neighbourhood* and *extended neighbourhood* will be particularly keenly observed, as New Delhi increasingly jockeys for a position at the global high table.

Notes

1 For a more detailed discourse on ancient cultural linkages between the Indian subcontinent and what constitutes modern day Afghanistan, see L. Chandra, 'Afghanistan and India: Historico-Cultural Perspective', in K. Warikoo (ed.), *The Afghanistan Crisis: Issues and Perspectives*, New Delhi: Bhavana Books, 2002.
2 H. Pant, 'India in Afghanistan: A Test Case for a Rising Power?', *Contemporary South Asia*, Vol. 18, No. 2, 2010.
3 S. Aaron, 'Straddling Faultlines: India's Foreign Policy Towards the Greater Middle East', *CSH Occasional Paper* (French Research Institute in India), No. 7, 2003, p.75.
4 S. Muni, 'India's Afghan Policy Emerging from the Cold', in K. Warikoo (ed.), *The Afghanistan Crisis: Issues and Perspectives*, New Delhi: Bhavana Books, 2002, p.335.
5 R. Horn, 'Afghanistan and the Soviet-Indian Influence Relationship', *Asian Survey*, Vol. 23, No. 3, 1983, pp.145–46.
6 Ibid., pp.248–49.
7 V. Schofield, *Afghan Frontier: Feuding and Fighting in Central Asia*, London: Taurisparke, 2003, p.322.
8 K. Santhanam (ed.), *Jihadis in Jammu and Kashmir: A Portrait Gallery*, New Delhi: Sage, 2003, pp.315–16.
9 Muni, 'India's Afghan Policy Emerging from the Cold', op. cit., p.341.
10 S. Ramachandran, 'In Afghanistan, Pakistan's loss is India's gain', *Asia Times*, 1 February 2002.
11 For a more detailed overview of the Indian assistance programme in Afghanistan, see Ministry of External Affairs, *India and Afghanistan: A Development Partnership*, New Delhi: External Publicity Division, Ministry of External Affairs (India), 2009.
12 'India's Difficult Mission in Afghanistan', *Centre for Strategic and International Studies*, 9 July 2008, forums.csis.org.
13 For a detailed account of the historical and political linkages between Kashmir and Afghanistan, read K. Warikoo, 'Shadow of Afghanistan over Kashmir', in K. Warikoo (ed.), *The Afghanistan Crisis: Issues and Perspectives*, 2002.
14 Ibid., pp.361–62.
15 Ibid., p.367.
16 UNDOC, *World Drug Report 2009*, New York: United Nations, 2009, pp.54, 90.
17 I. Kiesow and N. Norling, 'The Rise of India: Problems and Opportunities', *Silk Road Papers*, January 2007, p.86.
18 Gustavson Associates, *Islamic Republic of Afghanistan: Preparing the Natural Gas Development Project*, Colorado: Gustavan Associates, December 2007, p.5.
19 J. Risen, 'US Identifies Vast Mineral Riches in Afghanistan', *New York Times*, 13 June 2010.
20 Ministry of External Affairs, *India and Afghanistan: A Development Partnership*, op cit., p.17.
21 G. Srinivasan, 'Afghan Entry into SAARC Will Lead to $2 Billion Gain for Sub-continent', *The Hindu Business Line*, 29 March 2007.
22 Based on the author's personal experiences and interactions with Afghans in Kabul, as well as his trips to the south and east of the country between January and July 2010.
23 S. Tharoor, 'The Asian Century: India's Bollywood Power', *Project Syndicate*, 3 January 2008, www.project-syndicate.org.
24 BBC and ARD National Survey of Afghanistan, discussed in G. Langer, 'Frustration with the War, Problems in Daily Life Send Afghans' Support for US Efforts Tumbling', *ABC News*, 9 February 2009, abcnews.go.com.
25 M. Mazzetti and E. Schmitt, 'Pakistanis Aided Attack in Kabul, US Officials Say', *New York Times*, 1 August 2008.
26 '9 Indians Among 17 Dead as Taliban Bombers Attack Kabul', *The Times of India*, 26 February 2010.

27 Based on the author's extensive conversations with local Afghans in Kabul, Jalalabad and Kandahar from all walks of life. A large number of locals, especially in Jalalabad and Kandahar, spoke openly of what they perceived to be India's lack of investment in people like the ISI, which they viewed as being responsible for India's inability to pre-empt and effectively respond to attacks on its interests by Pakistan. Interestingly, religious minorities in Afghanistan, largely comprising Afghan Hindus and Sikhs who have family links in India, also see India as a soft state, albeit for a completely different set of reasons. They believe that, in spite of having spent vast sums of money in the reconstruction effort, New Delhi has been able to do precious little to safeguard their interests and secure their rights in Afghanistan.

28 'Taliban Issues Fresh Threats to Indians Working in Afghanistan', *Rediff News*, 1 July 2010, news.rediff.com.

29 'India, Afghanistan to Step Up Info Sharing to Fight Terror', *Outlook*, 21 January 2009.

30 'Import Dependence on Crude to Touch 94% by 2030: IEA', *Financial Express*, 22 January 2004.

31 I. Bagchi, 'Is India's Neighbourhood Set to Get Even More Dangerous?', *Times of India*, 6 February 2010.

32 'Pakistan Army Chief Denies Wanting to control Afghanistan', *East Asia Times*, 1 February 2010, www.eastasiantimes.com.

33 L. Doucet, 'Pakistan's Push for a New Role in Afghanistan', *BBC News*, 19 February 2010, news.bbc.co.uk.

34 'Al Qaeda Helping LeT Plot Terror Attacks In India: US', *Thai Indian News*, 4 December 2009, www.thaindian.com.

35 S. Singh, 'China's Afghan Policy: Limitations Versus Leverages', in K. Warikoo (ed.), *The Afghanistan Crisis: Issues and Perspectives*, New Delhi: Bhavana Books, 2002; M. Malik, 'Dragon on Terrorism: Assessing China's Tactical Gains and Strategic Losses Post September 11', Honolulu: Asia Pacific Center for Security Studies, October 2002.

36 'Will Adjustments in U.S. Anti-terror Strategy [Be] Successful?', *People's Daily/Xinhua,* 23 February 2009. Also M. Bhadrakumar, 'China Breaks its Silence on Afghanistan', *Asia Times*, 25 February 2009.

37 'US China Joint Statement', Beijing, 17 November 2009, www.whitehouse.gov.

38 T. Schaffer and A. Verma, 'A Difficult Road Ahead: India's Policy on Afghanistan', *South Asia Monitor Newsletter* (CSIS), 1 August 2010.

11

India and regional integration

David Scott

Introduction

India's involvement in regional integration is the focus of this chapter. This chapter starts with India's *immediate neighbourhood* (i.e. South Asia) and India's sense of identity within that region and with regard to the regional structure there, i.e. the South Asian Association of Regional Cooperation (SAARC). It then moves on to India's *extended neighbourhood* beyond South Asia (i.e. the Indian Ocean, the Bay of Bengal and East Asia), and India's sense of identity within those regions and with regard to their regional structures, i.e. the Indian Ocean Rim Association for Regional Co-operation (IOR-ARC) and Indian Ocean Naval Symposium (IONS), the Bay of Bengal Initiative for Multi-Sectoral Technical and Economic Cooperation (BIMSTEC— formerly Bangladesh, India, Myanmar, Sri Lanka, Thailand Economic Cooperation), East Asian Summit (EAS) and the Asia-Pacific Economic Cooperation (APEC). All of these involve India's sense and redefining of 'regions', and throw into question varying levels of integration. The words of Peter Jay come to mind, that 'good regionalism is good geopolitics; and bad regionalism is bad geopolitics'.[1] Such questions and shifts within India's sense of 'region' and regionalism involve questions of traditional geopolitics as well as *critical geopolitics*, in which 'region' and regionalism for India have been subject to construction and reshaping, the domain of International Relations (IR) *constructivism*.

South Asia (and SAARC)

India's clearest regional setting is within the subcontinent of South Asia, and its vehicle for regional integration is SAARC. If South Asia is defined geographically as the region bounded by the Hindu Kush-Himalayas on land and the Indian Ocean open waters, then India is immediately at the very heart of this area. It is no coincidence that the subcontinent is called the 'Indian' subcontinent. The question for India is how far that physical suggestion and geopolitical potential gets translated into actual geopolitical power actuality. The term 'hegemon' tends to have unattractive connotations, yet India's weight remains evident. If we take South Asia in the above geographical (Hindu Kush–Himalayas–Indian Ocean boundaries) or political (membership of SAARC) definition, then India looms large. In terms of geography, India covers around

75% of the landmass and the population of South Asia. In terms of location it has centrality: whilst it has borders with Pakistan, Nepal, Bhutan, Bangladesh and Sri Lanka, they do not have borders with each other. Consequently, relations within South Asia tend to be India-centred, be it positive or negative, with other bilateral relations between South Asian states being much less evident, in comparison. This gives India clear regional advantages, yet it also gives it regional disadvantages as smaller states either try to obstruct India, balance against India, seek to counterbalance with other South Asian states against India, or seek countervailing external (e.g. the People's Republic of China) help from outside the region. India's own actions towards South Asia have gone through three phases, and have led to the creation and progression of SAARC.

Initially, India's involvement with South Asia was limited, indeed neglected. India's relations with Pakistan were important, but highly negative. Instead, Jawaharlal Nehru, India's first Prime Minister (1947–64), who was also Minister of External Affairs, pursued a path of engagement with the world, a foreign policy that stressed morality and ethics, and which concerned itself with global issues like non-alignment and global nuclear disarmament. Nehru's involvement in South Asia was limited to establishing Indian treaty consolidation in the Himalayas, with Bhutan (1949), Sikkim (1950) and Nepal (1950); treaties which left a degree of Indian pre-eminence existing there in varying degrees, even whilst India's 'Forward Rights' inherited in Tibet were being lost to a resurgent China. Having consolidated a local Himalayan pre-eminence, Nehru tended to pursue a fairly limited involvement there, a degree of neglect. Sri Lanka was also neglected by India, as were the Maldives. Pakistan remained the bitter foe whose religious principles of national formation in 1947 had cut across Indian secular-geographical principles of national formation, the foe who had an ongoing territorial dispute with India over the province of Kashmir, and the foe with whom India went to the first of its several wars in 1949. The only sign of co-operation there was at a functional level was the Indus Waters Treaty of 1961. India's relations in South Asia remained bilateral, with no regional mechanisms in place for integration. As for regional integration, there had been some desultory conversations of it at the Asian Relations Conference in New Delhi in April 1947, the Baguio Conference in the Philippines in May 1950, and the Colombo Powers Conference in April 1954, but nothing came of them. Instead, the region settled down to ongoing India–Pakistan friction.

Interestingly enough, the most evident sign of India exerting itself in South Asia was with its forcible occupation of the Portuguese enclave of Goa, which was 'liberated' in 1961. The arguments used by Nehru were ones that seemed to give a pre-eminence to India, with Nehru invoking the earlier Monroe Doctrine to evoke his own doctrine, dubbed the Nehru Doctrine:

> The famous declaration by President Monroe of the United States [stated that] any inter-ference by a European country would be an interference with the American political system. I submit that [...] the Portuguese retention of Goa is a continuing interference with the political system established in India today. I shall go a step further and say that any interference by any other power would also be an interference with the political system of India today[...] It may be that we are weak and we cannot prevent that interference. But the fact is that any attempt by a foreign power to interfere in any way with India is a thing which India cannot tolerate, and which, subject to her strength, she will oppose. That is the broad doctrine I lay down.[2]

Unfortunately for Nehru's assumptions, India's strength may have been enough to eject Portugal from Goa, under the Nehru Doctrine, but it was not enough to stop China's growing presence in South Asian affairs, which was evident along the Himalayan sub-region, and manifest in China's unexpected, traumatic victory over India in the 1962 war. Nehru's successors were to draw hard lessons from this.

Nehru died in 1964, feeling bitterly betrayed by what he saw as Chinese treachery. After the short transition premiership of Lal Bahadur Shastri (1964–66), Nehru's daughter Indira Gandhi took over as leader of the Congress Party. During her time in politics she served as Prime Minister (1966–77, 1980–84), before her assassination at the hands of disgruntled Sikhs, whereupon her son Rajiv Gandhi took over as Congress leader and Prime Minister (1984–89), before his assassination at the hands of disgruntled Tamils. Indira Gandhi changed the focus of Indian foreign policy and its security focus. Instead of Nehru's neglect of South Asia and focus on globalist *soft power* morality, Indira Gandhi concentrated much more on South Asia and focused on an IR *realism-hard power-realpolitik*. Politically, Nehru's emphasis on the Non-Aligned Movement (NAM) gave way to Indira Gandhi's much closer relationship with the USSR, signalled by their 1971 Treaty of Peace, Friendship and Co-operation. Militarily, Nehru's relative neglect of India's armed forces gave way to a building up of India's military might. As such, 'bilateralism became the guiding principle of Indian foreign policy', rather than the shaping of any regional/multilateral structures for, and in, South Asia.[3]

Security-wise, this South Asia focus of Indira Gandhi was underpinned by what came to be dubbed the Indira Doctrine, whereby outside intervention in South Asian affairs was to be averted, 'the principle became a matter of faith for Indian foreign policymakers'.[4] It had two important planks:

> India will not tolerate external intervention in a conflict situation in any South Asian country, if that intervention has any implicit or explicit anti-Indian implication. No South Asian government must therefore ask for military assistance with an anti-Indian bias from any country. If a South Asian country genuinely needs external help to deal with a serious internal conflict situation, or with an intolerable threat to a government legitimately established, it should ask help from a number of neighboring countries including India. The exclusion of India from such a contingency will be considered to be an anti-Indian move on the part of the government concerned.[5]

Instead, local bilateral solutions were to be sought, in effect with India's involvement and indeed leadership, and based on Indian 'perceptions' of whether or not an anti-India bias was in play.

Application of the Indira Doctrine was seen in 1971 when India's intervention in the attempted breakaway of East Pakistan by Bengali nationalists enabled the setting up of an independent Bangladesh, in the wake of a relatively short but decisive military decapitation of Pakistani military forces by India. The 1971 India–Pakistan war transformed South Asian geopolitics and left India more than ever in a position of *hard power* military supremacy over its rival Pakistan, and in South Asia generally. Other examples of this relatively hard-nosed application of Indian power came with military intervention in the Sri Lankan civil war (1971).

Paradoxes abounded thereon, though, with the Indira Doctrine. The 'contradictions' between India's global policy and its regional approach were real.[6] Thus, 'at the international level, India rejected the notions of balance of power and exclusive spheres of influence; within the region it clung to them'.[7] Consequently, 'India was strongly opposed to intervention by major powers in the internal affairs of weaker ones, but within the subcontinent it had to perform the function of a provider of security to smaller nations and their regimes'.[8] Whilst 'India was all for multilateralism at the global level, in the region it insisted on bilateralism', in which

India would have the advantage on account of its inherent size and weight.[9] All in all, Raja Mohan pointed out that 'India seemed to move effortlessly between the roles of protestor at the global level and that of manager of the security order within the region', so that whilst 'its ambassadors were relentless critics of the international system in the global fora, within the region its envoys were transformed into proconsuls and viceroys in neighbouring capitals'.[10] Amidst such contradictions there was no room for any multilateral regionalism, no room for any South Asian regional integration structure, or organizational set-up, other than India's bilateral application of its own power advantages.

Indira Gandhi's assassination in 1984 brought her son Rajiv into power and under him the Indira Doctrine (sometimes called the Rajiv Doctrine) remained intact: bilateral arrangements for the region, with India playing the lead role. Examples of this included his decision to dispatch an Indian Peace-Keeping Force (IPKF) to Sri Lanka (1987–90); to send military forces to the Maldives in 1988 (Operation Cactus) to restore the toppled government to power; and to impose a trade embargo on a landlocked Nepal in 1989. However, a decade later and the question can be asked, why did India not go to Sri Lanka's rescue in May 2000 when the island's leadership begged it to intervene to save nearly 40,000 soldiers who were close to being captured by the separatist Liberation Tigers of Tamil Eelam (LTTE)? Devotta wondered if 'India's disinclination to get involved, even as Pakistan, China and Israel provided arms to Sri Lanka, raises the question of whether the country is still committed to the Indira Doctrine (which operates as India's equivalent of the United States' Monroe Doctrine in South Asia)', to which his argument was that 'domestic pressures, especially those emanating from Kashmir and the country's northeast, may have left India militarily overextended, especially during the late 1990s, and thereby prevented the country from flexing its military capabilities in the region as it did in the 1980s'.[11]

A different regional framework was seen with the formation of SAARC in 1985. The impetus for this came from Bangladesh, but India accepted its formation. However, its role was low key.

A change of direction in Indian policy towards South Asia was signalled by Inder Gujral (foreign minister and then Prime Minister), who announced in 1996 what came to be known as the Gujral Doctrine—namely, that the 'Government's Neighbourhood Policy now stands on five basic principles: firstly, with neighbours like Nepal, Bangladesh, Bhutan, Maldives and Sri Lanka, India does not ask for reciprocity but gives all it can in good faith and trust'.[12] What is, of course, interesting is that Pakistan was not included in this listing, their relationship remaining 'tormented' indeed, to use Gujral's own admittance.[13]

In the light of this 'friendly, co-operative mould', the Indian Government responded positively towards a strengthening of SAARC's role. Foreign secretary meetings began in 2002, with heads of government summits in 2004. The question arises, though, of how successful, and how important an avenue for Indian foreign policy SAARC has been? In many ways SAARC has been a disappointment. As one Indian commentator put it in 2010, 'whatever the officials may say, the fact remains that the record of the organisation has nothing concrete to boast of'.[14]

In terms of security SAARC has not involved itself in India's security issues, primarily the disputes with Pakistan over Kashmir. India remains keen to keep it as a bilateral issue between itself and Pakistan, to be resolved between them and not by any outside organization like SAARC (or indeed the UN): 'with or without SAARC India enjoys a central position in the economic and foreign policies of the neighbouring countries and conducts its relations bilaterally. It has the geographical advantage to shape bilateral policy without involvement of any third country', or organization like SAARC.[15] The other security issue, transnational terrorism, has received some SAARC treatment in the shape of the SAARC Regional Convention on Suppression of Terrorism (1997), but the failure of states like Pakistan to legislate internally on it has nullified much of its 'regional' value for India.

Meanwhile, SAARC's primary goal of fostering economic co-operation has not really worked. Intra-SAARC trade remains meagre. The seventh SAARC Summit meeting at Dhaka in 1993 saw the signing of the SAARC Preferential Trading Arrangement (SAPTA), with a South Asia Free Trade Agreement (SAFTA) signed at the 12th SAARC Summit in 2004. This SAFTA was to be implemented in 2006, but only in a gradual way, and with sensitive items exempted. South Asia's intra-regional trade as a share of total trade has continued to limp along at around 5% in the 1980s and 1990s and into the present, with SAARC having made little statistical difference. Such continuing low figures stand in contrast to the EU intra-trade figure of around 60% and Association of Southeast Asian Nations (ASEAN) figures of around 25%. In terms of India, SAARC remains marginal. Ratna and Sidhu summed it up in 2008 as, in straightforward terms, 'India's trade with its immediate neighbourhood of SAARC India's trade with its neighbouring countries has not been very impressive, both in terms of volume and as a percentage of its global trade'.[16] Having taken an already low 3.52% share of India's trade in 2003/04, it declined still further to a 2.83% share by 2007/08. For 2009/10 SAARC accounted for 4.69% of India's exports, and an even more lowly 0.57% of its imports.

Not surprisingly, Indian commentators can be dismissive of SAARC: 'regional interactions both in terms of movement of human beings or of goods, is minimum. Whatever success there may be in terms of economic exchange is perhaps not because of SAARC but despite it'.[17] India's leadership seems well aware of these SAARC limitations. Natwar Singh, foreign minister in 2004, felt that:

> Many pessimists would dismiss SAARC as a talking shop whose priorities are all mixed up. Detractors will point to the vast differences in geographical size, economic indicators, and diversity of economic and political systems as hurdles to integration. They would not be entirely wrong. SAARC will be 20 years old next year. It should be in the full maturity of its youth, ready to take on new challenges and directions. Yet, in fact it has yet to consolidate as an organization. At the recent SAARC meeting in Islamabad, we made a strong statement that it was time that SAARC departs from its endless round of meetings, seminars, and conferences, and moves to collaborative projects that bring tangible results to our peoples.[18]

A change of government brought little alteration to this analysis of SAARC's failure, and others' success. Manmohan Singh's sense of SAARC has been damning enough: 'it is however a fact that South Asia has not moved as fast as we all would have wished. We have only to see the rapid integration within ASEAN and its emergence as an important economic bloc in Asia to understand the opportunities that beckon'.[19] The only trouble is that such sentiments suggest a readiness for India to look elsewhere for success, to other regions as it were.

A further problem with SAARC has been political, that is to say, China's involvement with it. Here China's push for 'observer' status was initially resisted by India, but eventually was conceded in 2005, in the wake of pressures from other SAARC members for such an arrangement, and as a trade-off for acceptance of a (pro-India) Afghanistan as a full member. Nevertheless, some commentators saw China's presence in SAARC as a (negative) extra-regional influence, thereby in effect tearing up India's own Monroe Doctrine.[20] This push by China into South Asia has further spurred India to seek an active role in regions adjoining South Asia, and not to be left out of moves towards regional integration in such areas outside South Asia.

From 'South Asia' to 'southern Asia'

India's initial sense of 'region', a sense from which policy priorities can be shaped, may initially have been focused around 'South Asia' (subcontinent settings of SAARC), but in recent years India's sense of *region* has developed, and from that India's sense of regional organizations and regional integration in which to involve itself. In doing so, they have responded to concerns of Indian commentators in 1997 that 'India should break out of the claustrophobic confines of South Asia'.[21] In such a vein, the Bharatiya Janata Party (BJP) Minister of External Affairs, Jaswant Singh, announced in Singapore in 2000 that 'South Asia was always a dubious framework for situating the Indian security paradigm', for 'India's parameters of security concerns clearly extend beyond confines of the convenient albeit questionable geographical definition of South Asia'.[22]

One sign of this is a nudge from the region being considered as 'South Asia' or the region being seen as a wider 'southern Asia': 'Indian strategic experts have been reviving the geographical concept of "Southern Asia" to define India's role and context, thereby widening the geographical limits of its strategic neighbourhood to include states outside the SAARC area'.[23] Not only strategic commentators, but also India's politicians have been quite deliberately expanding the sense of what India's region actually involves:

> Our engagement with our neighbours is, as I am sure you realize, multi-pronged. It is at the same time conducted bilaterally, regionally under the ambit of SAARC, and through what one might call sub-regional or even trans-regional mechanisms such as BIMSTEC, which includes some SAARC members and some ASEAN ones, or IOR-ARC, which pulls together 18 countries whose shores are washed by the Indian Ocean, including some South Asian nations and several on other continents.[24]

Accordingly, India's sense of 'region' within which it operates and shapes its foreign policy has shifted to include overlapping and wider areas, namely the Indian Ocean, the Bay of Bengal, and Pacific Asia/East Asia, to which we can turn.

The Indian Ocean (and the IOR-ARC, IONS)

The 1990s saw India embrace moves towards a wider regionalism, not focused on India's bilateral focus (Indira Doctrine) on the South Asia region, but rather on India's multilateral role within the Indian Ocean region (IOR). Consequently, as part of its Gujral Doctrine embrace of multilateralism and regionalism, India joined the IOR-ARC in 1995. Admittedly this economics-based view of regional structuring languished in subsequent years. Partly this was because of the relative economic insignificance of the Indian Ocean basin states, and partly because of drift as other major Indian Ocean littoral players like South Africa and Australia looked elsewhere for their own respective regional engagement—South Africa to Africa, and Australia to the Asia-Pacific. The organization still exists, but its importance for India has never really been established.

A more recent development, and one that perhaps now engages India more, is the IONS. This was set up by India in 2008, and is deliberately modelled on the West Pacific Naval Symposium (WPNS). Interestingly enough, whilst India is a member of the WPNS, China is not a member of the IONS, with India blocking such an appearance by China. Instead, the IONS serves as a potential avenue for Indian leadership in the IOR, albeit unofficially. India's drive in fostering the creation of this organization is part of its 'Look South' policy, its maritime rediscovery of the Indian Ocean, the Indian Ocean as India's backyard, the Indian Ocean as somehow 'India's Ocean'—all reflecting Panikkar's sense of 'making the Indian Ocean truly Indian'.[25] India's naval chief, Sureesh Mehta, explained that 'many navies of the Indian Ocean Region look to India to promote regional maritime security', in effect to show some regional leadership.[26] Chinese sources were certainly quick to report the comments by Rear Admiral Pradeep Chauhan, Assistant Chief of Naval Staff, that the IONS would 'obviate the dependency on extra regional players in the region', and thereby enable India to take a lead and show its clear regional pre-eminence.[27] Whilst official statements about the IONS were fairly bland, a 'non-hegemonistic, cooperative consultative gathering', Indian media sources were clear enough that 'with India's growing clout [...] the navy has floated a maritime military bloc' for the Indian Ocean, led in effect by India.[28]

Bay of Bengal (and BIMSTEC, etc.)

India's regional setting is as much to do with the Bay of Bengal as with South Asia. After all, the entire western littoral of the Bay of Bengal consists of India's long eastern seaboard, and the eastern littoral of the Bay of Bengal is dominated by India's sprawling Nicobar and Andaman island chains, which sit on choke point exit (the Strait of Malacca) from the Bay of Bengal into South-East Asia. This also gives India much of the Exclusive Economic Zone for Bay of Bengal waters, much more than any other Bay of Bengal littoral state.

One trans-regional forum for India's involvement has been BIMSTEC, set up in 1997 by Bangladesh, India, Myanmar, Sri Lanka and Thailand, with Nepal and Bhutan joining in 2004. For India, BIMSTEC has the advantages of SAARC without the disadvantages (Pakistan), and represents a bridge between South Asia and South-East Asia (Myanmar, Thailand). India's sense was clear at the first BIMSTEC Summit in 2004, that 'we see BIMST-EC as a collective forum for giving full expression to the widely felt need to rediscover the coherence of our region based on the commonality of linkages around the Bay of Bengal', in which 'we consider our participation in BIMST-EC as a key element in our "Look East Policy" and long standing approach of good neighbourliness towards all our neighbours – by land and sea'.[29] Another trans-regional forum in which India is involved is the Mekong-Ganga Cooperation (MGC), which was set up in 2000 to bring together India and five South-East Asian nations, namely Thailand, Viet Nam, Laos, Cambodia and Myanmar, but not China, despite its Mekong headwaters and tributaries.

A further framework shaped by New Delhi has been India's hosting of the MILAN exercises since 1995, organized from India's Far Eastern Naval Command (FENC) at Port Blair in the Andaman islands. These exercises in the Bay of Bengal initially involved five nations—India, Sri Lanka, Thailand, Singapore and Indonesia. The number of navies participating in the MILAN exercises has gradually increased over the years, from five in 1995, seven in 1997, seven in 1999, eight in 2003, nine in 2005, to 13 in 2008. In the 2010 MILAN exercises Sri Lanka, Bangladesh, Myanmar, Thailand, Malaysia, Singapore, Indonesia, Brunei, the Philippines, Viet Nam, Australia and New Zealand again joined India. Neither Pakistan nor China was invited to participate.

East Asia (and the EAS, etc.)

India's 'Look East' policy, in mark-1 (South-East Asia) and mark-2 (Australasia, Oceania, East Asia), has taken India out of its South Asia setting into that of East Asia/Pacific Asia and the Pacific Ocean. This underpins comments from India's leadership that:

It is important to recognize manifest political and economic realities, when we try to tackle the crucial issues of growth and security. As home to 1 billion people, India has to be integral to any regional process pertaining to the Asia Pacific. We have a constructive and multi-faceted relationship with every major country of the region. This is also true of India's relations with ASEAN's East Asian neighbours [...] India's belonging to the Asia Pacific community is a geographical fact and a political reality. It does not require formal membership of any regional organization for its recognition or sustenance.[30]

With this in mind, India has forged membership links in various regional organizations in the western Pacific/East Asia/Asia-Pacific settings.

In part, this has involved India in close links with the ASEAN, with which there is far greater trade, and with which India is a Dialogue Summit partner. This also involves India in membership of the ASEAN Regional Forum (ARF), which links Pacific Rim countries and India with ASEAN. Such linkages have pulled India into the emerging Asia-Pacific, or rather Pacific Asia/East Asia settings. India has been an observer member of the WPNS since 1998, and is currently seeking full membership. It has also had observer status in 2006, 2008 and 2010 with the RIMPAC exercises held by the USA and other Pacific Rim nations (though not China), and will in all likelihood join as a full participant. Questions of regional definitions continue to crop up, as *The Hindu* put it:

> One technical hurdle is the APEC stipulation that 'an applicant economy should be located in the Asia-Pacific region'. It is for India to emphasise the hyphenated nature of this region and draw attention to an important plus. As a founder-participant in the evolving EAS process, India is already privy to the inter-state affairs of the Pacific-bordering East Asia. APEC membership will be a logical follow-up, with potential benefits to both sides.[31]

India is seeking full membership of APEC, where the moratorium of expanding members ended in 2010.[32]

Here, one important development within the Asia-Pacific has been the move towards East Asian regionality, through the mechanism of the EAS, which first met in 2005. This is seen as the driving force for some sort of East Asian Community to evolve. India was keen to be involved, for which it received strong support from Japan but initial obstruction from China. Nevertheless, India was invited and has settled down as one of the leading players at subsequent EAS summits. For India, EAS participation in this 'regional architecture for greater cooperation and economic integration', was 'a reflection of the increasing significance of the eastern orientation of India's foreign policy and our quest for closer engagement with countries of South-East Asia and East Asia'.[33] For Singapore's Lee Kuan Yew, the invitation had a simple aim, 'India would be a useful balance to China's heft'.[34]

Conclusions

Old-fashioned politics seem to underpin much of India's role in regional integration. Within South Asia, SAARC remains a weak channel for regional integration. India's very strength, and sheer size, within South Asia and SAARC means that other states keep looking out of the region: 'most South Asian countries have actively perceived their main security threat to be India. Accordingly, South Asian states have actively sought military, economic and diplomatic assistance from external [extra-regional] powers to offset India's influence. In such an environment, regional accommodation policies have become increasingly difficult'.[35] Conversely,

David Scott

India's own sense of economic opportunity, as well as challenging or constraining China outside South Asia, is leading China into a wider sense of regionality. In terms of 'regionality', a subcontinental mindset is being replaced by wider perceptions of region by India.

Notes

1 P. Jay, 'Regionalism as Geopolitics', *Foreign Affairs*, Vol. 58, No. 3, 1979.
2 J. Nehru, *India's Foreign Policy: Selected Speeches, September 1946–April 1961*, Delhi: Government of India, 1961, pp.113–15.
3 S. Kochanek, 'India's Changing Role in the United Nations', *Pacific Affairs*, Vol. 53, No. 1, 1980, p.53.
4 C. Raja Mohan, *Crossing the Rubicon*, New Delhi: Penguin, 2003, p.239.
5 B.S. Gupta, 'The Indian Doctrine', India *Today*, 31 August 1983, p.20. See also D. Hagerty, 'India's Regional Security Doctrine', *Asian Survey*, Vol. 31, No. 4, 1991.
6 Raja Mohan, *Crossing the Rubicon*, op. cit., p.240.
7 Ibid., p.239.
8 Ibid.
9 Ibid.
10 Ibid., pp.239–40.
11 N. Devotta, 'Is India Over-extended? When Domestic Disorder Precludes Regional Intervention', *Contemporary South Asia*, Vol. 12, No. 3, 2003, p.365.
12 I. Gujral, 'Significance of an Independent Foreign Policy', 14 October 1996, in *Continuity and Change. India's Foreign Policy*, London: Macmillan, 2003, pp.108–9, with Gujral using the phrase 'Gujral Doctrine'.
13 Ibid., p.109.
14 P. Nanda, 'SAARC – Expect No Miracles', *India Defence Review*, 3 May 2010.
15 S. Pattanaik, 'SAARC at 25: Time to Reflect', *IDSA Comment*, 7 May 2010.
16 R. Ratna and G. Sidhu, 'Making SAFTA a Success: The Role of India', *Research Report* (Commonwealth Secretariat), 2008, p.19, www.thecommonwealth.org.
17 D. Banerjee, 'SAARC – Helping Neither to Integrate Nor Look East', 25–26 September 2006, sueztosuva.org.au.
18 K. Singh, 'Address by EAM Mr. K. Natwar Singh at the Special Session of the National Seminar on "Historical Perspective of SAARC and prospects for South Asian Economic Union" at IIC', 23 July 2004, meaindia.nic.in.
19 M. Singh, 'Statement by the Prime Minister Dr. Manmohan Singh at the Inaugural Session of the 15th SAARC Summit', 2 August 2008, meaindia.nic.in.
20 Raja Mohan, 'SAARC Reality Check: China Just Tore Up India's Monroe Doctrine', *Indian Express*, 13 November 2005; Raja Mohan, 'Beijing in SAARC', *Indian Express*, 21 April 2010.
21 B. Gupta, 'India in the Twenty-first Century', *International Affairs*, Vol. 73, No. 2, 1997, p.309.
22 J. Singh, 'Speech', June 2000, in S. Siddique and S. Kumar (eds), *The 2nd ASEAN Reader,* Singapore: Institute of Southeast Asian Studies, 2003, p.464.
23 S. Singh, 'India and Regionalism', in *Regionalism in South Asian Diplomacy*, Stockholm: SIPRI Policy Paper, No. 15, February 2007, p.31.
24 S. Tharoor, 'India's Vision of Peace, Security and Development in South Asia', 11 January 2010, meaindia.nic.in.
25 K. Panikkar, *India and the Indian Ocean. An Essay on the Influence of Sea Power on Indian History,* London: George Allen & Unwin, 1945, p.84.
26 Sureesh Mehta, cited in '29 Nations to Attend Indian Navy's Maritime Symposium', *Indo-Asian News Service*, 21 January 2008.
27 'Indian Ocean Naval Symposium to be Held in India', *Xinhua*, 12 February 2008.
28 'Indian Navy Floats Maritime Military Bloc', *Financial Express* (Delhi), 9 February 2008.
29 M. Singh, 'Prime Minister's Speech at the Inaugural BIMST-EC Summit', 31 July 2004, www.bimstec.org.
30 A.B. Vajpayee, 'India's Perspective on ASEAN and the Asia Pacific Region', 9 April 2002, www.aseansec.org.
31 'India and APEC', *The Hindu*, 13 January 2007.

32 K. Modi, 'India: APEC's Missing Piece?', *CACCI Journal*, Vol. 1, 2008.
33 M. Singh, 'PM's Statement on Departure to Philippines for the 5th India–ASEAN Summit and the 2nd East Asia Summit', 13 January 2007, pmindia.nic.in.
34 K.Y. Lee, 'Lee Kuan Yew Reflects', *Time*, 5 December 2005.
35 K. Dash, *Regionalism in South Asia*, London: Routledge, 2008, p.77.

Part 3

India's 'extended neighbourhood'

12

Looking east 1: South-East Asia and ASEAN

Anindya Batabyal

Introduction

India's engagement with the South-East Asian region in the post-Cold War period has assumed significant proportions and remains one of the top priorities of the country's foreign policy.[1] India has consequently become one of the central pillars and players in South-East Asia at the dawn of the 21st century.

Initiated in the early part of the 1990s, India's 'Look East' policy has been directed to the region through the Association of Southeast Asian Nations (ASEAN). Though it is claimed that the Look East policy encompasses the entire Asia-Pacific region, its primary focus was undoubtedly on South-East Asia during the first phase of this policy that lasted until recently. It appears that during the second phase, India, apart from consolidating its relations with South-East Asia, is looking beyond at the larger Asia-Pacific region. India has been a full dialogue partner of ASEAN since 1995 and a summit-level partner since 2002.[2] India has also been a member of the ASEAN Regional Forum (ARF) since 1996, a founding member of the East Asian Summit (EAS) since 2005 and a member of the Asia Europe Meeting (ASEM) since 2006. While working its way through incremental stages to reach the status of ASEAN summit-level partner, Indian diplomacy also adopted the parallel strategy of enrolling in the ASEAN system through bilateral, regional and sub-regional means. Membership in these multiple groupings enabled India to cultivate varied linkages with ASEAN member states.

This article will focus primarily upon India's emerging political, economic and strategic links with the South-East Asian region as part of its Look East policy. The first part of this chapter will analyse the genesis of India's Look East policy in the early part of the 1990s. The second part of the chapter will critically look into the emerging economic co-operation between India and ASEAN. The third part of the chapter will analyse the emerging security co-operation between India and ASEAN, including India's role in the ARF. The fourth part of the chapter will dwell on the evolving ties between India and two sub-regional organizations: the Bay of Bengal Initiative for Multi-Sectoral Technical and Economic Cooperation (BIMSTEC), formed in 1997, and the Mekong Ganga Cooperation (MGC) forum, formed in 2000.

Genesis of the 'Look East' policy

Despite India's geographical proximity to South-East Asia, sharing over 1,600 km of land boundary with Myanmar and maritime boundaries with Myanmar, Thailand and Indonesia, South-East Asia was hardly a priority area in Indian foreign policy before the 1990s.

India was not among the countries that enthusiastically welcomed the formation of ASEAN in August 1967; India's ambivalent attitude towards ASEAN stemmed from the new Asian body's pronounced pro-Western orientation.[3] This led India to wonder about the organization's true purpose, especially in the context of the British Government's decision at that time to withdraw militarily from east of the Suez and the uncertain US role in Indo-China. ASEAN members were, anyway, initially lukewarm to any idea of India's membership in the regional association for individual reasons. Indonesia, the natural and de facto leader of the organization, feared that if India became a member it would dominate the organization. Coupled with this, India's strong anti-Chinese feelings, particularly after the Sino–Indian border conflict of 1962, might have created an adverse impact on Singapore's majority ethnic Chinese population if India at that time had been admitted as a member of ASEAN. Furthermore, Thailand and the Philippines were opposed to India's non-aligned foreign policy and were overtly pro-USA.

Moreover, after the signing of the Indo-Soviet Treaty of Peace, Friendship and Co-operation by India in 1971, the ASEAN states were suspicious of the USSR's role in determining India's foreign policy towards the region in general, and Viet Nam in particular. After Viet Nam's military intervention in Kampuchea in December 1978, India, by its decision to recognize the Heng Samrin regime in Kampuchea backed by Viet Nam forfeited whatever little goodwill it enjoyed in the ASEAN region at that time.[4] Such Cold War postures created a distance between India and ASEAN for a long time until the world bipolar structure collapsed in the late 1980s, ushering in a new era of regional equations.

The cumulative impact of the political and strategic changes that followed the end of the Cold War and the adoption of market reforms by the Congress (I) Government in India headed by P.V. Narasimha Rao (1991–96) led to a gradual transition in Indian-ASEAN relations. It was during this time that the Congress Government in India initiated the Look East policy, with the aim of re-ordering India's relations with the states in the South-East Asian region. The ASEAN states openly supported the economic reforms initiated by Rao to liberalize the Indian economy, expecting greater compatibility and economic synergies between the two sides. Many ASEAN states were attracted by the economic opportunities that a huge market like India offered after the decision to liberalize the Indian economy was taken. India was, in turn, attracted by the economic vitality of South-East Asia: 'India had to go beyond the confines of the South Asian Association for Regional Cooperation (SAARC) if it had to reap the benefits out of the economic potential of the South East Asian region and establish itself as a regional power'.[5]

While the economic reforms initiated in India were still in their infancy, it is of significance that ASEAN accorded sectoral dialogue partner status to India in January 1992 in the areas of trade, investment and tourism. India obtained the status of full dialogue partner of ASEAN in 1995, which underscored ASEAN's readiness to engage India in the various sectors of the dialogue partnership, as opposed to its former reticence to deal with India in certain limited areas. India also became a summit-level partner of ASEAN from 2002 onwards. Moreover, alongside closer economic co-operation with India, ASEAN was eager to engage India in discussions on politico-security issues as well. Following the award of full dialogue partner status, India was admitted to the ARF in 1996.

Backed by defence co-operation agreements with a number of countries, regular top-level political exchanges and thriving economic interaction, India is emerging as an important player in the South-East Asian and the wider Asia-Pacific region. For India, the Look East policy is aimed at greater economic alignment with, and a political role in, the dynamic Asia-Pacific region in general, and the South-East Asian region in particular. India clearly saw South-East Asia as a region where political, strategic and economic conditions could enable it to play a significant role.

India–ASEAN economic co-operation

Economics is at the heart of India's foreign policy (the Manmohan Doctrine) and is one of the instruments of its thrust towards ASEAN. As India's Prime Minister Manmohan Singh put it at the 2009 India-ASEAN Summit, 'the ASEAN region is synonymous with dynamic economic growth [...] India's engagement with the ASEAN is at the heart of our Look East Policy. We are convinced that India's future and our economic interests are best served by greater integration with our Asian partners in ASEAN.[6]

Since the initiation of the Look East policy, India has made significant progress in cultivating a multifaceted relationship with ASEAN on one hand, and its member states on the other. In the economic realm, the Look East policy provided a tremendous encouragement to economic ties between India and the ASEAN member states, resulting in the constitution of a number of institutional mechanisms to promote economic exchanges. The earlier Joint Trade Committees with the ASEAN states were upgraded as Joint Business Commissions, and an India-ASEAN Business Council and ASEAN-India Joint Management Committee were formed.

After India became a full dialogue partner of ASEAN in 1995, the ASEAN-India Joint Co-operation Committee and ASEAN-India Working Group on Trade and Investment were set up. An ASEAN-India Fund was created to promote trade, tourism, science and technology, and other economic activities. From virtually little or no investment from South-East Asia in the early 1990s, Malaysia and Singapore emerged as the 10th and 11th in terms of approved investment received by India by 2002. Thailand was in the 18th position and Indonesia and the Philippines were in the 33rd and 35th positions, respectively, in terms of approved foreign investment in the same year. Together, by 2002, these five countries accounted for nearly 5% of total approved foreign investment in India. Singapore continues to be the single largest investor in India among the ASEAN countries for foreign direct investment (FDI) inflows into India, and the second largest among all countries. The cumulative FDI inflow to India from Singapore during April 2000–April 2009 was around US $7,900m., rising to $3,450m. in 2008/09 alone.

The progress between India and ASEAN with regard to bilateral trade is equally impressive. India's trade grew fastest with South-East Asia compared with any other region between 1991 and 1997. While ASEAN exports kept the momentum, there was a considerable slowdown in imports as a result of the Asian financial crisis in 1997–98. However, imports by ASEAN, which temporarily slowed in the wake of the Asian financial crisis, again started to pick up from 2000 onwards. It is important to note that the two-way trade between India and the ASEAN countries witnessed an approximate six-fold increase from the level of $5,900m. in 1997 to more than $38,370m. in 2007/08. ASEAN has now emerged as India's fourth largest trading partner. In 2009/10 ASEAN accounted for $25,800m. of India's imports (an 8.95% share), whilst accounting for $18,110m. of India's exports (a 10.13% share). The biggest trade partner for India in the ASEAN countries is Singapore, with total bilateral trade during 2009/10 between India and Singapore standing at $14,050m.; Malaysia comes second, at $8,010m.

133

Not to be left off the Free Trade Area (FTA) bandwagon that swept across South-East Asia, India put across concrete plans to increase economic interaction and integration through institutional arrangements. At the second India–ASEAN summit, held at Bali in October 2003, both parties signed the India–ASEAN Comprehensive Economic Co-operation Agreement (CECA), alongside a bilateral Framework Agreement for Establishing a Free Trade Area between India and Thailand.[7] Under the India–ASEAN CECA, areas of economic co-operation identified included trade facilitation, trade financing, customs co-operation, agriculture, forestry and fisheries, services, mining and energy, science and technology, information and communication technology (ICT), transport and infrastructure, manufacturing, and human resource development. An Early Harvest Programme (EHP) was introduced to accelerate the implementation of the CECA. The timing of the signing of the CECA was significant. It was worked out hardly a year after the first summit between the two sides at Phnom Penh in 2002, and as the People's Republic of China was seriously holding talks with ASEAN on its own version of a free trade agreement. At the same time, in around September 2002, discussions were going on between ASEAN and Japan for the conclusion of an FTA between both sides. A sense of urgency to catch up with the East Asian giants like China and Japan, which were striking closer multilateral instruments of co-operation with ASEAN, was evident in the Indian move to sign the CECA in October 2003.

Further progress was evident in August 2009, when India and ASEAN signed an FTA in goods at Bangkok. The India–ASEAN FTA in goods will integrate the two globally important economic blocs for mutually beneficial economic gains. It was stated that mutually agreed tariff liberalization would gradually cover 75% of their two-way trade, beginning from January 2010. Under the FTA, India has incorporated 489 items from agriculture, textiles and chemicals in the negative list, meaning these products will be kept out of duty reductions. The India–ASEAN FTA in goods became operational from January 2010 onwards. India and ASEAN are at present negotiating agreements on trade in services and investment, which are expected to be signed in the future.

A year after the ASEAN–India CECA was signed, another landmark agreement, the ASEAN–India Partnership for Peace, Progress and Shared Prosperity Agreement, was signed by both sides at the Vientiane summit in November 2004.[8] The agreement reached between India and ASEAN at Vientiane provided a roadmap for the consolidation of India's relations with the South-East Asian states. It is a blueprint that draws up a comprehensive set of long-term objectives along with an Action Plan containing a package of proposals concerning multi-sectoral areas of co-operation between India and the ASEAN states. The areas of co-operation in the economic field include trade and investment, finance, energy, science and technology, research and development, human resource development, pharmaceuticals and health, agriculture, tourism and culture, small and medium-sized enterprises, and increased people-to-people contacts. In most of the areas mentioned in the Vientiane Agreement, co-operation between India and ASEAN had already started, more at the bilateral than at the multilateral level. The Vientiane Agreement committed India and her ASEAN partners to reiterate their full support for the implementation of ASEAN Concord II, leading to the formation of a more integrated ASEAN Community comprising the ASEAN Security Community, ASEAN Economic Community and the ASEAN Socio-Cultural Community. By such commitment, India agreed to integrate itself into the still-evolving ASEAN system.

The Vientiane Agreement was a miniature version of the ASEAN–India Vision 2020 prepared by the ASEAN think tanks ahead of the summit at Vientiane in November 2004. The energy sector was visualized by the Vision 2020 document as a promising area of mutual engagement and, with it, five broad strategies envisaged the promotion of oil and gas co-operation, namely joint exploration in the region, joint ventures for exploration in third countries, an ASEAN-India gas grid, an ASEAN-India Association of oil and gas companies, and exchange of experiences in non-conventional energy (solar, wind, geo-thermal).

India is already involved in the oil and gas sector in Myanmar, Malaysia, Viet Nam and Indonesia. ONGC Videsh Limited (OVL), the international arm of India's Oil and Natural Gas Corporation Limited, and the Gas Authority of India Limited (GAIL), both publicly owned, are engaged in joint exploration of gas in Myanmar's A1 and A3 blocks off the Rakhine coast (formerly the Arakan coast). These two Indian energy giants acquired a 30% stake in this block, along with the (Republic of) Korean companies KoGas and Daewoo. GAIL is also working in Viet Nam through a joint venture to construct the South Con Gas Plant, while OVL is involved in oil and gas exploration project with Vietnam Petroleum and BP Exploration (UK). Competition and friction with China is apparent in both the Vietnamese and Myanmar fields. India also imports petroleum from Malaysia, for example, with the Indian Oil Corporation (IOC) signing a contract with the Malaysian oil giant Petronas in June 2007 to purchase 1.5m. tons of crude oil. Indonesia, the world's largest exporter of liquefied natural gas and an oil producer, with most of the gas reserves located in central Sumatra, invited Indian companies to explore its hydrocarbons and construct gas pipelines from Indonesia to third countries. In July 2000 IOC signed a memorandum of understanding with the Indonesian oil company Pertamina to explore and buy oil and gas as well as modernize the refineries in the archipelago.

Infrastructure is another area where high levels of co-operation between India and the ASEAN states are taking place. This sector is capital-intensive, expert-guided and technology-driven. The liberalization of the Indian economy and the demand for global integration have goaded India into recognizing infrastructure as a national economic priority. In civil aviation the country has achieved tremendous progress in expanding domestic and global air connectivity. Malaysian companies were involved in the construction of a new airport at Hyderabad. India has emerged as the largest market for the Malaysian construction industry and major project participation by Malaysian companies includes the Mumbai-Pune expressway, Chennai by-pass road in Tamil Nadu, and the ongoing country-wide Golden Quadrilateral road project. Like Malaysia, Singapore is also a major investor in India's construction industry. Considering India's rapid drive to develop the infrastructure base in the country, the ASEAN countries will be active partners in this sector. Similarly, India is a major builder of railway lines in the South-East Asian states and its prospects for being a significant partner in building railway infrastructure in the region are high. Indonesia, Malaysia, Myanmar and Thailand are all major beneficiaries of Indian railway technology.

India-ASEAN security co-operation

The ARF constitutes a vital institutional link through which India has tried to consolidate its political and strategic ties with the ASEAN states. The ARF was formally launched at the Bangkok ASEAN summit in July 1994. The ARF provided India with an opportunity to explain some of its policies and break the isolation that resulted from its alliance with the former USSR during the Cold War. Many ASEAN countries viewed India, which joined the ARF in 1996, as a possible counterweight to future Chinese expansionism in the South-East Asian region.[9] Many government leaders and diplomats in South-East Asia are of the opinion that as an emerging power, India has a great role to play in the region. This factor was also one of the important reasons that made India attain the summit-level partner status with ASEAN in 2002. The first India-ASEAN summit took place in 2002, with India acceding to the ASEAN Treaty of Amity and Cooperation in Southeast Asia (TAC) in 2003.

This strategic importance of India for the ASEAN states was very much evident after the nuclear tests conducted by India and Pakistan in May 1998. The nuclear tests in South Asia became a focal point of discussion at the Manila ARF meeting in July 1998, which was attended by major powers like the USA, China, Japan and Australia. Apart from Viet Nam, which categorically endorsed India's position on the issue of nuclear tests, several other ASEAN states regretted the tests. Countries like Thailand, the Philippines and Japan, in particular, took a hard-line stance against India on the nuclear tests and wanted India to be condemned for carrying out the tests. However, the absence of a consensus among the ARF members on the issue of condemning India and Pakistan worked in India's favour. In the period immediately prior to the Manila ARF meeting in July 1998, India had been successful in clarifying its stand on the nuclear tests to the ARF member states. The joint communiqué issued at the end of the ARF meeting was moderate and it merely deplored the series of nuclear tests in South Asia. The final ASEAN position was largely shaped by Indonesia, which attacked the double standards and hypocrisy of the Western states, while countries like Singapore and Malaysia played a central role in ensuring that India was not isolated at the ARF. China's demand that the ARF express strong support for the UN Security Council Resolution condemning the nuclear tests in South Asia was rejected. Even Thailand and the Philippines fell in line with the common ASEAN position on the nuclear tests. While the ASEAN states were not prepared to do anything that would resemble a stand against China, they were also reluctant to let India down and displayed genuine concern for its security.

There is no denying the fact that the China factor, too, started to weigh heavily in several ASEAN quarters particularly after the closure of the US bases in the Philippines in 1992 and the emergence of the territorial disputes in the South China Sea as a major cause of concern, with China strongly maintaining its claims over the disputed area. While China has achieved greater economic integration with the region, there still remains apprehension over the strategic role it will play in the future. Although India has explicitly refuted the idea of becoming a counter-balancing power vis-à-vis China, it did not seem to be averse to the idea of using South-East Asian worries to advance its political and strategic interests in the region.[10] India, along with ASEAN, is particularly concerned about the growing Chinese influence in strategically located Myanmar. Contrary to previous perceptions, many South-East Asian states have begun to look upon India as a power that could play a kind of balancing role in the region, as Lee Kuan Yew delicately put it, to 'keep the center in ASEAN, India would be a useful balance to China's heft'.[11] Many scholars are of the view that India's entry into the ARF in 1996 was primarily a result of common interests that existed between the ASEAN states and India regarding perceptions of the threat posed by China. The upshot of the convergence of political and strategic interests between India and the South-East Asian states was the basis of a new strategic interaction between India and several South-East Asian states at the bilateral level.

India has also entered into bilateral defence pacts with most of the South-East Asian states facilitating the sale of technology, training personnel and joint military exercises. The degree of India's military co-operation is greater with the ASEAN states than with its immediate neighbours in South Asia. Their mutual security concern is guided by two broad factors: reconciling US military supremacy in the Asia-Pacific and balancing China's ascendancy in the region. Shedding the earlier Cold War suspicions of India's naval expansionism, the ASEAN countries are near unanimous in welcoming an Indian strategic role in the region, barring certain diplomatic qualms entertained by individual countries. Security co-operation between India and the ASEAN states is governed by military diplomacy, the naval forces being the prime instrument of building synergies. The regular deployment of the Indian Navy into the South China Sea since 2000 has been a not unwelcome feature for the South-East Asian states, though causing some concern to China. Both India and the ASEAN states have shown equal interest in sharing defence experience, know-how and material. In fact, India has far greater military resources to share with the ASEAN states than vice-versa. Simultaneously, India's ability to offer defence capabilities to the South-East Asian states has also enabled her to gain larger strategic space in the region.

Beginning with bilateral military initiatives and then through membership of the ARF and multilateral military exercises like MILAN, India has succeeded in gaining the security confidence of the South-East Asian states. In January 1991 the former Malaysian Prime Minister Mahathir bin Mohammad confidently declared that Malaysia did not feel threatened in any way by India. This was in sharp contrast to the apprehensions previously expressed by both Malaysia and Indonesia about Indian expansionist designs in South-East Asia in the 1980s. In 1992 the Malaysia-India Defence Committee was set up. Defence dialogue between India and Singapore began in the early 1990s, and by 1993 the navies of both states were engaged in joint naval exercises. A Memorandum of Understanding was signed between India and Viet Nam on bilateral defence co-operation in 1994, when the then Indian Prime Minister P.V. Narasimha Rao visited Hanoi. Bilaterally, while the economic partnership is growing steadily, defence co-operation has accelerated to the point of signing a strategic partnership between the two states during the visit of Vietnamese Prime Minister Nguyen Tan Dung to India in July 2007. By 1995 the Indian-sponsored multilateral naval exercise, MILAN, had engaged the key Malacca littoral states (Indonesia, Malaysia and Singapore) in the Andaman Sea. The significance of these military initiatives demonstrated some of the ASEAN states' readiness to accept India as a strategic partner in the unfolding, but as yet uncertain, post-Cold War geopolitical landscape in South-East Asia.

Particular noticeable defence interactions have developed between India and Singapore, beginning with joint naval exercises in 1993. These were followed up in successive years, including Singapore's participation in Madad-98, a multilateral search and rescue exercise launched by the Indian Navy. Singapore was the first among the South-East Asian states to become operationally involved with the Indian Navy, with their SIMBEX exercises taking place mostly in the Bay of Bengal, but also in the South China Sea at times. A bilateral defence agreement between India and Singapore was concluded in 1998. An important military operation that followed the 1998 defence agreement was the 11-day anti-submarine joint warfare exercise between the two navies in the Andaman Sea, which was independent of Singapore's participation in MILAN. Singapore had the rare distinction of being offered training facilities at Kochi, India's southern naval command, and gaining access to India's National Missile Testing Range on the eastern seaboard to test her guns and missiles. India-Singapore bilateral naval intercourse spans a wide range of operations that include search and rescue operation drills, anti-submarine warfare tactics, counter-mining exercises, interoperability of forces, anti-terrorism measures and exchange of naval information on such threats as piracy, poaching, etc. In 2003 both sides signed an upgraded bilateral Defence Co-operation Agreement, which sought to deepen the ongoing military co-operation, facilitate personnel exchanges, defence courses, intelligence sharing, etc. As part of this latest agreement, both countries conducted interoperability between the Indian Air Force and Singapore Air Force. The Singapore and Indian air forces also conducted joint air exercises at Gwalior in 2004 and in the same year participated in the multinational air exercises in Alaska, conducted by the US Air Force. Singapore is the only ASEAN state that is engaging with Indian tri-services. The tiny city-state of Singapore, strategically located at the cross roads of the South-East Asian and Asia-Pacific regions, is the ideal springboard for India.

With Indonesia, a bilateral agreement on Co-operative Activities in the Field of Defence was signed during former Indian Prime Minister Atal Behari Vajpayee's visit to the country in 2001, which facilitated functional co-operation in the area of defence. Military interaction gathered further momentum under the Indonesian President Susilo Bambang Yudhoyono, who emphasized a plan of action and strategic partnership on inter-state defence co-operation during his visit to New Delhi in 2007. A bilateral Defence Co-operation Agreement was signed between India and Indonesia, following which the first ever joint defence co-operation committee meeting took place at New Delhi in June 2007. Among other factors, Indonesia's latest security initiatives are guided by concern over China's ascendancy in the South-East Asian region and China's expanding military co-operation with the military regime in Myanmar.

Moreover, India's role in combating non-conventional security threats to the ASEAN states is well recognized, although this mutually beneficial relationship is more evident at the bilateral level than at the multilateral level. In fact, India's Minister of External Affairs offered a package at the 14th ARF meeting in 2007 to design and conduct training modules on maritime security, geared at anti-piracy, search and rescue, offshore and port security, anti-smuggling and drugs control and anti-poaching operations. In its attempt to further consolidate security ties with ASEAN after the terrorist attacks on the USA on 11 September 2001, India signed a Joint Declaration with ASEAN in October 2003 at the Bali Summit for Cooperation to Combat International Terrorism.[12] The Declaration clearly rejects any attempt to associate terrorism with any religion, race or nationality, and regards acts of terrorism in all its forms and manifestations committed wherever, whenever and by whomsoever. Further, India and the Philippines signed an Extradition Treaty in March 2004. India also signed a Treaty on Mutual Legal Assistance in Criminal Matters with Thailand in 2004 and with Singapore in June 2005. In 2005 a Memorandum of Understanding was signed between India and Thailand on joint maritime patrols to prevent piracy and smuggling in the Andaman Sea. An Extradition Treaty between India and Thailand was also signed. Further, an agreement was reached on mutual co-operation to handle prominent leaders of Indian insurgent outfits hiding in Thailand. Similarly, India and Myanmar, during the visit of the Indian defence minister to Myanmar in 2007, agreed to launch joint army operations to flush out north-eastern Indian insurgent camps located inside Myanmar's territory. Earlier, both India and the Myanmar Government had co-operated to conduct two counter-insurgency offensives, Operation Leech and Operation Golden Duck, to fight militant groups and their networks along the India–Myanmar border.

India's bilateral and multilateral engagement with the ASEAN states essentially is a function of her wider strategic objectives in South-East Asia and the Asia-Pacific region. ASEAN remains integral to India's overall strategic arrangement in the South-East Asian and the wider Asia-Pacific region. Undoubtedly, China is at the core of Indian assessment of the regional strategic environment and Indian diplomacy has played on the fears entertained by most of the states in the region of an economically and militarily rising Chinese power. Through a prudent and subtle assimilation of political, economic and military tactics, which avoids a direct anti-China alliance, axis or coalition, India is consolidating her position in the South-East Asian and Asia-Pacific region as a countervailing or 'balancing' power to China.[13] Almost all the states in the region are worried about the rise of China, although they refrain from admitting this openly.

Such a perception also brings India and the USA together to check China's rapid rise in South-East Asia. Both the USA and India also agree on a number of other strategic objectives that include combating terrorism and piracy, protection of the Sea Lines of Communication (SLOCs), anti-drugs drives, safety of energy and mercantile transportation, etc. The geopolitical range of mutual convergence spans from the Persian Gulf, Indian Ocean, Malacca Straits and beyond, up to the South China Sea.

However, such strengthening US-Indian military-security links in the Asia-Pacific region will not fail to affect India's political and strategic ties with ASEAN. The manner in which India is building strong partnerships, individually and collectively with the non-ASEAN powers such as the USA, Japan and Australia, may cast a shadow over India-ASEAN relations in the future. The Australia-India-USA-Japan quadrilateral grouping formed in 2007 could constitute an outer ring around the ASEAN security framework, although such a forum has yet to design its form and content. One of the important drivers for this quadrilateral grouping was to hedge against China and to counter its so-called 'string of pearls strategy', and undertake decisive measures to meet threats to the security of the Asia-Pacific region. Close military co-operation is already taking place between the members of this group and they have conducted joint military exercises in the Indian *and* Pacific Ocean waters, though Australia showed some hesitation over continuing such a format. Whether such non-ASEAN groups will in future complement ASEAN or override its regional identity will also influence India's relations with ASEAN. The ASEAN members, perhaps with the exception of Singapore, will not unanimously and openly endorse the quadrilateral group, since they do not want to invite Chinese ire. Further, there is the possibility of such an evolving four-power framework undermining ASEAN's own central role in regional multilateral security frameworks. ASEAN has always insisted on remaining in the driver's seat in both the ARF and the EAS. As part of her Look East policy, it remains to be seen how far India will perform a balancing act of deepening and consolidating its links with the ASEAN states and simultaneously building up strong linkages with the Pacific Rim powers further east like Australia, Japan and the USA.

India and sub-regional co-operation in South-East Asia

BIMSTEC

BIMSTEC is a sub-regional arrangement established in 1997, of which India is a member. As a sub-regional group, BIMSTEC assumes significance in more than one sense. It is the first ever regional arrangement that was established by some of the members from the SAARC and some of the ASEAN member states, thereby symbolizing growing recognition of naturally contiguous areas and development and action plans. BIMSTEC also filled the geopolitical void that used to exist between ASEAN and SAARC. BIMSTEC broadly identified sub-regional co-operation in six areas, namely trade and investment, technology, transport and communication, energy, tourism, and fisheries. Each member country is entrusted with the responsibility of co-ordinating a particular area of sub-regional co-operation, for instance India with technology and Myanmar with energy.

As part of its Look East policy, India played a prominent role in the initial formation of BIMSTEC (then called the Bangladesh, India, Myanmar, Sri Lanka and Thailand Economic Cooperation, changing to the current name in 2004) in 1997. At the February 2004 meeting of the organization, Bhutan and Nepal were added as new members. The July 2004 BIMSTEC summit declaration reflected the collective will of the member states to carry forward the BIMSTEC vision of mutually beneficial sub-regional co-operation through specific projects. A Framework Agreement for the creation of a BIMSTEC free trade area was also signed during the 2004 summit.[14] However, India's efforts towards creating this sub-regional grouping were motivated by both economic and strategic considerations.

Apart from promoting economic co-operation, India is keen to expand the scope of BIMSTEC to include political and security matters as well. As far as strategic considerations were concerned, by actively encouraging other states to be a part of this grouping, India sought to combat the escalating Chinese influence in Myanmar and other member states, through increased economic co-operation in the field of trade and investment, communications and transport, tourism, energy projects, and fisheries among the member states. It is interesting to note that on the sidelines of the BIMSTEC ministerial meeting in February 2004, India agreed to fund a feasibility study for the conversion of the Myanmar port Dawei into a deep-sea facility.

It is also worth noting that besides focusing on issues relating to trade and commerce, the July 2004 BIMSTEC summit declaration called upon the member states to join hands in combating international terrorism. The member states agreed not to allow their territory to be used by terrorist groups for launching attacks against friendly governments. A significant step in this direction was the setting up of a Joint Working Group on Counter-Terrorism. At the second BIMSTEC Summit held in New Delhi in November 2008, the Summit Declaration recognized the threat that terrorism posed to peace, stability and economic progress in the region, and emphasized the need for close co-operation to combat all forms of terrorism and transnational crimes. There, leaders of the BIMSTEC member states recorded satisfaction with the finalization of the BIMSTEC Convention on Combating International Terrorism, Transnational Organized Crime and Illicit Drug Trafficking.

MGC

India floated the MGC Forum with the signing of the Vientiane Declaration in November 2000.[15] The MGC had been approved in principle by the six states (India, Myanmar, Viet Nam, Laos, Cambodia and Thailand) at the ASEAN meeting in Bangkok in July 2000. Under its co-operative framework, tourism, culture and education were given precedence, while transport, communications and infrastructure were identified for the next phase. The basic thrust of the MGC Forum is to promote economic development of the Mekong region by developing the infrastructural facilities there. For India, MGC offers immense scope for creating linkages with the Mekong countries by connecting them to the relatively less developed Indian north-eastern region. The MGC is yet another forum for India to engage with the military regime in Myanmar. However, it would be puerile to ignore the wider strategic objectives behind the signing of the Vientiane Declaration. For both India and China the Mekong states provide strategic accessibility into the heartland of the Asia-Pacific. In an editorial that appeared in the *Bangkok Post*, it was stated that the real benefits of the MGC Forum might not be its content but the counterbalance it provides to the South-East Asian states against the increasing influence of China in the region.[16]

It is important to note that a few months before the signing of the Vientiane Declaration, China, too, signed a Mekong sub-regional agreement of co-operation, in April 2000, with Laos, Myanmar and Thailand. India, Viet Nam and Cambodia were not part of this group. Like India, developing the Mekong region is also of strategic advantage to China. It is important to recognise that both India and China are simultaneously engaged in separate regional groups in the Mekong basin and their timing is more than coincidental. Both India and China are keen to cultivate closer political, economic and strategic links with the states of the Mekong basin for gaining political and economic rewards. For India, close political relations with the states of the Mekong region will facilitate strategic access to the dynamic hub of the Asia-Pacific rim. Such a relationship will also promote India's bargaining power with the affluent and assertive original five ASEAN states. It appears that the MGC could help India balance China's policy involving gaining access to the Indian Ocean through its south-western province of Yunnan, Myanmar and Bangladesh as part of its perceived objective of encircling India. In fact, China's exclusion from the MGC Forum appears to be the Indian answer to China's opposition to the enlargement of ASEAN +3 (ASEAN plus China, Japan and the Republic of Korea).

Conclusions

The Look East policy has been the cornerstone of the country's new foreign policy initiative since the end of the Cold War. It is multidimensional in its objectives and reflects a new-found desire on the part of India to play a pre-eminent role in the affairs of South-East Asia and the Asia-Pacific region, which constitutes a part of India's *extended neighbourhood*. Despite enormous progress being made since the early 1990s, India still lags far behind China and the USA in terms of geopolitical and economic importance in the South-East Asian region.

In terms of trade and investment, there is a growing realization in the South-East Asian states that, despite China's greater attractiveness, India is an expanding economy and is one of the largest emerging markets for products and services in the world. Therefore, it would be too risky to excessively depend on China. There is no doubt that ASEAN has served one of India's major objectives of the Look East policy, which is reaching out to the wider Asia-Pacific region. As far as the security landscape of South-East Asia and the Asia-Pacific is concerned, it is quite evident that the USA will continue to act as the pre-eminent power and will try to maintain the strategic balance in the region. Most significantly, improved relations between India and the USA have also helped to facilitate India's relations with the ASEAN member states, given that most ASEAN states (with the exception of Myanmar and, to a lesser extent, Laos, Viet Nam and Cambodia) have close and cordial ties with the USA.

Moreover, in building relations with the ASEAN states, India enjoys certain political advantages. Unlike China or Japan, there is no historical baggage to worry about invasion or interference by India. In contrast to China, India also does not have any security problem with any of the South-East Asian states. In fact, some of the South-East Asian states consider India to be uniquely placed to play a kind of balancing role so that the region does not come under the influence of any one Great Power. Therefore, it is not without significance that following the first India-ASEAN summit in 2002, India was described as the 'western wing' of the ASEAN jumbo. India, the ASEAN states and many other states in the Asia-Pacific region share concerns about China's growing military build-up and economic clout. This mutual concern among India, the South-East Asian states and the states of the Asia-Pacific region provides India with the appropriate political and strategic space to implement its Look East policy, through which one of its aims is to balance China in Asia. While both sides would refrain from admitting so in public, it seems quite natural that the lengthening shadow of the Chinese dragon in South-East Asia will prove to be an important stimulus for greater interaction between India and the ASEAN states in the immediate future.

Notes

1 See K. Sridharan, *The ASEAN Region in India's Foreign Policy*, Dartmouth: Aldershot, 1996; G.V.C. Naidu, 'Wither the Look East Policy: India and Southeast Asia', *Strategic Analysis*, Vol. 28, No. 2, April–June 2004, p.332; G.V.C. Naidu, 'India and Southeast Asia: An Analysis of the Look East Policy', in P. Rao (ed.), *India and ASEAN: Partners at Summit*, New Delhi: Knowledge World Publishers, 2008, pp.131–32.
2 P.V. Rao, 'India and ASEAN: Summit Partnership', in P.V. Rao (ed.), *India and ASEAN: Partners at Summit*, op. cit., pp.4–7.
3 See K. Sridharan, 'India and ASEAN: The Long Road to Dialogue', *The Round Table*, No. 340, October 1996, p.467.

4 Ibid., pp.469–70. Also see F. Grare, 'In Search of a Role: India and the ASEAN Regional Forum', in F. Grare and A. Mattoo (eds), *India and ASEAN: The Politics of India's Look East Policy*, New Delhi: Manohar, 2001, pp.124–25.

5 C. Kuppuswamy, 'India's Look East Policy – A Review', *Papers* (SAAG), No. 3662, 12 February 2010.

6 M. Singh, 'PM's Statement at the 7th India–ASEAN Summit', 24 October 2009, pmindia.nic.in.

7 India-ASEAN, *Framework Agreement on Comprehensive Economic Cooperation Between the Republic of India and the Association of Southeast Asian Nations*, 8 October 2003, www.aseansec.org; India-ASEAN, *Agreement on Trade in Goods Under the Framework Agreement on Comprehensive Economic Cooperation Between the Association of Southeast Asian Nations and the Republic of India*, 13 August 2009, www.aseansec.org; India-Thailand, *Framework Agreement for Establishing a Free Trade Area Between the Republic of India and the Kingdom of Thailand*, 9 October 2003, commerce.nic.in.

8 India-ASEAN, *ASEAN-India Partnership for Peace, Progress and Shared Prosperity*, 13 November 2004, www.aseansec.org.

9 A. Acharya, 'Will Asia's Past Be Its Future', *International Security*, Vol. 28, No. 3, Winter 2003/04, pp.150–51; F. Yahya, 'India and Southeast Asia: Revisited', *Contemporary Southeast Asia*, Vol. 25, No. 1, 2003, p.100.

10 G.V.C. Naidu, 'Wither the Look East Policy', op. cit., p.338. Also see S. Sundararaman, 'India and ASEAN', *The Hindu*, 19 November 2002.

11 K.Y. Lee, 'Lee Kuan Yew Reflects', *Time*, 5 December 2005.

12 India-ASEAN, *ASEAN-India Joint Declaration for Cooperation to Combat International Terrorism*, 8 October 2003, www.aseansec.org.

13 A. Batabyal, 'Balancing China in Asia: A Realist Assessment of India's Look East Strategy', *China Report*, Vol. 42, No. 2, 2006, pp.179–97.

14 India-BIMSTEC, *BIMST-EC Summit Declaration*, Bangkok, 31 July 2004, www.bimstec.org.

15 V. Jayanth, 'The Mekong Ganga Initiative', *The Hindu*, 28 November 2000.

16 For further details, see M. Uniyal, 'India's Look East Policy Hits Pay Dirt in Southeast Asia', *Asia Times*, 21 November 2000.

13

Looking east 2: East Asia and Australasia/Oceania

Walter C. Ladwig, III

Introduction

Building on the discussion in the previous chapter of India's role in South East Asia, this chapter looks *beyond* to India's relations with the nations of East Asia and the Pacific. This geographic space is characterized by the influence of both a status quo Great Power (the USA), the bilateral alliances and forward military forces of which greatly shape regional security dynamics, and a rising regional power (the People's Republic of China). Since both the USA and China have such extensive economic and security ties with many countries in East Asia/Australasia it is difficult to discuss regional dynamics there without reference to them. However, since India's relations with both of these countries are taken up elsewhere in this *Handbook*, these two 'elephants in the room' will be pushed to the background of the discussion in this particular chapter.

India's role in the broader Asia-Pacific region is not one that is widely recognized—even by some regional specialists. For example, in a recent academic text on the politics of the region, India merits only a few passing references and is described merely as a country that 'interacts with the Asia-Pacific in various ways'.[1] Although it would be a significant mistake to overlook or discount the role that India is playing in this region, such omissions are somewhat understandable. From a geographic standpoint, India does not border the Pacific Ocean and it is only through its far-flung Nicobar and Andaman island territories that it is even adjacent to the key maritime choke points linking the Indian and Pacific Oceans. For those who narrowly conceive of East Asia stretching in an arc from Myanmar to Japan on the basis of race or a mythical quasi-Confucian culture, India would not appear to 'belong'. In terms of security linkages, India has traditionally had little involvement with either of the two key security issues in the region: the China–Taiwan dispute and the Democratic People's Republic of Korea's (North Korea) quest for nuclear weapons. Finally, from an economic standpoint, at present India's economic linkages with the region do not approach the depth or breadth that the nations of East Asia and Australasia have among themselves. While all of these factors may appear to be good reasons for not considering India's role in the region, to do so would be a mistake. A steadily expanding economy, paired with a growing partnership with key regional actors, is positioning India to have a dynamic impact on the emerging economic and security architecture of the Asia-Pacific.[2]

Going beyond South East Asia

The desire to play a significant role in Asia certainly existed among India's post-independence leadership. As Jawaharlal Nehru argued in the mid-1940s, 'the Pacific is likely to take the place of the Atlantic in the future as the nerve centre of the world. Though not directly a Pacific state, India will inevitably exercise an important influence there'.[3] However, with India embroiled by internal security challenges, external conflicts with Pakistan and China, and constrained by the so-called Hindu rate of growth, it would be several decades before Nehru's words could be legitimately echoed by his successors. Yet, in 2002 Prime Minister Vajpayee could declare that 'India's belonging to the Asia Pacific community is a geographical fact and a political reality', and that the region was 'one of the focal points of India's foreign policy, strategic concerns and economic interests'.[4]

After its initial success with the Association of Southeast Asian Nations (ASEAN), India moved into phase two of its 'Look East' policy, which encompasses a region 'extending from Australia to East Asia'.[5] Indian officials envisioned playing 'an ever-increasing role' in this *extended neighbourhood* that had been extended still further eastwards. Simultaneously, India expanded the range of issues on which it would engage East Asian nations from trade to wider economic and security issues, representing a further 'strategic shift in India's vision', one predicated on the understanding that 'developments in East Asia are of direct consequence to India's security and development'.[6] India's engagement with this broader region is a foreign policy priority that has been embraced by successive Bharatiya Janata Party (BJP) and Congress governments.

In some respects, the perceptions that India has not traditionally been part of the Asia-Pacific region could actually work to its advantage. While historical animosity colours the bilateral relations of many nations in the region, India is free from such baggage. Furthermore, in a part of the world where rival claims to maritime zones and border disputes are widespread, Delhi lacks any territorial disputes with the nations of the region. Despite Chinese efforts to curtail its influence, India gained political acceptance in its bid to be recognized as an Asia-Pacific power in 2005 when it was invited to attend the inaugural East Asian Summit (EAS)—an effort some believed would be the stepping stone to the formation of an East Asian Community (EAC) to mirror the European Community.[7] Support for India's inclusion in the EAS 'to serve as a counterbalance to China' came from South-East Asian nations such as Singapore, Indonesia and Thailand, as well as from Japan and the Republic of Korea (South Korea)—all of which championed India's participation despite objections from China.[8] While some Indian commentators view their nation's inclusion in Asia-Pacific regional forums as 'a recognition of [India's] fast growing economic and political clout', analysts taking a realistic view of events in Asia recognize that India was not invited to attend the EAS based on its economy alone, but also to prevent Beijing from dominating the institution.[9] In looking east beyond South-East Asia, India has developed links with East Asia, Australasia and Oceania.

East Asia

In East Asia, the dynamics of India's bilateral relations with South Korea, Japan and Taiwan are impacted by the common experience of having China as a neighbour.

South Korea

Signs of India's growing links with South Korea were formally evidenced in the Agreement on Long Term Cooperative Partnership for Peace and Prosperity, signed during the visit of

President Roh to India in October 2004. The framework included economic co-operation and expanded trade ties, as well as a foreign policy and security dialogue that promotes bilateral defence co-operation.[10]

Given that both states fought wars with China and face significant security challenges from revisionist 'partitioned' neighbours, it may be surprising that India's burgeoning relationship with South Korea is one that is driven by economics rather than geography or deep historical ties. In the early 1990s South Korea was actually one of the first countries to respond to India's attempts to open its economy to East Asia. There has been an average annual growth rate in their trade of 23.5% for more than a decade and a half. From a meagre US $530m. in 1992/93, bilateral trade between Asia's third and fourth largest economies expanded to a high of $12,630m. in 2008/09, before a slight slip back to $12,000m. in 2009/10 as a result of the global economic slowdown. Unsatisfied with this progress, in 2010 Indian and South Korean leaders announced a goal of expanding bilateral trade to $30,000m. by 2014. Towards that end, after three and a half years of negotiation, a free trade agreement (FTA) between India and South Korea, called the Comprehensive Economic Partnership Agreement (CEPA), entered into force on 1 January 2010. Intended to eliminate 85%–90% of tariffs on bilateral trade by 2019, as well as liberalize foreign direct investment (FDI) and facilitate trade in services such as information technology, law, engineering and finance, the agreement already saw a 70% increase in bilateral trade in the first quarter of 2010. At present India's exports to South Korea are primarily mineral oils, raw ore and cotton, while it imports electrical machinery, steel and nuclear energy-related technology. South Korea is also a top-10 source of FDI in India. The $12,000m. project undertaken by South Korean steel giant Posco at Paradip in Orissa to construct an integrated mining and steel production plant is the single largest foreign investment in India ever, as well as the largest foreign investment ever undertaken by a South Korean firm.

Although not as extensive as their economic co-operation, Indo-South Korean ties have extended into the military realm as well. India conducted joint naval exercises with the South Korean navy in 2000, 2004 and again in 2006. Although often overlooked, the South Korean Navy possesses a sizeable complement of surface combatants and submarines, comparable to the navies of France and the United Kingdom. May 2007 marked the first ever visit by a South Korean defence minister to India. This was coupled with expanded political ties as New Delhi and Seoul established a 'long-term co-operative partnership for peace and prosperity' that is intended to take Indo-Korean relations to 'a higher level'. The framework included economic co-operation and expanded trade ties, as well as a foreign policy and security dialogue that promotes bilateral defence co-operation. The two sides also signed a Memorandum of Understanding on joint defence production with the possibility of collaboration on self-propelled guns, armoured vehicles and smaller naval vessels such as minesweepers and frigates.

From a geostrategic perspective, Seoul and New Delhi are beginning to find a convergence of interests in key areas, much of which is China-related. Seoul is particularly concerned that China's on-going military build-up will enable it to dominate the sea lanes of the South China Sea—a development that would significantly undercut South Korea's political independence from its giant neighbour. As a result, Seoul has actively supported India's naval presence in maritime Asia to offset China's regional power. Despite Chinese opposition, South Korea has championed India's inclusion in East Asian regional forums like the EAS. New Delhi and Seoul are also united in their concerns about the proliferation of nuclear weapons and missile technology in their respective sub-regions. These worries also converge in China, which has aided both Pakistan and North Korea with their weapons of mass destruction (WMD) programmes.

145

Subsequent co-operation between Islamabad and Pyongyang in a 'nukes-for-missiles barter trade' reinforces the perception that India and South Korea face a common challenge. Finally, as the world's fifth largest importer of oil—the majority of which comes from the Gulf—South Korea shares India's abiding interest in the security of the sea lanes of the Indian Ocean that link energy supplies to markets in Asia.

As a concrete sign of the importance India attaches to the bilateral relationship, it hosted South Korean President Lee Myung-bak as the guest of honour for the 2010 Republic Day celebration. During the course of Lee's visit to India, the two sides announced an upgrade of their relationship to a 'strategic partnership', which will involve enhanced co-operation on nuclear non-proliferation, regular high-level military exchanges and increased collaboration between the two navies on sea lane security in the Indian Ocean.[11] Accords were also signed on technology co-operation in areas such as space and information technology, and South Korea offered India further assistance with civil nuclear technology to meet its growing energy needs. Visits to South Korea by India's Minister of External Affairs in June 2010 and its Minister of Defence in September 2010 reinforced such security convergence.

Japan

Unlike many countries in Asia, India bears no historical animus towards the Japanese. Since recovering from the diplomatic fallout over India's 1998 nuclear tests, Tokyo and New Delhi's shared interests in restraining the scope of China's influence in Asia, as well as their 'deep interest in tackling regional and global security challenges', have led to a strengthening of increasingly significant defence ties that one overly exuberant South Asian commentator has termed an 'Asia-Pacific alliance between India and Japan'.[12] Although it has been increasingly common to focus on China as the leading power in East Asia, it should not be forgotten that Japan's economy is larger than China's (though being overtaken in 2010) or India's and, with a defence budget that exceeds $40,000m., its military is among the most advanced in the world. In particular, Japan's Maritime Self-Defence Force is easily the most capable indigenous navy in the Asia-Pacific, and 'will likely continue to "outclass" those of regional rivals for the foreseeable future, in spite of recent modernization efforts within the Chinese navy and air forces'.[13]

A host of factors are driving enhanced co-operation between India and Japan. They share a similar desire to see a multi-polar Asia that is stable and secure. Both nations are also heavily dependent on oil from the Gulf and have shared concerns about the security of sea lanes in the western Indian Ocean and South China Sea. On a geopolitical level, they can both be considered potential rivals to China for primacy in the broader region. As Japan continues to evolve into a 'normal' nation willing to undertake a regional military role, tensions—both historic and strategic—continue to plague its relations with China. The military build-up undertaken by Beijing in the past decade has concerned both Japan and India. Japanese politicians have been quite explicit about the fact that India's presence in East Asia provides a needed balance to China's influence.[14] In an effort to forestall competition from its southern and eastern neighbours, China has attempted to prevent both Japan and India from gaining equal international status by opposing expansion of the UN Security Council to include the two nations, resisting the legitimization of India's nuclear arsenal, and attempting to block India's participation in pan-Asian regional forums. Such clumsy efforts have only had the effect of driving New Delhi and Tokyo closer together.

This is not to suggest that ties between India and Japan are driven strictly by realist geopolitical considerations. Among the rising powers of Asia, both Japan and India are established democracies while China remains an autocratic state. As a 2006 editorial in Japan's largest daily newspaper argued, 'India is an extremely important partner with which Japan can shape a new international order in East Asia because the two countries share common values of freedom and democracy'.[15] Former Japanese Prime Minister Shinzo Abe had emphasized the importance of institutionalizing liberal values such as human rights, the rule of law, and democracy in Asia. This focus dovetailed nicely with enhanced ties with the world's largest democracy. The notion of relying on shared principles to support strategic dialogue reached a high point in May 2007, when, at a meeting of the ASEAN Regional Forum (ARF), senior leaders from Japan and India joined their counterparts from the USA and Australia for consultations among the 'democratic quad' in Asia.[16] Support for the initiative was short lived, and although the successive Aso Government in Tokyo continued to prioritize values-based diplomacy, the new Labor Government in Australia made it clear in early 2008 that it did not favour a renewal of the dialogue for fear of antagonizing Beijing and 'the quad' fell by the wayside, though bilateral and trilateral links between the four participants continue to strengthen.

On the military level, following an agreement to strengthen co-operation between the two navies, India and Japan conducted reciprocal naval exercises in the Indian Ocean and the Sea of Japan in 2005.[17] The following year, the service chiefs of all three branches of the Japanese Self-Defence Forces made official visits to India, while the Indian Minister of Defence, Pranab Mukherjee, visited Tokyo for consultations with his counterparts, which produced an agreement to promote defence exchanges between the two countries. During Prime Minster Singh's visit to Japan in December 2006, the two countries established a framework to transform their relationship into a strategic partnership that would impact all aspects of interstate ties from trade and investment to defence co-operation.[18] This was followed by a 2008 Joint Declaration on Security Cooperation between Japan and India, which the two nations claim will form an 'essential pillar for the future architecture' of security in Asia.[19] These protocols commit both sides to information exchange and policy co-ordination on regional affairs in the Asia-Pacific region and on long-term strategic and global issues. This marks only the second such security agreement that Japan has entered into and it is only India's third after the USA and Australia. To further co-operation, the Indian Chiefs of Naval Staff and Army Staff visited Japan for conferences with their counterparts in 2008 and 2009, respectively.

The most visible example of Indo-Japanese security ties occurred in mid-April 2007 when the first ever multilateral exercise featuring India, Japan and the USA took place off of Tokyo Bay, featuring four Japanese guided missile destroyers, two American destroyers, and an Indian destroyer, corvette and tanker. A reciprocal exercise, *Malabar 07-2*, also involving Australia and Singapore, was held in the Bay of Bengal in September 2007. Featuring three aircraft carriers, 28 surface vessels, 150 aircraft and over 20,000 personnel, the five-day naval exercise was one of the largest ever held in the region. *Malabar 2009* held in the eastern sea of Okinawa in late April 2009 brought together 10 vessels from the Indian, Japanese and US navies in six days of exercises, marking the second time that the three navies had operated together in the western Pacific.

Commenting on the significance of enhanced Indo-Japanese ties, then-Prime Minster Abe suggested that this would become Japan's 'most important bilateral relationship in the world'.[20] This is a bold pronouncement given the importance of Japan's security alliance with the USA; however, India appears to be putting similar weight on the bilateral relationship. As former Indian external affairs minister Lalit Mansingh has noted, 'if we are forced to choose between China and Japan, my bet will be on Japan'.[21] A number of Japanese and Indian scholars have assessed that the intensifying strategic partnership between Delhi and Tokyo is part of a concerted effort to build an Asian regional order that counters China's increasing power.[22]

147

In the economic realm, Indo-Japanese ties have expanded considerably over the past decade. India looks to Japan as a significant partner for co-operation in the fields of science and technology. Since 2000, Japan has been the seventh largest source of FDI in India. In 2009, for the first time, Japan's investment in India ($5,220m.) exceeded its investment in China ($3,650m.), which signals an expansion of future economic interaction between the two countries. In the logic of comparative advantage, India's abundance of labour and steadily increasing human capital pairs nicely with Japan's capital-intensive but labour-scarce economy. Having been the first recipient of Japanese aid in 1958, India is also the leading recipient of Japanese overseas development aid. For example, Tokyo has supported major infrastructure projects within India, most notably the Delhi to Mumbai industrial corridor, which seeks to create a 1,483-km global manufacturing and transport corridor that spans six states. Since 2007, India and Japan have been undertaking negotiations on an FTA, known as the CEPA, which Prime Minister Singh hopes to have completed for signing by the time of the next annual summit at the end of 2010.

Given this trajectory of Indo-Japanese ties, there was deep apprehension in Delhi over the political earthquake that took place in Tokyo in late August 2009 when the ruling Liberal Democratic Party (LDP) was voted out of office for the first time since the Second World War. The Democratic Party of Japan (DPJ) leader and new Prime Minister, Yukio Hatoyama, had made no secret of his priority of building relations with China and fostering pan-Asian co-operation, which left a large question mark hanging over the future of Indo-Japanese ties—particularly since, in contrast to previous years, the DPJ's election manifesto in 2009 made scant reference to India. Consequently, it was an important sign that Hatoyama was eager to visit Delhi in December 2009 for the annual prime ministerial summit—the only annual prime ministerial-level dialogue Japan has with any country. The 2009 meeting resulted in the announcement of a New Stage of Japan-India Strategic and Global Partnership, which seeks to deepen bilateral co-operation on economic, regional and global issues as well as an action plan to concretely advance the security co-operation agreed to in 2008 in areas such as maritime security disaster management and disarmament.[23] That did much to signify that Hatoyama's 'Asia-centric' vision included India and that Indo-Japanese ties command bipartisan support in Tokyo. With Hatoyama's sudden resignation and replacement by finance minister Naoto Kan, uncertainty has again returned. The relationship is likely to undergo a shift of emphasis, with concerns about China, geopolitical rivalry and shared democratic values being downplayed in favour of economic linkages and deepening co-operation in existing areas.

Despite the great public enthusiasm, there are reasons to be somewhat more circumspect when examining Indo-Japanese ties. Economic engagement between the two countries has failed to keep pace with the development of security ties. Trade between the two nations has been increasing, from $6,540m. in 2005/06, to $7,470m. in 2006/07, $10,190m. in 2007/08, $10,910m. in 2008/09 and $10,360m. in 2009/10. Nevertheless, it remains relatively low, given sizes of economies and markets, with Indo-Japanese trade only one-third the size of Sino-Indian trade and less than one 20th of Sino-Japanese exchange. While India and Japan have established a bilateral trade target of $20,000m. for the end of 2010, Japan's continuing anaemic economic growth could prove a serious obstacle to deeper economic relations between the two nations. From an Indian perspective, there is also a significant imbalance to the trade, with India primarily exporting minerals and raw materials, while importing electronics, pharmaceuticals and heavy machinery. In terms of the relative importance of the export market to each country, Japan is India's 10th largest export destination, while India is only Japan's 26th most important market. Given that implementation of the Comprehensive Nuclear Test Ban Treaty (CTBT) has been a key objective of successive Japanese governments, which do not appear satisfied by India's voluntary moratorium on nuclear testing, nuclear non-proliferation issues are likely to continue to plague Indo-Japanese ties. In the medium term, these issues are more likely to be a minor irritant than a deal breaker. However, it is not clear what Japan's reaction would be if India felt compelled to test nuclear weapons again. Nevertheless, given the negligible diplomatic or security engagement between India and Japan during the many decades of the Cold War, the deepening of Indo-Japanese ties during the past 10 years should be considered an important development.

Taiwan

Having been an early supporter of the People's Republic of China in its bid to join the UN, India's scrupulous adherence to a 'one-China' policy limited diplomatic interaction with Taiwan until the mid-1990s. However, the economic imperatives of forging ties with a top 25 world economy as part of Look East led to the establishment of bilateral ties in 1995 through 'unofficial' consular offices (called 'cultural centres') in New Delhi and Taipei. India's foray into north-east Asia was taking place at the same time that the Taiwanese Government was actively attempting to diversify its international economic linkages away from mainland China, which accounts for more than two-thirds of its overseas investment, and more towards South-East Asia and beyond. As with Japan, interest in closer ties with India is also driven by the upswing in India's relations with the USA, a recognition that the South Asian giant can help ensure that Asia is not dominated by a single nation, and the belief that the democratic character of both governments provides a solid foundation for a future relationship.

Despite active efforts to promote economic, cultural and scientific exchanges, Indian leaders have attempted to avoid any official high-level contact between serving government officials of the two nations. On the other hand, unofficial contacts have been steadily growing. For example, parliamentarian and former defence minister George Fernandes visited Taiwan in 2004, while during a reciprocal visit the same year, former senior officials in the Taiwanese Ministry of Foreign Affairs met with former Prime Minister Gujral and former Deputy Prime Minister Advani. The following year, a group of Taiwanese legislators met with Indian parliamentary counterparts from the *Lok Sabha* in New Delhi. In 2007 then-Kuomintang (KMT) leader and subsequent Taiwanese President Ma Ying-jeou visited New Delhi, where he met with serving Indian government ministers and opposition leaders in an effort to expand scientific and economic co-operation with India. Ma was the first leader of the KMT party to visit India since 1942.

While the Taiwanese Government has been promoting India as an attractive alternative to the mainland for investment, its efforts to expand economic linkages have so far had only modest results. India's trade with Taiwan has been increasing in recent years, from $2,010m. (2005/06), to $2,590m. (2006/07), $4,160m. (2007/08), $4,370m. (2008/09) and $4,500m. (2009/10), but this still made up a fairly modest 0.96% of India's overall trade. Although India accounts for only roughly 1% of Taiwan's imports and exports, it stands as the 15th largest destination for Taiwanese exports as well as the 15th largest importer to Taiwan. India primarily exports minerals, cereals and cotton to Taiwan with mineral fuel oils accounting for slightly less than one-half of its total exports. Imports from Taiwan are primarily diesel fuel, electronic machinery and plastic. Taiwan views India's favourable demographics and technological competence as potential engines of growth, making it potentially a huge market as well as a major investment destination. Apropos of that, in 2007 Taiwan's Council for Economic Planning and Development set a goal of India becoming a top-10 trade partner by 2015. To that end, India and Taiwan have been undertaking talks over the last several years aimed at the establishment of an FTA between the two countries.

149

Australasia and Oceania

India's wider engagement with the Asia-Pacific includes two Commonwealth developed states, Australia and New Zealand, as well as Oceania—the myriad, mostly small Pacific island microstates of the Pacific Basin.

Australia

In looking East, India has also turned its gaze south-eastwards. For much of the 2000s it appeared that Indo-Australian relations had recovered significantly from the diplomatic crisis perpetuated by India's 1998 nuclear tests. A series of annual bilateral talks, begun in 2001, that focused attention on common security interests led to a renewed appreciation of the role that both countries could play in maintaining regional security.[24] As the Indian strategist C. Raja Mohan argued in 2003, Australia possessed untapped potential as an economic and strategic partner for India.[25] For its part, the Australian Government of John Howard recognized the important role that India could play in shaping the security architecture of the wider Asia-Pacific region: 'increasingly, we are looking to our west and observing India's growing political and economic weight and India is looking east seeking to forge stronger links with our region. The indications are that India is set to become one of Australia's most important regional and bilateral partners'.[26] Under Howard, Australia strongly supported India's entry into the ARF and publicly backed India's bid for a seat on the UN Security Council.

Since the election of Kevin Rudd's Labor Party in 2007, Indo-Australian relations have plateaued. A Mandarin-speaking sinophile, Rudd made relations with China the priority of his foreign policy, while his party's strong position on the Nuclear Non-Proliferation Treaty (NPT), lack of support for the US-India-Japan-Australia quadrilateral dialogue, put it at odds with New Delhi on these issues. Diplomatic tensions were exasperated by a series of violent attacks on Indian students in Australia in 2009 and 2010, which provoked widespread outrage in India and overshadowed recent gains in Indo-Australian ties. Following Rudd's surprise ousting as Prime Minister, Indo-Australian relations can only improve. His successor, Julia Gillard, who visited India in 2009 as Deputy Prime Minister, has emphasized the importance of strengthening bilateral relations with India and is unlikely to hold relations with New Delhi hostage to Sino-Australian ties.

In contrast to the political ups and downs of the last several years, steady progress has been made in the economic realm. Bilateral trade grew from \$5,769m. (2005/06), to \$7,920m. (2006/07), \$8,970m. (2007/08), \$12,540m. (2008/09) and \$13,800m. (2009/10), making India Australia's eighth largest trading partner and fastest growing export market. Since 2007 India and Australia have been undertaking a joint feasibility study of the merits of entering into an FTA—the results of which were expected by the end of 2010. With the balance of trade heavily favouring Australia, India imports gold, copper ore and wool, while exporting gemstones and textiles.

In the security realm, bilateral agreements between the two nations have emphasized their 'common interests on a number of important issues, including the Asia-Pacific and Indian Ocean regions'.[27] This recognition of mutual interests led to a series of agreements in 2006 and 2007 on joint naval exercises, enhanced maritime security co-operation, increased military exchanges, and joint training of the two nations' armed forces.[28] The year 2007 also saw the visit of both the Australian defence minister and the Chief of the Australian Defence Force to India. Defence co-operation between the two countries also extends to research and development of military technology, as well as collaboration on counter-terrorism efforts. After postponing twice, Prime Minister Rudd made a visit to India in November 2009, during which the two countries announced a 'strategic partnership'. Notably, India and Australia both also have 'strategic partnerships' in Asia with Japan, South Korea and the USA. The Joint Declaration issued by the two sides pledges co-operation in areas such as maritime security, counter-terrorism and a continued defence dialogue as well as 'policy coordination on regional affairs in the Asia region', which is a diplomatic euphemism for shared concerns over China's growing power.[29]

Nuclear issues are an important aspect of Indo-Australian security ties because Australia has 23% of the world's uranium reserves. Nuclear co-operation received a significant boost when the Government of John Howard decided to follow George W. Bush's Administration's lead in extending de facto recognition of India's nuclear status—which would allow India to purchase uranium from Australia.[30] However, this policy was reversed by the Labor Government, which has repeatedly insisted that India must join the NPT before it could ever buy Australian uranium. The refusal to honour Howard's commitment was viewed as a snub to India which, despite its unwillingness to sign the NPT, actually has an impeccable non-proliferation record—unlike many of the 'legal' nuclear powers. Despite this policy, Australia did support India's efforts to obtain a waiver from the Nuclear Suppliers Group (NSG) that would allow it to purchase uranium elsewhere. Labor leaders have been somewhat coy on this issue, leading some Australian analysts to believe that Australia will eventually supply uranium to India.[31] Despite this uncertainty and the present tensions in the relationship, Indo-Australian security ties remain more robust than either nation's bilateral defence co-operation with China—the ongoing military modernization of which was described by Australia's 2009 Defence White Paper as a potential 'cause for concern'. With enhanced security ties to both Japan and Australia, India has assimilated itself with what Mohan calls the 'northern anchor' and 'southern anchor' of US military presence in Asia.[32]

New Zealand

Although separated by a considerable distance, India and New Zealand can be said to have common roots in their shared historical links to the United Kingdom, parliamentary style of government and democratic character. While New Zealand maintained cordial relations with India for long periods during the Cold War, India-New Zealand ties were significantly harmed by India's 1998 nuclear tests. The High Commissioner of New Zealand was withdrawn in protest and a resolution strongly condemning the tests sailed through parliament with the support of all political parties. In subsequent years, questions about India's nuclear programme and its accession to the NPT and Comprehensive Test Ban Treaty (CTBT) dogged several high-profile visits, including that of then-Minister of External Affairs Jaswant Singh to New Zealand in 2001 and Prime Minister Helen Clark's 2004 visit to India, the first by a New Zealand head of government in nearly two decades.

In more recent years, New Zealand's strong commitment to both the existing structure of nuclear non-proliferation agreements and eventual nuclear abolition has caused tension in its relations with India. At the NSG meetings in 2008, when India and the USA were seeking the blessing of nuclear suppliers for their nuclear deal, New Zealand played an active role in attempting to block the waiver that would allow the selling of nuclear technology to India unless Delhi signed further restrictions. While New Zealand eventually lifted its objections after being personally lobbied by President Bush, Wellington's hard-line, anti-nuclear stance earned it the opprobrium of India's hyperbolic media.[33]

Economic interactions between the two countries are modest with bilateral trade totalling $754m. for 2009/10. India was New Zealand's 13th largest export destination and 24th largest trading partner. India imports coal, wool, wood pulp and machinery, while exporting gem-stones, jewellery and textiles. Despite the relatively small size of the economic relationship, the two countries commenced negotiations on an FTA in February 2010, which, according to New Zealand's High Commissioner to India, 'will be very important for putting a much more dynamic nature into the relationship'.[34]

Although India and New Zealand share interests in cultivating relations with China while remaining close to the USA and ensuring the security of sea lanes in the Indian Ocean, their defence co-operation has been as modest as their economic linkages. As befitting a nation in the Pacific, defence interaction has occurred primarily in the naval realm. In June 2006 the New Zealand frigate *Te Mana* made port calls in Kochi and Mumbai and the New Zealand Chief of Navy agreed with his Indian counterparts to undertake joint exercises. The following month, the frigate INS *Tabar* conducted joint exercises with the New Zealand Royal Navy as Vice-Admiral Sereesh Mehta, the chief of Eastern Naval Command, paid a reciprocal visit to Auckland. In 2007 a pair of New Zealand frigates visited Port Blair in the Andamans after conducting passage exercises with the Indian Navy. The same year, the New Zealand Defence Minister visited Delhi to meet with his counterpart and representatives of the Indian Navy to deepen defence co-operation between the two nations. In February 2010 the New Zealand navy sent observers to the Indian Navy's seventh biennial MILAN exercises in the Andaman Sea, which saw the participation of 10 other regional navies.

Despite this modest history, there may be reasons to be optimistic about Indo-New Zealand ties in the future. The right-of-centre National Party Government that took office in late 2008 appears to both support and welcome India's increased role in the Asia-Pacific—particularly as a balance to China. The Wellington Government recently introduced the Sir Edmund Hillary Prime Ministerial Fellowship for the express purpose of bringing Indian political leaders to New Zealand. The first recipient was the Congress party's General Secretary, Rahul Gandhi, who visited in February 2010. In welcoming Gandhi, New Zealand's Prime Minister was quite forthright in stating that India is a 'priority' relationship for his Government.[35] For its part, India by-passed a career civil servant to appoint Admiral Suresh Mehta, the former head of the Indian Navy and one of the bright lights of the Indian strategic community, as its new High Commissioner to New Zealand. Such developments may indicate the start of a new chapter in Indo-New Zealand relations.

Pacific Basin

India's primary interaction with the small island states of the southern and middle Pacific, Oceania, comes via its dialogue partner status with the Pacific Islands Forum (PIF), which it has held since 2003. The PIF is a regional organization linking the Cook Islands, the Federated States of Micronesia, Fiji, Kiribati, the Marshall Islands, Nauru, Niue, Palau, Papua New Guinea, Samoa, the Solomon Islands, Tonga, Tuvalu and Vanuatu, as well as Australia and New Zealand. India's focus in its engagement with the PIF micro-states is development and human resource capacity-building. Grants-in-aid provided by India fund projects in areas of local priority such as renewable energy, water and waste management, while India's technical expertise assists critical local industries such as coconut production and provides aid to Fiji's sugar industry to help it diversify into biofuels. India also sponsors training courses for regional diplomats and civil servants in practical areas such as public finance management, and has created scholarships for youths from PIF countries to study in India. Excluding Australia and New Zealand, India's economic interaction with the PIF nations is quite small: in 2008 bilateral trade totalled $355m. with them as a whole, with the large majority of that being with Papua New Guinea.

Of particular note are Indo-Fijian ties. India's relations with the most developed of the Pacific island states are heavily coloured by the tensions that exist between ethnic Fijians, who make up approximately 57% of the country's population, and the 37% of the Fijian populace that is of Indian decent—the latter of whom are heavily represented in the educational, professional and entrepreneurial sectors of the economy. Since the late 1980s Fiji has experienced a series of coups that ousted governments led or backed by Indo-Fijians. India's position as a champion of sanctions against these unelected Fijian regimes within the UN and the Commonwealth further harmed diplomatic relations. Ironically, a 2006 coup against a Fijian nationalist government led India to increase its interaction with Fiji, particularly as neighbours Australia and New Zealand downgraded their ties.

Since 2006 India has established a regular dialogue with the Fijian military government and Fiji's interim Prime Minister visited India in an unofficial capacity in 2009. New Delhi has used its engagement with the interim Government to emphasize the need for peace and harmony among Fiji's major communities as well as an early return to democracy in the island nation. India's re-establishment of linkages to Fiji can also be seen in geostrategic terms, particularly since the military Government has turned to China for support after having been expelled from both the Commonwealth and the PIF.

Constraints on India's role in the Asia-Pacific

In considering India's present and future role in East Asia and Australasia/Oceania, it is necessary to also discuss the factors that could constrain India's ability to engage with the region on a more robust basis. By most measures, phase two of the Look East policy must be judged a success. Nevertheless, India still faces a number of challenges in its efforts to project its influence into the Asia-Pacific region. At the grand-strategic level, there are questions about India's ability to articulate and implement a coherent long-term national security strategy, with its political establishment having some difficulty approaching defence and foreign policy issues in a systematic manner. Furthermore, there is not necessarily support for a robust Asia-Pacific role across the political spectrum. After vigorous protests by the Left parties over the multilateral nature of the 2007 *Malabar* exercise, the Indian Government did not include Australia or Japan in the 2008 version in an attempt to appease those parties that had recently withdrawn their support from the country's governing coalition.[36] Although the present Congress-led Government is not reliant on the Left parties, the vagaries of coalition politics in India can never be fully discounted.

A second challenge to Delhi's ability to focus its attention on the Asia-Pacific comes from India's *immediate neighbourhood*, which contains several weak countries that run the risk of becoming 'failed states'. Furthermore, India's tense relationship with its nuclear-armed neighbour, Pakistan, has long been the central concern of Indian foreign and defence policy. Although successive Indian governments have taken active steps to move government attention away from a single-minded focus on this sub-continental rivalry, Islamabad's continued support for terrorism within India and the very real threat of 'state failure' in Pakistan necessarily draw India's attention westward. Similarly, the continued economic and political challenges facing the small, fragile states on India's periphery—such as Bangladesh, Sri Lanka and Nepal—require attention that could otherwise be given to expanding its influence in the Asia-Pacific.

Though not insurmountable, India's political establishment faces a number of obstacles, ranging from domestic politics to regional instability, which could handicap India's ability to expand its economic and political influence in East Asia and Australasia/Oceania.

153

Conclusions

After nearly half a century of 'confinement' to the subcontinent, India is increasingly making its presence felt across East Asia and the Pacific through a forward-leaning foreign policy that marries robust political engagement with the cultivation of enhanced economic ties. Free from the historical animosities that colour many bilateral relationships in the region, New Delhi has the ability to pragmatically engage both great and medium powers in a constructive manner. In pursuing these strategic ties, New Delhi lends its military and economic power to a regional security order that can enhance stability in Asia by presenting any single power with a series of structural constraints that may persuade it that attempts to dominate the region are unlikely to succeed. The eastward focus, which has been a cornerstone of India's foreign policy since the end of the Cold War, is part of a broader effort to assert itself on the world scene. Through its Look East policy and associated military engagement with key regional powers, India has clearly signalled an ambition to play a leading role in the international politics of the broader Asia-Pacific region. Although it will be some time before India's economic and political influence matches the full extent of its regional ambition, it is clear that India is already much more than a state that merely 'interacts with the Asia-Pacific in various ways'.[37]

Notes

1 D. McDougall, *Asia-Pacific in World Politics*, Boulder: Lynne Reinner Publishers, 2007, p.7.
2 For recent discussions see H. Pant, 'India in the Asia-Pacific: Rising Ambitions With an Eye on China', *Asia-Pacific Review*, Vol. 14, No. 1, 2007; D. Scott, 'Strategic Imperatives of India as an Emerging Player in Pacific Asia', *International Studies*, Vol. 44, No. 2, 2007; W. Ladwig, 'New Delhi's Pacific Ambition: Naval Power, "Look East," and India's Emerging Influence in the Asia-Pacific', *Asian Security*, Vol. 5, No. 2, 2009.
3 J. Nehru, *The Discovery of India*, London: Meridian Books, 1956, p.550.
4 A.B. Vajpayee, 'India's Perspective on ASEAN and the Asia Pacific Region', 9 April 2002, meaindia. nic.in.
5 Y. Sinha, 'Resurgent India in Asia', 29 September 2003, www.meaindia.nic.in. Also C. Raja Mohan, 'Look East Policy: Phase Two', *The Hindu*, 9 October 2003.
6 K.N. Singh, 'Inaugural Address at the 7th Asian Security Conference', 27 January 2005, www.idsa.in; E. Ahamed, 'Reinforcing "Look East" Policy', 17 January 2006, mea.gov.in.
7 M. Malik, 'China and the East Asian Summit: More Discord than Accord', *Paper* (Honolulu: Asia-Pacific Center for Security Studies), February 2006. India's observer status with the West Pacific Naval Symposium (WPNS) and RIMPAC naval exercises, its membership of the Pacific Armies Management Seminar, and its attempts to join Asia-Pacific Economic Cooperation (APEC), are other signs of this institutional thrust in the Asia-Pacific.
8 'East Asia Summit: In the Shadow of Sharp Divisions', *People's Daily*, 5 December 2005.
9 Kuppuswamy, 'India's Look East Policy', *Papers* (SAAG), No. 3662, 12 February 2010. A similar point is made in Malik, 'China and the East Asian Summit', op. cit., p.3.
10 R. Sharma, 'India, South Korea Join Hands Against Terrorism', *The Tribune*, 7 October 2004.
11 India-South Korea, *India-Republic of Korea Joint Statement: Towards a Strategic Partnership*, 25 January 2010, meaindia.nic.in. Also 'Why the South Korean President's Visit is Important', *News* (Rediff), 22 January 2010.
12 R. Srinivasan, 'An Indo-Japanese Strategic Alliance', *News* (Rediff), 26 April 2005, in.rediff.com. The term 'alliance' remains sensitive, though, in Indian politics. See also D. Brewster, 'The India-Japan Security Relationship: An Enduring Security Partnership?', *Asian Security*, Vol. 6, No. 2, 2010.
13 Richard J. Samuels, 'New Fighting Power: Japan's Growing Maritime Capabilities and East Asian Security', *International Security*, Vol. 32, No. 3 (Winter 2007/2008), p.111.
14 See the comments of Keizo Takemi, Member of the House of Councillors and Minister in Shinzo Abe's Government: 'when we think about the framework of the Asia-Pacific region as a whole, we see that India is a geopolitically essential presence [...] Japan and India are alike in having a certain wariness of China. From the viewpoint of maintaining a balance in the region as a whole, this also leads to

thinking about a new mechanism of security cooperation', in 'Japan's Role in an Asian Community', *Annual Report*, Tokyo: Sasakawa Peace Foundation, 2003, pp.25–26.

15 'Japan-India Partnership Vital in East Asia', *Yomiuri Shimbun* (Tokyo), 15 December 2006.

16 Interestingly, it was reported that Delhi was initially 'lukewarm about the quad until Beijing began lobbying against it, leading India to sign on enthusiastically', D. Twining, 'Playing the America Card', *The Weekly Standard*, Vol. 13, No. 3, 1 October 2007.

17 P. Gupta, 'Looking East: India Forges Closer Ties with Japan', *Force*, Vol. 3, No. 3, 2005.

18 L. Mansingh, 'India-Japan Relations', *Issue Brief* (ICPS), No. 43, January 2007.

19 India-Japan, *Joint Declaration on Security Cooperation between Japan and India*, 22 October 2008, www.mofa.go.jp.

20 Cited in S.D. Naik, 'India-Japan Ties–Moving to the Next Level', *The Hindu Business Line*, 2 January 2007.

21 Mansingh, 'India-Japan Relations', op. cit.

22 G. Nishiyama, 'Japan PM Visits India, Eying Trade and China', *Reuters*, 21 August 2007; R. Sharma, 'India-Japan Ties Poised for Advance as Both Nations Eye China', *The Asia-Pacific Journal*, 6 September 2010.

23 India-Japan, 'New Stage of Japan-India Strategic and Global Partnership', 29 December 2009, www.mofa.go.jp. Also India-Japan, 'Action Plan to Advance Security Cooperation Based on the Joint Declaration on Security Cooperation between Japan and India', 12 December 2009, meaindia.nic.in.

24 A. Bergin, 'Benefits for Both Sides in Close Ties with India', *The Australian*, 22 August 2001.

25 Raja Mohan, 'Look East Policy: Phase Two', op. cit.

26 J. Howard, 'Australia's Engagement with Asia—A New Paradigm?', 13 August 2004, www.asialink.unimelb.edu.au.

27 'India-Australia Strategic Dialogue', Australian High Commission (New Delhi), 30 August 2001, www.india.embassy.gov.au.

28 'Australia Inks First Defence Pact With India', *Report* (India Defense), No. 1452, 7 March 2006, www.india-defense.com; M. Dodd, 'India Defence Ties to be Tightened', *The Australian*, 4 June 2007.

29 India-Australia, 'India-Australia Joint Declaration on Security Cooperation', 12 November 2009, meaindia.nic.in. For analysis see B. Chellaney, 'New Australia-India Security Accord: Asia's New Strategic Partners', *Japan Times*, 10 December 2009; D. Brewster, 'The Australia–India Security Declaration: The Quadrilateral Redux?', *Security Challenges*, Vol. 6, No. 1, 2010.

30 K. Kapisthalam, 'Australia and Asia's Rise', *Australian Journal of International Affairs*, Vol. 60, No. 3, 2006, p.371.

31 J. Malhotra, 'Australia Evolving its Position on Uranium Sales to India?', *Business Standard*, 23 March 2010.

32 C. Raja Mohan, 'The Asian Balance of Power', *Seminar*, No. 487, March 2000, www.india-seminar.com.

33 For example, S. Guha, '3 Nations Hold Out at NSG, India Faces Delay', *DNA* (Mumbai), 22 August 2008.

34 R. Holborow cited in N. Lakshman, 'India, New Zealand Plan to Begin Free Trade Pact Talks Next Year', *The Hindu*, 11 December 2009.

35 'India is a Priority, New Zealand PM Tells Rahul Gandhi', *Indo-Asian News Service*, 16 February 2010.

36 'Antony Nixes Expansion of India-US Malabar Naval Exercise', *Indo-Asian News Service*, 24 September 2008.

37 McDougall, *Asia-Pacific in World Politics*, op. cit., p.7.

14

Looking south: Indian Ocean

James R. Holmes

Introduction

As Indians gaze southward, they see the vastness of the Indian Ocean, an expanse criss-crossed by vital Sea Lines of Communication (SLOCs) and teeming with traditional and non-traditional challenges. Indians appear conflicted about the sea. India was an inward-looking, decidedly terrestrial civilization for many centuries. Indeed, during the age of Hindu rule, Indian kings made a conscious choice to withdraw from the sea. They forbade oceanic voyages in the 14th century, ostensibly to prevent an outflow of mathematicians and philosophers to Baghdad, the intellectual centre of south-west Asia. The subcontinent ultimately fell under the rule of Central Asian nomads who imprinted their land-bound habits of mind on Indian traditions and culture, reinforcing Indians' indifference to maritime matters.

Yet India clung to its national independence for many centuries, despite repeated land invasions. It co-opted and absorbed its conquerors. Not so with seaborne invaders. Portuguese mariner Vasco da Gama dropped anchor along the Indian coast at the end of the 15th century. Starting with da Gama, European seafarers progressively deprived India of control of the high seas in the Indian Ocean. At last, during the age of British rule, India lost its independence altogether. Defeat concentrates the mind. Accordingly, India bestirred itself following independence from Great Britain, launching into a fitful but determined effort to build a 'blue-water' navy, by definition aimed at operating in the far, deeper reaches of the Indian Ocean.[1] On a visceral level, then, Indians accept the importance of managing their maritime environs, but with little seagoing past to draw on, they have little vocabulary of their own to guide this unfamiliar project.

To compound the difficulties they face, events are unfolding in the Indian Ocean with dizzying velocity. Neighbouring China—another traditional land power rising to eminence and casting its gaze seaward—has set out to build a formidable fleet of its own. To fuel economic development, Beijing is eyeing the security of SLOCs traversing the Indian Ocean, which convey oil, gas and other raw materials to users in north-east Asia. For its part, the US Navy, which has underwritten maritime security in Asia since 1945, may be entering an age of 'elegant decline', to borrow from *Atlantic Monthly* columnist Robert Kaplan. The US sea services have rededicated themselves to primacy in maritime Asia, but the stark reality of economic stagnation and skyrocketing procurement costs has cast doubt on whether Washington can still sustain a preponderant fleet—and thus its role as the self-appointed custodian of security in the world's oceans.

In this time of transition, the pace of change swiftly renders any snapshot of Indian maritime strategy and forces moot. Rather, this chapter seeks to erect an analytical framework that helps students of Indian maritime strategy ask the right questions about the right things. One helpful framework is the indices of *sea power* set forth by Imperial German Vice-Admiral Wolfgang Wegener. Vice-Admiral Wegener was Imperial Germany's most gifted naval thinker. A seagoing officer, he offered an acid critique of the naval command's handling of strategy and operations during the First World War. Sea power, said Wegener, is a product of 'strategic position' (a geographical factor), the fleet (a tactical factor), and the nation's 'strategic will' to the sea (an ideational cultural factor), which 'breathes life into the fleet' and concentrates political and naval leaders' energies on bettering the nation's strategic position.[2] Wegener's *Naval Strategy of the World War* now ranks among the classics of sea power. His algorithm offers a useful way to analyse Indian maritime prospects as it looks south. A seagoing India will do the things Imperial Germany neglected to do, leveraging its unique geography, nurturing strategic will to the sea among key constituencies, husbanding its resources, and constructing a fleet to support New Delhi's strategic goals. Also incorporated in this chapter are insights from the works of sea-power theorist Alfred Thayer Mahan, who identified six determinants of would-be maritime nations' fortunes on the high seas, namely a) geographical position; b) physical conformation; c) extent of territory; d) number of population; e) national character; and f) policy and nature of government institutions.[3]

Assessing 21st-century India through the prisms of long-dead thinkers like Wegener and Mahan might appear quixotic, but it is eminently fitting. The reconfiguration of power in Asia today represents a historical anomaly, with India and China—two venerable land powers that share a common frontier and a past marked by enmity—concurrently crafting 'blue water' navies and strategies for using them. Not only do Wegener and Mahan furnish durable insights, but the *fin de siècle* era they inhabited represents the closest parallel to today. Then, as now, the system was in transition. New sea powers like the USA, Imperial Germany and Imperial Japan were ascending to Great Powerdom, within a system superintended by a 'weary titan', Britain and its Royal Navy. Whether and how Britain would manage potential challengers was the central question. Its performance was uneven at best. Whether the USA can do better in coaxing rising powers like India into a durable international order remains to be seen.

In the light of Wegener and Mahan, this chapter examines three main questions:

- *India's strategic position.* Geographic features impose bounds on maritime strategy, but strategic geography is nevertheless an intensely interactive field of endeavour. Past sea powers have sought not only to safeguard their shores but to find outposts overseas, providing additional strategic depth and supporting merchant and naval shipping. Whether India can exploit and improve its strategic position bears investigating.
- *Indian 'strategic will' to the sea.* Strategic will among the government, the populace and the armed forces constitutes both the enabler for, and the measure of, any nation's seaward enterprise. Seagoing peoples constantly strive to improve the nation's strategic position and the fleet that supports it. Consequently, gauging Indian resolve represents a critical step toward discerning how New Delhi will seek to manage India's aquatic surroundings.
- *The Indian navy fleet.* Rather than attempt a detailed net assessment of the Indian Navy, a force that finds itself in perpetual flux, the chapter briefly reviews New Delhi's progress

toward buying or building the ships and weaponry that comprise a 'blue water' navy, as well as procurement practices and the outlook for the indigenous defence-industrial base. A general overview will help India-watchers track the navy's progress and project future developments.

Strategic position

C. Raja Mohan offers a useful device to structure this survey of Indian Ocean geography, bearing in mind that strategic geography involves, to quote Prussian military theorist Carl von Clausewitz, a dynamic and innately interactive collision of 'living forces'.[4] Raja Mohan declares that 'India's grand strategy divides the world into three concentric circles', rippling out from the subcontinent. The first encompasses India's immediate environs, the second continental Asia and the Indian Ocean basin, and the third the entire globe.[5] We can set aside the third circle, to keep this analysis oriented toward how Indians look southward—toward the sea. How New Delhi might bolster its position in its Indian Ocean *extended neighbourhood* is the question.

The 'inner circle'

First, consider the inner circle, the Indian subcontinent and its immediate surroundings. India has to cope with challenges both on land and at sea. Like other land powers looking seaward, India finds itself pulled in different directions by continental and maritime interests. Mahan noted that land powers must guard against contiguous neighbours. The rigours of land defence siphon off resources that otherwise might go into industrial production, maritime industries, the merchant marine and the navy—Mahan's 'pillars' of sea power. For this reason, concluded the sea-power theorist, continental nations find it exceedingly difficult to make themselves into great sea powers. This would seem to rule out sea power for India, flanked as it is by neighbouring Great Power China and perennial antagonist Pakistan.

Furthermore, nations endowed with ample resources tended to look inward—further distracting attention from nautical pursuits. From a geographic standpoint, India ranks somewhere between the Kaiser's Germany, for which geography was a curse, and the USA, for which it was a blessing. Lord George Curzon, the last British viceroy of India, ranked the sea as the most daunting of all natural frontiers. The subcontinent is, in effect, an enormous peninsula jutting out into the Indian Ocean. It enjoys easy access to the sea lanes from its lengthy coastlines, although it lacks the plentiful bays, harbours and inland waterways that helped make the USA a maritime nation with which to be reckoned. Curzon ranked mountains the third most imposing feature, behind deserts. 'Backed as they are by the huge and lofty plateau of Tibet', however, 'the Himalayas are beyond doubt the most formidable natural Frontier in the world.'[6] India's setting clearly is not as favourable as the USA's, but mountain ranges and the sea represent a considerable barrier against maritime and overland threats.

Geography, then, mitigates the multiple demands of land and sea defence of which Mahan wrote, granting New Delhi considerable liberty of action on the high seas. Indeed, as George Tanham observes, Indians regard the subcontinent as a strategic unit bounded by the Hindu Kush, the Himalayas and the Indian Ocean.[7] This way of thinking persists even though air power and ballistic missiles have abridged the value of even the most imposing natural defences. India must maintain powerful land and air forces to hedge against China, keep Pakistan in check, and tend to internal security. Even so, New Delhi can turn its attention to the sea without undue fear of forfeiting its security on land.

The 'middle circle'

Next, consider how India surveys the Indian Ocean basin. This is where the Indians' maritime destiny will play out for the foreseeable future, barring unforeseen circumstances—say, a plunge in US maritime power coupled with a militant China—that compel New Delhi to project influence beyond the region. Choke points, islands and naval bases preoccupy Indian strategists gazing around the Indian Ocean region.

K.M. Panikkar, post-independence India's leading geopolitical thinker and the so-called Grandfather of the Indian Navy, credited a still older lineage from the Portuguese nobleman Dom Alfonso de Albuquerque and Albuquerque's strategy for using naval power to control the Indian Ocean. In turn, Panikkar waxed strongly about India's role, for example: a) 'to the Indian ocean, then we shall have to run as our ancestors did'; b) 'Indian interests have extended to the different sides of this Oceanic area [...] Her interests in the Indian Ocean, based as they are on the inescapable facts of geography, have become more important than ever before'; c) 'the future of India will undoubtedly be decided on the sea'; d) 'the waters vital to India's security and prosperity can be protected [...] with the islands of the Bay of Bengal with Singapore, Mauritius and Socotra, properly quipped and protected and with a navy based on Ceylon security can return to that part of the Indian Ocean which is of supreme importance to India'; e) 'unless, therefore, distant bases like Singapore, Mauritius, Aden and Socotra are firmly held and the naval air arm developed in order to afford sufficient protection to these posts, there will be no security or safety for India'; and f) 'the primary responsibility lying on the Indian Navy to guard the steel ring created by Singapore, Ceylon, Mauritius and Socotra'.[8]

Albuquerque's vision remains influential among Indian thinkers and practitioners, from Panikkar down to the present. India's 2007 Maritime Military Strategy document, New Delhi's most authoritative public statement of how it sees the nautical milieu and intends to respond to it, observed:

> Portuguese Governor Alfonso Albuquerque had in early 16th century opined that control of the key choke points extending from the Horn of Africa to the Cape of Good Hope and the Malacca Strait was essential to prevent an inimical power from making an entry into the Indian Ocean. Even today, whatever happens in the IOR [Indian Ocean Region] can affect our national security and is of interest to us.[9]

Taking its cue from Albuquerque, New Delhi is acutely conscious of choke points: narrow seas like the Straits of Malacca, Lombok, Sunda, Hormuz and Bab el-Mandeb, through which shipping enters and exits the Indian Ocean. Notes the 2004 Indian Maritime Doctrine, 'India sits astride [...] major commercial routes and energy lifelines', criss-crossing the Indian Ocean region.

New Delhi can radiate influence toward some of these narrow seas with ease. Outlying Indian possessions like the Andaman and Nicobar islands sit athwart the approaches to the Strait of Malacca. The Arabian/Persian Gulf lies not far from India's western coastline, conferring influence over sea traffic with what amounts to a bay or inlet in the Indian Ocean. Officialdom acknowledges the importance of such features and connects geography with sea power, exercised either by the Indian Navy fleet or by shore-based forces operating along the subcontinent's west coast. Geography may not be fate, but the 2004 Indian Maritime Doctrine states bluntly that Indians are 'in a position to greatly influence the movement/security of shipping along the SLOCs in the IOR provided we have the maritime power to do so. Control of the choke points could be useful as a *bargaining chip in the international power game, where the currency of military power remains a stark reality*' [my emphasis].[10]

If India benefits from forward bases, Indian thinkers worry that competitors like China will establish naval bases of their own. The notion that China is fashioning a 'string of pearls'—a Mahanian base network—is now a matter of conviction for many Indian strategists.[11] Such a network would lay the groundwork for the first Chinese naval presence in the region since the Ming Dynasty six centuries ago. Indeed, Beijing has inked a series of agreements with nations around the Indian Ocean littoral to develop port facilities that could act as staging bases for Chinese warships. Gwadar, in western Pakistan along the approaches to the Strait of Hormuz, has occasioned the most debate in Indian strategic circles—despite its exposed position, scant resources, and dubious prospects for defence against sea-launched air or missile strikes in wartime.[12]

It bears noting that Chinese commentators do not themselves talk in terms of a string of pearls; the phrase actually was coined in a Booz Allen report drawn up for the US Department of Defense in 2005, titled, appropriately enough, *Energy Futures in Asia*. It was probably inspired by an Indian participant in the Booz Allen workshop, before being popularized by Bill Gertz, a reporter for the *Washington Times*.[13] In turn, New Delhi leapt at it, interpreting Chinese basing rights as signs of incipient *encirclement*, its strategic nightmare. Many Indians see the modest Chinese naval deployment off Somalia in 2009 as the first step onto a slippery slope to a full-blown Chinese presence along the 'string of pearls'. Sober-minded Indian analysts now trace a 'rivalry arc' enclosing maritime Asia.[14] It none the less remains to be seen whether China's bid for Indian Ocean bases is part of a concerted strategy or simple opportunism.

How India appraises opportunities and challenges in the second geographic circle warrants close monitoring. Leading indicators of Indian maritime strategy include the importance affixed to geographic features like Gwadar, Sri Lanka, the Maldives and the Seychelles. India has shaped wider-ranging defence agreements, and frequent naval deployments (its strategic 'footprint') further south to the Maldives, Seychelles, Mauritius, Mozambique and South Africa.[15] Evidence of alarm over Chinese advances in the Indian Ocean could presage a more assertive, more heavily armed Indian approach to regional affairs—engaging strategic will and inducing New Delhi to accelerate its naval development. If Indians look with equanimity on the Chinese presence, this will betoken increasing confidence in the nation's capacity to manage the oceanic setting.

'Strategic will' to the sea

Geography, then, provides the setting within which regional dynamics will play out. However, as Clausewitz teaches, competitive human endeavours involve an interactive clash of wills manifest at times in dark passions like rage, spite and fear. Mahan, too, concentrated on the human dimension, pronouncing 'national character' and the 'character of the government' as two critical determinants of a nation's suitability for sea power.[16] For Wegener, a nation's strategic will to the sea represented the enabler for its quest for strategic position. Friedrich Nietzsche's writings on the will to power, which were part of the zeitgeist in *fin de siècle* Germany, evidently inspired the term.

This calculus is, in part, a function of *strategic culture*—the history, traditions and habits of mind that shape how a society pursues the goals it deems worth pursuing, within the bounds set by geography. Memories of British rule and the sea power that upheld it run deep among Indians. This is part of the British bequest to contemporary India. Recalls Panikkar, 'Great Britain sailed the seas of the Indian Ocean as an absolute mistress' on the eve of the First World War, despite challenges from Germany, Japan and the USA; 'her power was overwhelming at every point, and no nation or combination of nations could have contested her authority in the slightest degree'.[17] Fortifying Singapore, at the junction between the Indian Ocean and the South China Sea, only reinforced British control of maritime traffic.

The Second World War left Indians even more acutely aware of their nation-state's vulnerability to seaborne perils. Starting in early 1942, Imperial Japan besieged and overran Singapore from the landward side, destroyed Royal Navy units at Trincomalee, on Ceylon, and thus forced entry into South Asian waters. Worse still, the British Commander-in-Chief confessed that he could do nothing to keep the Imperial Japanese Navy from landing anywhere it wanted along the Indian coastline. Japanese submarine operations in the Arabian Sea exacted a heavy toll on merchant shipping, showing how exposed the Indian subcontinent was and remains to undersea warfare. This may help explain the vehemence with which Indian naval officials today reject any Chinese move to forward-deploy nuclear submarines to the region.[18]

In short, the Second World War shattered illusions about the Indian Ocean's protected status, thrusting naval strategy wholesale into questions of Indian foreign policy. 'A true appreciation of Indian historical forces', concluded Panikkar in 1945, 'will show beyond doubt, that whoever controls the Indian Ocean has India at his mercy', owing to India's lack of other outlets to the sea and its dependence on sea trade for commercial and economic vitality—the top priority for any government.[19]

Another strand in Indian strategic culture suggests that New Delhi will exhibit the same stubborn resolve that drove Great Britain. Indian sea power specialists strike a prickly attitude toward real or perceived encroachment in the Indian Ocean region. They look to the 19th-century USA as one model for how a non-aligned Great Power can manage its geographic surroundings to fend off external threats. In particular, they look to the Monroe Doctrine, the 1823 foreign policy statement that proclaimed the Western Hemisphere off-limits to European territorial expansion or a restoration of European political control over US republics that had won independence from the imperial powers. In practical terms, an Indian Monroe Doctrine would erect a joint defence of South Asia against Great Power encroachment from without, much as the USA saw its Monroe Doctrine as a joint defence of North and South America against predatory European empires.

While they will not try to implement it mechanically, any more than the USA did, Indians regard the Monroe Doctrine as one paradigm for foreign policy and strategy.[20] Think back to founding Prime Minister Jawaharlal Nehru's 1961 speech justifying the use of force to evict Portugal from Goa:

> Even some time after the United States had established itself as a strong power, there was the fear of interference by European powers in the American continents, and this led to the famous declaration by President Monroe of the United States [that] any interference by a European country would be an interference with the American political system. I submit that [...] the Portuguese retention of Goa is a continuing interference with the political system established in India today. I shall go a step further and say that any interference by any other power would also be an interference with the political system of India today [...] It may be that we are weak and we cannot prevent that interference. But the fact is that *any attempt by a foreign power to interfere in any way with India is a thing which India cannot tolerate, and which, subject to her strength, she will oppose. That is the broad doctrine I lay down* [my emphasis].[21]

Nehru's statement is extraordinarily rich, implying considerable determination on New Delhi's part to make itself South Asia's preponderant maritime power. Several themes are worth stressing:

- First, while a European presence on the Indian landmass was the prime mover for his doctrine, Nehru took the opportunity to warn *any* external power against taking *any* action, anywhere in the region, that New Delhi might construe as a threat to the Indian political system. His injunction against outside interference laid the intellectual groundwork for a policy aimed at regional primacy. Indeed, his 'broad doctrine' represented a more sweeping ban on external meddling than the doctrine framed by James Monroe and John Quincy Adams, who made no attempt to disturb existing European holdings in the hemisphere and did not proscribe European interference unless it reinstated European political control.
- Second, notwithstanding the wide scope of his principles, Nehru acknowledged realities of power and geography. Like Monroe's USA, Nehru's India remained weak by most measures. Even so, the Prime Minister wanted New Delhi to enjoy the discretion to implement his doctrine with greater vigour when Indian national power grew—opening up new political vistas and supplying Indian leaders with new instruments of statecraft.
- Third, while expelling the Portuguese presence from the subcontinent was his immediate concern, Nehru implied that India could enforce his precepts beyond the subcontinent. It was up to future prime ministers to decide how far beyond. Prime Ministers Indira and Rajiv Gandhi did just that, invoking his doctrine to justify diplomatic or military intervention in such places as Sri Lanka, Nepal and the Maldives. C. Raja Mohan matter-of-factly states that the Monroe Doctrine is part of Indian Grand Strategy: the 'Indian variation of the Monroe Doctrine, involving spheres of influence, has not been entirely successful in the past, but it has been *an article of faith* for many in the Indian strategic community' [my emphasis].[22]
- Fourth, Nehru asked no one's to articulate a hands-off doctrine. His doctrine—like the Monroe Doctrine before it—was not international law, which derives its force from the consent of states. Instead it was a unilateral statement of purpose to which New Delhi would give effect as national interests demanded and as national power permitted. India drove the Portuguese from Goa, affixing an exclamation point to Nehru's words.

Over time, if the US case is any indication, fellow Indian Ocean powers may silently acquiesce in India's Monroe Doctrine, lending it a kind of quasi-legal standing, or at least an air of permanence. However, their acquiescence will depend on whether New Delhi can replicate the US example, fortifying its comprehensive national power and thus its capacity to make good on its claim to regional leadership. A weak India would stand little chance of fulfilling Nehru's vision of a beneficent Great Power. Should Indians ultimately align their strategic aspirations with sufficient maritime capabilities, however, then their interactions with other sea powers could very well assume a bellicose character.

A competitive nautical environment is especially likely if extra-regional powers refuse to acquiesce in Indian ambitions, or if New Delhi's presumptions about its dominant place in the Indian Ocean predispose Indians to cast the intentions of other interested actors in the dimmest possible light. Combining worst-case thinking with strategic will to the sea and a strong navy could leave New Delhi intent on becoming a regional strongman like Grover Cleveland's USA, or a regional cop like Theodore Roosevelt's USA. Tracking how New Delhi assesses its prerogatives, threats and opportunities in the subcontinent's environs, and the capacity of partners like the US Navy will let India-watchers glimpse the future of Indian policy and strategy at sea.

The fleet

A critical mass of elite thinkers and officials seems set on developing sea power, and they appear determined to manage events in the Indian Ocean basin, reinforcing and improving the nation's strategic position in that part of their *extended neighbourhood*. Wolfgang Wegener would salute their élan. However, political resolve is not everything. Hardware does matter. Whether the Indian Navy, indigenous maritime industries and foreign suppliers can supply the wherewithal for a great navy remains to be determined. Consequently, it bears asking: Does India possess adequate reserves of human capital to support its seaward enterprise? Additionally, how readily can the necessary skills and infrastructure be manufactured where they do not already exist?

Mahan offers help with these questions. No matter how steadfast a society's desire to take to the sea, it needs a corps of mariners, shipwrights and other technical experts. Mahan observed that Great Britain, his model for sea power, boasted an advantage in 'staying power' on the high seas. Seamanship was critical, but it was 'various handicrafts which facilitate the making and repairing of naval material' that represented the foundation for a vibrant fleet, along with 'kindred callings' that 'give an undoubted aptitude for the sea from the outset'.[23] India is determinedly striving to create its own defence-industrial base. The Indian Navy formally embraces this concept, stating in its *Maritime Military Strategy* that it will 'remain committed to the concept of self-reliance and indigenization'.[24] Having been denied military-relevant technology during the era of British rule and subsequently during the Cold War, New Delhi would ideally like to meet all of its defence needs through domestic production. Plans in 2010 for India to induct 32 new ships into its Navy over the next decade envisaged three being built in Russia, two in Italy, and the remaining 27 in India. The Indian Government insists on technology-transfer clauses in many foreign defence contracts, and it often demands licensed production in India. This is the only way to hedge against cut-offs of arms transfers in times of crisis or war.

The twin goals of indigenization policy are autonomy for Indian foreign and security policy and technological progress for the defence sector. New Delhi is loath to see its liberty of action abridged through dependence on foreign suppliers, either for arms, or for parts, spares and service for items it has already purchased. At times this goal clashes with India's desire to expedite military modernization. Some foreign governments, particularly the US Government, restrict transfers of high technology. While Washington may be willing to sell a particular item, it commonly balks at releasing production technology or revealing sensitive technologies like source codes used to manufacture an item.

If New Delhi in turn refuses to purchase such items, it may deny itself the most advanced capability on the market, hampering its efforts to achieve military primacy in the Indian Ocean region. The Indian Navy and its civilian masters factor in such considerations while pursuing the nation's maritime ambitions. Fortunately from their vantage point, the security environment remains fairly hospitable, allowing them to take a leisurely approach to modernization. This element of Indian maritime strategy bears watching as an indicator of future developments.

The Indian Navy, like its sister services, has suffered from resource shortfalls since independence. The Government allocated new resources to the armed services following the disastrous 1962 border war with China. At the same time, the Government began to conduct systematic defence planning—to an extent. Five-year defence plans were drawn up for each of the armed services. Until 1997, however, every such plan was deferred or restructured before it was completed, owing largely to resource constraints. In 1964 a base force for the Indian Navy was established, with a force goal of 54 principal combatant vessels. The navy has never reached this goal, again because of resource shortfalls.[25]

The reasons for this strategy-policy mismatch are three. First, as Rahul Roy-Chaudhury documents, five-year plans were little more than wish lists compiled by the services, divorced from broader security goals. Second, the framers of these plans paid little heed to resource limitations. Even if the services' plans had been realistic, the shortfalls and crises bedevilling the

Indian economy throughout the 1960s, 1970s and 1980s would have rendered them inert. Third, the Indian Navy has traditionally been the 'Cinderella Service', as Admiral Arun Prakash put it ruefully.[26] New Delhi has regarded overland threats—China and Pakistan—as the primary threats to the subcontinent. Funding shortfalls have been the fleet's lot.[27] The Army and Air Force have routinely received more than double the budget share allotted to the Navy. Occasional budget increases rarely lasted long enough for the Navy to reach its goals in terms of numbers, types and sophistication of its platforms.[28]

Currently, the Indian Navy ranks fifth in size among world fleets, well ahead of Pakistan but shy of China. The fleet is founded on an assortment of patrol and coastal craft and combat-logistics ships alongside principal surface combatants, submarines, mine-warfare vessels and amphibious ships. Some units have exceeded their service lives and will see limited duty until they are replaced. In the long term, force-structure plans do call for increasing the fleet to over 160 ships by the year 2022, including three aircraft carriers, 60 major combatants, and close to 400 aircraft.[29] This should boost India to fourth or third among world navies. In the interim, though, the Indian Navy may actually shrink in the short term as older vessels are retired while replacements are built or purchased—incurring the delays typical of new combat systems.

Numbers of major platforms represent neither the sole nor necessarily even the best measure of combat power, but they do supply a way to approximate India's current and desired maritime capabilities. New Delhi makes no bones about its plans for a 'blue water' fleet centred on aircraft carriers. The Indian Navy's attempt to procure or build carriers and their escorts offers a representative sample of the opportunities and obstacles it confronts in surface, subsurface and aerial warfare. Accordingly, I use this as a proxy for the overall fleet-building effort.

A three-carrier fleet is the Indian leadership's goal. Factoring in refits and workups, this ensures that one-to-two vessels will be combat-ready at any time. In 2010 the Navy's one flat-top was the 1950s-vintage *Viraat* (ex-HMS *Hermes*). The Navy inked a deal with Russia in 2004 to buy the decommissioned Russian Navy carrier *Admiral Gorshkov*.[30] Renamed *Vikramaditya*, this 45,000-ton ship will carry 16 MiG-29K multirole aircraft and a mix of six Kamov-28 and -31 helicopters. The second carrier, known as the Indigenous Aircraft Carrier, will be a modest 37,000-ton ship. It will join the fleet in around 2015. It is designed as a STOBAR (short-takeoff, barrier-arrested recovery) ship and will carry 12 MiG-29Ks. The third carrier, another Indian-built unit, will displace 64,000 tons. It will be outfitted with steam catapults, a technology currently found only in the US Navy. It is slated for delivery in 2017.

Delays and technical setbacks have beset the carrier programme, however. The Russian Government doubled the price of the *Gorshkov/Vikramaditya* after discovering that the ship needed more work than originally thought, with delivery rescheduled from 2008 to the end of 2012. India was compelled to overhaul the *Viraat*, extending its service life to maintain a single-carrier fleet. The big-deck indigenous carrier will doubtless encounter delays of its own as Indian companies master the intricacies of building very large ships. Developing or importing catapults promises to be an especially thorny challenge.

The remainder of India's 'blue water' surface fleet consists of an assortment of destroyers, frigates and corvettes. The fleet is evolving beyond Soviet-built vessels from the 1970s and 1980s. Stealthy ships co-designed by Russian and Indian shipbuilders and constructed at Indian yards make up a growing proportion of the force. Ships designed and built entirely in India are starting to appear. New Delhi has also taken to issuing requests for information to Western shipbuilding companies, indicating its willingness to incorporate Western hulls into its fleet. The systems and armaments installed in Indian warships represent a mix of indigenous Indian designs, Russian designs tailored to Indian needs, and Western designs.

Integrating unlike hardware manufactured in different countries is a stubborn challenge that will not abate any time soon. Fleet composition will become increasingly modern over time as, for instance, 1980s-era *Rajput*-class destroyers (a modified Soviet *Kashin* design) undergo replacement by Project 15A *Kolkata*-class destroyers. The *Kolkata*s feature stealth characteristics, reducing their radar cross-section to elude detection. Their combat-systems suite will emphasize land attack. Similarly, India plans to construct 12 *Project 28* corvettes that specialize in anti-submarine warfare. Newer surface combatants feature significant upgrades in stealth, computers and communications, and offensive punch. Many are being fitted with lethal, extended-range cruise missiles like the supersonic Brahmos. The surface fleet—like the rest of the Indian Navy—will be a force with which to be reckoned in coming years, in and across the Indian Ocean.

Conclusions

Indian sea power remains a work in progress. Geography has blessed the subcontinent with impressive natural defences, a central position in the Indian Ocean, adjoining important SLOCs, and the capacity to assert a measure of control over the narrow seas by which seagoing traffic enters and exits the Indian Ocean. While a critical mass of Indian officialdom and the political elite appears intent on building up sea power to let New Delhi assume its role as the preponderant power in the Indian Ocean region, the tendency to look inward—as Mahan feared the USA would—still persists. A host of questions about the Indian Navy persist, surrounding not only hardware, but strategy and doctrine, tactical and operational proficiency, and seamanship. To gaze through a glass darkly, it behoves us watch these determinants of India's capacity to transact business in the great waters of the Indian Ocean, which some Indian naval advocates see as indeed 'India's Ocean'.[31]

Notes

1 D. Scott, 'India's Drive for a "Blue Water" Navy', *Journal of Military and Strategic Studies*, Vol. 10, No. 2, 2008.
2 W. Wegener, *The Naval Strategy of the World War* (1929), rep. Annapolis: Naval Institute Press, 1989, pp.xxvii, 96–100.
3 A. Mahan, *The Influence of Sea Power Upon History* (1890), rep. Gretna: Pelican, 2003, pp.28–29.
4 C. von Clausewitz, *On War*, in M. Howard and P. Paret (ed. and trans.), Princeton: Princeton University Press, 1976, pp.75, 77.
5 C. Raja Mohan, 'India and the Balance of Power', *Foreign Affairs*, Vol. 85, No. 4, 2006, p.18.
6 G. Curzon, *Frontiers*, 2nd edn, Oxford: Clarendon, 1908, p.18.
7 G. Tanham, *Indian Strategic Thought: An Interpretive Essay*, Santa Monica: RAND, 1992, p.v.
8 K. Panikkar, *India and the Indian Ocean. An Essay on the Influence of Sea Power on Indian History*, London: George Allen & Unwin, 1945, pp. (in order of quotations) 84, 16, 84/94, 16, 15, 90–91 and 95. His title deliberately echoes Mahan's earlier *The Influence of Sea Power on History*. Panikkar also cautioned against the naval policy of a resurgent China. All of these considerations re-emerge for current Indian naval strategy. Similar sentiments and geopolitical speculations in K. Vaidya, *The Naval Defence of India*, Bombay: Thacker, 1949.
9 Indian Navy, *Freedom to Use the Seas: India's Maritime Military Strategy*, New Delhi: Ministry of Defence, May 2007, p.59.
10 Indian Navy, *Indian Maritime Doctrine*, New Delhi: Ministry of Defence, 2004, p.64.
11 G. Khurana, 'China's String of Pearls in the Indian Ocean and its Security Implications', *Strategic Analysis*, Vol. 32, No. 1, January 2008.
12 I. Rehman, 'China's String of Pearls and India's Enduring Tactical Advantage, *IDSA Comment*, 8 June 2010.

13 B. Gertz, 'China Builds Up Strategic Sea Lanes', *Washington Times*, 18 January 2005.

14 G. Khurana, 'China-India Maritime Rivalry', *Indian Defense Review*, Vol. 23, No. 4, 2009.

15 D. Scott, 'Indian "Footprints" in the Indian Ocean: Power Projection for the 21st Century', *Indian Ocean Survey*, Vol. 2, No. 2, 2006; D. Berlin, 'India in the Indian Ocean', *Naval War College Review*, Vol. 59, No. 2, 2006. In 2010 a four-ship, two-month deployment to the South-East Asian littorals including the Strait of Malacca was matched by a four-ship, two-month deployment to the African littorals, including the Cape of Good Hope.

16 Mahan, *Influence of Sea Power Upon History*, op. cit., pp.50–89.

17 Panikkar, *India and the Indian Ocean*, op. cit., pp.74–76.

18 From the author's discussions with Indian naval officials, US Naval War College, May 2008.

19 Panikkar, *India and the Indian Ocean*, op. cit., p.83.

20 Discussed in J. Holmes and T. Yoshihara, 'Strongman, Constable, or Free-Rider? India's "Monroe Doctrine" and Indian Naval Strategy', *Comparative Strategy*, Vol. 28, No. 4, 2009.

21 J. Nehru, *India's Foreign Policy: Selected Speeches, September 1946–April 1961*, Delhi: Government of India, 1961, pp.113–15.

22 C. Raja Mohan, 'What If Pakistan Fails? India Isn't Worried…Yet', *Washington Quarterly*, Vol. 28, No. 1, 2004–05, p.127. Also C. Raja Mohan, 'Beyond India's Monroe Doctrine', *The Hindu*, 2 January 2003. See C. Raja Mohan, 'SAARC Reality Check: China Just Tore Up India's Monroe Doctrine', *Indian Express*, 13 November 2005, for China's entry/involvement in South Asian affairs, including observer status with its regional organization, the South Asian Association for Regional Cooperation (SAARC).

23 Mahan, *Influence of Sea Power Upon History*, op. cit., p.46.

24 Indian Navy, *Maritime Military Strategy*, op. cit., p.115.

25 R. Roy-Chaudhury, *India's Maritime Security*, New Delhi: Knowledge World, 2000, p.125.

26 A. Prakash, 'India's Maritime Strategy', *USI Journal*, Vol. 137, No. 568, April 2007.

27 Roy-Chaudhury, *India's Maritime Security*, op. cit., p.125.

28 H. Pant, 'India in the Indian Ocean: Growing Mismatch Between Ambitions and Capabilities', *Pacific Affairs*, Vol. 82, No. 2, 2009.

29 'Indian Navy Chief Admiral Sureesh Mehta Spells Out Visions 2022', *India Defense*, 10 August 2008, www.india-defense.com.

30 A. Nativi, 'Fleet Dreams: Delays Plague India's Effort to Expand its Navy', *Defense Technology International*, 1 April 2008.

31 See Scott, 'India's "Grand Strategy" for the Indian Ocean: Mahanian Visions', *Asia-Pacific Review*, Vol. 13, No. 2, 2006; J. Holmes, A. Winner and T. Yoshihara, *Indian Naval Strategy in the 21st Century*, London: Routledge, 2009.

15

Looking west 1: Iran and the Gulf

Mukund Narvenkar

Introduction

The first breakthrough in the new era of India's foreign policy in the 1990s saw an eastwards shift, a new 'Look East' foreign policy to engage South-East Asia. In more recent years, under Manmohan Singh (2004–present) this has been complemented by a westwards shift, a 'Look West' policy to engage with Iran and the Arabian/Persian (depending on whose side one was on) 'Gulf'.[1] This Look West policy is the focus of this chapter.

An option or a compulsion?

Whilst a Look West policy was an 'option' for India at the initial time after independence, it has now become an 'imperative' in its foreign policy. India has vital strategic interests in the Arabian Sea zone that includes the natural extensions like the Gulf and the Red Sea, with their respective choke points of the Strait of Hormuz and the Bab el Mandeb. India's strategic interests involve fast-growing trade (see Table 15.1).

They also involve 'energy security', caused by the growing importance for India of natural gas and oil resources, which give a boost in the importance of the reserves found in this energy-rich region (see Table 15.2).

Such trade, and especially energy, considerations give India a strategic imperative (in its own right and as a major regional power), to help secure Sea Lines of Communication (SLOCs) that pass through this zone, and which bring in trade and energy flows.

The role of extra-regional powers in the region has been long running. After the Second World War the United Kingdom continued to have interest in the Gulf before leaving it in 1971, with the USA then assuming the responsibility of defending pro-Western governments. During the Cold War the USSR had its geopolitical vision (along with the USA) of access to the warm water ports and oil fields of the Middle East, which failed with the defeat in Afghanistan. The sudden collapse of the USSR (in 1991), which was a major trading partner of India, combined with the First Gulf War (1990–91), which left a high point in oil prices, caused a balance of payments crisis for India.

Table 15.1 India's imports and exports to the Gulf and Iran, 2008–09 (US $m.)

Countries	India's exports	India's imports
Bahrain	286.52	1,442.82
Iran	2,534.01	12,376.77
Iraq	437.43	7,709.94
Kuwait	797.50	9,593.74
Oman	779.04	1,205.46
Qatar	674.37	3,498.91
Saudi Arabia	5,110.38	19,972.74
United Arab Emirates	24,477.48	23,791.25
Total	35,096.73	79,591.63

Source: Directorate-General of Commercial Intelligence and Statistics, http://dgft.delhi.nic.in.

Table 15.2 Oil and gas proved reserves of the Gulf (2009)

Countries	Oil reserves in billion barrels	Gas reserves in trillion cubic feet
Saudi Arabia	262.3	240
Iran	136.3	974
Iraq	115.0	112
Kuwait	101.5	55
United Arab Emirates	97.8	214
Qatar	15.2	911
Bahrain	0.1	3
Total	728.2	2509

Source: Directorate-General of Commercial Intelligence and Statistics, http://dgft.delhi.nic.in.

In the 1990s India moved forwards with its new foreign policy and economic liberalization. After the Soviet collapse, India saw new markets available in the Gulf (and Iran) to engage with economically. Meanwhile the USA built up its military strength in the region, so as to support its own economic interests in the region. In order to enhance the mobility of US forces and to provide logistical support, additional base facilities were sought and acquired in Oman and Bahrain. Today the USA has a presence in every country of the Gulf apart from Iran, something of a *Pax Americana* within which Indian interests (have to?) operate.[2] Apart from defending its own vital economic and strategic interests, the USA had also assumed the responsibility of safeguarding the interests of its allies (Western Europe and Japan) by ensuring them uninterrupted supply of oil from the Persian Gulf region. Accordingly, safe and free passage through the SLOCs in the Gulf remains vital for the USA, as indeed they do for India also.

Such factors have also shaped the growing Chinese interest in the region: 'energy security' considerations driven by China's growing need (like India) to import oil and gas, and to improve maritime trade with the region. For Harsh Pant, the Chinese arrival shows that 'China is starting to make its presence felt in Iran in a big way. It is now Iran's largest trading partner and is undertaking massive investments in Iran, rapidly occupying the space vacated by Western firms. India is right to feel restless about its own marginalisation in Iran despite its [India's] civilisational ties with the country'.[3] For India, already looking northwards and eastwards and encountering the People's Republic of China, in looking southwards and eastwards it is also encountering a Chinese-driven arrival in yet another part of India's *extended neighbourhood*: in the Gulf and Iran, the two parts of India's Look West policy to which we can now turn.

The Gulf

India and the relations with the Gulf are very old, and can be traced back to ancient times in both the cultural and economic domains. Relations flourished with more maritime links with the region, which were carried out by various traders from India as well as from the Gulf. They dominated Gulf maritime trade before the Europeans arrived in the early 19th century, and made it their ground of conflicts and opportunities. Meanwhile, India had also fallen under the sway of British control. On the one hand, the volume of trade between the Gulf and India diminished; on the other hand, the British presence in the Gulf was to some extent controlled from British India and underpinned by manpower from British India. In political terms, British foreign policy in the Gulf was carried out through the Persian Gulf Residency (PGR). Before 1857 the PGR had been a subdivision of the East India Company, whilst from 1858 onwards it came under the jurisdiction of the British India administration. In economic terms the Indian rupee was also the currency used in Kuwait, Bahrain, Qatar, the Trucial States and Oman, as provided by the Reserve Bank of India up to 1959. In military terms, Indian manpower was mobilized in the Second World War and deployed in Bahrain, and in large numbers (around 700,000) in Kuwait and Mesopotamia.

Post-independence, India revitalized its historical links with the Gulf region, with its 'strategic' significance increasingly recognized by India.[4] Pranab Mukherjee encapsulated India's economic and political concerns in the Gulf: 'beyond the immediate region, India has vital interests in the Gulf [...] the Gulf forms parts of our strategic [extended] neighbourhood', as an 'important source of energy, home to over 3.5m. Indians, and a major trading partner. Parts of it are also a source of ideology, funding and recruits to the cause of Islamic radicalism and terrorism'.[5] Such has been India's push into the Gulf that Harsh Pant argues that 'the international community and the West in particular has been obsessed with New Delhi's ties with Tehran and has tended to ignore India's much more substantive engagement with the Arab Gulf states [...] the significant stakes that India has in the Arab Gulf often go unnoticed'.[6] India's interests and presence in the Gulf revolve around various issues, namely the expatriate Indian community, economic-energy links, and maritime security-diplomacy.

Indian expatriates in the Gulf

When it comes to any conflict in the Gulf, India faces a major challenge because of its dependence on energy sources, and the safety and security of Indian migrants in the region. The discovery of oil and manpower shortages in the Gulf precipitated phenomenal labour migration to the region. Given the population pressure and bleak economic prospects at home, Indian labourers flocked to the Gulf in search of employment and higher wages. The presence of Indian labourers dates to 1935, when the Bahrain Petroleum Company (BAPCO) imported labour from India. Indians now comprise the largest expatriate community in the Gulf countries, which counts more than 3m. in the region, distributed accordingly between the United Arab Emirates (UAE, around 1.5m.), Oman (0.6m.), Kuwait (0.6m.), Bahrain (0.3m.), Qatar (0.2m.), with another 1.4m. in Saudi Arabia. Over 42.5% of the workforce in the UAE are Indians.

Two comparative trends can be seen.[7] First, unlike in the 1970s and 1980s when nearly 90% of Indians in the Gulf were blue-collar workers, today over 35% of the Indian expatriate workforce are white-collar professionals specializing in fast-moving fields such as the services and information industries. India's economic high-tech rise is reflected in the increasingly high-level economic appearance of Indians in the Gulf, where professionals and technically qualified Indians are engaged in huge numbers in the knowledge-based economic sectors such as Dubai Internet City, Dubai Media City and the Jebel Ali Free Zone (JAFZ). Second, unlike in other regions, Indian expatriates in the Gulf have a higher propensity to remit the money they earn. Gulf expatriates account for almost 30% of total remittances flowing back to India. It thus has become important that India maintains cordial relations with the Gulf countries and fosters general stability, so that there is no hindrance to such Indian economic activities in the Gulf.

Economics and energy

In the wake of economic reforms in India, and subsequent economic growth in the late 1990s, Gulf countries showed greater interest in strengthening their bilateral and commercial relations with India. Apart from the oil and gas market, Indian companies have established various ventures in different sectors such as management and consultancy services, construction projects, telecommunications, computer software and hardware engineering, manufacturing of detergent and pharmaceuticals. One basic complementarity was apparent: 'I see India's requirement for energy security and that of the Gulf countries for food security as opportunities that can be leveraged to mutual advantage'.[8] A framework agreement for economic co-operation was signed between India and the Gulf Cooperation Council (GCC) in August 2004. March 2006 saw the first joint ministerial meeting of the six-state GCC and India. Final negotiations for a Free Trade Agreement were started in January 2006, and set for signature in 2010.[9] Some Indian commentators argue that 'it is time for India to look beyond trade and business, and engage the GCC in political, security and strategic fields'.[10] The Gulf region has increased in relative economic importance for India. Bilateral trade between India and the GCC countries exceeded US $100,000m. in 2009 making GCC, as a bloc, India's largest trading partner. Within that, India-UAE trade of $7,190m. in 2003/04, a 5.6% share of India's overall trade, increased to $48,270m. in 2008/09, a 9.87% share of India's trade, though dropping back slightly to $43,470m. in 2009/10, or a 9.31% share of India's trade.

Energy requirements are the main area of exposure for India in the region, where 'a pattern of interdependence is emerging between India and the GCC due to their strategic position and central role in the current energy security discourse'.[11] Quite simply, 'the Gulf countries are crucial to the energy requirements of India, particularly oil'.[12] One-third of the world petroleum reserves are in the Gulf. With the growth of the offshore oil and gas industry, there has arisen an interest in its military utility and its defence. In the Gulf Wars of the 1980s, 1991 and 2003 there were naval clashes around oil rigs. Availability of oil in the Persian Gulf region has been the main factor responsible for enhancing the strategic importance of this region. Most of the Indian requirement for oil and gas was imported from the Persian Gulf. In this energy setting, India's ONGC Videsh Limited (OVL) has a 100% exploration share of Qatar's Najwat Najem field, and a 100% share of Iraq's Block 8 field.

Maritime security and maritime diplomacy

India's economic sea trade route has been laid down in history. All the treasures of the ancient and modern world were borne across the warm waters that stretch from the Arabian Peninsula to the shores of India. In the global strategic environment, India is an up-and-coming country with its fast-growing economy, stable democratic policies and expanding maritime dominion.

The world order has started to change from Europe-centric to Asia-centric, with India as a major player in the region, with more responsibility for securing the SLOCs, which are the lifeline of India's constant economic growth.

The threat of terrorism-related activity in the marine environment has drastically increased since the terrorist attacks on the USA on 11 September 2001. In the past there have been attacks on US ships in the Gulf, and *jihadist* piracy activities in the Strait of Malacca. In 2010 the Indian Minister of Home Affairs, P. Chidambaram, made the argument that 'it [*jihadist* terrorism] is not just from across the border in Pakistan but extends beyond to the Middle-East also. We have to redefine what cross-border terrorism means'.[13] Terror operatives in the Gulf have had a far more significant role in orchestrating several of the recent terror attacks in India than was known until recently: funding the serial blasts in Bangalore in 2008; assisting in the escape of its mastermind, Tadiyantavide Naseer, to Bangladesh; and probably playing a significant role in the Mumbai terrorist attacks on 26 November 2008.[14] The terrorist attacks on Mumbai in 2008 raised many questions about the security of the sea routes, given that terrorists entered from across the Arabian Sea. As a country with strong maritime forces in the region, India has to maintain a close maritime watch in the region for the safe passage of international maritime trade. The Indian Minister of Defence, A.K. Anthony, commented, whilst inaugurating an International Maritime Search and Rescue Conference (IMASRCON) in 2008, 'the region already faced a menace from sea pirates and [the] terror threat has [the] dimension of bringing in non states actors as well as agents of transitional crime', calling for greater international vigil to ward off these threats.[15] In short, India has to maintain strategic relations with the Gulf, in part to combat potential terrorist threats in the future.

As an emerging maritime power, from New Delhi's perspective, key security considerations include maintaining the accessibility of the Arabian Sea and flows into and out of the Strait of Hormuz. The large Islamic population on the shores of the sea and in its hinterland, the oil wealth of the Gulf and the key Strait of Hormuz are of importance for India's maritime security expansion in the region. Like the Government, the Indian Navy has also been Looking West into the Gulf.[16] The maritime forces work as part of foreign policy, with India's naval diplomacy showing the flag, showing sea power, deterring and attracting. The presence of Indian maritime forces in the Gulf and in its vicinity has been welcomed by international trading companies.

Goodwill visits have brought the Indian Navy into the Gulf on various occasions. The visit of India's aircraft carrier *INS Viraat* and two other ships to the UAE in March 1999 set the scene. A substantial three-week deployment by the Indian Navy took place in September–October 2004, involving two destroyers, *INS Mumbai* and *INS Delhi*, the advanced missile frigate *INS Talwar*, as well as *INS Kulish*, *INS Pralaya*, *INS Sindhuraj* and the support tanker *INS Aditya*. Their visit to Oman, Bahrain, Iran and the UAE was rightly interpreted by Chinese sources as Indian 'efforts to use its navy to project power' outside its own immediate coastal waters.[17] Altogether, around 40 Indian naval vessels were dispatched to Oman and the Gulf during 2005/07. August 2007 saw another powerful five-ship Indian flotilla deployed into the Gulf, with port calls at Muscat (Oman), Qatar, Abu Dhabi, Manama (Bahrain), al-Jubail (Saudi Arabia), before going across to Djibouti. December 2007 saw further dispatches of Indian warships to the UAE.

As elsewhere, naval diplomacy forms a prominent part of India's wider diplomatic projection, with Pranab Mukherjee explaining to an audience in the UAE in May 2008 that 'the steady expansion of our political and economic ties, the interactions between our security and defence personnel and the visits of our naval ships have added a new dimension to our relationship'.[18] The India-Oman *Thammar Al Tayyib* joint exercise has been a regular naval feature since 2003.

It was in this vein that when Sureesh Mehta took over as India's Chief of Naval Staff, his first trip overseas was to Abu Dubai in the UAE in February 2007, accompanied by talk of further Indian naval projection into the region. During Manmohan Singh's trip to the Gulf in November 2008, his visit to Oman saw agreement on strengthening maritime exercises, whilst his visit to Qatar saw a defence maritime co-operation pact signed alongside discussion of increased liquid gas supplies, an unsurprising blend of energy security considerations with defence considerations, and general presence.

Iran

Iran's role deserves discussion in its own right: 'our relations with Iran are a fundamental component of our 'Look West' policy'.[19] Links can be traced back to 4000 BC, when the Gulf was ruled by the Median, Achaemenid, Seleucid and Parthian Empires and later by the Sassanid Empire. During the period of the Sassanid Empire, Persia and north-western India (which was ruled by the Kushans and then Kushano-Sassanians) were deeply engaged in political, economic, cultural and religious intercourse. The coming of Islam brought further Iranian influences into India, including the widespread and long-running presence of Persian as a widely used language at the medieval and Mughal courts in India. In modern, post-colonial times, geographical proximity and economic complementarities have thrown open fresh opportunities for greater interaction between India and Iran.

The geostrategic importance of Iran in the Gulf is vital for India as it connects the Gulf to the Arabian Sea through its narrow Strait of Hormuz. Besides this, Iran is a growing regional player with a drive to acquire nuclear weapons. Iran shares coastlines along the Gulf to the south and the Caspian Sea to the north, with significant energy reserves in both areas. Since Iran is a major regional player, its foreign policy objective in the Gulf and in its immediate region of the Arabian Sea will have crucial implications for the security of the entire region, and for India. Indo-Iranian relations can be explained from their political, economic and strategic aspects.

Political aspects of Indo-Iranian relations

The relationship between India and Iran is far-reaching and multidimensional. The two states have recognized that they have a lot more to share and offer to one another. Their strategic partnership emerged in the first decade of the 21st century. The visit of Indian Prime Minister Atal Bihari Vajpayee to Tehran in April 2001 resulted in the signing of six agreements regarding co-operation in trade, technology and the energy sector, which marked the new beginning of revitalized relations between the two countries.[20] It also brought the signing of the Tehran Declaration (2001), which was echoed two years later in the Iranian President's trip to India and the New Delhi Declaration (2003). The talks were of a new 'axis' in the making, with a strategic partnership proclaimed by the two states.[21] However, such international political convergence does not detract from the concerns that India continues to have over Iran's theocratic and potentially unstable domestic political regime.[22]

Economic aspects of Indo-Iranian relations

India and Iran have had economic interactions with each other since time immemorial, from the ancient trade in cotton, textiles, indigo and food grains like rice, Malabar pepper, cardamom, ginger, cinnamon and coconut, to modern world trade like oil and gas. Post-1947 India had substantial economic links with the Shah's Iran, though the turmoil of the 1979 Iranian Revolution disrupted such economic relations. Subsequently, the prolonged war with Iraq weakened Iran considerably and brought about a severe economic crunch. Iran was in need of broadening economic relations, with India being a more natural and additionally productive economic partner than most other countries in the region. Much of Indo-Iranian economic co-operation centres on the ever-increasing hydrocarbons trade. In terms of primary energy like coal, oil, natural gas, nuclear and hydro electricity consumption, India is the sixth largest energy consumer in the world. Indian bilateral trade has increased in recent years, rising from $1,640m. in 2004/05 to $14,900m. in 2008/09, this being a 0.84% share of India's overall trade, and increasing to a 3.05% share in 2008/09, with Iranian hydrocarbons exports to India constituting most of this trade. Amidst the global recession Indo-Iranian trade fell slightly to $13,400m. in 2009/10, or a 2.87% share.

Iran is a major partner for India in its energy security.[23] This has been a recurring theme during the past decade. It was no surprise that the Tehran Declaration flagged this up: 'the geographical situation of Iran and its abundant energy resources along with the rapidly expanding Indian economy and energy market […] create a unique complementarity which the sides agree to harness for mutual benefit'.[24] It was again no surprise that the New Delhi Declaration affirmed how:

India and Iran have a complementarity of interests in the energy sector which should develop as a strategic area of their future relationship. Iran with its abundant energy resources and India with its growing energy needs as a rapidly developing economy are natural partners. The areas of cooperation in this sector include investment in upstream and downstream activities in the oil sector, LNG/natural gas tie-ups and secure modes of transport.[25]

Upstream and downstream activities involve India finding and then importing Iranian energy resources. The Indian leadership in the summer of 2010 was again emphasizing this complementarity:

Iran is a country extremely important to India from the perspective of energy security. There is a natural complementarity between the needs of energy-hungry India which hopes to grow at a rate of 8–10% in the coming years and Iran which is home to third largest proven oil reserves and second largest gas reserves. Iran is […] located relatively close to India permitting transportation of oil and gas at relatively low cost over sea as well as land.[26]

Transportation by sea is the avenue for by-passing Pakistan's potential obstructionism. Consequently, Iran's energy reserves in its Caspian and Gulf areas have involved Indian companies trying to gain direct access in terms of exploration and exploitation. Thus, in January 2004 India's OVL gained a 10% stake in the Yadavaran field, with India agreeing to buy 7.5m. metric tons of liquefied natural gas (LNG) from Iran each year for 25 years. This was, though, over-shadowed in October 2004, when Iran negotiated a $70,000m. deal with Sinopec, giving the Chinese company a 51% stake in the field's development. India was slightly compensated, as OVL gained a 100% stake in the Jeyfr oil field, with its estimated capacity of 30,000 barrels per day, although this was transferred in 2006 to Belorusneft, the national oil company of Belarus, with OVL seeking a doubling of its Yadavaran holding in compensation. The OVL-Hinduja consortium has been keen to develop the Azadegan oil field in Iran, which is projected to hold over 40,000m. barrels of oil. Further success was gained in an exploration service contract for the offshore Farsi Block gas fields, which was won by an OVL-led consortium consisting of OVL (40% share, and the operator), Indian Oil Corporation (IOC, 40% share) and Oil India Ltd (OIL, 20% share). By 2007 these explorations had revealed large reserves, estimated at over 12,800,000m. cu ft.

An OVL-Hinduja combination, set up in 2006, is eyeing the large South Pars field in Iran, with gas from this field due to feed the proposed Iran-Pakistan-India (IPI) pipeline, a pipeline that would in future provide India with Iranian natural gas.[27] However, there has been slowness in the IPI process because of the ongoing tussle and lack of trust between India and Pakistan. There has been immense pressure on India from the USA, which has opposed the pipeline as it would provide Iran with oil revenue that could undermine UN Security Council, European Union and US sanctions against the Iranian nuclear programme.

Strategic aspects of Indo-Iranian relations

The role of Pakistan in Indo-Iranian relations

Pakistan lies in between India and Iran. As such, it can make or break the proposed IPI gas pipeline, which is one reason why alternatives have been sought by India and Iran.[28] Pakistan also lies athwart the maritime routes between Iran and India, and is potentially able to disrupt them. Generally (Sunni) Pakistan has had bad relations with both India and (Shi'a) Iran. Such strategic logic, which Kautilya would have recognized, of 'my enemy's enemy being my friend' has brought these two non-contiguous states together.[29] In addition, both Iran and India have been against Pakistan's involvement and influence in Afghanistan through the Pakistani Inter-Services Intelligence (ISI) links with the Taliban.

Both Iran and India have concerns over the role of Gwadar, which was built as a deep water port with significant Chinese financial assistance. Its location near the mouth of the Gulf and at the opposite end of the strategic choke points of the Strait of Hormuz and the Gulf of Oman enhances its strategic importance. Iran's concerns are economic, with Gwadar's potential as a rival to Iran's nearby deep water port of Chabahar. India's concerns are partly energy-related. Given India's growing need for energy, supplied from the Gulf and Iran via the Arabian Sea, the dangers of being blocked by Pakistan operating out of Gwadar become of concern for New Delhi, since Pakistan's Navy would find it easier to operate closer to the Gulf. Other military concerns are also in play for India. During times of crisis, in the event of a war with India, the port of Gwadar would provide strategic depth to Pakistan's commercial and military vessels, with the Pakistani navy able to move its naval assets away from any Indian naval and air threat. In addition to Pakistani threats out of Gwadar, India also has further concerns about Gwadar enabling long-range naval operations by the Chinese Navy, heightened by China's Gulf of Aden operations using Gwadar as a berthing and resupply port during operations in 2009–10.

Iran as an entry to Central Asia

In the contemporary world it is important for India to have access to Central Asian energy and markets. Iran is significant for India in its own energy right, but also as a connecting gateway to other regions like Central Asia and its resources, the domain of traditional geopolitics. As India's Minister of External Affairs put it, Iran 'has the potential of being a transit country for supply of third country energy to India given its increasing links in this field with the landlocked countries of Central Asia [...] These projects, if realized, have the potential of making Iran an important element of a large energy corridor stretching from Central Asia to India'.[30] Whilst China sees Pakistan as its energy corridor for energy from the Middle East, able to circumvent India, India sees Iran as its own energy corridor for energy from Central Asia, able to circumvent Pakistan.

India's involvement with Iran has brought sustained Indian interest in building up Chabahar. India's Minister of External Affairs was clear enough in summer 2010 on its wider implications:

> I would like to mention, in particular, the Chabahar Port Project, and the need for accel-erating our joint efforts to fully realize the potential of the Port as well as the associated railway project. These are projects that are in the common interest of India, Iran and Afghanistan, but also the countries of Central Asia. Improving the connectivity of Chaba-har Port to the Zaranj–Delaram Highway (which was built with Indian assistance despite terrorist threats and with the sacrifice of Indian and Afghan lives, and has transformed the economy of Nimroz Province in Afghanistan) [...] will help India transport its goods [...] to Afghanistan, Central Asia and beyond. This project is thus at the heart of the common vision that India and Iran have for Afghanistan and the region as a whole, of increased and easier flow of goods, and creation of a network of transport routes and energy pipelines.[31]

Pakistan's role is the notable absence, with Iran's Chabahar (backed by India) serving as a rival to Pakistan's Gwadar (backed by China). Consequently, India, Iran and Afghanistan are keen to have access to new sea and road routes through Iranian ports. This development will give straight access to Indian goods to Central Asian markets through Afghanistan and Iran.

Another Central Asia-related aspect of India's relations with Iran is the International North-South Corridor (INSC) pipeline route. This was flagged up in the Tehran Declaration:

> They [India, Iran] agreed to accelerate the process of working out an appropriate scheme for the pipeline options and finalising the agreement reached on LNG. The sides reaffirm their commitment to strengthen transport and transit cooperation. In this context and in line with the proper implementation of Inter-governmental Agreement of International North-South Corridor between Iran, India and Russia and Agreement on International Transit of goods between Iran, India and Turkmenistan, they agree to encourage the businessmen and traders of the two countries to better utilise the said corridors.[32]

Potentially this cuts out not only an unstable Afghanistan, but also a potentially unfriendly Pakistan, with energy able to be shipped directly to India by the short maritime route if need be.

Iran's quest for nuclear 'power'

Iran's quest for nuclear power involves Iran's claims that it is merely trying to develop nuclear energy, amidst suspicions that it is seeking nuclear capacity in order to develop nuclear weap-ons. Although Iran is a member of the Nuclear Non-Proliferation Treaty (NPT), UN inspec-tors have found enriched uranium in environment samples, increasing US suspicion that Iran is developing nuclear weapons. Although the Iranian Government had categorically ruled out any intention of acquiring nuclear weapons, India remains concerned about the hard-liner theo-cratic nationalists who have been ruling Iran for over two decades. This all poses problems for India amidst a US drive to have tougher and tougher sanctions imposed on Iran, and talk of possible military action. The USA has been wary, indeed concerned, about Indian links with Iran.[33] US hostility towards Iran places India in the awkward position of having contradictory pressures from its two strategic partnerships: that with the USA and that with Iran. It is a delicate and uncomfortable 'tightrope' along which India has to walk.[34]

To some extent India has given way to such US pressure. On the grounds of being a responsible nuclear nation, in the September 2005 International Atomic Energy Agency (IAEA) vote, India voted to hold Iran in 'non-compliance' of its safeguards obligation, when major nuclear countries like China and Russia chose to remain absent. Manmohan Singh may have argued in parliament that 'India's vote on the IAEA does not, in any way, detract from the traditionally close and friendly relation we are privileged to enjoy with Iran [...] we have every intention of ensuring that no shadow is cast on these bonds',[35] but such a shadow was cast again in the following IAEA vote in February 2006, when India voted in favour of referring Iran to the UN Security Council, due to its apprehension of Iran's growing uranium enrichment capability leading to the development of nuclear weapons. However, there has been some distancing subsequently by India. Amidst talk of further sanctions in 2010, India demurred:[36]

> All concerned should adopt a flexible approach to achieve a comprehensive solution to all issues. India has always supported dialogue and avoidance of confrontation. The IAEA continues to provide the best framework for addressing technical issues related to the Iranian nuclear programme. We are justifiably concerned that the extra-territorial nature of certain unilateral sanctions recently imposed by individual countries [the USA], with their restrictions on investment by third countries [India] in Iran's energy sector, can have a direct and adverse impact on Indian companies and more importantly, on our energy security and our attempts to meet the development needs of our people.[37]

India could play a very important role between Iran and the Western powers, making the case for peaceful dialogue, but the question is, does India have any real say in Iran's nuclear programme, and will the USA/Western powers take India into consideration when pursuing any peace process with Iran? This is a worrying situation wherein India has to be able to convince the Western powers as well as Iran—the two mutual enemies, but both partners with India. Any future military escalation between the USA (possibly including Israel) and Iran will put the region *and* India's interest into jeopardy.

Conclusions

India, Iran and the Gulf region are likely to become increasingly interconnected. Both India and Iran may need to readjust or consider their relations in the context of the pulls and pressures experienced in their respective relationships with other players. Energy is going to play a very important role in building new relationships with India and the Gulf. Economic benefits, technological expertise and cultural exchange of thoughts will continue, and deserve strengthening. Iran will continue to operate in India's foreign policy for the safety and security of oil and gas, new prospects in Central Asia, technological benefits, and India's expertise in the region and its quest for global power. On the one hand, Iran also needs to make friends, as well as co-operate with other countries to break out of its present isolation, with India potentially able to play an important role in getting Iran to join the mainstream of world polity. India also needs friends in the Islamic world, such as the Gulf countries and Iran, to counter Pakistani hostility in the region.

Notes

1 C. Raja Mohan, 'India's "Look-West" Policy', *The Hindu*, 17 June 2004; Prime Minister's Office, 'PM Launches "Look West" Policy to Boost Cooperation with Gulf', 27 July 2005, pib.nic.in.

2 A. Pasha, 'Pax Americana in the Gulf Region. Implications for India's Quest for Energy Security', in S. Malakar (ed.), *India's Energy Security and the Gulf*, Delhi: Academic Excellence, 2006.

3 H. Pant, 'Turbulent Times for Indo-Iranian Ties', *Business Standard*, 30 May 2010.

4 S. Pradhan, 'Indo–Gulf Relations: Mapping Strategic Dimensions', *Gulf Asia Bulletin*, No. 5, August 2008.

5 P. Mukherjee, 'India's Strategic Perspective', Carnegie Institute, 27 June 2005, www.indianembassy.org.

6 H. Pant, 'India Looks Beyond Tehran in the Gulf', *Rediff News*, 17 March 2010, news.rediff.com.

7 See S. Pradhan, 'India's Economic and Political Presence in the Gulf: A Gulf Perspective', in A. Sagar and G. Kemp (eds), *India's Growing Role in the Gulf*, Washington: The Nixon Center, 2009.

8 Pranab Mukherjee, cited in M. Janardhan, 'Gulf Eyes Oil-for-Food Pacts', *Asia Times,* 21 June 2008.

9 S. Pradhan, 'India and the Gulf Cooperation Council (GCC): An Economic and Political Perspective, *Strategic Analysis*, Vol. 34, No. 1, 2010.

10 S. Pradhan, 'India and Gulf Cooperation Council: Time to Look Beyond Business', *Strategic Analysis*, Vol. 34, No. 2, 2010, p.409.

11 Z. Ahmed and S. Bhatnagar, 'Gulf States and the Conflict between India and Pakistan', *Journal of Asia Pacific Studies*, Vol. 1, No. 2, 2010, p.260. Also S. Malakar (ed.), *India's Energy Security and the Gulf*, Delhi: Academic Excellence, 2006; S. Pradhan, *India, GCC and the Global Energy Regime: Exploring Interdependence and Outlook for Collaboration*, New Delhi: Academic Foundation, 2008.

12 A. Rehman, 'Gulf, A Crucial Factor in India's Energy Requirements for Development', in S. Malakar (ed.), *India's Energy Security and the Gulf*, Delhi: Academic Excellence, 2006.

13 'Cross-border Terror Extends Beyond Pak: PC', *Indian Express*, 12 May 2010.

14 J. Joseph, 'LeT's Gulf Arm Funded 26/11, Bangalore blasts?', *Times of India*, 15 May 2010.

15 'Defence Minister Warns of Maritime Terror', *PTI* (Press Trust of India), 11 March 2008.

16 B. Raman, 'Indian Navy Begins to Look West', *Papers* (SAAG), No. 2128, 9 February 2007.

17 'India Deploys Warships in Gulf Region', *Xinhua*, 12 September 2004.

18 Pranab Mukherjee, 'India's Foreign Policy and India-Gulf Relations', 12 May 2008, www.meaindia.nic.in.

19 N. Sisodia, 'Speech by Foreign Secretary at IDSA-IPIS Strategic Dialogue on India and Iran: An Enduring Relationship', 5 July 2010, meaindia.nic.in. Also D. Berlin, 'India-Iran Relations: A Deepening Entente?', *Special Assessment* (Asia-Pacific Center for Security Studies), October 2004; C. Fair, 'Indo-Iranian Ties: Thicker than Oil', *Middle East Review of International Affairs*, Vol. 11, No. 1, 2007.

20 M. Khan, 'Vajpayee's Visit to Iran: Indo-Iranian Relations and Prospects of Bilateral Cooperation', *Strategic Analysis*, Vol. 25, No. 6, 2001.

21 H. Pant, 'India and Iran: An "Axis" in the Making?', *Asian Survey*, Vol. 44, No. 3, 2004, though somewhat sceptical. Also T. Schaffer and S. Fawzi, 'India and Iran: Limited Partnership and High Stakes', *South Asia Monitor,* No. 114, 20 December 2007; H. Pant. 'India-Iran Ties: The Myth of a "Strategic" Partnership', 1 February 2008, casi.ssc.upenn.edu.

22 D. Twining, 'India's Relations With Iran and Myanmar: "Rogue State" or Responsible Democratic Shareholder?', *India Review*, Vol. 7, No. 1, 2008.

23 F. Afrasiabi, 'Iran Holds Key to India's Energy Insecurity', Asia Times, 30 April 2008.

24 India-Iran, *Text of Tehran Declaration*, 10 April 2001, pib.nic.in.

25 India-Iran, *The New Delhi Declaration*, 25 January 2003, meaindia.nic.in.

26 N. Sisodia, 'Speech by Foreign Secretary at IDSA-IPIS Strategic Dialogue on India and Iran: An Enduring Relationship', op. cit.

27 See A. Sahay and J. Roshandel, 'The Iran–Pakistan–India Natural Gas Pipeline: Implications and Challenges for Regional Security', *Strategic Analysis*, Vol. 34, No. 1, 2010, pp.74–92.

28 R. Sengupta, 'India-Iran Gas Pipeline: A Transit Challenge', *News* (Rediff), 22 January 2003, www.rediff.com.

29 E. Ehrari, 'As India and Iran Snuggle, Pakistan Feels the Chills', *Asia Times*, 11 February 2003; R. Zeb, 'The Emerging Indo-Iranian Strategic Alliance and Pakistan', *Central Asia-Caucasus Analysis*, 12 February 2003, www.cacianalyst.org.

30 N. Sisodia, 'Speech by Foreign Secretary at IDSA-IPIS Strategic Dialogue on India and Iran: An Enduring Relationship', op. cit.

31 Ibid. Also D. Roy Chaudhury, 'India Push to New Iran Port for Access to Afghanistan', *India Today*, 26 July 2010.

32 India-Iran, *Text of Tehran Declaration*, op. cit.

33 J. Larkin and J. Solomon, 'As Ties Between India and Iran Rise, U.S. Grows Edgy', *Wall Street Journal*, 24 March 2005.

34 H. Pant, 'A Fine Balance: India Walks a Tightrope between Iran and the United States', *Orbis*, Vol. 51, No. 3, 2007; C. Fair, 'India and Iran: New Delhi's Balancing Act', *Washington Quarterly*, Vol. 30, No. 3, 2007; P. Kumaraswamy, 'Delhi: Between Tehran and Washington', *Middle East Quarterly*, Vol. 15, No. 1, 2008.

35 M. Singh, 'PM's Suo Motu Statement on Iran', 17 February 2006, pmindia.nic.in.

36 'India With Non-Western Powers to Oppose Iran Sanctions', *Indian Express*, 17 April 2010.

37 N. Sisodia, 'Speech by Foreign Secretary at IDSA-IPIS Strategic Dialogue on India and Iran', op. cit.

16

Looking west 2: Beyond the Gulf

P.R. Kumaraswamy

Introduction

The Middle East and North Africa, generally referred to as West Asia and North Africa (WANA) in official nomenclature, is a critical region for India.[1] Over the centuries India has had strong political, cultural, economic, often religious and energy-related contacts and inter-actions with this region. In the early part of the 20th century Indian nationalists recognized the importance of the region when they made common cause with their Arab counterparts, especially over the Palestinian question. The region's importance has only increased since then. Within the Middle East, the Gulf sub-region attracted an importance primarily and even exclusively because of its energy resources and the resultant economic opportunities. Hence, much of India's interest and attention was dominated by the oil-rich Gulf region, marginalizing other sub-regions such as the Fertile Crescent and the Maghreb.

India's sense of westwards *extended neighbourhood* has now, though, been extended still further beyond the Gulf into the further reaches of the Middle East/West Asia. This underpinned India's readiness to use its naval capacity to evacuate Indian nationals from Beirut, Lebanon in the summer of 2006, with Manmohan Singh explaining to the Indian parliament that in rescuing Indian nationals, it had been shown that 'West Asia is our extended neighbourhood and tensions in that region affect our security and our vital interests'.[2] Here, if one is looking for tangible shifts in India's post-Cold War world view and signs of maturity in its foreign policy, then one has to look beyond the Gulf region. More than any other country or region, Israel has symbolized a fundamental shift in India's foreign policy outlook. By breaking with the past and abandoning its historic baggage, India ushered in a new approach to its international relations. The zero-sum approach of the Cold War gave way to a nuanced policy that is based less on rhetoric and more on hard political calculations on the part of India.

The sudden disappearance of the Cold War global ideological schism created more problems for India's Middle East policy than is commonly recognized. Overnight it put an end to the traditional pro-Soviet policy that India had pursued towards the Middle East since the early 1950s.

Normalization with Israel

Normalization of diplomatic relations with the Jewish state was the most visible manifestation of the post-Cold War foreign policy of India. More than four decades after the formation of Israel, India established full diplomatic relations with the country in January 1992. This move signalled India's new non-ideological approach to foreign policy.

An initial formal Indian recognition of Israel had come as far back as September 1950, but a host of developments had prevented immediate normalization, even though an assurance to this effect was given when the Israeli diplomat Walter Eytan visited India in early 1952 and met Prime Minister Jawaharlal Nehru. Initially, financial constraints and lack of personnel prevented India from implementing Nehru's assurances of full normalization, including a resident mission in Tel-Aviv. Israel's collaboration with imperialism as manifested during the Suez war and Nehru's growing friendship with Gamal Abdel Nasser gradually diminished the prospects of full normalization. What began as a pro-Arab policy gradually transformed into a policy of unfriendliness, if not hostility, towards Israel. Beginning with his yielding to Arab political pressures on the eve of the Bandung Conference of April 1955, Nehru played a critical role in Israel's exclusion from the emerging bloc of Non-Aligned Movement and other Third World forums. Gradually, India intensified anti-Israeli rhetoric in its Middle East policy, as in November 1975 when New Delhi endorsed the infamous UN General Assembly Resolution 3379 that equated Zionism with racism.

The disappearance of the USSR, the end of the Cold War and the emergence of US hegemony all reduced international animosity towards Israel. US domination also meant the erstwhile advisories of Israel had to come to terms with the international clout of Israel's most friendly power. Political miscalculations of the Palestinians during the Kuwait crisis also meant that the regional animosity towards Israel lost some of its rationale.

These seismic changes in the Middle East compelled India to revisit its Middle East policy that had been anchored on Arab socialism, secularism and Soviet friendship. Driven by traditional reluctance and dithering, India began to slowly transform its policies and priorities in the Middle East. India not only had to co-habit with US domination but also engage rising conservatism in the region. In practical terms this meant devising a policy that was driven more by economic calculation than political rhetoric, which was the thrust of the Manmohan Doctrine anyway.[3]

India's unfriendliness became untenable in the wake of Yasser Arafat's willingness to seek a negotiated settlement with Israel. Continuation of the status quo would have earned India the reputation of being overzealous. The rationale of its Israel policy had collapsed, and there was an added danger of it becoming counter-productive to its desire to have closer ties with the West, especially the USA. Reversal of its four-decade policy towards Israel provided an opportunity for the Indian leadership to signal a clean break from the past and herald a new dynamism in its foreign policy.

Normalization of relations contained a US angle. Since the late 1940s Washington had been pressurizing New Delhi to abandon its unfriendliness towards Israel. The absence of Indo–Israeli relations figured prominently in many high-level meetings between Indian and US leaders. It was widely believed that it was only due to US pressure that Prime Minister Indira Gandhi resisted the temptation to close down the Israeli consulate in Bombay (now Mumbai) in 1982, following a controversial interview by the Israeli Consul-General in which Yosef Hassin accused India of competing with Pakistan to curry favour with the Arabs. For a long time 'block politics' provided India with sufficient leeway to resist US pressure tactics. Post-Cold War US pre-eminence was different. Having been forced to find ways of improving its relations with Washington, New Delhi began looking for ways to convey the new direction of its foreign policy. Normalization of relations with Israel proved to be the most effective means of conveying this new message. Dithering in a deep economic crisis and acute foreign exchange shortage, its ability to pursue economic reforms also depended heavily upon Washington's support and backing in various international financial institutions, including the World Bank. Thus, on 29 January 1992, on the eve of Prime Minister Narasimha Rao's visit to New York to attend the special summit session of the UN Security Council, India announced normalization of relations with Israel. Reflecting on this linkage, one keen observer of the region lamented that although the establishment of 'full diplomatic relations with Israel was a correct decision […] to do so under American pressure was unwise'.[4]

Since 1992 relations between India and Israel have flourished in a host of areas, including political contacts, economic interactions, cultural exchanges and, above all, military co-operation. After some initial hesitation, India began adopting an unapologetic attitude towards its new-found friendship with Israel. There was a series of high-level political visits between the two countries, including the visit of Israel's foreign minister in May 1993, President Ezer Weizman in December 1996, and foreign minister Silvan Shalom in February 2004. The high point of the bilateral ties was the visit of Prime Minister Ariel Sharon in September 2003. At that time not many friends of Israel were willing to host the maverick leader. Despite public protests from left-wing parties and Muslim groups, the visit was a watershed in Indo-Israeli relations. Despite initial misgivings, the Leader of the Opposition and President of the Congress party, Sonia Gandhi, met the Israeli leader, thereby signalling a broad national consensus regarding bilateral ties with Israel. From the Indian side, however, there were not many high-level visits until 2000, when Minister of Home Affairs L.K. Advani and Minister of External Affairs Jaswant Singh visited Israel. Reciprocal visits of India's President and Prime Minister are yet to take place.

At the same time, from the Indian side a host of other central ministers have visited Israel. On at least two occasions the visit of the defence minister has been cancelled owing to upheavals in the region. This, however, has been compensated by the active involvement of various state governments in promoting closer ties with Israel. Unlike the central Government, the state governments in India are less concerned about political controversy and calculation, and are driven more by the need to promote economic welfare of their respective states. This, in turn, makes the state governments look up to Israel for assistance in a host of areas such as agriculture, horticulture, irrigation, water management, arid cultivation, de-desertification, health care, etc. Indeed, since 1992 various state governments ruled by right-wing, left-wing and centrist parties have entered into a host of economic co-operation agreements with Israel.

The Communist Party of India (Marxist) (CPI (M)) was not far behind. Its critical political attitude towards Israel has not hampered the party from seeking closer economic co-operation with Israel. Indeed, in the summer of 2000 veteran communist leader and Chief Minister of West Bengal Jyoti Basu visited Israel. This was his last foreign visit as Chief Minister before he relinquished office. At around the same time his party colleague and later Speaker of the *Lok Sabha* (lower house of parliament) Somnath Chatterjee led a business delegation to Israel to promote investment opportunities in his home state of West Bengal. These two visits marked a diplomatic coup for Israel and indicated a larger Indian consensus on normalization. In short, political differences do not cloud economic interests, even for puritans like the CPI (M).

Ironically, in the wake of the outbreak of the al-Aqsa *intifada* (uprising) in September 2000, the Indian left had been demanding downgrading of closer ties with Israel. Some had even gone to the extent of demanding the recall of the Indian ambassador from Tel-Aviv. During 2004–08 the left-wing parties were instrumental in the continuation of the United Progressive Government under Prime Minister Manmohan Singh. Capitalizing on this unique situation and vulnerability of the Congress party, the left-wing parties hoped, demanded and clamoured for a 'course correction' vis-à-vis Israel. They were hoping that the Congress-led Government would 'undo' some of the pro-Israeli measures taken by the Bharatiya Janata Party (BJP)-led Government during 1998–2004. Much to the chagrin and disappointment of the left-wing parties, the Union Government was not prepared for any radical moves but, on the contrary, intensified close ties with Israel.

On the economic front, bilateral trade has grown in the last two decades; standing at less than US $100m. on the eve of normalization, it reached $3,854m. in 2009/10. If one excludes the hydrocarbons trade, this makes Israel one of India's principal trading partners in the Middle East. The flip side of this is that much of their two-way trade is dominated by diamonds, as Indian companies import raw diamonds and export them back to Israeli companies as polished, finished products. At the same time, bilateral economic co-operation also encompasses joint ventures and two-way investments in areas such as drip irrigation and medicine. Of late, Israel has been investing in various infrastructure projects in India.

The most important area of Indo-Israeli co-operation, however, revolves around the military arena, something that both countries are extremely reluctant to discuss publicly. In just over a decade after normalization, Israel emerged as a significant player in India's security calculations.[5] In recent years India has overtaken other potential markets such as Turkey and emerged as the largest market for Israeli arms exports. For its part, Israel is seen as the second largest defence supplier after Russia. Principal defence co-operation covers areas such as arms upgrading, small arms, border management, naval patrol, intelligence co-operation and counter-terrorism. India's search for advanced technology and Israel's demand for larger markets to economize its defence research are complementary. Both countries are seeking technological independence and qualitative superiority over their adversaries. Some of the major defence deals involving both countries since 1992 include: the Barak anti-missile system; the upgrade of ageing MiG fighter planes; fast patrol attack craft; radars and other surveillance equipment; night-vision hardware; and border fencing. Of all military-related deals with Israel, the purchase of three Phalcon advance airborne early warning systems at an estimated cost of $1,100m. was a major development. In the past, the USA vehemently opposed Phalcon sales to the People's Republic of China, and forced Israel to cancel the economically lucrative and politically important deal. However, as the left-wing parties were demanding that the Government abandon closer military ties with Israel, in July 2007 the Indian Government approved a $2,500m. programme to jointly develop defence systems against air missiles. Above all, amidst the controversy over Iran's nuclear ambitions, in March 2007 India launched an Israeli spy satellite into orbit. While actual quantum of Israeli exports remains controversial, in May 2007 defence minister A.K. Antony informed the Indian parliament that defence purchases from Israel during 2002–07 had been over $5,000m.

Furthermore, heads of various branches of the military, as well as the security establishments, have been visiting one another periodically. There is a structured, regular and ongoing consultation between the national security establishments of both countries. There is an institutional consultation mechanism between the two foreign ministries, and both countries have Joint Working Groups dealing with terrorism and defence production. Indian naval vessels have been making periodic port calls to Israel. Reflecting its changed attitude towards Israel and the Middle East peace process, India contributed troops to the UN Interim Force in Lebanon (UNIFIL) in Lebanon in November 1998 and joined the UN Disengagement Observer Force (UNDOF) along the Israeli–Syrian border in March 2006.

Closer military ties between the two countries once again highlight the importance of the USA in shaping Indo-Israeli ties. In the early years it was believed that Israel was critical to the improvements in Indo-US relations. Developments after 1992 indicated a different trend. Rather than Israel helping India to improve its relations with the USA, as was commonly hoped, Washington has been enhancing Indo-Israeli relations. Understanding and support from Washington are critical if India is to avoid the path that Sino-Israeli relations took after both countries normalized relations in 1992. Rather than enhancing closer military ties, US pressure forced the Jewish state to reduce, curtail and eventually abandon its military sales to China. It is in this context that one should view the controversial statement by India's National Security Advisor, Brajesh Mishra, at a dinner hosted by the American Jewish Committee in May 2003. According to him, these three countries 'have some fundamental similarities. We are all democracies, sharing a common vision of pluralism, tolerance and equal opportunity. Stronger India-US relations and India-Israel relations have a natural logic'.[6] A US veto, for example, would have scuttled the Indo-Israeli Phalcon deal.

There were other factors that worked in favour of India's strengthening ties with Israel. The 1993 Oslo Agreement enabled some Arab countries to establish low-level diplomatic ties with Israel, while the powerful Gulf Cooperation Council (GCC) abandoned secondary boycotts against Israel. Moreover, most Middle Eastern countries had no qualms about Indo-Israeli ties. After some displeasure in the immediate aftermath of Rao's decision, most countries pursued bilateral ties with India as if there were no Israel factor. Indeed, India's relations with the Middle East improved substantially *after*, rather than *before* 1992. India's economic growth and the resultant political clout resulted in many Middle Eastern countries looking at India favourably, attracted by the economic opportunities that India could provide and unconcerned about burgeoning Indo-Israeli ties. Contrary to fears and apprehensions, Arab and Islamic countries were not prepared to hold their bilateral ties with India hostage to the Israel factor. Even the Islamic Republic of Iran, known for its anti-Israeli rhetoric under President Mahmoud Ahmadinejad, pursued closer ties with India as if there were no Indo-Israeli partnership. There was one notable exception, though: Egypt. Marginalized regionally following the emergence of oil-rich Arab countries in the Gulf, the most populous Arab country took time to come to terms with Indo-Israeli ties.[7] In other words, while Israel was not responsible for the improvements in Indo-Arab ties, one can safely conclude that normalization of relations has not hampered the ability of Arab and Islamic countries to pursue closer political, economic and energy ties with India.

The Palestinian issue

Since the early 1920s the Indian nationalists and, later, the leaders of independent India consistently adopted a pro-Arab position in their attitude towards Jewish nationalism and Israel. Strong currents of anti-imperialism, opposition to religion-based nationalism propounded by the Muslim League in India, and the Congress party's concerns to win over the domestic Muslim population all resulted in Indian nationalists adopting an overly pro-Arab position vis-à-vis the Zionist demand for a Jewish 'national home'.[8] Elected to the UN Special Committee on Palestine (UNSCOP) in 1947, India recommended federalism as the solution for the Palestinian–Jewish divide. Not only did India oppose the partition plan for Palestine endorsed by the majority of members of the UN in November 1947, but a few months later it even opposed Israel's membership into the world body.

By the late 1950s opposition to Israel and commitments to the Palestinians became the main plank upon which India sought to promote its interests in the Arab world. Its policy was based on the twin principles of supporting the Arabs and Palestinians in their conflict with Israel, and of endorsing the pro-Soviet socialist states in the region. The former was an integral part of the

Congress party's foreign policy since the early 1920s, while the latter enabled India to identify itself with the secular Arab leaders who were also opposed to the US-led military alliance politics that involved Pakistan. A tacit convergence began to emerge between the two streams. The friendship between India's first Prime Minister, Nehru, and Egyptian leader Nasser symbolized this trend. The Arab secularism, anti-imperialism and socialism of Nasser was enamoured by Nehru, and paved the way for closer political ties which manifested at the Bandung Conference of 1955 and during the Suez crisis the following year. This bonhomie with Egypt continued at least until the Arab defeat in the June war of 1967 and the consequent emergence of religious conservatism in the Middle East.

India further strengthened its political ties with the Palestinian leadership. In 1975 it recognized the Palestine Liberation Organization (PLO) as the sole and legitimate representative of the Palestinian people. This paved the way for an official Palestinian presence in India, and in March 1980 India granted full diplomatic recognition to the PLO by upgrading its office to that of an embassy endowed with all diplomatic immunities and privileges. In November 1988 India became one of the first countries to recognize the newly proclaimed State of Palestine. While the Israeli consulate was languishing in Mumbai since 1953, the PLO had full diplomatic presence in the national capital. The Palestinian leader, Arafat, not only became a frequent visitor to India but was received as a head of state. While India refused to endorse the extremist positions in the region that called for the destruction of the state of Israel, its support of the Palestinian cause was manifested in its endorsement of the need for Palestinian self-determination and independent statehood.

The status quo was shattered by the end of the Cold War and a host of other developments that took place in 1990. Arafat's mishandling of the Kuwait crisis considerably weakened the Palestinian leadership and his support for Saddam Hussain during the crisis alienated the PLO from the principal players in the region such as Saudi Arabia, Kuwait and Egypt. This led to the marginalization of the Palestinian issue in Middle Eastern politics. The pro-Saddam Hussain stance taken by the Palestinian leadership during the Kuwait crisis meant that the PLO, and especially Arafat, became a *persona non grata* in influential Arab capitals. Many saw Arafat's stand during the crisis as a collaboration with the Iraqi occupiers—an act they were unwilling to forgive. In practical terms, this meant that India could no longer promote its interests in the Middle East, especially among the Gulf states, by playing up its support for the Palestinians.

The disappearance of the USSR, traditionally known for its pro-PLO policy, a few months later weakened the diplomatic leverage of the Palestinians. As a precondition for co-hosting the Madrid conference in October 1991, Moscow restored full diplomatic ties with Israel. These developments compelled the PLO to abandon its armed struggle and seek a negotiated political settlement with Israel. Its political vulnerability was exposed when the PLO agreed to go to Madrid as part of the joint Jordanian-Palestinian delegation, rather than as an independent delegation representing the Palestinians. The rising diplomatic fortunes of Israel became clear when China discovered the virtues of the Jewish state and began moving towards normalization.

Normalization with Israel did not imply that India had abandoned its traditional support for the Palestinians. As such, India walks a 'tightrope' between these two actors.[9] India has not modified any of its core principles regarding the Palestinian question and it continues to support the political rights of the Palestinians and their inalienable right to self-determination and statehood. The formation of an independent Palestinian state co-existing with Israel, New Delhi feels, is a pre-condition for lasting peace in the Middle East. Its recognition of the PLO as the sole legitimate representative of the Palestinians was not modified by its decision to normalize relations with Israel. Since 1992 it has received the Palestinian President Yasser Arafat, and later his successor Mahmud Abbas, as heads of state. Following the 1993 signing of the Declaration of Principles (DoP) in Washington between Israel and the PLO, India opened a mission in the Gaza Strip, later relocated to Ramallah in the West Bank. Underscoring its independent status, the Indian Mission to the Palestinian Authority reports directly to the foreign office in New Delhi and not to the Indian embassy in Israel, located in Tel-Aviv. On all major issues concerning the peace process, India remains at odds with the Jewish state. Much to Israel's consternation and displeasure, on key issues such as Jerusalem, settlements, borders and refugees, normalization has not brought about any significant changes in India's position.

At the same time, there have been subtle shifts in India's posture. Normalization clearly indicated India's willingness to move away from its traditional zero-sum game paradigm. Prior to normalization, support for the Palestinians and Arabs meant India adopting an unfriendly posture towards Israel. Even maintaining normal diplomatic ties with the Jewish state was perceived to be an unfriendly act towards the Palestinians or a dilution of India's commitment towards the Arabs. The end of the Cold War and regional shifts in the Middle East forced India to abandon the past and recognize a new reality: it was possible and necessary to maintain normal and even friendly ties with both rival parties if India was to be taken seriously. Even if it is not in a position to play the role of mediator, India's interests will be better served only if it maintains normal ties with *all* parties to the Middle East conflict.

Pakistan's role

The substantial shift in India's policy towards Israel and significant improvements in its relations with the Arab and Islamic countries were possible because of one other development: India de-linking Pakistan from its Middle East policy. Since the early 1920s India's attitude towards the region has been dominated and shaped by this factor. Even before Partition, pre-1947, the domestic rivalry between the Congress party and Muslim League dominated the concerns of the Indian nationalists towards the Middle East. Both were competing for the support and loyalty of the Indian Muslims and hence Middle Eastern issues such as the Khilafat and Palestinian questions dominated the foreign policy agenda. This compelled the Indian nationalists to view the Palestinian question through an Islamic prism.

Following Partition and independence in 1947, the Middle East became the battleground for Indo-Pakistani rivalry. During much of the Cold War years, India's Middle East policy was Pakistan-centric and was devoted to countering, balancing, minimizing and, if possible, nullifying Pakistan's diplomatic influence in the region. If Pakistan played up its Islamic credentials, India harped on secularism and consistent support for the Palestinians. Indeed, as highlighted by the controversy surrounding the first Islamic summit conference in Rabat in September 1969, the Middle East witnessed an intense Indo-Pakistani Cold War. For a while India had the upper hand, largely due to the preponderance of secular Arab nationalism led by Nasser. This, however, did not last long. The Arab debacle in the June 1967 war meant not only the marginalization of secular nationalism but also the resurgence of conservatism. Formation of the Organization of the Islamic Conference (OIC) significantly enhanced Pakistan's diplomatic gains in the Middle East, and the principal players in the region supported Pakistan during its wars with India in 1965 and 1971.

Indo-Pakistani rivalry manifested itself more acutely in the prolonged Indian refusal to normalize relations with Israel. India feared that Pakistan would make political capital out of ties with Israel. This, too, prevented India from establishing full diplomatic ties soon after its recognition of Israel in 1950. Moreover, India bowed to Pakistan's pressures and agreed to exclude Israel from the Afro-Asian Conference in 1955, at Bandung.[10]

However, the post-Madrid rise in Israel's diplomatic fortunes greatly nullified Pakistan's ability to score 'brownie points'. Arab endorsement of a political settlement through direct negotiations with Israel weakened any arguments against India talking to Israel, especially when there were no bilateral disputes to settle. India recognized that excessive focus on Pakistan or demanding that its interlocutors choose between the two South Asian neighbours was not always effective. Demanding that third parties minimize their commitments to Islamabad might even impede these countries from taking India seriously. One of the significant outcomes of the post-Cold War economic progress of India has been its aspiration for Great Power status. Confidence in its economic growth has emboldened its leaders to seek a place for India under the sun. In practical terms, this means that India is beginning to see itself more as an Asian power rather than an actor confined to impoverished South Asia. If its claims of Great Power status are to be taken seriously by others, then it will have to minimize its perennial competition and rivalry with its neighbour. India cannot be seen as an Asian power when its radar of political imagination fails to cross South Asia.

In the Middle East it has also meant India learning another lesson. The countries of the region view Pakistan primarily through an Islamic prism. As highlighted by King Abdullah of Saudi Arabia during his state visit to India in January 2006, they see India as a 'friend' and Pakistan as a 'brother'. This would continue to be the dominant attitude of the major countries of the region. It thus became prudent for India to shift the focus to bilateral issues rather than pursue a Pakistan-dominated policy towards the countries of the Middle East. While it is too early to call this a paradigm shift, there are indications that Pakistan figures less prominently in India's relations with the countries of the Middle East than during the Cold War.

Energy concerns (Saudi Arabia and elsewhere)

India's post-Cold War policy towards the Middle East has also been dominated by its search for energy security. Steady economic growth since the early 1990s has rapidly increased India's energy consumption and imports. While domestic oil production remains stagnant, its imports have increased rapidly. Crude oil imports have gone from about one-third of domestic consumption in the 1970s and 1980s to over two-thirds of domestic consumption. There is a general consensus that India's hydrocarbon import dependency will soon reach alarming levels. According to the Paris-based International Energy Agency, by 2030 as much as 87% of India's oil requirement will have to be met by imports.[11] According to India's Planning Commission, current import dependency of about 72% 'is growing rapidly'.[12]

This growing gulf between consumption and domestic production had forced India to adopt a sustainable energy security policy. This, in practical terms, means assured supply of hydrocarbons at affordable prices. It is in this context that one must view growing ties between India and Saudi Arabia.

At the ideological level, there is little in common between the Saudi brand of *Wahhabi* Islam and the secularism pursued by India. Nevertheless, energy security concerns have led both countries to take a new look at one another. This explains the high-profile visits between the leadership of the two countries. Since the visit of foreign minister Jaswant Singh to Riyadh in January 2001, there have been a number of political contacts between the two. These have generated the India-Saudi Arabia New Delhi Declaration (2006) and the Riyadh Declaration: A New Era of Strategic Partnership (2010).[13] It was no surprise that Manmohan Singh prefaced his 2010 trip with the simple comment that 'the Kingdom is India's largest and most reliable supplier of our energy needs from the region': true enough, since Saudi Arabia *is* India's largest crude oil supplier and contributes nearly one-third of India's total oil imports.[14] Largely driven by growing oil imports, India's total trade with Saudi Arabia surged to just over $25,000m. in 2008/09, though dropping back a little to just over $21,000m. in 2009/10. As highlighted by foreign minister Pranab Mukherjee during his own visit to that country in 2008, India sees Saudi Arabia as a potential partner in its massive infrastructure development projects, which require about $500,000m.–600,000m.[15]

At the same time, India's energy-driven calculations are not confined to Saudi Arabia and the Gulf region alone. Energy interests have brought India closer to Sudan, a country ravaged by prolonged civil war and sectarian violence. The departure of Western oil companies owing to internal instability has provided an opportunity for India's Oil and Natural Gas Corporation (ONGC). This state-owned company has invested over $2,000m. in Sudan, and is involved in the production and distribution of hydrocarbon resources in Sudan, shipped down the Red Sea to India. Indo-Sudanese ties mark a significant departure from the past patterns of India's foreign policy. Under normal circumstances it would be unthinkable for India to be involved so closely with a country that is amidst serious internal turmoil and at the receiving end of international criticism, condemnation and even isolation over the human rights situation in the Darfur region. However, growing demands for hydrocarbons have compelled India to sidestep other concerns and quietly capitalize on the lucrative Sudanese energy market.[16] Its energy interests in that country also resulted in the muted Indian reaction to the Darfur crisis and reminded the world that when it comes to energy security, India would not shy away from pursuing a path that might not be popular and may even be at odds with Washington.[17] Sudan is also a classic example for greater co-operation between India and China. The Greater Nile Petroleum Operating Company (GNPOC), for example, is a joint venture comprising the ONGC, which holds a 25% share, the China National Petroleum Corporation (CNPC), which holds a 40% share.

Further up the Nile, India's bilateral ties with Cairo got a boost when Indian oil companies made inroads into the Egyptian energy market. OVL has a 70% share in Egypt's North Ramadan field in the Gulf of Suez. At the top end of the Red Sea, the Suez Canal was specifically included in government definitions of India's *extended neighbourhood*: 'an extended neighbourhood for India which stretches from the Suez Canal to the South China Sea and includes within it West Asia'.[18] Coming out through the Suez Canal into the eastern Mediterranean, India not only has its defence links with Israel, it also has an economic presence in Syria, where the state-owned ONGC and CNPC jointly made a successful bid for stakes in the Petro-Canada operations, securing a 38% stake at $573m. This venture came under some criticism from the USA owing to the George W. Bush Administration's policy of isolating Syria.[19]

Conclusions

India is yet to evolve a coherent regional policy towards the Middle East. Deep internal divisions and prolonged lethargy have prevented New Delhi from adopting a holistic policy towards this region. This larger problem was compounded by the region's special complications. The prolonged Arab–Israeli conflict meant that normalization of relations with Israel could not be divorced from the periodic surges in violence. This has forced New Delhi to differentiate bilateral relations from the peace process and to pursue one relation independent of the other. This has enabled India to pursue closer ties with Israel, including in the military-security arena, without being unduly worried over the reaction of the Arab and Islamic countries. In a way, it has successfully sought and secured closer ties with Israel as well as its principal adversaries in the region. This was partly due to the demise of the ideological divide, but mostly due to India's emerging economic clout and importance. Seen in this wider context, at least with regard to the Middle East, political rhetoric is less relevant than economic and strategic calculations. Driven by the rising expectations of its growing middle class, India has embarked upon a policy that is governed more by economic rationale and less by political slogans. Indeed, if its policy towards Saudi Arabia is dominated by energy calculations, its policy towards Israel is governed more by military-security calculations. A successful pursuance of both these tracks will be a continuing challenge for India's Middle East policy beyond the Gulf.

Notes

1 Though 'West Asia' has been the official Indian nomenclature, 'Middle East' is the expression used by the countries of the region and is increasingly becoming popular even within India. Hence this chapter uses 'Middle East' rather than 'West Asia'.
2 M. Singh, 'PM's Suo-Motu Statement in Parliament Regarding the Situation in Lebanon', 27 July 2006, pmindia.nic.in.
3 M. Singh, 'Speech by Prime Minister Dr. Manmohan Singh at *India Today* Conclave, New Delhi', 25 February 2005, meaindia.nic.in.
4 M. Agwani, 'Inaugural remarks', in K.R. Singh (ed.), *Post-War Gulf Implications for India*, New Delhi, 1993, p.3.
5 For ongoing discussions, see P.R. Kumaraswamy, *India and Israel: Evolving Security Partnership*, Ramat Gan: BESA Center for Strategic Studies, 1998; F. Naaz, 'Indo-Israel Military Cooperation', *Strategic Analysis*, Vol. 25, No. 4, 2000; P.R. Kumaraswamy, 'India and Israel: Emerging Partnership', in S. Ganguly (ed.), *India as an Emerging Power*, Portland: Frank Cass, 2003; H. Pant, 'India, Israel Partnership: Convergence and Constraints', *Middle East Review of International Affairs*, Vol. 8, No. 4, 2004; R. Nair, *Dynamics of a Diplomacy Delayed: India and Israel*, Delhi: Kalpaz, 2004; 'India-Israel to Ramp up Military Ties, *Times of India*, 10 December 2009.
6 B. Mishra, 'Address by Shri Brajesh Mishra, National Security Advisor of India at the American Jewish Committee Annual Dinner', 8 May 2003, meaindia.nic.in.
7 The tension was manifested in the manner in which India conferred the Jawaharlal Nehru Award of International Peace upon President Hosni Mubarak in 1997, but it was only in November 2008 that Mubarak chose to come to India to receive the award in person: P.R. Kumaraswamy, 'Mubarak's Chutzpah – Cairo Treating India With Contempt', *New Indian Express*, 14 April 2008.
8 L. Gordon, 'Indian Nationalist Ideas about Palestine and Israel', *Jewish Social Studies*, Vol. 37, Nos. 3–4, 1975.
9 H. Mishra, 'India Walks Israeli-Palestinian Tightrope', *Asia Times*, 10 February 2008.
10 M. Brecher, *India and World Politics: Krishna Menon's View of the World*, London: Oxford University Press, 1968, p.79.
11 *IEA World Energy Outlook 2005: Middle East and North Africa Insights*, Paris: International Energy Agency, 2004, p.254.
12 Government of India, *Draft Report of the Expert Committee on Integrated Energy Policy*, New Delhi: Planning Commission, 2005, p.10.
13 India-Saudi Arabia, 'New Delhi Declaration', 7 January 2006, meaindia.nic.in; India-Saudi Arabia, 'Riyadh Declaration: A New Era of Strategic Partnership', 28 February 2010, www.pib.nic.in.
14 M. Singh, 'Prime Minister's Statement Prior to his Departure to the Kingdom of Saudi Arabia', 27 February 2010, meaindia.nic.in. For coverage of this visit, see S. Roy, 'Prime Minister Manmohan Singh in Saudi Arabia, 27 February–1 March 2010', *India Speaks-Special*, New Delhi: Middle East Institute, No. 4-S, 8 March 2010.
15 MEA, 'Briefing Points by Official Spokesperson on External Affairs Minister's Visit to Saudi Arabia', 19 April 2008, meaindia.nic.in.
16 S. Dutta, 'India's Oil Investments Safe in Sudan', *Times of India*, 5 August 2004; 'India, Sudan Ink Deal on Expanding Energy Ties', *Indo-Asian News Service*, 8 December 2009.
17 N. Ray, 'Sudan Crisis: Exploring India's Role', *Strategic Analysis*, Vol. 31, No. 1, 2007.
18 Y. Sinha, '12th SAARC Summit and Beyond', 3 February 2004, meaindia.nic.in.
19 S. Varadarajan, 'US Tells India to Back Off Syria Oil Deal', *The Hindu*, 28 January 2006.

17

Looking west 3: Africa

Ajay Dubey

Introduction

India and Africa are two shore neighbours. It is this geographical proximity, India looking westwards across the navigable Indian Ocean, that made the peoples of the two regions known to each other. Beginning with early colonial days, the free and voluntary relations of the past gave way to colonial needs and preferences. The present relations, between independent, self-respecting regions, were formally established only after both sides got independence. The 21st century has seen a renewed initiative of India with the India-Africa Forum Summit (IAFS) in 2008. Some similar initiatives have been taken by other Asian countries, like the People's Republic of China, Malaysia and Japan. Many observers call it a 'new scramble for Africa' by Asian countries to acquire African raw materials and energy resources.[1]

However, a historical examination of Indo-African relations shows that India's interest and intense engagement is not new; it is multidimensional. Africa is a continent consisting of 54 countries and India's relations with Africa are therefore heterogeneous, complex and diverse. Nevertheless, this chapter will focus on broader aspects of Indo-African relations, in which the historical goodwill of India is being translated now into economic and political co-operation.[2] In this context, this chapter will discuss Indo-African relations in distinct phases of history and then focus on the emerging areas of present engagement between the two regions.

Historical connections

Shared history embedded in ancient contacts

Contacts between India and Africa can be traced back to ancient times when Indian merchants from its western seaboard traded along the eastern littorals of Africa. The Indian Ocean was the connecting factor in this trade relation. The seasonal reversal of monsoon winds in the Indian Ocean was very helpful for the traders, who utilized it for navigation. The influence of Indian architecture on the African kingdom shows the level of trade development between the two civilizations. References in Vedic scriptures, as well as the travelogues and navigators' diaries, further attest to the fact that strong relations existed between the two ancient cultures. The *Periplus* (a Greek guidebook for sailors written about 2,000 years ago) mentions that trade existed between the Indian shores and Africa. Ibn Battuta in his account observes the presence of Africans known as *habshis* in the imperial armies of the Indian Kings. A large number of Africans came during medieval times and formed a major section of Muslim armies. They reached the highest positions in the army and their own forts. They settled along the western coast of India and were called *siddis*. This African diaspora in India predates the later indentured diaspora of India in Africa.

Colonial expansion and strengthening of India-Africa relations

The phase of European colonial expansion in Africa and India, however, brought an end to this traditional long-range trading system. This period of shared colonial rule led to migration of a substantial number of Indians, with a large number of People of Indian Origin (PIOs) taken to African countries in different capacities—as indentured workers, railway workers, artisans and slaves. This forced migration was part of the British policy to take Indian labourers all over the world to replace black slaves after their emancipation. The people of Indian origin not only greatly contributed to the host country, but also forged an inextricable link between India and Africa. Indian leaders before independence and later in the Government of India actively engaged themselves in the cause of PIOs.

It is in Africa that, for the first time, an Indian leader, Mahatma Gandhi, raised the issue of discrimination of PIOs in a big way. The discriminatory treatment in a racially structured society of South Africa drew Gandhi into active politics during his stay in Natal in 1893–1914. The period witnessed the first flowering of his approach of *satyagraha*, or non-violent resistance to tyranny. Gandhi's experience of discrimination in South Africa left an abiding influence in the identification of India with the freedom-loving peoples of Africa. His philosophy, which he successfully put into practice to achieve India's independence, inspired a generation of African leaders—including Kwame Nkrumah of Ghana, Obafemi Awolowo of Nigeria, Julius Nyerere of Tanzania, and Kenneth Kaunda of Zambia—in their own national liberation campaigns.[3]

Afro-Asian resurgence, anti-colonialism and anti-racism

While Gandhi was a common icon for Indo-African relations, it was Jawaharlal Nehru who gave the relationship its political structure. During his time as Prime Minister, Nehru was instrumental in shaping and defining major policy objectives and commitment to the Afro-Asian resurgence in which India and especially Nehru tried to emerge as a leader of ex-colonial countries. Under him, India took a definite diplomatic stand on many African issues. First, he supported the decolonization of African states, which he considered a continuation of India's own decolonization. It was largely based on his personal commitment to the process of Afro-Asian resurgence. Second, he took a firm stand against racial discrimination in South Africa and broke off India's diplomatic and trade relations with the racist regime. For African countries still under colonial rule during this period, both were relevant to Africa's immediate concerns of decolonization and democratization. The Bandung Conference (1955) and the Afro-Asian Peoples' Solidarity Conference of Cairo (1958) demonstrated these Afro-Asian perceptions of each other. India's engagement with Africa, its diplomacy and interactions in the Non-Aligned

Movement (NAM), the United Nations, the Commonwealth, and Afro-Asian organizations were mainly on the lines of anti-colonialism and anti-racism. Nehru also took a categorical stand on issues on people of Indian origin settled in Africa, and made it clear that they must identify with the local majority community and should not seek any special privilege over the natives in the country of their adoption.

The low ebb of the 1960s

However, early hopes of a more intensive Indo-African partnership went into a low ebb in the 1960s. Indian policy was unrealistic, overestimating the role Africa was going to play due to its numerical strength and underestimating the importance and priority that Africans attached to issues like decolonization and racial equality. India failed to realize that such issues like peaceful co-existence, highly relevant and important though they were for India, had to be integrated with African impatience for decolonization. In support for African decolonization, India was branded as having a softer attitude towards colonial powers. Indian insistence on non-violent struggles against colonialism, its advocacy of 'peaceful co-existence' and moderate stand on issues like the Mau Mau rebellion, the Algerian war of independence and the Congolese civil war, did not appeal to Africans. On the other hand, the Chinese militancy and advocacy for armed struggle did appeal to Africans.[4] Furthermore, India's Anglo-centric view resulted in no time limit being fixed for colonial withdrawal,[5] and the gulf caused between Indian settlers and Africans by colonialist propaganda that India was attempting to end white domination to replace it with Indians, brought differences out into the open. During the Indo–Chinese War of 1962 India was isolated; very few African countries supported India and many adopted an openly unhelpful attitude.[6] The Cairo Conference of Non-Aligned Countries (1964) exposed Indian isolation, with Africa taking the dominant control of the NAM.[7]

The result of this was that by the mid-1960s India's advantages as a beacon of decolonization in Africa, as one of the founders of the NAM and a leader of Afro-Asian resurgence, had been let down during the Indo–Chinese War by those very peoples whose demands it had championed. The situation for India became more alarming when it observed that African countries belonging to and professing the aiims of non-aligned groups were ready to accept Chinese claims and versions of events.

The issue of India's policy towards Indian settlers in Africa was another factor that did not augur well with African leaders. India had taken the exclusive issue of the discrimination of Indian settlers in South Africa to the UN. Blacks, who suffered worse discrimination in South Africa, were initially not included in the Indian resolution moved in the UN under Article 10 of the UN Charter. This caused great misgivings among Africans. Admittedly, Nehru had made it clear that 'in many parts of Africa – East, West, South – there are considerable number of Indians, mostly business people. Our definite instructions to them and to our agent in Africa are that they must always put the interest of indigenous population first. We want to have no vested interests at the expense of population of those countries'.[8] However, in the aftermath of the Chinese attack of 1962 he talked of the 'dual loyalty' of Indian settlers in Africa. They were supposed to stand up beside India when India was in crisis.[9] During the 1964 Africa Safari, Indira Gandhi also called these overseas Indian settlers 'Ambassadors of India'.

By the end of the 1960s India had a tough politico-diplomatic task to overcome the growing isolation in Africa. It was time for India to reconsider its relations with Africa. Its policy-makers in New Delhi adopted a less ambitious national policy, focusing instead on building their country's defence sector and securing its *immediate neighbourhood*.

South-south engagement

In the aftermath of the Chinese attack in 1962, India stopped treating African countries as a bloc and became more selective in its friendship. It started integrating the priorities of African countries and was able to convince African countries, to a certain extent, of the importance and relevance of its own stand and views on different issues. International situations and India's achievements at home played an important role in India's move to befriend African countries. India won the 1971 war with Pakistan, thereby liberating Bangladesh. The Sino–Soviet conflict and the Cold War enabled India to sign the 1971 Treaty of Peace, Friendship and Cooperation with the USSR. Indian diplomacy scored points by obtaining the support of one superpower against the other without being an ally of either. The success of India's 'Green Revolution' and achievement of self-sufficiency in food grains production demonstrated Indian economic and managerial capability. India's explosion of its nuclear device in 1974 restored its military confidence and raised its status as a military power. The launching of the *Aryabhata* rocket launcher in 1975 again placed India among the leading scientific and technological countries of the world. With newly acquired self-confidence, Indian policy became more proactive towards the African countries. For India it was the planned, systematic and persistent attempt of its policy pursuits that took the problems in its stride and exploited the favourable circumstances that came its way. India again became a power to which Africa turned for help and assistance, and as a model for development.

Under these changed domestic and international circumstances, Indo-African relations showed noticeable changes compared with the earlier period. The most important change was in the field of India's economic diplomacy towards the African states. The ever-growing industry and need to keep its balance of trade kept Indian economic diplomacy at the forefront of its foreign policy. Therefore, economic diplomacy, a secondary objective to the political imperatives of the 1960s, became the primary objective by the 1970s. The previous policy to make friends in Africa and to gain their diplomatic support on various issues shifted to the creation and cultivation of gainful economic links. This was in tandem with the increasing realization among developing countries of the need for economic co-operation under a south-south umbrella. India utilized its diplomatic strength in international forums like the UN, NAM and 'Group of 77', to develop south-south co-operation. Both the African states and India underlined the need for economic co-operation among themselves. It was at the Lusaka Summit (1970) that the Indian Prime Minister, Indira Gandhi, articulated and gave the call for south-south co-operation. She pledged Indian technology and human resources for this. Politically, by the early 1970s most of the African colonies had become independent except Rhodesia, Namibia and South Africa. For the newly independent countries, the priority was to consolidate their freedom by accelerating economic development.

On the issue of the struggle for liberation, India worked closely with the African countries in their fight against apartheid in South Africa and Namibia. India accorded diplomatic status to the African National Congress (ANC) in 1967 and the South-West African People's Organization (SWAPO) in 1985. Apart from diplomatic support, it added material assistance, but the material assistance remained meagre due to India's own limitation on giving more in those terms. However, the diplomatic initiatives were so vigorously pursued by India that they bridged the gap of less material assistance and projected India as a champion and uncompromising fighter against colonialism and racism. India also made contributions to the UN Fund for Namibia, UN Institute for Namibia, and UN Educational and Training Programme for South Africa. At the Harare NAM Summit in 1986 the Indian Prime Minister, Rajiv Gandhi, was chiefly responsible for the establishment of the Action for Resisting Invasion, Colonialism and

Apartheid (AFRICA) fund. The purpose of the AFRICA fund was to enable the NAM to help all the victims of apartheid in South Africa, Namibia and in the frontline states. According to one estimate, India provided Rs36m. by 1977–78, while India's initial contribution to the AFRICA fund was Rs500m., which included private and individual contributions of Rs25m.[10]

In the 1970s, on the issue of the Indian diaspora, Indira Gandhi advanced a policy of engagement which was resented by Africans. When Kenya and Uganda initiated the Africanization process, the Indian Government's sympathy and concern for people of Indian origin was resented.[11] India's intervention at that time was perceived as interference in internal affairs. This had policy implications. There was a realization of the fact that Africa did not reciprocate India's support for the African liberation movements by giving fair treatment to the people of Indian origin.[12] India had to revert to the policy of disengagement with the PIOs. Subsequent governments until the late 1990s continued this policy. Further, India's hesitation in welcoming the expelled Indians back into its fold, in turn made the PIOs realize the limits of Indian policy towards them and the fact that they were left to their own fates in their adopted countries.

In short, while Indian foreign policy during much of the Cold War did not have significant direct impact on unfolding developments in Africa, its political commitment to the NAM and its emphasis on south–south co-operation led to increased Indian exports to Africa. The balance of trade, which was in favour of Africa, shifted in favour of India until petroleum imports from Africa increased. This was resented by African countries as a new pecking order rather than south–south co-operation. However, consistent diplomatic support for African nationalist movements left India well positioned to take up its engagements across the continent and forge new ties, as it has done in recent years under globalization.

Current dynamics

Globalization: emerging areas of co-operation

In the post-Cold War era, with the end of apartheid in South Africa, one of the major rationales of solidarity no longer exists. The shared ideologies of NAM and anti-colonialism no longer remained the rallying points of interaction between India and Africa. The relationship was being shaped by the fundamental changes that took place in both India and Africa. On the one hand was India's rise as an economic power, its vibrant democracy, its integration into the world economy; on the other hand was a democratizing Africa, its rapid economic growth rates and its continental integration. Their ability to help one another is far greater today than it was in the past. There is a desire to work on their complementarities and build a partnership based on equality, mutual respect and mutual benefit. The focus has now shifted to economic emancipation and collective dreams of sustainable development, and interaction is now moving beyond government to governmental exchange to embrace the people at large.

The move is towards intensifying collaboration on bilateral, continental and global issues. Africa is co-operating with India at a continental, regional and bilateral level. The partnership at various levels is aimed at strengthening south–south co-operation, as there is a desire by both Africa and India to see each other prosper and gain a just place on the global stage. At the pan-African level India stepped up its relations with the African Union (AU), which was formalized by the IAFS in April 2008, and its Delhi Declaration.[13] The Indian Government argued that this Delhi Declaration and the IAFS was 'a defining moment in the India-Africa relationship'.[14] India views the AU as embodying the spirit of resurgent Africa and has been fully supportive of its programmes and objectives. India is now not just an observer, but a 'dialogue partner' with the AU. Given India's current relations with the AU, there are enormous possibilities for further co-operation, both economic and political, in the context of a multi-polar and globalized world. The 'democracy deficit' in the UN is clear to both India and Africa. Both India and Africa feel that they deserve permanent representation on the UN Security Council, and would support each other. Both sides have been broadly working together for UN reform and are now ready to strive to make the UN more representative and democratic. They also stand together on other critical issues, such as multilateral trade negotiations, reforms of international financial institutions, climate change and the fight against terrorism.

At the regional level India is engaged in constructing relations of partnership with regional organizations. India made good progress in developing co-operation with regional organizations within Africa like the Common Market for Eastern and Southern Africa (COMESA), the East African Community (EAC), the Southern Africa Development Community (SADC), and the Economic Community of West African States (ECOWAS), and is expecting to make similar progress with others. India has lines of credit available with the East African Development Bank, the Preferred Trade Area/Agreement (PTA) bank for the COMESA region, the West African Development Bank (BOAD) and, most recently, a line of credit of US $250m. to the ECOWAS Development Bank in West Africa, to help finance sub-regional projects. At the bilateral level, India is intensifying collaboration with African countries in sectors like agriculture, food and energy security, trade and technology.

Both regions understand the strategic importance of the other. India assumes immense significance for Africa's developmental goals in terms of trade, investment, entrepreneurial skills, military power, and educational and research training. Meanwhile, Africa's potential in terms of energy resources, minerals, raw materials and geostrategic location has strategic value for India. Such an understanding has led to emerging areas of co-operation, which include the economic field, energy sector, human resources development and capacity building, security and maritime co-operation.

Economic co-operation

Africa acknowledges India's economic growth and finds the Indian model relevant. India provides Africa with opportunities in different areas, having launched a number of initiatives for closer co-operation with Africa, which include the Focus Africa programme to increase trade with the continent and the Techno-Economic Approach for Africa India Movement (TEAM-9) initiative in 2003 to enhance co-operation with western and central African countries. India's bilateral (non-oil) trade with Africa has grown exponentially, from $3,000m. in 2000/01, to $29,300m. in 2008/09. During the 10-year period of 1998–2008, while imports have risen from $2,900m. to $20,500m., exports have increased from a mere $394m. to $5,400m. What is significant, is that the balance of trade has again shifted in favour of Africa, and Africa's share of India's overall trade has increased from 5.8% in 2002/03 to 8% in 2006/07. A region-wide analysis of India–Africa trade shows that India's trade with the western African region has risen most (due to increased imports of petroleum products), followed by that with southern Africa, northern Africa and eastern Africa. India is, however, mindful of the need to provide greater market access to imports from Africa. In accordance with its commitment at the World Trade Organization (WTO), it has decided to extend a duty-free preferential tariff scheme on 92% of import items for the 34 least developed countries in Africa.[15]

The Government of India is also working with the Indian private sector in forging project partnerships. The India-Africa project partnership conclaves held over the years reflect the growing investment and trade complementarities. It provides greater avenues for African countries to seek investment flows from the Indian private sector. The Indian Government is impressing upon Indian industry and Indian entrepreneurs that they should have non-exploitative engagements and build new co-operative partnerships with Africa. Indian industry is realizing the importance of Africa, especially in commercial terms. In the last few years private sector investment has acquired much greater visibility. It is giving the relationship a new dimension and advantage. Indian investors are respected because they are known for generating employment, transferring technology, contributing to intra-African trade, fulfilling domestic demand and enhancing foreign exchange earnings through exports. These investment flows are matched by a commitment by the Government of India made at the IAFS 2008 for up to $5,400m. in new lines of credit over a five-year period. However, there are challenges as to whether the Indian multinationals operating in Africa behave differently from the Western multinationals, and if they can be equal partners in Africa's development process. As far as the Indian Government is concerned, to facilitate economic engagement it has been providing financial assistance to various trade promotion organizations, export promotion councils and apex chambers in the form of market development assistance under the Focus: Africa programme, and even increasing lines of credit for executing projects in African countries.

Human resources development and capacity building

India's technological capabilities and developmental experience are germane to Africa's socio-economic development. One of the strong focuses of the current Indian partnership with Africa is the empowerment of people through capacity building and human resources development, specifically highlighted under the India–Africa Framework of Cooperation agreed at the 2008 IAFS. India recognizes Africa's need for human resources development in overcoming the gap for development in indigenous capacities. By adopting a people-centric development approach in Africa, India differentiates itself from other players: this is an approach that combines the use of lines of credit with deployment of Indian expertise to create assets in Africa. A major issue is how India is going to reciprocate by policy and acts that are qualitatively different from traditional buyers in Africa. India has proposed to support human resources development, market access and food security, which India can provide. Local skills development is part of many Indian projects.

Consequently, India has augmented its development package for Africa. India's support of the New Partnership for Africa's Development (NEPAD) initiative since its inception in 2001 is another step indicative of its efforts to assist Africa in achieving its development goals. India has committed $200m. to NEPAD to increase economic interaction with Africa. The aim has been to forge closer economic co-operation in the fields of mining, agro-processed products, motor vehicles and components, and information and communication technology (ICT). As announced at the 2008 IAFS, India doubled its financial package for development of the continent to $5,400m. over the next five years. It pledged another $500m. in projects related to capacity building and human resources development. It increased scholarships and the number of training slots for African students under the Indian Technical and Economic Cooperation (ITEC) programme. Africa is now the largest recipient of India's ITEC programmes.

The 1,600 training positions offered under the ITEC programme to Africa have become important avenues of capacity building, which in turn contribute to the fulfilment of developmental goals in so many countries. India seeks to establish an India–Africa Institute of Information Technology, India–Africa Institute of Foreign Trade, India–Africa Institute of Educational Planning and Administration, India–Africa Diamond Institute, 10 Vocational Training Centres and five Human Settlement Institutes in Africa. The Pan-Africa e-Network, costing over

$100m., is a particular project that illustrates India's commitment to share its progress in the information technology sector and bridge the digital divide. The project aims to promote tele-education and tele-medicine in all 53 members of the AU. Senegal has been designated by the AU as the hub for the entire project.

One further high-tech aspect of India's economic co-operation with the African countries has been offering its growing space expertise, technology and facilities at its Thumba launch station. This was shown in the PSLV-C15 Indian rocket being used at Thumba, in July 2010, to launch an Algerian satellite, amidst comments by K.R. Sridhara Murthy (the Managing Director of Antrix Corporation Ltd, the commercial and export arm of the Indian Department of Space) that, 'we are hopeful of tapping the market in Africa as more firms are establishing telecom and television networks there. Our rates are competitive compared to other players in the business of commercial launches'.[16] However, as one Indian commentator noted, 'particularly with regard to Africa, this launch needs to be viewed beyond commercial interests. Africa is a region of special geopolitical importance to India […] With this launch it could be said that India has started using "space diplomacy" as a foreign tool in Africa'.[17]

Energy co-operation

Energy co-operation is now one of the prominent areas of economic partnership between India and Africa. It is one of the prime drivers of the current relationship. India's economy is projected to grow at a rate of somewhere between 8% and 10% annually over the next two decades.[18] Currently, the country is the fifth largest consumer of energy in the world, accounting for some 3.7% of total global consumption. One-third comes from traditional sources of fuel, including wood, dung, crop residue, biogas and waste. However, with increased growth India is expected to overtake Japan and Russia to become the world's third largest consumer (after the USA and China), and these new needs can hardly be expected to be met by the traditional sources used by many households on the subcontinent. India needs to expand its energy supply to sustain its growth levels. In order to diversify its energy sources, it is investing in energy assets overseas. In this context Africa's energy resources are very significant for India. Almost one-quarter of India's crude oil imports are sourced from Africa. The Oil and Natural Gas Corporation Videsh Limited (OVL) has large overseas investment of over $2,000m. in Sudan. It has also acquired stakes in Senegal and other African countries like Côte d'Ivoire, Libya, Egypt, Nigeria and Gabon. For its energy requirements India is willing to share with Africa its expertise in exploration, distribution, refining, storage and transportation. Indian investment in this sector directly assists the building of a trained and skilled local workforce capable of efficiently running the assets. Of course, running such assets presupposes state stability, which brings us to the question of Indian support for UN stabilization efforts in Africa through UN peace-keeping operations

UN peace-keeping operations in Africa

India has played an active role in UN peace-keeping operations in Africa since the first mission to the former Belgian Congo in 1960. Since the end of the Cold War, India has put its military at the service of global order, contributing troops to numerous UN peace-keeping operations, many in Africa, and recognized in the appointment in May 2010 of Atul Khare as UN Assistant Secretary-General for Peacekeeping Operations. India has contributed nearly 100,000 troops, who are experienced in low-intensity conflict: in Mozambique (ONUMOZ, 1992), Somalia (UNOSOM, 1993–95, UNOSOMII), Rwanda (UNAMIR, 1994), Angola (1995, UNAVERM,

MONUA) and Sierra Leone (UNAMSIL, 1999–2000). More recently, Indian troops were deployed along the Ethiopia–Eritrea border (UNMEE), in the Democratic Republic of Congo, and in Sudan (2007). India also responded to the call by the UN Secretary-General for increased representation of female personnel in field Missions by providing the first full 'Female Formed Police Unit' for peace-keeping work in Liberia in 2007. This Unit has been successful in reaching out to women and children, besides performing its normal peace-keeping functions. The professionalism and involvement of the Indian troops in local community-related projects has been a feature of such operations.

Military security co-operation

Alongside such multilateral UN frameworks, India has been involved in its own bilateral military-security links with African countries. India provides military training to officers of various African defence forces, another important component of India's Africa policy. Africa lacks military training institutions, having thus to send its military officers abroad for training. Since the 1960s India has provided military training to a number of African countries, primarily from Anglophone Africa. The training covers fields such as security and strategic studies, defence management, artillery, electronics, mechanical, marine and aeronautical engineering, anti-marine warfare, logistics management and qualitative assurance services. During the last decade and a half, over 1,000 officers from 13 African countries have been provided withtraining by the Indian Army.

Maritime co-operation is a noticeable component of India's current engagement with Africa. In the Indian Ocean, piracy, smuggling, drugs- and arms-trafficking and terrorism all threaten the security of the Sea Lines of Communication (SLOCs). Frequent acts of piracy in the waters off Somalia during 2009–10 made those maritime stretches the most dangerous for merchant shipping in the world, including for Indian ships. At the regional level the Intergovernmental Authority on Development (IGAD) East Africa/Horn of Africa sub-region has significant importance for India for maritime security in the Indian Ocean. India's involvement and contribution, particularly in peace consolidation and post-conflict reconstruction in both Somalia and southern Sudan, have been a sign of India's interest in regional security and stability. India's deployment, at the end of 2008, of naval ships into the waters off Somalia to combat Somalia-based pirates was another sign of this. This was why Manmohan Singh told the Combined Services Conference in 2004 that 'our strategic footprint covers the region bounded by the Horn of Africa [...] Awareness of this reality should inform and animate our strategic thinking'.[19]

The Indian Navy regularly engages in naval exercises and naval diplomacy along the African littoral, and at the national level over the past few years India has deepened security and diplomatic co-operation with various AU members like South Africa, Mozambique, Madagascar, Mauritius and the Seychelles. Naval diplomacy and showing the flag has become an established feature of India's presence along the African littoral during the past decade, with a rising number of units deployed and with greater frequency. Naval involvement in the Marine Electronic Highway (MEH) being set up along the East African littoral from South Africa up to the Seychelles is another way to foster links with those AU members of MEH.[20]

Links with South Africa have partly been at the commercial maritime end of things. Amidst rising trade (around $7,500m. in 2008/09), the two countries entered into an agreement in March 2006 to improve co-operation in merchant shipping and related activities, with the agreement providing for the facilitation of Indian companies to establish joint ventures in the field of sea-based transportation and ship-building/repairs. Naval co-operation between India and South Africa was already apparent by 2000.[21] The Indian Air Force in 2004 conducted combined exercises with its South African counterpart. Indian Mirage 2000 fighters were deployed from north-central India and flew, aided by newly acquired Il-78 aerial tankers, to South Africa via Mauritius. India and South Africa conducted combined naval drills off the South African coast in June 2005. The formation of IBSA (India, Brazil, South Africa) saw further trilateral naval IBSAMAR exercises in South African waters in 2008 and 2010.

Given the fact that the African east coast is in India's strategic maritime *neighbourhood*, India aims for greater maritime presence (naval deployments and naval diplomacy), and stronger ties, with the African countries to secure those SLOCs.[22] In such a vein, four Indian warships—INS Delhi, INS Talwar, INS Godavari and INS Aditya—paid port calls to Mombasa (Kenya), Dar es Salaam (Tanzania), other east African ports, Madagascar and Mauritius during a two-month deployment from July to September 2008. Indian naval vessels were deployed off Maputo (Mozambique) to provide protection for the AU summit of 2003 and the World Economic Forum in 2004. Such extension was formalized in March 2006 with the India–Mozambique Memorandum of Understanding, under which India agreed to mount ongoing maritime patrols off the Mozambique coast. India set up in Madagascar its first listening post on foreign soil in July 2007.[23] In strategic terms, it could serve as a small base between India and the important shipping lanes of Mozambique.

India currently provides maritime security for AU island states like Mauritius and the Seychelles. Their logic has been mutual interests, as India's naval chief Arun Prakash explained: 'Mauritius, Seychelles and Comoros are friendly and well disposed to us. However, their security remains fragile, and we cannot afford to have any hostile or inimical power [China?] threatening it'.[24] Indian ships also became a regular feature in Mauritius, with agreement for India to monitor its Exclusive Economic Zone (EEZ) in 2003 and 2005. Currently, India is seeking a long-term lease of the Agalega islands in Mauritius.[25] Similar arrangements were made with the Seychelles, with their Memorandum of Understanding drawn up in 2003 for India to patrol her territorial waters. This was strengthened in 2010 to include the Seychelles' wider EEZ, increasingly under threat from Somalia-based pirates.[26]

Thus it was that the four-ship, two-month deployment in August–September 2010 of INS Mysore, INS Tabar, INS Ganga and INS Aditya involved them carrying out anti-piracy duties, patrolling the EEZs of the Seychelles and Mauritius, and visiting Kenya, Tanzania and Mozambique, before participating in the IBSAMAR trilateral exercises in South African waters.

Conclusions

India and the African countries are devising new parameters for an enhanced and enlarged relationship appropriate to their new role in a changing world. This new dimension in the India-Africa relationship has been a response to the challenge of globalization, and what has emerged is immense opportunities for mutually beneficial co-operation.

The model of co-operation into which India and the African countries are entering has emerged from the success of the IAFS held in New Delhi in April 2008. The co-operation mechanism is clearly one seeking mutual benefit through a consultative process. India does not wish to demand certain rights or projects in Africa; however, it wants to contribute to the achievement of Africa's development objectives as devised by African partners. Besides the consultative process and the spirit of friendship, sharing knowledge and experience is another aspect that makes many African countries relate to India. The sharing of experience on political institutions and human resources development is an important aspect of India's non-intrusive support to the development of democratic institutions in many African countries. Such factors may indeed give India the 'advantage over China' in their simultaneous, and fairly competitive, presence in Africa.[27]

The introduction of multilateralism into Indian-African relations through a multi-tiered co-operative partnership framework has brought transparency in decision making and reflects India's respect for its African partners. Out of the substantial funds committed for capacity building in Africa at the 2008 IAFS, one-half will be channelled through AU-led decisions and a similar amount is committed to the bilateral and regional tiers. The action through the AU was concretized through the announcement of a Joint Action Plan in March 2010, in which India shared the decision making on the allocation of resources, the creation of training programmes and the establishment of 19 institutions in Africa with the AU Commission and member states. This is an important feature of India's new model of engagement with Africa.

Indian-African relations over the years have witnessed various changes, moving from a period of high political, emotional and moral solidarity, to a more material, concrete and developmental approach. Indo-African diplomatic relations by the mid-1960s had reached a very low ebb. Indian policy was unrealistic in perceiving both the role Africa was going to play due to its numerical strength and sense of solidarity, and the importance and priority that Africans attached to issues like decolonization and racial equality, though India provided increasing support to African liberation movements both for decolonization and an end to racism. During the early period, India's support was not strong in material terms. Although during the 1970s and 1980s material assistance was added to Indian diplomatic efforts, they remained meagre due to India's own limitation for giving more in those terms. However, diplomatic alertness and initiative were so vigorously pursued that they bridged the gap of material assistance and projected India as a champion and uncompromising fighter against colonialism and racism. However, although Indian diplomacy did succeed in filling the gaps in Indian desires and its effective role in African liberation struggles, how far did it actually succeed in providing a coherence to India's economic relations within the emerging south-south concept?

India had added an economic dimension to its diplomacy and policy toward Africa by the mid-1960s. Selective and aggressive initiatives for friendship through economic diplomacy did help India, and through its ITEC and other programmes, India started to counter the growing Chinese economic diplomacy in the Third World, a competition that has re-emerged in recent years in Africa. Under the umbrella of the NAM, this economic focus became the main policy driver for India, and other diplomatic endeavours became supportive and adjunct to it in Africa. However, the economic relations that emerged in the context of Indian initiatives in the umbrella of south-south links were not very equitable, at least in trade. Indo-African growing trends in economic areas demand that in the light of India's past experiences, India should be sensitive to African concerns and expectations.

The current interactions call for partnership and south-south solidarity, and focus on economic empowerment and sustainable development in Africa. They show signs of both expanding and deepening, but if the growing trends under the Indian private sector in Indo-African economic relations do not distinguish themselves qualitatively from north-south relations, then it will create problems for Indian moves in Africa. The economic relations of India with Africa under globalization are gainful for India, but they have to be qualitatively different from north-south relations as far as African perceptions are concerned. The question remains: can India translate its historical and cultural goodwill along with its credentials as a fast developing ex-colonial country into a competitive edge to push its new economic agenda formulated under the IAFS 2008?

Notes

1 S. Naidu, 'India's Engagement in Africa: Self Interest or Mutual Partnership?', in R. Southall and H. Melber (eds), *The New Scramble for Africa: Imperialism, Investment and Development in Africa*, Scottsville, South Africa: University of KwaZulu-Natal Press, 2009.
2 E. Mawdsley and G. McCann, 'The Elephant in the Corner? Reviewing India-Africa Relations in the New Millennium', *Geography Compass*, Vol. 4, No. 2, 2010.
3 A. Gupta, 'India and Africa South of the Sahara', in B. Prasad (ed.), *India's Foreign Policy*, New Delhi: Vikas, 1979, p.269.
4 Tanzania's foreign minister, Oscar Kambona, said in the early 1960s that he and others thought that India's leadership of Asia was decadent and that China was an emergent force. Quoted in D. Kimche, *The Afro-Asian Movement: Ideology and Foreign Policy of the Third World*, Jerusalem: Israel University Press, 1973, p.246.
5 During the Belgrade NAM summit India did not want to fix any date for ending colonialism in Africa because it felt it would be unrealistic, while Sukarno wanted it to be two years, Nkrumah insisted on 31 December 1962, and Mali wanted it to be 'immediate'. Later, India suggested it be 'speedy' and improved this to 'immediate', which was finally accepted. See G. Jansen, *Afro-Asia and Non-alignment*, London: Faber, 1966, p.299.
6 M. Kumar, 'Reactions and Attitudes of African Countries to the Chinese Aggression on India', in V. Grover (ed.), *International Relations and Foreign Policy of India*, New Delhi: Deep & Deep, 1992.
7 Krishna Menon said, 'We became camp followers there [...] Our personality did not make any impact on the conference or on the delegates'. See M. Brecher, *India and World Politics – Krishna Menon Views of the World*, London: Oxford University Press, 1968, p.226.
8 See H. Chhabra, *India and Africa. Saga of Friendship*, New Delhi: Government of India, 1986, p.15.
9 A. Gupta, 'India and Asians in East Africa', in M. Twaddle (ed.), *Expulsion of Minorities: Essays on Ugandan Asians*, London: Athlone Press, 1975, p.130.
10 MEA, *Foreign Affairs Record*, New Delhi: Ministry of External Affairs, April 1973, pp.161–162.
11 See A. Dubey, 'Indo-Africa State Relations', *Africa Quarterly*, Vol. 37, Nos. 1–2, 1997, pp.51–55.
12 Ibid.
13 India-Africa, *Delhi Declaration* (India-Africa Forum Summit 2008), 9 April 2008, indembkwt.org.
14 P. Mukherjee, 'Address by External Affairs Minister at the India-Africa Business Luncheon', 9 April 2008, meaindia.nic.in.
15 R.I. Singh, 'India, Africa Ready to Embrace Global Destiny', 15 January 2006, meaindia.nic.in; inc. 'Modern India seeks to collaborate with a resurgent Africa to create a new world order. Ideology, redolent of an earlier era of a shared struggle against colonialism and imperialism, has been tempered with pragmatism and a sober realization of new challenges facing both India and Africa as they get ready to take their place under the global sun'.
16 'Indian Space Scientists to Tap Africa Market', *Asian Age*, 13 July 2010.
17 A. Lele, 'Successful Launch of PSLVC15', *IDSA Comment*, 16 July 2010.
18 See T. Poddar and E. Yi, 'India's Rising Growth Potential', in *BRICS and Beyond* (Goldman Sachs Global Economics Paper, No. 152), Washington: Goldman Sachs, 2007, pp.9–13. This followed on from D. Wilson and R. Purushothaman, *Dreaming with BRICs: The Path to 2050* (Goldman Sachs Global Economics Paper, No. 99), Washington: Goldman Sachs, 2003.
19 M. Singh, 'PM's Address at the Combined Commanders Conference', 26 October 2004, pmindia.nic.in.
20 'India to Join Marine Highway Project in Africa', *Wall Street Journal*, 24 March 2009.
21 R. Beri, 'Indo-South Africa Defence Cooperation', *Strategic Analysis*, Vol. 23, No. 10, 2000.
22 A. Vines and B. Oruitemeka, 'India's Engagement with the African Indian Ocean Rim States', *Africa Programme Paper* (London: Chatham House), No.1/08, 2008.
23 M. Pubby, 'India Activates Listening Post on Foreign Soil: Radars in Madagascar', *Indian Express*, 18 July 2007.
24 A. Prakash, 'Emerging India: Security and Foreign Policy Perspectives', 1 September 2005, indiannavy. nic.in. For India–China rivalry in the Seychelles and Mauritius, see C. Raja Mohan, 'Circling Mauritius', *Indian Express*, 11 February 2009; 'Sino-Indian Rivalry in the Western Indian Ocean', *ISAS Insights* (Singapore), No. 52, 24 February 2009.
25 Sidhartha, 'India Eyes an Island in the Sun', *Times of India*, 26 November 2006.
26 'India and Seychelles to Increase Cooperation for Maritime Security in IOR', *Frontier India*, 19 July 2010.
27 C. Xavier, 'India's Strategic Advantages Over China in Africa', *IDSA Comments*, 30 June 2010.

18

Looking north

Central Asia and the Shanghai Cooperation Organisation

Emilian Kavalski

Introduction

Analysis of the nascent international agency of regional powers that have global intentions has become a topic of growing significance in the study of world affairs—a development facilitated by the break-up of the Cold War order, which has allowed a number of actors to extend their international roles and outreach. India features prominently among those actors and its agency in global life is subject to growing public, policy and scholarly scrutiny. Its relations with Central Asia contributed to this increasing interest in the practices of India's 'enlightened self-interest' in its *extended neighbourhood*.

India's outreach to Central Asia offers insight into the country's *strategic culture* and the modes of security governance that it fashions. The region, thereby, becomes a prism for teasing out both the underpinnings of New Delhi's external strategies and the discourses through which they are articulated owing to India's encounter with the Central Asian agency of other international actors—especially Russia and the People's Republic of China. In other words, the region provides a transformative context for assessing the emerging roles and attitudes of India's global agency. At the same time, it also reveals that Russia and China are increasingly becoming the 'significant others' on the horizon of India's Asian outlook.

In Indian foreign policy parlance, the country's aspirations in Central Asia have been brought together under the narrative framework of the 'Look North' policy.[1] As its appellation suggests, the constructs of the Look North policy indicate a desire to emulate India's 'Look East' approach to South-East Asia, seen elsewhere. On the one hand, just like in the case of its relations with South-East Asia, the narratives of the Look North policy intend to demonstrate India's ability to 'break out of the claustrophobic confines of South Asia'.[2] On the other hand, unlike the Look East policy, the Look North approach to Central Asia has remained mostly a discursive platform for Indian pundits and commentators rather than an actual government strategy.

Thus, it has to be noted from the outset that this chapter undertakes an assessment of the narrative construction of India's involvement in Central Asia, revealing something of the 'mythmaking and international relations of a rising power'.[3] The chapter proceeds with an outline of the discursive modalities of the Look North policy. The investigation draws attention to the significance of the post-Cold War trajectories of India's foreign policy-making on its relations with Central Asia. This contextualization makes possible the engagement with the narratives of India's confrontation with the growing significance of the Shanghai Cooperation Organisation (SCO) in Central Asia. In particular, the encounter with the SCO reveals the complex attitudes informing India's relations with Russia and China in the post-Cold War period. The chapter concludes by demonstrating the relative lack of *influence* in India's Central Asian agency. The contention is that New Delhi's international image has few appealing attributes that regional states in Central Asia might be tempted to emulate.

The narrative outlines of India's Look North policy

During a visit to Turkmenistan in September 1995, the then Prime Minister P.V. Narasimha Rao announced that 'for India', Central Asia was an area 'of high priority, where we aim to stay engaged far into the future. We are an independent partner with no selfish motives. We only desire honest and open friendship and to promote stability and cooperation without causing harm to any third country'.[4] Rao's proclamation offers a glimpse into the discursive genesis of the Look North policy.[5]

Most commentators insist that India's engagement with Central Asia is a function of the country's historical interactions with the region. Thus, the 'long-standing historical ties encompassing the political, cultural, economic, and religious dimensions' form the premise for the current international relations between New Delhi and the region.[6] Yet, alongside these proclamations of extensive historical associations, observers have also acknowledged that, while 'Central Asia is closer to New Delhi then Chennai or Bangkok, Tashkent and Almaty ring a distant bell when the names pop up in casual conversations'.[7] Such attitudes indicate that even after the break-up of the USSR, New Delhi only very gradually began to develop an understanding of Central Asia's importance to the dynamics of South Asian affairs. This realization seems to have been one of the underlying features in the transformation of India's post-Cold War foreign policy.

In this context, the articulations of India's Look-North to Central Asia have come to stress the need for a 'proactive and meaningful policy that accords top priority to the region'.[8] Thus, the narrative exploitation of the legacies of the past by the Indian foreign policy elite discloses a strategy that aims 'to remind the new generation in Central Asia that India is not new to them but rather a very old friend'.[9] Consequently, India is presented as a model for Central Asian states. It is claimed that, in their search for 'support and constructive cooperation',

> India stood as an attractive direction to relate to. India was not only a multiethnic, multicultural, resilient society with vast experience of managing delicate intra-ethnic relations, but also a secular and democratic polity. [At the same time], India was geographically distant, but culturally and historically close, without any record of an intrusive or aggressive behaviour towards the newly emerged Central Asian republics.[10]

Such statements indicate that the Look North policy did not emerge in a vacuum, but was profoundly implicated by the post-Cold War trajectories of India's foreign policy-making. The formulation of a country's international interactions offers discursive platforms for the manifestation of national self-positioning on the world stage and the re-contextualization of historical narratives to the exigencies of the present. The following sections sketch out these dynamics.

India's engagement in Central Asia before 1998

It has to be remembered that, while nearly universally perceived as an opportunity for pro-moting different visions of 'new world orders', for India the crumbling of the Berlin Wall represented 'the loss of an entire world'.[11] New Delhi's external outlook had to confront sev-eral predicaments: a) on a pragmatic/policy level, India had to formulate a new international strategy in the absence of its erstwhile ally—the USSR—while at the same time acknowledging the failure of (Nehruvian) non-alignment; b) on a conceptual/strategic level, India's foreign policy-making became frustrated by the increasing tension between 'militarism' (i.e. coercive international stance) and 'moralism' (i.e. co-operative international stance). Consequently, India's policy-making anxiety in the immediate post-Cold War environment attests to the inability to meaningfully accommodate the desire for a more assertive role on the global stage while lacking the confidence that it *can* and *should* do so.[12]

Thus, the 'post-Cold War blues', which infected India's international affairs during the 1990s, made India's relations with Central Asia one of the most conspicuous aspects of its foreign policy ambiguity during this period. The uncertainty dominating New Delhi's outlook had two important implications:

> One was that there emerged a new Central Asia, independent and sovereign, freed from the control of the former Soviet Union, and looking forward to a greater and dynamic engagement with the rest of the world, particularly Asia. The second was a sort of crisis of confidence in India's foreign policy perspective resulting from the collapse of the Cold War framework of global politics and the consequent erosion of the former Soviet Union as a source of foreign policy support.[13]

However, India's failure to engage Central Asia more convincingly in this period is an out-come not only of the 'post-Cold War blues', but also of the formulation of New Delhi's external relations *in reaction to* Pakistan's foreign policy strategies. In 'Indian perceptions', Pakistan has 'vested interests' in pursuing a 'quest for strategic depth vis-à-vis India in Central Asia'.[14] The assertion is that the 'philosophy [of Pakistan's interactions with the region] appears to have always focused on a prescriptive approach as to what *should* happen in or to the Central Asian states within the overall backdrop of deep antagonism against India'.[15] India's Look North to Central Asia has therefore extended a *non-Pakistani* alternative to the region.

Thus, for the better part of the 1990s the 'ill-conceived [and] ill-executed treatment [of Central Asia] as a counterpoise between India and Pakistan' has tended to befuddle New Delhi's foreign policy-making.[16] In particular, the framework of India's Look North policy illustrates New Delhi's inability to obviate both the legacy of mistrust between India and Pakistan as well as the very real barrier posed by Pakistan-occupied Kashmir (PoK). Thus, while 'neither India nor Pakistan is an immediate neighbour of Central Asia', the export of the conflict between New Delhi and Islamabad to Central Asia can be described as an 'avoidable small game'.[17] Moreover, the policy attitudes that dominated India's strategic thinking on Central Asia for much of the first post-Cold War decade indicated that New Delhi's foreign policy outlook was influenced by the constraints of its South Asian context. Thus, for most of this period, India's foreign policy formulation remained in the grips of conceptual tensions, strategic uncertainty and geopolitical limitations, which hampered the extension of a coherent policy towards Central Asia.

India's engagement in Central Asia after 1998

India's '"forward" Central Asian policy' in the post-1998 period is seen 'as an integral component of its growing military, nuclear, and economic power'.[18] It is also a component of its growing energy needs.[19] However, some Indian commentators argued that, despite the proclamations of the region's 'historical belonging' to India's 'strategic neighbourhood', New Delhi was 'not giving sufficient attention to Central Asia'; consequently, 'good intentions have not been converted into substantive relations'.[20] The stated overarching objective of India's Look North policy is the promotion of 'peace and mutual prosperity'.[21] This intent, however, has been buttressed by the twin ambition of (a) maintaining 'the democratic and secular ethos' of the region, because it 'binds India and Central Asia together'; and (b) evolving 'measures that would safeguard the stability and integrity of Central Asian republics and save them from getting divided and opposing one another'; in addition, whilst confirming the pragmatism of its post-1998 foreign policy, India has engaged in strategic bilateral relations in Central Asia in an attempt to overcome its marginalization in the region.[22] The following sections outline these three approaches.

Experience of managing diversity within a secular and democratic polity

Indian commentators have noted that the (violence accompanying the) dissolution of the USSR and the Federal Republic of Yugoslavia has 'eroded the legitimacy of multi-ethnic, multi-lingual, and multi-religious states'.[23] This observation informs the (tacit) conviction that India is one of the remaining countries that share the characteristic features of the now defunct socialist federations. Consequently, such a realization underpins the responsibility of its foreign policy-making to assert the viability of India's state-building project by demonstrating the relevance and experience in successfully managing its internal diversity through the institutional arrangements of a secular and democratic polity. In other words, India is not 'multicultural by accident', but 'multicultural by design'.[24] Consequently, India's strategic objective in the region is to 'work for the rise and consolidation of democratic and secular polities in Central Asia, because the spill-over of the rise of religious extremism may threaten India's own internal stability and security'.[25]

Indian efforts and expectations, however, have been frustrated by the realization that the Central Asian republics 'were ill-prepared for independence'.[26] Although 'conversant in the art of governance', they suffered from a pronounced democratic deficit that hinders the establishment of 'long-term political and strategic vision' for their development.[27] In this setting, 'state failure remains a concern in New Delhi'.[28] Indian commentators list multiple (and often contradictory) rationalities in their explanation of the weakness of democratic practices in the region. Governments there remain 'undemocratic, dictatorial, authoritarian [...] the Central Asian scenario throws little awesome prospects for any radical departure from the present'.[29] Such awareness of the pervasive uncertainty of Central Asian affairs is deeply engrained in the narratives of the Look North policy and informs the encouragement of frameworks for regional co-operation.

Encouraging regional co-operation in Central Asia

Intertwined with the narrative modalities of secularism and democracy, the Look North policy also stresses the significance of regional co-operation to the stability and prosperity of Central

Asia. The proposition of Indian commentators is that 'India should try [to] forge a collective security arrangement and a collective project for the development of all the countries of the region regardless of their policy slants in favour of this or that Great Power'.[30] This insistence on the unity of Central Asian states reflects Indian perceptions of the pragmatic benefits from (even a rudimentary form of functional) co-operation which 'transforms conventional aspirations into more open, dynamic, and wider practices of peaceful coexistence, collective responsibility, and development'.[31] The fear is that, without regional integration, history might repeat itself and Central Asia may lose 'its creative capacity [just like it did] during the sixteenth century, owing to its internecine warfare, internal instability, and external aggressive policy'.[32]

In this respect, there seems to be a significant level of disappointment among Indian commentators that 'the political leadership of these countries has been unable to evolve a mind-set that could be truly characterized as [Central Asian]'.[33] Such a failure tends to be explained through the pursuit of narrow personal gains by nepotistic members of the state elite, which (more often than not) are disguised under the narrative cloak of (ethno-)national interests. Thus, commentators have noted that the failure of Central Asian states to establish a robust framework for regional co-operation illustrates their weak structures of governance.

The regionalization implicit in the discourses of the Look North policy exposes a conviction that it is India's 'purpose to engage more vigorously with an independent Central Asia through cultural structures'.[34] In this respect, some Indian commentators have suggested that the alleged 'homogeneity [of the region] is quite deceptive' and hinders the comprehension of the 'diversity, which is articulated in many different ways' in the convoluted dynamics of Central Asian politics.[35] Thus, the suggestion is that India needs to accompany its regionalizing approach with 'country-specific' strategies targeting the individual Central Asian republics. This understanding informs the discussion of India's bilateral relations with regional states in the following section.

India's strategic bilateralism in Central Asia

As already suggested, the narratives of the Look North policy indicate a desire to encourage the regional co-operation of the Central Asian states. Such proclamations notwithstanding, India's involvement in the region has been paralleled by a significant level of bilateral relations in an attempt to overcome the constraints imposed by its latecomer status in Central Asian affairs. In this respect, it is Tajikistan that—to all intents and purposes—has become the centrepiece of New Delhi's strategic bilateralism in Central Asia.

The construction of Tajikistan as India's 'gateway to Central Asia'[36] is of complex provenance in the narratives of the Look North policy. The hackneyed point of departure seems to be the observation of a 'millennia-old', 'civilizational relationship between Tajikistan and the Indian subcontinent'.[37] Strategically speaking, however, it is the shared perception of external threats that appears to motivate India's bilateral relations with Tajikistan. Indian commentators explain that the civil war that ravaged the country during the 1990s has been '*caused* by a skilful exploitation of the inter-regional/inter-clan rivalries by forces of Islamic fundamentalism supported by the Pakistan-backed Mujahideen in Afghanistan'; i.e., it was 'a spill-over of the victory of the Mujahideen armed groups in Afghanistan. The jobless Afghan *jehadis* found employment both in Tajikistan and in the Indian state of Jammu and Kashmir'.[38] Thus, India responded with logistic and military support for the anti-Taliban Northern Alliance through Tajikistan.

Such assistance has been articulated as a strategy for 'strengthening Tajikistan's secular forces in their war against Islamic fundamentalism'.[39] For instance, there have been allegations that India's military outposts in the country were set up as early as the mid-1990s.[40] Framed as an offer of 'humanitarian assistance', in 2000 India formally acknowledged the establishment of a military hospital on the Tajikistan–Afghanistan border at Farkhor, and the widening of a military air-strip near Dushanbe for transport aircraft.[41] More recently, India—still 'quietly, very quietly'—deployed at least one helicopter squadron at its Ayni air-base in Tajikistan to bolster its already existing rapid-response capabilities.[42]

The discourses of the Look North policy legitimize this military outreach by maintaining that 'the nation's strategic interests lie far beyond [its] borders'—a realization that is 'compelling New Delhi to consider the possibility of sending troops abroad *outside of the UN framework*'.[43] Thus, India's military presence in Tajikistan becomes one of the most conspicuous indications of the presumed assertive logic of its post-1998 foreign policy. In this respect, India's involvement in Central Asia exposes an underlying 'revisionist' foreign policy stance—through which New Delhi aims to *revise* the existing patterns in its international environment in order to facilitate the exercise of its own agency.[44]

Thus, the intense ties with Tajikistan reveal India's attempt to carve out a space for its stakes in Central Asia. At the same time, such bilateral relations do not demonstrate a socializing propensity that might become the cornerstone of a more encompassing community of practice in the region. What has been particularly frustrating for the proponents of the Look North policy is that, while India's longing for closer relations with Central Asia has largely remained unfulfilled, other actors in the meantime have managed to establish themselves as important partners to the region. The following section details the complex context of such an encounter in India's Central Asian policy.

Shanghaied into co-operation? Indian attitudes towards the SCO

The nuclear confidence of India's post-1998 foreign policy has endeavoured to project the image of a self-aggrandizing state capable of charting its course in the uncertain currents of global politics. However, while Looking North towards Central Asia, India has quickly recognized that it is not the only international actor striving to assert its agency in the region.

It is the awareness of this dynamic context that has made Indian observers particularly perplexed by the seemingly rapid emergence of the SCO as an increasingly sophisticated institutional architecture for Central Asian affairs. The development of the SCO has confirmed the viewpoint that the region has become the host of a 'new great game'.[45] The former ambassador, Kishan Rana, seems to offer one of the clearest explanations of what Indian commentators have in mind when they use this term:

> Visualize a three-dimensional, multiplayer chessboard, where a move by each protagonist produces eddies and backflows that affect all the others, and prompt counter-movements. Factor into this, the time as a fourth dimension, which takes this analogy beyond easy description. [Central Asia] resembles such a turbulent, volatile, and unpredictable scene owing to the mix of cooperation [and] contestation that marks virtually each bilateral relationship. The situation is all the more unpredictable because of the absence of fixed mooring points. [The region] thus offers a heady mix of bilateral, regional, and Great Power diplomacy, in which the players weave bewildering nets of connections and counter arrangements. Some of the emerging developments appear contradictory, understandable only in a fluid context.[46]

In recognizing the SCO's uniqueness, some have gone as far as to assert that it is emerging as '*the principal basis for strategic interactions* between Central Asia and the big and medium powers that surround the region'.[47] New Delhi's relations with the SCO, therefore, backstop the debate on 'whether India has an ambition for creating an area of influence' in the region.[48]

In this respect, India's gaining of SCO observer status in 2005 has been interpreted by some commentators as an indication of India's ability to '*dilute* Chinese and Russian influence' in Central Asia.[49] At the same time, others have praised New Delhi for 'choosing to maintain some political distance from the ambitious goals [that] Beijing and Moscow have for the organisation'.[50] Such statements reveal that Indian attitudes towards the SCO are influenced by the persisting tensions between continuity and change, convergence and divergence, and co-operation and conflict underpinning New Delhi's Central Asian outlook. This oscillation is simultaneously confounding and timely. It is confounding because of the enthusiasm and conviction with which opposing standpoints are propounded, very often by the same commentators! At the same time, it is timely because it reveals a diverse range of options for the Indian state elite to address the complexity of both Central Asian affairs and global politics.

The contention here is that Indian perceptions of the SCO make conspicuous New Delhi's shifting attitudes towards other international actors which would not necessarily be elicited from the country's bilateral relations with those actors. The discussion of the SCO in the narratives of the Look North policy has zoomed-in on India's encounter with the Central Asian agency of Russia and China. The following sections address this dynamic.

The SCO and India's encounter with Russia in Central Asia

Indian perceptions of the SCO's activities in Central Asia reveal attitudes towards Russia that present a more complex picture of the relations between New Delhi and Moscow than their bilateral interactions suggest. On the one hand, Russian support for India's inclusion as an observer in the SCO (and seemingly currently for India's full membership)[51] confirms the perception that the two countries have a shared interest in the stability of Central Asia. This then underpins the awareness that 'Russia would like India to become a big player in the region as a balancing factor for both the American and Chinese presence'.[52]

On the other hand, many Indian commentators assert that Moscow no longer has the over-bearing presence in Central Asia that it once had. In this respect, the perceived weakness of Moscow's foreign policy stance towards Central Asia has clashed with the assertiveness of New Delhi's post-1998 external relations. Thus, their interactions within the SCO framework have convinced some observers that 'beyond oil and arms sales, India finds little common ground with Russia'.[53] At the same time, Moscow's willingness to involve third parties—in particular China—in its Central Asian interactions have confirmed Russia's 'loss of its [Central] Asian republics'.[54]

For Indian commentators, therefore, the SCO epitomizes an alliance between Russia and China, which confirms that from Moscow's point of view 'China is a more fitting partner for Russia's multifaceted interests in Central Asia than India'.[55] A significant part of Indian hostility towards Russia's involvement in the region, therefore, derives from Moscow's departure from its usual framework of foreign policy behaviour. Thus, the patterns of divergence in India's encounter with Russia in Central Asia reveal that owing to the exigencies of domestic and global politics, there is very little degree of certainty regarding the future trajectories of New Delhi's interactions with Moscow. What appears certain, however, is that the glory days of the Cold War 'special relationship' between the two countries have petered out.

The SCO and India's encounter with China in Central Asia

For many Indian commentators, China's ability to establish the SCO in 2001 has become one of the clearest indications of the post-Cold War dynamism of Central Asian affairs. The SCO

has thereby enhanced the visibility of 'China's economic and political interests in the region [...
in the] politics of oil and gas', in which India lost out to China over competition for Kazakhstan
energy in 2005.[56] In this setting, India's encounter with the SCO has provoked distinct images
of Beijing's regional agency—ranging from a threat, through a partner, to a model. Although
not necessarily complementary, such diverse representations cohabit simultaneously within the
narratives of the Look North policy.

Perhaps the most interesting image of China, provoked by India's confrontation with the
SCO, is that of a model. A number of commentators have suggested that New Delhi's
encounter with Beijing's agency in Central Asia has produced the image of 'China as a role
model' for India's external relations.[57] The realization is that Beijing's experience provides
useful instruction for New Delhi's own engagement in the region. Thus, the consideration of
SCO in the narratives of the Look North policy suggests that if India is to become the Great
Power that it proclaims to be, it needs to learn from (if not emulate) the model set up by
Beijing.

A number of these 'lessons' relate to the structure, process and content of India's relations
with the region. Thus, in contrast to India, China's initiatives in Central Asia indicate the
development of a sophisticated 'holistic view' of foreign policy-making, which 'embeds the
state firmly within the interstate system as an organic and inseparable part, linking the fate even
of the inside of the state to the fate or nature of its outside'.[58] Indian perceptions of the SCO,
therefore, have provoked a desire to emulate Beijing's ability to 'establish quickly an international reputation for being able to look after itself [and, thus] become a "Great Power", whereas
India's potential remains unrealized'.[59] Consequently, encounter with Beijing's involvement in
Central Asia has produced diverse assessments of the SCO within the narratives of India's Look
North policy, all of which tend to reflect the difficulties in articulating a foreign policy strategy
in a complex world.

Conclusions

The discussion of the narratives of the Look North policy confirms New Delhi's foreign policy
desire that India becomes 'a kind of a model' for other countries'.[60] The proclivity towards a
discursive projection of India as a blueprint for Central Asian development has become a
defining feature of the Look North policy. Yet, as demonstrated, the confrontation with the
reality of Central Asian interactions and the involvement of other international actors—especially China—makes conspicuous that New Delhi has little (if any) influence in the region. Not
surprisingly, therefore, India's perception of the strengthening of the Beijing-based SCO has
further aggravated New Delhi's irritation at international, and regional, acceptance of China as
being the next global power. Thus, despite the proliferation of discourses on India's rise to
global prominence, the absence of a readily available Indian 'vision' of global politics prevents
New Delhi from living up to the expectations generated by such narratives.

The absence of a meaningful power of attraction (*soft power*) has undermined India's international engagement with Central Asia. This has been reflected in 'India's noticeable absence'
from Central Asian politics.[61] It is also reflected in India's weak position in what Shen considers
'India's absence from ideological energy diplomacy in Central Asia', in which 'India lacks a
unique ideology to increase its influence in Central Asia', and 'India therefore remains a Great
Power candidate in the region rather than a Great Power status holder'.[62] The discussion of the
narratives of the Look North policy has demonstrated that the discursive construction of India's
current external affairs does not project a specific (if any) vision of world order that would
distinguish it from the other participants in the 'new great game'. Consequently, the

international identity of New Delhi has no distinct attributes that regional actors in Central Asia might be tempted to emulate. The implication, then, is not only that India might remain a 'rising power' for longer than its pundits portend, remaining in 'the class of countries that are always emerging but never quite arriving'.[63] In other words, the analysis of India's relations with Central Asia still does not seem to offer a convincing response to the query of whether India *can change enough* to become a pole of attraction in an international environment marked by extreme turbulence, and a regional environment marked by multiple presences of outside actors.[64]

Notes

1 S. Bal, *Central Asia: A Strategy for India's Look-North Policy*, New Delhi: Lancer Publishers, 2004.

2 B. Gupta, 'India in the 21st Century', *International Affairs*, Vol. 73, No. 2, 1997, p.309.

3 E. Kavalski, *India and Central Asia: The Mythmaking and International Relations of a Rising Power*, London: I.B. Tauris, 2010.

4 Quoted in N. Joshi (ed.), *Central Asia: The Great Game Replayed. An Indian Perspective*, New Delhi: New Century Publications, 2003, p.110.

5 Although it ignores the growing energy considerations surrounding Central Asia, and India's energy competition there with China.

6 S. Bal, *Central Asia*, op. cit., p.4.

7 A. Bhattacharya, 'The Fallacy in the Russia-India-China Triangle', *Strategic Analysis*, Vol. 28, No. 2, 2004, pp.358–61.

8 N. Joshi, 'India's Policy Toward Central Asia', *World Focus*, Vol. 28, No. 335/336, 2007, p.445.

9 B. Jain, *Global Power: India's Foreign Policy, 1947–2006*, Lanham: Lexington Books, 2008, p.210.

10 N. Joshi (ed.), *Central Asia*, op. cit., p.106.

11 N. Menon and A. Nigam, *Power and Contestation: India since 1989*, London: Zed Books, 2007, p.166.

12 C. Raja Mohan, *Crossing the Rubicon: The Shaping of India's New Foreign Policy*, London: Palgrave Macmillan, 2004, p.208.

13 N. Joshi (ed.), *Central Asia*, op. cit., p.102.

14 N. Joshi, 'Geopolitic Perspectives on Central Asia: An Indian View', in J. Roy and B. Kumar (eds), *India and Central Asia: Classical to Contemporary Periods*, New Delhi: Concept Publishing, 2006, p.150.

15 S. Bal, *Central Asia*, op. cit., pp.332–33.

16 J. Singh, *Defending India*, New York: St Martin's Press, 1999, p.111.

17 G. Dietl, 'Quest for Influence in Central Asia: India and Pakistan', *International Studies*, Vol. 34, No. 2, 1997, p.134. Also S. Akbarzadeh, 'India and Pakistan's Geostrategic Rivalry in Central Asia', *Contemporary South Asia*, Vol. 12, No. 2, 2003.

18 B. Jain, *Global Power*, op. cit., p.210.

19 S. Blank, 'India's Quest for Central Asian Energy', *Eurasia Daily Monitor*, Vol. 2, No. 40, 2005.

20 K. Santhanam and R. Dwivedi (eds), *India and Central Asia: Advancing the Common Interest*, New Delhi: Anamaya Publishers, 2004, pp.18–19.

21 E. Kavalski, *India and Central Asia*, op. cit., p.89.

22 S. Ashopa, 'India and Post-Soviet Asia: An Appraisal of India's Central Asia Policy', in J. Roy and B. Kumar (eds), *India and Central Asia*, op. cit., p.188.

23 K. Santhanam and R. Dwivedi, *India and Central Asia*, op. cit., p.24.

24 N. Manohoran, quoted in E. Kavalski, *India and Central Asia*, op. cit., p.90.

25 N. Joshi (ed.), *Central Asia*, pp.98–99.

26 Ibid., p.69.

27 R. Sharma, 'Political System and Democratic Discourse in Central Asia: A View From Outside', in J. Roy and B. Kumar (eds), *India and Central Asia*, op. cit., p.125.

28 A. Gupta (ed.), *Strategic Stability in Asia*, Aldershot: Ashgate, 2008, p.115.

29 P. Dash, 'Central Asia: Tulips Have Different Hews', in J. Roy and B. Kumar (eds), *India and Central Asia*, op. cit., pp.190, 204.

30 S. Ashopa, 'India and Post-Soviet Asia: An Appraisal of India's Central Asia Policy', op. cit., p.188.

31 R. Sharma (ed.), *India and Emerging Asia*, New Delhi: Sage, 2005, pp.134–35.

32 N. Joshi (ed.), *Central Asia*, op. cit., p.260.

33 N. Behera quoted in E. Kavalski, *India and Central Asia*, op. cit., p.94.

34 Ibid., p.97.

35 R. Sharma, 'Political System and Democratic Discourse in Central Asia', op. cit., p.123.

36 M. Singh (ed.), *India and Tajikistan: Revitalizing a Traditional Relationship*, New Delhi: Anamika Publishers, 2003, p.153.

37 Ibid., pp.30–37.

38 Ibid., pp.39–40, emphasis added.

39 C. Raja Mohan, 'Indian Foreign Policy', *World Focus*, Vol. 28, No. 335/336, Nov.–Dec. 2007, p.395.

40 R. Bedi, 'India and Central Asia', *Frontline*, Vol. 19, No. 19, 14–27 September 2002.

41 M. Singh (ed.), *India and Tajikistan*, op. cit., pp.201–02.

42 R. Pandit, 'Indian Forces Get Foothold in Central Asia', *Times of India*, 17 July 2007. Also R. Pandit, 'India Closely Watching Oil Interests', *Times of India*, 17 July 2010.

43 C. Raja Mohan, 'Indian Foreign Policy', op. cit., p.395, emphasis added.

44 C. Raja Mohan, *Crossing the Rubicon*, op. cit., p.80.

45 N. Joshi (ed.), *Central Asia*, op. cit. India, of course, has its own Great Game with China, which is being played in Central Asia (e.g. Jen-kun Fu, 'Reassessing a "New Great Game" between India and China in Central Asia', *China & Eurasia Quarterly*, Vol. 8, No. 1, 2010), and across Asia and the Indian Ocean (e.g. D. Scott, 'The Great Power "Great Game" Between India and China: "The Logic of Geography"', *Geopolitics*, Vol. 13, No. 1, 2008).

46 K. Rana, *Asian Diplomacy*, Oxford: Oxford University Press, 2007, pp.211–13.

47 S. Varadarajan, quoted in E. Kavalski, *India and Central Asia*, op. cit., p.156, emphasis added.

48 S. Asopa, *Struggle for Spheres of Interest in Trans-Caucasia-Central Asia and India's Stakes*, New Delhi: Manak Publications, 2006, p.90.

49 R. Bedi, 'India and Central Asia', op. cit., emphasis added.

50 E. Kavalski, *India and Central Asia*, op. cit., p.97.

51 'Russia Backs India's Case for SCO Membership', *Times of India*, 12 June 2010.

52 B. Jain, *Global Power*, op. cit., p.214.

53 A. Gupta (ed.), *Strategic Stability*, op. cit., p.117.

54 D. Lak, *The Future of a New Superpower*, New York: Viking, 2008, p.266.

55 B. Jain, *Global Power*, op. cit., p.126.

56 R.G. Gidadhubli, 'Politics of Oil and Gas in Central Asia – Conflicts and Co-operation', *Dialogue*, Vol. 6, No. 2, October–December 2004, p.170.

57 N. Joshi (ed.), *Central Asia*, op. cit., p.20.

58 M. Bhattacharjea, quoted in E. Kavalski, *India and Central Asia*, op. cit., p.162.

59 G. Deshpande and A. Acharya (eds), *Crossing a Bridge of Dreams: Fifty Years of India and China*, New Delhi: Tulika, 2001, p.464.

60 S. Dutt, *India in a Globalized World*, Manchester: Manchester University Press, 2006, p.205, emphasis added.

61 M. Bhadrakumar, quoted in E. Kavalski, *India and Central Asia*, op. cit., p.205.

62 S. Chen, 'Great Power Politics: India's Absence from Ideological Energy Diplomacy in Central Asia', *China and Eurasia Forum Quarterly*, Vol. 8, No. 1, 2010, pp.96, 103. Having lost out to China over Kazakhstani energy, India remains interested in mooted pipeline projects to access Turkmenistani energy, namely the TAPI (Turkmenistan-Afghanistan-Pakistan-India) and INSC (International North South Corridor, down from the Caspian to Iran's port of Chabahar) projects, though TAPI is threatened by Afghanistan's instability and potential Pakistani obstruction.

63 S.K. Mitra, 'The Reluctant Hegemon: India's self-perception and the South Asian strategic environment', *Contemporary South Asia*, Vol. 12, No. 3, September 2003, p.402.

64 U. Kachru, *Extreme Turbulence: India at the Crossroads*, New Delhi: Harper Collins, 2007, p.14.

Part 4
India's Great Power relations

19

India's relations with Russia

Gulshan Sachdeva

Introduction

During the March 2010 visit of the Russian Prime Minister Vladimir Putin to New Delhi, the Indian Prime Minister Manmohan Singh described Russia in fulsome terms:

> Relations with Russia are a key pillar of our foreign policy, and we regard Russia as a trusted and reliable strategic partner. Ours is a relationship that not only stands independent of any other, but whose significance has grown over time. Our partnership covers areas such as defence, civil nuclear energy, space, science and technology, hydrocarbons and trade and investment.[1]

During discussions, bilateral economic as well as regional security issues were top of the agenda. Putin's India visit was also watched very carefully in many Western capitals as this was happening immediately after the London Conference, where the Western alliance had been working on exit strategies in Afghanistan. The Putin visit was seen by many in India as a precursor to any hedging strategy involving Russia, India, Iran and the Central Asian republics against the possibility of a Taliban return in Afghanistan. Since the signing of their Declaration on Strategic Partnership in October 2000, this had been the subsequent 11th summit meeting. Similar to earlier meetings, five more agreements were signed in March 2010. Apart from multi-billion-dollar arms deals, an inter-governmental agreement on broad-based co-operation in atomic energy and a 'road map' for future co-operation were also signed. Similar to the last few summits, strategic congruence, defence purchases, hydrocarbons and nuclear power dominated the agenda. The visit obviously gained more significance because of a changing strategic scenario in India's *neighbourhood*. This chapter aims to analyse how *and* if, to use Manmohan Singh's phrase, its 'significance has grown over time', in a relationship that first took shape in the days of the old USSR.[2]

Historical background

Historically, the USSR under Stalin (Iosif Dzhugashvili), was suspicious of the genuineness of India's independence and non-alignment. However, Indo-Soviet bonhomie started with

Jawaharlal Nehru's visit to the USSR in June 1955 and the Nikita Khrushchev/Nikolai Bulganin visit to India in December 1955. This was also the time when the Congress party in India was affirming its belief in state planning and a 'socialistic pattern of society', and Nehru was playing a leading role in the Bandung Conference (1955) of 29 Afro-Asian nations.[3] During the same period, the USSR began to use the instruments of aid, trade and diplomacy in developing countries, to limit Western influence.[4] Subsequently, Indo-Soviet relations flourished over the decades in the metallurgy, defence, energy and trade sectors. During the India–China war in 1962, the USSR tried to be neutral between what it called 'brother China' and 'friend India', with the People's Republic of China seeing this as a betrayal of international communist solidarity on the part of the USSR, and a factor that reflected and further exacerbated the growing Sino–Soviet split. In the early 1970s both Indian and Soviet leaders looked on the emerging US-Chinese rapprochement as a serious threat to their security. Their response had been in 1971 with the Indo-Soviet Treaty of Peace, Friendship and Cooperation, which provided immediate consultation in case of military action against parties to the Treaty.[5] During the India–Pakistan war in 1971, the USSR took a firm position in favour of India and sent ships to the Indian Ocean to counter any move by the USA, which had already sent its 7th Fleet ships into the Bay of Bengal. The results of the 1971 Indo–Pakistani war and emergence of Bangladesh established a trusted partnership between India and the USSR. During the 1980s both Rajiv Gandhi and Mikhail Gorbachev advocated a nuclear-free world. However, after the Soviet invasion of Afghanistan in 1979, India was also confronted with a dilemma of how to preserve its non-aligned credibility without jeopardizing its relations with the USSR.

In the initial post-Soviet period, bilateral relations in the 1990s went through a period of uncertainty when Russia was preoccupied with domestic economic and political issues, and with its relations with the USA and Europe.[6] Now India had to deal with a new Russia which was Eurocentric, economically dependent on the West, and neither had the interest nor the resources for Third World regimes.[7] President Boris Yeltsin, during his visit to Delhi in 1993, tried to recreate the spirit of old friendship with a new Treaty of Friendship to replace the old India-Soviet 1971 treaty. However, the fundamental character of the Treaty was transformed and in case of any threat to peace, the new Treaty vaguely called for regular consultations and co-ordination.[8] Although Yeltsin described India and Russia as 'natural partners', he was careful not to give the impression of a 'special relationship'.[9] Although relations were restored to respectable levels, the early years (1991–96) of 'benign neglect' of India by Russia left a deep mark on Indian policy-makers.[10]

The situation changed when the new Russian Prime Minister Yevgeny Primakov (1998–99) started shifting from the previous pro-Western Russian foreign policy. To strengthen his country's relations with old allies, Primakov visited India in 1998 and pushed proposals for creating a Russia-India-China (RIC) strategic triangle, although RIC coherence remains questionable for some Indian commentators like Abanti Bhattacharya: 'the development of a strategic triangle would be unrealistic. The reasons can be easily found in the mutual suspicion between India and China'.[11] The new Russian leadership under Vladimir Putin (president, 2000–08) reversed the Yeltsin-era drift in India-Russia bilateral relations, signed the Declaration on Strategic Partnership with India in 2000 and established the institution of annual summit meetings.[12] Moscow realized that, as a Eurasian power, an active Russian role and influence in dynamic Asia would be limited without a solid partnership with old friends like India.

Indian commentators welcomed Putin's comment in his 2004 visit, that 'India is our strategic privileged partner [...] And speaking from the point of view of geographical representation [...] India is number one', as recognition of India's own rise:

The emphasis is to be interpreted both in the geopolitical context and also in the military context. In terms of geo-political interpretation one could say that Russia accords primacy to India in the Indian sub-continent and all that it implies. In the military context it stresses that Russia recognizes India not only as a strategic partner but also as a 'privileged strategic partner'. If this is Russia's emphasis truly, then the long range prospect of Russia-India strategic cooperation is pregnant with exciting prospects.[13]

Despite its improving relations with the USA, China and Europe, India also did not want to abandon its time-tested relationship with Russia. In a world dominated by a single power (the USA), both the Indian and Russian vision of a multipolar world coincided. The issue of terrorism has also brought the countries together. Within South Asia, Russia has consistently supported India on the issue of Kashmir unconditionally over time or regime change and opposed its internationalization.[14] These issues continue to be reiterated at their Summit Declarations. Another point that both the partners have been emphasizing after every important meeting is that their partnership is neither against any third country nor at the expense of their relations with other major powers, understandable given Russia's strategic links with China and India's with the USA.

State linkages

Since 1992 about 15 summit meetings have taken place and about 135 agreements have been signed between the two countries. To improve their economic relationship, an Indo-Russian Inter-Governmental Commission on Trade, Economic, Scientific, Technological and Cultural Cooperation (IRIGC-TEC) has been working towards promoting bilateral co-operation. The Commission covers 11 joint working groups, namely: trade and economic co-operation; pharmaceuticals; petroleum; the coal industry; metallurgy; science and technology; cultural co-operation; information technology; power and energy; the environment and natural resources; and co-operation with the regions. In the 15th meeting of IRIGC-TEC, held in Moscow in October 2009, a new trade target of US $20,000m. by 2015 was agreed.

As already mentioned, a major turning point in their bilateral relationship was their formal Declaration on Strategic Partnership between Republic of India and the Russian Federation, signed during Putin's visit to India in October 2000.[15] Broadly, this agreement meant enhanced co-operation in the political, economic, defence and cultural fields. It talked of 'deepening and diversifying cooperation in sectors such as metallurgy, fuel and energy, information technology, communications and transport, including merchant shipping and civil aviation', and of 'further development of cooperation in banking and finance, and improving credit and insurance facilities'.[16] There was mention of simplifying rules and procedures for travel by entrepreneurs and businessmen of both countries. It was also agreed to jointly explore the possibilities of regional trading arrangements with third countries. Since then, summit meetings are taking place almost every year with many more agreements signed every year. The crux of all these summit meetings and accompanying declarations has been common positions on major global issues like international terrorism and desire for a multipolar world and close bilateral relations. These summits have been a very useful platform for formulating common positions and responses to emerging global political and economic issues.

However, what do these Summit declarations actually mean in real terms? There are many ways of looking at these developments. Every time the summit meeting takes place, the diehard proponents of old Indo-Soviet/Russian friendship emphasize the need to look at these agreements and declarations as a testimony of a time-tested, mutually beneficial friendship. They even go one step further and suggest that, along with Russia, India should forge solid friendships with other like-minded countries including China to soft *balance* some of the negative trends of a unipolar world, dominated by a single economic and military power.

However, many people in the new generation of Indians, who have entered the business or academic professions in the post-Soviet period, have somewhat different impressions about these summit meetings and declarations. They argue that countless bilateral meetings have taken place since 1992, and a plethora of agreements have been signed between the two countries. Various inter-governmental commissions and committees are also working to improve bilateral relations. In addition, both the countries are in an avowedly 'Strategic Partnership'. Yet, despite all this rhetoric, India's exports to Russia have remained lower than countries like Bangladesh, Nigeria, Kenya, Thailand, Israel and Viet Nam. In today's Russia about 70% of the economy is in the private sector, yet India has not moved beyond public sector and government declarations. So it is argued that India needs to strengthen the commercial component of its relationship through the linkages between the dynamic sectors of Indian industry, commerce and services and the newly emerging Russian private sector. In the absence of this relationship, it is argued that 'strategic partnership' may soon start losing its charm.

There is truth in both arguments. Even 20 years after the Soviet collapse, India's relations with Russia were still in transition, particularly in the commercial field. After some disruption, both have been able to restore and improve their political linkages. In the economic and academic fields, however, most old India-Soviet linkages have broken and new India-Russia links have not developed to the same extent. Both governments, including their summit meetings, have recognized this challenge.

It could be argued that, under new circumstances, business in both countries is no more the business of the governments. Therefore, it is up to the private sector to take advantage of conditions created by these agreements. Despite this, these high-level visits could have been used more effectively to promote Indian economic interests in Russia. Compared with India, Russians have done good business during these visits. Russia has a comparative advantage in the arms industry and India has purchased arms worth billions of dollars during these visits. Nine annual summit meetings over nine years were good opportunities for special bilateral economic relationships to have been created, even under entirely different circumstances. In 2005/06 trade still stood at a relatively modest $2,760m. In 2006 a Joint Study Group was set up to work out a programme for increasing bilateral trade to $10,000m. by 2010, and to explore the possibilities of a Comprehensive Economic Cooperation Agreement (CECA) between the two countries. The group submitted its lacklustre report in July 2007.[17] Except for the recommendation of a CECA, there were few specific recommendations. Subsequently, a Joint Task Force between the Indian Ministry of Commerce and Industry and the Russian Ministry of Economic Development was set up in February 2008 to monitor progress on a CECA, but with few concrete results emerging from the exercise. Trade by 2008/09 had increased to $5,420m., but fell back to $4,550m. in 2009/10, some way off the earlier target set for $10,000m. by 2010.

Defence linkages

There are estimates that about 800 Russian defence production facilities are kept in operation by Indian defence contracts.[18] Although China used to be the number one arms importer from Russia, India has emerged as number one since 2007. Some analysts have argued that, in arms exports, geopolitical and economic factors will eventually force Russia to make a choice between China and India, a contest that India will probably win.[19]

India's major purchases from Russia over the last 18 years have been varied and extensive, including aircraft (MIG 29, MIG 29 SMT, SU 30K, SU MK1), helicopters (Mi-17, Mi-18, etc.) and air-defence systems (AK 630 30mm, etc.). In June 2010 the Cabinet Committee on Security cleared another deal of more than $3,000m. to buy an additional 42 Sukhoi-30 MKI fighters from Russia. The deal came on top of the 230 aircraft already contracted from Russia in three deals worth a total of $8,500m. The initial contract was for 50 fighters, at $1,460m. In 2000 the Government contracted the licensed production of 140 fighters by Hindustan Aeronautics Limited. Then another 40 were added to the contract.[20] Some purchases have been of artillery and armoured vehicles (256M Tunguska), engines, sensors and a variety of missiles. Maritime purchases have been noticeable, including frigates (Talwar stealth class), submarines (Kilo/Sindhughosh), nuclear submarines (Akula-2 lease) and an aircraft carrier (the delayed Gorshkov purchase originally due for handover in 2008–09, now scheduled for handover at the end of 2012). Joint production has seen India also starting to produce a significant portion of armaments at home, including Brahmos missiles, T72M1 tanks, radars, anti-ship and anti-tank missiles, etc. Most tanks and aircraft are also being assembled in India. In 2009 the two countries agreed on a new military technical co-operation agreement for the period 2011–20. The new programme covers both ongoing projects, such as the Su-30 MKI fighter plane and the T-90 tank production in India, and 31 new projects, which include a fifth-generation fighter aircraft, the multi-role transport aircraft and a new multi-role helicopter. Under this programme India hopes to further shift from the buyer-seller relationship to joint design, development and production.

India also has a long tradition of collaboration in space with the USSR/Russia. Thumba Equatorial Rocket Launching Station was set up with Soviet help and many Indian experimental and remote sensing satellites were launched with Soviet co-operation. In 1990 India entered into a $350m. contract agreement with Russia to supply the cryogenic engines and technology for their manufacture within the country. Russia earlier agreed to provide India with the technology, but then reversed the decision after it signed the Missile Technology Control Regime agreement with the USA. The USA objected to giving India the technology because of its potential use for nuclear missiles. Commercial and political factors later compelled Russia to sell the rocket engines while withholding the technology. Soon afterwards Indian scientists were able to develop Indian engines. Currently, both countries collaborate on many space projects, which include India's unmanned lunar space flight project (Chandrayaan-2), the human space flight project and the development of the Indo-Russian Student Satellite, Youthsat. Russia has also agreed to provide India with access to signals from its Global Navigation Satellite System (GLONASS).

Commercial linkages

One important point of the old Indo-Soviet friendship was a special bilateral trade and economic relationship. Although this arrangement had many of the usual weaknesses, like corruption and patronage transactions in low-quality products, it helped many small and medium-sized private Indian companies to become exporters. After the disintegration of the USSR, this relationship was badly damaged. Economic transformation in Russia from a centrally planned economy to a market economy in 1992 coincided with the policies of economic liberalization in India. These developments changed the nature and character of foreign economic relations in both countries. Therefore, despite having solid economic and trade relations in the past, most Russian and Indian companies are still struggling to adjust in each other's markets. Economic relations are still surviving mainly because of defence purchases and some public sector investments by India. Commercial initiatives are slow to take advantage of Russian economic transformation. Despite good intentions, both governments have been unable to facilitate any major economic initiative which could have given a new direction to bilateral commercial ties.

Background of trading linkages

Since 1953, when the first trade agreement took place, seven long-term agreements have been signed between the two countries up to the collapse of the USSR. This bilateral trade was conducted through a specific system of trade and payment called the Rupee Trade System, based on annual plans. The important point of the system was payments in non-convertible currency. The trade turnover between the two countries increased from less than 2 crores in 1953 to about 8,000 crores in 1990–91. In 1990–91 more than 16% of Indian exports went to the USSR and about 6% of imports came from there.

One of the most striking characteristics of the Soviet centrally planned economy was that it had created a system of exchange in non-convertible currencies with many of its trading partners. This trade behaviour existed not only with the Council for Mutual Economic Assistance (CMEA) countries, but also with some other friendly countries like India. The value of exchange between the Russian rouble and Indian rupee currencies was arrived at through periodic bureaucratic negotiations.

Most of the ideologically-motivated scholars in India regarded this arrangement as a Soviet version of bilateral aid. The mainstream academia in India also declared that India had 'derived substantial benefits from its trade with the socialist world'.[21] In the late 1970s and early 1980s a few scholars in India had already warned that, despite short-term gains, this type of arrangement would harm long-term requirements of efficiency and growth.[22] After initial industrialization, India had problems of importing further machinery either for joint production for third countries or for the exclusive production for the socialist bloc. India did not want Soviet participation in those areas where it could get markets of its own. It also did not want 'captive units', the production of which could not be exported anywhere else but to the Soviet bloc and could give the Soviets the possibility of dictating terms.[23] Except for a few works, academia in India by and large did not bother to critically examine this pattern. The whole arrangement reflected political imperatives rather than economic rationality. After the Soviet break-up, the new policy elite in Russia also found these 'irrational' arrangements with developing countries unaffordable. The haste with which bilateral payment arrangements were scrapped in favour of payments in convertible currencies indicated that Russian and Indian policy-makers considered such bilateral arrangements undesirable under the new economic policy regimes in both countries.[24]

After the collapse of the USSR, the Indian and Russian Governments renegotiated the entire trade regime. The 1993 agreement terminated the traditional rupee trade arrangement and mandated all bilateral trade transactions to be conducted on a hard currency basis. However, with this agreement the issue of repayment of civilian and military loans taken by India from the former USSR also came up. Finally, after prolonged negotiations, the rouble credit was denominated in rupees and a repayment schedule was drawn up. The agreement provided for an annual repayment of about the equivalent of $1,000m. in rupees to Russia over a period of 12 years starting from 1994, with smaller amounts for a further period of 33 years. The rupee debt funds were to be used by the Russian side for import of goods and trade-related services from India. The rupee debt funds are maintained in a central account with the Reserve Bank of India. Under a three-year perspective plan, which came to an end in 1997, a part of the rupee debt funds was allocated for the import of tea, tobacco, soya meal and pharmaceuticals to designated Russian agencies. The balance was either auctioned or allocated to various states or importing organizations in Russia. In January 1998 this mechanism was replaced with a weekly auction of rupee debt funds conducted by the Vnesheconombank (Bank for Foreign Economic Affairs). During 1999 allocations made for the import of pharmaceuticals and medical equipment from India were utilized by several ministries in Russia. Between 2000 and 2006 the utilization of rupee funds continued through the auctions. In 2007 it was agreed that India's restructured rupee debt would be invested in Russian projects in India. According to Indian finance ministry sources, in December 2007 India still owed $1,970m. in debt to Russia under this category.

Contemporary trading ties

As a result of these changes, contemporary trade between India and Russia is based on payments in freely convertible currencies. All Russian exports to India follow the new system. However, in the 1990s about two-thirds of Indian exports were financed through the renegotiated rupee debt-repayment mechanism. As a result of all these economic policy changes, traditional actors in Indo-Russian trade and other economic relations like the public sector units and state trading corporations are no longer as relevant as they used to be in the Soviet era. Sections of the Indian private sector, which used to get away with selling many products of questionable quality under the bilateral system, also found it difficult to adjust to the radically changed economic and commercial environment in Russia, driven by market forces.

Although Indo-Russian trade has improved in the last few years, it has hovered around a 1% share during the first decade of the century. In quantity terms, although its volume has gone up from $905m. in 1995/96 to $4,547m. in 2009/10, it is still a very small sliver of India's trade; indeed, it was a 1.98% share in 1995/96, declining to a 0.97% share in 2009/10. Of course, statistics may not reveal the full story. Some imports from Russia, particularly metal, metal scrap, fertilizers, paper and paper products, may be sourced through international suppliers and are not reflected in these official figures. Similarly, many Indian goods enter Russia via 'shuttle trade' or through third countries. Still, this will not significantly change the broader picture. Russian trade figures have also included some of the arms exports in commercial trade figures in the last few years. Main items of traditional exports from India are pharmaceuticals, tea, coffee, ready-made garments, cotton, tobacco, edible preparations, iron and steel, etc. Recently, some non-traditional items like machinery have also shown some growth. Imports from Russia include iron and steel, fertilizer, wheat, minerals, chemicals, paper, rubber, copper, nickel, nuclear machinery, project goods, etc. Apart from goods, services trade may also become more significant in coming years. According to the Russian Central Bank, India and Russia had about $680m. in services trade in 2008. Russian services exports are mainly associated with construction and maintenance of equipment. In the last two years, services trade has moved in favour of India, with Indian exports in this category increasing from $90m. in 2003 to about $500m. in 2008.

Investment linkages

In the energy sector India's state public sector Oil and Natural Gas Corporation (ONGC) is active in Russia. In 2001 ONGC Videsh Limited (OVL) acquired a combined 20% interest in the Sakhalin-1 project. From 2006 this project started to generate positive cash flow. During 2008/09 ONGC's share of production was 1.853m. metric tons of oil and 0.372 billion cubic metres of gas. In 2009, at a total cost of $2,100m., OVL also completed the acquisition of seven blocks in the Tomsk region of western Siberia, previously held by a United Kingdom-listed company, Imperial Energy. At present, this Tomsk acquisition produces oil mainly from two fields and has its own infrastructure including pipeline network, field processing facilities and connections to the Transneft pipeline system.

The Indian ICICI Bank has opened its subsidiary ICICI Bank Eurasia in Russia, with branches in Moscow and St Petersburg. TATA Motors launched a project to assemble its light-duty trucks at Russia's Urals Automobile and Motors plant and assembling plant for buses at Volzhanin and Samotlor. The SUN group has also invested in Russia's food and real estate industries. Similarly, pharmaceutical companies like Dr Reddy's Laboratories Ltd and Lupin Ltd have investments in Russia. Berger Paints has also started operations in Russia. Carborundum Universal has purchased an 84% share in Russia's Volzhsky Abrasive Plant in the Volgograd region. The GMR Infrastructure has participated in a tender for the reconstruction and maintenance of St Petersburg's Pulkovo Airport. Other companies that are exploring possibilities for investment in Russia include GAIL, Indian Oil, Coal India, Reliance and Tata Tea.

Similarly, a few Russian companies are active in the Indian market. Silovyie Mashiny and Tekhnopromeksport are providing equipment and technical assistance for the construction of the Sipat thermal power plant in Chhattisgarh, Bihar and Uttar Pradesh. Two 1,000-megawatt nuclear power plants in Kudankulam, Tamil Nadu, are being constructed with the help of Russian Atomstroiekspor. In March 2010 both agreed on the construction of two more reactors (units five and six) at Kudankulam and two reactors at Haripur in West Bengal during India's 12th Five Year Plan period, 2012–17. Their agreement also outlined the timeline for the steps to be taken for the construction of Kudankulam units three and four, and called for progressive indigenization of supplies for units five and six at Kudankulam. For all six reactors at Kudankulam, Russia will provide the equipment and components, while Nuclear Power Corporation of India will build them.

The Russian AFK Sistema owns a 73% share in the Indian telecom operator Shyam Telelink. It is constructing a pan-Indian transmitting network, Shyam. The Russian VTB bank has also started operations in India. Sberbank also intends to enter the Indian market. The numerous other infrastructure companies that are already operating in India include Transstroi and Tsentrdorstroi (road construction), Elektrostal and Tyazhpromeksport (metallurgical industry) and Stroitransgaz (gas pipeline). A joint venture between Russian truck-maker KamAZ and India's Tatra Vectra Motors is nearing completion. The unit will produce Kamaz-6540 dump trucks of over 25 metric tons and Kamaz-5460 prime movers. Zarubezhneftegaz is doing exploration work along with GAIL in the Bay of Bengal. Russia's GidroOGK and India's SUN Group launched a joint venture called RusSUNHydro in 2009, with the newly formed company planning to participate in hydro electric projects in India. At the India-Russia Summit in 2007 a decision was made to establish a joint India–Russia titanium product facility. In February 2008 Russia's State Property Committee, the St Petersburg-based engineering company Tekhnokhim Holding and India's Saraf Group agreed to set up a plant in Orissa. The Russian share in the project is 55%, which is expected to be financed through Indian outstanding debts to Russia. Overall, however, Russian investment in India remains minuscule. According to the Indian Ministry of Commerce and Industry, total foreign direct investment (FDI) from Russia during the period between April 2000 and March 2010 was about $373m., which was 0.34% of total FDI inflows to India during that period.

Conclusions

Except for a very brief period in the early 1990s, India's relations with Russia have been based on mutual trust and confidence. In the mid-1990s relations were restored to respectable levels which have been further strengthened since the signing of their 'strategic partnership' in 2000. Currently, the main pillars of this relationship are strategic congruence, defence ties, nuclear power and hydrocarbons. The trouble for Indian policy-makers is that these areas still remain skewed in favour of Russia.[25]

The major challenge for both India and Russia is how to sustain this relationship in the absence of dynamic commercial ties. Future bilateral economic relations will depend on Russia's importance to India's developmental needs and vice versa. In the past, the USSR played an important role in India's industrialization process. It had a comparative advantage in sectors like steel, which was central to its needs. India now has to assess where Russia has a comparative advantage. So far, India has been able to develop linkages in defence production, the oil and gas sector and in nuclear energy. Indian industry has already identified areas of mutual interest, namely information technology, pharmaceuticals, telecommunications, financial services, hydro-carbons, energy and power, oil and gas, food processing, financial consultancy, management services, textiles and diamond processing. The problems are well known, however, including lack of information, visa problems and logistical issues. Still, very little attempt has been made to address these issues. There was a lot of hope that a Eurasian north–south trade corridor would be able to tackle some of the transportation problems. Owing to low trade volumes, however, the trading community has not yet developed this route. The strong political will in both countries to improve bilateral economic relations could have been converted into real economic gains if some imaginative initiatives had been taken, particularly when the Russian economy was booming between 2000 and 2007. With the global economic slowdown impacting in 2008/09, things have become more complicated for increasing India-Russia economic links, with trade declining from $5,420m. in 2008/09 to $4,550m. in 2009/10.

Current Indo-Russian commercial relations are certainly not commensurate with existing potential. In the last few years India has signed bilateral trade deals with many partners and many are under negotiation. However, until Russia joins the World Trade Organization (WTO), it is highly unlikely that India and Russia will be able to sign any significant bilateral trade and economic co-operation agreements. In the last two decades the Indian and Russian economies have moved far from each other. With no major breakthrough, Indian and Russian economic ties will continue to depend on the arms trade, and nuclear and energy industry linkages. Russian exports to India are likely to be from the extraction industries and limited Indian exports will continue to be from low-volume, high-value and high-profit sectors.

It is clear now that defence ties constitute the core of bilateral relations. Russia has provided the most advanced aircraft, tanks, rocket launchers, missiles, frigates and submarines to India. Through licensed production of arms, missiles and aircraft, India is slowly developing its own defence industry. There have been problems in defence supplies concerning product support, cost escalations, delays in delivery and incomplete transfers of technology. Still, substantial arms imports continue to come from Russia. With a changing foreign policy orientation in India, the importance of arms imports from Russia may see a declining trend in coming years. There was some uneasiness in Russia when India signed a Strategic Partnership with the USA in 2006, and there was talk of Russia being elbowed out as India's main arms supplier, particularly in the midst of troubled negotiations during 2008–10 over the sale of the Admiral Gorshkov aircraft carrier. Nevertheless, overall Russia remains an important factor in Indian foreign policy debates. Moreover, at the broadest level, the Indian elite believes that a strong Russia is important for maintaining a desired international equilibrium, both supporting the idea of multipolarity and a rule-based international system, within which India can continue its rise. This remains India's basic 'strategic synergy'.[26]

Gulshan Sachdeva

Notes

1 M. Singh, 'PM's Statement at the Joint Press Conference with his Russian Counterpart', 12 March 2010, pmindia.nic.in.
2 V. Chopra (ed.), *Significance of Indo-Russian Relations in 21st Century*, Delhi: Kalpaz Publications, 2008.
3 R. Thakur and C. Thayer, *Soviet Relations with India and Vietnam: 1945–1992*, Delhi: Oxford University Press, 1993.
4 R. Menon, 'India and the Soviet Union: A New Stage of Relations', *Asian Survey*, Vol. 18, No. 7, 1978.
5 S. Lounev, 'Soviet-Indian Relations (1955–71): The Birth of a Friendship', in P. Dash and Andrei M. Nazarkin (eds), *Indo-Russian Diplomatic Relations: Sixty Years of Enduring Legacy*, New Delhi: Academic Excellence, 2008.
6 S. Pandey, 'India in the Russian Foreign Policy Debate', in P. Sahai (ed.), *India-Eurasia: The Way Ahead*, Chandigarh: Centre for Research in Rural and Industrial Development, 2008.
7 R. Thakur, 'The Impact of the Soviet Collapse on Military Relations with India', *Europe Asia Studies*, Vol. 45, No. 5, 1993.
8 S. Jha, 'India and Russia: Challenges of Rediscovering the Past Linkages', in Shamsuddin (ed.), *India and Russia: Towards Strategic Partnership*, New Delhi: Lancer Books, 2001.
9 V. Dutt, 'Indo-Russian Relations: An Overview', in V. Chopra (ed.), *Indo-Russian Relations: Prospects Problems and Russia Today*, Delhi: Kalpaz Publications, 2001.
10 D. Ollapally, 'Indo-Russian Strategic Relations: New Choices and Constraints', in S. Ganguly (ed.), *India as an Emerging Power*, London: Frank Cass, 2003.
11 A. Bhattacharya, 'The Fallacy in the Russia-India-China Triangle', *Strategic Analysis*, Vol. 28, No. 2, 2004. Also G. Boquérat and F. Grare (eds), *India, China, Russia: Intricacies of an Asian Triangle*, New Delhi: Centre de Sciences Humaines, 2004; H. Pant, 'Feasibility of the Russia-China-India "Strategic Triangle". Assessment of Theoretical and Empirical Issues', *International Studies*, Vol. 43, No. 1, 2006. Nevertheless, foreign minister-level meetings of the three were held in 2005 ('promotion of multi-polarization' in their communiqué), and a heads of government summit in 2006, subsequently repeated with eight RIC meetings in 2007–09.
12 K. Sibal, 'Why Putin Needs to be Thanked', *Analysis* (Observer Research Foundation), 12 March 2010, www.observerindia.com.
13 S. Kapila, 'Russia Rekindles Strategic Partnership with Russia', *Papers* (SAAG), No. 1180, 7 December 2004.
14 A. Chenoy, 'India and Russia: Allies in the International System', *South Asian Survey*, Vol. 15, No. 1, 2008.
15 V. Chopra (ed.), *Indo-Russian Relations: Prospects Problems and Russia Today*, Delhi: Kalpaz Publications, 2001.
16 India-Russia, *Declaration on Strategic Partnership between Republic of India and the Russian Federation*, 3 October 2000, www.rusembassy.in.
17 India-Russia, *Report of the India-Russia Joint Study Group*, July 2007, commerce.nic.in.
18 I. Khripunov and A. Srivastava, 'Russian-Indian Relationship: Alliance, Partnership, or?', *Comparative Strategy*, Vol. 18, No. 2, 1999.
19 T. Zarzecki, 'Arming China or Arming India: Future Russian Dilemma', *Contemporary Strategy*, Vol. 18, No. 3, 1999.
20 J. Joseph, 'Rs 15000 Crore Sukhoi Deal Cleared', *Times of India*, 26 June 2010.
21 D. Nayyar (ed.), *Economic Relations between Socialist Countries and the Third World*, London: Macmillan, 1975, p.xi.
22 Jayashekar, 'India's Trade with the Soviet Bloc: Growing Dependence and Commodity Inconvertibility', *Problems of Non-Alignment*, Vol. 1, No. 2, 1983.
23 E. Valkenier, *The Soviet Union and the Third World: An Economic Bind*, New Delhi: Allied Publishers, 1986, p.142.
24 P. Sen, 'Hard Goods and Soft Currencies: A Note on Bilateral Payment Arrangements', *Working Paper* (New Delhi: Planning Commission), No. 2, 1999.
25 A. Shukla, 'India-Russia Ties: Strong but with Irritants', *News* (Rediff), 18 March 2010, www.rediff.com.
26 P. Dash and A. Nazarkin (eds), *India and Russia: Strategic Synergy Emerging*, Delhi: Authorpress, 2007.

20

India's relations with the European Union

Rajendra K. Jain

Introduction

India has a multi-dimensional relationship with the European Union (EU), its largest trading partner, a major source of foreign direct investment (FDI), a significant donor, an important source of technology, and home to a large and influential Indian diaspora. India no longer regards the EU as a mere trading bloc, but as an increasingly important political actor in world politics with a growing profile and presence.

Historical background

India took little interest in the movement for European unification during the first years of Indian independence. The European Economic Community (EEC), the predecessor to the EU set up in 1957 under the Treaty of Rome, was remote from Indian concerns. There were no statements by the Indian Government or any references to it in debates in the Indian parliament until the United Kingdom expressed its intention to apply for membership of the Common Market in 1961. The question of India's relations with the EEC then took on a new urgency, especially as it came at a time when India's balance of payments had deteriorated sharply.[1] Prime Minister Jawaharlal Nehru argued that the EEC would deepen Cold War divisions, widen the gap between the rich and poor countries, and weaken the Commonwealth of Nations.

Nevertheless, India recognized the importance of the nascent EEC and was among the first developing countries to establish diplomatic relations in 1962. Indian efforts to establish a new, post-colonial relationship with the Community proved a challenging task since, apart from the 'associated' overseas countries and territories of the member states, the Treaty of Rome contained no references to the rest of the Third World. Indian policy-makers deplored the fact that the EEC Council of Ministers made 'no conscious attempt' in the early years to evolve a development policy towards developing countries; instead the EEC was much too preoccupied with its internal problems, with negotiations for its enlargement, and therefore remained content to follow a limited policy in the framework of old colonial relationships of its member states.[2]

During the 1961–63 negotiations for the United Kingdom's entry, the EEC was compelled briefly to envisage future arrangements between the enlarged EEC and Commonwealth developing countries. India sought an Association Agreement similar to the one that the Mediterranean countries and the African, Caribbean and Pacific (ACP) countries had concluded with the EEC. However, this was ruled out for 'non-associables' like India lest these concessions were extended to all developing countries.

With the collapse of negotiations for the United Kingdom's entry into the EEC in January 1963, India and the Commonwealth countries, the *Times of India* editorial observed, had 'every reason to thank God and de Gaulle' for the collapse.[3] It led to an abatement of the threat of disruption of Indo-British trade for some time, but the challenge of defining the EEC's relations with developing countries remained. Relations with other developing countries would continue to be governed by the EEC's Common Commercial Policy.

For a decade (1963–73), Indian efforts focused on securing better market access for India's major exports and alleviation of its chronic trade deficit with the EEC, which was the largest it had amongst all its trading partners. This was dealt with on a product-by-product basis by the conclusion of annual agreements on the suspension, in whole or in part, of the customs duty. Though the EEC introduced the Generalised System of Preferences (GSP) in 1971, India felt that the GSP was not structured to solve the specific problems created for India by its loss of preferential access to the British market. Many of India's main exports, including jute, coir, cotton textiles and tobacco, were either excluded from the scheme or else subject to special arrangements.

With the United Kingdom's admission into the EEC in 1973, the enlarged Community had to decide on the arrangements to be concluded with the developing countries of the Commonwealth. The EEC was in no position to take on the burden of financial aid to countries as populous as India. Under the Joint Declaration of Intent, annexed to the United Kingdom's Treaty of Accession (1973), the EEC agreed to examine with the Asian Commonwealth countries 'such problems as may arise in the field of trade with a view to seek appropriate solutions'. India was the first country to take advantage of this offer. However, member states, even those with past colonial connections with India, had no real interest in alleviating India's difficulties. India was perceived as 'Britain's baby' and it was up to the British to act in its favour.[4]

The agreement the EEC was initially offering India lacked even 'a core'; it was 'all packaging'.[5] The EEC was reluctant to agree to any sweeping programme of economic, industrial and financial co-operation lest it open the door to a host of similar agreements with other developing Asian and Latin American countries. The five-year non-preferential Commercial Cooperation Agreement (CCA) that India eventually signed in 1973 was the result of the diplomatic acumen of K.B. Lall, the then Indian Ambassador to the EEC. The agreement contained no new tariff concessions, but provided both a focus and a contractual basis for India-EEC relations. India was not particularly jubilant about the CCA; it felt that it was the best it could get under the circumstances. Nevertheless, the CCA constituted a big step forward by the EEC and set the pattern for similar agreements with other South Asian countries. However, conscious development of trade opportunities for India continued to be assigned only 'a low priority'.[6] Nevertheless, a series of useful trade development and trade promotion programmes were launched, and an expert study was commissioned to identify shortcomings and recommend ways to overcome them.

After the conclusion of the 1973 CCA, India repeatedly urged the EEC to work out a new 'doctrine' covering the EEC's overall relationship with India rather than tackling matters each time in a piecemeal fashion. India took the initiative in 1978 and sought to expand the scope of the 1973 agreement by the conclusion of a new non-preferential economic and commercial agreement in June 1981, which expanded co-operation to more sectors.

The 1990s

With the end of the Cold War, the EEC (which became the EU in 1993) no longer had to look at India through the lens of Cold War equations. Moreover, India was becoming pro-gressively more interesting. Its policy of liberalization and economic reforms launched in 1991 with consistently high growth rates, acquisition of nuclear weapons in 1998, and steadily improving relations with the USA all led to recognition of India as a potential global player by the EU. In the post-Cold War era India pursued a pragmatic foreign policy, shed most of the ideological baggage, and accorded greater priority to the West as a market and a source of technology and FDI.

In the early 1990s India urged an overhaul of its co-operation agreement with the EU and an upgraded political dialogue, since the EU was not merely another trading area, but increasingly was becoming the collective diplomatic centre for Western Europe. A wide-ranging 'third-generation' agreement on Partnership and Development was signed on 20 December 1993 to encompass economic, technological and cultural co-operation, development and investment. The Joint Statement on Political Dialogue (1994) sought to achieve 'a closer and upgraded rela-tionship', and expressed the resolve of India and the EU to reinforce and intensify their mutual relations in the political, economic, technological and cultural fields. The European Commis-sion pushed for stronger links in its Communication on EU–India Enhanced Partnership (1996).[7]

The institutional architecture between India and the EU is now quite multilayered. Apart from the Joint Commission and Sub-Commissions, troika ministerial meetings have been held since 1982. Other institutional mechanisms include Senior Officials Meetings, meetings between the European Commission and Indian planners, bilateral meetings in the margins of multilateral forums, working groups of specialists (on subjects like export controls, terrorism experts and consular affairs), the India–EU Round Table, the India–EU Energy Panel and its working groups, a Security Dialogue, macro-economic dialogue on financial co-operation, a dialogue on human rights, and a science and technology steering committee. Annual summits have taken place since 2000.[8] Parliamentary exchanges began with the setting up of a South Asia Delegation in the European Parliament. A separate India Delegation was established in September 2009 to reflect the strategic partnership. The Indian parliament also set up a 22-member Parliamentary Friendship Group for Relations with the European Parliament in June 2008.

Indian perceptions

The Indian elite's perceptions of the EU have been and continue to be essentially conditioned by the Anglo-Saxon media, which impedes a more nuanced understanding of the processes and dynamics of European integration, as well as the intricacies and roles of EU institutions. For the Indian policy-maker, the EU is not an easy political animal to deal with, partly because of the rotating presidencies, proliferating regulations and so on seen with the EU. India, like many of the EU's other strategic partners, is clearly more comfortable with national bilateral frameworks. While there is some clarity regarding policies of EU member states, it is often difficult to say what EU policy is. Most stakeholders in India feel that India's democratic polity and shared values do not necessarily earn it any brownie points in Europe, that the EU, including the European think-tank community, continues to have a fixation with the People's Republic of China, and that most senior EU officials feel India 'is getting there, but not quite arrived'.[9]

225

More perceptive Indians feel that when it comes to India/South Asia there continue to be three kinds of people in the EU: those who are otherwise very well informed and knowledgeable, but who do not try to understand South Asia because others have tried it before and failed to do so; those who neither understand anything, nor wish to understand anything; and then a small minority of those who have the courage and perseverance to make an effort to understand the more complex problems of India and wish to do something about it. Relations with India are still driven by 'very small circles' in Brussels. In the first circle are those that have substantial economic stakes—primarily the 'Big Three' (France, Germany and the United Kingdom). When push comes to shove, they are the ones that bring the requisite energy to move things forward in an increasingly heterogeneous Union. In the second circle are those member states that have interests in certain sectors, but that do not quite have the big picture. In the third circle are the remaining member states, which broadly feel that if some things are good for others, it is fine with them. The Nordic countries have generally been viewed as the 'moral superpowers'.

'Strategic partnership'

The Joint Declaration of the first India–EU summit (June 2000) resolved that the EU and India should build 'a new strategic partnership' in the 21st century, founded on shared values and aspirations. The European Commission's Communication, An EU-India Strategic Partnership (June 2004), proposed to develop a strategic partnership with India in four key areas: a) co-operation, especially in multilateral forums, on conflict prevention, the fight against terrorism and non-proliferation of weapons of mass destruction; b) strengthened economic partnership through strategic policy and sectoral dialogues; c) development co-operation; and d) fostering intellectual and cultural exchanges.[10] A 46-page Commission Staff Working Document annexed to the Communication proposed over 100 actionable points in various sectors, the great majority of which concerned trade and commerce. In its first-ever strategy paper on relations with an outside entity, India responded with a detailed 31-page response to the Commission's Communication.[11] The 'strategic partnership' (upgraded) relationship was specifically endorsed at the fifth India-EU summit in 2004. There seemed a sense between them by 2005 that 'India-EU relations have grown exponentially from what used to be a purely trade and economic driven relationship to one covering all areas of interaction'.[12] A new Political Declaration and a Joint Action Plan (JAP) divided into four sections (political, trade and investment, economic policy, and cultural and academic) was adopted at the next India-EU summit in September 2005.[13] The revised JAP in September 2008, titled Global Partners for Global Challenges, added 40-odd items to the 100-odd items already contained in the original JAP.[14]

The EU's 'strategic partnership' with India is one of the nine that the EU has world-wide and one of the 30 that India has with other countries. The term 'strategic partnership' is an extremely elusive and elastic concept. Some call it a kind of 'honorary degree' conferred on key international players; others call it a 'charade'.[15] For the EU, a 'strategic partnership' comprises a common template in terms of annual summits, a Joint Plan of Action with a laundry list of actionable areas, and an incrementally increasing number of sectoral and policy dialogues that could foster an internal dynamic to gradually generate deliverables. For India, its strategic partnership with the EU raised the relationship to a new level where one can have broad-ranging discussions on bilateral, regional and global issues. These consultations, which now encompass around 45 issue areas, have enabled the two sides to better understand and appreciate each other's positions, perspectives and perceptions.

Political dialogue: convergence and divergence

There are fundamental differences between India and the EU on many issues because they are at different levels of development, because they come from two different milieux, and because they have different geographical and geopolitical priorities. Indian perspectives are shaped by its historical experiences and current realities, which include the fact that it lives in a very difficult and dangerous neighbourhood surrounded by failed or failing states, and confronts a variety of external threats and challenges. Despite exhortations to identify possible synergies and initiatives to promote human rights and democracy, there has in practice been little co-ordination on any of these goals.[16]

There is some convergence in policy and practice between the EU and India on questions of multilateralism and global governance, but that convergence has notable and significant limitations. There are basic differences in both perceptions and interests between India and the EU in many fields, including trade, development, climate change, the International Criminal Court, globalization, humanitarian intervention, etc. On most issues that matter to India, like enlargement of the UN Security Council and civilian nuclear energy, the EU either has no common policy or is unable to formulate one. Though the EU and India have shared objectives in most South Asian countries, they are often unable to calibrate their foreign policies to work there. India feels that the EU is a marginal player when it comes to the security milieu in South Asia.

India does not seek to replace, but democratize, existing structures of global governance and increase its role in decision-making. India has been consistently advocating a more democratized, more representative and more credible UN system and has sought membership as a permanent member of a reformed UN Security Council. To most stakeholders in India, Europe is clearly over-represented but is in no hurry to reduce such over-representation. Most of the existing financial and trade rules of the current international architecture reflect the power realities at the end of the Second World War in which India was a recipient rather than a framer of norms. India has been a beneficiary of these rules, but has long been a victim of them. In recent years, there has been a basic and increasing contestation about the content, value and scope of norms between the developed and developing countries. Europe often presents the normative agenda in a way that seeks to undermine the competitive advantage of developing countries. India wants to play a greater role in the making of new rules of the international economic and financial system.

Nevertheless, on most issues of substance, India's broad interests as a rising major power are consonant with those of the other major powers. In the military-political arena, India shares a common interest with other major powers in preventing the spread of weapons of mass destruction and terrorism, in fostering maritime security and stabilization of weak states, and in coping with health hazards and pandemics. Co-operative relations with them are likely to grow despite differences over specific issues. India will continue to strongly favour the development of multilateral regimes to regulate international trade and politics. In 2007 the EU, along with several other major world powers, gained official observer status in the South Asian Association for Regional Cooperation (SAARC), which reflects keen EU interest in the SAARC experiment.[17] However, unlike the foreign ministers of China, Japan and the Republic of Korea (South Korea), the European Commission was not represented at the 14th SAARC summit held in New Delhi; instead the EU delegation was led by the German Ambassador to India. Another new forum for India to further develop its growing relations with both Asia and Europe is the 45-member Asia-Europe Meeting (ASEM), which New Delhi joined in 2007 and in which the EU's European Commission is one of the co-ordinators.

Rajendra K. Jain

Combating terrorism and security dialogue

A victim of terrorism since 1980, Indian officials had for years stressed the need for a frank and honest dialogue with the EU on terrorism. Despite recognition by the EU of terrorism as a problem and its member states' dislike for Pakistani adventurism in Kargil (1999), Europe was not willing to confront Pakistan on its 'sponsorship' of cross-border terrorism. During the first India-EU summit (June 2000), Brussels resisted attempts by India to bring terrorism onto the agenda on the grounds that it was an issue best left to direct talks between India and individual member states of the Union. Brussels also did not share Indian characterizations of Pakistan as either a 'failed state' or an 'epicentre of terrorism'.

After the terrorist attacks on the USA on 11 September 2001, the EU itself accepted that terrorism had to be henceforth among the topics of discussion and since then the topic has figured at each summit. Both sides continue to share concern at the scourge of terrorism, and a Joint Working Group on terrorism has been meeting in recent years. However, at the second India-EU summit (2001), there were difficulties in formulating the text of the Declaration Against International Terrorism. After the terrorist attack on the Indian parliament (December 2001), which brought India's threat to go to war with Pakistan and the mobilization of 1m. troops in South Asia in the summer of 2002, several EU leaders visited India in an attempt to defuse the situation. New Delhi was enraged at European efforts at the third summit, held in Copenhagen in October 2002, to pressurize India on talking to Pakistan and exercising restraint through aggressive public diplomacy and by the strident tone of Danish Prime Minister Anders Rasmussen. The larger EU member states pleaded ignorance, while the Danes denied this.

Unlike the EU, it was the USA that took the lead in compelling Pakistan to ban terrorist groups operating from Pakistani territory. Brussels followed suit and declared several terrorist outfits as terrorist organizations in April 2004, but European bureaucracies soon lost enthusiasm in continuing this time-consuming exercise. In October 2004 the Council expressed willingness to 'consider' the Commission's proposal for the inclusion of India in its list of priority countries for a strategic co-operation agreement with Europol—the EU's centralized police organization. In November 2009 the two sides agreed to advance the negotiations between Europol and the Indian authorities in order to conclude an agreement to 'reinforce cooperation in the field of counter-terrorism'.[18]

A security dialogue on global and regional issues has been held annually since May 2006. The security dialogue held in November 2008 shortly after the Mumbai attacks was more substantive and constructive than any of the previous ones, largely because India sought to proactively engage the Europeans. The first Council Working Group on Terrorism (COTER) troika with India took place on 11 June 2009.

Most co-operation between India and European countries has been on a bilateral rather than multilateral basis. In fact, because of disparate priorities most EU member states neither share the same urgency nor interest in co-operating with India. However, the prospects of practical, ground-level security co-operation with the Union are remote, since it is the member states that have the assets and competences, not the Union.

Economic relations

The EU is an extremely important trade partner for India, accounting for 20.1% of its total exports and 13.3% of its total imports in 2009/10. India accounts for a more limited but rapidly growing share of EU trade, with 2.4% of the EU's total exports and 1.9% of its total imports, and with India ranked 10th on the list of the EU's main trading partners in 2008, up from 15th in 2002. India–EU trade increased from US $1,640m. in 1973 to $5,700m. in 1980. Over the decade 1981–90, India–EU trade increased by about five times. With India's economic reforms kicking in in 1991, Indo–EU trade recorded an annual rate of growth of around 20% in 1990–94, with substantive annual growth subsequently maintained during the following decade, rising from $19,500m. in 1996/97, to $56,690m. in 2006/7, and to $82,080m. in 2008/9. Some downturn was seen in the overall trade figure of $75,380m. for 2009/10, reflecting a decline in 2009 as the global economic downturn cast a shadow on the trade performance of both sides. However, by the first half of 2010 trade was recovering, owing to India's resumption of high growth rates; meanwhile Indian exports to the EU were up 18% from the January–April 2009 figures, whilst Indian imports from the EU were up 28% from the January–April 2009 figures. Services-wise, in euro terms, India exported €2,500m.-worth of services to the EU in 2001, while EU services exports to India amounted to €2,400m.[19] EU services exports to India had increased to €9,000m. in 2008, whereas India exported services worth €7,400m.[20]

The EU has been the largest source of FDI inflows for India since the country began economic reforms in 1991. During August 1991 to September 2004, actual FDI from the EU to India was $6,720m., which accounted for 21.6% of total FDI in India.[21] EU investment flows to India gained significant momentum in 2007, doubling in euro terms to €5,400m. from €2,500m. in 2006. With the financial turmoil followed by a severe economic crisis hitting Europe, EU FDI into India declined to €900m. in 2008.[22] Meanwhile, FDI from India to the EU soared from zero in 2004 to €10,000m. in 2007, and to €2,400m. in 2008.

The EU is becoming a major destination for India's outward investment in a variety of sectors like steel, pharmaceuticals, automobiles, information technology and energy. Recent key purchases have included Tata Steel's acquisition of Corus in 2007, and the iconic Jaguar and Land Rover brands acquired by Tata Motors in 2008. Investment by Indian companies in Europe is mostly strategic in nature, seeking to either gain access to new markets or advanced technology. The United Kingdom remains the most attractive destination for FDI in Europe, accounting for over 50% all Indian FDI projects in the region.

Trade and investment agreement

The stalemate in the Doha Round (trade negotiation round of the World Trade Organization – WTO) prompted the European Commission to propose the conclusion of bilateral Free Trade Agreements (FTAs) with India, South Korea and the Association for Southeast Asian Nations (ASEAN). The Helsinki Summit (October 2006) endorsed the High Level Trade Group recommendation for the conclusion of a trade and investment agreement. Some EU member states had expressed a preference for a comprehensive partnership agreement instead of 'a standalone FTA'. India had no desire to get involved in discussions on a Partnership and Cooperation Agreement for the sake of 'coherence' and an upgrading of the 1994 Cooperation Agreement, an agreement which is still the legal framework for co-operation and satisfies the prerequisites for an FTA with the Union. India preferred a step-by-step approach, since negotiating a broad-based trade and investment agreement would be challenging enough without the inclusion of non-trade issues, and stressed the importance of being conscious of the danger of overloading the agenda and stalling the entire process.

The Council and the Representatives of member states meeting within the Council formally adopted a negotiating mandate for 'a new generation' FTA with India on 23 April 2007. Ten rounds of negotiations have so far been held since negotiations began in June 2007. There continue to be difficulties because of insistence by the Union including non-trade provisions like an environmental and social clause, differences over issues like intellectual property rights, government procurement, etc., and efforts by Brussels to link trade with climate and India's social sector performance. The Union cites the growing assertiveness and sensitivity of the European Parliament on these issues after the Treaty of Lisbon came into force in December 2009. India remains staunchly opposed to the inclusion of 'extraneous' non-trade issues in the talks. New Delhi has asserted that under no circumstances will it be willing to undertake any commitments over and above what it has already agreed to in the WTO, and that there are other forums, like the International Labour Organization (ILO), in which to address these issues. The two sides will eventually be able to find the appropriate language to deal with these issues. The European Parliament is not likely to own up to the responsibility of rejecting an agreement with India for which there is strong support

The new trade and investment agreement will set the parameters of the India–EU trading relationship for the coming decades. Given several contentious issues (e.g. intellectual property rights, government procurement, an agreement is likely to be signed sometime in 2011, although ratification processes could further delay its implementation. According to a July 2010 report by FICCI-Grant Thornton, India–EU trade, which totaled 68.9 billion euros, is expected to exceed 160 billion euros by 2015. This could, in turn, possibly make political differences more manageable because the overall relationship very often tends to get tainted by differences in the WTO.

Conclusions

After 10 summits, India and the EU are gradually getting used to working together. Rhetoric continues to be strong. Post-Lisbon, the EU sees India as a significant factor:

> We see India playing an increasingly important role across a wide range of global issues and problems. Buoyed by your strong economic growth you are engaged more and more on trade and climate change or regional and global security. I believe this is very welcome. So the EU and India have the chance to step up our co-operation – deepening and broadening it. And above all, making it more strategic. The world we live in demands we invest more in new forms of partnership. We have to stand together politically and economically.[23]

Despite shared values, the lack of shared interests on a number of issues will continue to limit co-operation. India and the EU have many common interests, but transforming them into co-ordinated policies has been rather elusive. Despite the ongoing dialogue and consultations between India and the EU on 45 or so issues, Brussels and the member states complain that they encounter problems of capacity and resources of India's Ministry of External Affairs. In turn, the EU's foreign policy coherence and institutional solidification remains an evolving situation for India to deal with, while the post-Lisbon setting of the European External Action Service gives a further peg with which India must engage.[24]

Some have even argued that the two sides ought to focus on a smaller number of long-term strategic priorities rather than cluttering the agenda. The EU is becoming more concerned (like India) with the rise of China and its increasing assertiveness on many issues, apart from the perennial problem of mounting trade deficits (a problem India also faces with China), which may fuel protectionist sentiments. However, despite a declaration of 'strategic partnership', India and the EU have different approaches to security and have not yet built a real structure for discussion on security issues. However, a working relationship has been established between the EU naval operation, ATALANTA, deployed in the Gulf of Aden to combat piracy and India's naval deployments there.

The driving force behind the relationship for the most part has been, is, and will continue to be, trade and commerce. Their mutual long-term interest is going to be in areas like scientific and technological co-operation, movement of skilled persons, etc. With India becoming a key destination for research and development, and for the outsourcing of segments of the manu-facturing process, and given its pool of scientific talent to foster innovation, there is great potential for partnership in cutting-edge technologies in a manner that combines India's strengths with European capabilities.

A worsening demographic profile with an ageing population is compelling the EU to address the problems and opportunities of in-sourcing highly skilled immigrants or outsourcing services. Since skilled immigrants seek a better location and conditions, European countries are now increasingly willing to conclude social security agreements with India, which could eventually pave the way for the conclusion of an EU-wide social security agreement. India and the EU are exploring the possibility of concluding a Labour Mobility Partnership Agreement (which India has already signed with several Gulf countries) to facilitate 'legal' and 'orderly migration' of the workforce from India to European countries and vice versa.

Hopefully, the future will witness the broadening, deepening and intensification of civil society dialogue between India and the EU as well as greater intellectual and elite interaction. While both display a growing willingness to discuss and engage, they need to re-profile and re-orient their mindsets in order to tap into the vast untapped potential of their relations.

Notes

1 India's modest surplus of Rs 50 m. (US $10 m.) in 1950 with the EEC Six had been transformed into a trade deficit of approximately Rs 1,350 m. ($281 m.) in 1960. This deficit was thrice the value of Indian exports to the Community. No other country had a deficit of that order with the Community.

2 D. Singh, 'India and the European Community: Development Co-operation in the UNCTAD Context', *Studia Diplomatica*, Vol. 29, No. 4, 1976, pp.444–45.

3 Editorial, *Times of India*, 5 February 1963.

4 R. Abhyankar, 'India and the European Union: A Partnership for All Reasons', *India Quarterly*, Vol. 65, No. 4, 2009, p.395.

5 M. Subhan, 'An "Empty Shell" for India', *Far Eastern Economic Review*, 30 April 1973, p.55.

6 K. Lall and W. Ernst and H. Chopra (eds), *India and the EEC*, New Delhi: Allied Publishers, 1984, p.xvi.

7 European Commission, *EU-India Enhanced Partnership,* COM(96) 275 final, Brussels: European Commission, 26 June 1996.

8 India-EU, 'EU-India Partnership in the 21st Century', 28 June 2000, www.delind.ec.europa.eu. This first summit Joint Declaration included phrases like 'the EU and India are important partners in the shaping of the emerging multipolar world'.

9 See R. Jain, 'The European Union and China: Indian Perceptions and Perspectives', in G. Wiessala, J. Wilson and P. Taneja (eds), *The European Union and China: Interests and Dilemmas*, Amsterdam: Rodopi, 2009; R. Jain, 'The European Union and the Rise of China and India', in J. Marques, R. Seidelmann and A. Vasilache (eds), *Asia and Europe: Dynamics of Inter- and Intra-Regional Dialogues*, Baden–Baden: Nomos, 2009.

10 European Commission, *An EU-India Strategic Partnership*, COM(2004) 430 final, Brussels: European Commission, 16 June 2004.

11 Ministry of External Affairs, *EC Communication Titled 'An EU-India Strategic Partnership' – India's Response*, 27 August 2004, Ministry of External Affairs, meainida.nic.in. See E. Kavalski, 'Venus and the Porcupine. Assessing the European Union-India Strategic Partnership', *South Asian Survey*, Vol. 15, No. 1, 2008, for analysis of these key documents.

12 India-EU, *The India-EU Strategic Partnership. Joint Action Plan*, 7 September 2005, p.1, www.delind.ec.europa.eu. Also S. Ramchandran, 'The Expanding EU-India Relationship', *The Hindu*, 5 July 2005, 'The growing fascination with India is evident from the fact that it has now been made one of the EU's strategic partners. The single-minded focus on China and the Asian tigers has been replaced with the recognition that India matters in the long run'.

13 India-EU, 'Political Declaration on the India-EU Strategic Partnership', 7 September 2005, www.delind.ec.europa.eu; India-EU, *The India-EU Strategic Partnership. Joint Action Plan.*

14 India-EU, *Global Partners for Global Challenges: The EU-India Joint Action Plan (JAP)*, 29 September 2008, www.eeas.europa.eu.

15 C. Jaffrelot, 'India and the European Union: The Charade of a Strategic Partnership', March 2006, www.ceri-sciencespo.com.

16 R. Jain, *The European Union and Democracy Building in South Asia*, Stockholm: International Institute for Democracy and Electoral Assistance, October 2009.

17 See R. Jain, 'The European Union and SAARC: The First Enlargement and After', in S.-H. Park and H. Kim (eds), *Regional Integration in Europe and Asia: Legal, Economic, and Political Perspectives*, Baden-Baden: Nomos, 2009.

18 India-EU, *India-EU Joint Statement*, 6 November 2009, paragraph 12, www.eeas.europa.eu.

19 Delegation of the European Commission to India, *The European Union and India*, New Delhi: Delegation of the European Commission to India, 2005.

20 Eurostat, 'An EU27 Surplus in Trade in Goods with India of 2.1 billion in 2008', *News Release*, No. 157/2009, 4 November 2009.

21 Delegation of the European Commission to India, *The European Union and India*, op. cit.

22 Eurostat, 'An EU27 Surplus in Trade in Goods with India of 2.1 billion in 2008', op. cit.

23 Speech by Catherine Ashton, EU High Representative for Foreign Affairs and Security Policy and Vice-President of the European Commission, 'EU-India Relations Post-Lisbon: Cooperation in a Changing World', India International Centre, Speech/10/336, 23 June 2010, europa.eu.

24 A. Mukhopadhyay, 'The EEAS and the EU-India Strategic Partnership', *IDSA Comment*, 22 July 2010.

21
India's relations with China

Harsh V. Pant

Introduction

According to most political observers, the global political architecture is undergoing a transformation, with power increasingly shifting from the West to the East, in what has been called the 'Asian Century'. The two most populous nations on the earth, the People's Republic of China and India, are on their way to becoming economic powerhouses and are shedding their reticence in asserting their global profiles, all of which makes their relationship of still greater importance to the international system. The future of this Asian Century will to a large extent depend upon the relationship between the two regional giants, China and India, and the bilateral relationship between China and India will define the contours of the new international political architecture in Asia and the world at large. The importance of their relationship has not been lost on China and India. In one of his meetings with the Indian Prime Minister, at the 2004 Asia-Europe Meeting (ASEM), the Chinese Premier, Wen Jiabao, was reported to have remarked that 'when we shake hands, the whole world will be watching'. As of today, however, the trajectory of the Sino-Indian relationship remains as complex as ever to decipher, despite some positive developments in the last few years. This chapter examines the evolution of Sino-Indian ties over the last few decades and the constraints that continue to inhibit this relationship from achieving its full potential.

Initial encounters

As two ancient civilizations, India and China have had cultural and trade ties since at least the first century. The famous Silk Road allowed for economic and trade ties to develop between the two, with the transmission of Buddhism from India to China giving a further cultural dimension to the relationship between the two neighbours. The political ties between China and India, however, remained underdeveloped.

Independent India's first Prime Minister, Jawaharlal Nehru, saw anti-imperialist friendship between the two largest states of Asia as imperative if interference by the two external superpowers was to be avoided.[1] Solidarity with China was integral to Nehru's vision of Asian leadership. After the People's Republic of China was established in 1949, and India established diplomatic ties with it in 1950, India not only advocated China's membership at the UN but also opposed attempts to condemn China for its actions in Korea. Yet the issue of Tibet soon emerged as the major bone of contention between China and India. China was suspicious of Indian designs on Tibet, which India sought to allay by supporting the Seventeen-Point Agreement between Tibetan delegates and China in 1951, which recognized China's sovereignty over Tibet and guaranteed the existing socio-political arrangements of Tibet. India and China signed the famed Panchshila agreement in 1954, which underlined the Five Principles of Peaceful Co-existence as forming the basis of their bilateral relationship.[2] These principles included mutual respect for each other's territorial integrity and sovereignty; mutual non-aggression; mutual non-interference in each other's internal affairs; equality and mutual benefit; and peaceful co-existence. These were the heydays of Sino-Indian ties, with the *Hindi-China bhai-bhai* ('the Indians and Chinese are brothers') phrase a favourite slogan for the seeming camaraderie between the two states.

However, this was not to last for long. Soon the border dispute between China and India escalated and led to the 1962 Sino-Indian war.[3] Though a short war, it was to have a long-lasting impact on Sino-Indian ties. It demolished Nehru's claims of Asian solidarity, and the defeat at the hands of the Chinese psychologically scarred the Indian military and political elites. It led to China developing close ties with India's neighbouring adversary, Pakistan, resulting in what is now widely considered an 'all-weather' friendship. China supported Pakistan in its 1965 and 1971 wars against India and helped in the development of its nuclear weapons arsenal. Meanwhile, the Indian nuclear weapons programme was accelerated in light of China's testing of nuclear weapons in 1964.

The border issue continues to be a major obstacle in Sino-Indian ties, with minor skirmishes at the border continuing since 1962. As China and the USA came closer after their rapprochement in 1972, India gravitated to the USSR to balance the Sino-US-Pakistani axis. It was in 1988 that the then Indian Prime Minister, Rajiv Gandhi, turned over a new leaf in Sino-Indian ties, when he went to Beijing and signed an agreement that aimed to achieve a 'fair and reasonable settlement while seeking a mutually acceptable solution to the border dispute'.[4] The visit saw a Joint Working Group (JWG) set up to explore the boundary issue and examine probable solutions to the problem.

However, bilateral relations between India and China touched their nadir in the immediate aftermath of India's nuclear tests in May 1998. China had been singled out as the 'number one' security threat for India by India's defence minister just before the nuclear tests.[5] After the tests the Indian Prime Minister wrote to the US President justifying Indian nuclear tests as a response to the threat posed by China:

> We have an overt nuclear weapon state [China] on our borders, a state which committed armed aggression against India in 1962. Although our relations with that country have improved in the last decade or so, an atmosphere of distrust persists mainly due to the unresolved border problem. To add to the distrust that country has materially helped another neighbour of ours [Pakistan] to become a covert nuclear weapons state.[6]

Not surprisingly, China reacted strongly, with diplomatic relations between the two countries plummeting to an all-time low.

However, after more than a decade, relations between the two countries, at least superficially, seem to be on a much firmer footing, as they have tried to reduce the prospect for rivalry and expand areas of co-operation. The visit of the Indian Minister of External Affairs to

China in 1999 marked the resumption of high-level dialogue, as the two sides declared that they were not a threat to each other. A bilateral security dialogue was also initiated, which has helped the two countries to openly express and share their security concerns with each other. Both China and India continue to emphasize that neither side should let differences act as an impediment to the growth of functional co-operation elsewhere between the two states. India and China also decided to expedite the process of demarcation of the Line of Actual Control (LAC), and the JWG on the boundary question, set up in 1988, has been meeting regularly. As a first step in this direction the two countries exchanged border maps on the least controversial Middle Sector of the LAC. More recently, both nations agreed Political Parameters and Guiding Principles for the Settlement of the India-China Boundary Question (2005), broad principles to govern the parameters of any dispute settlement. China has expressed its desire to seek a 'fair' resolution to the vexed boundary issue on the basis of 'mutual accommodation, respect for history, and accommodation of reality'.[7]

Diplomacy of declarations

Former Indian Prime Minister Atal Bihari Vajpayee visited China in June 2003, the first visit by an Indian premier in a decade. The Joint Declaration signed during this visit expressed the view that China was not a threat to India.[8] The two states appointed Special Representatives in order to impart momentum to border negotiations that have lasted now for more than 20 years, with the Prime Minister's principal secretary becoming India's political-level negotiator, replacing the India-China JWG. India and China also decided to hold their first joint naval and air exercises. More significantly, India acknowledged China's sovereignty over Tibet and pledged not to allow 'anti-China' political activities in India. For its part, China seemed to have finally acknowledged India's 1975 incorporation of the former monarchy of Sikkim, by agreeing to open a trading post along the border with the former kingdom and later by rectifying its official maps to include Sikkim as part of India.[9] After being closed for 60 years, the Nathu La pass, a traditional trading post between Tibet and Sikkim, was reopened in 2006. High-level political interactions have continued unabated since then. The two states have set up institutionalized defence consultation mechanisms to reduce suspicion and indentify areas of co-operation on security issues.

Soon after assuming office, the Manmohan Singh Government made it clear that it was for closer ties with China and would continue to work towards improving bilateral relations with the country. India's former national security adviser, J.N. Dixit, wrote that 'the Congress will continue the process of normalizing, strengthening and expanding India's relations with China, which is the most important factor affecting Asian security and stability'.[10] In his first address to the nation, Prime Minister Manmohan Singh also emphasized the carrying forward of the process of further development and diversification of Sino-Indian relations.[11]

When Singh visited China in 2008, the two states signed a Shared Visions on the 21st Century declaration, 'to promote the building of a harmonious world of durable peace and common prosperity through developing the Strategic and Cooperative Partnership for Peace and Prosperity between the two countries'.[12] Support for the earlier Agreement on Political Parameters and Guiding Principles for the Settlement of the China-India Boundary Question (2005) was reiterated. The two sides have decided to elevate the boundary negotiations to the level of a strategic dialogue, with plans for a hotline between the Indian Prime Minister and the Chinese Premier as a means to remove misunderstanding and reduce tensions at the earliest opportunity. Their public vision suggested that this relationship would have 'a positive influence on the future of the international system'.[13]

The global structural imperative

At this international system level, India and China have found some real convergence of interests. Both share similar concerns about the international dominance of the USA, the threat of fundamentalist religious and ethnic movements in the form of terrorism, and the need to accord primacy to economic development. India and China have both expressed concern about the USA's use of military power around the world, and both were publicly opposed to the war in Iraq. This was merely a continuation of the desire of both states to oppose US hyperpuissance ever since the end of the Cold War.

Both China and India, much like other major powers in the international system, favour a multipolar world order wherein US unipolarity remains constrained by the other 'poles' in the system. China and India zealously guard their national sovereignty and have been wary of US attempts to interfere in what they see as domestic affairs of other states, be it Serbia, Kosovo or Iraq. Both took strong exception to the US air strikes on Iraq in 1998, the US-led air campaign against Yugoslavia in 1999, and more recently the US campaign against Saddam Hussain; both India and China argued that these violated the sovereignty of both countries and undermined the authority of the UN system. China and India share an interest in resisting interventionist foreign policy doctrines emanating from the West, particularly the USA, and display conservative attitudes on the prerogatives of sovereignty.

China and India have co-ordinated their efforts on issues as wide ranging as climate change, trade negotiations, energy security and the global financial crisis. Both nations favour more democratic international economic regimes. It is being argued that the forces of globalization have led to a certain convergence of Sino-Indian interests in the economic realm, as the two nations become even more deeply engaged in the international trading economy and more integrated in global financial networks.[14] They have strongly resisted efforts by the USA and other developed nations to link global trade to labour and environmental standards, realizing clearly that this would put them at a huge disadvantage vis-à-vis the developed world, thereby hampering their drive towards economic development, the number one priority for both countries. Both have committed themselves to crafting joint Sino-Indian positions in the World Trade Organization (WTO) and global trade negotiations in the hope that this might provide them with greater negotiating leverage over other developed states. They would like to see further liberalization of agricultural trade in the developed countries, to tighten the rules on anti-dumping measures and ensure that non-trade-related issues such as labour and the environment are not allowed to come into the WTO. Both have fought carbon emission caps proposed by the industrialized world and have resisted Western pressure to open up their agricultural markets.

The attempt by India and China in recent years has been to build their bilateral relationship on the basis of their larger world view of international politics. As they have found a distinct convergence of their interests on the world stage, they have used it to strengthen their bilateral relations. They have established and maintained regular reciprocal high-level visits between political leaders. There has been a real attempt to improve trade relations and to compartmentalize intractable issues that make it difficult for their bilateral relationship to move forward.

India and China have strengthened their bilateral relationship in areas as distinct as cultural and educational exchanges, military exchanges, and science and technology co-operation. Some military co-operation, something unthinkable a few years back, now takes place, with Indian and Chinese militaries conducting joint exercises. Economic relations between the two have been burgeoning, with China now India's largest trading partner. It was former Chinese Premier Zhu Rongji who suggested that the combination of Chinese hardware and Indian software would be irresistible to the global market. Bilateral trade has recorded rapid growth from a trade volume of US $265m. in 1991 to $42,440m. in 2009/10, or 9.1% of India's overall trade—45,950m. and an 11.8% share if Hong Kong is included. Its pace continues to accelerate, with India–China bilateral trade reaching $32,000m. in the first half of 2010. In addition to trade and interaction in the information technology sector, India facilitates China's economic development by exporting raw materials and semi-finished goods, as well as shipping Chinese cargo oversees. Chinese companies, for their part, have just begun to tap into India's ever-expanding consumer market by exporting electrical machines, home appliances, consumer electronics and mechanical goods. The two nations are also evaluating the possibility of signing a Comprehensive Economic Cooperation Agreement and a Free Trade Agreement, thereby building on strong complementarities between the two economies.

The number one priority for China's leadership today is economic growth and social stability. China's focus is going to be on maintaining its high rates of economic growth in coming years. China's political leadership is a product of the 'evolutionary policies' of Deng Xiaoping, which emphasize economic growth and orderly governance. China can be expected to continue on its current economic trajectory and to shape its foreign policy accordingly. India's focus is also on economic development at present, though its democratic political institutional structure ensures that consensus will elude India on the desirable route to economic development and modernization.

Global co-ordination and bilateral tensions

At the global level, the rhetoric is all about co-operation and, indeed, the two sides have worked together on climate change and global trade negotiations and in demanding a restructuring of global financial institutions in view of the global economy's shifting centre of gravity.

At the bilateral level, however, ties deteriorated to such an extent in 2009 that China took its territorial dispute with India all the way to the Asian Development Bank, where it blocked an application by India for a loan that included development projects in the Indian state of Arunachal Pradesh, which China continues to claim as part of its own territory. Buoyed by the perception that the Administration of US President Barack Obama plans to make its ties with China the centrepiece of its foreign policy in light of growing US economic dependence on China, China has displayed a distinctly more aggressive stance vis-à-vis India. China's lack of support for the US-Indian civilian nuclear energy co-operation pact, which it tried to block at the Nuclear Suppliers Group, and its obstructionist stance to bringing those behind the November 2009 terrorist attack in Mumbai to justice have further strained ties.[15]

Sino-Indian frictions are growing and potential for conflict remains high. There is rising alarm in India because of frequent and strident claims being made by China along the LAC in Arunachal Pradesh and Sikkim. Indians have complained that there has been a dramatic rise in Chinese cross-border 'intrusions' into the Indian territory over the last two years, most of them along the border in the region of Arunachal Pradesh, the Indian state that China refers to as *Zangnan* 'Southern Tibet'. China has upped the ante on the border issue. It has been regularly protesting against the Indian Prime Minister's visit to Arunachal Pradesh in 2009, asserting its claims over the territory. What has caught most observers of Sino-Indian ties by surprise is the vehemence with which Beijing has contested every single recent Indian administrative and political action in the state, even denying visas to Indian citizens of Arunachal Pradesh. India's Minister of External Affairs was forced to go on the record that the Chinese Army 'sometimes' intrudes on its territory, though he added that the issues were being addressed through established mechanisms. The recent rounds of boundary negotiations have been a disappointing failure, with a growing perception in India that China is less than willing to adhere to earlier political understandings on how to address the boundary dispute. Even the rhetoric has degenerated to the extent that a Chinese analyst connected to China's Ministry of National Defence claimed in a 2009 article that China could 'dismember the so-called "Indian Union" with one little move' into as many as 30 fragments.[16]

The fundamental underpinnings of the Sino-Indian bilateral relationship remain highly uncertain. China has tried hard to maintain a rough 'balance of power' in South Asia by preventing India from gaining an upper hand over Pakistan. China has consistently assisted Pakistan's nuclear weapons and ballistic missile programmes to counterbalance India's development of new weapons systems. India's preoccupation with Pakistan reduces India to the level of a regional power, while China can claim the status of an Asian and world power. It is instructive to note that even as India and China share similar concerns regarding Islamist terrorism in Kashmir and Xinjiang, respectively, China has been rather unwilling to make a common cause with India against Pakistan.

China's rapid economic growth in the last decade has given it the capability to transform itself into a military power. Its rapidly modernizing military is a cause of great concern for India. China's military may or may not be able to take on the USA in the next few years, but it will surely become the most dominant force in Asia. India is concerned about the opacity that seems to surround China's military build-up, with an emerging consensus that Beijing's real military spending is at least double the announced figure. The official figures of the Chinese Government do not include the cost of new weapons purchases, research or other big-ticket items for China's highly secretive military and, as a result, the real figure may be much higher than the revealed amount. Whatever Chinese intentions might be, consistent increases in defence budgets over the last several years have put China on track to become a major military power and the power most capable of challenging US predominance in the Asia-Pacific. While China's near-term focus remains on preparations for potential problems in the Taiwan Strait, its nuclear force modernization, its growing arsenal of advanced missiles, and its development of space and cyberspace technologies are changing the military balance in Asia and beyond. As China becomes more reliant on imported oil for its rapidly growing industrial economy, it will develop and exercise military power projection capabilities to protect the shipping that transports oil from the Persian Gulf to China. The capability to project power would require access to advanced naval bases along the sea lines of communication, and forces capable of gaining and sustaining naval and air superiority.

China's assistance to Myanmar in constructing and improving port facilities on two Cocos islands in the Bay of Bengal and the Andaman Sea may well be the first step to securing military base privileges in the Indian Ocean, potential listening posts for gathering intelligence on Indian naval operations, and a forward base for future Chinese naval operations in the Indian Ocean.[17] China's increasing naval presence in the Indian Ocean is occurring at the same time as Indian naval expansion has relatively slowed.[18] This could have great strategic consequences, because India's traditional geographic advantages in the Indian Ocean are increasingly at risk with any deepening Chinese involvement in Myanmar.

China has also been actively occupying islands, reefs and islets throughout the highly disputed South China Sea, occasionally resulting in skirmishes with rival claimants in the region. Interestingly, the Indian Navy has also been regularly deploying in the South China Sea since 2000. Moreover, China blocked India's membership in the Asia-Pacific Economic Cooperation (APEC) organization, and India became a member of the Association of Southeast Asian Nations (ASEAN) Regional Forum (ARF) despite China's opposition. China has been non-committal on India's membership in the Shanghai Cooperation Organization (SCO) and has obliquely warned against India's military presence in Central Asia. It was again China that drafted the condemnatory UN Security Council Resolution 1172 after India's nuclear tests in 1998.

For its part, India seems to have lost the battle over Tibet to China, despite the fact that Tibet constitutes China's only truly fundamental vulnerability vis-à-vis India. India has failed to limit China's military use of Tibet despite its great implications for Indian security, even as Tibet has become a platform for the projection of Chinese military power.[19] India's tacit support of the Dalai Lama's government-in-exile has failed to have much of an impact either on China or on the international community. By 2010 even the Dalai Lama seemed ready to talk to the Chinese, probably because he realized that in a few years Tibet might be overwhelmed with the Han 'Chinese' population and Tibetans themselves might become a minority in their own land.

Conversely, reports of Chinese intrusion across the Sino-Indian border appear time and again, especially across the eastern sector of the LAC in Arunachal Pradesh, with China continuing to lay claim to 90,000 sq miles of land in Arunachal Pradesh and not recognizing Arunachal Pradesh as part of Indian territory.[20] The opening up of the Nathu La trade route that connects Tibet and Sikkim was also fraught with dangers, because there were concerns that threats to the internal security of India posed by China could get worse with this opening. Moreover, the hopes of high trade flows through Nathu La have proved to be meagre trickles instead. India-China trade is overwhelmingly conducted via the sea, and is trade in which there has been a growing disadvantage for India in the past decade. A trade deficit for India with China of just over $4,100m. in 2005/06 had become a trade deficit of just over $19,200m. in 2009/10, in which China's exports to India of $30,824m. overshadowed India's much smaller exports to China of $11,617m.

Meanwhile, even though China has solved most of its border disputes with other countries, it is reluctant to move ahead with India on border issues. No results of any substance have been forthcoming from the Sino-Indian border negotiations even as the talks continue endlessly and the momentum of the talks itself seems to have flagged. So far, only the maps of the Middle Sector of the LAC, the least controversial part of the boundary, have been exchanged, and those, too, yet require confirmation. China has adopted shifting positions on the border issue, which might be a well-thought out position to keep India in a perpetual state of uncertainty. In the Indian context, China is ready for an early settlement of the border dispute *if* India concedes strategic territory. China's claims along the LAC also seem to be growing and may, therefore, indicate the reluctance so far to exchange maps on the western (Aksai Chin) and eastern (Arunachal Pradesh) sectors. With China controlling about 35,000 sq km of territory in Aksai Chin in the western sector and laying claim to almost all the 90,000 sq km of Arunachal Pradesh in the eastern sector, no early resolution of the boundary dispute is in sight. For its part, China sees a close Indo-US relationship as an attempt by the USA to encircle China, especially as it comes along with increasing US military presence and influence in Central and South Asia after the terrorist attacks on the USA on 11 September 2001. China has reacted strongly against the idea of a 'democratic quad' consisting of India, Japan, Australia and the USA, as manifested in their joint military exercises in the Bay of Bengal in September 2007.

India's growing challenge

India's challenge remains formidable. It has not yet achieved the economic and political profile that China enjoys regionally and globally, but it is increasingly bracketed with China as a rising power, emerging power or even a global superpower. The Indian elite, who have been obsessed with Pakistan for more than 60 years, have found suddenly a new object of fascination.

India's main security concern now is not the increasingly decrepit state of Pakistan but an ever more assertive China, which is widely viewed in India as having a better ability for strategic planning. The defeat at the hands of the Chinese in 1962 has psychologically scarred the elite perceptions of China and they are unlikely to change in the near future. China is viewed by India as a growing, aggressive nationalistic power, the ambitions of which are likely to reshape the contours of regional and global balance of power with deleterious consequences for Indian interests.[21] Whilst Indian policy-makers continue to believe that Beijing is not a short-term threat to India, they believe it needs to be watched over the long term, with Indian defence officials increasingly warning in rather blunt terms about the disparity between the two Asian powers. India has been warned by its former Naval Chief that the country neither has 'the capability nor the intention to match China force for force' in military terms, while the former Air Chief has suggested that China posed more of a threat to India than Pakistan.[22]

It may well be that the hardening of the Chinese posture toward India has been a function of its own sense of internal vulnerability, but that is hardly a consolation to Indian policy-makers who have to respond to Indian public opinion that increasingly wants the nation to assert itself in the region and beyond. India is rather belatedly gearing up to respond with its own diplomatic and military overtures, setting the stage for Sino-Indian strategic rivalry.

The rise of China is a major factor in the evolution of Indo-Japanese ties, as is the USA's attempt to build India into a major balancer in the region. Both India and Japan are well aware of China's not-so-subtle attempts at preventing their rise. It is most clearly reflected in China's opposition to the expansion of the UN Security Council to include India and Japan as permanent members. China's status as a Permanent Member of the Security Council and as a nuclear weapons state is something that it would be loath to share with any other state in Asia. India's 'Look East' policy of active engagement with ASEAN and East Asia remains largely predicated upon Japanese support, whilst generating Chinese ambivalence. India's participation in the East Asia Summit was facilitated by Japan, but initially resisted by China. While China has resisted the inclusion of India, Australia and New Zealand in ASEAN, Japan has strongly backed the entry of all three nations.

Recent convergence in the strategic priorities of India and the USA, as well as Japan, notwithstanding, it is unlikely that India would openly become a part of the US-led alliance framework against China. Like most states in the Asia-Pacific, India would not want to antagonize China by ganging up against it. Yet India is the country that will be and already is most affected by a rising China. China is a rising power in Asia and the world and as such will do its utmost to prevent the rise of other power centres around its periphery, like India, which might in the future prevent it from taking its rightful place as a global player. China's 'all-weather friendship' with Pakistan, its attempts to increase its influence in Nepal, Bangladesh and Myanmar, its persistent refusal to recognize parts of India such as Arunachal Pradesh, its lack of support for India's membership of the UN Security Council and other regional and global organizations, and its unwillingness to support the US-India nuclear pact—all these point towards China's attempts at preventing the rise of India as a regional and global player of major import. With India's recent rise as an economic and political power of global significance, Sino-Indian ties are now at a critical juncture, with India trying to find the right policy mix to deal with its most important neighbour.

The Sino-Indian security dilemma

The two sides are locked in a classic International Relations (IR) *security dilemma*, whereby any action taken by one is immediately interpreted by the other as a threat to its own interests.[23]

China has always viewed India as a mere regional player and has tried to confine India to the periphery of global politics. It was being argued a few years back that India was not on China's radar, as the country had set its eyes much higher. Today, the rise of India poses a challenge to China in more ways than one—the most important being ideological. The success of the Indian developmental model poses a significant challenge for the Chinese regime. As the story of India's success is being celebrated across the world, especially in the West, it is no surprise to see China becoming edgier in its relationship with India. It is notable that only after the USA started courting India did Chinese rhetoric towards India undergo a slight modification. Realizing that a close US-Indian partnership would change the regional balance of power to its disadvantage, China has started tightening the screws on India. It has further entrenched itself in India's *immediate neighbourhood* of South Asia, even as Sino-Indian competition for energy resources has gained momentum around India's *extended neighbourhood* and beyond. The development of infrastructure by China in its border regions with India has been so rapid and effective, and Indian response so lackadaisical, that the Indian member of parliament from Arunachal Pradesh was forced to suggest in sheer exasperation that the Government should allow Arunachal Pradesh to get a rail link from China, as even 60 years after independence India has failed to connect his state with the nation's mainland. India, in response, is now trying to catch up with China by improving the infrastructure on its side of the border areas. It has deployed two additional army divisions, and heavy tanks, and has ramped up its air power in the region, which is a bone of contention between India and China. Amidst such military build-ups and forward deployments on land and at sea, tensions are inherent.[24] Unless managed carefully, the potential for such incidents turning serious in the future remains high.

Conclusions

Both China and India are rising at the same time in an Asia-Pacific strategic landscape that is in flux. India is still 'grappling with an uneasy relationship' vis-à-vis China, amidst their simultaneous ascent in the global inter-state hierarchy and in mostly the same region of the world.[25] Even as they sign documents with high-sounding words year after year, the distrust between the two is actually growing at an alarming rate. Economic co-operation and bilateral political as well as socio-cultural exchanges are at an all-time high, yet this has done little to assuage their concerns vis-à-vis each other's intentions. Despite the rhetoric of a new phase in the relationship, the problems between India and China are substantial and complicated, with no easy resolution in sight. India and China are two major powers in Asia with global aspirations and some significant conflicting interests. The geopolitical reality of Asia ensures that it will be extremely difficult, if not impossible, for *Hind-China* ('Indians and Chinese') to be *bhai-bhai* (brothers) in the foreseeable future.

Notes

1 M. Krasna, 'Three Main Stages in the Development of Sino-Indian Contacts During the Indian Freedom Movement', *Archiv Orientalni*, Vol. 49, No. 3, 1981.
2 India-China, *Agreement between the Republic of India and the People's Republic of China on Trade and Intercourse Between Tibet Region of China and India*, 29 April 1954, www.commonlii.org.
3 For a detailed account see S. Hoffmann, *India and the China Crisis*, Berkeley: University of California Press, 1990. Also the earlier account by N. Maxwell, *India's China War*, London: Jonathan Cape, 1970, quite critical of Nehru and his 'Forward Policy'.
4 India-China, 'Joint Press Communiqué', 23 December 1988, www.fmprc.gov.cn.
5 'China is Threat No.1, Says Fernandes', *Hindustan Times*, 3 May 1998.

  6 A.B. Vajpayee, 'Letter' [to William Clinton], *New York Times*, 13 May 1998.
  7 A. Joseph, 'Wen to Seek Resolution of Border Dispute', *Indian Express*, 15 March 2005.
  8 India-China, *Declaration on Principles for Relations and Comprehensive Cooperation Between the People's Republic of China and the Republic of India*, 23 June 2003, www.fmprc.gov.cn.
  9 A. Baruah, 'China Keeps its word on Sikkim', *The Hindu*, 7 May 2004.
 10 J. Dixit, 'A New Security Framework', *The Telegraph* (Kolkata), 17 May 2004.
 11 M. Singh, 'Address to the Nation', 24 June 2004, meaindia.nic.in.
 12 India-China, *A Shared Vision for the 21st Century of the People's Republic of China and the Republic of India*, 15 January 2008, www.fmprc.gov.cn.
 13 Ibid. It also had something of particular interest to India: 'The Indian side reiterates its aspirations for permanent membership of the UN Security Council. The Chinese side attaches great importance to India's position as a major developing country in international affairs. The Chinese side understands and supports India's aspirations to play a greater role in the United Nations, including in the Security Council'.
 14 J. Clad, 'Convergent Chinese and Indian Perspectives on the Global Order', in F. Frankel and H. Harding (eds), *The India-China Relationship: What the United States Needs to Know*, New York: Columbia University Press, 2004.
 15 On China's role in trying to scuttle the nuclear deal, see H. Pant, 'The US-India Nuclear Pact: Policy, Process, and Great Power Politics', *Asian Security*, Vol. 5, No. 3, 2009.
 16 The essay, under the pseudonym *Zhanlue* ('Strategy'), appeared in August 2009 on *China International Strategy Net*, www.iiss.cn, a 'patriotic' website focusing on strategic issues. See D. Rajan, 'China Should Break up the Indian Union, Suggests a Chinese Strategist', *Papers* (SAAG), No. 3342, 10 August 2009.
 17 For a discussion of the strategic relevance of Myanmar for China vis-à-vis India, see C. Bhaskar, 'Myanmar in the Strategic Calculus of India and China', in K. Bajpai and A. Mattoo (eds), *The Peacock and the Dragon: India-China Relations in the 21st Century*, New Delhi: Har-Anand Publications, 2000.
 18 H. Pant, 'India in the Indian Ocean: Mismatch Between Ambitions and Capabilities', *Pacific Affairs*, Vol. 82, No. 2, 2009.
 19 A balanced analysis of the Tibetan problem in Sino-Indian relations can be found in J. Garver, *Protracted Contest: Sino-Indian Rivalry in the Twentieth Century*, Seattle: University of Washington Press, 2001, pp.32–78. For the very different perceptions of India and China regarding the boundary question, see pp.100–09.
 20 A. Joseph, 'We Don't Recognize Arunachal Pradesh: China', *Press Trust of India*, 25 July 2003. More generally, see D. Scott, 'Sino-Indian Territorial Issues: The "Razor's Edge"?', in H. Pant (ed.), *The Rise of China: Implications for India*, New Delhi: Foundation Books, 2011.
 21 On Sino-Indian competition, see H. Pant, 'India in the Asia Pacific: Rising Ambitions with an Eye on China', *Asia-Pacific Review*, Vol. 14, No. 1, 2007; D. Scott, 'The Great Power "Great Game" between India and China: "The Logic of Geography"', *Geopolitics*, Vol. 13, No. 1, 2008; 'India, China Engage in Great Game in Indian Ocean', *Indian Express*, 6 April 2010.
 22 R. Singh, 'China Now Bigger Threat than Pak: IAF Chief', *Hindustan Times*, 23 May 2009; S. Mehta, 'India's National Security Challenges', 10 August 2009, maritimeindia.org.
 23 J. Garver, 'The Security Dilemma in Sino-Indian Relations', *India Review*, Vol. 1, No. 4, 2002; J. Holslag, 'The Persistent Military Security Dilemma between China and India', *Journal of Strategic Studies*, Vol. 32, No. 6, 2009.
 24 This was underlined in a reported incident in 2009 when an Indian Kilo class submarine and Chinese warships, on their way to the Gulf of Aden to patrol the pirate-infested waters, reportedly engaged in rounds of manoeuvring as they tried to test for weaknesses in the other's sonar system. The Chinese media reported that its warships forced the Indian submarine to the surface, which was strongly denied by the Indian Navy.
 25 H. Pant, *The China Syndrome: Grappling with an Uneasy Relationship*, London: HarperCollins, 2010. Also J. Holslag, *China and India: Prospects for Peace*, New York: Columbia University Press, 2010.

22

India's relations with the USA

David Scott

Introduction

In 2000 US President William (Bill) Clinton stood up in the Indian parliament and extolled the ideational values, in this case 'democracy', that united India and the USA.[1] India was the world's biggest democracy in population terms, and the USA was the world's biggest democracy in power terms. In their subsequent Joint Statement, India-US Relations: A Vision for the 21st Century (2000), both countries stressed these values shared in common, and looked forward to 'a day of new beginnings' in relations between the two countries.[2] The irony is that from the 1950s through to the 1990s India and the USA were rather estranged, yet a decade later India was indeed 'crossing the Rubicon' in establishing close defence-military-strategic links with the USA, with the People's Republic of China as a third-party (unstated) consideration.[3] The Indian-US relationship now looks set to be a central one for the emerging international system of the 21st century. This chapter looks at their estrangement and then their convergence.

Cold War estrangement

Ironies abound in their relationship. Take, for example, the last days of British colonialism. Winston Churchill may have famously said that he had not become Prime Minister in order to preside over the death of the British Empire, yet it was US pressure, by Franklin D. Roosevelt, that played its part in pushing Britain to retreat from India, its 'jewel in the crown'.[4] The USA should have been in pole position as India took its place as an independent state, proudly proclaiming the virtues of democracy, yet instead it was a situation of 'estranged democracies' for the following decades.[5]

Divergent alignments

Even as an independent democratic India emerged, external politics were pulling apart the otherwise natural convergence that their internal politics (democracy) would have suggested. By 1947 the world was sliding into the Cold War. On the one hand stood the USA, looking for allies and commitment and swiftly engaged in building up alliances (the North Atlantic Treaty Organization—NATO, the Central Treaty Organization—CENTO, and the Southeast Asia Treaty Organization—SEATO), which would encircle and contain the USSR. Its logic was that if states were not with it then they were against it. On the other hand, India refused to align itself with either the US or Soviet camp. For the USA there was no third way, however, and Nehru's advocacy of non-alignment was viewed at best as weak and hypocritical, and at worst as giving the advantage to the USSR.

Even whilst India resolutely proclaimed the virtues of non-alignment, its adversary Pakistan was quick to align with the USA and its alignment systems, joining CENTO and SEATO on either side of India, as it were. US military supplies to Pakistan in the 1950s may have been seen as strengthening Pakistan as an anti-communist bulwark, but for India it was an enabling device for Pakistan to try and maintain strategic parity with India. As Nehru put it in 1954, 'this granting of military aid by the United States to Pakistan creates a grave situation for us in India [...] it adds to our tensions'.[6] Such logic continues down to the present.

Some of the rhetoric could still be invoked. First Lady Jacqueline Kennedy Onassis' visit to India in 1962 saw the spell of Camelot cast over India, and Jawaharlal Nehru suitably entranced. However, whilst Nehru did, in effect, tear-up his non-alignment distance and ask for US military aid amidst the military debacle against China, the reluctance of the USA to commit itself to any significant assistance meant a continuation of the rather cool nature of US-Indian relations. Conversely, US relations with Pakistan worried India, with ongoing concerns expressed by India: 'the Government of India regrets the decision of the United States Government to undertake supplies of spare parts of lethal weapons to Pakistan [...] the reactivation of Pakistan's military machine, which the US decision will necessarily bring about, will pose a threat again to India'.[7] Such coolness in relations between India and the USA was compounded by India's tilt towards the USSR that took place in the 1960s and 1970s. One of the reasons for the Sino-Soviet split had been Moscow's support of India's position in the lead up to war, with Soviet military supplies being a significant factor in the rebuilding of India's military strength after 1962. Nehru's advocacy of centrally planned economies saw him closer to Soviet-style economics than to US-style deregulated capitalism.

Nehru's daughter, Indira Gandhi, continued this tilt toward the USSR, signified in the Treaty of Peace, Friendship and Cooperation that they signed in 1971. From India's point of view, the USSR was the major power giving it support, whilst for Pakistan it was the USA (and China). Such entanglements were on show in 1971 when the USA supported Pakistan, not wishing to see India's power advantages further strengthened in South Asia at the expense of Pakistan. India's sense of US hostility was palpable: 'the United States Government is still side-stepping the central issue [Pakistani domestic suppression] and is responding with flagrant injustice in attempting to pin the major responsibility for the present conflict on India'.[8] Indira Gandhi felt that, 'our relationship as a whole has been uneasy over a long period of time. To our grave concern, U.S. policy as it developed impinged seriously on our vital interests [...] in regard to Bangladesh and during the December war, the United States openly backed Pakistan'.[9] The US position was that, 'this has been a full-scale invasion in East Pakistan, and it must stop' (George Bush), and that, 'it is the US view that India's recourse to military action was unjustified' (Henry Kissinger).[10] Consequently, elements of the US 7th Fleet were sent into the Bay of Bengal, complete with aircraft carrier, to put pressure on India. Such pressure was, though, countered by firm diplomatic support and signs of Soviet readiness to deploy its own military muscle to block such US moves.

India continued to show worries over the US naval presence in the region. In 1974 it was a question that 'we are deeply concerned at the continuing presence of the US naval task force in the Indian Ocean which is confirmed by the arrival of the aircraft carrier "Kitty Hawk"'.[11] India also felt that it was not being taken seriously by the USA.[12] In the world of the 1980s, the Cold War II period, India saw threats from extra-regional superpowers as particularly posed by the USA, with New Delhi decrying US military moves in the Indian Ocean, including the setting up of military base facilities on Diego Garcia.

> India noted with increasing concern that an area in which the two countries appeared to be following divergent policies was the continuing military build-up by the United States in the Indian Ocean area […] The build-up included the expansion of the Diego Garcia base and the reported decision that it would be built up as a major air, naval and perhaps nuclear facility […] and the plans of the USA for the creation of a rapid deployment force of 110,000 personnel for use primarily in the Indian Ocean. Reports about [US] seeking of fuelling, re-stocking and rest and recreation facilities at littoral ports and attempts to acquire base facilities have caused serious concern to the Government of India and other non-aligned states.[13]

The USA saw India as providing assistance to the Soviet deployment from Vladivostok to Viet Nam and into the Indian Ocean, the so-called 'Arc of Crisis'. The unwillingness of India to denounce the Soviet move into Afghanistan in 1979 was seen as further grounds of difference between the two states.

In contrast, of course, Pakistan's firmly anti-Soviet position over Afghanistan brought it support, and military supplies, from the USA. India's position was clear, it was unhappy, just as Nehru had been back in 1954. Its attempts in 1982 to block US sales to Pakistan were unsuccessful:

> The US decision to supply sophisticated arms to Pakistan ostensibly as a reaction to the Soviet intervention in Afghanistan, aroused apprehensions in India. In the past, India had more than once been a victim of Pakistani aggression. The possibility of the introduction of a new generation of armaments into the sub-continent, heightened the fears based on past experience. The concern of the Government of India about the US decision was, there-fore, conveyed adequately to the United States at various levels but unfortunately without result […] The passage of the proposals on the security assistance to Pakistan through the US Congress which confirmed the Administration's decision, cast a shadow over bilateral relations which showed no signs of lifting at the year end.[14]

India continued to be concerned about US (and Chinese) military aid to Pakistan. As for the USA, it viewed India with coolness at best. In 1992 the US position was that, 'we should dis-courage Indian hegemonic aspirations over the other States in South Asia and on the Indian Ocean'.[15] The following year, US officials were stressing, 'let me make it very clear. We are not seeking a strategic relationship with India'.[16] The irony there is that that was precisely the trajectory of US-Indian links.

Post-Cold War convergence

The post-Cold War period posed new challenges for India and the USA. For India, the break-up of the USSR in effect removed its previous close ally with which it had a Treaty of Peace, Friendship and Cooperation, but also removed the ideological battleground that had seen India tilting towards a USSR with which the USA was in competition. The collapse of the USSR also left India potentially more isolated within the international system. For the USA, the collapse of the USSR had indeed removed its Cold War foe, against which it had constructed alliances and judged other countries like India. However, whilst the Cold War period had seen a strategic logic bringing the USA and China together against a common Soviet threat, the removal of the USSR removed that logic and left China as the emerging rival power to the USA. India's own problems with China (territorial disputes and so forth) remained as keen as ever. India's own rise in Asia was bringing it increasingly up against an equally (or even more strongly) rising China. Classic International Relations (IR) *balance of power* (Kenneth Waltz) factors would have suggested a China-India balance against the USA. Instead, Stephen Walt-style *balance of threat* factors of aggregate power, offensive capabilities, perceived offensive intentions and geographical proximity seemed more important for India, particularly on account of the last two (perceived offensive intentions, geographical proximity), to balance instead with the USA against China.

Such considerations were already affecting how India and the USA regarded each other. The US Administration of Bill Clinton (1993–2001) was quick enough to move towards India, with Clinton's 'Community of Democracies' providing some of the ideological underpinnings for this. Some initial steps were signalled in the Agreed Minute on Defense Cooperation, which was signed in January 1995, a 'first important step' with its talk of 'gradually increasing cooperation in defense research and production', which 'begins the process for deepening and strengthening the security relations between India and the United States of America [...] significant and really historic because we have now been more than four decades absent that kind of security relationship'.[17] However, the pace was slow. As the US Secretary of Defense, William Perry, put it, 'in India, I stressed that arms sales were simply not on the agenda. I did say that we would look for ways of gradually increasing cooperation in defense research and production, but I emphasized that this will not be an area for immediate or bold steps'.[18] US supplies to Pakistan continued, as they still do, to complicate relations with India: 'the Government of India deeply regrets [...] the US decision to take no action on the clandestine acquisition by Pakistan of 5,000 ring magnets for its nuclear weapons programme, and indeed to continue uninterruptedly with its transfer of sophisticated US arms to Pakistan'.[19]

An important turning point was the election of the Bharatiya Janata Party (BJP) in 1998. Their first decision of substance was to press ahead with nuclear testing, Pokhran-II. The US response was quick: 'this week I want to speak to you about a matter of grave concern to the United States and the international community, India's nuclear test explosion. These tests were unjustified and threaten to spark a dangerous nuclear arms race in Asia. As a result, and in accordance with our laws, I have imposed serious sanctions against India, including an end to our economic assistance, military financing', albeit lifted by November 1998.[20]

By then, Atal Bihari Vajpayee had been quick to make a play for stronger Indian-US relations in September 1998. In his speech, 'India, USA and the World' to the Asia Society he argued that they were 'estranged democracies', in which US preference for relations with Pakistan and China had blinded it to the role that India could play. His vision was one where, 'Indo-US ties based on equality and mutuality of interests is going to be the mainstay of tomorrow's stable, democratic world order'. The stress on a democratic world order is an interesting slant pointing not just to US-Indian domestic politics of democratic pluralism, but also to a more democratic international system, where US unipolarity was giving way to multipolarity (what some would call the 'democratization of international relations'). He went on, 'India and the US are natural allies in the quest for a better future for the world in the 21st century'. Raja Mohan sees it as 'simple in its conception but a breathtaking departure from India's traditional foreign policy of non-alignment and anti-American and anti-Western orientation', a 'brazen pitch for an alliance with Washington'.[21]

Clinton's own trip to India in 2000, at the end of his presidency, gave further momentum to this rapprochement. His comments to a Joint Session of the Indian parliament soothed Indian sensibilities, especially his comments that, 'we welcome India's leadership in the region', and 'we want to take our partnership to a new level'.[22] Amidst the emphasis of democracy and human rights inspiration of Gandhi in the USA, the economic take-off of India was also a feature noted by him:

> You liberated your markets, and now have one of the 10 fastest growing economies in the world [...] Americans have applauded your efforts to open your economy, your commitment to a new wave of economic reform[; such that] we are proud to support India's growth as your largest partner in trade and investment. And we want to see more Indians and more Americans benefit from our economic ties, especially in the cutting fields of information technology, biotechnology, and clean energy. The private sector will drive this progress.[23]

What was significant in this late Clinton setting was that their relationship still seemed to be a matter of *soft power* values (democracy, pluralism) and *hard power* (economics), but with *hard power* military-security issues much less evident. A sense of 'estranged democracies' was giving way to 'engaged democracies'.[24]

Anti-terrorism

One element pulling them closer together was not the state-level challenge of China, but the transnational threat of terrorism. India for some time had been warning about the dangers of *jihadist* acts of violence, erupting across Kashmir during the 1980s but also targeting the rest of India, as with the Mumbai bombings of 1993 which saw 250 people die. The hijacking of Indian Airlines IC 814 brought discussion and the setting-up of an Indo-US Joint Working Group on terrorism in February 2000, wherein the two countries agreed to share experiences, exchange information and co-ordinate approaches and action.[25] As part of its assistance to India, the USA offered to give anti-terrorism training for inter-departmental co-ordination, crisis response and consequence management.

Under the presidency of George W. Bush (2001–09), the USA faced its own outrages, notably the terrorist attacks of 11 September 2001 at the hands of al-Qa'ida. India was quick to give full support, including transit facilities, as the USA moved against the Taliban regime in Afghanistan that had hosted al-Qa'ida. Manmohan Singh's visit to the USA in November 2001 gave him the opportunity to express the fullest and strongest support for the USA. The joint Indian-US statement noted that, 'since September 11, the people of the United States and India have been united as never before in the fight against terrorism. In so doing, they have together reaffirmed [...] the importance of further transforming the US-India relationship [...] they noted that both countries are targets of terrorism, as seen in the barbaric attacks on 11th September in the United States and on 1st October in Kashmir'.[26] The importance for India was the linking of Kashmiri 'terrorism' to terrorism elsewhere.

On 20 December 2001, following the attack on the Indian parliament, the USA placed the *Jaish-e-Mohammed* and *Lashkar-e-Taiba* on all three US terrorist lists: the Foreign Terrorist Organizations (FTO) list, the Specially Designated Global Terrorists (SDGT) list, and the Terrorist Exclusion List. In addition, it called upon Pakistan to take steps to crack down on terrorism emanating from Pakistan, and to take decisive action against *Lashkar-e-Taiba* and *Jaish-e-Mohammed* and other terrorist organizations, their leaders, finances and activities.

India could continue to express concern over US unwillingness to name Pakistan as a 'state sponsor of terrorism'.[27] On the one hand, Pakistan's previous support of the Taliban Government had left uncertainties over Pakistan's position after the terrorist attacks on the USA. Nevertheless, Pakistan's position as the immediate front-line state for operations in Afghanistan gave it leverage over the USA, which continued to need Pakistan's assistance more than it needed India's in the immediate efforts to curb Taliban and al-Qa'ida operatives in Pakistan. Potentially, it also enabled Pakistan to try to trade its assistance to the USA over taking action against Taliban/al-Qa'ida forces in Pakistan for the USA taking a more pro-Pakistan position over Kashmir.

Nevertheless, India could project itself as standing shoulder to shoulder with the USA in the global 'war on terrorism'.[28] Such a line-up was helped by a reference by Osama bin Laden in an audio message on *Al Jazeera* on 23 April 2006, wherein he spoke of a 'Crusader-Zionist-Hindu' conspiracy.[29] The bombings carried out across Mumbai in November 2008 strengthened their common anti-*jihadist* concerns. The fact that the Mumbai bombers had entered India from Pakistan strengthened India's attempts to get the USA to distance itself more from Pakistan.

Defence convergence

The most significant development in recent years has been the convergence between India and the USA in security-military areas. This has taken India far from the days of Nehru and Indira Gandhi with their campaigns for non-alignment and for getting the USA out of the Indian Ocean.

Even as the Clinton Administration was coming to an end, the incoming Republican Administration under George W. Bush was dreaming of recasting the international system. His prospective National Security Council (and later Secretary of State) adviser, Condoleezza Rice, was already talking of constraining China: 'China is not a "status quo" power but one that would like to alter Asia's balance of power in its own favor. That alone makes it a strategic competitor' for the USA, but also for India.[30] Her take was to note that the USA, 'should pay closer attention to India's role in the regional balance. There is a strong tendency conceptually to connect India with Pakistan and to think only of Kashmir or the nuclear competition between the two states. But India is an element in China's calculation, and it should be in America's, too. India is not a Great Power yet, but it has the potential to emerge as one', and one able to join the USA in balancing China.[31]

Such strategic logic dominated US-Indian relations during the Bush presidency and was reciprocated by both BJP- and Congress-led governments in India. By the time of Vajpayee's visit to the USA, in the aftermath of the 2001 attacks, India and the USA were talking of creating a 'strategic partnership' between the two countries. Indian commentators like Ganguly could talk of 'the start of a beautiful friendship' in 2003, with January 2004 seeing the US-Indian Next Steps in Strategic Partnership (NSSP) initiative being launched.[32] The following year saw the launching of the Indian–US Global Democracy Initiative (GDI). Such a strategic convergence was seen by hard-headed Indian commentators as 'inevitable', driven by common geopolitical imperatives and common *balance of threat* analyses directed at China.[33] Neither India nor the USA wished to pursue hard containment or antagonistic rejection of China; both were trying to engage with China where possible. However, as part of their mutual hedging strategies towards China both were ready to strengthen their own security relationship, to engage in elements of unstated but apparent balancing as well towards China. The terminology being used by 2002 was of, 'a more robust military partnership'.[34] This involved their talk, and substance, by 2002, 'of the impressive growth in military cooperation between India and the

United States [...] But the long-term goal is much more ambitious, and is based on strategic, diplomatic and political cooperation'.[35] From India's point of view, geopolitical extension of power was indicated in the agreement in 2002 for Indian ships *INS Sharda* and *Sukanya* to take over from the USA in escorting ships through the Straits of Malacca.

With regard to alignment, the key development was the Defence Agreement drawn up in 2005 between the two countries. This defence convergence had real teeth to it, amidst growing deliberate moves to foster inter-operability of forces. It has involved India in purchasing powerful and advanced weapons from the USA. At sea, India's purchase of USS Trenton (commissioned in 2007 as INS *Jalasha*, the second biggest vessel in the Indian fleet) gave India long-range, amphibious deployment capabilities for Indian Ocean operations, whilst the 2009 agreement to purchase the latest Boeing P-8 AWAC planes gave further long-range tracking capabilities. In the Indian Ocean, Indira Gandhi's 1980s strictures against US presence have given way to continued and substantive co-operation. The MALABAR exercises are but one of an extensive and varied range of bilateral exercises (e.g. COPE) with the USA in which India is now regularly involved. A particularly interesting variant was the MALABAR-1 exercises, which took place between the Indian and US Navies in the Western Pacific in 2007. MALABAR-2 was equally interesting, later that year, in which units from Japan, Australia and Singapore joined the Indian and US Navies in the Bay of Bengal, to China's disquiet. Such defence-military convergence was also echoed in the Joint Declaration in 2005 to co-operate over nuclear energy, with the USA lifting its previous restrictions on nuclear trade, with domestic and international legislation completed by 2009.

Conclusions

US-India strategic co-operation is set to run into the 21st century.[36] The context for this is India's rise within the international system. The Indian leadership, looking at the new Barack Obama Administration, judged that, 'the new US Administration has, indeed, focused on continuity in the bilateral relationship. In this, is the inherent recognition of India's place in the world, our regional role, and our demonstrable economic strength and potential'.[37] The US Quadrennial Review (2010) was equally clear about India's impact:

> As the economic power, cultural reach, and political influence of India increase, it is assuming a more influential role in global affairs. This growing influence, combined with democratic values it shares with the United States, an open political system, and a commitment to global stability, will present many opportunities for cooperation. India's military capabilities are rapidly improving through increased defense acquisitions, and they now include long-range maritime surveillance, maritime interdiction and patrolling, air interdiction, and strategic airlift. India has already established its worldwide military influence through counterpiracy, peacekeeping, humanitarian assistance, and disaster relief efforts. As its military capabilities grow, India will contribute to Asia as a net provider of security in the Indian Ocean and beyond.[38]

In geopolitical terms, there seems to be an unofficial shift taking place as the USA shores up its position in the Western Pacific (e.g. Guam), but starts to stand to one side to see India assume a greater role in the Indian Ocean as, indeed, a 'net provider of security'.

A lot of this recent US-India convergence has been because of their common concerns about China. As India's Minister of External Affairs, Nirupama Rao, gently alluded to in her 2010 address, 'The United States and India: Charting the Future Course':

The rise of China is of course observed with close attention in our region. China's demonstrable economic strength and its growing military capabilities are a matter of fact and we must incorporate such factors into our calculus of the emerging 21st century scenario in the Asia Pacific. This is where a mature and evolving dialogue between India and the United States will be of considerable relevance in clarifying approaches to the regional situation and the policy approaches of roles of our two countries in these new [China-related] circumstances.[39]

However, both partners remain concerned not to forego engagement links with China, with which they both have bigger trading links.[40] India is concerned about the USA playing the 'India card' to gain concessions from China, before then dropping India, whilst the USA is also concerned about India playing the 'US card' in order to gain concessions from China, before then dropping the USA.

At the regional (Asia and the Indian Ocean) level, the long-term logic of Walt's *balance of threat* pulls India and the USA together, though at the global level the logic of Waltz's *balance of power* in the long term pulls India together with other powers like Russia, China and Brazil (the BRIC formation), to replace US unipolarity with multipolarity. The common position of India and the USA as democracies does, however, provide a substantial ideational base for long-term co-operation, whilst geopolitically their respective spheres and strategic backyards do not particularly overlap, leading Rao to not inaccurately sum up that, 'our collaboration and cooperation will be indispensable for shaping the character of the 21st century', in which 'we share common values and common strategic interests'.[41]

Notes

1 W. Clinton, 'Remarks to a Joint Session of Parliament in New Delhi', 22 March 2000, in *Public Papers of the Presidents of the United States. William J. Clinton. 2000–2001*, Washington: Office of the Federal Register, National Archives and Records Service, 2001, Book 1, p.514.
2 India-US, *India-US Relations: A Vision for the 21st Century*, 21 March 2000, pib.nic.in.
3 N. Gaan, *India and the United States. From Estrangement to Engagement*, Delhi: Kalpaz, 2007; C. Raja Mohan, *Crossing the Rubicon. The Shaping of India's New Foreign Policy*, New York: Palgrave Macmillan, 2004.
4 G. Hess, *America Encounters India, 1941–47*, Baltimore: John Hopkins University Press, 1971.
5 D. Kux, *India and the United States: Estranged Democracies 1941–1991*, Washington: National Defense University Press, 1992.
6 J. Nehru, 'Statement to Parliament', 1 March 1954, in *Selected Works of Jawaharlal Nehru*, Second Series. Vol. 25, New Delhi: Jawaharlal Nehru Memorial Fund, 1999, p.341.
7 'Statement of the Government of India on the Resumption of US Arms Supplies to Pakistan', 12 April 1967, in R. Jain (ed.), The *United States and India 1947–2006. A Documentary Study*, Delhi: Radiant Publisher, 2007, p.297.
8 'Statement by Indian Representative Samar Sen in the UN Security Council', 5 December 1971, in R. Jain (ed.), *The United States and India 1947–2006. A Documentary Study*, op. cit., p.50.
9 I. Gandhi, 'India and the World', *Foreign Affairs*, Vol. 51, No. 1, 1972, pp.74–75.
10 G. Bush, 'Statement by US Representative Bush in the UN Security Council', 5 December 1971', and H. Kissinger, 'Background Briefing by National Security Adviser Henry Kissinger', 7 December 1971, in R. Jain (ed.), *The United States and India 1947–2006. A Documentary Study*, op. cit., pp.50, 51.
11 S. Singh, 'Swaran Singh's Statement on Entry of a Nuclear Powered Aircraft Carrier in the Indian Ocean', 12 March 1974, in R. Jain (ed.), *The United States and India 1947–2006. A Documentary Study*, op. cit., p.67.
12 B. Nayar, 'Treat India Seriously', *Foreign Policy*, No. 18, Spring 1975.
13 Ministry of External Affairs, *Annual Report, 1980–81*, New Delhi: Ministry of External Affairs, 1981, pp.37, iv.
14 Ministry of External Affairs, *Annual Report, 1981–82*, New Delhi: Ministry of External Affairs, 1982, p.28.

15 'Classified Policy Document Prepared by American Defene Department in Consultation With the National Security Council and President Bush', 8 March 1992, in R. Jain (ed.), *The United States and India 1947–2006. A Documentary Study*, op. cit., p.84.

16 J. Malott, 'Statement by Principal Deputy Assistant Secretary of State for South Asian Affairs, John R. Malott', 19 May 1993, in R. Jain (ed.), *The United States and India 1947–2006. A Documentary Study*, op. cit., p.315.

17 W. Perry, 'Statement by U.S. Secretary of Defense William J. Perry After the Signing of the Agreed Minute on Defense Cooperation', 12–14 January 1995, in R. Jain (ed.), *The United States and India 1947–2006. A Documentary Study*, op. cit., p.317.

18 'Statement by Defence Secretary Perry', 31 January 1995, in R. Jain (ed.), *The United States and India 1947–2006. A Documentary Study*, op. cit., p.319.

19 'Press Release Issued in New Delhi on US Policy to Pakistan's Nuclear Programme', 14 May 1996, in R. Jain (ed.), *The United States and India 1947–2006. A Documentary Study*, op. cit., p.401.

20 W. Clinton, 'Clinton's Radio Address to the Nation', 17 May 1998, in R. Jain (ed.), *The United States and India 1947–2006. A Documentary Study*, op. cit., p.411.

21 C. Raja Mohan, *Crossing the Rubicon. The Shaping of India's New Foreign Policy*, op. cit., pp.49–50.

22 W. Clinton, 'Remarks to a Joint Session of Parliament in New Delhi', op. cit., p.514.

23 Ibid.

24 K. Bajpai and A. Mattoo, *Engaged Democracies: India-US Relations in the 21st Century*, New Delhi: Har-Anand Publications Pvt Ltd, 2000.

25 P. Rajeswari, 'Terrorism—an Area of Cooperation in Indo-US Relations', *Strategic Analysis*, Vol. 24, No. 6, 2000. See S. D'Souza, 'Indo-US Counter-Terrorism Cooperation: Rhetoric Versus Substance', *Strategic Analysis*, Vol. 32, No. 6, 2008, for potential gap between rhetoric and substance.

26 'India-US, 'Joint Statement on Vajpayee's Visit to Washington, D.C.', 9 November 2001, in R. Jain (ed.), *The United States and India 1947–2006. A Documentary Study*, op. cit., p.128.

27 'US, India and Terrorism', *The Tribune* (editorial), 9 December 2002.

28 G. Parthasarthy, 'Global Fight Against Terrorism', *The Tribune*, 27 September 2001; C. Raja Mohan, 'Towards a Global War Against Terrorism', *The Hindu*, 13 September 2001. Also B. Raman, 'Global Terrorism: India's Concerns', *Papers* (SAAG), No. 2021, 12 November 2006.

29 For an analysis of the message, see B. Raman, 'Bin Laden Targets India', *Papers* (SAAG), No. 1776, 25 April 2006.

30 C. Rice, 'Promoting the National Interest', *Foreign Affairs*, Vol. 79, No. 1, 2000, p.56.

31 Ibid.

32 S. Ganguly, 'The Start of a Beautiful Friendship: The United States and India', *World Policy Journal*, Vol. 20, No. 1, 2003.

33 S. Kapila, 'India-USA Strategic Partnership: The Advent of the Inevitable', *Papers* (SAAG), No. 120, 22 April 2000.

34 D. Camp, 'Speech by Deputy Assistant Secretary of State for South Asia', 3 April 2002, in R. Jain (ed.), *The United States and India 1947–2006. A Documentary Study*, op. cit., p.330.

35 C. Rocca, 'Address by Assistant Secretary of State Christina B. Rocca', 14 May 2002, in R. Jain (ed.), *The United States and India 1947–2006. A Documentary Study*, op. cit., p.332.

36 S. Ganguly, B. Shoup and A. Scobell, *US-Indian Strategic Cooperation into the 21st Century*, London: Routledge, 2006.

37 N. Rao, 'The United States and India: Charting the Future Course', 12 January 2010, meaindia.nic.in.

38 *Quadrennial Defense Review Report*, Washington: Department of Defense, 2010, p.60.

39 N. Rao, 'The United States and India: Charting the Future Course', op. cit.

40 With regard to trade with India, China overtook the USA in 2005/06, with US $42,440 m. (India–China) and $39,710 m. (India–USA) in 2009/10. The volume of US-China trade was larger, at $369,220 m. in 2009/10, consisting of $304,410 m. in Chinese exports to the USA and $64,810 m. US exports to China. In 2009/10 India's overall trade with the USA involved a small surplus, with $19,530 m. in exports to the USA, compared with $16,980 m. in imports from the USA.

41 N. Rao, 'The United States and India: Charting the Future Course'. Also C. Raja Mohan, 'Rising India: Partner in Shaping the Global Commons?', *Washington Quarterly*, Vol. 33, No. 3, 2010.

Part 5
India and global issues

23

India and the Indian diaspora

Ajay Dubey

Introduction

The diaspora is now recognized as an international influencer. Apart from its role in economic development, it plays an important role in bilateral relations between the host country and country of origin. It has emerged as a major driver for the foreign policy of countries with substantial overseas communities. Globalization enables it to serve as a resource both for the host and home country. It has created an environment for communities to look beyond rigid national boundaries for economic and cultural needs. Even developing countries have matured now to permit extraterritorial loyalties. Many of them are using their own diaspora abroad as well as the diaspora within their territory as an important resource to realize their national objectives. Cheaper and faster means of communication at a global level provide opportunities for different diaspora to network and come together. The emerging scientific and technological advancement and global media have further enabled the different diaspora and states to engage with each other.

India has its own particular global diaspora of over 25m., spread over 196 countries. It includes foreign citizens of Indian origin, termed 'people of Indian origin' (PIO), and Indian passport holders who are based in foreign countries, termed 'non-resident Indians' (NRI). The Indian diaspora includes particularly significant groups in the Gulf (over 3m.) and in North America (around 4m.) consisting of various ethnic, linguistic and religious groups, reflecting the cultural diversity of India. Indian migration itself is widely varied in terms of historical context, causes and consequences, as well as in terms of social characteristics, such as level of education, caste and class, place of origin, religion and language.[1] Indian migrants migrated in different bursts and numbers. During ancient times they went as merchants and explorers from western India to Africa and the Middle East. From south-eastern India they migrated to Burma (now Myanmar), Indonesia and other countries of South-East Asia. A section of this Indian diaspora derived its livelihood from international trade, maintaining international kinship and economic networks. During this phase Indians also migrated to the Far East and South-East Asia as part of the cultural spread of Buddhism, and some south Indian rulers like the Cholas sent successful expeditions to the region. However, they are now more or less a lost diaspora.

The bulk of Indian migration took place during the colonial period, when the previous small-scale movement of Indian people turned into a mass migration.[2] They went broadly in three different capacities, namely (a) the indentured worker in sugar colonies of the Caribbean, Oceania and Africa; (b) the *Kangani/ maistry* system to Malaysia and Ceylon (now Sri Lanka); and (c) free passenger Indians. The free Indians (called 'passenger Indians') went in a small number as traders, money lenders, etc. to anglophone, francophone and lusophone territories. In the latest phase, during the 20th century, Indians immigrated as skilled workers to industrialized nations in Europe, North America and Oceania, as well as semi-skilled workers to the Middle East. However, the latter were not given citizenship.

There are various ways in which the Indian diaspora is classified. The 'old diaspora' refers to all those who went before the independence of India, while the 'new diaspora' refers to those who went after independence. The old diaspora forms the bulk of the total Indian diaspora, migrating to Malaysia, Mauritius, Trinidad and Tobago, Fiji, Guyana and Suriname. The term PIO is used for those who have taken local citizenship, whether coming from the new or old diaspora. There are PIOs who went to countries in the Caribbean, Africa, Fiji, etc., and who migrated after a few generations to Europe, North America or Australia, and are called 'twice migrants'. Indians living overseas who still have an Indian passport, even if they are overseas for many years, are the NRIs. Over 5m. Indians in the west Asian countries are in this category.

All these categories will be examined in this chapter, which aims to study the changes and continuity in the evolution of Indian policy towards the Indian diaspora. This includes examining the imperatives, experiences, experiments and attempts by the Government of India to engage the Indian diaspora.

India's policy towards its diaspora

Indian policy towards the Indian diaspora has continued to evolve since colonial times, through the Cold War period, to the present day.

The pre-independence period

During the colonial period the Indian National Congress (INC), the vanguard party of the Indian struggle for freedom, had concerns about Indians overseas. Indians operated under an indentured worker system, taken up under colonial rule to replace slave labour. The INC sent several delegations and workers to inspect the treatment of indentured Indian workers, protesting against colonial government policies and asking for improved status and conditions for indentured workers. Indian nationalists of all shades demanded improvements in working and living conditions of Indians settled abroad. The cause of Indians overseas was advocated by nationalist leaders, such as Gopal Krishna Gokhale, Mahatma Gandhi, V.S. Srinivasa Shastri, Jawaharlal Nehru, H.N. Kunzru, Acharya Kripalani and Ram Manohar Lohia. They repeatedly stressed the need to safeguard the interests of the people who had to leave the shores of India to cater for the economic interests of the United Kingdom. In Mauritius and Fiji, Mahatma Gandhi sent Manilal Doctor, while coming back from South Africa, to mobilize them.[3] He advised them to actively participate in local politics and to demand a legitimate share in the governance and economy of their new home.

Indians also used the Indian diaspora around the world to push the cause of Indian independence. They were exhorted to identify with the Indian cause, as only a free India could hope to protect and safeguard their interests, and were visualized by Gandhi as a segment of emerging Indian independence opinion, a policy of *identification* in other words. One strand of Congress opinion (comprising C.F. Andrew, Shastri, Kunzru, M.M. Malaviya and B.G. Gokhale) was mainly concerned with discrimination of overseas Indians in Africa and elsewhere, and wanted for them a parity with local white settlers. They visited worker recruitment centres and talked to workers about their problems. In succeeding years, the issue of discrimination of Indians in South Africa became a sentimental issue for Indian nationalists, given Mahatma Gandhi's earlier efforts there.

Jawaharlal Nehru, who from 1930 shaped the foreign policy of India within the INC, had different views. Nehru had long visualized the clash of interests of Indians overseas with local inhabitants. In 1927 he prepared a paper, *A Foreign Policy of India*. In this paper, for the first time, he categorically outlined the policy of the INC regarding Indian settlers in other colonial countries, the role that India wanted them to play in their country of adoption, and the kind of support that they could expect from India. He asked in the paper, 'what is the position of Indians of foreign countries to-day?', and argued that the overseas Indians had gone there as 'a hireling of exploiter' British Government.[4] However, he suggested elsewhere that, 'an Indian who goes to other countries must co-operate with people of that country and win for himself a position by friendship and service [...] Indians should co-operate with Africans and help them, as far as possible and not claim a special position for themselves'.[5]

Nehru represented the left wing of the Congress party. He differed from the conservative wing, whose demands were confined to the betterment of Indians overseas. Nehru believed in co-operation between Indians and natives, advocating Indian support to a combined struggle of Indian settlers and natives in which the native cause would be paramount. As an exception, Nehru extended special support to Indian settlers in South Africa, reflecting Gandhi's earlier work there. In a message to the INC in Natal, Nehru wrote in 1939: 'India is weak today and cannot do much for her children abroad but she does not forget them and every insult to them is a humiliation and sorrow for her. And a day will come when her long arm will shelter and protect them and her strength will compel justice for them'.[6] It is this duality between Nehru's policy and the presence of two wings (conservative and left) in Congress which helps us to understand the changes and continuities in Indian policy towards Indian overseas communities.

Post-independence period

Immediately after India's independence, the Indian Government was not in a position to assist in obtaining full justice for Indian settlers abroad. In fact, the problems of PIOs in different countries were so diverse, the positioning and status so different and the reach of India so varied, that a nascent Indian state did not find itself equipped or strong enough to address the diaspora issues head on.[7] Besides, Nehru had other priorities like the mobilization of Afro-Asian countries to keep them away from Cold War rivalries.[8] For such mobilization, the issues of the PIOs were not to be emphasized.

Thus, during the 1950s and the best part of the 1960s, establishing any special relationship with the diaspora was not a priority of India's foreign policy. Independent India gave them little recognition, except the advice that they should strive hard to be the best citizens of their countries of adoption. Nehru did not deviate from his strongly held policy on Indian settlers abroad. His world view was guided by respect for national sovereignty, amicable international relations, non-interference in the internal affairs of other nations, and the pursuit of non-alignment. He adopted a policy of 'active dissociation' towards the Indian diaspora. Expressing his views in the constituent assembly of India on 8 March 1948, Nehru said:

Now these Indians abroad what are they? Are they Indian citizens – are they going to be citizens of India or not? If they are not, then our interest in them becomes cultural, humanitarian and not political. Either they get the franchise of the nationals of the other country or treat them as Indian minus franchise and ask for them the most favourable treatment given to an alien.[9]

He advised Indian immigrants, 'if you can not be, and if you are not friendly to the people of that country, come back to India and do not spoil the fair name of India'.[10] Nehru made it clear in 1950 that, 'in many parts of Africa – East, West, South – there are considerable number of Indians, mostly business people. Our definite instructions to them and to our agents in Africa are that they must always put the interest of indigenous populations first. We want to have no vested interests at the expense of the population of those countries'.[11] He expressed the same view repeatedly, saying of Indians abroad, 'if they adopt the nationality of that country we have no concern with them. Sentimental concern there is, but politically they cease to be Indian national'.[12] Nehru was very clear that any overt move by the Indian Government to support the PIOs in overseas communities would do more harm than good to them. He was not, though, against people-to-people contacts or non-governmental association.

However, during his worst political crisis, Nehru also talked about dual loyalty of Indians overseas. During the Indo–Chinese war (1962), contributions were welcomed from Indians living in East Africa to help boost its defence efforts. When questioned on this, Nehru told a foreign journalist that, 'Indians overseas have dual loyalty, one to their country of adoption and [the] other to their country of origin'.[13] Conversely, India deplored it as an act of disloyalty when it found that Indians abroad were selling and promoting Chinese-made goods to the cost of Indian goods. Nevertheless, between 1960 and 1966 the gulf between India and Indian settlers abroad widened, as India came to believe that Indians were more of an obstacle than an asset in its diplomatic relations with Africa. In India's post-1962 diplomatic strategy it seemed a matter of fewer consequences if PIOs were to face some degree of discrimination overseas.

Nehru's policy of exhorting Indians to identify themselves with locals in Asia and Africa was not based only on his ideological commitment. In Kenya the presence of Indian settlers was larger than the European community, and European settlers wanted to keep Kenya as a 'white man's country'. A strong anti-Indian campaign was being pursued by whites in Africa, with several riots breaking out in Kenya, Uganda and South Africa involving Indians and Africans during 1944–49. If the African struggle were weakened and divided, there was every likelihood that white Kenyan settlers would have extended a South African model in East Africa. There-fore, it was necessary that Indian settlers join hands with blacks in opposing white settlers, even if thus sacrificing their short-term gains. The Caribbean Indians were so far off, that despite knowing about their problems and marginalization by the black diaspora community as well as by the colonial rulers, they were ignored by the Indian Government. Unlike the problems of Indians in Ceylon or Burma, the issues of Indians in the Caribbean created little pressure from the Indian leadership or the masses back home. The distance and absence of connectivity with India led to a noticeable neglect of the Indian diaspora in the Caribbean. The Nehru period saw the suppression, subjugation and marginalization of the Indian diaspora globally because Indians had, with a few exceptions, a minority status. Rivals and opponents of Indians in the host country noticed India's policy of active dissociation. They found the Indian diaspora helpless and unsupported by its mother country.

The policy that the Indian diaspora should focus itself on the countries where they had set-tled and to which it should be loyal started to change in the latter half of the 1960s, especially after Indian isolation following the Indo–Chinese war of 1962. In 1964, during Indira Gandhi's tour of the African countries, she continued to emphasize the loyalty and full contribution of

Indian settlers to the societies in which they lived, but she made it a point not to miss out Indian settlers, leaders and members of the community, even if they were small in number. She also called Indian settlers 'ambassadors of India'. Similarly, while touring Fiji, Mrs Gandhi said, 'I feel like a mother concerned about the welfare of a married daughter who has set up home far away'.[14] This was a subtle departure from the earlier Nehru policy of active dissociation, as Indian settlers now became a useful instrument for generating goodwill towards India. Their unofficial position as 'ambassadors of India' implied that they were no longer excluded from policy considerations of India. This shift became more noticeable in many areas when Mrs. Gandhi became Prime Minister of India in 1966. By the second half of the 1960s there was an increasing realization that overseas Indians, whatever passport they might hold, should not be left completely outside India's policy. This also suited India's economic diplomacy in developing countries, where Indian settlers had the requisite capital and network to share with Indian economic initiatives in those countries.

Testing pro-diaspora policy

During the 1970s and 1980s Indians surfaced globally as a literate and skilled diaspora that created no problems for their host countries. The oil boom of the 1970s also enabled a large number of Indian low-paid workers, the NRI diaspora, to go to the Gulf region in large numbers, where they remained employed for a long period, even though they had no chance of settling or acquiring local citizenship.[15] As a result, they were obliged to repatriate all their earnings and savings to India. This benefited India's foreign exchange reserves, which were a scarce resource at that point in time. The Government of India moved strongly on this, creating better banking for the repatriation of foreign exchange and raising the interest rates on foreign exchange deposits. It took up the issue of the welfare of its migrant workers in west Asian countries and introduced a policy of compulsory registration of recruitment agents of labourers to avoid the exploitation and deportation of the workforce. Given the economic and political importance of these workers, the Indian policy-makers took an increasing interest in them. This class of the Indian diaspora maintained and continuously nurtured links with India.

In comparison with the NRI component of the Indian diaspora, the experience of PIO communities was very different. During this period, Indian policy-makers continued to follow a 'hands-off' policy so far as migrants to the USA, Europe and regions outside west Asia were concerned. India also tried to test its pro-diplomacy policy in 1967, when Jomo Kenyatta started a policy of Africanization in Kenya. It backfired badly, as it did also in the face of Idi Amin's expulsion of East Africa Indians from Uganda in 1972. The advent of the Bharatiya Janata Party (BJP) Government to power in 1977 saw some policy changes. It reiterated that Indian foreign policy would try and attain the right balance between pursuing its diplomatic goals and the issues concerning overseas Indians.

Globalization and a policy of 'pro-active association'

Since the early 1990s, the relationship between India and the Indian diaspora has dramatically changed. The adoption of the Structural Adjustment Programme (SAP) in 1990 and preponderance of Indians in the global IT revolution played a very important role in that change.[16] The emergence of the new Indian elite in the Western world during the 1980s (especially in the USA, Canada and the United Kingdom), resulted in India showing a keen interest in the new diaspora in order to attract their remittances and investment. Most importantly, India's collapsing economic system in the early 1990s led to a foreign exchange crisis. The

Government realized that it had to change its economic strategy very quickly. The crisis brought to the fore the country's relationship with Indians overseas, especially NRIs, as India weighed its options on how to increase the flow of foreign currency into the country again.

India started to take a proactive interest in Indians overseas. NRIs in North America and Europe were then seen as the cash-rich diaspora who could be approached to help the country by parking their funds in overseas Indian bank accounts. Successful attempts were made to secure the involvement of the affluent NRIs in setting up industries and to tide over the foreign exchange crisis through attractive financial instruments, like Resurgent India Bonds which tapped into US \$4,200m. in 1998.[17] The double launch of those bonds enabled India to continue economic reform without recourse to IMF loans and conditions. This was a clear and crucial demonstration of diaspora power.

The buoyancy in the Indian economy was clearly visible in the second half of the 1990s, and restored the faith of a large section of the Indian diaspora in the Indian economy. In turn, India realized the importance of its diaspora and started a dialogue with expatriate Indians.[18] The international fame and stature acquired by Indians abroad also enhanced the status of the diaspora in the eyes of its mother country. Their industry, enterprise, educational standards, economic strength and professional skills were widely acknowledged within India.

These developments brought about a remarkable shift in the Indian Government's policy towards the Indian diaspora. From the policy of active dissociation, there was a shift to a policy of pro-active association with the Indian diaspora. Under the new economic policy of the Narasimha Rao Government, a number of special concessions were made to encourage NRIs to invest in the Indian stock exchange, set up new industrial ventures or deposit their savings in Indian banks. Admittedly, the break from the Nehru tradition did not happen quickly enough, as there remained blockages associated with repatriation of profits amidst bureaucratic 'red tapism'.[19] Nevertheless, all this made it clear that India was engaging its diaspora who had left in the post-independence period, mostly to developed countries. The NRIs, therefore, became synonymous with the new diaspora who had gone to advance their economic standing, and not those who left the country as indentured labourers, petty traders or free passengers under colonial rule. The latter group was not much focused on, as far as economic priority was concerned. The attention towards the older diaspora was largely cultural, patchy and patronizing, whereas the new concern of India was largely economic and political.[20]

Under the changed domestic and international situation, India decided to urgently and seriously engage its diaspora. When the BJP came to power in 1998, the Government extended the policy of cultural support to the diaspora both at the state and civil society level, something of a policy U-turn.[21] In contrast to Nehru's policy of active dissociation of overseas Indians from Indian foreign policy, the BJP stood for a pro-active and overt association with the Indian diaspora for foreign policy objectives. The NRIs were in greater focus, as they were encouraged even more than before to invest in India, with general relaxation across the board for them. India's overt association policy helped to organize the first ever conference of parliamentarians of Indian origin in New Delhi, organized by the Indian Council of International Co-operation. This shift was clearly visible by 1999, when the Chennai Declaration of the BJP stated:

> We believe that the vast community of NRIs and PIOs also constitute a part of the great Indian family. We should endeavour to continually strengthen their social, cultural, economic and emotional ties with their mother country. They are the rich reservoir of intellectual, managerial and entrepreneurial resources. The government should devise innovative schemes to facilitate the investment of these resources for India's all round development.[22]

The Indian diaspora policy acquired greater momentum with the BJP-led Indian Government taking new initiatives to engage the diaspora. In his address to the sixth Convention of the Global Organisation of People of Indian Origin (GOPIO) in Delhi, in January 2001, India's Prime Minister communicated candidly enough about his Government's plan: 'We do not merely seek investment and asset transfer. What we see is a broader relationship; in fact, a partnership among all children of mother India so that our country can emerge as a major global player'.[23] Vajpayee added that his Government would assist the overseas Indian community in maintaining its cultural identity and in strengthening the emotional, cultural and spiritual bonds that bind them to the country of their origin, but that the Government would always encourage PIOs to keep 'their political commitment to their adopted countries'.[24] The GOPIO convention was attended by around 200 delegates from several countries.

The Singhvi Committee recommendations and implementation

Vajpayee established a committee headed by L.M. Singhvi, a BJP member of parliament, to suggest policy recommendations on the Indian diaspora to the Government. The Singhvi Committee consequently produced a report recommending certain initiatives to engage with Indians overseas, including: a) improvement of the PIO card scheme; b) observation of Pravasi Bharatiya Divas (non-resident/diaspora Indian day) on 9 January (the day Mahatma Gandhi returned to India from South Africa) every year; and c) setting up the institution of a Pravasi Bharatiya Samman Award (PBSA) award for eminent PIOs and NRIs.[25] Apart from such general recommendations, the other issues that were covered included special PIO counters at airports, the welfare of Indian women married to NRIs/PIOs, and problems of overseas Indian labour. There were also sector-wise recommendations under the headings of culture, economic development, tourism, education, health and the media. There were various spin-offs arising from the Singhvi Committee recommendations.

Pravasi Bharatiya Divas

Pravasi Bharatiya Divas, set up in 2003, was the first step towards the implementation of the Singhvi Committee report. It had 1,904 foreign delegates, including the Prime Minister of Mauritius, and 1,200 domestic delegates. For Singhvi this meant that, 'today, by common consent, the Indian diaspora is a force to reckon with and constitute what I termed long ago as the national reserve and resource of India', whilst for the Minister of External Affairs, Yashwant Sinha, it reflected two converging trends whereby, 'I believe that we have every reason to be optimistic about India, the Indian diaspora, and our partnership. Today is only the beginning [...] The Indian diaspora has today come into its own. Similarly, India too has arrived on the world stage'.[26] Manmohan Singh's address to the third Pravasi Bharatiya Divas (2005) was soaring:

> If there is an Empire today on which the sun truly cannot set, it is the empire of our minds, that of the children of Mother India, who live today in Asia, Africa, Australia, Europe, the Americas and, indeed, on the icy reaches of Antarctica. Our honoured Chief Guest today, His Excellency Jules Rattankoemar Ajodhia is the Vice President of distant Surinam, that lies half the globe away! [...] Yet, there is a unifying idea that binds us all together, which is the idea of 'Indian-ness'.[27]

The January date for the Pravasi Bharatiya Divas has a symbolic significance, for it was on 9 January 1915 that Gandhi, often called the first Pravasi Bharatiya, returned to India after two decades in South Africa where he led a struggle for Indian freedom. On 9 January representatives of Indians overseas (both PIOs and NRIs) assemble together, with the Government of India conferring Bharat Samman decorations on the high-profile ones among them, and new policy pronouncements are made. This buttresses the varied Pravasi Bharatiya Divas gatherings also held around the world.[28]

The Pravasi Bharatiya Samman Award

The highest honour conferred on overseas Indians, the PBSA is conferred by the President of India as part of the Pravasi Bharatiya Divas Conventions organized annually since 2003. The award is made to an NRI or PIO who has excelled in their field, or has established and run an organization or institution that has enhanced India's prestige in the country of residence.

The PIO card

On the basis of an interim report by the Singhvi Committee, the Government of India announced the PIO card scheme, which provided substantial advantages to PIOs compared with other foreign nationals, whereby by paying a one-time fee of $1,000, they could get multiple entry visas for 20 years. PIO cardholders have almost all the commercial rights of an Indian citizen, except in the case of the purchase of agricultural property. The card provides visa-free access to India, with cardholders having many rights similar to NRIs except voting rights. In response to the long and persistent demand for 'dual citizenship', particularly from the Indian diaspora in North America and other developed countries, the Government started the Overseas Citizenship of India (OCI) scheme. At the 2006 Pravasi Bharatiya Divas in Hyderabad, Prime Minister Manmohan Singh presented the first OCI card, also referred to as the 'dual citizenship card'. It is available to the diaspora in all countries allowing dual citizenship, except Pakistan and Bangladesh.

Post-2004 diaspora measures

The Congress-led Government that succeeded the BJP Government has carried the process further for strengthening ties with the diaspora, establishing a fully fledged Ministry of Overseas Indian Affairs under a separate Minister. The new MOIA introduced several measures, like posting welfare officers in Indian missions, establishment a 24-hour helpline, the provision of legal advice in the Indian missions in the Gulf, and a toll-free phone number for women. The MOIA has also signed a Memorandum of Understanding and agreements with several Gulf countries to safeguard the interests of Indian workers there.[29]

Overseas Indian Facilitation Centre

The Government also launched an Overseas Indian Facilitation Centre, a one-stop shop to help overseas Indians invest in India. It intends also to establish a Diaspora Knowledge Network by creating a database of overseas Indians who would act as a knowledge diaspora and whose knowledge resources could be utilized through the ICT platform. The main objectives of the Network are: to build sustainable development institutions into a brain trust or brain circulation that will help identify innovative projects on the ground in various sectors in India; and to find suitable partners among the transnational Indian community for market-based solutions.

'Know India' programme

The Know India Programme is a project of the MOIA that aims to associate closely with the younger generations of the Indian diaspora. It provides a unique forum for students and young professionals of Indian origin to share their views, expectations and experiences, and bond closely with contemporary India. This includes a three-week comprehensive orientation programme organized by the MOIA and implemented in partnership with a state government and through the logistical support of the Nehru Yuva Kendra and the Confederation of Indian Industry.

Scholarship programme for diaspora children

The objective of the scholarship programme, introduced in the academic year 2006/07, is to make higher education in India accessible to the children of overseas Indians and promote India as a centre for higher education studies. Under the scheme, 100 PIO/NRI students are awarded a scholarship of up to $3,600 per annum for undergraduate courses in engineering, technology, humanities, liberal arts, commerce, management, journalism, hotel management, agriculture, animal husbandry and others.

Gender issues

The MOIA has also taken a series of steps for the welfare and well-being of Indian women going to other countries to work in different capacities. Special attention has been paid to cases reported by Indian women deserted/abandoned by their NRI husbands. The Ministry has started a scheme to provide legal and financial assistance to such Indian women. Several inter-ministerial meetings, seminars and awareness campaigns have been organized, and efforts have been made to incorporate overseas Indian women's associations to help such Indian women find a solution to their problems.

Tracing roots

The MOIA also launched a 'tracing roots' scheme in October 2008. Under this scheme, the Ministry facilitates PIOs in tracing their ancestral roots in India. For this purpose, the Ministry has signed a Memorandum of Understanding with an organization called INDIROOTS. PIOs who wish to trace the roots of their ancestors in India can do so with the help of this programme.

Besides these, other policy instruments devised are the India Development Foundation, which helps channel contributions from NRIs to philanthropic activities in India in a wide range of activities; and the establishment of the NRI/PIO University, the Internship Programme for Diaspora Youth, aiming to associate closely with the younger generation of the Indian diaspora. Furthermore, the Ministry intends to leverage the resource of prominent youth organizations with an all-India profile, such as Nehru Yuva Kendra Sangathan, for meaningful engagement with diaspora youth during India's development process, as well as reinforcing the cultural, emotional and professional ties with their country of origin.

Conclusions

The Indian Government's interaction with the diaspora is in line with global trends. The global view of migrants has been changing in recent years, with migrants no longer perceived as economic refugees. Today, Indians overseas, particularly in developed countries, are seen as a potential resource for the country due to their success and achievement in the countries of their adoption. With 25m. PIOs, India is no longer restricted to the subcontinent. They may be just over 2% of India's population, but their estimated collective resources are substantial. The diaspora has gained in importance over the years, and the more prosperous overseas communities have acquired substantial political influence in their adopted countries and have emerged as useful assets for their home countries.

A growing and rising India needs to engage its diaspora for its global positioning, with Vasant Moharir's sense at the Pravasi Bharatiya Divas—Europe of, 'the role of Indian Diaspora in accelerating India's transition as a Global Power'.[30] India's diaspora policy needs to treat its Indian diaspora as a 'strategic' resource. It needs to have policies and instruments for engaging its diaspora globally, which would give it global visibility and goodwill. An assessment of India's diaspora policy would show that it has acquired greater momentum and magnitude, but it is still both lopsided and short-sighted. The narrow focus on the dollar-rich diaspora in North America is not broad enough. A global focus on the Indian diaspora will give India strategic assets and opportunities to play a global role in times to come. The captive Indian diaspora in west Asia and the opportunities for Indian workers in the Association of Southeast Asian Nations (ASEAN) countries gets only cosmetic policy support. The real issues facing these sectors and the opportunities in the regions are not being addressed either by engaging these countries or by policy support. Some of the Indian diaspora is in non-anglophone regions like the francophone and lusophone areas. There is no policy designed and extended to those whose identity and culture have been eroded substantially under the assimilative policies of France. There is a strong urge in these communities to restore their identity and link with India. In countries like Malawi, where indentured Indians went, even today they are stateless and need and support from India. They do not even figure in the bulky official report of the Singhvi Committee. Indian policy needs to design a strategy and set of initiatives to broaden its focus and include the PIOs who form the bulk of its diaspora. In this context, India can learn from the experiences of other countries with a large diaspora. In other words, a comparative understanding of the diaspora as a player in international relations and as a resource for home and host countries will provide a better insight into a new diaspora policy for India.

Notes

1 C. Bhat, *India and the Indian Diaspora – A Policy Issue*, University of Hyderabad: Department of Sociology, 1998.
2 See J. Mangat, *A History of the Asians in East Africa*, Oxford: Oxford University Press, 1969; H. Tinker, *A New System of Slavery*, London: Oxford University Press, 1979; K. Sadhu, *Indians in Malaya: Some Aspects of their Immigration and Settlement 1786–1957*, Oxford: Oxford University Press, 1969; Y. Ghai and D. Ghai, *The Asian Minorities of East and Central Africa*, London: Minority Rights Group, 1971.
3 H. Tinker, 'Odd Man Out: The Loneliness of the Indian Colonial Politician. The Career of Manilal Doctor', *Journal of Imperial and Commonwealth History*, Vol. 2, No. 2, 1974.
4 J. Nehru, 'A Foreign Policy of India', 19 September 1927, in S. Gopal (ed.), *Selected Works of Jawaharlal Nehru*, New Delhi: Orient Longman, Vol. 3.
5 Ibid., pp.353–68.
6 J. Nehru, 1939, *Selected Works of Jawaharlal Nehru*, New Delhi: Orient Longman, 1976, p.618; cited in government press release, K. Rana, 'Overseas Indians', *Features* (Press Information Bureau), 13 January 2003, pib.nic.in, written by Rana with regard to the first Pravasi Bharatiya Diwas gathering held in January 2003.
7 C. Heimsath and L. Mansingh, *A Diplomatic History of Modern India*, Bombay: Allied Publishers, 1971, p.302.
8 See A. Dubey, 'Nehru and Africa in Afro-Asian Solidarity', *Ind-Africana*, Vol. 2, No. 2, 1989.

9 J. Nehru, 'India Keeps Out of Power Blocs', 8 March 1948, in *Independence and After: A Collection of Speeches, 1946–1949*, New York: The John Day Company, 1950, pp.221–22.

10 Ibid, p.222.

11 H. Chhabra, *India and Africa. Saga of Friendship*, New Delhi: Government of India, 1986, p.15.

12 J. Nehru, 'Reply to Debate on Foreign Policy in Lok Sabha', 2 September 1957, in *India's Foreign Policy: Selected Speeches, September 1946–April 1961*, New Delhi: Government of India, 1961, p.130.

13 See A. Gupta, 'India and Asians in East Africa', in M. Twaddle (ed.), *Expulsions of Minority: Essay on Ugandan Asians*, London: Athlone Press, 1975, p.134.

14 Cited in R. Thakur, 'India and Overseas Indians', *Asian Survey*, Vol. 25, No. 3, 1985, p.356.

15 A. Rahman, *Indian Labour Migration to the Gulf*, New Delhi: Rajat, 2001.

16 A. Dubey, 'Changing Salience of the Relationship Between the Indian Diaspora and India', *Diaspora Studies*, Vol. 1, No. 2, 2008.

17 C. Bhat, 'India and the Indian Diaspora – A Policy Issue', Hyderabad: Department of Sociology, University of Hyderabad, 1998.

18 A. Gangopadhyay, 'India's policy towards its Diaspora: Continuity and change', *India Quarterly*, Vol. 61, No. 4, 2005.

19 Ibid.

20 B. Parekh, 'The Indian Diaspora', in J. Motwani and M. Cosine (eds), *The Global Indian Diaspora: Yesterday, Today and Tomorrow*, New York: Global Organization of People of Indian Origin, 1993, pp.8–9.

21 A. Dubey, 'Comparative Understanding Needs to be Arrived At', *Foreign Affairs Journal*, Vol. 3, No. 2, 2008.

22 BJP, 'Chennai Declaration', 1999, cited in M. Chitkara, *Rashtriya Swayamsevak Sangh. National Upsurge*, New Delhi: A.P.H. Publishing Corporation, 2004, p.410.

23 A.B. Vajpayee, 'Prime Minister Vajpayee's Speech at the Inauguration of the International Convention of the Global Organisation of People of Indian Origin', 6 January 2001, meaindia.nic.in.

24 Ibid.

25 Government of India, *Report of the High Level [Singhvi] Committee*, New Delhi: Ministry of External Affairs, 2001, www.indiandiaspora.nic.in.

26 'Theme Presentation by Dr L.M. Singhvi, Chairman, Organizing Committee of the Pravasi Bharatiya Divas', and 'Address by Mr Yashwant Sinha, Minister for External Affairs of India', Proceedings of the Pravasi Bharatya Divas, Inaugural Session, 9–11 January 2003, pp.16 and 15–16, respectively, www.indiandiaspora.nic.in/ch2.pdf.

27 M. Singh, 'PM's Inaugural Speech at Pravasi Bharatiya Divas', 7 January 2005, pmindia.nic.in.

28 V. Lal, 'India in the World: Hinduism, the Diaspora, and the Anxiety of Influence', *Australian Religious Studies Review*, Vol. 16, No. 2, 2003.

29 J. Sharma, 'Poised to Play an Important Role', *Foreign Affairs Journal*, Vol. 3, No. 2, 2008.

30 V. Mohahir, 'India Rising: The Role of Indian Diaspora in accelerating India's transition as a Global Power', Pravasi Bharatiya Divas—Europe, 19 September 2009, www.indiawijzer.nl.

24

India and international terrorism

Arpita Anant

Introduction

The al-Qa'ida attack on the USA on 11 September 2001 heralded a decade in which Indian concerns with terrorism were highlighted at the international level. Analysts argued that al-Qa'ida and its linkages with the Taliban meant that 'the headquarters of international terrorism has moved from West Asia to the Subcontinent'.[1] The Indian discourse on international terrorism is clearly reflective of its concerns with cross-border terrorism perpetrated by terrorist groups based in Pakistan with connections to al-Qa'ida. More recently, the appearance of support groups based in Nepal, Bangladesh, Bhutan and Sri Lanka has resulted in the spread of terrorism from specific geographic locales to urban centres in India.[2]

Indian security analysts expressed their alarm at the first reference to Kashmir by Osama bin Laden, in an audio message on *Al Jazeera* on 23 April 2006, when he spoke of a 'Crusader-Zionist-Hindu' conspiracy.[3] Such analysts asserted that *jihadist* organizations affiliated to the International Islamic Front (IIF) had been active in Jammu and Kashmir since 1993. Since 1998 al-Qa'ida's imprint was felt in India in the form of *jihadist* suicide terrorism in Jammu and Kashmir. Al-Qa'ida's modus operandi in terms of use of improvised explosive devices (IEDs), *fidayeen* suicide attacks, self-fabricated explosives, use of the internet (for communication, propaganda and other operational purposes), and use of mobile phones as trigger devices, all became visible in India. Also the selection of soft targets, civilians, economic and strategic infrastructure, was seen as being akin to the al-Qa'ida mode of operation.

As a region that has experienced terrorism for several decades, various scholars and security analysts have analysed the nature of terrorism in India and South Asia. According to S.D. Muni, there are four distinct characteristics of terrorism in South Asia. First is the terrorism-conflict link. Conflicts rooted in political marginalization, socio-economic deprivation, discrimination, caste, religious, regional and cultural suppression, and neglect cause terrorism.[4] Second is the politics-terror nexus, witnessed in Pakistani (especially Inter-Services Intelligence—ISI) support to terrorist groups that work against India, or Sri Lankan President Ranasinghe Premadasa's covert support of the Liberation Tigers of Tamil Eelam (LTTE) against the Indian Peace-keeping Force in Sri Lanka. Third is the use of force by groups and the state use of force to counter terrorism. Finally, there is the external dimension of terrorism, characterized by exploitation of local insurgencies by neighbouring countries, spillovers into neighbouring areas, bilateral and multilateral co-operation, and third-party mediation by donor countries between governments and the terrorist organization.[5] According to Ayesha Siddiqa, there are two types of terrorism in South Asia: first, terrorism induced and conducted in partnership with global terrorist networks; and second, acts of violence in pursuance of the rights of people.[6] Among the first category are included terrorist groups in Pakistan and Bangladesh with links to al-Qa'ida. These groups also support the ISI-sponsored religious war in Jammu and Kashmir.[7] The second category contains certain groups in India, Nepal and Sri Lanka. In such analyses, the international connection is conspicuous.

Within India, the external connections of terrorist groups active in Jammu and Kashmir have been highlighted often. Scholars have argued that Pakistan and Afghanistan have had a tremendous influence on the Islamist transformation of the insurgency in Kashmir.[8] Quoting the 1993 report of the US House of Representatives Research Committee entitled *The New Islamist International*, K. Warikoo argues that in addition to providing logistical support, Pakistan's ISI runs organizations like *Hizb-e-Islami*, *Harkat-ul-Jihad* and *Jamaat-i-Islami* (in Pakistan), *Hizb-e-Islami* and *Jamiat-i-Islami* (Afghanistan), and *Hizbul Mujahideen* (Kashmir). All these had become part of the Popular International Organization (PIO) led by Hassan al-Turabi. At the peak of militancy in Kashmir, several organizations had a clearly Islamist agenda, including the Islamization of the province's socio-political and economic set-up, a merger with Pakistan, and unification of the '*ummah* [Muslim world] community'. Two organizations, *Tehrik-i-Ahyay-e-Khilafat* and *Tehrik-e-Khilafat-e-Islamia* that were in existence in 1992 even advocated the establishment of an Islamic Caliphate. In the north-eastern states of India, where terrorism is characterized by tribal groups acting against the state, one tribal group acting against another tribal group, and tribal groups acting against non-tribal groups, the external linkages impact through criminal networks, illegal migration of Bangladeshis, and Islamist militancy.[9] Using data from the University of Maryland's *Global Terrorism Database II* for the period 1998–2004, it has been argued that the fatalities caused by terrorist attacks are linked to the attack type and attack group. In this period India suffered the highest number of terrorist incidents (784 out of 7,184 world-wide), and fatalities (3,008). Bombings, followed by armed assaults, have resulted in the most casualties. Among the known perpetrators, Islamist groups have caused the most fatalities, most of them in Jammu and Kashmir, followed by fatalities in the north-east.[10]

The external connection is also emphasized by police officials who have been involved in controlling the drugs menace in the region. In their study on the working of the Golden Triangle and the Golden Crescent in India, they dwell at length on the negative forces unleashed by globalization, which have had a tremendous impact.[11] The long sea borders of India and the porous border with several countries, including Myanmar, also add to the external dimension of the terrorist threat in India.[12]

The transnational nature of terrorism in the region has had an impact on inter-state relations in South Asia. State sponsorship of terrorism and the victim state's response has increased bilateral tensions between India and her neighbours, namely Pakistan, Bangladesh, Sri Lanka, Nepal and Bhutan. It has also been instrumental in increasing the role of the USA as a regional player.[13] S.D. Muni firmly concludes that narco-terrorism, money-laundering, illegal small arms, state support to non-state groups and migrants are all instances of 'subaltern globalization' that are a menace to the state, inter-state relations and the subalterns in South Asia.[14]

India and international terrorism

An analysis of the debate in India in the aftermath of the 2001 terrorist attacks on the USA reveals an attempt to place the Indian experience in an international context, accompanied by the lament that India's tragedy was never acknowledged by the Western world. Thus, Manoj Joshi argued that until the catastrophic events of 11 September 2001, the Mumbai blasts of 1993, which left 250 dead, were the worst acts of urban terrorism.[15] This tragedy and the role played by Pakistan did not even find mention in the *Patterns of Global Terrorism* report of the USA.

In an interview given to the *Pioneer*, in the wake of the attacks on the USA, Lal Krishna Advani (the Minister for Home Affairs) argued that the Western nations were for once realizing that a democratic and law abiding country like India was also a victim of international terrorism: 'even the Western countries are realising how, in the name of jihad, militants are killing innocent children, men and women in Kashmir', and as a country that respects human values, 'India is now a front-runner in the war against terrorism'.[16] Given its long-term collaboration with Uzbekistan, Tajikistan and Iran, strategic thinkers also saw an opportunity for India to play a crucial role in Afghanistan in safeguarding the interests of the Uzbek, Tajik and Hazara (Shi'a) minorities.[17]

Pragmatists, however, cautioned against an over-zealous response to the international campaign on the basis of an acceptance of Indian concerns. They argued that the necessities of geopolitics made Pakistan critically important for the USA. India, therefore, would never be able to ensure that the USA named Pakistan as a 'state sponsor of terrorism'. In these circumstances, it would be best for India to put together an alternative alliance of countries that shares its priorities, such as Russia, Sri Lanka and Israel.[18] By 2002, the mismatch between Indian and US perspectives on terrorism was being debated openly in India.[19]

Some argued that, given the distinct Indian ethos, India should not compete with Pakistan to be the front-line state in the war against terrorism. Instead, India could lead the way by defining the nature of the international campaign against terrorism. Such a campaign could evolve around some 'important elements' like terrorism as a crime against humanity, terrorism as being indivisible, a comprehensive and integrated approach to dealing with terrorism, vulnerability of democratic governments and their way of life and freedom to international terrorism, no justification of terrorism on the ground of *jihad* or struggle for freedom, and a campaign against terrorism is not a campaign against any religion.[20]

India had actively worked towards building a consensus on international terrorism in the UN. India's initiative resulted in the UN General Assembly's adoption of the Declaration on Measures to Eliminate International Terrorism in 1994, which for the first time recognized the need for states to refrain from supporting terrorism and state obligation to persecute or extradite perpetrators of acts of terrorism. In 1999 the General Assembly adopted a resolution on Measures to Eliminate International Terrorism, mainly to discuss India's draft convention on terrorism. The resolution 'calls upon States to refrain from financing, encouraging, providing training for or otherwise supporting terrorist activities'.

The Indian Draft Comprehensive Convention for Combating International Terrorism (CCIT) was presented to the 51st (1996/97) session of the UN General Assembly.[21] Indian efforts were rewarded when, after initially ignoring the Convention, the UN General Assembly decided to take it up for discussion in September 2000. By then it had also been revised to include provisions from the International Convention for the Suppression of Terrorist Bombings (1997) and the International Convention for the Suppression of the Financing of Terrorism. India actively pursued countries during bilateral meetings and in multilateral organizations for the adoption of the CCIT. This initiative was supported by the Non-Aligned Movement (NAM), G-8, G-15, Commonwealth Heads of Government Meeting (CHOGM) and the European Union (EU). Similarly, during the visit of the Indian President to the People's Republic of China, China's support was also solicited.

At the UN, the draft CCIT was taken up for consideration in various rounds of negotiations: one in 2000, two in 2001, and another in 2002. The need for a CCIT was explained by H.E. Kamlesh Sharma, Permanent Representative of India to the UN, in October 2001 thus: 'Planes were hijacked, but the cluster of Conventions on hijacking provides for action only against the hijackers; on September 11 they killed themselves with their victims. Passengers were taken hostage, but the cluster of Conventions against hostage taking also provides for action only against the hostage-takers; on September 11, they killed themselves with their victims'. Similarly, planes were used as bombs, whereas the Conventions have a precise definition of an explosive. No action is envisaged 'against those who supported, instigated or harboured the terrorists'.[22]

As of 2003, the Working Group had accepted Articles 6–9 of the Indian Draft pertaining to extra-territorial jurisdiction of the victim state, blocking seeking of safe havens/asylum by perpetrators of violence, and state responsibility for suppression of terrorism. Article 2 of the Draft on definition of acts of terrorism and principle responsibility of the commander under whose control the subordinates commit a crime was revised and redrafted and was pending adoption. The debate on Article 18 on the role of military force when there is a disagreement whether the perpetrator of violence is a terrorist or a freedom fighter was ongoing. By March 2010 a Draft had been ironed out and was on the table, although India's envoy Hardeep Puri was still noting that 'there remain two outstanding issues that still needed to be resolved dealing with what kind of armed struggle, for instance a liberation movement, would not be called a terrorist act, and secondly would military forces be within the scope of the convention'.[23]

Eleven existing pieces of domestic legislation identified unlawful or criminal activities as acts of terrorism.[24] In compliance with UN Security Council Resolution 1373 (Threats to International Peace and Security Caused by Terrorist Acts), passed in the wake of the attacks in September 2001, India has undertaken several measures to combat terrorism. These are reported to the UN Counter Terrorism Committee (CTC) periodically.[25] India adopted the Prevention of Terrorism Ordinance (POTO) in October 2001.[26] In March 2002 India adopted the Prevention of Terrorism Act, a comprehensive piece of counter-terrorism legislation that replaced the POTO. It criminalizes fund-raising for terrorist activities. Terrorist crimes not committed in India nor affecting India's interests, but perpetrated from Indian soil were already punishable under the UN Security Council Act (1947), with assets of terrorist organizations listed by the UN Sanctions Committee under Resolutions 1267, 1333 and 1390 also able to be frozen using provisions of the same Act. To prevent and punish incitement of terrorism, the Unlawful Activities Prevention Act (1967) was amended in 2004. The Government also promulgated the Prevention and Suppression of Terrorism (Implementation of Security Council) Order (2004), to strengthen action against non-profit organizations.

Illicit financial transactions are sought to be controlled through the Directorate of Enforcement (which monitors the Foreign Exchange Management Act), the Central Board of Direct Taxes (which monitors the evasion of income tax), and the Directorate of Revenue Intelligence (which monitors violations of customs laws and proceeds deriving from smuggling activities). The latter works in liaison with enforcement agencies in India such as the Central Economic Intelligence Bureau, Income Tax Department, Enforcement Directorate, Narcotics Control Bureau, Directorate-General of Foreign Trade, Border Security Force, Central Bureau of Investigation, Coast Guard, state police authorities and Customs and Excise Commissions. It also maintains a close liaison with the World Customs Organisation, Brussels, Regional Intelligence Liaison Office, Tokyo, Interpol and foreign customs administrations. Several mechanisms are in place to prevent the use of *hawala* (remittance) money for financing terrorism. The administrative, investigative, prosecutorial and judicial authorities are provided with specific training for preventing and suppressing the financing of terrorism. Such training is imparted at the National Police Academy at Hyderabad, the Military Intelligence Training School and Depot at Pune, the Central Bureau of Investigation Academy at Ghaziabad, the Intelligence Bureau Central Training School at New Delhi, and the National Judicial Academy at Bhopal. The Prevention of Money Laundering Act (2003) criminalizes money laundering. The Central Economic Intelligence Bureau (CEIB), set up in 1985, receives and analyses reports from various agencies related to suspicious economic transactions. In the banking system this task is performed by the regional and national headquarters of banks under the aegis of the Reserve Bank of India. The Foreign Exchange Management Act (1999) makes *hawala* transactions illegal. Only registered wire transfer services are allowed to operate foreign money transfer service schemes and Indian agencies with which tie-ups are permitted are also listed. The Financial Intelligence Unit (FIU-IND) in the Department of Revenue of the Ministry of Finance was set up in 2004.

Most states in India have set up anti-terrorist cells, special operations groups, or special task forces to deal with terrorism. A Multi-Agency Centre (MAC) in the Ministry of Home Affairs co-ordinates all counter-terrorism efforts. A Joint Task Force has been set up within the Intelligence Bureau to co-ordinate the intelligence of central and state police forces. Also it gathers information from the subsidiary MACs in the different Indian states. Security on the borders has been stepped up by the establishment of the Border Guard Forces.

It is, though, interesting to note that India refused to take assistance from the UN's Counter-Terrorism Committee Executive Directorate (CTED) and several other multilateral forums, as India considered that it had considerable expertise suited to its own peculiar requirements. Moreover, there is clearly stated Indian preference for bilateral arrangements and agency-to-agency co-operation. Here, India has offered to provide technical assistance to other countries in the training of immigration officials, computerization of immigration systems, setting up of financial intelligence units, analysis of intelligence related to money laundering and terrorist financing, technology for analysis of financial information, and the like.

India's concerns regarding misuse of nuclear material are reflected in its domestic laws. Illegal possession of arms and acquisition of radioactive material is punishable under the Indian Arms Act (1959) and Indian Atomic Energy Act (1962). On the international level, at India's initiative the UN General Assembly also adopted a resolution in 2000 on Reducing Nuclear Danger. In several of its presentations to the UN's Sixth Committee on International Terrorism, India favoured early adoption of the Convention against Nuclear Terrorism. India signed the Convention on Physical Protection of Nuclear Weapons and it also co-sponsored the Resolution on the Code of Conduct for Safety and Security of Radioactive Sources adopted by the General Assembly of the International Atomic Energy Agency (IAEA). To prevent export of dual-use technologies that could be used for manufacturing weapons of mass destruction, there is a list of special chemicals, organisms, materials, equipment and technologies (SCOMET). The Indian Register of Shipping is responsible for the implementation of the International Ship and Port Facility Security (ISPS) code. On 24 July 2006 India signed the 2005 International Convention for the Suppression of Acts of Nuclear Terrorism. Supporting its decision, it was argued that 'India shares the objective of the International Convention for the Suppression of Acts of Nuclear Terrorism, which demonstrates the resolve of the international community to deny terrorists access to nuclear materials and enhances international cooperation between states in devising and adopting practical measures for prevention of acts of nuclear terrorism and for the prosecution and punishment of their perpetrators'.[27]

The 2010 Nuclear Security Summit vindicated India's position on international terrorism by making the connection between international terrorism and clandestine proliferation. The communiqué issued by the Summit 'commits the participating countries', which included Pakistan, to co-operate effectively to 'prevent and respond to incidents of illicit nuclear trafficking', and agree to 'share, subject to respective national laws and procedures, information and expertise through bilateral and multilateral mechanisms in relevant areas such as nuclear detection, forensics, law enforcement and the development of new technologies'.[28]

International co-operation in combating terrorism

Indian efforts to get greater international appreciation of its terrorism challenge were sought to be achieved by a clear articulation of the al-Qa'ida connection to Pakistan-based groups. Thus, condemning the car-bomb attack on the Jammu and Kashmir assembly by *Jaish-e-Mohammad*, India pointed to its leader Masood Azhar's links to al-Qa'ida and asserted that, 'at a time when the democratic world has formed a broad and determined coalition against international terrorism, India cannot accept such manifestations of hate and terror from across its borders. There is a limit to India's patience'.[29] In doing so, the Government was cautious not to compromise the Indian position on non-involvement of third parties in resolving the Kashmir issue and, therefore, no external assistance of any kind was sought.

Given the transnational linkages of terrorism, there was recognition in the Indian strategic community that counter-terrorism strategies should be multi-pronged and include foreign policy initiatives, an overall national posture and the use of military force. At the national level a need was felt for better intelligence gathering, media management and military initiatives, including pre-emptive strikes and creation of security zones. At the regional level a need was felt for co-operation, capacity building, addressing the audience and creating an understanding of the larger purpose. At the international level, a need was felt for measures to deal with tools/ weapons of terrorism, mercenaries and stateless terrorists, and to arrive at an acceptable definition and international norms for dealing with terrorism.[30] After the 2001 attacks on the USA this understanding was further reinforced given the nature of international terrorism. It was argued, for instance, that there was an urgent need for national, regional and international organizations that could pre-empt and prevent terrorism by way of collecting, sharing and collating information.[31]

Given the complex nature of the challenge, the Government set up an Inter-Agency Group on Counter-Terrorism comprising representatives of the Ministries of External Affairs, Home Affairs, Defence, Finance, the National Security Council Secretariat and concerned government agencies. Its aims were:

a) to articulate a clear and specific Indian stance on global terrorism;
b) to communicate accurate, substantial and credible information/ intelligence to friendly governments;
c) to advise Government on information/ queries/ responses arising out of inputs from foreign governments;
d) to advise Government on both domestic and foreign media responses to terrorist activities; and
e) to advise Government on requirements for both direct and indirect interaction with foreign interest groups on terrorism-related issues.[32]

In order to strengthen international co-operation against terrorism, India set up Joint Working Groups with several countries. In addition, three types of bilateral treaties have been entered into: agreements to combat terrorism and organized crime, narcotic drugs offences, etc., extradition treaties, and treaties on mutual legal assistance in criminal matters.

India is also party to multilateral arrangements and agreements. It co-operates with INTERPOL by supporting and using its Red Corner Alerts. They facilitate exchange of operational information and development of joint programmes to combat organized crime and terrorism. There are 34 countries with which such co-operation is underway, including Australia, Belgium, Bhutan, Bulgaria, Canada, China, Egypt, Fiji, France, Germany, Hong Kong, Israel, Italy, Kazakhstan, Kyrgyzstan, Myanmar, Nepal, the Netherlands, Oman, Papua New Guinea, Romania, Russia, Singapore, Sri Lanka, Sweden, Switzerland, Tanzania, Thailand, Tunisia, Turkey, the United Arab Emirates, United Kingdom, USA and Uzbekistan. India's multilateral initiatives have been channelled through the UN (discussed above), the EU, the South Asian Association for Regional Cooperation (SAARC), the Bay of Bengal Initiative for Multi-Sectoral Technical and Economic Cooperation (BIMSTEC, formerly the Bangladesh, India, Myanmar, Sri Lanka, Thailand Economic Cooperation) and the Asia-Europe Meeting (ASEM) forums.[33] In addition, India joined the Financial Action Task Force (FATF) as an observer in 2006 and as a full member in June 2010. India is also a member of the Asia-Pacific Group on Money Laundering.

Two important countries with which co-operation on terrorism has been put in place are the USA and Pakistan. US-Indian convergence on the issue had already been seen with the series of dialogues held since September 1999, in the aftermath of the Indian Airline Flight IC-814 hijacking.[34] In the first meeting of the Indo-US Joint Working Group on Terrorism in February 2000, the two countries agreed to share experiences, exchange information and co-ordinate approaches and action, including co-operation and implementation of the US Anti-terrorism Assistance programmes. During the same year, the two countries also established the Indo-US Joint Working Group of legal experts on terrorism. Also, as part of its assistance to India, the USA offered to give anti-terrorism training for inter-departmental co-ordination, crisis response and consequence management. The terrorist attacks of September 2001, and the USA's 'Long War' on terrorism, heightened this convergence.[35] Prime Minster Atal Bihari Vajpayee's visit to the USA in November 2001 pushed this convergence further, in which US-Indian co-operation was widened to include investigations into the terrorist attacks and intelligence sharing on terrorist groups and networks. In January 2002 the Director of the US Federal Bureau of Investigation (FBI), Robert S. Mueller, visited India. The two sides discussed sharing information and technical collaboration through the bilateral Mutual Legal Assistance Treaty. In the regular meetings of the Joint Working Group held since then, this bilateral US-Indian co-operation has been strengthened.[36]

After substantial international (i.e. US) pressure in the aftermath of the 2001 terrorist attacks, and the attempted attack on the Indian parliament on 13 December 2001, Pakistani President Pervez Musharraf gave a commitment in January 2002 that Pakistan would not allow its territory to be used for any terrorist activity anywhere in the world and that no organization would be allowed to indulge in terrorism in the name of Kashmir. He reiterated his resolve in his addresses to the nation in May 2002 and June 2002. However, after initial reduction, infiltrations were soon back to pre-commitment levels.[37]

Following renewed assurances from Musharraf to prevent use of Pakistani territory for anti-India groups, on 6 January 2004, the Composite Dialogue between the two countries was put in place. The first round of the Composite Dialogue in June–August 2004 concentrated on eight issues: Siachen, Sir Creek, Tulbal navigation project, terrorism and drugs-trafficking, economic and commercial co-operation, promotion of friendly exchanges, peace and security (including confidence-building measures), and Jammu and Kashmir. At the end of August 2005 the two countries decided to co-operate on intelligence sharing, and at the end of March 2006 they exchanged a list of wanted people.

Bilateral meetings on the issues of terrorism and drugs-trafficking have been held regularly. In the second round of the meeting both sides underlined the need for co-operation between India's Central Bureau of Investigation (CBI) and Pakistan's Federal Investigation Agency (FIA). They also noted with satisfaction the continuing co-operation and exchange of information between narcotics-control agencies of both countries and agreed to put in place an understanding between them. Their Memorandum of Understanding aimed to have a regular institutional mechanism in place to intensify mutual co-operation and liaison on drugs-control matters. In addition to these areas, in the third round of meetings they agreed on the need to take measures to check human-trafficking, illegal immigration and counterfeit currency.

At the meeting between the Indian and Pakistani leaders on 16 September 2006 in Havana, Cuba, both leaders decided to put in place a Joint Anti-Terrorism Mechanism, to identify and implement counter-terrorism initiatives and investigations, and to exchange information investigations on either side related to terrorist acts and prevention of violence and terrorist acts in the two countries. The foreign minister-level talks held in November 2006 concluded with an agreement to set up a three-member anti-terrorism mechanism headed by the Additional Secretary (International Organizations) of the Ministry of External Affairs of India and the Additional Secretary (UN and European Commission) of the Ministry of Foreign Affairs of Pakistan. Its mandate was to consider counter-terrorism measures, including the regular and timely sharing of information.

It is interesting to note that the breakthrough in bilateral co-operation with Pakistan came at the end of the near failure of the regional initiatives of SAARC, through which India tried to get the co-operation of its neighbouring countries in preventing cross-border terrorism. India is party to the SAARC Convention on Suppression of Terrorism, which came into force in August 1988. The SAARC Convention defined acts of terrorism that would *not* qualify as political offences. It also gave extra-territorial jurisdiction to nations to punish perpetrators of terrorist acts and made it obligatory for member countries to adopt domestic legislation that criminalizes terrorism. Such laws were enacted by India, Sri Lanka, Nepal and Bhutan, but not by Pakistan. In 1993 India also enacted the SAARC Convention (Suppression of Terrorism) Act, to give effect to the Convention and as part of India's fight against 'the menace of global terrorism'.[38] The Government took up the issue of misuse of territories of neighbouring countries by terrorists with Bhutan, Bangladesh, Nepal, Myanmar and Thailand.[39] Subsequently, in 2004, SAARC adopted the Additional Protocol to the SAARC Regional Convention on Suppression of Terrorism. However, the ineffectiveness of the SAARC Convention was apparent, reflecting lack of action and intent; SAARC was designed to leave contentious issues of a bilateral nature, and the SAARC Convention was meant to be operationalized on a bilateral basis. Also, SAARC did not have a focused and intense agenda and was rendered ineffective due to political interference.[40]

International recognition of India's concerns regarding terrorism

As early as October 1999, a delegation of ambassadors from France, Portugal, Finland, Germany and the European Commission visited Jammu and Kashmir. The delegation met government officials, political leaders and a cross-section of people in the state to assess the prevailing situation there. The delegation assessed the impact of cross-border terrorism in the state, with the finger pointed to Pakistan's 'sponsorship' of cross-border terrorism there and elsewhere in India.

In the aftermath of the hijacking of the Indian Airlines Flight IC-814 in December 1999, India's Minister of External Affairs contacted his counterparts in several countries, including neighbouring countries, member countries of the UN Security Council, and governments of nations that had passengers on the hijacked flight. The Minister also spoke to his counterparts in many countries. As a result, pledges of co-operation, support and statements of condemnation of this act were received from all quarters. Countries like China also strongly condemned all acts of terrorism, and in the declaration of the Shanghai-5 Defence Ministers' Meeting in March 2000, the countries resolved not to tolerate ethnic separatism, religious fundamentalism and terrorism. The hijacking also led to a bilateral agreement between Italy and India.

At a hearing of the International Relations Committee of the US House of Representatives on 12 July 2000, the US State Department Coordinator for Counter-terrorism said that Pakistan was allowing its territory to be used by terrorist groups, but stopped short of making a legal determination of Pakistan as a 'state sponsor of terrorism'. During US President William (Bill) Clinton's visit to India in March 2000, he condemned the killing of 35 Sikhs in Jammu and Kashmir, and tried to get Pakistan to commit to cracking down on terrorist groups on its soil. During his subsequent visit to Pakistan in March 2000 President Clinton raised 'the need for Pakistan to intensify efforts to defeat those who inflict terror'.[41]

The 2000 Patterns of Global Terrorism Report, compiled by the US State Department, recorded Pakistan's continued support to the insurgency in Kashmir. On 20 December 2001, following the attack on the Indian parliament, the USA placed *Jaish-e-Mohammed* (JeM) and *Lashkar-e-Taiba* (LeT) on all three US terrorist lists—the Foreign Terrorist Organizations (FTO) list, the Specially Designated Global Terrorists (SDGT) list and the Terrorist Exclusion List (TEL). In addition, it called upon Pakistan to take steps to crack down on terrorism emanating from Pakistan and to take decisive action against the LeT and JeM and other terrorist organizations, their leaders, finances and activities. The White House notice issued on the same day described the LeT as the armed wing of the Pakistan-based religious organization, *Markaz-ud-Dawa-wal-Irshad*.

Alan Kronstadt's Congressional Research Study of 2003 clearly stated that terrorism in Kashmir was supported by groups like LeT and others that are based in Pakistan, and which have been officially designated by the US as 'foreign terrorist organizations'. In addition, this Congressional Research Study also declared the Al-Akhtar Trust in Pakistan to be a terrorist support organization funding al-Qa'ida and Taliban activities. Dawood Ibrahim was designated a global terrorist.[42] The 2003 Patterns of Global Terrorism Report recognized that the extremist violence in Jammu and Kashmir was fuelled by infiltration across the Line of Control. Besides retaining the designation of Pakistan-based groups such as LeT, *Harkat-ul Mujahideen* and JeM as terrorist organizations, the USA has, in the 2003 Report, added others, such as *al-Badr Mujahideen*, *Hizb-ul Mujahideen* and *Jamiat ul-Mujahideen*, to its lists of terrorist organizations. However, the initial US response to the Nadimarg massacre in Jammu and Kashmir in March 2003 came as a surprise to India. Rather than outright condemnation of the massacre, the US State Department merely urged India to resume 'dialogue' with Pakistan. However, the subsequent US-British statement on 27 March was more pointed, condemning the Nadimarg massacre, calling on Pakistan to end infiltration across the Line of Control in Kashmir, and urging Pakistan to do its utmost to discourage acts of violence by militants in Jammu and Kashmir.[43]

At the international level, in 2002 the G-8 Summit urged Pakistan to prevent terrorists from operating from its soil. In response to the terrorist attacks on Mumbai on 11 July 2006, the G-8 Summit, the Chairman of the Council of the Heads of State of the Commonwealth of Independent States, the Chairman of the African Union and other international organizations formally expressed their willingness to take all necessary measures against such terrorists, their organizers and sponsors. As a result of the growing international recognition of the seriousness of international terrorism and India's diplomatic efforts, several countries became more sympathetic to the problem of cross-border terrorism. International reaction, sympathy and support to India in the wake of the terrorist attacks in Mumbai on 26 November 2008 are testimony to this.

Conclusions

Although India had been facing the threat of international terrorism for several decades, her concerns were taken seriously only in the aftermath of the 11 September 2001 attacks on the USA. This was reflected in increasing international support for the Indian draft Comprehensive Convention on International Terrorism at the UN. In the years that followed, India took the lead in formulating and sponsoring several important conventions and declarations on various aspects of international terrorism. In compliance with the resolutions of the Counter Terrorism Committee, India's internal mechanisms for dealing with the terrorism (legal, institutional and operational) challenge were strengthened. Despite India's diplomatic initiatives, however, the consequences of state sponsorship of terrorism are yet to be appreciated fully by the international community.

Notes

1 C. Raja Mohan, 'Towards a Global War Against Terrorism', *The Hindu*, 13 September 2001.
2 B. Raman, 'Global Terrorism: India's Concerns', *Papers* (SAAG), No. 2021, 12 November 2006.
3 For an analysis of the message, see B. Raman, 'Bin Laden Targets India', *Papers* (SAAG), No. 1776, 25 April 2006. Also 'Al Qaeda Claim of Kashmir Link Worries India', *International Herald Tribune*, 14 July 2006.
4 S. Muni, 'Responding to Terrorism: An Overview', in S. Muni (ed.), *Responding to Terrorism in South Asia*, New Delhi: Manohar Publishers, 2006, p.452. Also P. Ramana, 'Data Paper on Terrorism. I. South Asia', in S. Muni (ed.), *Responding to Terrorism in South Asia*, op. cit.
5 S. Muni, 'Introduction', in *Responding to Terrorism in South Asia*, op. cit., pp.11–29, 473–90.
6 A. Siddiqa, 'Terrorism in South Asia', in S. Muni (ed.), *Responding to Terrorism in South Asia*, op. cit.
7 Ibid., p.340.
8 K. Warikoo, 'Religious Extremism and Terrorism in Kashmir', in M. Singh (ed.), *International Terrorism and Religious Extremism: Challenges to Central and South Asia*, New Delhi: Anamika 2004.
9 A. Upadhyay, 'Terrorism in the North-East: Linkages and Implications', *Economic and Political Weekly*, Vol. 41, No. 48, 2006.
10 V. Borooah, 'Terrorist Incidents in India, 1998–2004: A Quantitative Analysis of Fatality Rates', *Terrorism and Political Violence*, Vol. 21, No. 3, 2009.
11 G. Shah and R. Dixit, *Narco-Terrorism*, New Delhi: Siddhi Books, 1996.
12 R. Suri, 'Indian Security and the Threat of Terrorism', *Agni*, Vol. 10, No. 111, 2007.
13 S. Muni, 'Terrorism and Interstate Relations in South Asia', in S. Khatri and G. Kueck (eds), *Terrorism in South Asia: Impact on Development and Democratic Process*, New Delhi: Shipra Publication, 2003.
14 I. Ahmed, 'Contemporary Terrorism and the State, Non-State, and the Interstate: Newer Drinks, Newer Bottles', in S. Khatri and G. Kueck (eds), *Terrorism in South Asia: Impact on Development and Democratic Process*, op. cit.
15 M. Joshi, 'Fight Against Terrorism Has to be Indivisible', *Economic Times*, 13 September 2001.
16 L.K. Advani, 'Combating Terrorism', interview, *The Pioneer*, 15 September 2001.
17 G. Parthasarthy, 'Global Fight Against Terrorism', *The Tribune*, 27 September 2001.
18 N. Pani, 'Servility Does Not Pay in the War Against Terrorism', *The Economic Times*, 5 October 2001.
19 'US, India and Terrorism', *The Tribune*, editorial, 9 December 2002.
20 M. Dubey, 'Global Campaign Against Terrorism', *The Hindu*, 26 September 2001.
21 The salient features of the CCIT are as follows: a) all states have a responsibility not to support terrorist acts and/or provide any assistance, training, safe haven, etc.; b) all states should adopt measures to ensure that terrorist acts within the scope of the Convention are under no circumstances justified by considerations of political, philosophical, ideological, racial, religious or other similar nature; c) all states

should take all practicable measures to prohibit the establishment and operation of terrorist installations and training camps; and d) terrorists should either be prosecuted or extradited.

22 K. Sharma, 'Statement in the United Nations', New York, 3 October 2001, in K. Gupta (ed.), *International Terrorism: World Viewpoints, Volume 5: Response of India, Pakistan and the US*, New Delhi: Atlantic Publishers, 2002, p.219.

23 Cited in 'India Ready with Text of Convention Against International Terrorism', *The Hindu*, 22 March 2010.

24 These are the Indian Penal Code 1860, the Code of Criminal Procedure 1973, the Arms Act 1959, the Explosives Act 1884, the Explosives Substances Act 1908, the Indian Telegraph Act 1885, the Armed Forces (Special) Powers Act 1958, the Unlawful Activities (Prevention) Act 1967, the Anti-Hijacking Act 1982, the Merchant Shipping Act 1948, and the United Nations Security Council Act 1947.

25 Notable among them are UN Security Council, *Report by India to the Counter-Terrorism Committee pursuant to Resolution 1373* (2001), S/2000/1278, 27 December 2001; UN Security Council, *Security Council Resolution 1373 (2001): Supplementary Report Submitted by India*, S/2002/883, 7 August 2002; UN Security Council, *Response to CTC Questions*, S/2003/452, 21 April 2003; UN Security Council, *Government of India: Fourth Report to the Counter-Terrorism Committee*, S/2004/451, 3 June 2004; UN Security Council, *Fifth Report of the Government of India to the Counter-Terrorism Committee*, S/2007/196, 11 April 2007.

26 Terrorist organizations proscribed under the POTO, as per criteria set in its Section 18, are: Babbar Khalsa International, Khalistan Commando Force, Khalistan Zindabad Force, International Sikh Youth Federation, Lashkar-e-Taiba, Pasban-e-Ahle Hadis, Jaish-e-Mohammad, Tehreek-e-Furqan, Harkat-ul-Mujahideen, Harkat-ul-Ansar, Harkat-ul-Jihad-e-Islami, Hizb-ul-Mujahideen, Pir Panjal Regiment, Al-Umar-Mujahideen, Jammu Kashmir Islamic Front, United Liberation Front of Assam, National Democratic Front of Bodoland, People's Liberation Army, United National Liberation Front, People's Revolutionary Party of Kangleipak, Kanleipak Communist Party, Kanglei Yaol Kanlge Lup, Manipur People's Liberation Front, All Tripura Tiger Force, Liberation Tigers of Tamil Eelam, Student's Islamic Movement of India, and Deendar Anjum.

27 Ministry of External Affairs, 'India Signs International Convention for the Suppression of Acts of Nuclear Terrorism', 25 July 2006, meaindia.nic.in.

28 DNA, 'India's Position on International Terrorism Vindicated at Summit', *Daily News & Analysis*, 14 April 2010, www.dnaindia.com.

29 Ministry of External Affairs, 'India Condemns Terrorist Attack on J&K State Assembly', *Press Release*, 1 October 2001, www.indianembassy.org.

30 T. Kartha, 'Countering Transnational Terrorism', *Strategic Analysis*, Vol. 23, No. 11, 2000.

31 A. Karim, 'Challenges of International Terrorism', *Security and Society*, Vol. 1, No. 1, 2004. For more on the Indian perspective see P. Chari and S. Chandran (eds), *Terrorism Post 9/11: An Indian Perspective*, New Delhi: Manohar Publishers, 2003.

32 J. Singh, 'High Level Group on Counter Terrorism', reply to Unstarred Question No. 1795, 28 November 2001, Lok Sabha, meaindia.nic.in/searchhome.htm. For the strategy, tactical aspects and concepts of counter insurgency in India, see N. Asthana and A. Nirmal, *Terrorism, Insurgencies and Counter-Insurgency Operations*, Jaipur: Pointer Publishers, 2001.

33 P. Mukherjee, 'Intervention on Counter-Terrorism at the ASEM Meeting', 30 May 2007, meaindia.nic.in.

34 P. Rajeswari, 'Terrorism—an Area of Cooperation in Indo-US Relations', *Strategic Analysis*, Vol. 24, No. 6, 2000.

35 T. Hoyt, 'India and the Challenge of Global Terrorism: The "Long War" and Competing Domestic Visions', in H. Pant (ed.), *Indian Foreign Policy in a Unipolar World*, New Delhi: Routledge, 2009.

36 Though S. D'Souza, 'Indo-US Counter-Terrorism Cooperation: Rhetoric Versus Substance', *Strategic Analysis*, Vol. 32, No. 6, 2008, warns of a gap between substance and rhetoric.

37 V. Khanna, 'Continuation of Terrorism by Pakistan', 13 March 2003, Rajya Sabha, meaindia.nic.in.

38 A. Panja, 'Menace of Global Terrorism', 15 March 2000, Lok Sabha, meaindia.nic.in.

39 A. Panja, 'Terrorism Issue with Neighbouring Countries', 17 May 2000, Lok Sabha, meaindia.nic.in.

40 R. Tripathi, 'SAARC Convention on Suppression of Terrorism: An Agenda for Relocation', in O. Mishra and S. Ghosh (eds), *Terrorism and Low Intensity Conflict in South Asian Region*, New Delhi: Manak Publication, 2003, pp.175–87.

41 A. Panja, 'US Stand on Terrorism', 26 April 2000, Lok Sabha, meaindia.nic.in.

42 K. Kronstadt, *International Terrorism in South Asia*, CRS Report for the Congress, 3 November 2003.

43 G. Parthasarthy, 'Terrorism is the Core Issue', *The Pioneer*, 8 May 2003.

25

India and the United Nations

Sreeram Chaulia

Introduction

> Our institutions of global governance, centred on what may be called the UN system, were designed
> for the most part at the end of the Second World War and reflected the politico–economic rea-
> lities of that age [...] There has been a sea change since then. Bipolarity has given way to multi-
> polarity [...] It is obvious that if the system was being designed today it would be very different
> [...] India, as the largest democracy in the world and an emerging economy that has achieved the
> ability to grow rapidly [...] will continue to strive for the reform of the United Nations to make it
> more democratic.[1]
>
> (Manmohan Singh)

> nations that are powerful and dissatisfied are usually nations that have grown to full power after
> the existing international order was fully established and the benefits already allocated.[2]
>
> (Abramo Organski)

International organizations during a 'power transition'

Rising powers present a classic problem to the international status quo because they aspire and
push to convert their lately acquired capabilities into greater recognition, prestige, and control
over rules, practices and institutions that guarantee world leadership. Carving out a prominent
place in international organizations, the executive arms of institutions, comes as a natural thirst
for states intent on converting their hard-earned superior power into legitimized and predictable
long-term domination. International Relations (IR) *constructivist* scholar Nicholas Onuf's insight
that 'rules create conditions of rule'[3] is, ironically, not lost upon the current era's emerging
powers, which are schooled in IR *realist* doctrines of foreign policy but are not loath to harnessing multilateral organizations for further accumulation of influence and agenda-setting privilege in a range of issue areas. The pioneers of IR *liberal institutionalism*, Robert Keohane and
Joseph Nye, had also correctly predicted in 1971 that transnational relations (cross-border
interactions where at least one non-state actor like an international organization or a

multinational corporation is involved) 'may redistribute control from one state to another and benefit those governments at the centre of transnational networks to the disadvantage of those in the periphery'.[4] Gaining voice and weight within international organizations has become both a 'symbolic' and 'substantive' measure of foreign policy success for states that are on the rise, especially those for which ambitions are not system-disruptive. Eduard Jordaan's definition of 'emerging middle powers' includes the behavioural trait of 'opting for reformist and not radical global change',[5] and it fits a number of contemporary states like India that are trying to raise their own importance within the existing international order instead of resorting to war or forming alternative systems with their own institutions. The onus on gaining eminence in international organizations and the concomitant pressure on their present elite members to accommodate the newcomers by giving them their due is thus a ubiquitous feature in world politics today.

Since a dissatisfied rising state can find enough avenues for satiating its burning desire to be one of the major powers in the current liberal multipolar world order, its foreign policy will be attuned to maximizing opportunities to find top spots and leverage in key international organizations. This is essentially one of the elements of grand strategy for what Andrew Cooper classifies as 'the big emerging powers' like India, which have left behind fellow middle powers in the last couple of decades due to sustained economic advances.[6] The moves that such emerging powers like India (as well as the People's Republic of China and Brazil) make at international summits are followed with interest in the media and by world governments, precisely because of the sense that a *power transition* is on and that these countries are playing it out in the portals of multilateral organizations in Geneva, New York or Washington, DC. India's approach to the UN and the responses it receives from the world body must be contextualized in this global background of movement of power towards multipolarity and the bid to democratize hitherto oligopolistic forums that rhetorically preached equality of all sovereign states. The first half of this chapter contains a history of India's relations with the UN in select security and political economy issue areas. The later part of the chapter homes in on the current scenario, wherein New Delhi is pushing desperately to be given more authority within the UN system. In the process, it aims to highlight the bitter realities of how accumulating power changes the attitude and behaviour of a state towards international organizations and vice versa.

Shifting attention, constant frustration

By virtue of being the so-called 'jewel in the crown' of the British Empire, India was one of only four non-sovereign territories that were founding members of the UN in 1945. Upon attaining independence, India brought to the UN its ideals of anti-colonialism, opposition to racial discrimination and non-alignment in the nascent Cold War, and tried to obtain a leadership position within the organization by appealing to the universal morals enshrined in the UN Charter. In the words of its globally conscious first Prime Minister, Jawaharlal Nehru, India would 'endeavour to play that role in its [the UN's] councils to which her geographical position, population and contribution towards peaceful progress entitle her'.[7] Nehru amassed *soft power* for India through diplomatic blitzes at the UN during the 1950s, immersing the Indian delegation in New York and Geneva in activities such as mediation to end the Korean War, the Vietnamese war of independence, and the second Arab–Israeli war over Suez. Nehru also committed Indian military personnel to sensitive UN peace-keeping missions in the Middle East, Africa and the Mediterranean, when the concept of multinational armies under UN aegis to preserve international peace was just taking off. Through an extremely active presence in important organs of the UN, India of the Nehru era seemed to be making up for its economic and military weakness through stellar institutional contributions to building the post-war world. While this strategy was never explicit, there was a realization up to the 1960s that India could only garner international recognition by investing energies in strengthening multilateral organizations like the UN rather than through typical IR *realism* self-help stratagems of bullying and exploitative behaviour that are the hallmarks of Great Powers.

None the less, Nehru's inherent internationalist faith in the UN and instinctive adherence to its principles proved costly on some occasions due to the power play inherent in an organization that had been crafted to accommodate and reward Great Powers of the time, such as his decision to refer Pakistan's intervention ('invasion') in disputed Kashmir to the UN Security Council in January 1948. The United Kingdom, which was hoping to avoid being seen as unfriendly to a Muslim state after the creation of Israel, used pressure tactics on its allies France, Canada and the USA to support the Pakistani viewpoint that Kashmir's accession to India was disputable and had to be put to the test of a plebiscite.[8] Nehru's hope that the UN would unconditionally instruct Pakistan to vacate the one-third portion of Kashmir that its tribesmen and army had occupied fell flat in the face of geopolitical manoeuvrings and cross-issue linkage. To this day, Indian strategic commentators and rightist critics of Nehru bemoan his cardinal mistake of taking the Kashmir dispute to a UN that was packed with pro-Pakistani partisan powers.[9] According to Brahma Chellaney, 'Nehru did not appreciate that the UN was an institution of power politics, not an impartial police force'.[10] As if a double reminder were needed that India was small fry in a UN dominated by crafty Great Powers divided into two ideological camps, New Delhi was disappointed to find that Security Council members the USA, United Kingdom and France tried to prevent it from forcibly absorbing the Portuguese colony of Goa in 1961.[11] But for the Soviet veto in favour of India, Goa could have become enmeshed in another Kashmir-like stalemate for decades, buffeted by the changing winds of Great Power alignments and preferences that were paralysing and hijacking the UN.

Nehru could have opportunistically capitalized on Cold War polarization at the UN to secure for India a Permanent Seat on the Security Council, but missed the boat twice in the 1950s to the perpetual dismay of future generations of Indians. In 1952 Washington offered India entry as the sixth Permanent Member, in order to keep China out of contention and to leave the Kuomintang of Taiwan in its place as the UN-recognized Chinese regime. Nehru, who was anxious then to accommodate Mao Tse Tung's China, rejected the offer on the grounds that it would sow divisions between New Delhi and Beijing, and would split Third World unity against Western neo-imperialism. In 1955 Soviet Prime Minister Nikolai Bulganin issued a similar offer that would have entailed bypassing Maoist China and would have made India a veto-wielding member of the Security Council. Again, Nehru insisted on a stage-by-stage admission process wherein, 'we should first concentrate on getting [communist] China admitted', and 'then the question of India might be considered separately'.[12] Whether the feelers from Washington or Moscow to promote India to a Permanent Member of the Security Council could have carried the day by obtaining consensus in the badly riven Cold War heyday is far from certain, but the burden of hindsight is wearisome for Indians who fret today about not yet succeeding in gaining entry into the 'P' (Permanent Member) category of the highest institution for overseeing world security.

Disillusionment with the UN and its perceived inability to take the side of justice, as India saw it, kept mounting after Nehru, especially in the context of India's wars with Pakistan in 1965 and 1971. An India facing increasingly hostile threats from its northern neighbours deliberately lowered its interest in the UN because the heavily politicized organization was unable to come to the rescue on New Delhi's core national security concerns. Stanley Kochanek has shown how, between 1962 and 1976, 'bilateralism became the guiding principle of Indian foreign policy', relegating the UN to just an 'arena for maintaining such contacts'.[13] The USSR's backing was much more crucial than a slow and rigged UN Security Council when India obtained its greatest strategic victory by breaking up Pakistan into two and carving out independent Bangladesh.

Once India had tested its first 'peaceful' nuclear device in 1974, the UN's non-proliferation agenda became another irritant that forced New Delhi to view some units of the organization with distaste as fronts for imposing discriminatory regimes instead of promoting universal disarmament. The higher onus placed on preventing horizontal rather than vertical proliferation of nuclear weapons by the Security Council-affiliated International Atomic Energy Agency (IAEA) kept India out of rule-making and rule-obeying functions on an issue that went on gaining momentum as central to global security. As a 'nuclear pariah' that was not recognized as a weapons power and which was barred from accessing atomic fuel and technology, India could only make occasional forays at the UN by tabling aspirational proposals for universal disarmament.[14] Non-proliferation continues to be a sore spot for India-UN relations because the organization's supreme minders happen all to be nuclear weapons states and are still eager to retain their oligopoly in weapons of mass destruction, the 'nuclear apartheid' argument advanced by Jaswant Singh in 1998.[15] When India tested five nuclear devices in 1998, citing concerns over China's existing nuclear capabilities, the UN Security Council 'strongly deplored' the action and the General Assembly expressed 'dismay and disappointment', confirming Indian convictions that the organization was barking up the wrong tree due to the manipulation of its priorities by some P-5 (the five Permanent Members of the Security Council) members.

For several decades India has been further peeved over what it considers the UN Secretariat's propensity to 'interfere' in the Kashmir dispute, as if the latter were dancing to the tune of Pakistan's brief of internationalizing the conflict. A conventionally superior power that controls two-thirds of Kashmir, India always prized a bilateral solution to the Himalayan region's fate that would relatively favour New Delhi over Islamabad. Dragging in the UN is a threat to India, which knows from past experience that the organization could become a smokescreen for hostile Great Powers to meddle in Kashmir and revive options like 'self-determination' for Muslim residents of Kashmir. In 1998, shortly after India and Pakistan conducted tit-for-tat nuclear tests, UN Secretary-General Kofi Annan deputed a three-member team to travel to South Asia and defuse tensions by encouraging dialogue. New Delhi reacted with characteristic defensiveness by declining to receive the visitors and reminding the UN that, 'there was no scope for a third-party involvement of any nature whatsoever in respect of India's relations with Pakistan'.[16] Indian defiance of the UN's good offices was repeated during the 1999 quasi-war for Kargil between nuclear-armed India and Pakistan, when Annan proposed deputing a special envoy to mediate. Prime Minister Atal Behari Vajpayee was determined to avoid a 1948-like fiasco. He 'summarily rejected' Annan's right to interfere in the matter and ordered Indian military operations to continue until all the Pakistani intruders were flushed out.[17] The memory of a UN that tended to apportion blame equally between aggressors and aggressed, either due to technical reasons of wishing to appear as a neutral international organization or owing to pushing and pulling by Great Powers with vested interests in South Asia, comes reflexively to Indian foreign policy-makers.

The continued presence of a UN Military Observer Group (UNMOGIP) along the India–Pakistan border to monitor cease-fire violations has not pleased India since 1972, when New Delhi extracted verbal promises from a war-defeated Islamabad to stick to purely bilateral avenues for mutual problems. Convinced that the UNMOGIP's *raison d'être* has expired, India restricts its activities on Indian territory and hosts it with utmost reluctance. In 2001 the thorny presence of unwelcome UN observers on the Indian side of Kashmir erupted in controversy when their Austrian chief publicly described the valley as a tormented place, accused India and Pakistan of indulging in 'political games', and went to the extent of commenting that the USA might have to get involved to resolve the vexing issue. India responded furiously and compelled the Austrian to issue an apology for 'stepping out of mission brief' and 'causing discomfort' to the authorities in New Delhi.[18] From the Indian perspective, a line had been crossed leading to a direct affront to its sovereignty.

Periodically, India also bristles at reports or remarks of UN offices that call for independent investigations into accusations of civilian killings in Kashmir by Indian army personnel. In 2008 the UN High Commissioner for Human Rights (UNHCHR) released a statement asking India to, 'comply with international human rights principles in controlling the demonstrators' during an upsurge in anti-India protests by Kashmiri Muslim outfits. New Delhi snapped back that the comments were 'uncalled for and irresponsible', and that the UN should be monitoring incidents in Kashmir where innocent civilians were being victimized by Islamist terrorists.[19] In July 2010 a release that the 'secretary general is concerned over the prevailing security situation there [in the Kashmir Valley] over the past month', brought immediate comments from India that this was 'gratuitous advice', and a UN semi-retraction that this was guidance rather than a statement on the part of Bang Ki-moon, and had been taken out of context by India.[20]

As countering terrorism turned into a central concern at the UN after the terrorist attacks on the USA on 11 September 2001, India has vigilantly opposed UN departments and branches that suggest that there are 'root causes' of terrorism, like socio-economic backwardness or identity-based discrimination and that they must be primarily redressed. In 2002 New Delhi warned the UN General Assembly against the UNHCHR's advisories seeking to provide justification for terrorist violence by causally linking it to absence of rule of law or self-determination.[21]

Comeback via counter-terrorism

As a longstanding sufferer of *jihadist* terrorism, India had drafted a Comprehensive Convention on International Terrorism (CCIT) as early as 1996 for the General Assembly committee, but it required a massive strike at the heart of the USA in 2001 for the issue to rise up the ladder of priorities. Sensing a global rule-making chance that had been denied to India in other domains of international security like nuclear weapons, New Delhi plunged headlong into redrafting its CCIT and winning consensus from other UN members to finalize a treaty that would buttress India's fight against violent *jihad* and embarrass its state sponsors. The US-led global 'war on terrorism' created a new normative environment at the UN which was amenable to stewardship on the issue by a rising power like India, which reminded everyone else that it was the worst victim of the scourge of terrorism. By March 2010 India had a 'text on the table' for adoption by the UN and was pressing for its adoption, canvassing far and wide in world capitals.[22] Counter-terrorism was thus seized upon by India in the last decade when the iron was hot at the UN level, displaying an activism for multilateral outcomes in the sphere of international peace and security that was missing since Nehru's days. The greater self-confidence India had acquired since being bracketed as one of the emerging economic power centres of the world was visible in its shepherding of the UN's incipient counter-terrorism regime. With India being taken more seriously in different world forums as an Asian giant that was growing at a respectable pace, the same UN system that had seemed unfair and captured by Great Powers for ages could now become a receptive institutional venue at which New Delhi might translate its steadily building strength into global governing power.

A causal relationship between a state's increasing power and the degree of its interest in shaping the agenda of international organizations is straightforward. However, it must be qualified by the caveat that preponderant powers might totally bypass institutional channels and not care for the collective opinion of the international community. The proclivity of the USA to go it alone in war and 'humanitarian intervention' began in President William (Bill) Clinton's second term, threatening the centrality of the UN Security Council as the ultimate arbiter of world order. Some Indian commentators, schooled in multilateral ethics, were shocked at New Delhi's apparent acquiescence at the turn of the millennium in the North Atlantic Treaty Organization's (NATO) bid to arrogate the term 'international community' and to undermine UN mechanisms.[23] The seeming absence of countervailing power against US unipolarity at that time may have, in fact, shaken India's customary deference to the UN on all non-India-related security problems. Washington went into unilateralist overdrive under President George W. Bush, putting paid to expectations at the end of the Cold War that a 'new world order' based on international law and organizations had arrived. However, it is worth noting that India rose in the last decade from a far lower baseline than the USA did during its post-Cold War 'unipolar moment'. The former lacked the military machine to pummel any of the sources of its external security threats into submission in the way the USA was trying in the 'war on terrorism'.

New Delhi's responses to repeated terrorist assaults traced to Pakistan have been marked by helpless restraint and agony rather than US-style frontal retaliation. Instead of turning the screws through proactive military moves that lacked UN sanction, New Delhi sought assurances from Washington that it would pressurize Islamabad to turn off the terrorist taps aimed at India.[24] Simultaneously, the Manmohan Singh Government tried to corner Pakistan at the UN level by bringing what it considered its dubious *jihad*-incubating foreign policy under the scanner of greater international scrutiny and disapproval. Lacking decisive policy instruments to silence Islamist extremism in its neighbourhood and having realized the traction of the US-Pakistani alliance for the war in Afghanistan, a power of India's medium stature saw value in championing UN-led global ripostes to the menace troubling it. Since the inter-related challenges of terrorism and warfare are not leaving the international limelight any time soon, one foresees that India's return to centre stage in this security issue area at the UN will last for some time and will roll back the post-Nehruvian decline in Indian involvement in the international organization. At the same time, the limitations of a counter-terrorism strategy that is merely institutional and not militarily punitive are nudging India into gaining an approval of sorts from the USA to prosecute retaliation on Pakistan or *jihadist* elements in Bangladesh if more spectacular terrorist attacks occur on Indian soil.[25] The bottom line since 1948 has been that India's security threats cannot be solved by banking on a UN that is the handmaiden of hostile or indifferent Great Powers.

South-South revival: elixir or burden?

Until now, we have chronicled the regional and global changes in power structure and normative climate that informed India's fluctuating interest in the UN's mandate to maintain international peace and security. It is equally important to examine the ups and downs in Indian–UN relations in the corollary sphere of international political economy. Assigned with the duty of accelerating the economic growth of poor countries, the UN system has spawned a wide variety of specialized agencies, funds and departments that cater to developmental themes and needs of the Global South. As a vastly populous developing country, India has been a recipient of billions of dollars of multilateral foreign aid disbursed through the UN's sub-organizations and affiliated international non-governmental organizations (NGOs) for poverty reduction and improvement of life indices. From 1958 onwards, the World Bank's Aid-to-India Consortium co-ordinated the bulk of loan transfers to India. Aid dependence on the UN family defined India's economic relationship with the world organization for decades during the country's long spell of a crawling 'Hindu rate of growth'. The fate of socialist planning of the economy until 1991, which was quixotically meant to foster self-sufficiency, was frequently tied to multilateral aid via UN pipelines. The utter failure of foreign aid-driven centralized planning was exposed by economist Shyam Kamath when he labelled India 'the World Bank's star patient' whose sickness could never be healed as long as Indian enterprises remained over-protected and uncompetitive.[26] Even after the Indian economy was unshackled in the last two decades, the World Bank harnessed deep connections within India's body politic, establishing direct relationships with state-level units of the Indian union and pumping in ever more aid. The anticlimax of India as a fast-growing emerging economy that is searching for a grander role in the world theatre but still stretching out a bowl as a top recipient of World Bank and UN Development Programme aid has been a national embarrassment that has not been felt by populist politicians in the country's provinces. Opinion-makers have argued forcefully for foreign exchange-flush India to disentangle itself from the international aid racket and gain in self-esteem as a rising power, but to little avail.[27]

A small grace is that, after the global economic crash of 2008, India (along with Brazil and China) started lending huge sums to the crisis-hit IMF and pressed for a quid pro quo of greater voting shares in international financial institutions.[28] UN development agencies have also stressed the importance of dynamic emerging economies like India taking charge of delivering investment, technology and expertise to poorer countries of the Global South, i.e. acting as donors within South-South co-operation frameworks.[29]

The rejuvenation of the South-South paradigm in the context of the booming BRIC (Brazil, Russia, India and China) economies of the last decade has an altogether new meaning and edge that was lacking when the concept was unveiled at the UN after decolonization under the banner of 'Third World' solidarity. India has its own phalanx of multinational corporations that have accumulated enough capital to venture outwards and seal significant mergers and acquisitions overseas, especially in distant parts of the Global South.[30] The vast potential for South-South trade and sharing of technical know-how between India, China, Africa and Latin America is being fulfilled 'BRIC by brick' and has provided a tangible basis for realizing the old dream of former colonized parts of the world uniting for mutual benefit. There is also a discernible attempt on the part of bigger and more progressive economies of the Global South to engage in multilateral economic institution-crafting that falls outside the range of the Bretton Woods system and related UN agencies. Venezuela's bold ALBA initiative, which breaks with the World Bank's capitalistic model of economic development, has Asian counterparts with China in the driver's seat of various currency swap agreements and preferential trading arrangements.

However, India has been a lot less active in proposals for forming an 'Asian Monetary Union' (AMU) or in imagining a world without neo-liberal financial institutions, due to its own post-1991 political class's proximity to free market values. New Delhi's reluctance to think outside the box, even after the existing global economic architecture failed to anticipate and mitigate the worst downturn since the Great Depression, is a product of India's deeper integration into the capitalist world system and deliberate attempt not to upset the upswing in its relations with the USA. Despite sloganeering in favour of a 'multipolar world' and 'democratization of international relations', India is no longer a radical state that can lead thought or action on ridding the Global South of foreign aid-dependency or neo-colonial forms of economic exchange with the Global North. It is now firmly within the incrementalist camp of emerging powers that seeks admission and distinction *within* extant institutions, including the UN's organs. The Indian (and to a lesser extent Brazilian and Chinese) projection is that the international system would automatically become fairer and more democratic if emerging economies were incorporated into positions of higher responsibility in pre-existing institutions. In other words, India prefers the current global institutional status quo in terms of substantive ideological orientation, but seeks changes in form, like membership and representation.

It bears a reminder that India of the 21st century is an entirely different kettle of fish from the firebrand socialist India that used to grab the soapbox inside some UN forums to seek a leftward turn for the world organization's priorities. As one of the paladins of the Non-Aligned Movement (NAM), India was the first to launch policy proposals in the 1960s at the UN Conference on Trade and Development (UNCTAD) for just and equitable relationships between exploitative Northern states and repressed Southern states on trade in raw materials and primary commodities. India was at the forefront of adoption by the UN General Assembly in 1974 of the motto, a 'New International Economic Order', to end neo-colonial economic practices by Great Powers in the Global South. Well into the 1980s, 'to use UNCTAD and other international economic institutions for securing more beneficial economic policies in favour of the interests of developing countries [...was] a fundamental objective of India's economic diplomacy'.[31] Since neo-Marxist dependency theory found a safe haven in UNCTAD, it was natural for socialist India to strive to be seen in the limelight in this intergovernmental body even when New Delhi had minimized involvement in the UN's Great Power-controlled security gatherings. As long as India self-identified itself as a tireless worker for justice on behalf of the Global South and an eager convener and mobilizer of the G-77 bloc inside the UN, its profile in the economic policy-making side of the organization was outstanding. Great Powers had monopolized the peace-and-security minding organs of the UN and left some freedom for articulators of the views of the Global South to give vent to their grievances via UNCTAD and the General Assembly, which were treated with contempt by Western states as glorified talking shops. India earned a reputation in these alternative UN venues up to 1991 as a moralistic grandstander that punched above its weight by using the bully pulpit. However, once the Indian economy privatized and the state jettisoned socialism in all but name, New Delhi invested less in pillorying the capitalist world system at the UN and spoke more avidly as a convert to economic globalization. In the unipolar world of the 1990s India did or said nothing at the UN that set it apart from the chorus about the inevitability of globalization and the benefits it would accrue.

This trend has accelerated in the new century, with India no longer singing the tune of New International Economic Order or burdening itself with the mantle of a born leader of the G-77 at the UN. It would be fair to argue, however, that a democratic transitioning market economy like India faces a global identity crisis that is neither socialist nor fully convinced of the virtues of untrammelled free markets. Treading a nebulous ground and unsure of itself, India has adopted a dual identity on international political economy. It shows signs of behaving like a mature capitalist Great Power that tries to promote its own corporations and trade interests world-wide through self-interested action, but retreats into the safety of numbers provided by the G-77 (as of 2010, it had UN member states) where it suits a particular issue area. For instance, India rediscovered some of its old 'Third Worldist' solidarity as a bargaining tool in multilateral negotiations for the stalled Doha Round of the World Trade Organization (WTO). Although a state that prefers to be on the right side of the USA on some foreign policy issues, India's commerce minister in 2007, Kamal Nath, dug in his heels with fellow developing countries against unfair Western subsidies at a WTO meeting, earning the ire of the US Trade Representative, Susan Schwab, as 'the villain of the piece' who scuppered the Doha Round.[32] Sensing a commonality of interests with an assertive group of states from the Global South, India has not hesitated to use the card of 'Third World' collective action to scuttle international economic deals that would hurt its exporters.

The UN-centred G-77 has thus found new non-UN bases in organizations like the WTO, which are arguably more consequential than UNCTAD or the General Assembly in the current age. If India's huffing and puffing inside the UN against an iniquitous world economy fetched some brownie points for it as a spokesperson for the Global South, it is today able to garner more attention and grudging respect from Great Powers at the WTO. The formation of small logjam-breaking diplomatic conclaves at the WTO like the G-4 (USA, EU, Brazil and India), speak to India's relatively enhanced status. Unlike the UN, where international laws are often bent to accommodate the whims of Great Powers, rules-based organizations like the WTO offer India a better chance to convert its economic preferences into policy. Indian trade lawyers have won several cases at the WTO's Dispute Settlement Body (DSB) against mightier forces like the USA and EU, an unthinkable outcome had the conflict raged inside the UN system. On trade issues, the trend of India devoting ever more resources to the WTO while downsizing its South-South advocacy inside the UN system is set to intensify as the country's trade profile and interests broaden.

However, the new issue domain of global environment policy that has risen up the ranks of key international concerns over the last decade necessitates a renewed engagement by India with the concerned segments of the UN. Unlike the WTO, there is no UN-independent international organization or regime to regulate and reverse the ticking time bomb of climate change. Inter-state efforts to co-ordinate a reduction in carbon emissions and transfer green technology to poor countries are being spearheaded by a UN Secretariat (the UN Framework Convention on Climate Change—UNFCCC) located in Germany and informed by the Intergovernmental Panel on Climate Change (IPCC), which was established by the UN Environment Programme (UNEP). The structure of global environmental decision-making and India's own position as a rapidly growing emerging economy predicted to expand its carbon footprint thus propelled New Delhi to engage wholeheartedly with the relevant UN offices. In 2010 the relationship between India and the IPCC hit rough weather, despite the fact that the Panel's head was an Indian scientist, R.K. Pachauri, who had been nominated by the Government of India and had been backed by the USA in 2002. India's environment minister, Jairam Ramesh, openly questioned the IPCC's projection of early disappearance of the Himalayan glaciers as 'not based on an iota of scientific evidence', and as scare tactics for which the Panel 'has to do a lot of answering'.[33] The Indian rebuff came close on the heels of an incident of compromised e-mails from the Panel's experts, which strengthened climate sceptics' claims that exaggeration and alarmism were being deployed by UN scientists to rush states into committing to deeper carbon emission cuts. As an important hold-out, along with China, on agreeing to mandatory emission cuts for developing countries, India is wary of scientific claims that entail severe adjustment costs and loss of competitiveness for its growing industries.

As in the case of trade talks, the Indian line is to adhere to the Global South position that there must be 'differentiated responsibilities' between the advanced industrialized polluters and late industrializers whose right to economic development should not be constrained by any international treaty. However, India finds itself in an odd bind when it invokes a joint Global South stance on climate change because the G-77 is itself split on this topic. Small island nations and least developed sub-Saharan African states are anxious for an ambitious international agreement that would force richer developing countries to cut emissions. When the BASIC group (Brazil, South Africa, India and China) entered into a face-saving Copenhagen Accord with the USA in December 2009 at the failed UN climate change Copenhagen Conference, and justified it as 'good for the entire developing world', the rest of the G-77 slammed what they considered a betrayal by their erstwhile leaders.[34] So, while India attempts to wear multiple hats at the UN, including that of Third World frontbencher on an *à la carte* basis, the strategy can backfire due to the complexity of new global problems and the differential rates of economic growth within the Global South. Ambiguity about India as a genuine representative of the G-77 at the UN is perhaps inevitable, but it is sure to leave New Delhi without a bell-wether portfolio in the organization.

The final frontier

India's concerted bid to be admitted as a veto-wielding 'P' member of the Security Council is the single most watched issue within the country when it comes to the UN organization as a whole. As the sanctum sanctorum and prime custodian of international law with more political powers than any other entity in the international system, the Security Council is a bull's eye for India to target. The demand for India's inclusion in a reformed Security Council keeps getting shriller as the country persists with large personnel contributions to UN peace-keeping missions and leapfrogs out of mediocre economic performance into an Asian giant with a pluralistic democratic political system to boot. However, entrenched resistance and mixed signals of existing P-5 members doused high hopes that India's long battle to be made a permanent member with veto power might finally fructify in around 2006.[35]

Since then, the process of enlargement has got stuck, with the USA never openly supporting India's candidature, and China reluctant to give a free pass to rivals like India or Japan to walk in with power parity. Apart from the stonewalling of some P-5 veto holders, Indian diplomacy has also struggled to secure endorsements from the prerequisite two-thirds of members of the General Assembly to carve out new permanent seats. All has not been smooth sailing for the G-4 frontrunners (India, Brazil, Germany and Japan) in cobbling together adequate bloc votes from within and beyond their own regions. Stefan Schirm has coined a telling phrase for the G-4's vain hunt: 'leaders in search of followers', i.e. rising powers that fail to convince their respective neighbouring states and regional organizations that their elevation will be a win-win proposition that would benefit said neighbouring states.[36] Pakistan and the rest of the Organisation of the Islamic Conference (OIC) countries remain barriers to India's race to find its cherished spot at the horseshoe table in New York, an objective reality that New Delhi cannot easily overcome.

Some diplomatic insiders suggest that India needs to show greater flexibility on key security issues for its Permanent Membership drive to regain momentum. Hints were dropped by US Senator John Kerry in the run up to the 2006 time-line for Security Council enlargement, that India must sign the Nuclear Non-Proliferation Treaty (NPT) for Washington to approve New Delhi's candidacy.[37] A former US arms control official repeated Kerry's arguments in 2009 that, 'resuming nuclear testing or not signing the CTBT [Comprehensive Test Ban Treaty] could affect its [India's] chances for a permanent seat in the UNSC'.[38] A former US career diplomat, Howard Schaffer, also recommended in 2009 that India's crusade for the seat should be seconded by the USA, 'in return for New Delhi agreeing to genuine and enforceable concessions on the Kashmir issue'.[39] More generically, the USA has hedged its bets on India as a reliable pro-Western partner and does not wish to encourage India's permanent entry into the Security Council without the assurance that it will side with US positions as assuredly as the United Kingdom and France do. For the same reason, the USA voted against India's high-profile candidate for the post of UN Secretary-General in 2006, Shashi Tharoor, and expended its diplomatic might to lobby for a putatively more pliable South Korean nominee, Ban Ki-moon.[40] The notion that there is a price to be paid in terms of national security or foreign policy autonomy for getting into the Security Council is unpalatable to India, which, as we saw earlier in this chapter, prioritizes territorial integrity over and above platitudes about adhering to UN resolutions or advice. Admittedly, India's home affairs minister, P. Chidambaram, has exuded confidence that the country's persistent diplomacy and economic vigour will propel it into the Security Council in this decade.[41] However, a more likely scenario is that India drops this ball for a more propitious moment and concentrates on other, more open international organizations that promise quicker returns and responsiveness to New Delhi's growing clout.

Conclusions

A UN Security Council without the constant attendance of India might be an anomaly that is eventually corrected, but the plenitude of international institutions in the contemporary world's thickset governance architecture means there is life outside the UN. India will do commendably if, while waiting for its red letter day in New York, it participates with gusto in new security and economic institutions like the Shanghai Cooperation Organization (SCO) and the East Asia Summit (EAS), which are sprouting in its *extended neighbourhood*. How India shuffles its deck at the G-20—which has been declared the premier international institution to manage the global economy—is going to be more widely followed than India's routine omissions and commissions inside the UN. The vicissitudes of international alliances, configurations and structures since colonized India's Ramaswamy Mudaliar signed the UN Charter in June 1945 prove beyond a doubt that the surest route to the hub of global policy-making emanates from a combination of national power accumulation and prescient foreign policy planning that dovetails the prevailing institutional ethos. If India understands its own capacities, grows in self-awareness of its peculiar strengths, and executes pointed actions that carry it from the semi-periphery to the centre of international institutions, the icing on the cake of a Permanent Seat in the UN Security Council will be the beginning, not the end, of a national quest to shape global governance for the planet.

Notes

1 M. Singh, 'The Vision of Emerging Powers—India', in *Compendium of the G-8 Summit*, 9 July 2009, L'Aquila, Italy; rep. 'PM's Vision of Emerging Powers in 21st Century', *Press Release* (PIB), 7 July 2009, pib.nic.in.
2 A. Organski, *World Politics*, New York: Alfred Knopf, 1958, p.328.
3 N. Onuf, 'Constructivism: A User's Manual', in V. Kubalkova *et al.* (eds), *International Relations in a Constructed World*, New York: M.E. Sharpe, 1998, p.63.
4 R. Keohane and J. Nye (eds), *Transnational Relations and World Politics*, Cambridge, MA: Harvard University Press, 1971, p.xxiii.
5 E. Jordaan, 'The Concept of a Middle Power in International Relations: Distinguishing Between Emerging and Traditional Middle Powers', *Politikon*, Vol. 30, No. 1, 2003.
6 A. Cooper, 'Middle Powers: Squeezed Out or Adaptive Into New Roles?', *Public Diplomacy*, Vol. 1, No. 1, 2009, p.29.
7 Cited in 'India and the UN', *India News*, Vol. 17, No. 31, 1978, p.1.
8 C. Dasgupta, *War and Diplomacy in Kashmir, 1947–48*, New Delhi: Sage Publications, 2002, p.111.
9 'Terrorism, Kashmir "Festering Sores" Due to Nehru's Mishandling: Advani', *Indian Express*, 15 February 2010.
10 B. Chellaney (ed.), *Securing India's Future in the New Millennium*, New Delhi: Orient Longman, 1999, p.545.
11 M. Fisher, 'Goa in Wider Perspective', *Asian Survey*, Vol. 2, No. 2, 1962.
12 J. Nehru, 22 June 1955, in *Selected Works of Jawaharlal Nehru*, Second Series, Vol. 29, New Delhi: Oxford University Press, 2002, pp.231; 1 August 1955, ibid., p.303.
13 S. Kochanek, 'India's Changing Role in the United Nations', *Pacific Affairs*, Vol. 53, No. 1, 1980, p.53.

14 R. Gandhi, 'A World Free of Nuclear Weapons', 9 June 1988, www.indianembassy.org. This speech, delivered by India's Prime Minister at the UN General Assembly, attained hallowed status in India as a legitimate alternative to the non-proliferation agenda. In 2008 the Indian Government officially commemorated the 20th anniversary of what New Delhi believes was a landmark proposal. Cf. P. Sharma, 'Government to Celebrate 20 Years of Rajiv Gandhi's Peace Plan', *Indo-Asian News Service*, 27 May 2008.

15 J. Singh, 'Against Nuclear Apartheid', *Foreign Affairs*, Vol. 77, No. 5, 1998.

16 'India Turns Away 3-Member UN Team', *News* (Rediff), 25 June 1998, www.rediff.com.

17 'PM Rejects UN Offer', *The Hindu*, 31 May 1999.

18 'UNMOGIP Chief Says Sorry to India', *Dawn*, 2 November 2001.

19 'India Rejects UN Kashmir Comment', *BBC*, 29 August 2008, news.bbc.co.uk.

20 S. Ramachandran, 'India Draws a Line over Kashmir', *Asia Times*, 10 August 2010.

21 'India Rejects UN Panel's Bid to Link Rule of Law, Terrorism', *Asia Africa Intelligence Wire*, 20 November 2002.

22 'India Ready With Text of Convention Against International Terrorism', *The Hindu*, 22 March 2010.

23 N. Koshy, 'Sidelining the United Nations', *Economic and Political Weekly*, 8 April 2000.

24 S. Chaulia, 'Is there a "Burns Effect" on Pakistan?', *Indo-Asian News Service*, 17 October 2006.

25 'India's Patience on Terror not Unlimited: Robert Gates', *IndoAsian News Service*, 20 January 2010.

26 S. Kamath, 'Foreign Aid and India: Financing the Leviathan State', *CATO Policy Analysis* (CATO Institute), No. 170, 1992.

27 S. Chaulia, 'India's Self-Confident Avatar', *The International Indian*, February 2008.

28 S. Verma, 'India's $10 Billion Loan to IMF Will Ensure Higher Quota, Voting Share', *Financial Express*, 2 October 2009.

29 J. Lamont, 'UN Seeks Emerging States' Help to Aid Poor', *Financial Times*, 9 March 2010.

30 P. Gammeltoft, 'Emerging Multinationals: Outward FDI From the BRICS Countries', *International Journal of Technology and Globalisation*, Vol. 4, No. 1, 2008.

31 N. Jayapalan, *Foreign Policy of India*, New Delhi: Atlantic Publishers, 2003, p.471.

32 J. Bhagwati, 'A Skewed Blame Game', *India Today*, 30 July 2007.

33 'India Criticises UN Warning on Himalayan Glacier Melt', *BBC*, 19 January 2010, news.bbc.co.uk.

34 J. Gupta, 'Four Countries Hold Up Copenhagen Accord', *Indo-Asian News Service*, 19 December 2009.

35 A. Gentleman, 'Annan Rebuffs India's Hopes for an Expanded UN Role', *New York Times*, 29 April 2005.

36 S. Schirm, 'Leaders in Need of Followers: Emerging Powers in Global Governance', *European Journal of International Relations*, Vol. 16, No. 2, 2010.

37 I. Basu, 'John Kerry: A Thorn in India's Side', *Asia Times*, 6 March 2004.

38 'India's Stance on CTBT Could Affect its UN Chances: US Expert', *Indo-Asian News Service*, 22 October 2009.

39 'US Should Offer UNSC Seat to India to Resolve Kashmir', *Indian Express*, 27 May 2009.

40 S. Guha, 'US Veto Ends Shashi Tharoor's Run for Top Job at the UN', *Daily News & Analysis*, 4 October 2006.

41 'Permanent Seat at Security Council This Decade: Chidambaram', *Business Standard*, 31 March 2010.

26

India and nuclear weapons

Chris Ogden

India is a nuclear weapon state [...] It is not a conferment that we seek; nor is it a status for others to grant. It is an endowment to the nation by our scientists and engineers. It is India's due, the right of one-sixth of humankind. Our strengthened capability adds to our sense of responsibility; the responsibility and obligation of power.[1]

(Atal Bihari Vajpayee)

Introduction

This chapter traces the role that nuclear weapons have played within India's international relations from her independence in 1947 to her emergence as a future Great Power at the beginning of the 21st century. During this period, nuclear weapons and nuclear technology became critical touchstones for India's leaders and policy-makers, serving as powerful emblems of the country's independence, its technological proficiency and gradual modernization. In terms of international relations, nuclear power is regarded as a tool with which India can achieve strategic autonomy, and provide self-sufficiency in her diplomatic, political and economic affairs. As India's first Prime Minister, Jawaharlal Nehru pondered 'what does independence consist of? – it consists fundamentally and basically of foreign relations'.[2] Nuclear power helps enable this vision of independence and encompassed Nehruvian principles of non-violence, non-alignment, peace, disarmament, self-reliance and development. In turn, nuclear weapons were a means with which to protect Indian territory from external forces, to secure her regional pre-eminence and to stake her claim to future influence in the international system.

While reflective of the aspirations and beliefs of her leaders, India's domestic and foreign policy concerning nuclear weapons came to be based upon a paradox centred on the concurrent 'pursuit of independence and a commitment to peace'.[3] Thus, on one hand the acquisition of nuclear technology could help alleviate the country's energy needs, sustain its economic development and provide (through nuclear weapons) an effective deterrent against the negative intentions of its neighbours and others. On the other hand, however, India's leaders remained resolutely pro-nuclear disarmament, arguing that the existence of *any* nuclear weapons threatened India's security and that of the world. These latter views reflected both the idealism and morality of Nehru and, in the early years of the Cold War, the aims of being non-aligned from either of the two superpowers. This paradox became manifest in Indian foreign policy through a strategic-scientific enclave that simultaneously pursued a dual approach of developing nuclear weapons *and* calling for global disarmament.

The chapter is split into three major sections. In the first section, I investigate the roots of India's nuclear programme post-independence until the late 1960s, and show how India's leaders pursued the dual-track policy of development (including weaponization) and disarmament. In turn, section two analyses how from the early 1970s to the late 1990s India continued to use this approach to try to relieve external pressures towards her from the USA, People's Republic of China and Pakistan. The third section then deals with the nuclear tests of 1998 and their aftermath, in particular India's increased international leverage but also the continuing paradox of maintaining her opposition to nuclear weapons while developing them. The chapter ends with some thoughts as to the continued role and importance of nuclear weapons (and nuclear technology) in defining the current and future trajectory of India's international relations.

Nuclear beginnings and the early Cold War

India's aspirations for a nuclear programme began before independence and were then consecrated through the creation of the Indian Atomic Energy Commission in 1948. Combining work at the Tata Institute of Fundamental Research (itself set up in 1945), Homi Bhabha was the founding chair of the Atomic Energy Commission and guided India's nascent nuclear development. In turn, and complementing his role as India's first Prime Minister and defence minister, Jawaharlal Nehru held responsibility for the Department of Atomic Energy (DAE) that had been created in August 1954. This had few, if any, institutional checks or balances and was open to little military influence, reflecting its technological rather than militaristic orientation.[4] The DAE would remain under the direct control of subsequent Indian prime ministers. Economic advancement initially drove India's nuclear considerations, which were simultaneously aimed at overcoming decades of colonial exploitation, developing India's technical infrastructure and garnering international prestige through a display of scientific prowess. As funding significantly rose in the earlier 1950s, India's leaders increasingly saw nuclear science as a way to ameliorate India's post-independence position and to signal her international resurgence.[5]

While India's nuclear programme helped to nurture India's industrial base through the skill of her physicists and mathematicians, it was also multi-faceted through its focus on the multiple uses of nuclear energy. Initially, the peaceful non-military uses of nuclear energy were prominent and mixed with the wider goal of universal nuclear disarmament. This approach confirmed a focus on India's economic development that eschewed military spending and an avoidance of the two superpower blocs, as manifested through India's leadership of the Non-Aligned Movement (NAM). Principles of *ahimsa* (non-violence) and *satyagraha* (truth-force—the doctrine used to describe non-violence) further supported the aim of achieving peaceful development. In turn, a world free of nuclear weapons would help to reduce the risk of existential nuclear conflict, protect South Asia from external influences, and enhance Indian security. Maintaining India's independence underpinned these notions through a 'refusal to accept any external controls and restraints instituted in a discriminatory way',[6] and a commitment to peaceful, non-military uses of nuclear technology.

India's nuclear development came to be described in terms of self-reliance and self-sufficiency, manifestations that called for the country's autonomy to be protected in all spheres. Whilst this autonomy primarily concerned civilian needs, awareness that nuclear weapons could be used for defence and deterrence also became noted within India's early international relations. Indeed, as

India–China relations began to deteriorate in the late 1950s a consensus developed among India's leaders that nuclear weapons could and should be developed if a commensurate nuclear threat from China was apparent.[7] Such threat perceptions would inculcate more military uses of India's nuclear potential and bolster her nascent independence. They also reflected the view that, from the very beginning, many of India's scientists and leaders knew that nuclear technology 'would bring nuclear weapons'.[8] This outlook then coupled with tensions between a moral antagonism towards nuclear weapons (including demands for disarmament) and a desire to be a Great Power. A nuclear capability often came to personify the latter, particularly in terms of avoiding any international isolation and also by creating a bargaining chip that challenged the hold on atomic technology by the veto-wielding P-5 (the USA, USSR, United Kingdom, France and China) Permanent Members of the UN Security Council (UNSC).

In the early Cold War period, however, India's focus remained more on technological advancement in terms of nuclear energy and associated economic benefits rather than with developing a nuclear arsenal. Thus, from 1955 onwards nuclear co-operation between India and several other governments (Canada, the USA, the United Kingdom and France) was established. These links led to the building of the APSARA research (light water) reactor in 1956, the first research reactor of its kind in Asia, and to the building of the CIRUS research (heavy water) reactor in 1960. By 1962 Indian scientists had begun producing their own heavy water and in 1965 they separated plutonium for the first time.[9] All these accomplishments represented key steps in the realization of India's nuclear energy industry, but also had possible dual usages, especially the manufacture of weapons-grade plutonium. In turn, in April 1954 in the Indian parliament Nehru had called for the prohibition and elimination of nuclear weapons, as well as a halt to all nuclear testing. These calls came in an era when nuclear tests were being held above ground and eventually contributed to the Partial Test Ban Treaty of 1963 whereby atmospheric testing was banned (although France carried out such tests until 1974 and China until 1980). The ban led to the ascendancy of underground testing.

By the beginning of the 1960s, several states—other than the USA, which had used nuclear weaponry in 1945 against Japan at Hiroshima and Nagasaki—had proven nuclear capabilities. These states were the USSR (which first tested in 1949), the United Kingdom (which first tested in 1952), and France (which first tested in 1960). Thus, four of the five powers with permanent vetoes on the UNSC, the P-5 powers, had nuclear weapons in their arsenals. After India was heavily defeated in the 1962 war with China, another dimension emerged concerning the research side of India's nuclear programme—that of developing India's 'nuclear option'. The nuclear option meant undertaking research towards the development and production of nuclear weapons and associated technology (such as missiles, bombs and triggering devices) for possible future use. Such an option would only be realized if and when India's security was under direct threat from another nuclear weapons-ready state, and was regarded as a pragmatic policy.[10] An underlying aspiration to become a Great Power state additionally heightened the sense among India's elite that having nuclear weapons equated to being a Great Power like the P-5 states. Having nuclear weapons would also thwart the need for any security guarantees from any external (nuclear) powers, thus allowing India heightened strategic autonomy.

China's nuclear tests at Lop Nor on 16 October 1964 confirmed India's perceived threat, and added credence to the notion that nuclear weapons were force equalizers that overcame military asymmetries between states. In addition, nuclear weapons became seen as a shortcut to a modernized defence force that would exponentially improve India's security. After Indian leaders failed to illicit nuclear guarantees from the USA and the USSR (whereby India could be protected with their nuclear capabilities), pressure grew for India's nuclear option to be realized and in 1964 Indian Prime Minister Lal Bahadur Shastri launched a programme to reduce the time in

Chris Ogden

which India could be weapons capable to six months.[11] Chinese threats of opening a second front during the 1965 India–Pakistan war reinforced this necessity, as did the emergence of close China-Pakistan ties aimed at limiting India's regional influence.[12] Post-1964 the nuclear debate in India thus became dominated by the threat posed by China, the cost of nuclear weaponization and the morality of having such weapons.[13]

At the same time, India's leaders continued to call for a complete ban on nuclear testing and began campaigning in 1965 for a universal non-proliferation treaty. Such a treaty would be based upon those states with nuclear arsenals giving them up in order to inspire 'would-be nuclear' states not to attempt development. Within the international community at large and the P-5 powers, China's 1964 tests had also underlined the need to prevent further proliferation. The resultant Nuclear Non-Proliferation Treaty (NPT) was signed on 1 July 1968 by the United Kingdom, the USA and the USSR, and came into force on 5 May 1970. However, rather than fulfilling India's aims of banning all nuclear weapons, the NPT split the world into Nuclear Weapons States (NWS)—defined as those that had tested prior to 1 January 1967 and who could keep their weapons—and Non-Nuclear Weapons States (NNWS)—which were banned from ever possessing or developing nuclear weapons. The terms of the NPT were then to be reviewed every five years from 1970 onwards. Opposed to a treaty that did not provide 'equal and legitimate security'[14] for all states, and in order to keep the nuclear option open, India refused to sign the NPT. As such, India's leaders maintained the policy that, 'unless everyone closes the nuclear door, it is not in India's interests to do so.'[15] The NPT also increased Indian distrust of the international community, as it threatened India's autonomy, development and long-term power aims.

From Pokhran I to the 1990s: India's nuclear option emerges

By the early 1970s the ambiguity of the 'nuclear option' had effectively merged India's anti-nuclear and pro-nuclear opinions whereby a nuclear bomb would be developed but not used. This ambiguity ensured that India's weaponization programme continued but simultaneously reassured those in India's elite who both wanted a nuclear weapons capability (the hawks) and those that did not (the doves). At the same time, moral arguments as to the legitimacy of having nuclear weapons had become supplanted, courtesy of the NPT, by arguments more concerned with the nuclear 'haves' and 'have-nots'. These arguments appeared to cast India as a second-rate power, and nuclear bombs increasingly came to symbolize the national power, strength and development that India's leaders craved. India's refusal to declare South Asia a nuclear weapons-free zone, as proposed by the USA, underscored these aspirations and India's policy direction.[16]

In turn, although India had fought a successful conflict with Pakistan in 1971 (which led to the creation of Bangladesh), and had signed the 20-year Treaty of Peace, Friendship and Cooperation with the USSR, India's regional security environment was deteriorating. This deterioration was typified by the US tilt to Pakistan in the 1971 war (during which the USA sent ships into the Bay of Bengal), by deepening China-Pakistan ties and, most critically, by the US-China rapprochement under Richard Nixon and Mao Tse Tung from 1972. These relations effectively created a China-Pakistan-USA united front against India and were strengthened by China's regional nuclear monopoly. Such factors combined with a variety of domestic pressures,[17] and India's Prime Minister Indira Gandhi (the daughter of Nehru) decided to carry out a nuclear test to demonstrate India's capability. With a sufficiently developed nuclear programme at hand and under the codename 'Smiling Buddha', India undertook her first nuclear test on 18 May 1974—a test described as a Peaceful Nuclear Explosion (PNE). This description copied

292

other PNEs by the USA and the USSR (so denoted as they were for ostensibly non-military purposes, such as economic development), but was widely classified by both Indian and external observers as a weapons test. The test also became known as Pokhran I, named after the site where the test took place in the Thar Desert in Rajasthan.

At the time there was a sense that the PNE 'impart[s] to Indians a sense of security and self-confidence',[18] and was emblematic of India's criticism of the P-5 powers and the NPT. While France congratulated India on her successful tests, and the USSR and China were more muted yet critical in their responses, the USA and Canada removed all nuclear ties and assistance. In turn, the USA introduced sanctions on all its economic and military aid to India. The severity of this response came from India's open challenge to the P-5's anti-proliferation regime, but also from the fact that US (and Canadian) reactors had been used to help produce the fissile material used in the PNE. As a non-signatory of the NPT, India was also not under International Atomic Energy Agency (IAEA) safeguards—a factor that increased international anger. Furthermore (and enhancing Indian perceptions of an international conspiracy against it), the PNE led to the creation of the London Suppliers Group (later renamed the Nuclear Suppliers Group—NSG). This group aimed to control the export and transfer of materials that could be used to produce nuclear weapons. It thus prevented India from gaining assistance with its nuclear programme (including nuclear reactors, components, international scientific contacts and exchanges), but also emboldened Indian self-sufficiency and nuclear autonomy by further accentuating the gap between India's aspirations and her actual place in the world.

Also of influence on India's decision to test in 1974 was Pakistan's nuclear programme. In the 1950s and early 1960s this programme had initially mirrored India's with an Atomic Energy Commission established in 1956 and little consideration given to the military uses of atomic energy. By the mid-1960s, however, this approach changed as Pakistan's leaders argued that parity had to be achieved with India, particularly after Pakistan's defeat in the 1965 war. Pakistani policy-makers also became concerned with the state's lack of 'strategic depth' (commonly defined as the distance between her borders and major cities/core industrial areas). This issue was amplified by the loss in 1971 of the eastern part of her territory (which then formed the newly independent Bangladesh). The 1971 war thus led to strategic asymmetries between Pakistan and India, and led Pakistan's leaders to urge the weaponization of the state's nuclear capabilities from 1972 onwards. In turn, India's 1974 PNE 'increased, Pakistan's nuclear resolve'.[19] The multiple crises between India and Pakistan in the 1980s and 1990s increasingly came to include a consideration of any possible nuclear dimension, especially after the outbreak of insurgency in Kashmir from 1989.[20]

With the USSR's invasion of Afghanistan in 1979, the importance of the US-Pakistan relationship was reaffirmed. Keen to prevent a Soviet success in Afghanistan, the USA vastly increased the amount of its aid to Pakistan, amounting to US $400m. in 1979 and $3,200m. over the six years from 1981 to 1987.[21] While some of this aid could be used to develop Pakistan's nuclear weapons programme, these concerns did not surmount the USA's primary geopolitical aim of lending as much support as possible to various *mujahideen* resistance groups in Afghanistan. The US focus on (and need for) Pakistan further undermined India's position as she became ranked behind Pakistan and China in US calculations concerning South Asia, despite the events of 1971 and 1974. Under these conditions and combined with its previous research, Pakistan was 'nuclear weapons capable' by the mid 1980s—a success aided by the work of Abdul Qadeer Khan, the head of its uranium enrichment programme. Reflective of a shared awareness of this mutual nuclear capacity, in December 1985 India and Pakistan signed a Nuclear Non-Attack Agreement that prohibited the targeting of nuclear facilities in the event of conflict.

Both sides also began testing ballistic missiles that were theoretically capable of carrying a nuclear warhead, underlining how the two states were sufficiently technologically developed to build a nuclear weapon. In February 1988 India tested *Prithvi*, a short-range ballistic missile with a range of 150 km and capable of carrying a 1,000-kg warhead. In February 1989 Pakistan then tested its battlefield range ballistic missile, *Hatf I*, with a range of 70 km and capable of carrying a payload of 500 kg. In turn, in May 1989 India tested *Agni*, a short-range ballistic missile with a maximum range of 800 km with a 1,000-kg warhead. From this period onwards, both sides would continue to advance their respective missile technologies, expanding their range and payload capacities, and thus increasing the susceptibility of Indian, Pakistani and Chinese cities to potential attack. In 1988 US officials reported that Pakistan had gained a nuclear weapon design from China, along with related missile technology.[22]

Despite these developments, India's diplomatic efforts to achieve unilateral nuclear disarmament continued, and included a new dimension of self-restraint whereby India would not test any further nuclear weapons. As such, in 1978 India pursued negotiations for an international agreement on prohibiting the use or threat of use of nuclear weapons; in 1982 she called for a 'nuclear freeze' to prohibit the production of fissile materials for weapons and in 1988 Prime Minister Rajiv Gandhi tabled an Action Plan at the UN for the phased elimination of all weapons within a specific timeframe.[23] India also supported plans for a Nuclear Weapons Convention akin to the Biological Weapons Convention (opened for signature on 10 April 1972 and entering into force on 26 March 1975), and the Chemical Weapons Convention (opened for signature on 13 January 1993 and entered into force 29 April 1997), both of which India signed.

However, as had been the case for the NPT, India refused to sign the Comprehensive Nuclear Test Ban Treaty (CTBT) that opened for signature in New York on 24 September 1996. India argued that the Treaty favoured the P-5 powers, did not carry forward the disarmament process and, therefore, effectively diminished India's nuclear potential.

By the 1990s India's nuclear weapons programme appeared to face an existential crisis. India's nuclear stance appeared as ambiguous 'recessed deterrence', and she remained one of the 'main NPT holdout states',[24] along with Pakistan and Israel. Still contending with international sanctions, it seemed that many international proliferation controls were India-specific and intended to threaten her strategic autonomy and Great Power emergence. Thus, Indian analysts talked of a US-EU-Japan (and even US-China) concert against India. When the CTBT's entry into force provisos (Article 14) opened up a final testing window from September 1996 to September 1999, such nuclear inequity appeared to be explicit, particularly after China and France tested nuclear devices in 1995. The indefinite extension of the NPT in 1995 only compounded these perceptions. International rebuffs towards India's attempts at restricting proliferation had, however, continued to spur Indian leaders towards nuclear (weapons) development.[25] The end of the Cold War also signalled the demise of the USSR as a reliable counterweight for India to use against the international system, along with a now less meaningful NAM. Unable to benefit from Soviet arms trading and political support, India was increasingly isolated in a world now dominated by the USA—a position that threatened her regional security and global influence.

Pokhran II: from outlier to mainstream

In 1998 a newly elected government led by the Hindu nationalist Bharatiya Janata Party (BJP) came to power. With policies that promoted the image of a powerful, resurgent and dynamic India to the world, the BJP had consistently advocated the induction of nuclear weapons in their election manifestos. In particular, they recognized the symbolic appeal of testing nuclear

weapons. As the new Minister of External Affairs, Jaswant Singh argued that international proliferation controls amounted to a 'nuclear apartheid' that cast South Asia and Africa outside of
the dominant global 'nuclear security paradigm'.[26] Such discrimination placed India in a position inferior to the Great Powers, often in association with Pakistan. This perspective linked
with the repeated calls from India's strategic enclave of analysts and academics to resume testing.
Although India had the appropriate scientific–military nuclear infrastructure in place, it was
often only US pressure (and intelligence) that had stopped any new tests, particularly in the
mid-1990s.[27] These factors coupled with the BJP's desire to test—often bolstered by their
nationalism and a need to establish the power of their governing coalition.

Several other regional, global and systemic factors were also in evidence by 1998. Thus,
analysts noted how India's strategic environment had deteriorated due to China's rapid economic rise, which made India-China relations asymmetrical and unbalanced. They also
remarked upon how the USA was reluctant to become a declining power (and therefore
wanted to force its strategic view on the world), how Pakistan had gained (covert) nuclear
parity with India, and also how India's own economic growth would allow her to withstand
new sanctions in the event of new testing.[28] Others saw the need for a new Indian world view
that shifted away from Cold War strategic calculations, particularly with the continued absence
of a nuclear guarantee.[29] Against this backdrop, amid great secrecy, and only two months after
coming to power and after new Pakistani missile tests (*Ghauri*) on 6 April, the BJP Government
under Prime Minister Atal Behari Vajpayee tested five nuclear devices on 11 and 13 May 1998.
Confirming their own capabilities and in response to domestic pressures, Pakistan carried out its
own nuclear tests at Chaghai Hills in Baluchistan on 28 and 30 May.

Codenamed Operation *Shakti* (strength), and often called Pokhran II (having used the same
test site as the 1974 PNE), India's 1998 nuclear explosions were the first overt tests since the
NPT had come into force in 1970. They also came at a time when several states had recently
renounced their nuclear programmes, including South Africa (in 1993), Argentina (in 1995) and
Brazil (in 1998), all of which then signed the NPT. For India's elite, the tests were not only
about challenging the international non-proliferation regime and declaring India's nuclear prowess to the world, but also about the ongoing validation of her nuclear programme and technological development.[30] Thus, the BJP could have simply declared India to be a nuclear
weapons state in 1988, but during Pokhran II tested a thermonuclear device that required an as
yet untested nuclear triggering device. These issues backed up the credibility and expertise of
India's scientific community (thus continuing the central scientific drive of India's nuclear programme that dated back to the 1940s) and ensured that India had a proven and credible nuclear
deterrent. Furthermore, the Indian Government saw nothing illegal with the tests because as a
non-signatory of the NPT and CTBT, Pokhran II did not flout any international conventions.
In turn, her leaders noted that India's total of six nuclear tests in 1974 and 1998 paled in
comparison with the more than 2,000 tests held by the P-5 powers since 1945.

Despite initial sanctions from the USA and Japan after the tests, and almost universal condemnation, Pokhran II resulted in India moving from an outlier of little significance to the
international mainstream. Not only did the tests result in a new assertion of Indian autonomy in
international affairs, but they also provided their own nuclear guarantee—thus removing any
need for dependence on external states. Indeed, the tests transformed her global relations,
especially through their explicit enunciation of India's desire for a Great Power role, which was
supported by her increasing economic and technological strength. This combination made India
a state *needed* by other countries. In turn, policy concerning UNSC recognition became more
prominent, with a permanent seat now seen as 'not a quest' but as 'India's rightful due'.[31] While
certainly less idealist, more belligerent and increasingly pragmatic, India's leaders still argued for

universal nuclear disarmament. India used its acquisition of nuclear weapons as a new point of leverage, stating that it would give up its own proven nuclear capabilities in any new non-proliferation regime. Therefore, the paradox at the centre of India's nuclear programme between weaponization and disarmament that had been present since independence continued.

Also characteristic of this paradox, India's National Security Advisory Board unveiled the state's Draft Nuclear Doctrine on 17 August 1999. The main elements of the doctrine were a no-first-use policy, non-use of nuclear weapons against non-nuclear weapons states, a moratorium on nuclear tests, the non-export of nuclear technology and working towards universal nuclear disarmament. Conservative in nature, the doctrine displayed a commitment to using 'strategic nuclear assets as instruments of retribution in case deterrence fails', rather than as tools of aggression.[32] Such a nuclear doctrine was regarded as conducive to strategic stability in South Asia, which reassured China and the USA in particular, and created the image of India as a responsible nuclear power. Building upon the 1999 Draft, India's nuclear command structure was made public on 4 January 2003. These doctrines also accompanied the comprehensive review of national security in 1999 (the first since independence) that introduced a Nuclear Command Authority (NCA) under the control of the Prime Minister and the new post of National Security Adviser.

The impact of the Pokhran II tests varied. At the regional level, relations appeared to worsen, lead to conflict and then stabilize with Pakistan, whilst deteriorating and then significantly improving with China.[33] The most important impact of the 1998 tests was on the Indo–US relationship. After initial anger at their deception, the 1998 nuclear tests forced US attention onto South Asia—particularly given India's significance as the largest military (and now nuclear) power between the USA's two major military presences in the Persian Gulf and East Asia. Likewise, Pakistan's own tests placed the region under greater scrutiny and were a spur for serious dialogue between envoys from both sides. Lasting eight months, this was the longest sustained dialogue between high-level Indian and US officials since 1963. Against the backdrop of nuclear proliferation (with the USA urging India to sign the CTBT), Kashmir, economics and the US sanctions that had been in place since 1974, the talks transformed a difficult relationship between the two sides into a co-operative one. Critically, the USA accepted the new significance of India in terms of its economy, nuclear capabilities, stable democracy and large middle class. However, misgivings over US ties with Pakistan and China continued to underpin Indian sentiments.

These developments formed part of Indian elite attempts to strategically lift India away from South Asia towards a greater global role—itself an ongoing goal associated with acquiring nuclear weapons—and to improve her security environment. Enhanced Indo–US relations also provided possibilities to obtain (nuclear) technology transfers, which could significantly aid India's economic development. Through the Agreed Principles of 21 March 2000, both sides resolved to have a closer and better relationship in all spheres (including nuclear), and with the arrival of President George W. Bush, the USA dropped all demands for India to sign the CTBT and join the related Fissile Material Cutoff Treaty (FMCT). Common experiences of terrorism (for the USA the attacks in September 2001 and for India the attacks in December 2001 on its parliament), a shared democratic basis and a newly vocal Indian diaspora in the USA also helped to improve US-Indian relations.[34] This improved relationship also paid other dividends, including a more neutral tilt by the USA towards Pakistan (particularly during the 1999 Kargil conflict) and de-hyphenating India and Pakistan when US policy-makers thought of South Asia, as well as heightened economic, political, cultural and military co-operation.

Improved Indo–US relations led to the signing of their Next Steps in Strategic Partnership (NSSP) of January 2004, which focused on the three-fold issue of civilian nuclear energy, civilian space programmes and high technology trade, with a dialogue on missile defence being added. Under the joint US-India Civilian Nuclear Cooperation announcement (July 2005), India agreed to separate its civil and military nuclear facilities and to have all its civil nuclear facilities placed under IAEA safeguards. This agreement gave India de facto nuclear recognition. After being passed in the US Congress (via the Hyde Act, which allowed the modification of Section 123 of the 1954 US Atomic Energy Act), it was then blocked from scrutiny in the Indian parliament, although only after Prime Minister Manmohan Singh survived a no-confidence vote in July 2008. Subsequently, in August 2008 the IAEA approved the safeguards agreement with India, and in September 2008 the NSG granted India a waiver, over Chinese obstruction, to give India access to civilian nuclear technology and fuel from other countries—developments that effectively allowed India to sidestep the requirements of the NPT. In October 2008 the deal was legislated as the United States-India Nuclear Cooperation Approval and Non-Proliferation Enhancement Act, ending the US sanctions on nuclear trade that dated from the 1974 PNE.[35]

Conclusions

With a consistent policy of nurturing her atomic capabilities since independence, by the beginning of the 21st century India's nuclear weapons programme was established and overt. Through the 1998 tests and the subsequent rapid developments in Indo-US relations, India had become a de jure nuclear state despite being outside international proliferation controls—giving her a unique international status. Displaying a proven nuclear weapons capability within a conservative and defensive doctrine, India had shown her technological and scientific prowess to the world. These capabilities had increased India's (and South Asia's) prominence and importance in international relations (especially for the USA) and further bolstered India's aspirations to become a Great Power. In turn, India's domestic nuclear energy programme benefited from the 1998 tests, as a decade later she surmounted the international safeguards that had at one time restricted her. Aiding her continued economic growth and energy security, the signing of civilian nuclear agreements with the USA, France and Russia confirmed the success of this trajectory and firmly placed her in the group of established nuclear powers.

However, what of the paradox of weaponization and disarmament underpinning India's nuclear policy? While India's leaders had rallied against the 'nuclear haves', with the 1998 tests and their aftermath India appeared to have joined the nuclear apartheid which it abhorred. Even though she has yet to join the NPT or CTBT, India enjoys the privileges of the P-5 powers whereby they do not need to have their military nuclear facilities monitored. India's leaders have displayed remarkable tenacity to get her to this position, but it is unclear whether they will continue to pursue India's disarmament goals or now acquiesce to an international regime which their country has effectively joined. This situation is compounded by India's growing strategic nuclear capabilities, most particularly its recent acquisition of a 'nuclear triad' that gives her the ability to launch nuclear weapons from land, air and sea. Such an ability puts India on a par with the USA, Russia and China. Continued missile development also resulted in the successful testing in February 2010 of the Agni-III, which with a range of 3,500 km is capable of hitting Beijing, and which made India China's clear strategic rival.

Thus, while India's leaders continue to talk of disarmament, the morality of such aims has diminished in the face of India acquiring atomic weapons. This change suggests not so much that India's nuclear paradox has been lost, but simply underlined as a multi-faceted tool with which she can continue to gain her aspiration to Great Power status. Indeed, some Indian analysts advocate vast increases in her nuclear arsenal to include 150–200 warheads, and even to offer other states protection under an Indian nuclear umbrella.[36] As such, India could choose to join the NPT as a nuclear weapons state, thus gaining parity with the P-5 powers and introducing a new commonality with them that could aid her geopolitical power aspirations and stated aim of reforming the UNSC through gaining Permanent Member status. Such NPT commonality with the USA, Russia and China could be used as a more convincing base for universal nuclear disarmament—although the nuclear capabilities of these states currently far exceed India's. Finally, in an age of growing multilateralism and globalized economics, nuclear weapons appear more symbolic than strategic—with economic strength, technological advancement and influence in international forums more likely indicators of current and future power potential. India's nuclear weapons may thus aid her international rise but appear unlikely to define it.

Notes

1 A.B. Vajpayee, '*Suo Motu* Statement by Prime Minister Shri Atal Behari Vajpayee in Parliament', 27 May 1998, www.indianembassy.org.
2 Nehru quoted in, K. Bajpai, 'India: Modified Structuralism', in M. Alagappa (ed.), *Asian Security Practice: Material and Ideational Influences*, Stanford: Stanford University Press, 1999, p.173.
3 N. Ram, *Riding the Nuclear Tiger*, New Delhi: LeftWord Books, 1999, p.vii.
4 G. Perkovich, *India's Nuclear Bomb: the Impact on Global Proliferation*, Berkeley: University of California Press, 1999, p.9. See also I. Abraham, *Making of the Indian Atomic Bomb: Science, Secrecy and the Post-colonial State*, London: Zed Books, 1998; R. Chengappa, *Weapons of Peace: The Secret Story of India's Quest to be a Nuclear Power*, Delhi: HarperCollins, 2000; N. Koshy, 'Nuclear Weapons and India's Foreign Policy', in R. Harshe and K.M. Seethi (eds), *Engaging with the World: Critical Reflections on Indian Foreign Policy*, Hyderabad: Orient Longman, 2001.
5 S. Cohen, *India: Emerging Power,* Washington: Brookings Institution, 2001; S. Ganguly (ed.), *India as an Emerging Power*, London: Frank Cass, 2003; O. Marwah, 'Indian Nuclear and Space Programmes: Intent and Policy', *International Security*, Vol. 2, No. 2, 1997.
6 N. Ram, *Riding the Nuclear Tiger*, op. cit., p.48.
7 D. Hagerty, *The Consequences of Nuclear Proliferation: Lessons from South Asia*, Cambridge: MIT Press, 1998, p.72.
8 R. Jones, *India's Strategic Culture*, USA: Defense Threat Reduction Agency SAIC, 2006, www.dtra.mil.
9 A. Kapur, *Pokhran and Beyond: India's Nuclear Behaviour*, Delhi: Oxford University Press, 2000, p.51.
10 See A.G. Noorani, 'India's Quest for a Nuclear Guarantee', *Asian Survey*, Vol. 3, No. 7, 1967.
11 D. Hagerty, *The Consequences of Nuclear Proliferation*, op. cit., p.73.
12 S. Ganguly, 'Explaining the Indian Nuclear Tests of 1998', in R.G.C. Thomas and A. Gupta (eds), *India's Nuclear Security*, London: Lynne Rienner, 2000, p.44.
13 See M. Reiss, *Without the Bomb: The Politics of Nuclear Non-Proliferation*, New York: Columbia University Press, 1988.
14 Government of India, 'Evolution of India's Nuclear Policy'.
15 R. Basrur, 'Nuclear Weapons and Indian Strategic Culture', *Journal of Peace Research*, Vol. 38, No. 2, 2001, p.195.
16 N. Ram, *Riding the Nuclear Tiger*, op. cit., p.50.
17 R. Thomas and A. Gupta, 'Introduction', in R. Thomas and A. Gupta (eds), *India's Nuclear Security*, London: Lynne Rienner, 2000, p.2.
18 S. Chaturvedi, 'Representing Post-Colonial India: Inclusive/Exclusive Geopolitical Imaginations', in K. Dodds and D. Atkinson (eds), *Geopolitical Traditions: A Century of Geopolitical Thought*, London: Routledge, 2000, p.226.
19 D. Hagerty, *The Consequences of Nuclear Proliferation*, op. cit., p.74.
20 P. Chari, P. Cheema and S. Cohen, *Four Crises and a Peace Process: American Engagement in South Asia*, Delhi: HarperCollins, 2008.
21 D. Hagerty, *The Consequences of Nuclear Proliferation*, op. cit., p.79.
22 Ibid., p.128.
23 R. Gandhi, 'A World Free of Nuclear Weapons', 9 June 1988, www.indianembassy.org.

24 R. Thomas and A. Gupta, 'Introduction', op. cit., p.5; K. Bajpai, 'India: Modified Structuralism', op. cit., p.184.

25 R. Menon, *A Nuclear Strategy for India*, New Delhi: Sage Publications, 2000; S. Ganguly, 'Explaining the Indian Nuclear Tests', op. cit., p.51; A. Kapur, *Pokhran and Beyond*, op. cit., p.190.

26 J. Singh, 'Against Nuclear Apartheid', *Foreign Affairs*, Vol. 77, No. 5, 1998, p.48. See also M.E. Ahrari, 'Growing Strong: The Nuclear Genie in South Asia', *Security Dialogue*, Vol. 30, No. 4, 1999; P. Bidwai and A. Vanaik, *South Asia on a Short Fuse: Nuclear Politics and the Future of Global Disarmament*, Delhi: Oxford University Press, 1999; S. Pande, *India and the Nuclear Test Ban*, New Delhi: Institute for Defence Studies and Analyses, 1996, pp.5–24.

27 C. Fair, 'Learning to Think the Unthinkable: Lessons from India's Nuclear Tests', *India Review*, Vol. 4, No. 1, 2005, p.23; K. Pant, 'Pokharan-II and Security Ramifications', in *Bharatiya Janata Party 1980–2005: Party Document – Volume 9, Achievements & Looking Ahead*, New Delhi: BJP HQ, 2005.

28 See S. Cohen, 'Why did India "Go Nuclear"?', in R. Thomas and A. Gupta (eds), *India's Nuclear Security*, London: Lynne Rienner, 2000; H. Synnott, *The Cause and Consequences of South Asia's Nuclear Tests. Adelphi Paper 332*, Oxford: Oxford University Press, 1999; K. Frey, *India's Nuclear Bomb and National Security*, London: Routledge, 2006.

29 S. Ganguly, 'Explaining the Indian Nuclear Tests', op. cit.

30 P. Chawla, '"We Have Shown Them That we Mean Business": Interview with Atal Bihari Vajpayee', *India Today*, 25 May 1998; D. Ollapally, 'Mixed Motives in India's Search for Nuclear Status', *Asian Survey*, Vol. 41, No. 6, 2001; K. Pant, 'Pokharan-II and Security Ramifications', op. cit., p.85.

31 J. Singh, 'Interview: Diplomat Minister', *The Times of India*, 24 July 2000.

32 A. Tellis, 'India's Emerging Nuclear Doctrine: Exemplifying the Lessons of the Nuclear Revolution', *NBR Analysis*, Vol. 12, No. 2, 2001, p.iii. Also V. Khanna, *India's Nuclear Doctrine*, New Delhi: Samskriti, 2000; V. Nair, 'The Structure of an Indian Nuclear Deterrent', in A. Mattoo (ed.), *India's Nuclear Deterrent: Pokhran II and Beyond*, New Delhi: Har-Anand, 1999; H. Pant, 'India's Nuclear Doctrine and Command Structure: Implications for Civil-Military Relations in India', *Armed Forces & Society*, Vol. 33, No. 2, 2007, p.249; R. Roy-Chaudhury, 'India's Nuclear Doctrine: A Critical Analysis', *Strategic Analysis*, Vol. 33, No. 3, 2009.

33 Z. Jian, 'II Reaction to the Draft Indian Nuclear Doctrine', *China Report*, Vol. 35, 1999; Y. Jing-Dong, 'India's Rise after Pokhran II: Chinese Analyses and Assessments', *Asian Survey*, Vol. 41, No. 6, 2001. Also W. Walker, 'International Nuclear Relations after the Indian and Pakistani Test Explosions', *International Affairs*, Vol. 74, No. 3, 1998.

34 A. Carter, 'America's New Strategic Partner?', *Foreign Affairs*, Vol. 85, No. 4, 2006; K. Chenoy and A. Chenoy, 'India's Foreign Policy Shifts and the Calculus of Power', *Economic and Political Weekly*, Vol. 62, No. 35, 2007.

35 S. Ganguly, B. Shoup and A. Scobel (eds), *US-Indian Strategic Cooperation into the 21st Century: More than Words*, London: Routledge, 2006; U.N. Gupta, *International Nuclear Diplomacy and India*, New Delhi: Atlantic, 2007; J.A. Kirk, 'Indian-Americans and the US-India Nuclear Agreement: Consolidation of an Ethnic Lobby?', *Foreign Policy Analysis*, Vol. 4, No. 3, 2008.

36 See B. Karnad, *Nuclear Weapons and Indian Security: The Realist Foundations of Strategy*, Delhi: Macmillan, 2002. For example, Karnad proposes that such a nuclear umbrella could be used to protect Viet Nam from China.

27

India and climate change

Uttam Kumar Sinha

Without a careful long-term strategy, climate change may undermine our development efforts, with adverse consequences, across the board, on our people's livelihood, the environment in which they live and work and their personal health and welfare. It is also a challenge which encompasses the interests of both present and future generations [...] Today, climate change, generated by the cumulative accumulation of greenhouse gas emissions in the atmosphere, through human economic activity, threatens our planet. There is a real possibility of catastrophic disruption of the fragile life-sustaining ecological system that holds this world together. Science is now unequivocal on this assessment.[1]

(Manmohan Singh)

Introduction

Climate change is an all-encompassing issue that directly touches upon human development and people's livelihood. It has effects in combination with other major issues and such interaction is impacting the international order. For much of the past decade climate change has shaped and dominated the international agenda and will increasingly be a game-changer in the future.

The science of climate change, blunt in its observation, points to the fact that the planet's climate system is being pushed beyond its carrying capacity by dangerous anthropogenic interference. However, the science has not positively converged with political decisions. In fact, as scientific evidence becomes far more noticeable, the politics of climate change is becoming stubbornly intractable. The search for a global solution to climate change based on 'common but differentiated responsibilities', the position taken by India and other countries like the People's Republic of China, has thus resulted in a political impasse.[2] This indeed is an entrenched irony of the international system. While states are prime movers of issues, they, however, tend to determine actions by perception of sovereignty, national interest and security. The science of climate change may have awakened us but the politics of it remain perennially divided and contested.[3] Characteristically, climate change has entered the realm of negotiations. Issues such as national action plans (rather than global binding commitments), leadership roles and historical responsibilities are determining countries' positions and, to a large extent, defining their foreign policy agenda.

For states, climate change fundamentally remains a challenge and a dilemma. It is difficult to overcome their natural inclination of being protectionist and to simultaneously frame stringent adaptation and mitigation policies to keep global warming below two degrees Celsius. The broad approach seems to imply a global emission 'peak' by 2015, followed by a low-carbon emission path that is expected to drop by 6% per year before reaching a desired '80% below 1990 levels' in 2050. This suggests that carbon dioxide (CO_2) concentrations would peak near 425 ppm. (parts per million) before they begin to decline. As global negotiations for the period beyond 2012 proceed—structured on the notable achievements in 1997 of the United Nations Framework Convention on Climate Change (UNFCCC) and its Kyoto Protocol—there is considerable uncertainty as to whether a 'Grand Deal', which failed in Copenhagen in December 2009, will ever come about, or what format a post-Kyoto regime will take beyond 2012.[4] Nevertheless, while there is uncertainty over the structure and the mechanism, the science continues to forewarn that global warming is continuing unabated.

This chapter will examine India's perceptions on the problem of climate change and its negotiating position. It will also evaluate the policies and actions that India has initiated, particularly post-Copenhagen, to contain the challenges of climate change.

India and climate change: perceptions and positions

India's position on climate change has been articulated with a conviction and determination probably unmatched in recent years on any other issue. Indian negotiators are known for saying that they did not create the climate problem, emphasizing at every meeting the inequity and injustice of expecting India to cut down its carbon emissions. This underpins India's acceptance of the 1997 Kyoto Protocol. As its government ministers argue, 'India stands by the UN Framework Convention Treaty on Climate Change and the Kyoto Protocol. This mechanism recognizes the "common but differentiated responsibilities" of the countries in the matter of reduction of green house emissions. The Convention also recognizes that as developing countries grow, their emissions are bound to increase'.[5]

At the heart of India's climate change stand is the argument that it must be allowed to pollute on a 'per capita basis' equal to the advanced industrialized countries. India has thus been propounding the 'per capita emissions' line. The 'per capita emissions' are central to India's position on carbon emissions reduction. This has formed the basis of India's criticism of the UNDP *Human Development Report* in 2007, which stipulated an 80% reduction in CO_2 emissions by developed countries and 20% reduction by developing countries by 2050, while also noting that, 'emissions of CO_2 from India may have become a matter of global concern for climate security'.[6] While it seems egalitarian, Montek Singh Ahluwalia, Deputy Chairman of the Planning Commission, thought that if 'per capita emissions' were considered then countries like India would still have to bear a bigger burden as per the UN Development Programme (UNDP) recommendation. Instead, he reasoned that developing countries should be allowed to increase their per capita emissions and the developed world should reduce them: 'you could say, for example, that the West has done most of the emissions for the last 140 years and the problem that we have is because of the total emissions that have been done in the last 140 years, so actually it shouldn't be per capita. We should be a little higher and they should be a little low because of all the damage that they have done'.[7]

Such a position immediately shifts the responsibility on to the shoulders of the developed countries to drastically cut emissions if the world is to meet the target of keeping global warming within the generally agreed 'safe limit' of two degrees Celsius, as determined by the Intergovernmental Panel on Climate Change (IPCC). It also allows India the space and time to grow at a sustained pace and strengthen its poverty alleviation and developmental programmes. However, even more significant for India, particularly when it comes to the international forum, is the assurance that, 'despite our developmental imperatives, our per capita GHG [greenhouse gas] emissions will not exceed the per capita GHG emissions of the developed industrialized countries'.[8] It reflects, on the one hand, a position of confidence and self belief in its economic policies and, on the other, a signal to the developed world that it will not be pressurized in the negotiations. This is carried forward in India's adaptation and mitigation policies, which state that, 'the most important adaptation measure is development itself'.[9] On mitigation, the 11th Five Year Plan is unequivocal: 'with a share of just 14 per cent of global emissions, any amount of mitigation by India will not affect climate change'.[10] The document calls for action by developed countries and a burden-sharing formula based on historic culpability, 'common but differentiated responsibilities' and the 'per capita emissions' principle.

The 'per capita emissions' argument has become a strong counter-response to the unsustainable consumption patterns of the rich industrialized nations and is in consonance with the UNFCCC, which recognizes the rights of developing countries to economic development and also the 'common but differentiated responsibilities' of different countries. Contrasting calculations have long been made. In 1991 it was the basic point made by Parikh that, 'only 25 per cent of the global population lives in the rich industrialised countries but they emit more than 70 per cent of the total global CO_2 emissions', and that 'Indian citizens emit less than 0.25 tonnes of carbon per year whereas a citizen of the USA, emits more than 5.5 tonnes'.[11] In the UNDP *Human Development Report 2007/2008*, India's CO_2 emissions per capita had gone up from a 1990 figure of 0.8 to 1.2, but still remained significantly below the figures for developed countries like the USA (20.6), Canada (20.0), Australia (16.2), Japan (9.9), and the Organisation for Economic Co-operation and Development (OECD) average of 11.5.[12] Such comparative figures add immediate legitimacy to the 'per capita emissions' stand, emphasizing the need for an equitable *and* efficient solution—equity in terms of equal allocation of global environmental space to all, and efficiency through a system of tradable emission quotas. This has framed India's long-standing argument that emissions by the poor who live on the margins of subsistence should be considered a basic human right and should not be counted when ascribing responsibilities for emissions reduction.

The tenets of India's argument and negotiations on climate change have consistently remained 'equity with social justice'—the right to develop and a need-based living. It draws inspiration from what Mahatma Gandhi, regarded as an apostle of human ecology, is widely cited as having said, that 'the earth provides enough for everyman's needs but not for everyman's greed'. The 'need' and 'greed' add contestation to the 'subsistence emissions' and 'lifestyle emissions' debate. Thus, the right to develop, right to utilize resources and not be penalized by international constraints is held by India. As Manmohan Singh put it:

> Our people have a right to economic and social development and to discard the ignominy of widespread poverty. For this we need rapid economic growth. But I also believe that ecologically sustainable development need not be in contradiction to achieving our growth objectives. In fact, we must have a broader perspective on development. It must include the quality of life, not merely the quantitative accretion of goods and services. Our people want higher standards of living, but they also want clean water to drink, fresh air to breathe and a green earth to walk on.[13]

India clearly feels that it is owed an incalculable ecological, social and economic debt by the industrialized, developed countries. The ecological debt also includes the illegitimate appropriation of the atmosphere and the planet's absorption capacity by the industrialized countries. The climate change debate in India has brought in a new set of dynamics and narratives where on the one side there is the politics of blame and on the other recognition of a shared dilemma and a growing need for action.

Energy challenges and climate change

For a rising economic power like India, the interplay between energy, environment and development policy is complex and challenging. There are issues of eradication of poverty and economic growth, on the one hand, and the sustainability of natural resources and energy choices on the other. India's development path with a projected growth rate of 8%–9% is inextricably dependent upon external fossil fuel supply and, in the absence of sufficient domestic oil resources, its quest for energy security is paramount.[14] While global mitigation strategies are still being deliberated, India's domestic strategy sets forth an approach towards a low-carbon economy, principally to reduce its dependency on fossil fuels without compromising its steady growth rate.

India's energy scenario in the coming decades will largely depend on the energy use choices. However, at any reduced level, fossil fuels will remain the dominant source of energy in any conceivable scenario up to 2030 and in all probability beyond. According to projections by the IPCC, India will experience dramatic increases in energy and greenhouse gas emissions in the world *if* it sustains an 8% annual economic growth rate or more, since its primary energy demand will then multiply at least three- to four-times its present levels. There is now a clear recognition that business-as-usual is no longer tenable.

India's Integrated Energy Policy, adopted in 2006, is a response to managing the energy agenda through various measures. Such measures include:[15]

- Promoting energy efficiency in all sectors
- Need for mass transport
- Encouraging renewables
- Accelerating nuclear and hydro electric power as clean energy
- Research and development in clean energy technologies
- Reforming energy markets to ensure price competition

The Integrated Energy Policy is bolstered by other relevant legislation, including the New and Renewable Energy Policy (2005), the Rural Electrification Policy (2006), the National Environment Policy (2006) and the Environment Impact Assessment (2006). However, the 11th Five Year Plan suggestion for faster and more inclusive growth, targeting 9%–10% from 2007–12, seems far too ambitious. Calculations suggest that India needs about 500 megawatts (MW) of power each week for the next 25 years to sustain the present growth rate of 8%. India's current installed power capacity is close to 145 gigawatts (GW), of which the overwhelming majority, 52%, comes from coal-based generation (76,299 MW), and with renewables, including hydro electricity, accounting for 34%.[16]

For a country of India's size and energy requirements, 145 GW is not sufficient. The growth rate will be undermined and compromised by the lack of available power. Increasing the installed power capacity to 225 GW by 2012 and then to 800 GW by 2030, along with the corresponding expansion of the energy infrastructure, would come at a huge cost. For India, finance for development is crucial and, therefore, it needs to be positively engaged in the multilateral forum. Such an expansion also implies a high CO_2 emissions rise, since much of it will continue to come from fossil fuel-based energy. The dilemma pertains to which energy pathways to take. The Planning Commission in its 2006 study noted that the projected CO_2 emissions from various different scenarios ranging from coal-dominant to low-carbon ones found a difference of nearly 35% between the best-case scenario and the worst. In the business-as-usual scenario emissions will rise from the present 1.2 gigtons (Gt) per capita per year, to 5.5 Gt per capita per year by 2031–32. In the best-case scenario, or low-emissions scenario, the rise would be to 3.9 Gt per capita per year.[17]

The emphasis for India needs to be on pursuing carbon abatement policies that minimize energy consumption and reduce dependency on oil imports. Not surprisingly the 11th Five Year Plan commits the country to reducing energy intensity per unit of GHGs by 20% from the period 2007–17. India's energy intensity level of 0.16 is below the world average of 0.21 and the US figure of 0.22, with Indian officials like R. Shahi arguing that, 'lowering the energy intensity of GDP [gross domestic product] growth through higher energy efficiency is important for meeting India's energy challenge and ensuring its energy security [...] there is room to improve and energy intensity can be brought down significantly in India with current commercially available technologies'.[18] It was significant in his exposition on energy policy that Shahi brought out the basic tensions surrounding climate change and India's position:

> However, it is important to keep the perspective in view. Per capita emission of carbon dioxide are the highest in high income countries [...] Development process will necessitate consumption of higher levels of energy. While discussing the concerns on issues like climate change and global warming, it will not be equitous to put together countries with comparatively low per capita emissions and whose large population are yet to see the fruits of development and respectable standard of living with countries which are already developed and have very high per capita income and still have ever growing energy consumption. Efforts should be to achieve a unit of human welfare with least possible energy consumption.[19]

Certainly there exists a large potential for energy saving. For example, one-third of total energy is used for domestic cooking purposes, thus efficient cooking processes are a high priority. Also the Bureau of Energy Efficiency (BEE) started an energy labelling programme for appliances in 2006, which is expected to lead to significant savings in electricity annually. While many of the measures are directed towards greater energy efficiency, price reforms and removal of subsidies to encourage a more carbon-friendly market, the crux of the problem lies in reducing fossil fuel energy or, in other words, focusing on clean energy options.

The National Action Plan on Climate Change (NAPCC), released by the Prime Minister in June 2008, is a plan of action and sets out key initiatives on energy and climate connect. The Prime Minister noted: 'our vision is to make India's economic development energy efficient. Over a period of time we must pioneer a graduated shift from economic activity based on fossil fuels to one based on non-fossil fuels and from reliance on non-renewable and depleting sources of energy to renewable sources'.[20] The NAPCC has eight 'missions':

- National solar mission
- National mission for enhanced energy efficiency
- National water mission
- National mission on sustainable habitat
- National mission for sustaining the Himalayan ecosystem

- National mission for green India
- National mission for sustainable agriculture
- National mission on strategic knowledge for climate change

The NAPCC identifies measures and mechanisms that link development objectives to addressing climate change effectively, with a clear focus on renewable energies that are scalable and sustainable. There is now traction in India's initiatives and investments on clean energy. India has the fourth largest installed wind energy capacity and is the second largest biogas producer. Under the 11th Five Year Plan a target of 14 GW–20 GW of additional renewable capacity are planned. Further, India actively supports the Clean Development Mechanism (CDM) under the UNFCCC and has effectively employed it.

India's vulnerability to climate change

In spite of the controversies questioning the credibility of the IPCC, especially over 'alarmist' projections and science concerning the extent of Himalayan glacier melt, the Indian Government regards the IPCC as an important scientific body, albeit not sacrosanct.[21] In spite of the head of the IPCC being an Indian, Rajendra Pachauri, apprehensions have always existed and more often than not been perceived on the basis of the IPCC being driven and dominated by the concerns of the industrialized world. The current leadership effort has been to build a network of scientific institutions in order to develop 'domestic' research capacities on climate issues, especially on glacial studies.

Nevertheless, there is growing recognition in India of the need for 'precautionary principles' based on the vulnerability and risks that climate change poses, and in this regard the IPCC findings have been instructive. According to the Ministry of Environment and Forests (MoEF) report of October 2007, India is already spending over 2% of its GDP on measures to adapt to the impact of climate variability. The costs are high, with some estimates that India could suffer a loss of 9%–13% of its GDP in real terms by 2100 in a no-change scenario, and the precautionary principles, therefore, gain much credence.[22]

The IPCC *2001 Report* projected for India a 2.7–4.3 degrees Celsius rise by 2080 and further predicted a sea-level rise up to 88cm by 2100 in the Indian subcontinent. The report stated: 'Rising sea levels could threaten coastal mangrove and wetland systems, and increase the flood risk faced by a quarter of India's coast dwelling population'.[23] In its *2007 Report* some of the IPCC projections for South Asia and India included the following:[24]

- Glacier melt in the Himalayas projected to increase flooding, followed by decreased river flows as the glaciers recede.
- Freshwater availability, particularly in large river basins, projected to decrease, which along with population growth and increasing demand could adversely affect more than 1,000m. people by 2050.
- Coastal areas, especially heavily populated mega-delta regions, will be vulnerable to increased flooding from the sea and rivers.
- Crop yields could decrease by up to 30% in South Asia by the middle of the 21st century, with the risk of hunger projected to be very high.

The above projections and findings underscore India's vulnerability to climate change that could severely test its governance and institutional resilience. It could, if not comprehensively dealt with, become a political challenge difficult to overcome.

However, while India is exposed to climate change risks, it has not yet ascertained how vulnerable it is to climate change. Risk is the probability of the event happening. Vulnerability is expressed by the negative effects of climate change and taken as an extreme form. India is vulnerable to the consequences of climate change like food shortages, droughts, flooding, disease outbreaks, alteration in maritime ecosystems, increased frequency of national disasters, melting of glaciers, degradation of coastal areas, migration leading to demographic shifts, etc. Agriculture will become increasingly sensitive to climate change, while concerns over emissions could lead to protectionism in international trade. As for the 700m. people in rural India who are dependent on the most climate change-sensitive sectors for their livelihoods—agriculture, forests and fisheries—the future will bring declining crop yields, degraded land, water shortages and ill health. The unexpected and extreme weather conditions accompanied by climate change will also render traditional weather knowledge useless.

Climate change and its impact on water resources are likely to emerge as a critical issue in India's relations with its neighbours. Seven of the world's major rivers originate in the Himalayan and Tibetan plateaux and are a source for about 40% of humanity living in China, India, Nepal, Bhutan, Myanmar, Bangladesh, Pakistan and other South-East Asian countries like Laos, Cambodia and Viet Nam. In the Indian neighbourhood, water relations (or water security) will be high on the political agenda. In Pakistan, anti-India propaganda routinely highlights how India is bent upon diverting the Indus waters and converting Pakistan into a desert. Bangladesh has also been critical of India on water-related issues. India's neighbourhood is unstable; fragile states will come under considerable stress and strain due to climate change. Tensions between India and Pakistan are likely to arise over water issues due to reduced flows in the Indus River Basin. Over-fishing could become an issue between India and Sri Lanka. India could face climate refugee inflows from neighbouring countries, particularly Bangladesh and the Maldives. Water issues are likely to assume greater salience in Sino-Indian relations as well, particularly in the context of reports that China is planning to divert the waters of Yarlung-Tsangpo, which originates from Tibet and flows into India as the Brahamaputra, to its northern territories.

Climate change will also have an impact on the war-fighting capabilities of the Indian military. Changing weather patterns will have to be factored into mission planning. The melting of snows and the accompanying flash floods could undermine the military's mobility, its communication facilities, stock levels and logistics. Simultaneously, the armed forces will be required to prepare new missions geared towards relief and rescue. The increasing frequency of natural disasters will require the armed forces to gear adequately to meet these disasters and they will also have to focus on immediate and long-term planning to meet the consequences of natural disasters.

The key ministry traditionally leading on domestic policy-making has been the Ministry of Environment and Forests, while the Ministry of External Affairs leads on international negotiations such as those under the UNFCCC. Over the years, other ministries with a mandate to help frame India's climate change policy have emerged. This has also led to overlapping objectives, particularly with ministries mandated with energy-related portfolios such as coal, power, petroleum and natural gas, and new and renewable resources. Interestingly, the Ministry of New and Renewable Energy (MNRE) is the first such in the world and draws its antecedence from the Commission for Additional Sources of Energy (CASE), which came about in the backdrop of the oil shocks of the 1970s. In order to create policy co-ordination and coherence, in June 2007 the Council on Climate Change was constituted under the direct chairmanship of the Prime Minister, to 'coordinate national action plans for assessment, adaptation and mitigation of climate change and to advise the Government on proactive measures that can be taken by India to deal with the challenge of climate change'. The military has also been closely involved in the protection and management of ecology. An ecological cell was established in the Army headquarters under the Quartermaster General Branch in the early 1990s, since which time the Indian Army has established eight Ecological Task Force (ETF) units and is probably the only army in the world with troops dedicated to greening arid deserts and barren mountains. The National Disaster Management Authority (NDMA), under the chairmanship of the Prime Minister, came into existence under the Disaster Management Act of 2005 and is the nodal agency for effective disaster management.

India as an emerging power

At the 1972 UN Conference on Human Environment in Stockholm, regarded as a prototype for the numerous other UN-sponsored global meets on environmental issues and which helped to establish the United Nations Environmental Programme (UNEP), Prime Minister Indira Gandhi lent credence to the 'South' developing countries' point of view by stressing the poverty of the developing countries as the single greatest contributor to environmental degradation. The Stockholm Conference also signalled India's formal entry into the global debate on environmental issues as a torch-bearer of the developing countries' right to develop. In the 1992 Rio Conference 'per capita equity' was the bedrock of India's international stance.

At the Copenhagen Summit in 2009 India, along with Brazil, South Africa and China (BASIC), emerged as key players in the negotiating process. Though fragmented in outlook, these leading developing countries share a common set of concerns around the developmental impact of climate change itself and, concurrently, a suspicion that the evolving regime on climate change is aimed at shifting an unfair burden of accountability for it onto them. Post-Copenhagen the growing gap between perspectives held by industrialized and emerging economies has increased, raising the spectre of a new North–South divide over climate change. While the emerging geopolitical alliance between the four large developing BASIC countries will seek to shape the future contours of negotiations on emission reductions, a counter-response can be equally expected, particularly towards China and India as global culprits for CO_2 emissions. In fact, the European Union (EU) refers to the two as 'advanced developing countries', trying to make a distinction that India and China should not take refuge in the developing world indices, but should have a new set of parameters to evaluate their particular responsibilities. Calculated backlashes from the industrialized countries, such as the use of environmental regulations as barriers to trade, will be likely and the imposition of such penalties could undermine vital developmental gains for the emerging economies.

India, as in the 1970s, will be central in recasting the relationship between the older industrialized and newer industrializing worlds. The prevailing approach to global governance, symbolized by the ad hoc inclusion of these countries through the G8 plus mechanism, has already given way to an institutionalized engagement in the form of the broadened membership of the G20. As Manmohan Singh told the G8 Summit, 'the quicker you reduce your emissions, the greater the incentive for us to follow [...] If we are to honestly address the climate change challenge, it is important that we recognize the right to equal sustainable development and historical responsibility'.[25] India, through the grouping, will echo its long-standing position on non-binding commitment on emissions cuts and call for the industrialized countries to adopt quantifiable targets commensurate with their historical impact on the global climate.

With a not-so-substantive Copenhagen Accord and a general inertia setting in, thinking beyond the Kyoto framework and exploring other multilateral arrangements is a likely outcome. The Asia-Pacific Partnership for Clean Development and Climate (APP), formed in 2005 with member countries including Australia, China, India, Japan, the Republic of Korea

(South Korea) and the USA, will draw considerable attention. A transregional grouping like IBSA (India, Brazil and South Africa) along with other developing countries like China could coalesce around carbon emissions and articulate a multilateral arrangement on 'restricting' emissions rather than 'reducing' them. In fact, IBSA + China constitutes the BASIC countries. Climate change was the subject of the BASIC summit in June 2010, in which suggestions to sideline the 'historic responsibility' obligations of existing developed Western countries were rejected.[26] Moreover, they are increasingly looking to less-developed areas of the world (and in some cases developed resource countries like Canada and Australia), to address their energy needs, especially through state-supported oil and coal exploration and commercial development of bio-fuels. Whether their complementary positions on climate change can help bridge their contrasting interpretation of global politics, however, will have to be seen.

Climate change debate post-Copenhagen

As the most populated democratic country, India has found the 'per capita equity' argument always appealing. Not only with the climate change debate, but on many other occasions, whether on financial contributions to the UN or seeking a Permanent Seat on the UN Security Council, India has projected its high population and unbridled growth convincingly. Such a position has been a matter of convenience and justification for not taking action that does not suit India's interests. However, the 'per capita emissions' stance, particularly in the post-Copenhagen period, has domestically generated a great deal of introspection, with frequent argument that a new and confident India needs to go beyond its narrow confinements and grandstanding and take the lead in climate change action. Others take a far more conservative view, arguing that the 'principle of equity' based on an 'equal per capita approach' is not only a principled position but has national consensus cutting across party lines. India's negotiators, having invested considerable diplomatic and lobbying effort, are sensitive to any counter views that they feel compromise the foreign policy of India.

Such negotiators believe that this consensus is being challenged by the Minister of Environment, Jairam Ramesh, who has often indicated that India should abandon the 'per capita approach'. According to Ramesh, 'this common but differentiated responsibilities argument can be given but the political economy in today's world being what it is [...] if we have superpower ambitions and superpower visions then that should take on superpower responsibilities, and superpower responsibilities include greater awareness on the international dimensions'.[27] It is a perceptive interpretation of the geopolitical reality. It is unlikely that India and China will be exempted from the CO_2 emissions reduction requirements in the post-2012 scenario, and likely that India will be called upon to make some modest reductions. This is instructive. India has not been an historic emitter and has thus justified its position on emissions cuts, but it will be a large future emitter, a fact that it cannot negate. For example, during the period 1990–2000 emissions in the USA grew by 16%, while in India they grew by 51%. The future will see a larger carbon footprint. What is at stake here for the critics of the Minister's approach is the damage to India's credibility in the negotiations and the importance of a national consensus on a major policy reversal that is approved by parliament.

The whole debate demonstrates the reviewing, revamping and re-examination of policies, arguments and strategies on climate change. This is vital, as interests change with a changing world. Many questions emerge: whether the 'per capita emissions' principle is a defensive stance today with a changing balance of power. How does India balance its domestic interests and yet contribute to its aspirations of a global emerging power? Does the 'per capita equity' need to be measured with India's own population, since the rich in India are as high in their consumption and carbon footprint as the average person in the industrialized world? Are 'per capita emissions' a justification of India's failure to deal effectively with climate change and a protective mechanism for the rich and affluent? Does looking away from the 'per capita' perspective herald a new thinking and put India at the forefront of contemporary states searching for solutions and breaking deadlocks on complex issues?

Conclusions

Climate change presents unprecedented challenges and opportunities for India. In the 1970s India's position was based on ideological preconception and linked to development and poverty. It was articulated with unmatched conviction. Since the 1990s the climate debate has been about projection, posturing and grandstanding. In recent times, particularly post-Copenhagen, there seems to be a rethink and re-evaluation that suggests that Indian policy-makers, along with business and industry, are responding to both the energy challenge and climate change challenge. India's 'per capita emissions' position has been heatedly discussed, and with increasing intensity domestically. Stressing emissions rights is one thing, but stressing other larger objectives of a climate-responsible development agenda is equally important both in operative and functional terms. India needs a new narrative that is bold and forward-looking and not trapped in regressive approaches.

Emissions rights cannot be situated outside the framework of equitable human development. India's argument on emissions rights is valuable to the extent of being allowed the space and time to develop, but it cannot be an excuse for not taking effective action to curb the dangers of climate change. India needs to ensure a conducive global environment for furthering its economic interests, enhanced trade and investment inflows, technology transfers and energy security. Politically, as the international system transitions to real multipolarity, existing power-holders may seek to freeze this move, to continue the existing inequities in the international order. To break such exclusivity, India needs to balance its stance on external climate change negotiations with its internal action plan. India should be seen as the change. Taking unilateral steps in mitigating emissions and setting voluntary targets for energy efficiency should convey the message that it is not a deal-breaker but a game-changer. The critical choice that India will have to make is when to join the emissions-reduction process, first on a voluntary basis and later with legally binding targets. For India, it will not be an either/or situation any more. It will necessitate a major shift of approach, strategy and, more importantly, a *mindset*.

Notes

1 M. Singh, 'Prime Minister's Speech on Release of Climate Change Action Plan', 30 June 2008, pmindia.nic.in. See also U. Sinha, 'Climate Change: Issues and Divides', *Strategic Analysis*, Vol. 33, No. 2, 2009, for general India-related analysis.
2 'It is very important that the provisions and principles of the Convention, especially common but differentiated responsibilities and respective capabilities, are respected in these negotiations and their outcomes in letter and spirit', quoted from M. Singh, 'Intervention at Major Economies Meeting on Climate Change', G-8 Summit, 9 July 2008, pmindia.nic.in.
3 For an interesting account of the science and politics of climate change, see A. Dessler and E. Parson, *The Science and Politics of Global Climate Change*, Cambridge: Cambridge University Press, 2006, pp.34–37.
4 The Copenhagen Accord adopted on 18 December 2009 laid down that: a) CO_2 emissions would be kept below two degrees Celsius, with efforts to 'peak' them as early as possible. No binding emission cuts were proposed; and b) developed countries commit to a goal of mobilizing jointly US $100,000m. a year by 2020 to address the needs of developing countries, especially with regard to mitigation, adaptation, capacity building, technology development and transfer.

5 R. Shahi, 'India's Strategy Towards Energy Development and Energy Security', Board of International Energy Agency, 12 December 2006, p.19, www.powermin.nic.in.
6 UNDP, *Human Development Report 2007/2008. Fighting Climate Change: Human Solidarity in a Divided World*, New York: United Nations Development Programme, 2007, pp.7, 44.
7 See Ahluwalia's interview, 'Everyone in the World Should Have an Equal Carbon Footprint. Pollution Per Person should be Equalised', *Indian Express*, 3 December 2009.
8 M. Singh, 'Intervention at Major Economies Meeting on Climate Change', G-8 Summit, 9 July 2008.
9 Statement by Kapil Sibal at the 95th Indian Science Congress, 2008.
10 Government of India, *Eleventh Five Year Plan 2007–2012*, New Delhi: Planning Commission, June 2008, p.205.
11 See K. Parikh, *Consumption Patterns: The Driving Force of Environmental Stress*, New Delhi: Indira Gandhi Institute of Development Research, 1991.
12 UNDP, *Human Development Report 2007/2008*, op. cit., p.69.
13 M. Singh, 'Prime Minister's Speech on Release of Climate Change Action Plan', 30 June 2008, pmindia.nic.in.
14 The *Eleventh Five Year Plan (2007–2012)*, op. cit., sets a target of 9% growth in the five-year period, reaching 10% by the end of the Plan.
15 Government of India, *Integrated Energy Policy: Report of the Expert Committee*, New Delhi: Planning Commission, 2006, pp.15–16.
16 Government of India, *India's Installed Power Capacity*, New Delhi Ministry of New and Renewable Energy, 2008.
17 Government of India, *Integrated Energy Policy*, op. cit., p.50.
18 R. Shahi, 'India's Strategy Towards Energy Development and Energy Security', op. cit., pp.5–6. The figure, cited by Shahi, is in terms of kgOE / $GDP PPP, i.e. kilograms of oil equivalent per dollar of GDP expressed in purchasing power parity terms.
19 Ibid., p.19.
20 M. Singh, 'Prime Minister's Speech on Release of Climate Change Action Plan', op. cit.
21 In 2010 the relationship between India and the UN's IPCC hit rough weather, despite the fact that Rajendra Pachauri, head of the IPCC, had been nominated by the Government of India. India's environment minister, Jairam Ramesh, openly criticized the IPCC's projection of early disappearance of the Himalayan glaciers as 'not based on an iota of scientific evidence', and being scare tactics for which the Panel 'has to do a lot of answering'. See 'India Criticises UN Warning on Himalayan Glacier Melt', *BBC*, 19 January 2010, news.bbc.co.uk.
22 Carbon Disclosure Project, *Report 2007. India*, p.12, www.cdproject.net. Also, 'India More Vulnerable to Climate Change', *Times of India*, 3 September 2008.
23 United Nations Intergovernmental Panel on Climate Change (UNFCCC), *Climate Change 2007: Synthesis Report. Summary for Policymakers – An Assessment of the Intergovernmental Panel on Climate Change*, New York: United Nations Intergovernmental Panel on Climate Change, 2007, p.13.
24 Ibid.
25 M. Singh, 'Intervention at Major Economies Meeting on Climate Change', op. cit.
26 N. Sethi, 'BASIC Meet on Climate Equity in June', *Times of India*, 3 May 2010.
27 M. Mehta, 'Per Capita Fig Leaves and Melting Glaciers – Will the Real Jairam Ramesh Please Stand Up?', 20 August 2009, www.climatechallengeindia.org.

28

India and outer space

S. Vijayasekhara Reddy

Introduction

After the USSR and the USA heralded the dawn of the space age in 1957, almost all countries took it for granted at the outset that major space programmes were beyond their financial scope. Even the industrialized nations of Europe, with the possible exception of France, shared this outlook. The Indian Prime Minister, Jawaharlal Nehru, stated in early 1960 that although India was 'high up in the list of advanced countries' in the field of atomic energy, it could not go far in space exploration because of its want of resources.[1] Yet the appeal of space remained strong, and this chapter sets out to analyse the appeal and implementation of such drives for India.[2]

Setting up India's space programme

In India the appeal of space was largely confined to the scientific community engaged in the various branches of upper atmospheric and geophysical sciences. As early as 1956 the physicist Vikram Sarabhai, who had played an active role in shaping the international science programme International Geophysical Year (IGY) in 1957–58, had called for establishing a research base in 'rockets and missiles', and from 1958–59 was engaged with the problems of setting up an organized space programme in the country. With international co-operation in the peaceful uses of outer space emerging high on the agenda of the UN and with the National Aeronautic and Space Administration (NASA) of the USA making concrete proposals for co-operation in space research at the third meeting of the Committee on Space Research (COSPAR) in early 1960, policy-makers in India began to think seriously about the relevance of space research for a developing country like itself. Convinced that space research and space technology had practical applications with significant implications for agriculture, education, industry and other areas of scientific endeavour,[3] that 'the subject of peaceful uses of outer space is likely to be of increasing importance in the near future',[4] and that it was a field in which international co-operation on an extensive scale may be brought about, the Government of India in August 1961 entrusted the Department of Atomic Energy (DAE) with the responsibility of conducting space research and its peaceful applications. In early 1962 the DAE set up the Indian National Committee for

Space Research (INCOSPAR) to help formulate and execute policies for peaceful uses of outer space. With the appointment of Sarabhai as the chairman of this committee, Indian space plans began to take concrete shape.

INCOSPAR initially planned to set up a programme of meteorological rocket sounding in collaboration with NASA, but when international scientific unions such as COSPAR as well as the United Nations Committee on the Peaceful Uses of Outer Space (COPUOS) came up with the proposals to accord UN sponsorship for international sounding rocket facilities in scientifically critical locations, India by virtue of its location on the geomagnetic equator offered to host such a facility. With the active support and assistance of the principal space powers, the USA and USSR, as well as France and the United Kingdom, India then established an international sounding rocket facility, the Thumba Equatorial Rocket Launching Station (TERLS), which became operational in November 1963 with the launching of a US *Nike Apache* rocket carrying a sodium vapour payload supplied by France.

Although India began its foray into space with a scientific research programme, from its inception the main thrust was on realizing the practical benefits of space research through self-reliant development of space technology. Homi J. Bhabha, the head of the DAE underscored this at a seminar organized by INCOSPAR in early 1963, when he said:

> Another and perhaps the most important reason for India going into space research was that there are many areas in which it is likely to yield results of great practical interest and importance in the near future, and we would once again be falling behind the advanced countries in practical technology if we were not to look ahead and prepare to take advantage of these new developments also [...] If we do not do so now, we will have to depend later on buying know-how from other countries at much greater costs.[5]

In the latter half of the 1960s the basic infrastructure necessary for a broad-based space programme was put in place under the leadership of Vikram Sarabhai, who was appointed head of the DAE upon the untimely death of Bhabha in 1966. Sarabhai also broadly outlined the objectives of the space programme. While the broad goals of the programme were to enable the country to leap-frog to a higher level of social and economic development, the specific social and economic objectives of the space programme related to the use of orbiting satellites for communications, in respect of telecommunications and television, meteorological observation and forecasting, and remote sensing of natural and renewable earth resources.

As in other national endeavours, 'self-reliance' was the main thrust of the strategy employed in the accomplishment of India's space policy objectives. The accent on attaining self-reliance in space technologies was further reinforced by the difficulties in acquiring critical space technologies from the industrialized nations. In early 1965, when India, which had already signed an agreement with Sud Aviation of France for the licensed production of a *Centaure* sounding rocket, approached the USA for the *Scout* rocket technology, the USA saw it as a step in the direction of acquiring ballistic missile capability and refused to supply the rocket technology. For a country like India, which had been seeking to maximize its independence in the international system, the denial of rocket technology raised concerns over the dependence of a national programme on launch services provided by advanced space powers. As Sarabhai pointed out in August 1968, in his address to the UN Conference on the Exploration and Peaceful Uses of Outer Space:

> The political implications of a national system dependent on foreign agencies for launching a satellite are complex. They are not negative in the present day world only in the context

of the coming together of the national interest of the launcher and the user nations. As long as there is no effective mutuality or interdependence between the two, many nations left with the ground segment would probably feel the need for some measure of redundant capability under complete national jurisdiction.[6]

The striking aspect here was his focus on the political national sovereignty considerations felt by India in relation to outside states. It was all part and parcel of India's wider concerns for 'strategic autonomy'.

In the latter half of the 1960s, therefore, the acquisition of indigenous capabilities in the entire spectrum of space technology, launch vehicles, satellites and supporting ground technology for space applications became a fundamental feature of the Indian space effort. The strategy that Sarabhai laid out for attaining self-reliance in space technology was one that combined strong domestic research and development (R&D) effort with import of technology from abroad. He stressed that leaders at the operative level of the programme must be committed and willing to stretch themselves to the fullest before asking for help from outside.[7] Guided by this principle, he developed the space programme with international collaboration by forging relationships with space organizations in the USA, France, the United Kingdom and the USSR.

The Space Science and Technology Centre (SSTC) that was established at Veli Hills in 1966–67 formed the core around which an extensive research and development infrastructure for designing, developing and constructing rockets and satellite payloads and instrumentation began to take shape. In the area of rocketry, with the basic infrastructure necessary for rocket construction becoming available from the licensed production of the *Centaure* sounding rocket, the DAE sought to acquire indigenous competence in the field by developing a series of one-stage and two-stage sounding rockets, called the *Rohini* series. Beginning with the *Rohini-75*, a small rocket weighing only 10 kg that was launched in November 1967, a number of sounding rockets, each with increasing diameter and payload capacity, were developed and launched. In the area of satellite communications India gained experience in building and operating ground satellite communication terminals from the Experimental Satellite Communication Station (ESCES) that was set up with funding from the UN Development Programme (UNDP). The DAE also organized experiments to demonstrate the development potential of television as well as remote sensing techniques, and conducted a series of system studies to define the overall system configuration for the satellite-based television broadcasting experiment that it proposed to conduct using NASA's *ATS-6* satellite. As a result of these activities, space research that was initiated by a small group of scientists expanded to include over 2,500 scientists from some 18 major institutions, universities and organizations by the end of the 1960s.

Institutionalized programme

Equipped with the basic capabilities to produce its own two-stage sounding rockets and sophisticated scientific payloads, in the early 1970s the DAE sought to acquire further capabilities to construct communication and remote-sensing satellites, as well as launch vehicles to orbit such satellites, by developing experimental satellites and launch vehicles. With space research and technology poised for a new phase of development, the Government of India considered it 'necessary to set up an organization, free from all non-essential restrictions or needlessly inelastic rules, which will have responsibility in the entire field of science and technology of outer space and their applications'.[8] Consequently, in June 1972 the Government set up a new policy-making body, the Space Commission, and handed over the subject of space research and its utilization (which had been held by the Department of Atomic Energy since

1961) to a newly created Department of Space (DOS). The DOS, directly under the charge of the Prime Minister, was made responsible for the execution of space activities in the country through the Indian Space Research Organization (ISRO), which had been set up in 1969. With this, the Indian space effort that began as an informal activity taken up by the DAE was transformed into an institutionalized programme with an assigned budget, time-bound goals, and specific projects in space applications and technology.

The newly established DOS initially focused on developing the necessary experience to enable the design, manufacturing and operational teams to make the best use of the technology available. To this end, it conducted a series of experimental missions in the fields of satellite technology, launch vehicles and space applications. In the area of satellite applications the DOS/ISRO gathered experience in running a satellite-based instructional television system by conducting a year-long experiment, the Satellite Instructional Television Experiment (SITE) during 1975–76. It used NASA's *ATS-6* geostationary satellite to beam educational television broadcasts directly to community systems in over 2,400 villages. The following year, the DOS initiated another preparatory experiment, the Satellite Telecommunications Experiment Project, using the Franco-German communications satellite *Symphonie*. This two-year (1977–79) experiment enabled the country to gather experience in operating and using a geostationary satellite for domestic telecommunications. ISRO also conducted experiments in remote sensing utilizing its own experimental satellites (*Bhaskara-I* and *Bhaskara-II*), which were launched by the USSR in 1979 and 1981. It built a station in Hyderabad to receive data from US *Landsat* earth resources satellites. This station later became the base of the Indian National Remote Sensing Agency (INRSA).

In the area of satellite technology ISRO built its first scientific satellite (*Aryabhata*), two experimental earth observation satellites (*Bhaskara-I* and *Bhaskara-II*) and an experimental communication satellite (*APPLE*—Ariane Passenger Payload Experiment) for launch aboard a test flight of the European Space Agency's *Ariane* launch vehicle in 1981. In building Indian capabilities in satellite technology, the USSR played a vital role. Both the *Aryabhata* and the *Bhaskara* satellites were developed by joint teams of Indian-Soviet scientists and engineers. An important feature of these experimental satellite projects was that they were not modelled after the early generation satellites of the space powers, but represented state-of-the-art technology.[9] The *APPLE* satellite, up-to-date in some of its features, incorporated the three-axis stabilization technology that was mastered by the USA and Europe only in the mid-1970s.

In the area of launch vehicles, in 1973 ISRO took up the development of a four-stage launch vehicle, the *SLV-3*. Between 1979 and 1983 ISRO conducted four experimental launches of the *SLV-3*, a small 23-metre solid-fuelled experimental rocket. Although the first launch of the *SLV-3* ended in failure, the second launch in 1980 succeeded in placing a small scientific satellite weighing 40 kg into near earth orbit. With this, India became a member of the select group of space-faring countries, joining the USSR, USA, France, People's Republic of China and the United Kingdom.

Since the early 1980s, which is generally described as the maximum spin-off stage of the Indian space programme, ISRO operationalized its space services, initially by utilizing the multifunctional Indian National Satellites (INSATs) constructed abroad, and later by developing its own INSAT and Indian Remote Sensing (IRS) satellites. ISRO also acquired indigenous capabilities to place its own remote sensing and communication satellites into sun-synchronous and geo-synchronous orbits, respectively. The INSAT system, which was established with the commissioning of the *INSAT-1B* satellite in 1983, initiated a major revolution in the communications sector. In 2010 a constellation of 11 indigenously built INSAT satellites with a total of about 211 transponders in the C, Extended C and Ku-bands provided services to not only sustain the communication revolution in telecommunications and television broadcasting, but also to play a vital role in weather forecasting, disaster warning, and search and rescue operations. The IRS satellite system, which became operational with the launch of *IRS-1A* in 1988, had 10 IRS satellites in operation in 2010, the largest civilian remote sensing satellite constellation in the world. The images provided by these satellites in a variety of spatial resolutions, spectral bands and swathes are being used for several vital applications covering agriculture, water resources, urban development, mineral prospecting, environment, forestry, drought and flood forecasting, ocean resources and disaster management.

In the 1990s India also acquired the capability to place its remote sensing satellites in sun-synchronous orbit. With the *SLV-3* establishing indigenous technologies relating to propulsion, aerodynamics staging, structural engineering, vehicle control and guidance, and mission management, in the early 1980s ISRO took up the development of the Polar Satellite Launch Vehicle (PSLV) to access the sun-synchronous orbit. The PSLV, a vehicle 10 times bigger than the *SLV-3*, incorporated complex technologies such as the strap-on motors and close-loop guidance system. Validating these technologies by constructing the Augmented Satellite Launch Vehicle (ASLV), ISRO carried out three developmental flights of the PSLV, beginning with its first launch in September 1993. With the first operational launch of the PSLV in September 1997 succeeding in putting a 1,250-kg remote sensing satellite, the *IRS-1D*, into sun-synchronous orbit, India's dependence on Russian launchers for orbiting its remote sensing satellites ended. With several improvements being made in subsequent versions of the PSLV, especially those involving thrust, efficiency and weight, the PSLV emerged as a workhorse for launching a variety of satellites into low earth- and sun-synchronous orbits, as well as unmanned lunar probes.[10] Its latest incarnation, the *PSLV-C15*, was successfully tested in July 2010 to launch an Algerian satellite, leading an Indian commentator to state that, 'this launch needs to be viewed beyond commercial interests […] with this launch it could be said that India has started using "space diplomacy" as a foreign tool'.[11]

The technological significance of PSLV also lies in the fact that it feeds directly into the first and second stages of the more powerful Geo-synchronous Satellite Launch Vehicle (GSLV) for launching communication satellites into higher orbits. The development of the GSLV with a cryogenic upper stage that was taken up in the late 1980s suffered a setback when Russia, coming under intense pressure from the Missile Technology Control Regime (MTCR), abrogated the 1991 deal to transfer cryogenic engine technology. The indigenous efforts to develop this engine began in 1996. In the meantime, ISRO used the cryogenic engines that were supplied by Russia without transferring technology, under the deal that was renegotiated with Russia in 1994. The first GSLV (*Mark 1*) was launched in 2001, putting an Indian satellite into orbit. Four more GSLV launches followed in 2003, 2004, 2006 (a failure) and 2007. In April 2010 the first flight of the *GSLV-D3 (Mark 2)*, incorporating the indigenously built cryogenic upper stage, ended in failure, pushing back ISRO's plan to attain complete self-reliance in orbiting its INSAT satellites, though a further launch attempt was envisaged for 2011.

Acquisition of technological capabilities

Although international co-operation played an important role in establishing the base for sounding rockets, satellite applications and satellite manufacture, the main thrust of Indian space policy has been on gaining indigenous competence in 'the essential components of space technology'.[12] This was prompted by the difficulties in acquiring critical space technologies from the industrialized nations. In the years after India conducted a Peaceful Nuclear Explosion (PNE) in 1974, its nuclear programme encountered problems due to stringent export control exercised by the industrialized nations. Anticipating similar problems with space technology, the DOS under the chairmanship of Satish Dhawan (1972–84), began to strategically plan and organize indigenous technology development.[13] Major initiatives to strengthen the domestic capabilities of industry and other national institutions were taken up. These included using existing capabilities as well as creating new capabilities in industry through technology transfer and technical assistance.

To begin with, the space programme had little or no industrial base to support it. In the 1960s much of the work was done in-house, including the development of equipment and hardware fabrication. In the 1970s, as a result of the expansion of activities associated with experiments in space technology and applications, ISRO made deliberate and sustained efforts to promote the participation of domestic industry in the space effort by instituting technology transfer. However, only a few industries accepted major responsibilities or committed themselves to the space projects. Throughout the 1970s industry's collaboration with the space programme was largely confined to the establishment of ground-based facilities, although it took up some fabrication work related to satellites and the *SLV-3*. With the projects taken up by ISRO in the 1980s (satellite services and development of operational satellites and launch vehicles) requiring gigantic facilities and new technologies, large industrial back-up became a necessity. However, the industry was reluctant to take up ISRO projects or absorb the know-how for products and processes generated by the space programme. Studies conducted by ISRO's research centres in the early 1980s identified the factors limiting the industry's participation in space projects as follows: the low volume and less repetitive jobs of ISRO; the rigorous quality and time standards set by the space establishment; and hesitation of industry to experiment with new materials and processes.[14] In an effort to lower the costs of the programme and share the burden of hardware and technical work with industry, DOS/ISRO adopted a range of policies such as aggressive promotion of technology transfers from ISRO laboratories and offering consultancy services to industry,[15] discouraging the Government from adopting liberal import policies,[16] and designing space products and services not only to meet domestic requirements but also international market requirements.[17]

As a result, by the end of the 1980s Indian industries emerged as sub-contractors for various ISRO projects. In the process ISRO's budget spent through the Indian industrial sector rose from 1% in the 1970s to over 60% by the 1990s. By summer 2010 over 500 industries were contributing a range of products and services to the Indian space effort.[18] With most of the fabrication work on rockets and hardware and about 20%–30% of fabrication work on satellites subcontracted to industry, ISRO emerged mainly as a research and development organization with end-to-end capability, from conceptualizing to realizing the space system—satellites, launch vehicles and associated ground systems.[19]

The expansion phase

Having acquired the capability to design and develop its own satellites and launch vehicles, and established the space systems (INSAT and IRS) that had become an important part of the country's developmental infrastructure, since the 1990s India has sought to commercialize space technologies and services as well as strengthen space sciences by taking up planetary missions. As has been seen, in the 1980s the DOS/ISRO began designing its products to meet the domestic and international market to stimulate the participation of Indian industry in the space endeavour. The forced indigenization efforts since the 1980s, as a result of the restrictions on technologies and components imposed by the MTCR and the escalation of the cost of space projects, have strengthened the urge to commercialize. In the 1990s India entered the international market to offer its products and services by establishing Antrix Corporation Limited as a commercial wing of the ISRO in 1992. Antrix initially began its earnings by providing services and data, but with the PSLV launcher proving its reliability and cost efficiency, Antrix began offering launch services for accessing low and polar orbits. Since 1999, when Antrix first launched a third-party satellite (the 100-kg South Korean satellite *Kistsat-3* and 45-kg German *DLR Tubsat*) along with ISRO's own, it has launched over 22 small and large foreign satellites, the heaviest one so far being the 350-kg Italian satellite *Agile* in 2007.[20] It has also begun to supply satellite subsystems and has established an alliance with Europe's leading satellite manufacturer, EADS Astrium, to jointly manufacture communication satellites using the INSAT Bus for selling in global markets.

Although India has been carrying out research in the fields of astronomy, atmospheric sciences and long-term climate research using sounding rockets, balloons and scientific satellites, in the early years of the new millennium the DOS/ISRO embarked on an ambitious planetary exploration, the flagship mission of which was *Chandrayaan*. This development was widely seen as a departure from the DOS's original vision of an application-driven programme, even if the mission 'can provide impetus to science in India, a challenge to technology and, possibly, a new dimension to international cooperation'.[21] The *Chandrayaan* mission, launched in October 2008, consisted of a lunar orbiter and an impactor. In addition to five indigenous instruments, the mission included six scientific payloads from NASA, the European Space Agency and Bulgaria. The mission was instrumental in the ISRO-NASA joint discovery of water molecules on the moon's surface, unattained by any of the previous missions of such nature. The follow-on mission, *Chandrayaan-2*, proposed to be launched in 2013, is being jointly developed with Russia. It will have an Indian orbiter and Russian lander and rover, and opportunities for scientific instruments from other countries. Meanwhile, the ISRO is also exploring the possibility of setting up an intermediate base on the moon so that it can help the space agency to explore other planets such as Mars and Jupiter from that platform.

Indian space programme: the security dimension

Space technology and its applications have enabled India to develop more autonomy in international relations and acquire greater control over its economy, as well as capacity for autonomous development. Equally important, they are providing a number of technology-related strategic choices to deal with the national security challenges facing the country, in which 'space security' has become a concern for India.[22]

Despite its civilian thrust, the Indian space programme had to contend with a significant military push. The diffusion of nuclear and advanced conventional weaponry in the country's immediate neighbourhood, particularly Pakistan and China with which India has had adverse relations, contributed to these pushes and pulls.[23] The first major push came in the mid-1960s when, in response to the nuclear explosion conducted by China in October 1964, the Indian Government revised its nuclear policy and reserved the option to go nuclear. In such a context, the nascent space programme gained wider support, as space activity came to be seen as an important element in the technological base for not only economic security but also military security.[24]

The continuing nuclear testing by China and advances made by that country in rocketry kept alive the debate on India's nuclear option and strengthened the advocates of military use of space technologies. In the 1970s the military potential of the civilian space programme came into sharper focus during the debate on the country's nuclear posture. That debate was sparked-off by the launch of a satellite by China in April 1970, a development which was widely seen in

India as evidence of the growing nuclear muscle of China. The demand for the nuclear deterrent capability vis-à-vis China was revived and gained widespread support. At a symposium in New Delhi called to review China's success in space in May 1970, scientists, defence experts, economists, political analysts and members of parliament decided by an overwhelming majority that the Government should revise its nuclear policy and produce the bomb immediately. When the Government of India outlined to the public the profile of a 10-year nuclear energy *and* space development programme in July 1970, which included among other things the development of an experimental satellite launch vehicle, the 'bomb-for-security' lobby saw it as a firm step towards nuclear weaponry. Although a separate missile development programme, the *Devils Programme*, was initiated in the defence sector in 1970–71, it was the space programme that had already established a modest infrastructure in rocketry, which continued to attract the attention of the 'bomb-for-security' lobby.

In this context, those who wanted the immediate or early establishment of nuclear deterrence vis-à-vis China called for accelerating the space launch vehicle project, the *SLV-3*, so that it could be developed into an Intermediate Range Ballistic Missile (IRBM) with the addition of an improved guidance system. Others who wanted a balanced development of rocketry called for close co-ordination between the missile development efforts in the defence sector and the civilian space programme, and between the DOS and defence ministry.

In the early 1980s, taking advantage of the growing technological capabilities within the country, the Government of India decided to establish design and production capabilities for guided missiles within the country to meet the perceived immediate and future needs of the armed forces of the country. That decision was strengthened by the belief that achieving self-reliance in critical technologies and weapon systems in a selective manner would not only meet the country's military security requirements but also reinforce and strengthen the country's capabilities in 'dual-use' technologies and, therefore, its development of high technology. The Integrated Guided Missile Development Programme (IGMDP) set up under the aegis of the Defence Research and Development Organization (DRDO), the primary source of all defence R&D within the country, was charged with the task of developing a variety of missiles. Utilizing the missile R&D base that was already present in the DRDO, and deriving sustenance and strength from the industrial and technological infrastructure established by the civilian space programme, the IGMDP achieved quick results. Within a short span of seven years the IGMDP developed a variety of guided missiles and established the country's capability for indigenous production of long-range ballistic missiles. Several of these missiles, including the nuclear-capable *Prithvi* and *Agni* missiles, have already been inducted into the armed forces since the 1990s, even as efforts are on to develop ballistic missiles with a longer range.

Conclusions

Since the late 1990s a new dimension to the military use of space technology has emerged on the security horizon. This arose as a result of the increasing use of space assets to complement and support military functions on the one hand, and the development of ballistic missile defence systems on the other. With the USA demonstrating the effectiveness of space assets for aiding military operations in the first Gulf War in 1991, the military functions of space assets are becoming increasingly attractive to space powers. At the same time, the incentive to deny the benefits of space assets to their adversary has also become strong among some space powers. The USA, Russia and China have proven capability to destroy space assets; several others have the capacity to disable these space assets through a range of technologies. In this scenario, the demand for military use of space technologies has gained ground. The Indian Air Force (IAF), which has been seeking to establish an Aerospace Command to leverage space technologies, received support from the Parliamentary Standing Committee on Defence in 2004. In early 2007, soon after China carried out a test in which it used a missile to destroy an old satellite in orbit, the IAF chief announced that India would build an Aerospace Defence Command (ADC) aimed at preventing possible attacks from space. Military analysts say that the Indian project will probably replicate the North American Aerospace Defence Command (NORAD), set up by the USA and Canada, which detects and tracks man-made objects in space.

Even as the IAF is pressing for the military use of space, the anti-satellite (ASAT) test by China in January 2007 added a new dimension to space security—the possibility of the weaponization of space. While there are concerns over the safety and security of the space assets that the country has so painstakingly built,[25] there is no consensus on how best to deal with the issue. On the one hand, the Minister of External Affairs, Pranab Mukherjee, warned that the international community was 'treading a thin line between current defence related uses of space and its actual weaponization', and called on 'all States to redouble efforts to strengthen the international legal regime for the peaceful use of outer space'.[26] At the same conference, Aerospace Power in Tomorrow's World, the Minister of State for Defence Production, Rao Inderjit Singh, said that the 21st century would belong to aerospace power and urged the creation of a 'vibrant' aerospace industry in India to create the necessary synergy: 'a robust civil programme can be used to transform the IAF into a dominant space power'.[27] On the other hand, the Minister of Defence, A.K. Antony, expressed concern about the emergence of anti-satellite weapons, a new class of heavy lift-off boosters and an improved array of military space devices in the neighbourhood, and wondered how long India could 'remain committed to the policy of non weaponization of the outer space'.[28] Meanwhile, the *Space Security Report* of the IDSA-Pugwash Society Working Group on Space Security noted with concern that 'India is one of the few countries where space capabilities have been developed primarily for developmental and societal progress with almost no dedicated capacity to meet the needs of the military or security establishment', and warned that this could 'prove to be a major vulnerability'.[29] Which of these approaches will eventually come to prevail in the near future will depend on how India defines its core security interests and advances in the field of space research. It will equally depend on how the other space powers, with their different levels of development of space and levels of assets, arrive at a consensus on space security.

Notes

1 Nehru cited in the *New York Times*, 6 January 1960.
2 See S. Reddy, 'India's Forays into Space. The Evolution of Its Space Programme', *International Studies*, Vol. 45, No. 3, 2008; K. Murthi and H. Madhusudan, 'Strategic Considerations in Indian Space Programme—Towards Maximising Socio-economic Benefits', *Acta Astronautica*, Vol. 63, No. 1–4, 2008; P. Bagla, 'India in Space: No Dream is Too Big for Us', *Economic Times*, 18 July 2010.
3 S. Dhawan, 'Manned Flight', *Seminar*, No. 5, November 1960. See also D. Kothari and A. Nagarajan, 'Exploration Prospects', *Seminar*, No. 5, November 1960.
4 Government of India (Department of Atomic Energy), *Annual Report 1960–61*, Mumbai (Bombay): Department of Atomic Energy, 1961, p.20.
5 Cited in G. Raj, *Reach for the Stars: The Evolution of India's Rocket Programme*, New Delhi: Viking, 2000, p.18.
6 Government of India, *Annual Report 1978–79*, Mumbai (Bombay): Department of Atomic Energy, p.37.
7 K. Chowdhary (ed.), *Science Policy and National Development: Vikram Sarabhai*, Delhi: Macmillan, 1974, p.30.
8 Cited in M. Rajan, *Indian Spaceflights*, Delhi: Publications Division, 1985, p.134.
9 The *Aryabhata* was as sophisticated as many satellites that were being flown by other countries at that time. Incorporating more than 12,000 active and passive electronic components in addition to 20,000 solar cells, *Aryabhata* was also the heaviest first launch ever attempted by any country. U. Rao, 'An

Overview of the Aryabhata Project', in U. Rao and K. Kasturirangan (eds), *The Aryabhata Project*, Bangalore: Indian Academy of Sciences, 1979.

10 A modified version of the PSLV, with stretched strap-on boosters, was used in October 2008 in the *Chandrayaan* mission to the moon, which included an orbiter and an impactor.

11 A. Lele, 'Successful Launch of PSLV-C15', *IDSA Comment*, 16 July 2010. In addition, it carried two Indian satellites, one Canadian satellite and one Swiss satellite.

12 S. Dhawan, 'Application of Space Technology in India', in *Prof. S. Dhawan's Articles, Papers and Lectures*, Bangalore: ISRO, 1997, p.134.

13 A. Baskaran, 'From Science to Commerce: The Evolution of Space Development Policy and Technology Accumulation in India', *Technology and Society*, Vol. 27, 2005, p.166.

14 'Indian Industry's Space Trek', *Business Standard* (New Delhi), 12 January 1986.

15 Under the Technology Consultancy Scheme initiated in 1982, ISRO began transferring product and process technologies covering a wide range of categories. Of the 150 technologies transferred, around 62% cater to spin-off applications and around 32% to the space applications market.

16 For instance, in January 1982 the DOS drew the attention of the Scientific Advisory Committee to the Cabinet to the impact of technology import policies on generation and utilization of domestic science and technological capabilities, and called for checking technology dumping by foreign countries, L. Sharma, 'Indigenous Efforts Get Raw Deal', *Times of India*, 26 January 1982.

17 S. Dhawan, the Chairman of the Space Commission, for instance, urged the industry to take part in evolving space technologies by pointing to the growing interest of many developing countries in remote sensing technologies and the opportunities for export of know-how, S. Dhawan, 'The 18th Sriram Memorial Lecture', in *Prof. S. Dhawan's Articles, Papers and Lectures*, op. cit., p.129.

18 U. Sankar, *The Economics of India's Space Programme – An Exploratory Analysis*, New Delhi: Oxford University Press, 2007.

19 M. Nair, 'Empowering the Bottom of the Pyramid from the Sky: A Case for Satellite-based Services', *IIMB Management Review*, Vol. 17, No. 13, 2005.

20 P. Molekhi, 'Payload Payback', *The Economic Times* (New Delhi), 18 July 2010.

21 DOS/ISRO Chairman, K. Kasturirangan, quoted in P. Chakravarty, 'India Craves the Moon to Crown its Space Odyssey', *Space Daily*, 12 March 2000, www.spacedaily.com.

22 K. Singh, 'India's Endeavour to Attain Space Security Asset', *Articles*, No. 3071, 15 March 2010, www.ipcs.org.

23 O. Marwah, 'Indian Nuclear and Space Programmes: Intent and Policy', *International Security*, Vol. 2, No. 2, 1997.

24 For instance, *Science and Culture*, an influential journal in science policy circles, observed that 'even without a bomb but with well-developed indigenous rockets and missile technology, electronics and radar technology, we can to some extent claim a feeling of adequacy in future situations that may arise', in 'China Joins Atomic Club: What Should India Do?', *Science and Culture*, Vol. 30, No.10, October 1964.

25 At a modest estimate, the value of India's space assets, in space and on the ground, is about Rs.100,000 crores or US $25,000m.; see K. Kasturirangan, 'The Emerging World Space Order', in A. Lele and G. Singh (eds), *Space Security and Cooperation*, New Delhi: Academic Foundation, 2009, p.33.

26 P. Mukherjee, 'Address by EAM at the Inaugural Session of the International Seminar on "Aerospace Power in Tomorrow's World"', 4 February 2007, meaindia.nic.in.

27 Singh cited in 'Preserve Outer Space from Weapons: India', *INS News*, 4 February 2007, news.boloji.com.

28 R. Rao, 'Will India Prepare for Space War?', *Article* (IPCS), No. 3038, 7 January 2010.

29 IDSA-Indian Pugwash Society Working Group, *Space Security – Need for a Proactive Approach*, New Delhi: Academic Foundation, 2009, p.70.

29
Postscript

David Scott

This *Handbook* was shaped during 2010, and presents something of a snapshot of how voices from inside and outside India perceive India's presence in the international system. In retrospect, what is noticeable is the way in which economy-energy drivers, the stuff of the Manmohan Doctrine, crop up across the *Handbook*. What is also noticeable is the way in which China crops up not just in the specific chapter on the India-China bilateral relationship, but also in most of the chapters dealing with India's *immediate neighbourhood*, *extended neighbourhood*, relations amongst global powers, and on global issues.

Meanwhile, two voices can be put forward in terms of India looking forward. One voice is that 'India has entered the 21st Century with greater self-confidence, vastly enhanced capacity for achievement, and soaring expectations […] remarkable progress […] Our vision is to make the 21st Century India's Century […] multipolar world order, with India as one of the poles'.[1] A second voice is that 'I said the emergence of India as a major global power is an idea whose time has come', in which 'I can assure you that tomorrow we will do you proud by the record of our performance in economic and social reconstruction of our country. I am convinced as I said a moment ago, that the 21st Century will be an Indian Century. The world will once again look at us with regard and respect'.[2] The first voice was the Bharatiya Janata Party (BJP) *Vision Statement* of 2004, while the second voice was the Prime Minister Manmohan Singh who won the elections of 2004. Despite the divisive domestic politics and despite their criticisms of each other, there was a common feeling between these political leaders that India is rising and will continue to rise. This simple structural fact is why this *Handbook* was created, to serve as a window onto that increasingly important factor in world affairs, India. Manmohan Singh's words of India being looked at with regard and respect are true enough; it is a matter of 'interest and significance' as well. India's rise and impact is set to be a big structurally-generated story for the 21st century.

Notes

1 Bharatiya Janata Party, *Vision Document 2004*, 2004, www.bjp.org.
2 'Charlie Rose Interviews Indian PM Manmohan Singh', Council for Foreign Relations, 27 February 2006, www.cfr.org; M. Singh, 'PM's Inaugural Speech at Pravasi Bharatiya Divas', 7 January 2005, pmindia.nic.in.

Select bibliography

Aaron, S. 'Straddling Faultlines: India's Foreign Policy Towards the Greater Middle East', *CSH Occasional Paper* (French Research Institute in India), No. 7, 2003.

Abhyankar, R. 'India and the European Union: A Partnership for All Reasons', *India Quarterly*, Vol. 65, No. 4, 2009.

Abraham, I. *Making of the Indian Atomic Bomb: Science, Secrecy and the Postcolonial State*, London: Zed Books, 1998.

Acharya, A. 'Will Asia's Past Be Its Future?', *International Security*, Vol. 28, No. 3, Winter 2003/04.

—— 'India and Southeast Asia in the Age of Terror: Building Partnerships for Peace', *Contemporary Southeast Asia*, Vol. 28, No. 2, 2006.

Ahmed, I. 'Contemporary Terrorism and the State, Non-state, and the Interstate: Newer Drinks, Newer Bottles', in S. Khatri and G. Kueck (eds), *Terrorism in South Asia: Impact on Development and Democratic Process*, New Delhi: Shipra Publication, 2003.

Ahmed, Z. and Bhatnagar, S. 'Gulf States and the Conflict between India and Pakistan', *Journal of Asia Pacific Studies*, Vol. 1, No. 2, 2010.

Ahrari, M. 'Growing Strong: The Nuclear Genie in South Asia', *Security Dialogue*, Vol. 30, No. 4, 1999.

Ajithkumar, M. *India Pakistan Relations: The Story of a Fractured Fraternity*, New Delhi: Kalpaz Publications, 2006.

Akbarzadeh, S. 'India and Pakistan's Geostrategic Rivalry in Central Asia', *Contemporary South Asia*, Vol. 12, No. 2, 2003.

Alagappa, M. (ed.). *Asian Security Practice: Material and Ideational Influences*, Stanford: Stanford University Press, 1998.

Ali, S. *The Fearful State: Power, People and Internal War in South Asia*, London: Zed Books, 1993.

Anoop, S. 'Regional Integration in South Asia: Chasing a Chimera?', *Regional Studies*, Vol. 18, No. 4, 2000.

Asher, M. 'India's Rising Role in Asia', *Discussion Paper* (RIS, New Delhi), No. 121, 2007.

Ashraf, T. 'Doctrinal Reawakening of the Indian Armed Forces', *Military Review*, Vol. 84, No. 6, November–December 2004.

Asopa, S. *Struggle for Spheres of Interest in Trans-Caucasia-Central Asia and India's Stakes*, New Delhi: Manak Publications, 2006.

Asthana, N. and Nirmal, A. *Terrorism, Insurgencies and Counter-Insurgency Operations*, Jaipur: Pointer Publishers, 2001.

Athwal, A. *India-China Relations: Contemporary Dynamics*, London: Routledge, 2008.

Bagla, P. *Destination Moon: India's Quest for Moon, Mars and Beyond*, New Delhi: HarperCollins, 2008.

Bajpai, G. 'India and the Balance of Power', in *The Indian Year Book of International Affairs*, Madras: Indian Study Group of International Affairs, 1952.

Bajpai, K. 'Indian Strategic Culture', in M. Chambers (ed.), *South Asia in 2020: Future Strategic Balances and Alliances*, Carlisle: US Army War College, 2002.

Bajpai, K., Chari, P.R., Cheema, P., Cohen, S. and Ganguly, S. (eds). *Brasstacks and Beyond: Perception and Management of Crisis in South Asia*, New Delhi: Manohar, 1995.

Bajpai, K. and Mallavarapu, S. (eds). *International Relations in India: Bringing Theory Back Home*, New Delhi: Orient Longman, 2004.

—— *International Relations in India: Theorising the Region and Nation*, New Delhi: Orient Longman, 2004.

Bajpai, K. and Mattoo, A. (eds). *Securing India: Strategic Thought and Practice*, New Delhi: Manohar Publishers, 1996.

—— *Engaged Democracies: India–US Relations in the 21st Century*, New Delhi: Har-Anand Publications Pvt Ltd, 2000.

Bal, S. *Central Asia: A Strategy for India's Look-North Policy*, New Delhi: Lancer Publishers, 2004.

Baru, S. *Strategic Consequences of India's Economic Performance*, New Delhi: Academic Foundation, 2006.

Baskaran, A. 'From Science to Commerce: The Evolution of Space Development Policy and Technology Accumulation in India', *Technology and Society*, Vol. 27, 2005.

Basrur, R. 'Nuclear Weapons and Indian Strategic Culture', *Journal of Peace Research*, Vol. 38, No. 2, 2001.

—— 'Nuclear Weapons and India-Pakistan Relations', *Strategic Analysis*, Vol. 33, No. 3, 2009.

Basu, R. *Globalization and Indian Foreign Policy*, Jaipur: Vital Publications, 2007.

Batabyal, A. 'Balancing China in Asia. A Realist Assessment of India's Look East Strategy', *China Report*, Vol. 42, No. 2, 2006.

Bedi, R. 'India and Central Asia', *Frontline*, Vol. 19, No. 19, 14–27 September 2002.

Behera, N. 'Re-imagining IR in India', *International Relations of the Asia-Pacific*, Vol. 7, No. 3, 2007.

—— (ed.). *International Relations in South Asia: Search for an Alternative Paradigm*, New Delhi: Sage Publications, 2008.

Beri, R. 'Indo-South Africa Defence Cooperation', *Strategic Analysis*, Vol. 23, No. 10, 2000.

Berlin, D. 'India-Iran Relations: A Deepening Entente', *Special Assessment* (Asia-Pacific Center for Security Studies), October 2004.

—— 'India in the Indian Ocean', *Naval War College Review*, Vol. 59, No. 2, 2006.

Berman, I. 'Israel, India, and Turkey: Triple Entente?', *Middle East Quarterly*, Vol. 9, No. 4, 2002.

Bhaskar, C. 'Myanmar in the Strategic Calculus of India and China', in K. Bajpai and A. Mattoo (ed.), *The Peacock and the Dragon: India-China Relations in the 21st Century*, New Delhi: Har-Anand, 2000.

—— 'Manmohan Doctrine and India's External Relations', *Comment* (IDSA), 16 March 2005, www.idsa.in.

Bhat, C. *India and the Indian Diaspora – A Policy Issue*, University of Hyderabad: Department of Sociology, 1998.

Bhattacharjea, M. 'India-China-Pakistan: Beyond Kargil – Changing Equations', *China Report*, Vol. 35, No. 4, 1999.

Bhattacharya, A. 'The Fallacy in the Russia-India-China Triangle', *Strategic Analysis*, Vol. 28, No. 2, 2004.

—— 'China and Maoist Nepal: Challenges for India', *IDSA Comment*, 23 May 2008.

Bidwai, P. and Vanaik, A. *South Asia on a Short Fuse: Nuclear Politics and the Future of Global Disarmament*, New Delhi: Oxford University Press, 1999.

Bisht, M. 'India-Bhutan Relations: From Developmental Cooperation to Strategic Partnership', *Strategic Analysis*, Vol. 33, No. 3, 2010.

Blank, S. 'India's Rising Profile in Central Asia', *Comparative Strategy*, Vol. 22, No. 2, 2003.

Blazevic, J. 'Defensive Realism in the Indian Ocean: Oil, Sea Lanes and the Security Dilemma', *China Security*, Vol. 5, No. 3, 2009.

Boesche, R. 'Kautilya's *Arthasastra* on War and Diplomacy in Ancient India', *Journal of Military History*, Vol. 67, No. 1, 2003.

Boquérat, G. and Grare, F. (eds). *India, China, Russia: Intricacies of an Asian Triangle*, New Delhi: Centre de Sciences Humaines, 2004.

Brecher, M. *India and World Politics: Krishna Menon's View of the World*, London: Oxford University Press, 1968.

Brewster, D. 'India's Strategic Partnership with Vietnam: The Search for a Diamond on the South China Sea?', *Asian Security*, Vol. 5, No. 1, 2009.

—— 'The India-Japan Security Relationship: An Enduring Security Partnership?', *Asian Security*, Vol. 6, No. 2, 2010.

—— 'The Australia–India Security Declaration: The Quadrilateral Redux?', *Security Challenges*, Vol. 6, No. 1, 2010.

Buzan, B. 'South Asia Moving Towards Transformation: Emergence of India as a Great Power', *International Studies*, Vol. 39, No. 1, 2002.

Cappelli, V. 'Containing Pakistan: Engaging the *Raja-Mandala* in South-Central Asia', *Orbis*, Vol. 51, No. 1, 2007.

Carter, A. 'America's New Strategic Partner?', *Foreign Affairs*, Vol. 85, No. 4, 2006.

Chander, P. *India & Pakistan Unending Conflict*, 3 vols, New Delhi: Aph Publishing Corporation, 2002.

Chandra, L. 'Afghanistan and India: Historico-Cultural Perspective', in K. Warikoo (ed.), *The Afghanistan Crisis: Issues and Perspectives*, New Delhi: Bhavana Books, 2002.

Chandramohan, B. 'Indo-Bhutan Joint Action Against Insurgents', *IDSA Comment*, 5 October 2009.

Chari, P. 'Civil-Military Relations in India', *Armed Forces and Society*, Vol. 4, No. 1, November 1977.

Chari, P. and Chandran, S. (eds). *Terrorism Post 9/11: An Indian Perspective*, New Delhi: Manohar Publishers, 2003.

Chaturvedi, S. 'Representing Post-Colonial India: Inclusive/Exclusive Geopolitical Imaginations', in K. Dodds and D. Atkinson (eds), *Geopolitical Traditions: A Century of Geopolitical Thought*, London: Routledge, 2000.

Chellaney, B. (ed.). *Securing India's Future in the New Millennium*, New Delhi: Orient Longman, 1999.

—— *Asian Juggernaut: The Rise of China, India and Japan*, New Delhi: HarperCollins, 2006.

Chen, S. 'Great Power Politics: India's Absence from Ideological Energy Diplomacy in Central Asia', *China and Eurasia Forum Quarterly*, Vol. 8, No. 1, 2010.

Chengappa, R. *Weapons of Peace: The Secret Story of India's Quest to be a Nuclear Power*, New Delhi: HarperCollins, 2000.

Chenoy, A. 'India and Russia: Allies in the International System', *South Asian Survey*, Vol. 15, No. 1, 2008.

Cherian, S. 'Tilting the Balance', *South Asia Intelligence Review*, Vol. 3, No. 18, 2004.

Chhabra, H. *India and Africa. Saga of Friendship*, New Delhi: Government of India, 1986.

Chitkara, M. *Rashtriya Swayamsevak Sangh. National Upsurge*, New Delhi: A.P.H Publishing Corporation, 2004.

Chopra, V. (ed.). *Indo-Russian Relations: Prospects Problems and Russia Today*, Delhi: Kalpaz Publications, 2001.

—— (ed.). *Significance of Indo-Russian Relations in 21st Century*, Delhi: Kalpaz Publications, 2008.

Chowdhary, K. (ed.). *Science Policy and National Development: Vikram Sarabhai*, Delhi: Macmillan, 1974.

Clad, J. 'Convergent Chinese and Indian Perspectives on the Global Order', in F. Frankel and H. Harding (eds), *The India-China Relationship: What the United States Needs to Know,* New York: Columbia University Press, 2004.

Cohen, S. 'Geostrategic Factors in India–Pak Relations', *Asian Affairs*, Vol. 10, No. 3, 1983.

—— *The Indian Army: Its Contribution to the Development of a Nation*, New Delhi: Oxford University Press, 1990.

—— 'Why Did India "Go Nuclear"?', in R. Thomas and A. Gupta (eds), *India's Nuclear Security*, London: Lynne Rienner, 2000.

—— *India: Emerging Power*, Washington: Brookings Institution Press, 2001.

Crossette, B. 'The Elephant in the Room', *Foreign Policy,* January/February 2010.

Curzon, G. *The Place of India in the Empire*, London: J. Murray, 1909.

Dabhade, M. 'India and East Asia: A Region Rediscovered', in H. Pant (ed.), *Indian Foreign Policy in a Unipolar World*, New Delhi: Routledge, 2009.

Dabhade, M. and Pant, P. 'Coping with Challenges to Sovereignty: Sino-Indian Rivalry and Nepal's Foreign Policy', *Contemporary South Asia*, Vol. 13, No. 2, 2004.

Dadwal, S. 'Energy Security: India's Options', *Strategic Analysis*, Vol. 23, No. 4, 1999.

Das, P.G. *The Elephant Paradigm–India Wrestles With Change*, New Delhi: Penguin, 2001.

Das, P.K. *New Heights in Indo-US Relations*, Jaipur: Raj Publishing House, 2005.

Das, P.S. 'India's Maritime Concerns and Strategies', *USI Journal* (New Delhi), Vol. 136, No. 565, 2006.

Dasgupta, C. *War and Diplomacy in Kashmir, 1947–48*, New Delhi: Sage Publications, 2002.

Dash, K. *Regionalism in South Asia*, London: Routledge, 2008.

Dash, P. and Nazarkin, A. (eds). *India and Russia: Strategic Synergy*, Delhi: Authorpress, 2007.

—— (eds). *Indo-Russian Diplomatic Relations: Sixty Years of Enduring Legacy*, New Delhi: Academic Excellence, 2008.

Datta, V. *India's Foreign Policy in a Changing World*, New Delhi: Vikas, 1999.

Deshpande, G. and Acharya, A. (eds). *Crossing a Bridge of Dreams: Fifty Years of India and China*, New Delhi: Tulika, 2001.

Devotta, N. 'Is India Over-extended? When Domestic Disorder Precludes Regional Intervention', *Contemporary South Asia*, Vol. 12, No. 3, 2003.

Dhar, M.K. *Mission to Pakistan – An Intelligence Agent in Pakistan*, New Delhi: Manas Publications, 2002.

Dhawan, S. *Prof. S. Dhawan's Articles, Papers and Lectures*, Bangalore: ISRO, 1997.

Dibb, P. 'Towards a New Balance of Power in Asia', *Adelphi Paper*, No. 295, 1995.

Dietl, G. 'Quest for Influence in Central Asia: India and Pakistan', *International Studies*, Vol. 34, No. 2, 1997.

—— 'New Threats to Oil and Gas in West Asia: Issues in India's Energy Security', *Strategic Analysis*, Vol. 28, No. 3, 2004.

Dittmer, L. (ed.). *South Asia's Nuclear Security Dilemma: India, Pakistan, and China*, Armonk: M.E. Sharpe, 2005.

Dixit, J. *Makers of India's Foreign Policy: Raja Ram Mohun Roy to Yashwant Sinha*, New Delhi: HarperCollins, 2004.

Dreze, J. and Sen, A. *India: Development and Participation*, New Delhi: Oxford University Press, 2002.

Drezner, D. 'The New World Order', *Foreign Affairs*, Vol. 86, No. 2, 2007.

D'Souza, S. 'Indo-US Counter-Terrorism Cooperation: Rhetoric Versus Substance', *Strategic Analysis*, Vol. 32, No. 6, 2008.

—— 'Jihad Beyond Jammu & Kashmir', *Strategic Analysis*, Vol. 33, No. 3, 2009.

Dubey, A. 'Nehru and Africa in Afro-Asian Solidarity' *Ind-Africana*, Vol. 2, No. 2, 1989.

—— 'Indo-Africa State Relations', *Africa Quarterly*, Vol. 37, Nos. 1–2, 1997.

—— 'Changing Salience of the Relationship Between the Indian Diaspora and India', *Diaspora Studies*, Vol. 1, No. 2, 2008.

—— 'Comparative Understanding Needs to be Arrived At', *Foreign Affairs Journal*, Vol. 3, No. 2, 2008.

Dutt, S. 'India and the Himalayan States', *Asian Affairs*, Vol. 11, No. 1, 1984.

—— *India in a Globalized World*, Manchester: Manchester University Press, 2006.

Dutt, V. *India's Foreign Policy*, New Delhi: Vikas, 1984.

Emirates Center for Strategic Studies and Research (ed.). *The Balance of Power in South Asia*, Reading: Ithaca Press, 2000.

Engardio, P. (ed.). *Chindia: How China and India are Revolutionising Global Business*, London: McGraw-Hill, 2006.

Fair, C. 'Learning to Think the Unthinkable: Lessons from India's Nuclear Tests', *India Review*, Vol. 4, No. 1, 2005.

—— 'Indo-Iranian Ties: Thicker Than Oil', *Middle East Review of International Affairs*, Vol. 11, No. 1, 2007.

—— 'India and Iran: New Delhi's Balancing Act', *Washington Quarterly*, Vol. 30, No. 3, 2007.

Feigenbaum, E. 'India's Rise, America's Interest', *Foreign Affairs*, Vol. 89, No. 2, 2010.

Fisher, M. 'Goa in Wider Perspective', *Asian Survey*, Vol. 2, No. 2, 1962.

Frankel, F. and Harding, H. (eds). *The India-China Relationship: Rivalry and Engagement*, Oxford: Oxford University Press, 2004.

Frey, K. *India's Nuclear Bomb and National Security*, London: Routledge, 2006.

Fu, J.-K. 'Reassessing a "New Great Game" between India and China in Central Asia', *China & Eurasia Quarterly*, Vol. 8, No. 1, 2010.

Gaan, N. *India and the United States: From Estrangement to Engagement*, New Delhi: Kalpaz, 2007.

Gandhi, I. 'India and the World', *Foreign Affairs*, Vol. 51, No. 1, 1972.

—— *Safeguarding Environment* (1984), rep. New Delhi: Indira Gandhi Memorial Trust, 1992.

Gandhi, P. (ed.). *India and China in the Asian Century: Global Economic Power Dynamics*, New Delhi: Deep & Deep Publications, 2007.

Gandhi, R. 'A World Free of Nuclear Weapons', 9 June 1988, www.indianembassy.org.

Gangopadhyay, A. 'India's policy towards its Diaspora: Continuity and change', *India Quarterly*, Vol. 61, No. 4, 2005.

Ganguly, R. *Kin State Intervention in Ethnic Conflicts: Lessons From South Asia*, New Delhi: Sage Publications, 1998.

Ganguly, S. *The Origins of War in South Asia: Indo–Pakistani Conflicts Since 1947*, Boulder: Westview Press, 1994.

—— 'Explaining the Indian Nuclear Tests of 1998', in R. Thomas and A. Gupta (eds), *India's Nuclear Security*, London: Lynne Rienner, 2000.

—— *Conflict Unending: India-Pakistan Tensions Since 1947*, New York: Oxford University Press, 2002.

—— 'The Start of a Beautiful Friendship: The United States and India', *World Policy Journal*, Vol. 20, No. 1, 2003.

—— (ed.). *India as an Emerging Power*, London: Frank Cass, 2003.

—— 'Will Kashmir Stop India's Rise?', *Foreign Affairs*, Vol. 85, No. 4, 2006.

—— 'Nuclear Stability in South Asia', *International Security*, Vol. 33, No. 2, 2008.

Ganguly, S. and Hagerty, D. *Fearful Symmetry: India–Pakistan Crises in the Shadow of Nuclear Weapons*, Seattle: University of Washington Press, 2006.

Ganguly, S. and Kapur, S. *India, Pakistan, and the Bomb: Debating Nuclear Stability in South Asia*, New York: Columbia University Press, 2010.

Ganguly, S. and Pardesi, M. 'Explaining Sixty Years of India's Foreign Policy', *India Review*, Vol. 8, No. 1, 2009.

Ganguly, S., Shoup, B. and Scobell, A. (eds). *US-Indian Strategic Cooperation into the 21st Century*, London: Routledge, 2006.

Garver, J. *Protracted Contest: Sino-Indian Rivalry in the Twentieth Century*, Seattle: University of Washington Press, 2001.

—— 'Asymmetrical Indian and Chinese Threat Perceptions', *Journal of Strategic Studies*, Vol. 25, No. 4, 2002.

—— 'The Security Dilemma in Sino-Indian Relations', *India Review*, Vol. 1, No. 4, 2002.

Gordon, S. *India's Rise to Power in the Twentieth Century and Beyond*, New York: St Martin's Press, 1995.

Grant, C. 'India's Role in the New World Order', in *Briefing Note* (Centre for European Reform), September 2008.

Grare, F. 'In Search of a Role: India and the ASEAN Regional Forum', in F. Grare and A. Mattoo (eds), *India and ASEAN: The Politics of India's Look East Policy*, New Delhi: Manohar, 2001.

Grover, B. *Sikkim and India: Storm and Consolidation*, Delhi: Jain. Brothers, 1974.

Gujral, I. *A Foreign Policy for India*, New Delhi: External Publicity Division, 1998.

—— *Continuity and Change: India's Foreign Policy*, London: Macmillan, 2003.

Gupta, A. 'India and Asians in East Africa' in M. Twaddle (ed.), *Expulsions of Minority: Essay on Ugandan Asians*, London: Athlone Press, 1975.

—— 'India and Africa South of the Sahara', in B. Prasad (ed.), *India's Foreign Policy*, New Delhi: Vikas, 1979.

Gupta, A., Kalyanaraman, S. and Behuria, A. 'India–Pakistan Relations After the Mumbai Terror Attacks: What Should India Do?', *Strategic Analysis*, Vol. 33, No. 3, 2009.

Gupta, B. 'The Indian Doctrine', *New Statesman* (New Delhi), 6 August 1983.

—— 'The Indian Doctrine', *India Today*, 31 August 1983.

—— 'India in the 21st Century', *International Affairs*, Vol. 73, No. 2, 1997.

—— 'No First Use Options', *Indian Express*, 17 January 2009.

Gupta, K. (ed.). *International Terrorism: World Viewpoints, Volume 5: Response of India, Pakistan and the US*, New Delhi: Atlantic Publishers, 2002.

—— *India-Pakistan Relations with Special Reference to Kashmir*, 4 vols, New Delhi: Atlantic Publishers & Distributors (P) Ltd, 2006.

Gupta, P. 'Looking East: India Forges Closer Ties with Japan', *Force*, Vol. 3, No. 3, 2005.

Gupta, S. 'Indo-Bhutan Relations', in Ramakant and R. Misra, *Bhutan Society and Polity*, 2nd edn, New Delhi: Indus Publishing, 1998.

Gupta, U. *International Nuclear Diplomacy and India*, New Delhi: Atlantic, 2007.

Hagerty, D. 'India's Regional Security Doctrine', *Asian Survey*, Vol. 31, No. 4, 1991.

—— *The Consequences of Nuclear Proliferation: Lessons from South Asia*, Cambridge: MIT Press, 1998.

—— (ed.). *South Asia in World Politics*, Oxford: Rowman and Littlefield, 2005.

—— 'India and the Global Balance of Power: A Neorealist Snapshot', in H. Pant (ed.), *Indian Foreign Policy in a Unipolar World*, New Delhi: Routledge, 2009.

Harshe, R. and Seethi, K. (eds). *Engaging with the World: Critical Reflections on India's Foreign Policy*, New Delhi: Orient Longman, 2005.

Heimsath, C. and Mansingh, L. *A Diplomatic History of Modern India*, Bombay: Allied Publishers, 1971.

Hess, G. *America Encounters India, 1941–47*, Baltimore: John Hopkins University Press, 1971.

Hiranandani, G. 'The Indian End of the Telescope: India and its Navy', *Naval War College Review*, Vol. 55, No. 2, 2002.

Hiscock, G. *India's Global Wealth Club: The Stunning Rise of its Billionaires and Their Secrets of Success*, Singapore: John Wiley & Sons, 2007.

Hoffmann, S. *India and the China Crisis*, Berkeley: University of California Press, 1990.

—— 'Rethinking the Linkage between Tibet and the China-India Border Conflict: A Realist Approach', *Journal of Cold War Studies*, Vol. 8, No. 3, 2006.

Hoge, J. 'A Global Power Shift in the Making', *Foreign Affairs*, Vol. 83, No. 4, 2004.

Holdich, T. *The Gates of India*, London: Macmillan, 1910.

Holmes, J., Winner, A. and Yoshihara, T. *Indian Naval Strategy in the 21st Century*, London: Routledge, 2009.

Holmes, J. and Yoshihara, T. 'Strongman, Constable, or Free-Rider? India's "Monroe Doctrine" and Indian Naval Strategy', *Comparative Strategy*, Vol. 28, No. 4, 2009.

Holslag, J. 'The Persistent Military Security Dilemma between China and India', *Journal of Strategic Studies*, Vol. 32, No. 6, 2009.

—— *China and India: Prospects for Peace*, New York: Columbia University Press, 2010.

Horn, R. 'Afghanistan and the Soviet-Indian Influence Relationship', *Asian Survey*, Vol. 23, No. 3, 1983.

Hoyt, T. 'India and the Challenge of Global Terrorism: The "Long War" and Competing Domestic Visions', in H. Pant (ed.), *Indian Foreign Policy in a Unipolar World*, New Delhi: Routledge, 2009.

Hymans, J. 'India's Soft Power and Vulnerability', *India Review*, Vol. 8, No. 3, 2009.

IDSA-Indian Pugwash Society Working Group. *Space Security, Space Security-Need for a Proactive Approach*, New Delhi: Academic Foundation, 2009.

Indian Navy (Integrated Headquarters). *Indian Maritime Doctrine*, New Delhi: Ministry of Defence, 2004.

—— *Freedom to Use the Seas: India's Maritime Military Strategy*, New Delhi: Ministry of Defence, 2007.

Jacques, K. *Bangladesh, India, and Pakistan: International Relations and Regional Tensions in South Asia*, New York: St Martin's Press, 2000.

Jain, B.M. *Global Power: India's Foreign Policy, 1947–2006*, Lanham: Lexington Books, 2008.

Jain, R. (ed.). *Soviet-South Asian Relations 1947–1978*, Oxford: Martin Robertson, 1979.

—— (ed.). *The United States and India 1947–2006. A Documentary Study*, Delhi: Radiant Publisher, 2007.

—— 'The European Union and China: Indian Perceptions and Perspectives', in G. Wiessala, J. Wilson and P. Taneja (eds), *The European Union and China: Interests and Dilemmas*, Amsterdam: Rodopi, 2009.

—— 'The European Union and the Rise of China and India', in J. Marques, R. Seidelmann and A. Vasilache (eds), *Asia and Europe: Dynamics of Inter- and Intra-Regional Dialogues*, Baden-Baden: Nomos, 2009.

Jayapalan, N. *Foreign Policy of India*, New Delhi: Atlantic Publishers, 2003.

Jayashekar. 'India's Trade with the Soviet Bloc: Growing Dependence and Commodity Inconvertibility', *Problems of Non-Alignment*, Vol. 1, No. 2, 1983.

Jha, R. *The Himalayan Kingdoms in Indian Foreign Policy*, New Delhi: Maitryee Publications, 1986.

Jha, S. *Uneasy Partners: India and Nepal in the Post-colonial Era*, New Delhi: Manas, 1975.

Jian, Z. 'Reaction to the Draft Indian Nuclear Doctrine', *China Report*, Vol. 35, No. 4, 1999.

Jones, R. *India's Strategic Culture*, USA: Defense Threat Reduction Agency SAIC, 2006.

Joshi, N. (ed.). *Central Asia: The Great Game Replayed. An Indian Perspective*, New Delhi: New Century Publications, 2003.

—— 'India's Policy Toward Central Asia', *World Focus*, Vol. 28, No. 335/336, 2007.

Kachru, U. *Extreme Turbulence: India at the Crossroads*, New Delhi: HarperCollins, 2007.

Kalyanaraman, S. 'Operation Parakram: An Indian Exercise in Coercive Diplomacy', *Strategic Analysis,* Vol. 26, No. 4, 2002.

Kamath, S. 'Foreign Aid and India: Financing the Leviathan State', *CATO Policy Analysis* (CATO Institute), No. 170, 1992.

Kamdar, M. *Planet India: The Turbulent Rise of the World's Largest Democracy*, London: Simon & Schuster, 2007.

Kapila, S. 'India–USA Strategic Partnership: The Advent of the Inevitable', *Papers* (SAAG), No. 120, 22 April 2000.

—— 'India-Israel Relations: The Imperatives for Enhanced Strategic Cooperation', *Papers* (SAAG), No. 131, 1 August, 2000.

—— 'Bangladesh-China Defence Co-operation Agreement's Strategic Implications', *Papers* (SAAG), No. 582, 14 January 2003.

—— 'Israel-India Strategic Cooperation and Prime Minister Sharon's Visit: The Added Dimension', *Papers* (SAAG), No. 777, 2 September 2003.

—— 'India's New "Cold Start" War Doctrine Strategically Reviewed', *Papers* (SAAG), No. 991, 4 May 2004.

—— 'Bangladesh Government in Denial Mode on Country's Talibanisation', Papers (SAAG), No. 1058, 15 July 2004.

—— 'Russia Rekindles Strategic Partnership with Russia', *Papers* (SAAG), No. 1180, 7 December 2004.

—— 'Indian Army Validates its Cold Start War Doctrine', *Papers* (SAAG), No. 1408, 7 June 2005.

—— 'The Strategic Significance of the New Delhi Declaration', *Papers* (SAAG), No. 1743, 14 March 2006.

—— 'China: The Strategic Reluctance on Boundary Settlement with India', *Papers* (SAAG), No. 2023, 13 November 2006.

—— 'European Union-India Strategic Partnership Reviewed', *Papers* (SAAG), No. 2661, 7 April 2008.

—— 'Saudi Arabia – India Diplomatic Overtures', *Papers* (SAAG), No. 3701, 4 March 2010.

Kapur, A. *Pokhran and Beyond: India's Nuclear Behaviour*, New Delhi: Oxford University Press, 2000.

—— *India – From Regional to World Power*, London: Routledge, 2006.

Kapur, S. 'India and Pakistan's Unstable Peace: Why Nuclear South Asia is Not Like Cold War Europe', *International Security*, Vol. 30, No. 2, 2005.

—— 'The Kashmir Dispute: Past, Present and Future', in S. Ganguly, A. Scobell and J. Liow (eds), *The Routledge Handbook of Asian Security Studies*, London: Routledge, 2010.

Karnad, B. *Nuclear Weapons and Indian Security: The Realist Foundations of Strategy*, New Delhi: Macmillan, 2002.

—— (ed.). *Strategic Sell-Out: Indian-US Nuclear Deal*, New Delhi: Pentagon Press, 2009.

Kartha, T. 'Countering Transnational Terrorism', *Strategic Analysis*, Vol. 23, No. 11, 2000.

Kautilya. *Kautilya's Arthasastra. Book VI*, tr. R. Shamasastry, Bangalore: Government Press, 1915.

Kavalski, E. 'Venus and the Porcupine. Assessing the European Union-India Strategic Partnership', *South Asian Survey*, Vol. 15, No. 1, 2008.

—— *India and Central Asia: The Mythmaking and International Relations of a Rising Power*, London: I.B. Tauris, 2010.

Kavic, L. *India's Quest for Security: Defence Policies, 1947–1965*, Berkeley: University of California Press, 1967.

Khan, M. 'Vajpayee's Visit to Iran: Indo-Iranian Relations and Prospects of Bilateral Cooperation', *Strategic Analysis*, Vol. 25, No. 6, 2001.

—— 'India-Pakistan Trade: A Roadmap for Enhancing Economic Relations', *Policy Brief* (Peterson Institute for International Economics), July 2009.

Khan, S.A. 'The State and the Limits of Counter-Terrorism-II: The Experience of India and Bangladesh', in I. Ahmed (ed.), *Understanding Terrorism in South Asia: Beyond Statist Discourses*, New Delhi: Manohar Publishers, 2006.

Khan, Y. *The Great Partition: The Making of India and Pakistan*, New Haven: Yale University Press, 2007.

Khanna, V. *India's Nuclear Doctrine*, New Delhi: Samskriti, 2000.

Khripunov, I. and Srivastava, A. 'Russian-Indian Relationship: Alliance, Partnership, Or?', *Comparative Strategy*, Vol. 18, No. 2, 1999.

Khurana, G. 'China's String of Pearls in the Indian Ocean and its Security Implications', *Strategic Analysis*, Vol. 32, No. 1, January 2008.

—— 'China-India Maritime Rivalry', *Indian Defense Review*, Vol. 23, No. 4, 2009.

Kiesow, I. and Norling, N. 'The Rise of India: Problems and Opportunities', *Silk Road Papers*, January 2007.

Kirk, J. 'Indian-Americans and the US-India Nuclear Agreement: Consolidation of an Ethnic Lobby?', *Foreign Policy Analysis*, Vol. 4, No. 3, 2008.

Kochanek, S. 'India's Changing Role in the United Nations', *Pacific Affairs*, Vol. 53, No. 1, 1980.

Koshy, N. 'Sidelining the United Nations', *Economic and Political Weekly*, 8 April 2000.

—— 'Nuclear Weapons and India's Foreign Policy', in R. Harshe and K. Seethi (eds), *Engaging with the World: Critical Reflections on Indian Foreign Policy*, Hyderabad: Orient Longman, 2001.

Krasna, M. 'Three Main Stages in the Development of Sino-Indian Contacts During the Indian Freedom Movement', *Archiv Orientalni*, Vol. 49, No. 3, 1981.

Kukreja, V. *Civil-Military Relations in South Asia: Pakistan, Bangladesh, and India*, New Delhi: Sage Publications, 1991.

Kumar, M. 'Reactions and Attitudes of African Countries to the Chinese Aggression on India', in V. Grover (ed.), *International Relations and Foreign Policy of India*, New Delhi: Deep & Deep, 1992.

Kumar, N. *India's Global Powerhouses: How They Are Taking On the World*, Cambridge: Harvard Business School Press, 2009.

Kumar, S. 'Nuclearisation of Tibetan Plateau and its Implications for India', *Article* (ICPS), No. 482, 13 March 2001.

Kumaraswamy, P. *India and Israel: Evolving Security Partnership*, Ramat Gan: BESA Center for Strategic Studies, 1998.

—— 'India and Israel: Emerging Partnership', in S. Ganguly (ed.), *India as an Emerging Power*, Portland: Frank Cass, 2003.

—— 'Delhi: Between Tehran and Washington', *Middle East Quarterly*, Vol. 15, No. 1, 2008.

—— *India's Israel Policy: From Nonrelations to Friendship*, New York: Columbia University Press, 2010.

Kundra, J. *Indian Foreign Policy: 1947–1954*, Groningen: J.B. Wolters, 1956.

Kuppuswamy, C. 'India's Look East Policy – A Review', *Papers* (SAAG), No. 3662, 12 February 2010.

Kux, D. *India and the United States: Estranged Democracies 1941–1991*, Washington: National Defense University Press, 1992.

Ladwig, W. 'New Delhi's Pacific Ambition: Naval Power, "Look East", and India's Emerging Influence in the Asia-Pacific', *Asian Security*, Vol. 5, No. 2, 2009.

Lak, D. *The Future of a New Superpower*, New York: Viking, 2008.

Lal, V. 'India in the World: Hinduism, the Diaspora, and the Anxiety of Influence', *Australian Religious Studies Review*, Vol. 16, No. 2, 2003.

Lall, K., Ernst, W. and Chopra, H. (eds). *India and the EEC*, New Delhi: Allied Publishers, 1984.

Lall, M. 'Indo-Myanmar Relations in the Era of Pipeline Diplomacy', *Contemporary Southeast Asia*, Vol. 28, No. 3, 2006.

Lele, A. 'Successful Launch of PSLVC15', *IDSA Comment*, 16 July 2010.

Mahbubani, K. *The New Asian Hemisphere: The Irresistible Shift of Global Power to the East*, New York: PublicAffairs, 2008.

Malakar, S. (ed.). *India's Energy Security and the Gulf*, Delhi: Academic Excellence, 2006.

Malik, M. 'The Proliferation Axis: Beijing-Islambad-Pyongyang', *Korean Journal of Defense Analysis*, Vol. 15, No. 1, 2003.

—— 'China and the East Asian Summit: More Discord than Accord', *Paper* (Honolulu, Asia-Pacific Center for Security Studies), February 2006, www.apcss.org.

—— 'War Talk: Perceptual Gaps in "Chindia" Relations', *China Brief*, Vol. 9, No. 20, 2009.

Mallik, D. *The Development of Non-Alignment in India's Foreign Policy*, Allahabad: Chaitanya Publishing House, 1967.

Mansingh, L. (ed.). *Indian Foreign Policy: Agenda for the 21st Century, Volume 1*, New Delhi: Konark Publishers, 2000.

—— 'India-Japan Relations', *IPCS Issue Brief*, No. 43, January 2007.

Marwah, O. 'Indian Nuclear and Space Programmes: Intent and Policy', *International Security*, Vol. 2, No. 2, 1997.

Mathur, C., Jurgen-Richter, F. and Das, T. *India Rising: Emergence of a New World Power*, Singapore: Marshall Cavendish Business, 2006.

Mathur, U. and Varughese, G. 'From "Obstructionist" to Leading Player: Transforming India's International Image', in D. Michel and A. Pandya (eds), *Indian Climate Policy: Choices and Challenges*, Washington: Henry Stimson Center, 2009.

Mattoo, A. (ed.). *The Peacock and the Dragon: India-China Relations in the 21st Century*, New Delhi: Har-Anand Publications, 2000.

Mawdsley, E. and McCann, G. 'The Elephant in the Corner? Reviewing India-Africa Relations in the New Millennium', *Geography Compass*, Vol. 4, No. 2, 2010.

Maxwell, N. *India's China War*, London: Jonathan Cape, 1970.

—— 'Sino-Indian Border Dispute Reconsidered', *Economic and Political Weekly*, Vol. 34, No. 15, 1999.

—— 'Forty Years of Folly: What Caused the Sino-Indian Border War and Why the Dispute is Unresolved', *Critical Asian Studies*, Vol. 35, No. 1, 2003.

Mazumdar, A. 'Bhutan's Military Action Against Indian Insurgents', *Asian Survey*, Vol. 45, No. 4, 2005.

McDonald, J. and Wimbush, S. 'India's Energy Security', *Strategic Analysis*, Vol. 23, No. 5, 1999.

McLeod, D. *India and Pakistan: Friends, Rival or Enemies?* Aldershot: Ashgate, 2008.

Mehra, M. *India: Emerging Leadership on Climate Change*, Washington: Heinrich Bolls Foundation, December 2008.

Mehta, A. 'Countering India's Maoist Insurgency', *RSIS Commentaries*, No. 74, 5 July 2010.

Mehta, S. 'India and the Soviet Union: A New Stage of Relations' *Asian Survey*, Vol. 18, No. 7, 1978.

Menon, N. and Nigam, A. *Power and Contestation: India Since 1989*, London: Zed Books, 2007.

Menon, R. *A Nuclear Strategy for India*, New Delhi: Sage Publications, 2000.

Meredyth, R. *The Elephant and the Dragon: The Rise of India and China, and What it Means for the Rest of Us*, New York: W.W. Norton, 2007.

Mishra, R. 'Nuclear and Missile Threats to India: China-Pakistan Nexus in South Asia', *Papers* (SAAG), No. 296, 17 August 2001.

Misra, A. *India-Pakistan Coming to Terms*, London: Macmillan, 2010.

Misra, K.P. (ed.). *Foreign Policy of India: A Book of Readings*, New Delhi: Thomson, 1977.

Mistry, D. 'A Theoretical and Empirical Assessment of India as an Emerging World Power', *India Review*, Vol. 3, No. 1, 2004.

Mitra, S. 'War and Peace in South Asia: A Revisionist View of India-Pakistan Relations', *Contemporary South Asia*, Vol. 10, No. 3, 2001.

—— 'The Reluctant Hegemon: India's Self Perception and the South Asian Strategic Environment', *Contemporary South Asia*, Vol. 12, No. 3, 2003.

Modi, K. 'India: APEC's Missing Piece?', *CACCI Journal*, Vol. 1, 2008.

Mohammed, A. 'India Matters', *Washington Quarterly*, Vol. 21, No. 1, 2000.

Motlagh, J. 'The Maoists in the Forest: Tracking India's Separatist Rebels', *Virginia Quarterly Review*, Vol. 84, No. 3, 2008.

Mukhopadhyay, A. 'EU-India Counter-Terrorism Cooperation: Post-Lisbon Prospects', *IDSA Comment*, 22 February 2010.

—— 'The EEAS and the EU-India Strategic Partnership', *IDSA Comment*, 22 July 2010.

Muni, S. *Pangs of Proximity*, New Delhi: Sage Publications, 1993.

—— 'India's Afghan Policy Emerging from the Cold', in K. Warikoo (ed.), *The Afghanistan Crisis: Issues and Perspectives*, New Delhi: Bhavana Books, 2002.

—— (ed.). *Responding to Terrorism in South Asia*, New Delhi: Manohar Publishers, 2006.

Muni, S. and Mohan, C. Raja. 'Emerging Asia: India's Options', *International Studies*, Vol. 41, No. 3, 2004.

Murthi, K. and Madhusudan, H. 'Strategic Considerations in Indian Space Programme – Towards Maximising Socio-economic Benefits', *Acta Astronautica*, Vol. 63, No. 1–4, 2008.

Naaz, F. 'Indo-Israel Military Cooperation', *Strategic Analysis*, Vol. 25, No. 4, 2000.

Naidu, G. 'India and the Asia-Pacific Balance of Power', *Strategic Analysis*, Vol. 25, No. 5, 2001.

—— 'Wither the Look East Policy: India and Southeast Asia', *Strategic Analysis*, Vol. 28, No. 2, 2004.

—— 'India and Southeast Asia: An Analysis of the Look East Policy', in P. Rao (ed.), *India and ASEAN: Partners at Summit*, New Delhi: Knowledge World Publishers, 2008.

Naidu, S. 'India's Engagement in Africa: Self Interest or Mutual Partnership?', in R. Southall and H. Melber (eds), *The New Scramble for Africa: Imperialism, Investment and Development in Africa*, Scottsville, South Africa: University of KwaZulu-Natal Press, 2009.

Nair, R. *Dynamics of a Diplomacy Delayed: India and Israel*, Delhi: Kalpaz, 2004.

Nair, V. 'The Structure of an Indian Nuclear Deterrent', in A. Mattoo (ed.), *India's Nuclear Deterrent: Pokhran II and Beyond*, New Delhi: Har-Anand, 1999.

Nanda, B. (ed.). *Indian Foreign Policy: the Nehru Years*, New Delhi: Vikas, 1976.

Nanda, P. (ed.) *Rising India: Friends and Foes*, New Delhi: Lancer, 2007.

—— 'SAARC – Expect No Miracles', *India Defence Review*, 3 May 2010.

Narlikar, A. 'Peculiar Chauvinism or Strategic Calculation? Explaining the Negotiating Strategy of a Rising India', *International Affairs*, Vol. 82, No. 1, 2006.

Nativi, A. 'Fleet Dreams. Delays Plague India's Effort to Expand Its Navy', *Defense Technology International*, 1 April 2008.

Nayar, B. 'Treat India Seriously', *Foreign Policy*, No. 18, Spring 1975.

Nayar, B.R. and Paul, T. *India in the World Order: Searching for Major Power Status*, Cambridge: Cambridge University Press, 2003.

Nehru, J. *The Discovery of India*, London: Meridian Books, 1956.

—— *India's Foreign Policy: Selected Speeches, September 1946–April 1961*, New Delhi: Government of India, 1961.

Niazi, T. 'China's March on South Asia', *China Brief*, Vol. 5, No. 9, 2005.

Noor, S. 'Pakistan-India Relations and Terrorism', *Pakistan Horizon*, Vol. 60, No. 2, 2007.

Noorani, A. 'India's Quest for a Nuclear Guarantee', *Asian Survey*, Vol. 3, No. 7, 1967.

Norbu, D. 'Tibet in Sino-Indian Relations: The Centrality of Marginality', *Asian Survey*, Vol. 37, No. 11, 1997.

Ollapally, D. 'India and the New "Asian" Balance of Power', *Strategic Analysis*, Vol. 22, No. 4, 1998.

—— 'Mixed Motives in India's Search for Nuclear Status', *Asian Survey*, Vol. 41, No. 6, 2001.

—— 'Indo-Russian Strategic Relations: New Choices and Constraints', in S. Ganguly (ed.), *India as an Emerging Power,* London: Frank Cass, 2003.

Panda, P. *Making of India's Foreign Policy: Prime Ministers and Wars*, New Delhi: Raj Publications, 2003.

Pande, I. (ed.), *India China: Neighbours Strangers*, London: HarperCollins, 2010.

Pande, S. *India and the Nuclear Test Ban*, New Delhi: Institute for Defence Studies and Analyses, 1996.

Pandey, S. 'India in the Russian Foreign Policy Debate', in P. Sahai (ed.), *India-Eurasia: The Way Ahead*, Chandigarh: Centre for Research in Rural and Industrial Development, 2008.

Panikkar, K. *India and the Indian Ocean: An Essay on the Influence of Sea Power on Indian History*, London: George Allen & Unwin, 1945.

Pant, G. *India: The Emerging Energy Player*, New Delhi: Pearson Longman, 2008.

Pant, H. 'India and Iran: An "Axis" in the Making?', *Asian Survey,* Vol. 44, No. 3, July/August 2003.

—— 'India-Israel Partnership: Convergence and Constraints', *Middle East Review of International Affairs*, Vol. 8, No. 4, 2004.

—— 'Feasibility of the Russia-China-India "Strategic Triangle". Assessment of Theoretical and Empirical Issues', *International Studies*, Vol. 43, No. 1, 2006.

—— 'Saudi Arabia Woos China and India', *Middle East Quarterly*, Vol. 13, No. 4, 2006.

—— 'India in the Asia-Pacific: Rising Ambitions With an Eye on China', *Asia-Pacific Review*, Vol. 14, No. 1, 2007.

—— 'India's Nuclear Doctrine and Command Structure: Implications for Civil-Military Relations in India', *Armed Forces & Society*, Vol. 33, No. 2, 2007.

—— 'A Fine Balance: India Walks a Tightrope between Iran and the United States', *Orbis*, Vol. 51, No. 3, 2007.

—— 'India and Bangladesh: Will the Twain Ever Meet?', *Asian Survey*, Vol. 47, No. 2, 2007.

—— 'India and Bangladesh: A Relationship Adrift', in M. Chatterji and B. Jain (eds), *Conflict and Peace in South Asia*, London: Emerald Publishers, 2008.

—— *Contemporary Debates in Indian Foreign and Security Policy: India Negotiates its Rise in the International System*, New York: Palgrave Macmillan, 2008.

—— 'Indian Foreign and Security Policy: Beyond Nuclear Weapons', *Brown Journal of World Affairs*, Vol. 25, No. 2, 2009.

—— 'Looking Beyond Tehran: India's Rising Stakes in the Gulf', in A. Sagar and G. Kemp (eds), *India's Growing Role in the Gulf*, Washington: Nixon Center, 2009.

—— 'India in the Indian Ocean: Growing Mismatch Between Ambitions and Capabilities', *Pacific Affairs*, Vol. 82, No. 2, 2009.

—— 'The US-India Nuclear Pact: Policy, Process, and Great Power Politics', *Asian Security*, Vol. 5, No. 3, 2009.

—— 'China's Naval Expansion in the Indian Ocean and India–China Rivalry', *The Asia-Pacific Journal*, No. 3353, 3 May 2010.

—— 'India in Afghanistan: A Test Case for a Rising Power?', *Contemporary South Asia*, Vol. 18, No. 2, 2010.

—— *The China Syndrome: Grappling with an Uneasy Relationship*, London: HarperCollins, 2010.

Pardesi, M. 'Deducing India's Grand Strategy of Regional Hegemony from Historical and Comparative Perspectives', *RSIS Working Paper* (Nanyang Technological University), No. 76, 2005.

Pardesi, M. and Ganguly, S. 'India and Energy Security: A Foreign Policy Priority', in H. Pant (ed.), *Indian Foreign Policy in a Unipolar World*, New Delhi: Routledge, 2009.

Parekh, B. 'The Indian Diaspora', in J. Motwani and M. Cosine (eds), *The Global Indian Diaspora: Yesterday, Today and Tomorrow*, New York: Global Organization of People of Indian Origin, 1993.

Parikh, K. and Gokam, S. *Consumption Patterns: The Driving Force of Environmental Stress*, New Delhi: Indira Gandhi Institute of Development Research (IGIDR), 1991.

Pasha, A. *India, Iran and the GCC States: Political Strategy and Foreign Policy*, New Delhi: Manas Publication, 2000.

Patil, S. 'India's China Policy in the 1950s: Threat Perceptions and Balances', *South Asian Survey*, Vol. 14, No. 2, 2007.

Patil, V. and Jha, N. (eds). *India in a Turbulent World*, New Delhi: South Asian Publishers, 2003.

Pattanaik, S. 'Indo-Nepal Open Border: Implications for Bilateral Relations and Security', *Strategic Analysis*, Vol. 22, No. 3, 1998.

—— 'SAARC at 25: Time to Reflect', *IDSA Comment*, 7 May 2010.

Paul, T. (ed.). *The India-Pakistan Conflict an Enduring Rivalry*, Cambridge: Cambridge University Press, 2005.

Perkovich, G. *India's Nuclear Bomb: the Impact on Global Proliferation*, Berkeley: University of California Press, 1999.

—— 'Is India a Major Power?', *Washington Quarterly*, Vol. 27, No. 1, 2003–04.

Pillai, K. (ed.). *Indian Foreign Policy in the 1990s*, London: Sangam Books, 1997.

Poddar, T. and Yi, E. 'India's Rising Growth Potential', in *BRICS and Beyond* (Goldman Sachs Global Economics Paper, No. 152), Washington: Goldman Sachs, 2007.

Poulose, T. 'Bhutan's External Relations and India', *International and Comparative Law Quarterly*, Vol. 20, No. 2, 1971.

Pradhan, B. 'Changing Dynamics of India's West Asia Policy', *International Studies,* Vol. 41, No. 1, 2004.

Pradhan, P. 'India and Gulf Cooperation Council: Time to Look Beyond Business', *Strategic Analysis*, Vol. 34, No. 1, 2010.

Pradhan, S. *India, GCC and the Global Energy Regime: Exploring Interdependence and Outlook for Collaboration*, New Delhi: Academic Foundation, 2008.

—— 'India's Economic and Political Presence in the Gulf: A Gulf Perspective', in A. Sagar and G. Kemp (eds), *India's Growing Role in the Gulf*, Washington: The Nixon Center, 2009.

—— 'India and the Gulf Cooperation Council (GCC): An Economic and Political Perspective', *Strategic Analysis*, Vol. 34, No. 1, 2010.

—— 'India and Gulf Cooperation Council: Time to Look Beyond Business', *Strategic Analysis*, Vol. 34, No. 2, 2010.

Prakash, A. *From the Crow's Nest: A Compendium of Speeches and Writings on Maritime and Other Issues*, New Delhi: Lancer Publishers, 2007.

—— 'India's Maritime Strategy', *USI Journal*, Vol. 137, No. 568, 2007.

Prasad, B. (ed.). *India's Foreign Policy: Studies of Continuity and Change*, New Delhi: Vikas, 1979.

Rahman, A. *Indian Labour Migration to the Gulf*, New Delhi: Rajat, 2001.

Rahul, R. *The Himalayan Borderland*, Delhi: Vikas Publishing House, 1970.

Raj, G. *Reach for the Stars – The Evolution of India's Rocket Programme*, New Delhi: Viking, 2000.

Raja Mohan, C. *Crossing the Rubicon: The Shaping of India's New Foreign Policy*, New Delhi: Penguin, 2003.

—— 'What If Pakistan Fails? India Isn't Worried…Yet', *Washington Quarterly*, Vol. 28, No. 1, 2004–05.

—— 'India and the Balance of Power', *Foreign Affairs*, Vol. 85, No. 4, 2006.

—— 'Balancing Interests and Values: India's Struggle with Democracy Promotion', *Washington Quarterly*, Vol. 30, No. 3, 2007.

—— 'Indian Foreign Policy', *World Focus*, Vol. 28, No. 335/336, 2007.

—— 'India's Strategic Challenges in the Indian Ocean and the Gulf', in *India's Grand Strategy in the Gulf*, Washington: The Nixon Center, 2009.

—— 'Sino-Indian Rivalry in the Western Indian Ocean', *ISAS Insights* (Singapore), No. 52, 24 February 2009.

—— 'Rising India: Partner in Shaping the Global Commons?', *Washington Quarterly*, Vol. 33, No. 3, 2010.

Rajadhyaksha, N. *The Rise of India: Its Transformation from Poverty to Prosperity*, New Delhi: Wiley India, 2006.

Rajagopalan, R. 'Neorealist Theory and the India-Pakistan Conflict', in K. Bajpai and S. Mallavarapu (eds), *International Relations in India: Theorising the Region and Nation*, New Delhi: Orient Longman, 2004.

Rajagopalan, R. and Sahni, V. 'India and the Great Powers: Strategic Imperatives, Normative Necessities', *South Asian Survey*, Vol. 15, No. 1, 2008.

Rajan, D. 'China Should Break up the Indian Union, Suggests a Chinese Strategist', *Papers* (SAAG), No. 3342, 10 August 2009.

Rajan, M. *Indian Spaceflights*, Delhi: Publications Division, 1985.

Rajeswari, P. 'Terrorism—an Area of Cooperation in Indo-US Relations', *Strategic Analysis*, Vol. 24, No. 6, 2000.

Ram, N. *Riding the Nuclear Tiger*, New Delhi: LeftWord Books, 1999.

Ramakant and Upreti, B. (eds). *India and Nepal: Aspects of Interdependent Relations*, Delhi: Kalinga Publications, 2001.

Raman, B. 'Bin Laden Targets India', *Papers* (SAAG), No. 1776, 25 April 2006.

—— 'Global Terrorism: India's Concerns', *Papers* (SAAG), No. 2021, 12 November 2006.

—— 'Indian Navy Begins To Look West', *Papers* (SAAG), No. 2128, 9 February 2007.

—— 'Gwadar, Hanbantona and Sitwe: China's Strategic Triangle', *Papers* (SAAG), No. 2158, 6 March 2007.

—— 'Pakistan as China's Force-multiplier Against India', *Papers* (SAAG), No. 3918, 11 July 2010.

Rao, P. (ed.). *India and ASEAN: Partners at Summit*, New Delhi: Knowledge World Publishers, 2008.

Rao, P.V.R. *India's Defence Policy and Organisation Since Independence*, New Delhi: The United Services Institution of India, 1977.

Rao, R. 'Will India Prepare for Space War?', *Article* (IPCS), No. 3038, 7 January 2010.

Rao, U. 'An Overview of the Aryabhata Project', in U. Rao and K. Kasturirangan (eds), *The Aryabhata Project*, Bangalore: Indian Academy of Sciences, 1979.

Ray, N. 'Sudan Crisis: Exploring India's Role', *Strategic Analysis*, Vol. 31, No. 1, 2007.

Reddy, S. 'India's Forays into Space. The Evolution of its Space Programme', *International Studies*, Vol. 45, No. 3, 2008.

Rehman, I. 'China's String of Pearls and India's Enduring Tactical Advantage', *IDSA Comment*, 8 June 2010.

Rosen, S. *Societies and Military Power: India and its Armies*, Ithaca: Cornell University Press, 1996.

Roshandel, J. 'The Iran-Pakistan-India Natural Gas Pipeline: Implications and Challenges for Regional Security', *Strategic Analysis*, Vol. 34, No. 1, 2010.

Rothermund, D. *India: The Rise of an Asian Giant*, New Haven: Yale University Press, 2009.

Roy, J. and Kumar, B. (eds). *India and Central Asia: Classical to Contemporary Periods*, New Delhi: Concept Publishing, 2007.

Roy-Chaudhury, R. *India's Maritime Security*, New Delhi: Knowledge World, 2000.

—— 'India's Nuclear Doctrine: A Critical Analysis', *Strategic Analysis*, Vol. 33, No. 3, 2009.

Sachdeva, G. 'India-China Economic Cooperation Through Growth Quadrangle', in K. Bajpai and A. Mattoo (ed.), *The Peacock and the Dragon: India-China Relations in the 21st Century*, New Delhi: Har-Anand, 2000.

—— *Economy of the Northeast: Policy, Present Conditions and Future Possibilities*, New Delhi: Konark Publishers, 2000.

—— 'India Ocean Region: Present Economic Trends & Future Possibilities', *International Studies*, Vol. 41, No. 1, 2004.

—— 'India and the European Union: Time to De-Bureaucratize Strategic Partnership', *Strategic Analysis*, Vol. 33, No. 2, 2009.

—— 'Regional Economic Linkages', in N. Joshi (ed.), *Reconnecting India & Central Asia: Emerging Security & Economic Dimensions*, Washington, DC: Central Asia Caucasus Institute (Johns Hopkins University), 2010.

Sadhu, K. *Indians in Malaya: Some Aspect of their Immigration and Settlement 1786–1957*, Oxford: Oxford University Press, 1969.

Sagar, A. and Kemp, G. (eds). *India's Growing Role in the Gulf*, Washington: The Nixon Center, 2009.

Sahadevan, P. 'India's Policy of Non-Intervention in Sri Lanka', in A. Raju (ed.), *India-Sri Lanka Partnership in the 21st Century*, New Delhi: Kalpaz Publications, 2007.

Sahay, A. 'The Iran-Pakistan-India Natural Gas Pipeline: Implications and Challenges for Regional Security', *Strategic Analysis*, Vol. 34, No. 1, 2010.

Sahgal, A. and Palit, P. 'The Singh Doctrine', *Armed Forces Journal*, Vol. 143, No. 10, 2005.

Sankar, U. *The Economics of India's Space Programme–An Exploratory Analysis*, New Delhi: Oxford University Press, 2007.

Santhanam, K. *Jihadis in Jammu and Kashmir: A Portrait Gallery*, New Delhi: Sage Publications, 2003.

Santhanam, K. and Dwivedi, R. (eds). *India and Central Asia: Advancing the Common Interest*, New Delhi: Anamaya Publishers, 2004.

Sanyal, S. *The Indian Renaissance: India's Rise After a Thousand Years of Decline*, New Delhi: Penguin, 2008.

Sawhney, P. and Sood, V. *Operation Parakram: The War Unfinished*, New Delhi: Sage, 2003.

Schaffer, T. and Fawzi, S. 'India and Iran: Limited Partnership and High Stakes', *South Asia Monitor*, No. 114, 20 December 2007.

Schaffer, T. and Verma, A. 'A Difficult Road Ahead: India's Policy on Afghanistan', *South Asia Monitor*, No. 144, 1 August 2010.

Schirm, S. 'Leaders in Need of Followers: Emerging Powers in Global Governance', *European Journal of International Relations*, Vol. 16, No. 2, 2010.

Schofield, V. *Kashmir in Conflict: India, Pakistan and the Unending War*, London: I.B. Tauris & Company, 2003.

Scott, D. 'India's "Grand Strategy" for the Indian Ocean: Mahanian Visions', *Asia-Pacific Review*, Vol. 13, No. 2, 2006.

—— 'Indian "Footprints" in the Indian Ocean: Power Projection for the 21st Century', *Indian Ocean Survey*, Vol. 2, No. 2, 2006.

—— 'Strategic Imperatives of India as an Emerging Player in Pacific Asia', *International Studies*, Vol. 44, No. 2, 2007.

—— 'India's Drive for a "Blue Water" Navy', *Journal of Military and Strategic Studies*, Vol. 10, No. 2, 2007–08.

—— 'The Great Power "Great Game" between India and China: "The Logic of Geography"', *Geopolitics*, Vol. 13, No. 1, 2008.

—— 'India's "Extended Neighbourhood" Concept: Power Projection for a Rising Power', *India Review*, Vol. 8, No. 2, 2009.

—— 'Sino-Indian Territorial Issues: The "Razor's Edge"?', in H. Pant (ed.), *The Rise of China: Implications for India*, New Delhi: Foundation Books, 2011.

Sengupta, J. *Non-Alignment: in Search of a Destination*, Calcutta: Naya Prokash, 1979.

Shah, G. and Dixit, R. *Narco-Terrorism*, New Delhi: Siddhi Boooks, 1996.

Shamsuddin (ed.). *India and Russia: Towards Strategic Partnership*, New Delhi: Lancer Books, 2001.

Sharma, A. 'India and Energy Security', *Asian Affairs*, Vol. 38, No. 2, 2007.

Sharma, J. 'Poised to Play an Important Role', *Foreign Affairs Journal*, Vol. 3, No.2, 2008.

Sharma, R. 'India-Japan Ties Poised for Advance as Both Nations Eye China', *The Asia-Pacific Journal*, 6 September 2010.

Sharma, R.R. (ed.). *India and Emerging Asia*, New Delhi: Sage, 2005.

Sharma, S. *Lal Bahadur Shastri: An Era of Transition in Indian Foreign Policy*, New Delhi: Kanishka, 2001.

Sherman, M. and Sondhi, M. 'Indo-Israeli Cooperation as a US National Interest', *Ariel Center for Policy Research (ACPR) Policy Papers*, No. 89, 1999.

Shukul, C. (ed.). *Indian Foreign Policy at Crossroads: A Conceptual Stocktaking of the Post-Cold War Period*, Ujjain: Madhya Pradesh Institute of Social Science Research, 1995.

Sidhu, W. and Yuan, J. 'Resolving the Sino-Indian Border Dispute: Building Confidence Through Cooperative Monitoring', *Asian Survey*, Vol. 41, No. 2, 2001.

Sikri, R. 'India's Foreign Policy in the Coming Decade', *Working Paper* (Institute of South Asian Studies, Singapore), No. 25, 25 September 2007.

—— *Challenge and Strategy. Rethinking India's Foreign Policy*, New Delhi: Sage, 2009.

Singh, J. 'Against Nuclear Apartheid', *Foreign Affairs*, Vol. 77, No. 5, 1998.

—— *Defending India*, New York: St Martin's Press, 1999.

—— 'Speech', June 2000, in S. Siddique and S. Kumar (eds), *The 2nd ASEAN Reader,* Singapore: Institute of Southeast Asian Studies, 2003.

Singh, K. 'India's Endeavour to Attain Space Security Asset', *Articles* (IPCS), No. 3071, 15 March 2010, www.ipcs.org.

Singh, K.R. (ed.), *Post-War Gulf Implications for India*, New Delhi: Lancers Books, 1993.

Singh, M. (ed.), *India and Tajikistan: Revitalizing a Traditional Relationship*, New Delhi: Anamika Publishers, 2003.

Singh, P. 'India-Nepal Relations: Rickety Roadmap', *World Focus*, Vol. 317, No. 27, 2003.

Singh, R.K. *India's Foreign Policy: The First Study in Continuity and Change*, New Delhi: Samiksha Prakashan, 2001.

Singh, S. 'India and Regionalism', in *Regionalism in South Asian Diplomacy*, Stockholm: SIPRI Policy Paper, No. 15, February 2007.

Singh, S.D. 'India and the European Community: Development Co-operation in the UNCTAD Context', *Studia Diplomatica*, Vol. 29, No. 4, 1976.

Sinha, S.K. 'The Chief of Defence Staff', *Journal of Defence Studies*, Vol. 1, No. 1, 2007.

Sinha, U. 'Climate Change: Issues and Divides', *Strategic Analysis*, Vol. 33, No. 2, 2009.

Sinha, Y. 'Diplomacy in the 21st Century', in A. Gupta, M. Chaturvedi and A. Joshi (eds), *Security and Diplomacy*, New Delhi: Manas Publications, 2004.

Sisodia, N. and Bhaskar, U. *Emerging India: Security and Foreign Policy Perspective*, New Delhi: Promilla, 2007.

Sobhan, R. 'The Need for Economic Integration', *South Asian Survey,* Vol. 13, No. 2, 2006.

Sridharan, E. 'Economic Cooperation and Security Spill-Overs: The Case of India and Pakistan', in M. Krepon and C. Gagne (eds), *Economic Confidence-Building and Regional Security*, Washington: Henry L. Stimson Center, 2000.

Sridharan, K. *The ASEAN Region in India's Foreign Policy*, Dartmouth: Aldershot, 1996.

—— 'India and ASEAN: The Long Road to Dialogue', *The Round Table*, No. 340, October 1996.

—— 'Regional Organisations and Conflict Management: Comparing ASEAN and SAARC', *Working Paper* (Crisis States Research Centre, National University of Singapore), No. 33, 2008.

Stewart-Ingersoll, R. and Frazier, D. 'India as a Regional Power: Identifying the Impact of Roles and Foreign Policy Orientation on the South Asian Security Order', *Asian Security*, Vol. 6, No. 1, 2010.

Stratfor. 'Bhutan: Counterinsurgency a Strategic Window for India', *Stratfor Report*, 18 December 2003.

Subrahmanyam, K. *Perspectives in Defence Planning*, New Delhi: Abhinav, 1972.

—— *Indian Security Perspectives*, New Delhi: ABC Publishing House, 1982.

Subramanian, N. 'India's Great Power Plans', *The Diplomat*, 29 March 2010.

Suri, R. 'Indian Security and the Threat of Terrorism', *Agni*, Vol. 10, No. 111, 2007.

Swami, P. *India, Pakistan and the Secret Jihad: The Covert War in Kashmir, 1947–2004*, London: Routledge, 2007.

Swamy, S. (ed.). *India's China Perspective*, New Delhi: Konrak Publishers, 2001.

Synnott, H. 'The Cause and Consequences of South Asia's Nuclear Tests', *Adelphi Paper*, No. 332, Oxford: Oxford University Press, 1999.

Tan, T. and Kudaisya, G. *Partition and Post-Colonial South Asia*, London: Routledge, 2008.

Tanham, G. *Indian Strategic Thought: An Interpretive Essay*, Santa Monica: RAND, 1992.

Tarapot, P. *Insurgency Movement in North Eastern India*, New Delhi: Vikas Publishing House, 1993.

Tellis, A. 'India's Emerging Nuclear Doctrine: Exemplifying the Lessons of the Nuclear Revolution', *NBR Analysis*, Vol. 12, No. 2, 2001.

—— *India's Emerging Nuclear Posture: Between Recessed Deterrent and Ready Arsenal*, Santa Monica: RAND, 2001.

—— *India as a New Global Power: An Action Agenda for the United States*, Washington: Carnegie Endowment for International Peace, 2005.

Thakur, R. 'India and Overseas Indians', *Asian Survey*, Vol. 25, No. 3, 1985.

Thakur, R. and Thayer, C. *Soviet Relations with India and Vietnam: 1945–1992*, Delhi: Oxford University Press, 1993.

Thomas, R. *India's Search for Power. Indira Gandhi's Foreign Policy, 1966–82*, New Delhi: SAGE, 1984.

Thomas, R. and Gupta, A. (eds), *India's Nuclear Security*, London: Lynne Rienner, 2000.

Tinker, H. 'Odd Man Out: The Loneliness of the Indian Colonial Politician. The Career of Manilal Doctor', *Journal of Imperial and Commonwealth History*, Vol. 2, No. 2, 1974.

Tripathi, R. 'SAARC Convention on Suppression of Terrorism: An Agenda for Relocation', in O. Mishra and S. Ghosh (eds), *Terrorism and Low Intensity Conflict in South Asian Region*, New Delhi: Manak Publication, 2003.

Twining, D. 'India's Relations With Iran and Myanmar: "Rogue State" or Responsible Democratic Shareholder?', *India Review*, Vol. 7, No. 1, 2008.

Upadhyay, R. 'De-Pakistanisation of Bangladesh', *Papers* (SAAG), No. 2199, 7 April 2007.

Vaidya, K. *The Naval Defence of India*, Bombay: Thacker, 1949.

Varshney, A. 'India's Democratic Challenge', *Foreign Affairs*, Vol. 86, No. 2, 2007.

Vines, A. and Oruitemeka, B. 'India's Engagement with the African Indian Ocean Rim States', *Africa Programme Paper* (London: Chatham House), No.1/08, 2008.

Vohra, P. and Ghosh, P. (eds). *China and the Indian Ocean Region*, New Delhi: National Maritime Foundation, 2008.

Wagner, C. 'From Hard Power to Soft Power? Ideas, Interaction, Institutions, and Images in India's South Asia Policy', *Heidelberg Papers in South Asian and Comparative Politics*, No. 26, 2005.

Walker, W. 'International Nuclear Relations after the Indian and Pakistani Test Explosions', *International Affairs*, Vol. 74, No. 3, 1998.

Warikoo, K. 'Shadow of Afghanistan over Kashmir', in K. Warikoo (ed.), *The Afghanistan Crisis: Issues and Perspectives*, New Delhi: Bhavana Books, 2002.

—— 'Religious Extremism and Terrorism in Kashmir', in M. Singh (ed.), *International Terrorism and Religious Extremism: Challenges to Central and South Asia*, New Delhi: Anamika Publishers, 2004.

—— (ed.). *Himalayan Frontiers of India: Historical, Geo-political and Strategic Perspectives*, London: Routledge, 2009.

Wirsing, R. *India, Pakistan, and The Kashmir Dispute*, New York: St Martin's Press, 1998.

—— 'The Kashmir Territorial Dispute: The Indus Runs Through It', *Brown Journal of International Affairs*, Vol. 25, No. 1, 2008.

Woodman, D. *Himalayan Frontiers. A Political Review of British, Chinese, Indian and Russian Rivalries*, London: Barrie and Rockliff, 1969.

World Bank. 'India-Bangladesh Bilateral Trade and Potential Free Trade Agreement', *Bangladesh Development Series Paper*, No. 13, 2006.

Wulbers, S. 'Identity Configurations in India-Europe Relations', in S. Wulbers (ed.), *EU India Relations. A Critique*, New Delhi: Academic Foundation, 2008.

Xavier, C. 'India's Strategic Advantage Over China in Africa', *IDSA Comment*, 30 June 2010.

Yahya, F. 'India and Southeast Asia: Revisited', *Contemporary Southeast Asia*, Vol. 25, No. 1, April 2003.

Yuan, J.-D. 'India's Rise after Pokhran II: Chinese Analyses and Assessments', *Asian Survey*, Vol. 41, No. 6, 2001.

Zaidi, S. 'Economic Confidence Building Measures in South Asia: Trade as a Precursor to Peace with India', in M. Ahmar (ed.), *The Challenge of Confidence Building in South Asia*, New Delhi: Har-Anand Publications, 2001.

Zaman, R. 'Kautilya: The Indian Strategic Thinker and Indian Strategic Culture', *Comparative Strategy*, Vol. 25, No. 3, 2006.

—— 'Strategic Culture: A "Cultural" Understanding of War', *Comparative Strategy*, Vol. 28, No. 1, 2009.

Zarzecki, T. 'Arming China or Arming India: Future Russian Dilemma', *Contemporary Strategy*, Vol. 18, No. 3, 1999.

Zeb, R. 'The Emerging Indo-Iranian Strategic Alliance and Pakistan', *Central Asia-Caucasus Analysts*, 12 February 2003.

—— 'Gwadar and Chabahar: Competition or Complementarity', *Central Asia-Caucasus Analysts*, 22 October 2003.

Zhang, G. 'The Rise of China: India's Perceptions and Responses', *South Asian Survey*, Vol. 13, No. 1, 2006.

Index